STRIVING WITH GRACE:
VIEWS OF FREE WILL
IN ANGLO-SAXON ENGLAND

AARON J KLEIST

Striving with Grace:
Views of Free Will
in Anglo-Saxon England

UNIVERSITY OF TORONTO PRESS
Toronto Buffalo London

© University of Toronto Press Incorporated 2008
Toronto Buffalo London
Printed in Canada

ISBN 978-0-8020-9163-5

∞

Printed on acid-free paper

BT
809
.K58
2008

Library and Archives Canada Cataloguing in Publication

Kleist, Aaron J
    Striving with grace: views of free will in Anglo-Saxon
England / Aaron J Kleist.

(Toronto Old English series)
Includes bibliographical references and index.
ISBN 978-0-8020-9163-5

1. Free will and determinism – Religious aspects – Christianity.
2. Free will and determinism – Early works to 1800.   3. Grace (Theology)
– Early works to 1800.   4. Religious thought – England – Middle Ages,
600–1500.   5. Christian literature, Latin (Medieval and modern) –
England – History and criticism.   6. English literature – Old English,
ca. 450–1100 – History and criticism.   I. Title.   II. Series.

BT809.K58 2008   233'.7   C2008-901560-6

University of Toronto Press acknowledges the financial assistance to its publishing program of the Canada Council for the Arts and the Ontario Arts Council.

University of Toronto Press acknowledges the financial support for its publishing activities of the Government of Canada through the Book Publishing Industry Development Program (BPIDP).

Contents

Acknowledgments

Without three things, the labours underlying the pages in your hand would have been to no avail: counsel, funding, and support. For the first I am indebted to Michael Lapidge; from him I learned that pages of research must lie behind every written word. My thanks also go to those who counselled from a distance, supplying invaluable data from their unpublished research: Timothy Graham, Petrus Tax, Teresa Webber, and Joseph Wittig. Most of all, however, I wish to thank Andy Orchard, who taught me that a written word need not show the pages of research behind it. Seldom have I found a man so gifted to be so selfless.

Funding to produce this extensive revision and augmentation of a Cambridge thesis has been provided by a Fellowship from the National Endowment for the Humanities and by Biola University, which graciously granted me a research leave in 2004; to Chris Grace, Linda Williams, and the distinguished members of Biola's Research and Development Committee, I am additionally obliged for generous subvention support. I am deeply grateful as well for the invitations extended by Simon Keynes and Michael Franklin to serve during my leave as Honorary Research Associate of the Department of Anglo-Saxon, Norse, and Celtic and as Visiting Scholar of Hughes Hall at the University of Cambridge.

That mainstay of research, however, the quiet of sanctuary from multifarious demands, has only come through the sacrifice of others. My extended family of Kleists and Misers have been a steadfast source of encouragement through the course of this endeavour. Benjamin Flemming came to the rescue in the eleventh hour of producing the index. Day to day, however, it has been the selfless efforts of my wife

that have made my research possible, epitomized by the gift of count-
less early mornings. To you, Amanda, I offer my admiration for the
labours underlying the pages in your hand.

Introduction

This is not a book primarily about theology, though theological issues are central to its focus. It is not a book primarily about translation, though how writers translated ideas across centuries is likewise a crucial concern. Rather, this work considers a fundamental question of human experience and ways in which writers have sought to resolve it: in this uncertain world filled with factors beyond our control, to what extent do our decisions and efforts make a difference? For Anglo-Saxon England, as for so much of the medieval West, the problem was compounded by a theistic tradition. Does the existence of a sovereign God, absolute in his control and in his knowledge of future things, make human choice and striving meaningless? Are we masters of our fate – to some extent, at least – or are we simply puppets acting out our empty parts?

For the Western church in the Middle Ages, it was Augustine of Hippo who formulated the official position on the issue, and it would not be unreasonable to presume that his influence on England would be pervasive. One of the few major studies of Anglo-Saxon theology, for example, Lynne Grundy's examination of the teaching of Ælfric of Eynsham, builds on the assumption that 'almost all the ideas contained within Ælfric's sermons are to be found in Augustine, who was either their originator or their refiner.'[1] While, as we shall see, Augustine's influence on Ælfric and on Anglo-Saxon England as a whole was in fact profound, rarely are matters among Anglo-Saxons so straightforward. Other Fathers with different perspectives also influenced English writers. The English blended patristic thought and added decidedly unorthodox ideas. Their primary sources were at times suspect or blatantly heretical – and yet they occasionally so revised their material that little heresy remained.

This work seeks to untangle the complex interplay of factors that produced strikingly different, if often complementary, explanations of free will in early England. Chapter 1 examines the work of Augustine as a benchmark against which later teaching may be measured. Beginning by surveying various catalysts for Augustine's thought – the Manichaeans, Donatists, Pelagians, and Semi-Pelagians – it outlines the changes in Augustine's view of free will over the course of his career. To determine which Augustine Anglo-Saxons may have known – the early Augustine, the mature Augustine, or a confusing mixture of the two – it attempts to reconstruct the knowledge of Augustine's works at various locations and points in English history. Through a study of the manuscript evidence and known sources for Anglo-Saxon works, it reveals whether the material available to the authors under consideration would have given a balanced, incomplete, or distorted view of Augustine's foundational teaching on the will.

Chapters 2 and 3 consider two Fathers who rivalled Augustine's impact on early England: Gregory the Great and the Venerable Bede. The one was a foreigner directly responsible for the establishment in England of Roman Christian practice and Benedictine monasticism; the other was an English luminary who drew on his predecessors' work and transmitted it to later Anglo-Saxon England. These sections discuss the Fathers' debt to and departure from Augustine's teaching on free will, reconstruct later English writers' potential knowledge of their works, and describe the Fathers' teaching on free will, particularly as transmitted in England from the time of Bede to the Conquest.

Chapters 4 and 5 examine two works that draw on one of the most important studies of free will to influence the Middle Ages, Boethius's *De consolatione Philosophiae*. First, there is the *Old English Boethius*, adapted into the vernacular by the scholar-king Alfred the Great. Chapter 4 gives an overview of Alfred's literary labours, sets Boethius in the context of the late Roman Empire, and discusses the treatment of free will in *De consolatione*. It notes the Neoplatonic framework of *De consolatione*, surveys continental and insular Christian commentaries on the work, and then turns to Alfred's twin versions of Boethius, investigating the radical ways in which Alfred alters his source and the teaching that results regarding free will. Second, there is the *Carmen de libero arbitrio*, a Latin poem produced by Lantfred, a continental monk at Winchester. Chapter 5 provides background regarding Winchester and the Benedictine Reform, sets forth what may be known of Lantfred and the evidence for his authorship of the poem, and considers his potential access to commentaries on *De consolatione*. It shows both his independence from these commentaries and his linguistic and conceptual debt to Boethius's work itself. Closely examining a central metaphor in the poem, moreover, it reveals the impact Lantfred's source has on his theology.

Chapter 6 addresses another text produced under the Benedictine Reform that draws on and is shaped by a theologically suspect source. The text is *De adiutorio Dei et libero arbitrio*, supervised and perhaps composed by Wulfstan the Homilist, archbishop of York. Its surprising source is John Cassian's *Collatio* XIII, the central statement of Semi-Pelagianism. The chapter sets forth the evidence for Wulfstan's authorship of the treatise before reviewing the origins of Semi-Pelagianism, the significance of *Collatio* XIII, and the particular importance of Cassian for Benedictines. Analysing *De adiutorio Dei* line by line, it then traces how the author selectively borrows from and adapts *Collatio* XIII, noting all the while the heterodox implications of the resulting thought. Finally, comparing *De adiutorio Dei* to Prosper of Aquitaine's Augustinian critique of Cassian's work, it finds that the author not only knew the suspect nature of his source but attempted to avoid questionable material therein by drawing only on passages that Prosper does not overtly condemn. As with the *Carmen de libero arbitrio*, therefore, while attempting to encourage its audience to righteous living, *De adiutorio Dei* introduces a Semi-Pelagian emphasis on human ability to a centre of the Benedictine Reform.

Chapter 7 concludes our inquiry with a study of arguably the most educated, prolific, and influential writer of late Anglo-Saxon England: Ælfric of Eynsham. It describes his pedagogical mission and commitment to presenting orthodox doctrine – teaching, that is, by recognized ecclesiastical authorities – discusses the importance of his chief work, the *Sermones catholici*, and underscores the work's profound debt to Augustine, Gregory, and Bede. Analysing the *Sermones* in detail, moreover, it considers cases where Ælfric draws on one or more of these Fathers, clarifying the ways in which he uses, adapts, blends, supplements, and selects among these sources. While this commitment to authoritative patristic teaching may distinguish Ælfric from his Benedictine contemporaries, the chapter also shows that Ælfric is not immune to relying on heretical texts. While no Semi-Pelagian, furthermore, and while consistently affirming a patristic view of humanity's need of God's grace, Ælfric just as consistently affirms the importance of human merit. The chapter thus reveals Ælfric to be not simply a mouthpiece of

Augustine or a mechanical reproducer of patristic thought. Like his fellow Anglo-Saxons who wrestle with the issue of free will, he proves to be a man with an individual theological perspective that gently shapes and supplements his source material. In consequence, his work, together with that of his fellows, testifies to their belief in the necessity of God's assistance, even as it demonstrates their determination to impact their world meaningfully through their efforts.

Caueat lector

Of the many shortcomings of a volume such as this, one in particular may trouble the judicious reader: the limits imposed on authors, works, and theology treated herein. In the first place, the study focuses on individuals writing in Anglo-Saxon England – or, in the case of Augustine and Gregory, writers foundational thereto. Lantfred, a visitor from the Continent, thus appears where Alcuin, an Anglo-Saxon writing on the Continent, does not – an unsatisfying state of affairs. Second, when assessing the extent to which earlier works were known to later Anglo-Saxons, far greater consideration is given to the possibility of direct knowledge of those works than to the potential for indirect transmission of texts – or, more nebulous yet, of concepts – in part or in paraphrase. In fact, however, avenues of intellectual influence on early England are both multifarious and difficult to precisely reconstruct: a snippet of patristic material reproduced imperfectly by a later writer, for example, might indicate knowledge of the patristic work as a whole, preserved in a faulty copy or by imperfect memory, or acquaintance only with that snippet through aural or written encounters with the quotation in a third-party source. Crucial though an understanding of ultimate sources may be, therefore, intermediate agents of intellectual transmission cry out for further examination. Third, the very concept of free will evokes an array of corollary theological conundrums: providence, divine foreknowledge, predestination, the origin of evil, and the fall of the angels as a precursor to human corruption. While our investigation touches on all these issues at points, it does not treat them in the detail their complexity so clearly warrants. The only excuse that can be offered for such deficiencies is the overriding demand of the subject of free will itself: a subject that even in our opening exploration of Augustine's corpus threatens to overrun its bounds. However limited the results, control on this question must be imposed. To the means by which I have sought to control my subject one may well object; should frustration drive others to more detailed inquiries, however, one feels that the results are not entirely unworthwhile.

Abbreviations

ASE	Anglo-Saxon England
Assmann	*Angelsächsischen Homilien und Heiligenleben.* Ed. B. Assmann. BaP 13. Kassel, 1889.
BaP	Bibliothek der angelsächsischen Prosa
Belfour	*Twelfth-Century Homilies in MS Bodley 343.* Ed. A.O. Belfour. EETS os 137. London, 1900.
Bethurum	*The Homilies of Wulfstan.* Ed. D. Bethurum. Oxford, 1957.
Brotanek	*Texte und Untersuchungen zur altenglischen Literatur und Kirchengeschichte.* Ed. Rudolf Brotanek. Hall, 1913.
CCCM	Corpus Christianorum, Continuatio Mediaevalis. Turnhout, 1966–.
CCSL	Corpus Christianorum Series Latina. Turnhout, 1953–.
Cetedoc	*Cetedoc Library of Christian Latin Texts.* CD-ROM. Louvain-la-Neuve, 1991. CLCLT-2
CH I	*Ælfric's Catholic Homilies: The First Series, Text.* Ed. P.A.M. Clemoes. EETS ss 17. Oxford, 1997.
CH II	*Ælfric's Catholic Homilies: the Second Series, Text.* Ed. M.R. Godden. EETS ss 5. London, 1979.
CSEL	Corpus Scriptorum Ecclesiasticorum Latinorum. Vienna, 1866–.

Diuers.quaest.	Augustine. *De diuersis quaestionibus lxxxiii.* Ed. A. Mutzenbecher, 11–249. CCSL 44A. Turnhout, 1975.
EETS	Early English Text Society
Fehr	*Die Hirtenbriefe Ælfrics in altenglischer und lateinischer Fassung.* Ed. B. Fehr. BaP 9. Hamburg, 1914.
Gneuss	Gneuss, Helmut. *Handlist of Anglo-Saxon Manuscripts: A List of Manuscripts and Manuscript Fragments Written or Owned in England up to 1100.* Tempe, 2001.
Grammar	*Ælfrics Grammatik und Glossar.* Ed. J. Zupitza. Berlin, 1880.
Hall	Hall, Thomas N. 'Wulfstan's Latin Sermons', in *Wulfstan, Archbishop of York.* Turnhout, 2004.
Hexameron	Ælfric. *Exameron Anglice, or the OE Hexameron.* Ed. S.J. Crawford. BaP 10. Hamburg, 1932.
Interrogationes	Ælfric. *Interrogationes Sigewulfi,* ed. G.E. Maclean, 'Ælfric's Version of *Alcuini Interrogationes Sigeuulfi in Genesin,*' *Anglia* 7 (1884): 1–59.
Irvine	Irvine, Susan. *Old English Homilies from MS Bodley 343.* EETS os 302. Oxford, 1993.
LS I and II	*Ælfric's Lives of Saints.* Ed. W.W. Skeat. EETS 76, 82, 94 and 114. London, 1881–1900. Repr. as two volumes 1966.
MGH	Monumenta Germaniae Historica
Napier	Napier, Arthur, ed. *Wulfstan: Sammlung der ihm zugeschriebenen Homilien nebst Untersuchungen über ihre Echtheit.* Berlin, 1967. Repr. from Berlin, 1883.
OEBoeth.	Alfred. *Boethius's Consolation of Philosophy.* Ed. W.J. Sedgefield. In *King Alfred's Old English Version of Boethius.* Oxford, 1899.
PG	Patrologia Graeca. Ed. Jacques-Paul Migne, 161 vols. Paris, 1857–86.
PL	Patrologia Latina. Ed. Jacques-Paul Migne, 221 vols. Paris, 1844–64.

SH I and II   *Homilies of Ælfric: A Supplementary Collection.* Ed. J.C.
Pope. EETS 259 and 260. London, 1967–8.

STRIVING WITH GRACE:
VIEWS OF FREE WILL
IN ANGLO-SAXON ENGLAND

CHAPTER ONE

A Doctrine Defined:
The Influence of Augustine

The theological influence of Augustine of Hippo is vast. From Anglo-Saxon England alone, some 107 manuscripts survive that contain material attributed to him – nearly a tenth of the surviving corpus as a whole.[1] On numerous subjects, his teaching for centuries provided the foundation for orthodox thought in the West, and as a result he plays a unique role in our inquiry. While to the modern academic it may be the sheer variety of Anglo-Saxon theological perspectives that is of interest, to some Anglo-Saxons theological correctness was more important than ideological diversity. Such was true for the figures treated in this work: while, as we shall see, the extent to which their teaching was Augustinian might have varied widely, all laboured to eschew error and to present salutary Christian doctrine. Gregory the Great showed his concern for right belief when he sent Augustine of Canterbury to turn England from paganism. The Venerable Bede took pains to refute works that had been condemned 300 years before. Alfred the Great, lamenting the ruin of learning through pagan invasion, personally invested himself in translating 'needful' books. Lantfred of Winchester devised elaborate metaphors to enjoin individuals to a proper understanding of and attitude towards God. Ælfric of Eynsham was emphatic in his efforts to combat contemporary doctrinal error. Wulfstan the Homilist said in no uncertain terms that the nation's fate depended on the rightness of human actions and belief. On the subject of free will, if any body of thought may be seen as the benchmark against which the doctrine of these men may be measured, it must be that which for the Second Council of Orange and thus (officially, at least) for the Catholic Church as a whole set the standard for orthodoxy in the Middle Ages: the theology of Augustine of Hippo.[2]

Catalysts for Augustine's Thought:
The Manichaeans, Donatists, Pelagians, and Semi-Pelagians

In August 430, the man who would come to be known as the Doctor of Grace lay on his deathbed reflecting on human responsibility.[3] Not far off was his library, with little cupboards holding some ninety-three volumes of his works – over 230 books, letters in their hundreds, and selections from thousands of sermons preached, a staggering testament to decades of controversy and theological engagement. Beyond the walls of Hippo were the Vandals, Arian invaders who were overwhelming the world of Catholic, Roman Africa for which Augustine long had laboured. Before him, however, on his walls he had hung four psalms on penance; in solitude by his own request, reflecting on his long life, on them he focused in preparation for the hereafter.

The issue of volition – the extent to which God and human beings are responsible for human choices – was one that had recurred in various forms throughout Augustine's life, in his writings against the Manichaeans, the Donatists, and most important, the Pelagians and Semi-Pelagians. Manichaeism, first of all, was a system of thought to which Augustine himself had turned early in his spiritual journey.[4] As a teenager studying in Carthage around 373, Augustine was inspired by a work of Cicero to seek after wisdom. Having been raised in a predominantly Christian house, he sought wisdom first in Christian teaching; he was repelled, however, by what he perceived as the inelegant style of scripture (in contrast with the Latin classics) and the anti-intellectualism of the African Church, which seems to have encouraged blind faith rather than awkward questions. The Manichaeans, by contrast, promised to lead adherents to the wisdom of God through reason, and to them he subsequently turned.

Drawing on the teachings of a third-century Mesopotamian sage named Mani, the Manichaeans viewed human beings as rational and spiritual beings created by God, a Good Principle perpetually at war with the Evil Principle responsible for creating the material world. One attraction of Manichaean thought for Augustine was that it offered a solution to a key question that had troubled him: what causes people to do evil? The Manichaeans' dualism exonerated God from culpability in this regard; on the contrary, God as the Good Principle was the antithesis of evil. Similarly, moreover, the Manichaeans absolved individuals from blame: as pure spirits imprisoned in material bodies, human beings' evil deeds do not proceed from the spirit's free choice but are determined by the evil, material part of their nature. This baser nature so dominates the good self that people do evil against their will. It would be nearly a decade before Augustine found himself dissatisfied with the Manichaean view, and a dozen years more until he turned his efforts towards confronting Donatism. Much would happen in the interim. In 383 he left Carthage for Rome, where influential Manichaean friends helped get him appointed professor of rhetoric in Milan. There he encountered the preaching of Ambrose, whose spiritual interpretation of the Bible renewed his interest in Christianity. Following his conversion in 386 and baptism by Ambrose the following Easter, Augustine eventually settled in his birthplace of Thagaste in northern Africa; among his works written here are some against the Manichaeans. In 391 he went to Hippo to found a monastery, but was appointed priest for the city by popular acclaim. Valerius, bishop of Hippo, ensured that Augustine would succeed him to the episcopate by having him appointed coadjutor in 395; Augustine's ascension duly followed with Valerius's death the following year. Even as a priest, however, Augustine addressed himself not only to ecclesiastical responsibility but to theological debate, for it was in these years that he engaged the Donatist controversy.

Following the Great Persecution of Diocletian in 303–5, a substantial part of the African Church sought to condemn clergy who had 'collaborated' with the oppressors by handing over copies of the Bible to be burned by pagan authorities.[5] In 311, charging that the bishop of Carthage had been ordained by such a collaborator, eighty African bishops declared his ordination invalid and elected another bishop in his place. This rival bishop was then succeeded by one who gave the movement its name: Donatus. The Catholic bishop was supported by Emperor Constantine, who sought to discourage schism, and opposed by the Donatists, who enjoyed widespread African support. By the time Augustine was ordained, the rift had lasted for eighty years, and in Hippo the Catholics found themselves in the minority. Among the questions raised by the debate were two with implications for the issue of volition. One question arose from the Donatists' denial of the validity of sacraments administered by impure agents: to what extent does the effectiveness of the sacrament depend on the divine power inherent therein as opposed to human intent (either of the administrator or the recipient of the sacrament)? Another issue arose from Augustine's increasing sanction of force after 405 in bringing schismatics back into the Catholic fold: if force brings about conversion, so that the will is effectively changed by an external agent, to what extent may the influence of divine grace be said to be responsible for human change? In 411 a conference at Carthage decided against the Donatist position; with the end of one controversy, however, another was to begin, for among the refugees from the Visigoths' sack of Rome in 410 was a monk from either Ireland or Britain named Pelagius.

For a number of years, Pelagius and disciples such as Caelestius had championed a rigorous asceticism that emphasized humanity's self-sufficient ability to achieve righteousness.[6] God, they maintained, does not command people to do what is beyond their ability; human beings' free will must thus be sufficient for them to fulfil God's commands. Pelagius acknowledges the need for grace, but defines grace as the gift of human capacity for moral choice and the subsequent instruction of the Law and of Christ. Through such gifts, Pelagius says, individuals have both the knowledge of God's requirements and the ability to carry them out. Adam's disobedience does not hamper his descendants; people's minds may become clouded or darkened through the yoke of habitual sins, but such impediments may be overcome by the illumination provided by scripture. Faith, then, is a meritorious human decision to which God responds by providing the grace of further understanding. As Eugène Portalié notes, however, Pelagius's emphasis on human ability carried with it a demanding yoke: 'Since perfection is possible for man, it is obligatory.'[7]

Caelestius was charged with heresy in Carthage in 411; Pelagius, averring that human will depends on 'grace,' was aquitted by a council in Palestine in 415. The African councils of Carthage and nearby Milevis responded by condemning both men the following year, and their fate was sealed when in 418 they were condemned by Pope Zosimus and exiled by the emperor. Far from being over, however, the Pelagian controversy now entered its second phase as a new figure took up Pelagius's banner: Julian, bishop of Eclanum, whom Peter Brown calls 'the most devastating critic of Augustine in his old age.'[8] Against this brilliant opponent, reiterating at greater length his criticism of Pelagian views of volition and grace, Augustine would write until his death in 430.

Some of Augustine's most important works on free will, however, were written during his final years in response to challenges that would develop into a heresy that would rage for at least a century: Semi-Pelagianism. The nascence of the debate may be traced to the pivotal years 426 and 427. A number of key texts were produced during this period, and it is difficult to determine which, if any, were written with an awareness of the others. During this time, first of all, monks from the north-African town of Hadrumentum sent a delegation to ask Augustine how his teaching on grace left room for human choice.[9] Augustine responded in 426 or 427 with two letters (*Epistulae* 214 and 215) and two books: *De gratia et libero arbitrio*, showing scripture's affirmation both of volitional freedom and the necessity of grace, and *De correptione et gratia*, addressing the question of predestination and the nature of grace before and after original sin.[10] Writing perhaps in response to these or previous Augustinian works, and certainly out of concern at persistent pockets of Pelagian belief,[11] a monk named John Cassian wrote *Collatio* XIII, a work which would form the centrepiece of Semi-Pelagianism.[12] In it, Cassian acknowledged that people required God's help to accomplish good, but affirmed that they could desire good and seek God's aid in bringing good to pass; such a desire comprised an independent, meritorious initiative to which God might respond with grace. Cassian's work was welcomed by monks in southern Gaul, who resisted what they perceived as Augustine's denial of human responsibility for or effort in salvation;[13] it was opposed, however, by two laymen named Hilary and Prosper of Aquitaine. Prosper, an ardent supporter of Augustine living in Marseilles, composed his own anti-Pelagian treatise to warn a fellow layman about this new, unorthodox teaching. Possibly before reading Cassian's text, but after recognizing that the reception of *De correptione* had only confirmed Gallic resistance, he wrote to Augustine himself, denouncing the dissenters' objection that 'remoueri omnem industriam tollique uirtutes, si Dei constitutio humanas praeueniat uoluntates.'[14] After another layman, Hilary, had voiced similar concerns about anti-Augustinian doctrines circulating in Gaul,[15] Augustine responded ca. 429–30 with *De praedestinatione sanctorum* and *De dono perseuerantiae*. Acknowledging that he had once thought of individuals' initial faith as their own contribution, he now argued that human beings are utterly dependent on grace: in a word, 'Quid autem habes quod non acceperis?'[16]

These were to be Augustine's last major contributions to the debate, and we have no evidence that Cassian responded to them. Neither Cassian's silence nor Augustine's death in 430, however, put an end to the controversy. Prosper and Hilary sought papal condemnation of Cassian's theology, only to be frustrated by his strong reputation and support in Rome. Having just completed a treatise against Nestorius at the request of Leo, archdeacon of Rome and later pope – one which included, moreover, an attack on Pelagianism – Cassian was a prominent and recognized defender of orthodoxy.[17] Pope Celestine responded cautiously, therefore, to Prosper's request: a letter was issued to the bishops of southeastern Gaul, commending Augustine and condemning 'novel' ideas, but mentioning no specific names or doctrines.[18] Prosper was not deterred. After reading *Collatio* XIII, in 432 he produced *De gratia Dei et libero arbitrio contra Collatorem*, a scathing, point-by-point denunciation of Cassian's text, which he viewed as almost completely heretical.[19] If Prosper's inflammatory style did little justice to the contents of the work or its moderate tone, it also did nothing to persuade Cassian's supporters. Semi-Pelagianism continued to be the dominant teaching on grace in Gaul for nearly a century.[20] In 529, however, the Second Council of Orange brought overt opposition to an end when it ruled on the Semi-Pelagian position. While not endorsing the whole of Augustine's thought, it did approve its core, affirming that 'Per peccatum primi hominis ita inclinatum et adtinuatum fuerit liberum arbitrium, ut nullus postea aut diligere Deum sicut oportuit aut credere in Deum aut operari propter Deum quod bonum est possit, nisi eum gratia misericordiae diuinae praeuenerit.'[21] With the confirmation of the Council's ruling by Pope Boniface II in 531, the church's official position was set: thenceforth, down through the Middle Ages, Augustine's teaching on free will as codified by the Council would constitute the standard for orthodox doctrine – even if in practice other voices would add to believers' understanding of the issue.[22]

The theology produced as a result of these controversies directly affected views on free will in Anglo-Saxon England. Gregory the Great, sixth-century 'apostle to the English,' would uphold the official censure of Semi-Pelagianism while himself departing significantly from Augustine's position. In the eighth century, the Venerable Bede, having initially employed Julian as a source, would join Augustine in attacking Julian's Pelagian thought. Towards the end of the tenth century, Ælfric of Eynsham would affirm Augustine's teaching on grace while drawing (perhaps unwittingly) on Pelagius's writings. A couple of decades thereafter, Wulfstan the Homilist, contemporary and commissioner of Ælfric's work, would authorize a study based on Cassian. But what was this Augustinian standard by which they might be measured?[23]

Augustine's Theology of Free Will: Overview

In the main, Augustine's vision of the Fall, grace, and freedom of choice was not one derived from his patristic forebears, who tended to speak more of human free will and responsibility than the inevitability of sin through humanity's corruption.[24] Rather, it was one he himself constructed in response to philosophical and theological challenges. Early on, the Manichaeans' deterministic view of evil caused him to emphasize the role of human will; in later works, the Pelagians' stress on humans' ability lead him to respond with emphasising grace. It is not accurate to say, however, that his opponents' arguments push Augustine into increasingly radical positions, so that by the end he has, as Portalié puts it, 'sacrificed freedom of the will on the altar of divine determinism.'[25] The central turning-point, in fact, comes towards the beginning of his career, in his first major work after being consecrated as bishop, *De diuersis quaestionibus ad Simplicianum* (396 AD). Gerald Bonner describes this work as an intellectual conversion-experience 'hardly less significant than his decision to seek Catholic baptism, in a garden at Milan in 386.'[26] It is here, Augustine says, that he first comes to understand Paul's message in I Corinthians: 'Quid autem habes quod non accepisti?'[27] The vital principle he gains is that God is responsible even for the beginnings of individuals' belief. With this tenet in place, most scholars agree that at this point the basic components of Augustine's theological system are complete.[28]

In his works before the episcopate, then, Augustine maintains that people have not only the capacity, but the unhindered ability to choose either good or evil. In the first book of *De libero arbitrio*, for example (388 AD), Augustine states that human culpability lies in failing to attain virtue that he could easily achieve simply by willing it.[29] Before the completion of the third book in 395, however, his views are challenged by his debates with the Manichaean, Fortunatus. Under pressure from Pauline texts that were to prove fundamental to his future work,[30] he is compelled to admit that only Adam possessed unhindered moral choice; fallen humans sin by necessity.[31] Nevertheless, he says, the fact that individuals' capacity for good is impaired does not mean that it is powerless. People may bind themselves through habitually choosing evil, so that it becomes more and more difficult to choose good; even so, they can believe in God and desire good through the free will God has given them.[32] When Augustine comes to study Romans 9 in his letter to Simplicianus, however, he places new emphasis both on the corrupting effects of the Fall and on the primacy of grace. Adam's disobedience has marred human nature: while people still have the capacity to choose good or evil, their desires are now such that they will inevitably – and voluntarily – choose evil.[33] They still have free will (*liberum arbitrium*), but have lost their freedom (*libertas*).[34] God's intervening grace thus is needed to enable individuals to choose good.[35]

Three further questions rise out of this new perspective: whence does the beginning of one's belief come, how does God influence the process, and does this influence irresistibly cause people to choose good? In regards to humans' belief, first of all, before his letter to Simplicianus Augustine seeks to correlate God's grace to some extent with human merit. In *Expositio quarundam propositionum ex epistola ad Romanos*, for example (394/395 AD), Augustine suggests that faith is not from God, but a voluntary response to God's universal call.[36] By the time he considers Romans 9 in *Ad Simplicianum* I.2.5 and 9, however, Augustine has been so struck by God's sovereignty and human helplessness that he rejects the proposition that individuals can believe on their own. By its very definition, he says, grace is gratuitous and cannot be given on the basis of any human merit – even an incipient flicker of good desire or the beginnings of faith. Rather, faith too must be the result of God's initiative: grace preveniently 'prepares' peoples' will.[37]

Second, how exactly does God bring people's faith about? Again, Augustine initially attempts to formulate a precise explanation, offering in *Ad Simplicianum* the theory of congruent vocation. The omniscience of God is such, Augustine says, that he knows how an individual will respond to any set of motivations.[38] Placed alone in a vault filled with gold, for example, with the certain knowledge that his actions will never be discovered, a person might gladly commit a theft that fear of punishment or social censure would otherwise restrain. As God can shape all events to fit his purposes exactly, therefore, he places individuals in situations to which he knows they will respond favourably. No force is used; he does not compel them to come to faith. Nevertheless, the circumstances in which God calls people are such that they will voluntarily and even joyfully believe.[39]

J.P. Burns has argued, however, that developments in Augustine's theology during the Donatist controversy lead him to view God's work more in terms of direct inspiration.[40] He notes four principles that come to affect Augustine's understanding of grace: first, just as the Spirit is responsible for the efficacy of the sacraments, so he may be responsible for the efficacy of preaching. Second, when schismatics or unbelievers are presented for baptism, the Spirit 'works a consecration which is contrary to their evil will and may even temporarily suspend the guilt of their sin.' Third, God sometimes changes hearts by force applied through the civil power. Finally, the salvation of infants by baptism alone provides not only a key example of gratuitous election but a new paradigm for conversion: just as God allows only some infants to be baptized, so he grants only certain adults the chance to hear the Gospel. [41] These principles in turn shape Augustine's response to Pelagius.

Burns posits three stages to Augustine's answer to the Pelagian claim that human beings, having been given the 'grace' of volitional capacity, are able on their own to initiate and achieve righteousness. In *De gratia Christi et de peccato originali* (418 AD), Augustine speaks of the efficacy of God's assistance in general without distinguishing between faith and good works (I.14.15). In his *Epistula ad Sixtum* later that same year, he attributes both individually to the work of the Spirit.[42] In *Contra duas epistulas Pelagianorum* (420 AD), however, pointing to Paul's conversion as his model, he asserts that God does not simply assist individuals' righteous initiative, but changes a heart that is in the very act of pursuing evil (I.19.37). Without denying that God may providentially manipulate the environment of human choices – the premise of congruent vocation – Augustine affirms that conversion is actually achieved through the Spirit's transformation of individuals' wills. Just as the Spirit inspires people's good deeds after conversion, then, so it is with faith: God moves rather than guides a person to Christ.[43]

Third, then, is it possible for human beings to resist this inward intervention? Again, Augustine views the freedom of individuals' wills as unimpaired throughout this process; at all times they may technically choose either obedience or rebellion.[44] It is their desire that is in question. The Spirit cannot make humans' desire 'neutral': by its very definition desire must be for something, and people will never be without some desire. The Spirit's inspiration, therefore, changes individuals' love of evil (*concupiscentia*) into a love for God (*caritas*).[45] Where this is their whole desire, there is no resistance; they are drawn, like a sheep to grass, to that which has become sweet to them.[46] Augustine notes that not all are thus called; there is a general call to all humankind in the testimonies of Creation and the Gospel, but this is not always accompanied by the Spirit's transformation of human hearts.[47] For those God does call in this way, however, faith is the inevitable result.[48]

The desire for good that people have at conversion by no means remains steadfast thereafter; to persevere, individuals must rely on the Spirit's transforming power. Even after conversion, human beings are marked by an inward struggle between flesh and spirit, the result of the lingering presence of concupiscence, which is not eradicated at baptism as is antecedent guilt.[49] In the *Confessiones*, Augustine describes this struggle as a conflict of two wills: the new one, still developing in its desire for God, being resisted by the old one, made strong by long indulgence.[50] Torn by competing desires, people choose good, but not wholeheartedly, and thus contribute to their own division. Augustine exhorts believers to struggle against their evil desires, warns that victory comes only through grace, and promises that in heaven the striving of flesh and spirit shall cease. Rather than merely having a will that is free, the elect will have a will that is truly freed – freed from any desire to do evil; freed for the freedom (*libertas*) of remaining permanently in righteousness.[51]

The Knowledge of Augustine in Anglo-Saxon England

The perspective on Augustine's thought offered by the lens of modern editions and modern scholarship, however valuable, must be treated with caution. Anglo-Saxons, the evidence would suggest, had far more limited access than we to Augustine's works, and our access to Anglo-Saxon evidence has been limited by the ravages of time. Four bodies of information may help to reconstruct as best we can which Augustinian works might have been known to Bede, Alfred, Lantfred, Wulfstan, and Ælfric, the Anglo-Saxon authors examined hereafter: first, Augustinian manuscripts surviving from the relevant centres; second, Augustine manuscripts surviving from England as a whole during these periods; third, Augustinian sources used by the various authors; and fourth, continental collections of Augustinian material known to at least one of these authors.

The first source of information is also the least helpful. From the region around Wearmouth–Jarrow prior to Bede's death in 735, no works by Augustine survive; the closest approximation we have is a fragment of *De consensu euangelistarum* possibly from Northumbria dating from the second half of the eighth century.[52] *De consensu* compares, collates, and argues for the harmony of the Gospel accounts, and is of limited help on the question of free will. From Winchester, similarly, we find no Augustinian works before the end of the tenth century – none, that is, that might have been known to Alfred, who died in 899; Lantfred, who worked there around the years 970–3; and perhaps even Ælfric, who left Winchester to become a monk of Cerne around 987. An altered excerpt from *Quaestiones euangeliorum*, a treatment of problematic phrases in

Matthew and Luke, appears in a late tenth century manuscript probably from Winchester.[53] No copies of Augustine remain from Cerne or Eynsham, Ælfric's next appointment, prior to Ælfric's death around 1010, nor from Worcester or York prior to Wulfstan's death in 1022.[54]

A better picture of the knowledge of Augustine in Anglo-Saxon England may be gleaned from the surviving evidence from England as a whole, even if such evidence cannot prove that our five authors knew these Augustinian texts. Besides the copy of *De consensu* noted above, extracts of Augustine appear in but one manuscript before 899.[55] From the period 900 x 1022, however – the years following Alfred up to Wulfstan's death – at least nineteen works by Augustine survive,[56] as well as three falsely attributed to Augustine.[57] The latter are beyond the scope of this study, Augustine's authentic corpus posing more than a sufficient challenge; nonetheless, such texts constitute a valuble point of consideration for future scholarship, inasmuch as they may have been perceived by Anglo-Saxons as Augustinian. Among the former, authentic works of Augustine, however, are six of particular importance to the Pelagian and Semi-Pelagian debate: *De natura et gratia*, written between 413 and 415 against Pelagius's *De natura* and affirming the need for grace to 'free' a nature that would otherwise choose only evil; *De perfectione iustitiae hominis*, written between 415 and 416 against Caelestius's assertion that it was both possible and obligatory for human beings to live without sin; *De gratia et libero arbitrio* and *De correptione et gratia*, both written in response to the monks of Hadrumentum; and *De praedestinatione sanctorum* and *De dono perseuerantiae*, written in response to Prosper and Hilary and the doctrines of the monks of Gaul. Only one copy of each of these works survives from Anglo-Saxon England before the late eleventh century, and all six are contained in a single manuscript: Salisbury, Cathedral Library 117 (s. x [prov. Salisbury]), a collection also containing Augustine's two letters to the monks of Hadrumentum and the letters of Prosper and Hilary to Augustine.[58] Gneuss describes the manuscript as a tenth-century work of Salisbury provenance,[59] placing it temptingly close to the world of Ælfric: Salisbury is but twenty miles from Winchester and thirty-five from Cerne. Nonetheless, it is unlikely that Ælfric would have known the manuscript. Teresa Webber believes that the manuscript is of continental origin, noting that it begins with a contents list in Uncial followed by texts in Caroline, and that its word separation is not very far advanced. In addition, she suggests that the manuscript was imported after Salisbury's foundation in 1075, rather than being part of the collection of the bishop of Sherborne, the site of the see before it moved to Salisbury. She states: 'The lack of any evidence of descendants of this manuscript elsewhere in England in the post-Conquest period might suggest that the manuscript came directly to Salibsury and stayed there, rather than being one of the number of imported exemplars that seem to have circulated round the country.'[60] No palaeographic evidence remains, therefore, to suggest that any of these major Augustinian works were known in Anglo-Saxon England during the lifetimes of our five authors.

A similar view is offered by source studies of the Anglo-Saxon authors under consideration. At least fifty works by Augustine have been proposed as sources for Bede;[61] among them is *Contra Iulianum* (421/422 AD), which Augustine directed against Julian along with *De nuptiis et concupiscentia* (419/421), *Contra duas epistulas Pelagianorum* (420/421), and his final work, *Contra Iulianum opus imperfectum* (428/430), left unfinished at his death. None of these other works against Julian appear to have been used by Bede, however, nor any of the treatises represented by the Salisbury collection. Fewer works still are thought to have been used by Alfred: aside from the *Soliloquia*, a version of which Alfred himself likely produced, only a couple of letters, the *Retractationes*, and *De ciuitate Dei* have been offered as probable sources.[62] The last of these texts, moreover, is the only Augustinian work posited by scholars as being used by Bede and Alfred in common. Lantfred's knowledge of Augustine may have been more extensive: his writings show the probable influence of five major works besides Augustine's letters and sermons, all of which were or may have been known to Bede.[63] Neither he nor Wulfstan, however, whose sermons reveal his knowledge of at least three works by Augustine, show familiarity with Augustine's later writings on free will.[64]

Aside from Bede, it is Ælfric that appears to draw most heavily on the African Father.[65] The *Sermones catholici*, Ælfric's most influential work, describes him as 'þone wisan Augustinum ... ðam ðe we wel truwiað to swa micelre deopnysse.'[66] Augustine is the first source Ælfric cites in his first series of *Sermones*, one to whom Ælfric refers explicitly nineteen times thereafter and on whom to some extent over half of his homilies draw.[67] He is also one on whom Ælfric relies for several discussions of free will. Despite Ælfric's clear exposure to Augustine, however, studies of Ælfric's sources have made apparent that – save for a couple of scant references – Ælfric draws on none of Augustine's major works on free will when composing the *Sermones*. Indeed, when one considers the thirteen proposed Augustinian sources for the *Sermones*, one is struck by the tentativeness of these attributions. Five of the works used by Bede appear here – *De doctrina Christiana, Enarrationes in psalmos, Enchiridion ad Laurentium, De Genesi ad litteram,* and *De trinitate* (not a certain source for Bede) – but all five have been described as possible rather than certain sources. Instead, much of Ælfric's material appears to have been derived from Augustinian sermons and selections from *Tractatus in euangelium Ioannis*, which Godden suggests Ælfric knew independently and 'consulted as a matter of course' when commenting on John's Gospel.[68]

In considering the implications of these lists of sources, of course, one does well to keep in mind the limitations of the evidence. Such lists are neither exhaustive nor always certain; they simply reflect scholars' best efforts to record 'substantive' parallels. Even when sources are unquestioned, moreover, they indicate merely which texts Anglo-Saxon authors used, not all those which they heard or read and by which they were influenced. To say that an Augustinian work is a probable or certain source, furthermore, does not mean that the whole would have been known by the Anglo-Saxon author in question. Godden cites Augustine's *Retractationes* as a probable source for Alfred's version of Augustine's *Soliloquies*, for example, but notes that the relevant passage from the *Retractationes* often appears as a prologue to manuscript copies of Augustine's *Soliloquies*; Alfred, therefore, need not have had access to the whole of this source.[69] Such caveats aside, however, the sources would seem to corroborate the evidence of surviving manuscripts: Augustine's major works on free will, such as those found in the Salisbury collection, may not have been known to our Anglo-Saxon authors.

Finally, in addition to the manuscripts surviving from the relevant centres, manuscripts surviving from England as a whole, and the sources used by the various authors, there are the continental collections of Augustinian material known to have been used by Ælfric: Paul the Deacon, Smaragdus, and Haymo of Auxerre.[70] The homiliary of Paul the Deacon, first of all (720–ca. 799), was a series of readings for the Sundays and feast days of the church year commissioned by Charlemagne at the end of the eighth century. Intended for use in the night office, the work was designed both to replace existing homiliaries, which often had errors in transcription and lections of dubious origin, and to introduce Roman custom into Gallic liturgy. The result was a collection whose quality of readings and breadth of coverage made it what Cyril Smetana has called 'a standard for the western church for eleven hundred years.'[71] As the collection is of complete, rubricated homilies, Ælfric would have known the authorship of the texts on which he drew. Second, there is Smaragdus's *Collectiones in Euangelia et Epistolas*, also known as the *Expositio libri comitis*. Another product of the Carolingian reform, this work too was a series of lections drawn from patristic sources, organized according to the liturgical year, and intended not for public preaching but for ecclesiastical use.[72] While Smaragdus compiles his homilies using extracts from multiple authorities rather than a single patristic source, the extracts are not intermingled but presented in discrete blocks, with their sources (usually) identified by abbreviations in the margins. As with Paul the Deacon, therefore, Ælfric would have known the source of the theology he found in Smaragdus. Such is not the case with the ninth-century homiliary of Haymo of Auxerre. Haymo blends, edits, and augments his sources with little care for attestation. As a result, Ælfric cites the Fathers directly when drawing on Paul the Deacon and Smaragdus, but must refer to Haymo by name given the latter's lack of attributed sources.[73] In identifying texts which Ælfric knew as Augustinian, then, the contents of Haymo need not be examined.

Of these collections, that of Paul the Deacon is the most important for our purposes. Along with Haymo and the anonymous hagiographic collection known as the Cotton-Corpus legendary, Paul the Deacon served as Ælfric's main source for his *Sermones catholici*: Ælfric used just under a hundred homilies from the collection for the *Sermones*, drawing primarily on works attributed to Augustine, Gregory the Great, and Bede; he continued to employ it, moreover, in homiletic works of his later career.[74] Ælfric does not cite Paul the Deacon in his list of authorities in his Latin preface to the first series of *Sermones*, directly listing such figures as Augustine, Gregory the Great, and Bede as sources instead (*CH* I.praef.15–16). Smaragdus, by contrast, appears in Ælfric's list as a source in his own right even though Ælfric uses him far less frequently than he does Paul the Deacon. Two reasons may be posited for the prominent reference: first, while not as weighty an authority as Church Fathers such as Augustine, Smaragdus was the author of a commentary on Benedict's *Regula* and a standard guide to monasticism, and thus perhaps a name of importance for Ælfric's monastic audience.[75] Second, whereas Paul the Deacon includes whole homilies or significant portions of patristic material whose authors he clearly identifies (if not always correctly), Smaragdus joins together series of short extracts or even phrases – over 500 all told, not all of which are identified in every manuscript of the *Collectiones*. The standard edition found in PL 102 is decidedly deficient in this regard: Migne records only 198 attributions, of which many are erroneous or misplaced. These attributions have been corrected and expanded in three studies by Alexander Souter, who records ninety-six entries for Augustine, eighteen that are questionable – marked 'A,' for example, in a manuscript – and one incorrectly attributed to Augustine; I have reproduced and expanded his list of Augustinian extracts in Appendix I, Table I.7.[76] Authors such as Ælfric, then, seeking for Augustinian source material for a particular passage or liturgical occasion, would find it far more easily in Paul the Deacon than in Smaragdus.

When one attempts to reconstruct what Augustinian content they would have offered Anglo-Saxons, however, both collections present their own sets of challenges. On the one hand, though as early as 1985 Helmut Gneuss stated that 'it should be one of the foremost tasks of future research to establish the version or versions of Paul's Homiliary employed in the late Anglo-Saxon period,' to date no study has established the precise form of Ælfric's copy of Paul the Deacon.[77] In its original form, the homiliary contained some 244 readings from patristic sources; a later medieval version printed in PL 95, however, shows considerable expansions and revisions, containing some fifty-four additional sermons. It is difficult to say with certainty, therefore, what Augustinian works Ælfric would here have encountered. In Smaragdus's *Collectiones*, the problem is still greater. As we have noted, different copies of Smaragdus's work identify his sources with varying consistency. Sometimes extracts from Augustine are given no label at all; sometimes Augustinian texts are attributed to other authors (Table I.8); sometimes others' work is mistakenly marked as Augustine's (Table I.9). Such difficulties aside, an analysis of what we may reconstruct from Paul the Deacon and Smaragdus reveals few additional Augustinian works beyond those used by Ælfric as sources. Most of the selections in Paul the Deacon are sermons and tractates, not books: the homiliary includes a few passages from *De ciuitate Dei* and *De diuersis quaestionibus,* but these seem not to have been used by Ælfric, even if known (Table I.1). The same pattern is found in the later version of Paul the Deacon: aside from more sermons and tractates, the only major difference is the inclusion of passages from *Enarrationes in psalmos* which Ælfric again did not employ (Table I.2). Smaragdus, by contrast, includes extracts from a number of works besides sermons and tractates: some fifteen in all, in addition to four letters; included among this material is one extract from *De praedestinatione sanctorum* (Table I.7). With this one exception, however, the witness of these collections appears to confirm the evidence of the extant Augustinian manuscripts and the sources used by Anglo-Saxon authors: Augustine's major works on free will, such as *De gratia et libero arbitrio*, *De correptione et gratia*, *De praedestinatione sanctorum*, *De dono perseuerantiae*, or even the early *De libero arbitrio* (on which we will have cause to comment), do not appear to have been known in Anglo-Saxon England.

The striking absence of such texts raises two crucial questions: First, given this gap, what sort of picture of Augustine's theology would Anglo-Saxon authors have received? Second, given the development of Augustine's theology over the course of his career, does this picture reflect Augustine's early thought, mature thought, or a confusing mixture of the two? Granted, no definitive answer can be given to such questions: the manuscript evidence, to begin with, is too fragmentary to reconstruct all works that were known to the authors under consideration. A beginning, however, may be made by examining those sources drawn upon by Bede, Alfred, Lantfred, Wulfstan, and Ælfric, including (in Ælfric's case) the collections of Smaragdus and Paul the Deacon.

Augustine's Theology of Free Will in Works Known to Bede

The Augustinian materials used by Bede are considerable – eleven major works at least, excluding the letters and sermons, with two other probable and three other possible sources. Some of these texts focus less on the issue of free will than do others; in some cases, Bede's knowledge of the work is still in question. Even with such considerations, however, drawing only on selections from Bede's library, it is possible to show that Bede would have had clear access to Augustine's teaching on volition. Such exposure he would have gained from one or more of the following: the *Confessiones*, *Enarrationes in psalmos*, *De Genesi ad litteram*, *De ciuitate Dei*, *Enchiridion*, or *De haeresibus*.

Confessiones

The *Confessiones*, Augustine's autobiographical exploration of the nature of God,[78] was widely popular in the Middle Ages and probably served as a source for Bede. In this work, written between 397 and 401, Augustine explores among other issues the contrast between his early beliefs and his Christian convictions. As a Manichaean, Augustine notes, he believed that human beings sinned by necessity, as a result of being corporeal, rather than admit that he 'sponte devia[uit], et poena erra[uit]' (turned aside by his own accord, and sinned as a punishment).[79] The year before his conversion, however, he wrestled with the possibility that free will, not physical compulsion, leads to human depravity (VII.3). Not long thereafter, he rejected the Manichaean position that there were two distinct natures in human beings at war with one another, acknowledging both his responsibility for evil and his inability to overcome it on his own (VIII.10–11). Ultimately, recognizing that his only hope was in God's great mercy, he encapsulated his understanding of grace with a classic statement to which Pelagius would react with outrage: 'Da quod iubes, et iube quod uis' (Give what you command, and command what you will).[80] As in the later *De ciuitate Dei*, the key to this interrelationship between the will and grace lies in human desires. Desire, or love, is like a weight that draws human beings to their natural place: just as stones plummet earthward and fire rises up, so the heart burdened by concupiscence draws individuals to evil while the heart inflamed by *caritas* draws individuals to righteousness (XIII.9.10). It is this enkindling of righteous desire that enables human obedience, and it is a desire that only God can give. As Augustine says, 'Dono tuo accendimur, et sursum ferimur' (By your gift we are inflamed and are borne upwards).[81] Both the initiative and fulfilment of righteousness are thus solely made possible by God.

Enarrationes in psalmos

Augustine composed his *Enarrationes in psalmos* over some thirty years, commenting on the first thirty-two Psalms by 392 and completing the whole by 420.[82] It was an influential work for more than one Anglo-Saxon author: Bede draws on it for his *Expositio Apocalypseos*, *In principium Genesis*, and possibly *Historia ecclesiastica gentis Anglorum*; Lantfred employs the work for his *Translatio et miracula S. Swithuni*; and Ælfric may cite from it in one of the *Sermones catholici*.[83] A few selections may serve to illustrate the text's importance for readers' understanding of free will.

Treating the lengthy Psalm 118, for example, Augustine returns repeatedly to this theme. In verse 80, where the Psalmist asks that his heart 'fiat perfectum' (would be faultless), Augustine praises the writer for praying for righteousness rather than presuming that he himself possessed it. Here, says Augustine with satisfaction, is found no 'audacia de libero arbitrio contra gratiam confidentis' (impudence of one relying on free will as against grace).[84] Such prayer does not precede divine intervention; first God's grace blots out past sins, then the Spirit helps people to fight against their evil desires, and then people are able to pray for further aid. As he says: 'Ita donata nobis regeneratione, adiuta conflictione, fusa precatione, fit cor nostrum immaculatum' (Thus, regeneration having been given us, our battle having been aided, prayer having been poured forth, our heart is made pristine).[85] Two further verses in Augustine's eyes reiterate this dependence on grace. Verse 112, on the one hand, sees the Psalmist turning (*inclinans*) his heart to obey God's laws. As the writer earlier calls on God to turn his heart towards his Word, however 'inclina cor meum ad testimonia tua,' Augustine states that we should understand obedience as the product both of 'diuini muneris et propriae uoluntatis,' God's gift and our own will.[86] Lest individuals should attribute too much to their own power, however, there is also verse 126. Here, as the Psalmist prays for understanding of God's laws, Augustine notes that the Law was given to humble the proud and those 'presuming on the freedom of their will' (de libertate sui arbitrii praesumentibus) so that, repentant, 'they might run by faith to aiding grace' (per fidem ad subuenientem currerent gratiam).[87]

Compared with such measured statements, Augustine's commentary on Psalm 78 might come as a bit of a shock. Noting that human beings are sick and in need of a healer, Augustine nonetheless stresses that their infirmity has not deprived people of free will. On the contrary, he explains, 'qui enim adiuuatur, etiam per seipsum aliquid agit' (he who is aided also does something through his own effort).[88] While he holds individuals responsible for their actions, however, and affirms the importance of using their will and strength righteously, Augustine is just as clear that such ability can achieve nothing good without grace. As he says regarding Psalm 138: 'Habemus liberum arbitrium; sed illo ipso libero arbitrio quantum possumus, nisi nos adiuuet ille qui iubet?'[89] The *Enarrationes in psalmos*, therefore, while exhorting people to righteous deeds, would leave its readers in no doubt as to their need of divine assistance.

De Genesi ad litteram

The biblical account of creation was a subject to which Augustine would repeatedly return. Between 388 and 389, a year or two following his baptism at Milan, he composed *De Genesi contra Manichaeos* to affirm a single Creator in contrast to the Manichaeans' dualistic vision of good and evil Principles. Dissatisfied with his allegorical approach in this work, in 393 he began *De Genesi ad litteram imperfectus liber*, a first attempt at a comprehensive historical treatment of Genesis that he would ultimately leave incomplete. In 401 he concluded his *Confessiones* with three books that offered both literal and allegorical expositions of Genesis 1. That same year, moreover, he undertook what has been called 'a kind of Augustinian *summa* on the subject of creation': *De Genesi ad litteram*, a study of the literal significance of the biblical account.[90] This work, which would take Augustine some fifteen years to complete, would prove a staple source for Bede's *In principium Genesis*, which in turn would be drawn on by Ælfric.[91] In it, Augustine addresses a subject conceptionally foundational to the corruption of the human will, though one to which this study cannot do justice: the demonic fall – or more precisely, the origin of evil in the aversion of Satan's will, particularly as considered in the problematic light of heavenly foreknowledge.[92]

In this work, Augustine suggests that unlike human beings, who must grow gradually in wisdom, angels from the moment of their creation apprehended all that would come to be made by gazing directly on and 'adhering in pure charity to' the eternal Word of God ('Mens uero angelica pura charitate inhaerens Verbo Dei' [IV.32; cf. II.8 and IV.24]). The angelic mind was thus able to grasp all things simultaneously ('omnia mens simul angelica potest' [IV.33]), so that the righteous angels had the blessed assurance of knowing that they would abide forever in God's truth (XI.17).[93] Augustine recognizes, however, that such foreknowledge raises a vexed question as regards Satan himself: did Satan foreknow that he would reject this truth, or was knowledge of his future hidden from him alone among the angels (XI.17)? For Augustine, the answer lies in the nature and timing of Satan's fall. On the one hand, Augustine is quick to defend God against any wrongdoing. Evil, to begin with, is not a nature with which individuals may be born, but a loss of the good. God created Satan good, with the ability to cling to the highest good – namely, Himself – though he also gave Satan the freedom to deprive himself of this good (VIII.14): Satan thus had the ability to stand fast in righteousness had he so willed (XI.16). From the very moment he was made, however, Satan was corrupted by delight in his personal power (XI.23), being proud of his own perceived superiority and then jealous of human beings who were made in God's image (XI.14). As John states: 'Ille homicida erat *ab initio* et in ueritate non stetit' (He was a murderer *from the beginning and did not stand in the truth* [John 8.44, emphasis mine]).[94] For Augustine, therefore, the problem of Satan's potential foreknowledge is resolved by the immediacy of Satan's fall: Satan's knowledge of sin was not an anticipation of an inescapable future, but an awareness of a dreadful present. God's knowledge, by contrast, both foresaw Satan's sin and took it into account: he created Satan good but free to fall knowing that he would use Satan's evil choices to bring about further good (XI.11 and 22). Part of that good would be the grace extended to human beings made corrupt through Satan's tempting of their progenitors. Here, God is revealed not simply as innocent of wrongdoing but as utterly responsible for righteousness. Augustine states: 'Quod attinet ad naturam iniqua sua uoluntate deprauatam, recursum per semetipsam non habet, sed per Dei gratiam, qua adiuuatur et instauratur ... quod reuertitur, qui reuertitur, non sibi tribuat, sed gratiae Dei' (As far as a nature corrupted by its own wicked will is concerned, it has no recourse in itself, but [only] in the grace of God, by which it is assisted and renewed ... That one who returns does return he should not attribute to himself, but to God's grace [IX.18]).[95]

De ciuitate Dei

De ciuitate Dei, written over the course of fourteen years (413–27), is a systematic criticism of the lingering paganism of an aristocratic intelligentsia that, like Pelagius, had come to Carthage after the sack of Rome.[96] Among the numerous subjects treated in the work are at least two of relevance to writers on free will in Anglo-Saxon England: God's foreknowledge and the consequences of the Fall.

Having denied in Book IV that the dominance of the Roman Empire should be attributed to pagan gods, and having dismissed in Book V the notion of Fate as related to the determinism of the stars, Augustine turns in V chapter 9 to the question of free will and divine foreknowledge: if God knows unfailingly all that will take place, how can people choose other than that which God has foreseen? As we will have cause to see in relation to Alfred's *Old English Boethius,* Augustine affirms both foreknowledge and freedom. Our free choices, he says, are among those things which God foresees: 'Ipsae quippe nostrae uoluntates in causarum ordine sunt, qui certus est Deo eiusque praescientia continetur.'[97] In this sense, God's knowledge does not determine human actions. At the same time, however, Augustine emphasizes God's sovereignty and influence

on human volition. God's will, supreme in power, 'uoluntates bonas adiuuat, malas iudicat, omnes ordinat; et quibusdam tribuit potestates, quibusdam non tribuit.'[98] Such does not mean that God is responsible for
evil: he is the one who bestows all ability, not all choices ('omnium
potestatum dator, non uoluntatum'). On the contrary, wicked wills are a
perversion of human nature, which God made good.

In Book XI, we gain additional insight into Augustine's view of divine
foreknowledge. XI chapter 21, examining God's creation of light in Genesis, considers the ramifications of the statement that God 'saw that it
was good' (Gen. 1.4). God's 'seeing,' Augustine says, is not a sudden act
of discovery but an eternal state of knowledge. Augustine does more
than simply assert God's omniscience; rather, he describes God's vision
in terms which – as we shall see when we come to Alfred's *Boethius* – are
evocative of the Neoplatonic language of Boethius's *De consolatione
Philosophiae*. God beholds simultaneously the past, present, and future,
Augustine says, for he apprehends them 'omnino incommutabiliter ...
stabili ac sempiterna praesentia' (altogether unchangeably ... in his stable and eternal present).[99] God's vision, moreover, goes hand in hand
with his sovereignty: just as the Unchanging One moves all temporal
things without any movement that time can measure, Augustine says,
so he knows all temporal events with a knowledge that time cannot
measure. Like V chapter 9, therefore, XI chapter 21 affirms that God
knows and 'moves' all things; nonetheless, Augustine maintains, God's
sovereignty preserves a role for the will.

The question of God's foreknowledge becomes all the more pressing
given the catastrophic consequences of the Fall. Though God foreknew
the evil that humans would choose, Augustine explains, he did not
deprive them of the power of free will, knowing also the good that he
would consequently bring about (XXII.1). Nonetheless, the Fall has had a
profound effect on human nature, and it is to this effect that Augustine
turns in XII chapter 22. Two choices, Augustine says, were offered to
humankind: they might obey God and receive eternal blessedness with
the angels as a reward, or use their free will proudly to disobey. On
choosing the latter, they joined not the ranks of angels but the ranks of
beasts, living as slaves to their appetite ('libidinis seruui').[100] In XIII chapter 14 he describes the situation more vividly: from humans' bad use of
free will, it says, there came 'series huius calamitatis ... quae humanum
genus origine deprauata, uelut radice corrupta, usque ad secundae mortis
exitium, quae non habet finem, solis eis exceptis qui per gratiam Dei liber-
antur, miseriarum connexione perducit.'[101] Humanity is thus enslaved to

its evil desires and without hope of righteousness, let alone salvation, apart from the unmerited intervention of divine grace. The judgment is poetic: having been unwilling to do good when they were capable of doing so, now, even if they desire to do good, people cannot carry it out (XIV.15). Now, however, even believers live in a state of division, with the spirit and the flesh warring with each other (XXI.15; Gal. 5.17). Thus XIV chapter 11 reiterates this portrait of humanity's state: depraved and enchained, it says, people have lost both their health and their freedom. This freedom, 'amissum proprio uitio, nisi a quo dari potuit, reddi non potest' (having been lost through its own fault, cannot be restored save by him who [originally] was able to bestow it).[102] To his chosen, however, such freedom God will give, ending the war between flesh and spirit with the gift of new spiritual bodies in heaven (XXII.21). There, moreover, God will provide a 'superior freedom' to human beings: while before they were free to sin or not to sin, in heaven humans will be able to sin no longer. Augustine's solution to this apparent paradox lies in human desires. Using an image developed in *De libero arbitrio* and the *Confessiones*, Augustine describes love as a gravitational mass (*pondus*) drawing the will to its natural place of rest: what individuals desire, that they will choose (XI.28).[103] Whereas on earth people's evil desires prevent them from doing good, however, in heaven sin will have no power to delight; human beings will choose only to do good, their desires having been changed by the grace of God (XXII.30).

Enchiridion

Composed between 421 and 423 in answer to questions posed by one Laurentius, the *Enchiridion* or 'Handbook' on the Christian life addresses such issues as humanity's purpose, the extent to which doctrine is a matter of reason and of faith, theological errors for Christians to avoid, and so forth. *Fontes Anglo-Saxonici* records only one possible use of the text by Bede, one certain quotation in Asser's Life of Alfred (suggesting that the text was at least known in Alfred's circle), one possible parallel in Ælfric's *Sermones catholici*, and three other borrowings in anonymous Anglo-Latin and Old English writers; a firmer borrowing by Ælfric is posited below.[104] If the *Enchiridion* were known to such authors, however, in it they would have found some of the clearest teaching on free will and grace outside of Augustine's later major treatises on the subject.

    Section 9, to begin with, presents a striking portrait of postlapsarian volition. Humans, chapter 30 states, are slaves – slaves that are 'free' only in the sense that they happily carry out the will of their master, sinful desire. By Adam's evil use of his free will, he destroyed (*perdidit*) his true freedom, which consisted in the ability to take pleasure in doing good. Until Christ sets someone free, asks Augustine, 'Quid boni operatur perditus, nisi quantum fuerit a perditione liberatus? Numquid libero uoluntatis arbitrio? Et hoc absit.'[105] Chapter 31 makes it plain that both faith and good deeds are gifts of God. Chapter 32 adds that even the power of free will is God's gift – the power by which people believe, hope, and love. Individuals' will and God's mercy work together, Augustine says, but the latter encompasses, transforms, and brings human will to pass. As the Psalmist affirms, 'Misericordia eius praeueniet me' and 'Misericordia eius subsequetur me' (Your mercy shall precede me … Your mercy shall follow me [Psa. 58.11 and 22.6]); that is, 'Nolentem praeuenit, ut uelit; uolentem subsequitur, ne frustra uelit' (It precedes the unwilling person to make him willing; it follows the willing person so that he wills not in vain).[106]

Section 28 comprises another set of expositions on the will that echoes Augustine's statements in *De ciuitate Dei*. Chapter 104 addresses God's foreknowledge and sovereignty: though God foresaw human disobedience, Augustine says, God arranged history so as to fulfil his good plans in spite of humanity's evil choices. Chapter 105 speaks of the nature of volition in the life hereafter. In heaven, while the righteous will no longer be able to choose evil, their inability will constitute no limitation on their will; rather, they will so desire happiness that they will find it impossible to desire sin. Just as they will have a better kind of immortality, where they will no longer be able to die, so they will be granted a superior kind of freedom. Chapter 106 underscores that the will itself, through which individuals accept God's salvation, 'nec omnino per seipsum, sed per solam Dei gratiam … liberatur' (is freed … not at all by itself, but solely through the grace of God).[107] Finally, chapter 107 concludes that even eternal life, the reward for good works, is wholly unearned, since individuals' righteous merits ('bona merita') are themselves God's gifts. What is salvation, therefore, but grace given for grace ('gratia pro gratia redditur')?

De haeresibus

De haeresibus, written in 428, was one of the last works Augustine composed before his death and as such offers an experienced perspective on Pelagianism. Bede appears to have drawn on the work for his *Expositio*

Apocalypseos, but to date no evidence suggests that *De haeresibus* was otherwise known in England before the late eleventh century.[108] Pelagianism is the last heresy the work addresses, the 'newest of all heresies' which Augustine still labours to combat (ch. 88). The Pelagians deny people's need for grace, says Augustine – or rather, they define grace merely as the gifts of free will, the Law, and the teaching of Christ. They deny original sin with its corrupting effect on human desires, and deny that love (*caritas*), the source of righteous living and the fulfilment of the Law, is given to people by God. In short, says Augustine, they claim that human beings by their own efforts can live sinless lives. Augustine does not refute each of these assertions at length, but sets against them a series of scriptural passages: it is Jesus who draws people from the dominion of darkness so that they might believe (cf. Col. 1.13); it is the Father who alone enables people to come to Christ (cf. John 6.66); it is the Spirit who pours *caritas* into people's hearts (Rom. 5.5). Faith, righteous desires, and good deeds are all thus due to grace rather than human effort.

The six works summarized above clearly demonstrate that the main tenets of Augustine's position on free will would have been known in some form to Bede, despite the apparent absence in England of Augustine's mature works on the subject. Indeed, as the above shows, the primacy of grace is a pounding refrain through Augustine's works; Bede would have been bombarded with the message of human need – as would other authors drawing on these works in Anglo-Saxon England.

Augustine's Theology of Free Will in Works Known to Alfred

In comparison with the library of Bede, fewer Augustinian works are known to have been used by Alfred. On the one hand, Alfred was probably familiar with *De ciuitate Dei*. In that work, he would have encountered not only descriptions of the effects of the Fall on human volition, but a key discussion of foreknowledge that would have ramifications for his version of Boethius. Two letters he also likely knew: *Epistula* 147, *De uidendo Deo*, on envisioning the immaterial God and treating the distinction between knowledge (sight) and faith, and *Epistula* 211, written to nuns disgruntled with their new prioress, on order and unity; unlike *De ciuitate Dei*, in neither is free will a major subject of consideration. Finally, there are the *Soliloquia*.

The *Soliloquia* are an important source for Alfred, as he selected the work as one of 'the most needful for people to know' and invested himself personally in its translation. This dialogue between Augustine and Reason on the nature of the self and of God is unusual among the texts known in Anglo-Saxon England in that it is one of Augustine's early compositions. Written between 386 and 387 just before his baptism 'in the months when he was teetering on the brink of the change from Roman rhetorician to Christian apologist,'[109] it predates by a year the first book of De libero arbitrio and predates by nearly a decade the sea-change in his views on volition. Remarkably, however, though it does not treat the issue of free will directly, the text offers a perspective largely consonant with Augustine's later emphasis on grace.

Augustine in the Soliloquia begins his quest for knowledge by appealing to God the Father, Son, and Holy Spirit, and to all the Trinity; these prayers suggest the extent to which Augustine sees himself as relying on God. It is God, Augustine acknowledges, who teaches people to distinguish good from evil; God who frees them from slavery to worldly desires; God who keeps them from succumbing to temptation; God who causes them to thirst for righteousness and then satisfies their thirst; God who cleanses and God who converts (conuertit [I.1.3]). Certainly individuals' virtuous choices play a part: without faith, hope, and love, Reason says, no soul can be healed so that it may see or understand God (I.6.12). Unless one perseveres in these virtues, moreover, human effort (looking) will not result in understanding (sight [I.6.13]). Reason does affirm that God will free from the darkness of confusion those who believe and pray to him (II.6.9), and Augustine insists that he is making the requisite effort: 'Credo, et quantum possum obtempero; plurimumque ipsum deprecor, ut plurimum possim' (I believe and submit as much as I can, and I entreat him exceedingly so that I might do the most I can).[110] Whence, however, does this faith come? The beginning of Book II may supply the answer, as Augustine begins his inquiry afresh by saying, 'Credamus Deum affuturum' (Let us believe that God will help us). 'Credamus sane,' Reason responds, 'si uel hoc in potestate [nostra] est' (Let us believe indeed, if even this is in our ability). 'Potestas nostra ipse est' (He himself is our ability), Augustine concludes.[111]

One should be careful in reading too much into such statements; Augustine is here more concerned with speaking humbly than speaking precisely about individuals' capacity for faith and deeds. As we have noted, moreover, addressing the issue directly some eight years later, he will argue that faith is human choice rather than God's gift. Revealing in this regard may be a comparison between his classic appeal in the *Confessiones* – 'Da quod iubes, et iube quod uis' (Give what you command, and command what you will) – with an analogous prayer here: 'Iube, quaeso, atque impera quidquid uis, sed ... sana et aperi oculos meos, quibus nutus tuos uideam ... et omnia me spero quae iusseris esse facturum.'[112] *Spero* is, of course, the major point of difference: the *Confessiones* convey no doubt as to the realization of God's gift, but rather a confidence that God will bring about the whole of human righteousness. Nonetheless, a reader already familiar with Augustine's later thought could easily read the *Soliloquia* in terms of that mature perspective.

Also significant for Alfred is the fact that the text also portrays God in distinctly Neoplatonic terms, using language similar to that found in Boethius's *De consolatione Philosophiae*, which Alfred likewise turns into Old English. It is through God's laws, for example, that 'motus instabilis rerum mutabilium ... semper ad similitudinem stabilitatis reuocatur' (the unstable movement of changeable things ... is always recalled to the imitation of stability).[113] Through these laws, too, 'arbitrium animae liberum est, bonisque praemia et malis poenae, fixis per omnia necessitatibus distributae sunt' (the soul's choice is free, and rewards are distributed to the righteous and punishments to the wicked by compulsions firmly fixed in all things).[114] We will have cause to explore the implications of such imagery in due course; for the present, however, suffice it to say that in addition to presenting Alfred with an orthodox perspective of humanity's need, the *Soliloquia* also set the will in a Neoplatonic framework.

Like Bede, Alfred likely had not read Augustine's mature works on free will; like Bede, his knowledge of Augustine's basic thought would not have suffered unduly as a result. *De ciuitate Dei* alone would have provided ample teaching on the subject, and from that teaching the *Soliloquia* would not have detracted. Had Alfred known more than an extract from the *Retractationes*, moreover, a text on which he alone among Anglo-Saxon authors seems at one point to have drawn,[115] a sketch even of Augustine's major works would have been available to him. The penultimate entry, for example, is *De gratia et libero arbitrio*, written against 'eos qui, cum defenditur Dei gratia, putantes negari liberum arbitrium, sic ipsi defendunt liberum arbitrium ut negent Dei gratiam, asserentes eam secundum merita nostra dari.'[116]

Augustine's Theology of Free Will in Works Known to Lantfred

While the perspective offered by Lantfred's *Carmen de libero arbitrio*, as we shall see, is predominantly Boethian rather than Augustinian,

Michael Lapidge's recent edition of Lantfred's primary work, the *Translatio et miracula S. Swithuni*, identifies a number of Augustinian texts known to this author. The two works certainly used by Lantfred, *De ciuitate Dei* and *Enarrationes in psalmos*, have been dealt with above; relying on them alone, Lantfred would have received a clear impression of Augustine's doctrine. The *Epistulae* and *Sermones*, a number of which will be considered under Ælfric's sources, would only have deepened this familiarity, though it is unclear as to how many of the letters and sermons Lantfred would have encountered.

Two works remain that Lantfred probably knew. *De trinitate*, first of all, written between 399 and 419, does not have volition as its focus; it does, however, set forth clear statements regarding human corruption and God's sovereignty. Humans, on the one hand, having destroyed their strength, cannot return to righteousness unless God calls them to repentance and forgives their sins (XII.11.16). Thereafter, God regenerates people by his grace (V.11.12 and XIII.16.21) so that they may imitate Christ in loving God (VI.5.7). This grace God gives freely, not on the basis of merit (IV.1.2), for merit too is the gift of God (XIV.15.21). In all things, Augustine concludes, the sovereignty of God is paramount: in heaven as on earth, God's will 'per cuncta diffundit, et utitur omnibus ad incommutabile arbitrium sententiae suae ... siue bonis per eius gratiam siue malis per propriam uoluntatem.'[117]

Second, there are the *Quaestiones in Heptateuchum*, composed as Augustine was finishing *De trinitate* around 419. Among the issues addressed by the work are two of particular relevance to our inquiry. First, there is the statement in Exodus that God 'hardens' Pharaoh's heart[118] – a difficult passage about which Augustine has some difficult words. To begin with, Augustine notes, God hardens Pharaoh's heart so that he might display his miraculous power; God uses the wicked, therefore, to bring about good. By no means did God make Pharaoh wicked; rather, that wickedess grew out of Pharaoh's own choice ('inoleuit ex arbitrio uoluntatis'). At the same time – and here Augustine touches carefully on a disturbing aspect of the Fall – the underlying, corrupt nature that prompted Pharaoh's choice was the result of Providence rather than volition: 'Qualitate mala ut huc uel illuc moueatur ... quae causae ut existant uel non existant, non est in hominis potestate; sed ueniunt ex occulta prouidentia, iustissima plane et sapientissima.'[119] Again, the fact that God's patience moved Pharaoh to resistance rather than submission was Pharaoh's own fault ('uitii proprii fuit'); nonetheless, the fact that Pharaoh by his own fault would resist

was due to God's dispensation ('dispensationis fuit diuinae'). Individ-·
uals' corrupt nature does not excuse them from their misdeeds: the
wicked may not have control over their evil impulses ('causae ... non
sunt in eorum potestate'), but their wicked actions proceed from their
own evil choices. When God says that he will harden Pharaoh's heart,
Augustine concludes, what he means is 'Quam durum sit demon-
strabo' (I will show how hard it is).[120]

The other passage, treating the commandments given to Moses, discusses the means by which humans become able to obey. Drawing on one
of his favourite passages on volition, Augustine affirms that both parties
are involved in the work of righteousness. On the one hand, it is God
who works in individuals both to will and to do ('Deus est enim qui operatur in uobis et uelle et perficere' [Phil. 2.13]); on the other hand, God
calls people to work out their salvation ('uestram salutem operamini'
[Phil. 2.12]). Individuals may thus be said to 'cooperate' with God ('Operatur ergo ille, cooperamur nos'), but only in the sense that their efforts follow and depend on God's initative – as Lantfred would have known
from *De trinitate, Enarrationes in psalmos,* and *De ciuitate Dei.*[121]

Augustine's Theology of Free Will in Works Known to Wulfstan

In addition to the *Tractatus* on John's Gospel, the theology of which
will be treated as part of Ælfric's sources, there were at least two works
by Augustine that Wulfstan knew in whole or in part: *De baptismo contra Donatistas* and *In Ioannis epistulam ad Parthos tractatus x.* The former
was written between 400 and 401 against the Donatists' denial of the
validity of sacraments administered by 'impure' agents. Part of the
importance of the Donatist controversy, as we have had occasion to
note, was the precedent it set for Augustine's understanding of the efficacy of grace in spite of human will. Just as in his mercy God 'supplied
what had been wanting' (quod defuerat compleuit) in the thief on the
cross, who had faith but had not baptism (cf. Luke 23.42–3), so God
supplies what is wanting in baptized infants who perish, who have the
sacrament but not faith.[122] In God's chosen, therefore, grace not only
brings about faith, but can do so with no assistance from human volition. By inference, moreover, just as heretics may receive the grace of
baptism against their will, one might conclude that grace may change
individuals' desires even in the face of their opposition.

The other work known to Wulfstan was Augustine's treatise on I
John, begun in 407 or 408 and completed between 415 and 416. Among

the passages treated herein is I John 3.3: 'Omnis qui habet spem hanc in ipso, castificat semetipsum, sicut et ipse castus est' (Everyone who has this hope [of salvation] in him purifies himself even as [Christ] is pure).[123] Look, Augustine says: the writer has not taken away free will, for believers are commanded to make themselves pure. At the same time, however, who purifies human beings but God? You purify yourself, explains Augustine, when 'adiungis uoluntatem tuam Deo' (you join your will to God), like the Psalmist who calls on God to be his helper – that is, to assist his righteous efforts (Psa. 26.9). Ultimately, however, the believer cannot attribute his righteousness to himself: 'Castificas te, non de te, sed de illo qui uenit ut inhabitet te' (You purify yourself not by yourself, but by him who comes to dwell in you).[124]

Wulfstan does not draw on the passages mentioned here for his work, and it is uncertain whether he knew them; the extract he uses from De baptismo speaks about wolves in the church and sheep without, imagery he no doubt found appealing. Nonetheless, had he encountered these texts in full, he would have found clear statements on Augustine's view of grace.

Augustine's Theology of Free Will in Works Known to Ælfric

The Two Exceptions

As with the four Anglo-Saxon writers above, the vast majority of Ælfric's known Augustinian sources suggest that to Ælfric Augustine's major works on free will would have been unknown. Two potential exceptions, however, ought to be considered. Smaragdus, on the one hand, includes one selection from De praedestinatione sanctorum: sections 15.31–16.32, which at least some Smaragdus manuscripts correctly identify as the work of Augustine. The subject is an odd one: here, in the process of arguing that the entirety of humanity's salvation is contingent on grace, Augustine points to the example of Christ's incarnation. Did the human nature which Christ assumed have any preceding faith or good deeds to merit being united with Christ's divinity? Augustine asks. In the same way, 'gratia fit ab initio fidei suae homo quicumque christianus' (it is by grace that any one from the beginning of his faith becomes a Christian).[125] Such grace is expressed in God's call: not his general call for people to be saved, but the call that itself brings faith about ('qua uocatione fit credens').[126] This passage from De praedestinatione is one of literally hundreds of patristic extracts packed together in Smaragdus, and as

Ælfric does not quote the text, there is no way of knowing whether he read it or whether his copy of Smaragdus even identified it as Augustinian. A similar uncertainty surrounds *De correptione et gratia* 11.28 and 13.39, two passages which Godden has cited as potential sources for Ælfric's major discussion of free will in *CH* I.7, his first homily for Epiphany.[127] Section 11.28, to begin with, addresses Adam's state before the Fall: God made people with free will, Augustine says, so that through obedience he could win the eternal blessing of being unable to sin, or through disobedience bring all of humanity under God's just condemnation. That some are saved is made possible solely by grace – gratuitous grace ('gratia fit, gratis fit').[128] Section 13.39, in turn, states that the number of the saved is fixed, that these have been 'called according to the purpose' [Rom. 8.28] – that is, given faith through God's irresistible call – and that their good works are evidence of their calling and salvation.[129] While such passages would be somewhat informative of Augustine's teaching on free will, however, it is uncertain as to whether Ælfric encountered them at all, let alone as part of a lost copy of *De correptione*. Even as he notes some similarities between between *CH* I.7 and these passages, Godden states that there is 'little that suggests a direct debt.' The relevant portion of 11.28, in fact, occasionally appears in Carolingian treatises on predestination, and while no evidence suggests that such served as Ælfric's immediate source, 'it seems likely that he knew it as a quotation or extract.'[130] If Ælfric did read these sections of *De praedestinatione* and *De correptione*, therefore, they would have taught that grace brings about faith, that God's call to his chosen is irresistible, that Adam's sin made it impossible for human beings to save themselves, and that they now rely on God's gratuitous intervention. These passages would probably have been the only parts of these works, moreover, that Ælfric would have known.

What view then would Ælfric have had of Augustine's teaching on the will? Examining the various extracts in Paul the Deacon and Smaragdus and the assorted texts known to Ælfric, we find that they address at least three key aspects of this issue: (1) original sin and the corruption of human nature, (2) the divine origin of faith, and (3) the divine origin of good works.

The Corruption of the Will

Examining the effects of the Fall on human moral capacity, first of all, the Augustinian selections in Paul the Deacon's homiliary are careful to state that human nature is corrupt rather than evil. This distinction is precipitated by a discussion of Christ's accusation to the Pharisees that 'Vos ex patre diabolo estis.'[131] Jesus does not here suggest, Augustine argues, that human beings are literally descended from a family of darkness and derived from the principle of evil, as the Manichaeans would have it. God made human nature good, and even now it is good in the sense of being derived from what is good rather than what is evil. Humanity's contribution, on the other hand, their choice of evil or 'evil will,' has corrupted this nature, so that like the Jews they become children of the devil by imitating him.[132] Rather than having two natures, then, which battle one another, Augustine maintains that people have a good nature which they voluntarily have made depraved.[133]

This said, the Augustinian texts on which Ælfric draws apart from Paul the Deacon suggest that individuals are marked by an inward division between the flesh and the spirit. The Lord's Prayer reflects this, Augustine says, for people petition God for his will to be done on earth, in their flesh, as it is in heaven, in their spirit (cf. Matt. 6.10). While God ultimately will bring about concord between the two, in this life the law of the flesh wars against the law of the mind.[134] Such division does not imply that people have latent righteous impulses that strive with darker desires. Augustine makes it clear that left to themselves, people will be entirely evil: 'Nemo habet de suo, nisi mendacium et peccatum.'[135] On the contrary, he says, the fact that individuals resist their fleshly cravings at all is due to God's grace: 'Sine dubio uinceris, si illum adiutorem non habueris.'[136]

In contrast to Ælfric's other sources, Smaragdus is less informative about the effects of the Fall on the will. One rare Augustinian extract that directly mentions free will is an explanation of Christ's parable of the plunder of the strong man's house (Matt. 12.29). Christ, Augustine says, comes into this world, which is subject to death and under the devil's power. By the 'stronger bonds' of his power, Christ frees his chosen from the devil's possession, in such a way that now, without the devil hindering, they may believe in Christ by their own free will.[137] While the passage reflects Augustine's mature understanding of humans' will as in bondage prior to the intervention of grace, it does not explain the nature of this bondage: that people are able in theory to choose good, but bound in practice by their inevitable tendency to choose evil – a tension Augustine expresses summarily elsewhere by saying that the will is 'liberum, sed non liberatum; liberum iustitiae, peccati autem seruum' (free, but not freed – free from righteousness, but enslaved to sin).[138] Even if the passage is vague as to the precise effects of the Fall, however, it does suggest that the Fall has crippled human beings' ability to believe.

The Divine Origin of Faith

This said, certain passages in Paul the Deacon may give the impression that faith derives from human effort rather than God's grace. One metaphor Augustine uses to describe conversion, for example, is that of fishing. For believers, Augustine notes, the word of God should be like a hook to a fish: 'Capit quando capitur.'[139] Here there is an active role for the fish: conversion, it would seem, depends on believers responding to the lure of the word. Peter's request to walk with Christ on the water is a similar case. On the one hand, Augustine does note that it is Christ's call that enables Peter to believe. Jesus commands, supports, and directs, and he who previously had been afraid jumps without hesitation onto the water.[140] At the same time, however, it is Peter who first asks Jesus to call him to come (Matt. 14.28). A third example is Christ's statement that the Father gives good gifts to his children, even as human beings do when asked for bread, an egg, or fish (Matt. 7.9–11 and Luke 11.11–13). The fish, Augustine says, represents faith. Just as a strong fish is not broken by the waves, so faith may remain strong through the trials and tempests of the world, if it is not eaten or corrupted by the devil.[141] The context of the parable suggests that it is human beings that ask for the gift of faith, not God who preveniently bestows it. None of these texts, however, specifies the source of inspiration for the actions of the characters involved. Nor is this surprising: when addressing topics other than free will, Augustine often presumes the influence of grace even when he does not take the time to mention it explicitly. When Augustine does turn specifically to the origin of faith, however, by no means does he suggest that belief is due to human initiative. Coming to Christ's assertion that 'Ei uero qui non operatur credenti autem in eum qui iustificat impium, reputatur fides eius ad iustitiam,'[142] Augustine affirms: 'Et ipsum credere in Christum, opus est Christi. Hoc operatur in nobis, non utique sine nobis.'[143] The exact manner in which Christ brings about faith, however, especially in such a way as to be 'non sine nobis,' is not here addressed.

The Augustinian texts apart from Paul the Deacon provide further detail in this regard. While they affirm that faith comes from God, they also note that individuals cannot be forced to believe against their will. People may be forced physically to do something, but they must believe voluntarily. Augustine explains that instead of the will being drawn to God by force, it is drawn by a love or desire for good (*caritas*), just as it previously has been drawn to sin by its love or desire for evil (*concupiscentia*). Even as sheep may be drawn by the promise of a leafy branch, so the soul is drawn to God by what it desires most: 'Quo currit trahitur, amando trahitur, sine laesione corporis trahitur, cordis uinculo trahitur ... Quid enim fortius desiderat anima quam ueritatem?'[144] While this last statement may seem incompatible with Augustine's stark view of humanity's fallen nature, Smaragdus notes that the Spirit transforms individuals' hearts so that they desire and are drawn to what is good. The way this transformation is described, moreover, reflects not so much Augustine's early idea of congruent vocation as it does his mature belief in the Spirit's inward inspiration: 'Quod intellegunt, intus datur, intus coruscat, intus reuelatur.'[145] Such grace is irresistible: as Christ says, 'Omnis qui audiuit a Patre et didicit uenit ad me.'[146]

One way in which Smaragdus discusses the origin of faith is in his depiction of God's enlightenment of human beings. Commenting on Christ's healing of the man born blind, for example (John 9.1–7), Augustine explains that the man represents the human race, blinded through the sin of Adam, from whom it inherits both death and sin.[147] This man is directed to wash in the pool of Siloam just as believers are directed to the washing of baptism; in doing so, they are set free from their sin and enlightened by Christ. Smaragdus makes the connection plain: 'Illuminatio fides [est].'[148] The same point recurs following Augustine's comments on John 1.12: 'Quotquot autem receperunt eum, dedit eis potestatem filios Dei fieri his qui credunt in nomine eius.'[149] Rather than reproducing Augustine's final restatement of the verse, Smaragdus interjects a striking variation from one of Augustine's later works: 'Ergo potestas, ut filii Dei fiant, qui credunt in eum, cum hoc ipsum datur eis, ut credat in eum.'[150] Smaragdus makes it clear, moreover, that this faith is not given based on any human merit: 'Gratia ... praeuenit nos, ut simus amici ex seruis, ideo nobis non subrepat superbia, quasi pro nostris meritis aliquid acciperemus, dum filii irae fuimus, nunc autem filii Dei per gratiam effecti sumus, sine qua nihil possumus facere.'[151] The grace of faith, therefore, is both gratuitous and prevenient.

The Divine Origin of Good Works

For Augustine, Christ's statement that 'Sine me nihil potestis facere' (Without me you can do nothing [John 15.5]) has bearing on human beings' righteous deeds as well as their faith. Granted, in Paul the Deacon the principle is sometimes obscured by passages exhorting individuals to repentance and good deeds. Augustine calls on people to 'Amplectimini ueritatem, *ut* accipiatis libertatem,' or 'Dele quod fecisti, *ut* Deus saluet quod fecit,' going so far as to say that he who does so 'cum Deo facit' (works with God).[152] On their own, such statements make it sound as though individuals' efforts somehow achieve their freedom and salvation. As Augustine later will make clear in *De correptione et gratia*, however, while human beings must be urged to change, it is God who brings change about. Here, for example, when Augustine emphasizes the need for repentance, he also notes that 'Peccatum tuum non tibi displiceret, nisi Deus tibi luceret, et eius ueritas tibi ostenderet.'[153]

Men's dependence on God is more explicit in Augustine's discussion of Christ's statement that 'Ego sum uitis uos palmites' (I am the vine; you are the branches [John 15.5]). Augustine stresses that the branches contribute nothing to the vine, but derive their life and subsequent growth from it. God does include the branches so that they contribute to the process, but it is God who enables them even to do this. While not mentioning the Pelagians by name, Augustine scoffs at those who assert that people of their own power are able to act righteously; this, he says, is entirely the work of the Divine Gardener.[154] Augustine notes that Paul himself does not attribute his apostolic endeavours to his own effort, saying rather that 'Gratia autem Dei sum id quod sum.'[155] When Paul goes on to say that this grace was not fruitless, but that he laboured more than the rest of the apostles, moreover, Augustine admonishes: 'Quasi tibi coepisti tribuere, quod paulo ante Deo dederas. Agnosce, et sequere: "Non ego autem, sed gratia Dei mecum."'[156]

While the texts in Paul the Deacon affirm God's role in good works, however, they explain neither the exact nature of God's work, nor how human efforts play a part. What can people contribute, if all is due to God? On the one hand, Paul calls upon believers to 'Cum metu et tremore vestram salutem operamini'; on the other, he acknowledges that 'Deus est enim qui operatur in uobis et uelle et perficere.'[157] Commenting on the passage, Augustine affirms that this is a work 'quod utique in illo, sed non sine illo Christus operatur' (which Christ certainly works in [man], but not without him).[158] He does not disclose, however, precisely how this may be so.

While the Augustinian extracts in Smaragdus have little to say on the divine origin of good works, the miscellaneous texts on which

Ælfric draws are firm on the matter. Love for God, or *caritas*, which is the fulfilment of the Law (Rom. 13.10), cannot be gained through human effort; it is instilled (*diffusa est*) into the believer's heart by the Spirit.[159] In consequence, people should not be daunted by the task of righteous living; rather, Augustine says, 'Nemo ergo dicat, "Quis illud potest?" Contendite haec implere in cordibus uestris. Tenete ut diligatis. Luctamini et uincetis.'[160] The reason why people may strive with confidence, however, is because 'Christus ibi uincit.'[161] To accomplish good, therefore, human beings should pray for God's help; indeed, God wants individuals earnestly to desire his intercession, so that his gifts should not be taken lightly. Prayer itself, however, comes from the Spirit's inspiration: 'Ipsum desiderium ipse insinuauit.'[162]

Augustine affirms that people depend on God not only for individual deeds, but for the lifelong perseverance necessary for believers – the importance and gratuity of which Augustine will argue at length in *De dono perseuerantiae*. Here, however, to those who admit that they received faith but think that they preserved it thereafter by their own power, Augustine is content to quote Psalm 126.1: 'Nisi Dominus custodierit ciuitatem frustra uigilat qui custodit eam.'[163] 'Labora, custodi,' he says, 'sed bonum est ut custodiaris. Nam custodire te non suffices.'[164] Similarly, when Paul, towards the end of his life, reflects that 'Bonum certamen certaui cursum consummaui,'[165] Augustine admonishes: 'Cursum consummasti: quo ducente, quo regente, quo iuuante? ... neque uolentis, neque currentis, sed miserentis est Dei.'[166]

Augustine's Theology as Known to Anglo-Saxon Writers: Summary

Augustine's teaching in the sources known to our five Anglo-Saxon writers may thus be summarized as follows: Human nature is not inherently evil, but has been corrupted by the Fall so that individuals struggle against fleshly desires. The fact that people struggle at all is due to grace; left to themselves, they will invariably choose evil. Augustine depicts humanity as bound and blind, needing Christ to free and illumine them before they can believe. God does not force people to believe; rather, through the Spirit's inward inspiration he changes individuals' desires so that they are drawn to him. From the beginnings of faith to perseverance in good works, therefore, the salvation of human beings is due to God. As Augustine says, 'Numquam fit a te, quod non ipse facit in te.'[167]

Our survey of passages on free will in the works above has by no means been exhaustive; in no way, moreover, does this chapter address the multifarious means by which Augustinian theology may indirectly have impacted Anglo-Saxon writers. Nonetheless, one conclusion does emerge from this discussion: remarkably, despite the absence in England of Augustine's major treatises on free will, the texts that were available to these authors present both a consistent and fairly complete picture of Augustine's mature teaching on grace. Granted, these writers may have been familiar with more of Augustine's work. Apart from direct quotations, moreover, we cannot guarantee that they read, understood, or remembered every relevant passage in their putative sources. Nor is it clear that they could have identified Augustine's early work had they encountered it, or that they expected developments in Augustine's theology rather than a uniform presentation of doctrine.[168] We can establish, however, that each of these authors had the resources to gain an accurate portrait of Augustine's thought. The question now is how they responded to it, especially in the face of competing influences. One such influence would undoubtedly have been the teaching of that Father whose influence on Anglo-Saxon England was likewise profound: Gregory the Great.

CHAPTER TWO

Cooperating with Grace:
Gregory the Great,
Apostle to the English

Perhaps the most widely read author in the Western church until the
revival of interest in Augustine's works in the twelfth century,[1] Gregory
the Great was a man whose impact on Anglo-Saxon England was profound, for it was he who was responsible for the mission of Augustine of
Canterbury in 596 which led to both the conversion of England to Roman
Christianity and the introduction of the Benedictine Order.[2] Ælfric,
for example, names Gregory the *Engliscre ðeode apostol* (Apostle to the
English);[3] he is an authority upon whom Ælfric draws in over half of
the *Sermones catholici* and to whom Ælfric refers more often than all the
other Fathers combined – even when one excludes the homily devoted to
Gregory's life and the Augustinian mission (*CH* II.9).[4] As we will see,
Ælfric was not alone in his knowledge and appreciation of this patristic
authority: all five of our Anglo-Saxon authors, in fact, had access to or
show familiarity with Gregory's writings. As all but Alfred were or were
heavily influenced by Benedictine monks, such acquaintance should
come as no surprise: though perhaps not a Benedictine himself, Gregory
played a key role in the growth of the movement, both through the
Augustinian mission and through his widely read account of Benedict's
life and miracles.[5] For Anglo-Saxon writers, therefore, Gregory was – at
least in theory – an authority to be reckoned with. That potential influence
has important ramifications for our authors' understanding of free will,
for Gregory departs significantly from Augustine in his view of volition.

Gregory as Monk, Politician, and Man of Action

In some ways, the world had changed little in 160 years. The Rome to
which Gregory the Great succeeded as bishop in 590 was a city in crisis –

a crisis all too reminiscent of Augustine's last days at Hippo.[6] Another Germanic tribe, the Lombards, had invaded Italy in 568; partly pagan, partly Arian, they had established footholds in regions near Rome and by 586 were again besieging towns and ravaging the countryside. Refugees flooded into the city; food and other resources grew scarce. Then in 589 the Tiber overflowed: houses were swept away, granaries were destroyed, and plague was loosed upon the land.

In many ways, Gregory's background and views paralleled other writers treated in this work. Like Augustine, he was a bishop who suppressed Donatists in Africa and wrote amid the attack of heterodox invaders. Like Boethius, whose writing Alfred would later adapt into Old English, he was related to the powerful Anicii family and appointed prefect, the highest civil administrator in Rome. Like Augustine, Lantfred, Wulfstan, and Ælfric, he was a monk – the first monk, in fact, appointed to the papal see – and a keen supporter of the Benedictine movement. Like Æthelwold, episcopal superior to Lantfred and Ælfric at Winchester, he incurred opposition by placing monks in key ecclesiastical positions. And like Wulfstan, he saw the trials inflicted upon the people as a divine punishment for their sins.

Gregory came to his ultimate office with skills honed by a series of other posts. As prefect in 573, he was responsible for providing for the security, finances, and food supply for the city – experience on which he would draw directly as pope. On his father's death in 574 or 575, however, he seemingly renounced the political life in favour of monasticism, dispossessing himself of his inherited wealth, turning his ancestral home into a monastery dedicated to St Andrew, and establishing six other monasteries on family estates in Sicily. His contemplative retreat was not to last: within three years, he was ordained a deacon, probably by Pelagius II (bishop of Rome, 578–90), who in 579 appointed him papal representative to the imperial court at Constantinople. There he remained until late 585 or early 586, living as part of a community of monks who had accompanied him from St Andrew's. Discussions with these monks at Constantinople would form the basis for Gregory's monumental *Moralia in Iob*.

While at court, Gregory appealed to Emperor Maurice (582–602), to whose eldest son he was godfather, for aid against the Lombards' attacks on Italy. Maurice was reluctant to sign a truce with the Lombards, fearing that such a move might be seen to 'legitimize' their presence in his lands. In 586, however, Maurice had his exarch or imperial representative in Italy pay a considerable sum to the invaders to secure a truce. The peace was not to last: hostilities continued after Gregory was recalled to Italy to serve as adviser to Pelagius II. As a result, when the latter's death to plague in 590 brought Gregory to the papacy, Gregory found himself facing a triple threat of disease, famine, and Lombard depredation – and this time the emperor did not help.

It is difficult to say to what extent Gregory's circumstances, like those of Augustine, influenced his theological writings; what is clear, however, is that in the absence of sovereign intervention, Gregory acted decisively on his own. On the one hand, even before his official consecration, Gregory took charge of the city, organizing a three-day series of penitential processions of clergy and laity to seek God's mercy in ending the plague. Next, having appealed in vain to the exarch for assistance, and over the exarch's protestations, around 593 Gregory independently arranged peace through a substantial payment to the Lombard king. Maurice (ironically) called Gregory's policy of conciliation foolish, but Gregory argued that, fearing God, he sought to avoid the destruction even of his enemies.[7] Throughout, moreover, up to his death in 604, Gregory sought to instruct his charges in the faith through a series of influential works.

Gregory as Preacher, Teacher, and Writer

Predominant among Gregory's writings are his biblical commentaries. The *Homiliae xl in Euangelia*, to begin with, is a collection of forty homilies or exegetical treatments of Gospel readings preached during Gregory's first years as pope (590–2). The first twenty were read on Gregory's behalf when he was prevented from preaching by ill health; the second twenty he preached directly, had transcribed, and then revised in 593. In terms of influence, they are arguably the jewel of Gregory's homiletic crown. Patricia DeLeeuw describes them as 'simple, straight-forward expositions ... which use *exempla* to illustrate their moral lesson and avoid complex exegesis and theology. Less solemn and more accessible than the homilies of Augustine,' they were 'used far more often than any other homily collection in the Carolingian world.'[8] If the *Homiliae in Euangelia* are pastoral works intended for popular address, however, another tone altogether is found in the *Homiliae in Ezechielem*, twenty-two homilies preached around 593 in the face of the Lombards' siege of Rome. Considering the symbolism of Ezekiel's vision of a new temple, Gregory offers his audience comfort as well as instruction, a peace gained through sublime contemplation.

Taken down stenographically at the time of address, the homilies were revised by Gregory eight years later. Two other commentaries survive at a slightly further remove, having been dictated from memory by a monk present at the original address: *Homiliae ii in Canticum Canticorum*, written perhaps in the early years of his pontificate, of which only a portion (treating Song of Songs 1.1–8) survives, and *In librum primum Regum expositionum libri vi*, written perhaps during his middle years as pontiff and treating I Samuel 1–16. Other works once preserved in a similar fashion apparently included Gregorian commentaries on Proverbs, the Prophets, and the Heptateuch, but these are lost to us. One work that has been seen as a commentary on all of scripture, however, given the numerous passages of exegesis interwoven therein,[9] is the *Moralia siue Expositio in Iob*. Based initially on a set of conversations with fellow monks at Constantinople, and revised at least through the mission of Augustine of Canterbury in 596, to which it refers (XXVII.11.22), it grew to a mammoth thirty-five books treating what some have called 'the totality of Christian doctrine from God the Creator to God the Rewarder.'[10] Drawing on Augustinian hermeneutical principles, the *Moralia* perhaps more than any other work established the fourfold system of biblical interpretation – understanding scripture as speaking on historical or literal, allegorical, tropological or moral, and anagogical or prophetic levels – as a standard for the Middle Ages.[11]

Less certain, though worthy of mention, are Gregory's contributions to the liturgy. Most important may be his influence on the so-called Gregorian Sacramentary, a book of prayers offered by the celebrant of the mass. The degree to which such liturgical material is original to Gregory is a matter of some debate: while scholars agree that he composed at least some of the prayers, perhaps during the period between 593 and 596, the earliest extant copy of the Sacramentary is an amalgamation of material that postdates Gregory by some two centuries. As such, the version reflects the complex process of revision to the Roman liturgy in the interim that tends to obscure its Gregorian core.[12]

In addition to the commentaries and his putative liturgical writings, three other works by Gregory survive. The first of these is the *Registrum epistolarum* or *Epistularum libri xiv*, a compendium of some 814 letters drafted by Gregory over the course of his pontificacy. Some are official in nature, relating to the conferment of offices, administration of papal estates, and so on; others impart spiritual direction. The question of authorship of this material should be approached with a certain degree of caution, however, as the final product may have been influenced by formulae or templates developed by the lateran chancery responsible for papal correspondence.[13] At least one of these letters was of particular importance for Anglo-Saxon England: the *Libellus responsionum* or series of replies by Gregory to questions posed by Augustine of Canterbury regarding the fledgling English church; preserved as *Epistularum libri xiv* XI.4.64, a version of the *Libellus* was also transmitted by Bede in his *Historia ecclesiastica gentis Anglorum* (I.27).[14] Second, there are the *Dialogorum libri iv*, written between 593 and 594 in the form of a conversation between Gregory and Peter the Deacon, Gregory's secretary and later biographer. The fourth book deals with Last Things: death, judgment, and the life hereafter – not inappropriate subjects given the devastations facing Rome at that juncture. The first three books, however, describe the lives and miracles of sixth-century saints, with the second book dedicated exclusively to Benedict of Nursia, founder of Benedictine monasticism. Along with Gregory's sponsorship of Augustine's mission to England, this work was a key factor in promoting the spread of the order, ensuring the widespread dissemination and influence of Gregory's writings as a result.[15] Finally, there is the *Regula pastoralis*, composed during the first months of his pontificate. Its four books discuss the selection of men for pastoral service, the virtues with which they ought to live, the appropriate methods for preaching to various types of people (forty in all), and the need for pastors to guard themselves against pride and personal ambition. Profoundly influential, the *Regula pastoralis* would be to clergy what Benedict's *Regula* was to his monks.

Not all the works have volition as their focus; some, indeed, seem hardly to touch on the subject. Few studies have been published, moreover, on Gregory's teaching on free will. Nonetheless, the consensus of those works available to our Anglo-Saxon writers appears to be that Gregory departs significantly from Augustinian thought: prevenient grace does not make humans irresistibly choose good, Gregory suggests, but enables them either to cooperate with or to reject God.

Gregory's Debt to and Departure from Augustine in His Theology of Free Will

Gregory's theology does far more than simply echo the principles of Augustine. Gregory's debt to the African Father is both pronounced and subtle, that of a faithful follower who nonetheless has his own perspective and concerns. 'Almost everything in him has its roots in Augustine,' Reinhold Seeberg states, 'and yet almost nothing is genuinely Augustinian.'[16]

Carole Straw likewise adds: 'Gregory's spirituality is often little more than variations of tradition; yet slight changes can be of great consequence ... This is particularly true of Gregory's relation to Augustine.'[17] It is also particularly true of Gregory's teaching on free will. Augustine's mature position lays absolute stress on the primacy of grace, so that any suggestion that individuals may do something righteous apart from God is necessarily heretical. For Gregory, however, an exhortation to righteous effort is fundamental to preaching.[18] While he affirms, therefore, that human will is so weak that it can accomplish nothing without God, Gregory does not say that it is without power altogether. People indeed require grace if they are to will good; nonetheless, having received it, their will is an original agent capable of cooperating with or rejecting God's grace. It is not merely the product of grace, as Augustine would have it, so transformed that it will inevitably obey. The result, as Jaroslav Pelikan puts it, is that 'the official Augustinianism of Gregory contained the possibility for subtle shifts from the doctrine of the sovereignty and necessity of grace ... to a reintroduction of the notions of merit and human initiative.'[19] Frederick Dudden summarizes it thus:

> In his doctrine of Grace, Gregory took up a position midway between pure Augustinianism and Semi-Pelagianism.[20] As against the former, he claimed some merit for man's consenting and co-operating will, and omitted the doctrines of irresistible grace and unconditional election. In opposition to the latter, he denied man's ability to initiate good, and gave the chief weight to the precedent and enabling grace of God.[21]

For readers respectful of both Church Fathers, therefore, this difference in thought inherently posed a potential interpretive challenge: when faced with analogous commentaries by both patristic writers – as Ælfric, at the very least, certainly was – which perspective, if either, would they choose? To the question of competing influences – a question made the more complex, as we shall see, by the writings of Bede, Boethius, Cassian, and Prosper – we will return in later chapters; first, however, we must clarify the extent to which Gregory was known in early England. How would his views have been transmitted to our Anglo-Saxon writers?

The Knowledge of Gregory in Anglo-Saxon England

In contrast to Augustine's vast corpus of writings, much of which appears not to have been known in Anglo-Saxon England, Gregory's few major works were consistently read and drawn upon down through the Anglo-Saxon period.[22] This trend may be demonstrated by turning again to four key bodies of information: Gregorian manuscripts surviving from the relevant centres, Gregorian manuscripts surviving from England as a whole during these periods, Gregorian sources used by the various authors, and continental collections of Gregorian material known to at least one of these authors.

In the first instance, in contrast to the dearth of early evidence for Augustine's works, material associated with Gregory survives from areas or centres associated with all five figures in our inquiry. We have two copies of the *Moralia* and possibly one copy of the *Dialogi* from Northumbria predating the death of Bede.[23] Three copies of Alfred's translation of the *Regula pastoralis* date from from Winchester prior to Alfred's death[24] and from Worcester prior to the death of Wulfstan.[25] Wulfstan's library at Worcester appears also to have contained copies of the *Dialogi* (both Gregory's original and the translation associated with Alfred's circle), the *Homiliae in Euangelia, Libellus responsionum*, and Latin *Regula pastoralis*.[26] Ælfric's libraries at Cerne and Eynsham are the only centres not represented, but then no pre-eleventh-century material from these centres survives save for London, British Library, Royal 7. C. xii, an early copy of Ælfric's First Series of *Sermones catholici* made at Cerne.[27]

When we expand our search to include Gregorian material throughout England during these periods, our list of texts expands somewhat. While copies of no works other than the *Moralia* and possibly the *Dialogi* predate Bede's death, eighteen manuscripts remain from the period ending with Alfred's death, including copies of the *Dialogi, Homiliae in Euangelia, Homiliae in Ezechielem, Moralia*, and *Regula pastoralis* (both Gregory's original and Alfred's translation).[28] Between Alfred's and Wulfstan's deaths, in addition to the works preserved at Worcester, we find copies of the *Moralia* and a selection of the *Registrum epistolarum*.[29]

Predictably, however, source studies suggest that more Gregorian texts were known to Anglo-Saxons than the extant manuscript evidence would indicate. In addition to the *Moralia* and *Dialogi*, copies of which may remain from Bede's Northumbria, Bede appears to have drawn on the *Homiliae in Ezechielem, In librum primum Regum expositionum libri vi, Homiliae ii in Canticum Canticorum*, the *Regula pastoralis*, portions of the *Homiliae in Euangelia*, and certain Gregorian letters.[30] As well as the *Regula pastoralis*, which he translated, and the *Dialogi*, a translation of which he commissioned from Wærferth, bishop of Worcester (872?–915?), Alfred likely knew the *Homiliae in Euangelia*.[31] Lantfred appears to have been familiar with the *Moralia, Homiliae in Euangelia, In librum primum Regum expositiones,* and some form of the *Epistularum libri xiv*.[32] Despite the presence of Gregory's works at Worcester, on the other hand, the extent to which Wulfstan knew Gregory at all remains unclear: source studies of Wulfstan to date have identified no Gregorian sources save for possible borrowings in one of Wulfstan's homilies.[33] Ælfric, by contrast, was familiar with up to four of Gregory's works.[34] His knowledge of Gregory's *Homiliae in euangelia* is attested by his heavy dependence upon them in the *Sermones*: Ælfric uses thirty-three of the forty homilies for his collection. The *Sermones* also draw on two if not three of the four books of the *Dialogi*, suggesting that Ælfric may have known the whole of the work; in one homily, indeed, he twice cites the *Dialogi* by name (*CH* II.21.115 and 177).[35] Two faint echoes of the *Regula pastoralis* may come from Alfred's version, which Ælfric is likely to have encountered at Winchester,[36] though it is difficult to believe that he had not read the Latin text as well. The evidence for Ælfric's knowledge of the *Moralia,* however, is somewhat more ambiguous.

On the one hand, when Ælfric came to write his homily on Job (*CH* II.30), one might expect him to have turned to the *Moralia* as a definitive reference on the subject. Godden, however, states that 'Ælfric's usual sources offer no precedent for this account of Job.'[37] Similarities between the *Moralia* and Ælfric's work have been noted: Lawrence Besserman points out parallels between the *Moralia* and *CH* II.30;[38] Arvid Gabrielson sees analogous passages in *CH* I.11 and 14,[39] John Pope cites the *Moralia* as a source for two of Ælfric's later homilies,[40] and Godden posits nine possible borrowings from the *Moralia* in *CH* I.31, I.34, I.40 and II.30. Few if any of the parallels are precise enough, however, to establish definitively Ælfric's knowledge of the text. One other passage from *CH* II.5 is a tempting candidate: in one of his most crucial statements on free will in the *Sermones*, Ælfric notes that 'Godes mildheortnys ús forestæpð. and his mildheortnys ús fyligð; Þa ða we wel noldon. ða forhradode godes mildheortnys ús þæt we wel woldon; Nu we wel willað. ús fyligð godes mildheortnys þæt ure willa ydel ne sy.'[41] One of the only other examples of such a concise formulation is found in the *Moralia,* where Gregory treats one of Augustine's favourite passages on the subject of volition: 'Quid autem habes, quod non accepisti?' (What do you have that you did not receive? [I Cor. 4.7]). Believers are doubly indebted to God, Gregory affirms, for it is God who 'et praeueniendo dedit eis bonum uelle quod noluerunt, et subsequendo concessit bonum posse quod uolunt.'[42] Unfortunately, however, an even closer parallel appears in Augustine himself: here, explaining the Psalmist's twin statements that 'Misericordia eius praeueniet me' and 'Misericordia eius subsequetur me' (His mercy shall precede me and His mercy shall follow me [Psa. 58.11 and 22.6]), Augustine states that 'Nolentem praeuenit, ut uelit; uolentem subsequitur, ne frustra uelit.'[43] Even if such references cannot establish that Ælfric had the *Moralia* in front of him when composing the *Sermones*, they may indicate that it was a work that Ælfric had read and occasionally recalled. For Godden, in the end, the evidence is sufficient: while the similarities suggest 'rather Ælfric's general familiarity with the *Moralia* than its immediate use,' Gregory's work was one which Ælfric 'evidently knew well.'[44] The issue is an important one, for perhaps in no other Gregorian work is the question of free will treated in greater detail.

Finally, there are the collections of Gregorian material found in Paul the Deacon and Smaragdus, the contents of which merely serve to corroborate the picture above. When we set forth the contents of the former and source all sixty-three authentic Gregorian extracts in the latter, it appears no wonder that Ælfric drew so freely on the *Homiliae in Euangelium*, nor that he would privilege the *Homiliae* over other Gregorian texts.[45] Thirty-two of the forty *Homiliae* were available in what Smetana has posited as the 'original' form of Paul the Deacon; thirty-nine appear in the later form of the homiliary preserved in PL 95.[46] No works by Gregory other than the *Homiliae* appear, moreover, in these collections. As one would expect, Smaragdus includes far smaller extracts of Gregory in his compendium (and fewer homilies – twenty-four in all), but here too nearly all his material comes from the *Homiliae*. One extract is from the *Dialogi*, two from the *Homiliae in Ezechielem*, and three from the *Moralia*, but these are the only exceptions. It would appear, in short, that while Ælfric may have read other works by Gregory – during his study at Winchester, for example – his primary immediate sources would have presented him primarily with exegesis of the Gospels.

Gregory's Theology of Free Will as Known to the Anglo-Saxons

To say that the above works may have been known to our Anglo-Saxon authors, however, does not mean that the works would have been informative on the subject of free will. While the issue does receive consideration in Gregory's far-ranging *Moralia in Iob*, for example, it is far less a concern in the *Dialogi* and *Regula pastoralis*. The *Homiliae in Euangelia*, from which Smaragdus supplies three scores of extracts, contains passages of more relevance to the topic, but the selections included by Smaragdus contain few references to free will, fewer that are correctly attributed to Gregory, and none that provide material to which Ælfric did not have access elsewhere.[47] One major difference, however, distinguishes Gregory's work from that of Augustine: while the African Father wrote over an extended period and developed considerably in his thought, Gregory produced most of his works in the first four to six years of his pontificacy (590–4/6).[48] Perhaps partly in consequence, Gregory's works show little development in doctrine.[49] In reconstructing Anglo-Saxons' knowledge of Gregory, therefore, the question is not whether particular works represent the pope's 'early' or 'mature' thought, but what they corporately teach on the issue of free will. Rather than surveying a wide spectrum of Gregory's writings, we may focus instead on those best known to our Anglo-Saxon authors: the *Regula pastoralis* and *Dialogi*, used by Bede, Alfred, and Ælfric, and likely present in Wulfstan's library; the *Homiliae in Euangelia*, available to Lantfred as well as to all the above; and the *Moralia in Iob*, known by Bede, Lantfred, and most likely Ælfric as well. To these authors, these four works would have conveyed at least four major aspects of Gregory's view of volition: humanity's corruption and the consequent tumult of their mind, human bondage and liberation, their blindness and enlightenment, and the origins of individuals' faith.

. *Corruption and the Divided Mind*

First, then, the Gregorian texts available to Ælfric present human beings as having been corrupted in their desires. One way in which such corruption is seen is the struggle between flesh and spirit that hamstrings even the believer's will for good. If Augustine describes this struggle as a binary conflict of two wills – the new one, developing in its desire for God, battling the old one, made strong by long indulgence[50] – Gregory employs more complex imagery. To begin with, Gregory notes that Adam was created upright and steadfast in his love for God, so that as long as he wished he would not swerve from it. Because Adam willingly chose change, however, human beings now bear the burdens of change unwillingly.[51] Gregory states that just as people's bodies are now harassed by hunger and disease, so their minds are torn between conflicting desires: when at rest they long for action; when busy, they pant for rest. They whirl between hope and fear, laughter and grief, desire and disillusion.[52]

Gregory's images reflect this confusing condition. At one point, following Jerome, he compares humans to the moon, which by its unceasing alteration reflects the instability of their mortal nature.[53] At another point, he describes humans' preoccupation with worldly things as a dense wood, the branches of which cut off both all sight of heaven and, paradoxically, the evil depths of their hearts.[54] Alternatively, he portrays humans' desires as a tumultuous crowd, an uproar of forbidden thoughts and memories of prior sins: here, though people strive through contemplation to concentrate on God alone, temptations urge them towards new sins even as memories of past failure threaten to drown their prayers.[55] As Gregory says in the *Moralia*:

> Tot itaque loca culmen mentis inclinant, quot subortae cogitationes unitatem bonae intentionis dissipant. Recta etenim mens staret, si uni cui debuerat cogitationi semper inhaereret. Recta mens staret, si non se in umeris motibus fluxa mutabilitate prosterneret.

> As many thoughts then as spring up and disperse the unity of good intention, so do as many places bend down the loftiness of the mind. For the mind would stand upright, if it always clung close to that one thought to which it ought. The mind would stand upright, if it did not, by its countless motions, debase itself in fluid change.[56]

In believers, however, God works to control the tumult of their desires. Indeed, for Gregory the contrast between the minds of the wicked and righteous is dramatic in this regard. Whereas the wicked soul without God is only able to fall – a position corresponding to Augustine's view of total depravity – holy people 'nullis procul dubio in corde tumultibus premuntur ... Solam namque aeternam patriam appetunt; et quia nulla huius mundi diligunt, magna mentis tranquillitate perfruuntur.'[57] Such a transformation is due solely to grace. In yet another image, for example, Gregory explains God's statement that he 'conclusit ostiis mare' (closes up the sea with doors [Job 38.8]). The sea, Gregory says, represents the human heart, surging with the force of various sinful desires. God restrains the sea, however, by inspiring people both with holy fear and love for God and their neighbour. This deterrent and goad serve as doors or as a bar over the heart, protecting people's virtues against the waves of temptation.[58] Put another way, Gregory affirms that God brings such order to believers' minds that where there was once a clamourous throng, God sits enthroned as a king with a host of virtues around him.[59] While people's wills are divided by their fleshly struggle, he concludes, by the Spirit's power they come to love what their flesh does not desire. Striving with the help of grace, they may ultimately become like Peter, who 'cruciatum martyrii nolendo uoluisset' (willed the torment of martyrdom even while he was unwilling).[60]

Bondage, Freedom, and the Cooperating Will

If Gregory follows Augustine in portraying the human struggle against the flesh as a result of the Fall, he is nonetheless far more concerned with individuals' sin than he is with that of Adam. This in turn is reflected in Gregory's depiction of human depravity. Gregory states, for example:

> In iniquitate namque concepti, et in delicto editi; per insitae corruptionis molestias pugnam nobiscum huc deferimus, quam cum labore uincamus ... Corruptionis namque malum, quod unusquisque nostrum ab ortu desideriorum carnalium sumpsit, in prouectu aetatis exercet; et nisi hoc citius diuinae formidinis manus reprimat, omne conditae naturae bonum repente culpa in profundum uorat.

> Being conceived in iniquity and born in sin, we bring with us into this world a contest, through the plague of innate corruptions, which we must · strive hard to overcome ... For the evil of corruption which each one of us has acquired from the springing up of his carnal desires, he exercises as he advances in years; and unless the hand of Divine fear speedily represses it, sin quickly swallows up all the goodness of created nature.[61]

In positing an original 'goodness of nature' (naturae bonum), Gregory does more than simply acknowledge, as Augustine does, that God made human nature good. Rather, as we shall see more fully in his teaching on enlightenment, Gregory envisages a process whereby people inherit the desire for evil at birth and bind themselves thereafter through their own evil habits. In this, he departs from Augustine's view of humanity's utter depravity.

One way in which Gregory describes the human condition is through an extended metaphor of a lioness that is lured into a pit. From that pit, he says, a tunnel leads to another pit in which there is a cage, and into this cage the lioness goes of her own free will. Thereafter, though the lioness may be drawn out of the pit, she cannot escape the cage that surrounds her. Likewise, Gregory explains, people fall from the freedom they once enjoyed when they seek to satisfy the cravings of their flesh. This is true not only in terms of the Fall of Adam, but in terms of believers' everyday experience, for they are constantly falling into the pit of pride. They become caged, Gregory says, when they continue to sin even after they have been rescued from the pit of condemnation, and as a result lack the power to do the things which they desire. Paradoxically, Gregory suggests that the cage thwarts people's desires for both good and evil, for he views the cage itself in multiple ways: first, it is the prison of human corruption that prevents people from accomplishing good; thereafter, it is the bonds of heavenly discipline that prevent believers from doing evil; and finally, it is the bars of self-discipline and humility by which believers guard themselves from pride.[62]

If Gregory presents a complex view of human bondage, so also does he present a complex view of their freedom. At times, Gregory's view seems largely Augustinian. Human beings are under the yoke of the devil's control, he says, until the Spirit anoints them 'gratia libertatis' (with the grace of freedom).[63] As with God's illumination of individuals (see below), this inspiration is swift: the Spirit, 'ruptis peccatorum nostrorum uinculis, citius nos ad libertatem nouae conuersationis ... perducit' (having burst the chains of our sins, leads us quickly ... to the liberty of our new life).[64] This does not mean that believers regain the original freedom of Eden: even when one 'prodire ad libertatem iustitiae nititur' (strives to go forth to the freedom of righteousness), he is still fettered by the corruption of the flesh.[65] Rather, Gregory explains, believers gain their freedom in three distinct phases.[66] First, he says, new converts may enjoy a period of freedom from their fleshly desires, as they experience the relief and joy of salvation. Second, lest they gain a false sense of confidence in their abilities, God allows them to be assaulted by various temptations. These are the more intense for believers as the devil redoubles his efforts to regain those he has lost. Finally, the elect reach the reward of heaven; here they are freed from temptation and gain the true 'libertate[m] uitae incorruptibilis' (freedom of a pure life).[67]

At other times, however, Gregory departs from Augustine, depicting human beings not as bound from birth as a result of Adam's sin, but free until they themselves submit to the devil's yoke – though even then they seem to retain some freedom to resist the tyranny of evil habits. Gregory states:

Quisquis se prauo desiderio subiicit, iniquitatis dominio *dudum libera* mentis colla supponit. Sed huic domino contradicimus, cum iniquitati quae nos
ceperat, reluctamur; cum consuetudini uiolenter resistimus, et desideria
peruersa calcantes contra hanc ius nobis libertatis ingenitae uindicamus.

Whoever yields himself up to bad desire, submits the neck of his mind, *till
now free*, to the dominion of wickedness. Now we withstand this master,
when we struggle against the evil whereby we had been taken captive
when we forcibly resist the bad habit, and treading under all forward
desires, maintain against the same the right of inborn liberty.[68]

Granted, Gregory may simply be presenting a general principle: it is
easier for people to resist their fleshly desires before they are enslaved
by habitual sin. In Augustine, however, there is no suggestion of an initial measure of freedom, let alone a 'ius libertatis ingenitae' (right of
inborn liberty), to which people can appeal. While Augustine agrees
that Christ 'frees' believers, it is clear that they are only on parole:
grace may suspend and even change people's evil desires, but in the
absence of grace, individuals will immediately revert to evil. Gregory,
by contrast, though he acknowledges the lingering presence of concupiscence, teaches that grace gives human beings a real freedom by
which they themselves may choose good. God 'uincula cordis soluit
ut ad uacationem paenitentiae mens nostra se erigat, et, carnis soluta
compedibus, in auctorem suum libera gressum amoris tendat.'[69]
Dudden puts it thus:

> While Augustine regards the co-operating will as a mere form under which
> grace unfolds itself – it being irresistibly determined from within so that its
> assent to the promptings of grace follows with certainty (the assent itself
> being a gift of grace) – Gregory attributes to it a real independence, in virtue
> of which, when once it is freed from the necessity of choosing evil, it can
> reject or co-operate with the grace that has freed it ... Thus, grace and free
> will are two independent, necessary factors in sanctification.[70]

Gregory himself puts it this way: 'Superna pietas prius ait in nobis
aliquid sine nobis ut, subsequente quoque nostro libero arbitrio,
bonum quod iam appetimus agat nobiscum.'[71] Grace comes first;
human consent follows; the two then work together (*agat nobiscum*).
When Gregory says that God 'praeueniendo dedit eis bonum uelle
quod noluerunt' (by preceding [men] enabled them to will the good

that they did not desire), therefore, he means not that God 'makes' people choose good, but that God makes people able to choose good. This ability implies a measure of freedom for the will that Augustine would not accept.

Gregory cites I Corinthians 15 on a number of occasions to illustrate the relationship between grace and the cooperating will. On the one hand, he says, in stating that 'Gratia autem Dei sum id quod sum,' Paul acknowledges that the elect are only righteous because God prevents them from sinning.[72] On the other hand, by saying that 'Gratia eius in me uacua non fuit, sed abundantius illis omnibus laboraui,' Paul shows that free will follows and yields its consent to grace.[73] At the same time, Paul is careful not to ascribe his labours to himself, adding, 'Non ego autem sed gratia Dei [mecum].'[74] Even so, Gregory concludes, Paul speaks of grace as 'mecum' 'ut et diuio muneri non esset ingratus, et tamen a merito liberi arbitrii non remaneret extraneus.'[75]

Gregory thus shows both parties at work. God may restrain believers from doing evil through the cage of his discipline, but individuals must also impose bars of self-control. God may free people from the devil's domination, but they must not forfeit their freedom by succumbing again to evil habits. God may free people's will to choose and do good, but individuals are responsible for accepting and acting on the grace they are given. Whatever virtue human beings may acquire, however, Gregory insists that they remember that their virtue is due to grace. As he says: 'Haec ergo dixi, ne quis in bono iam opere positus sibi uires boni operis tribuat.'[76]

Blindness and Illumination

A similar pattern is found in Gregory's treatment of human enlightenment. Like Augustine, Gregory describes people as blind as a result of the Fall.[77] He also says, however, that having focused on earthly things, people have lost inwardly the light of the invisible world 'quanto foras deformiter sparsa' (in proportion as it [their soul] was dissipated without) – that is, to the degree that it became/becomes wicked.[78] This is a revealing phrase, for in contrast to Augustine, Gregory does not depict humanity's blindness as absolute. Rather, focusing again on individuals' personal sin, he seems to suggest that people begin with some degree of understanding or sight, so that they become rather than are born blind.[79] Gregory says, for example, that each person is born in the daylight, though thereafter he 'in noctem nequissimae perpetrationis ruit' (rushes headlong into the night of the foulest practice).[80] People have healthy pupils, but their eyes become bleary, like one 'cuius sensum natura exacuit; sed conuersationis prauitas confundit' (whose sense nature has made keen, but whom a depraved habit of life confuses).[81] They are made in God's image, with the capacity of reason, so that each is 'naturae lege compellitur' (compelled by the law of nature) to distinguish between right and wrong.[82] While the Fall impairs humans' capacity for heavenly knowledge, therefore, it does not destroy it completely. William McCready notes, for example, that since God reveals himself through nature (Psa. 18.2–5 and Rom. 1.20), 'the same physical universe that drew us away from God can serve to call us back to him again.'[83] Recognizing that even the witness of nature may be beyond fallen humanity's ability to apprehend, moreover, God supplements this general revelation with the specific revelation of Christ. Wisdom, or Christ, 'semetipsam nobis quasi transeuntibus in mediis semitis fixit, ut uidelicet in eam, quam quaerere nolumus, impingamus.'[84] While people begin with the potential to see, however, they blind themselves and incapacitate their reason through their own disobedience. As Gregory says, 'Hoc ipsum namque malum quod agi menti se obicem ante oculum rationis interserit. Unde fit ut anima prius uoluntariis tenebris obsessa postmodum bonum iam nec quod quaerat agnoscat.'[85] In presenting human blindness as an acquired condition rather than an absolute state, Gregory's point is not to paint people in a positive light (so to speak); rather, it is to emphasize humanity's personal culpability: people cannot use their inherited weakness as an excuse for their own sin.

In keeping with this view of blindness as a progressive disease, Gregory also departs from Augustine in depicting blind humanity not as utterly corrupt but as able to desire and strain to see the light. Though people are no longer able to raise themselves to heavenly things, he notes, and generally lie prostrate in things below, sometimes a soul 'cum uero miris conatibus ab his exsurgere nititur' (with marvellous efforts strives to rise up [from the same]).[86] Though the unrighteous 'hac uita ... totis desideriis appetunt' (wholeheartedly pursue [the things of] this life), Gregory nonetheless affirms that 'plerique agere recta desiderant' (the greater number desire to do right).[87] While a person cannot muster the discipline needed for holiness, and will not succeed on his own, at times he 'resultare consuetudini quasi totis se uiribus parat' (seems to set himself with all his powers to make a stand against [evil] habit).[88] One crucial instance in which this is seen is in Gregory's exposition of the blind man outside Jericho (Luke 18.35–43).

Interpreting the blind man as the human race, which has become ignorant of the light of God's truth, Gregory observes that even while the
man is 'illuminandus' ([yet] to be enlightened), he recognizes his
need for healing, desires it, and perseveres in his petitions until he
receives sight.[89] Gregory presents the man's actions as an example for
all: 'Quisquis ergo caecitatis suae tenebras agnoscit ... clamet medullis
cordis ... dicens: "Jesu fili Dauid, miserere mei."'[90]

At the same time, Gregory acknowledges that it is only by God's
intervention that people desire to see the light. 'Per semetipsam,' he
says, 'in amore praesentis saeculi prostrata mens dormitat ... nisi diuinae gratiae aspiratione pulsetur'; 'Si manu subita superni respectus
excitamur, diu clausos mox eosdem ad ueritatis lucem oculos meritis
aperimus.'[91] Gregory defines the light of God, in fact, as 'gratia praeue-
niens quae si in nostro corde nequaquam gratuito consurgeret, profecto mens nostra in peccatorum suoum tenebris obscura remaneret.'[92]
While Gregory notes that this light comes generally to people through
Christ's incarnation, he also says that God restores the capacity of individuals to perceive their fallen state. To this end, Gregory variously
speaks of God illuminating (*illustrans*), irradiating (*irradians*), or kin-
dling (*succendens*) human minds.[93] Ultimately, of course, illumination
is a long process by which people come to know God; it begins, however, with a lightning-bolt. Gregory has no time for the subtleties of
congruent vocation: in his view, the Spirit 'humanum animum subito
ut illustrat immutat' (changes a human mind instantaneously to
enlighten it), as it did at Pentecost, reviving those who are dead in evil
habits like Lazarus from the grave.[94] Even as Saul is converted in the
very act of going to persecute the church in Damascus, Gregory says,
so it is with conversion in general: 'statim ... peccatricis mentis duritia
ab immobilitatis suae obstinatione permutatur' (instantly ... the obdu-
racy of the guilty soul is changed).[95]

Whereas Augustine views the Spirit's inspiration as inevitably efficacious, however, Gregory again insists that grace does not necessitate
human obedience.[96] The blind man outside Jericho may be an example
to human beings, but not all follow his example: like blind people sitting by the way (that is, Christ) who do not cry out for sight, individuals can come to believe in Christ's existence but have no desire for
God's light.[97] In the same manner, when treating the parable of the
Great Banquet (Luke 14.16–24), Gregory distinguishes between those
who are given understanding and choose to do good, and those who
refuse to do good in response to understanding.[98] Indeed, expounding

the analogous parable of the Wedding Feast (Matt. 20.2–14), Gregory notes that people can not only reject spiritual illumination, but oppose it so violently that they persecute God's messengers.[99] Those God enlightens thus have a real power for independent choice, either for good or evil.

Faith: Divinely Inspired and Meritorious

Gregory's depiction of enlightenment teaches, then, that God inspires human faith. Without God's prevenient and gratuitous gift of light, people will not open their eyes and desire to turn from the world to God. The primacy of grace was a point of some importance for Gregory, for, as we have had cause to note, earlier in the sixth century the Second Council of Orange had condemned the Semi-Pelagian view of faith as a meritorious human initiative. In the *Moralia*, Gregory strongly condemns those who suggest that individuals believe by their own power and are rewarded by God's grace thereafter. When God asks Job, 'Ubi eras quando ponebam fundamenta terrae?' for example,[100] Gregory explains that earth represents the soul of a just person, while the foundations of earth stand for faith. God lays this foundation in human beings when he breathes into their hearts the first cause of firmness, the fear of the Lord, so that individuals come to believe in him. On this foundation the edifice of virtues is then raised. People should remember their helpless origins, Gregory warns, lest they attribute their progress to their own power.[101]

This said, Gregory's teaching is not as straightforward in the *Homiliae*. Gregory notes, for example, that the Spirit was in the disciples' hearts to give them faith, but goes on to say that they received the Spirit's anointing because they deserved (*meruerunt*) it.[102] Again, he affirms that faith has merit (*meritum*) when it believes what it cannot grasp by reason, even to the point where it forms the basis for God's intervention: as Christ tells the blind man and the woman afflicted with bleeding, 'Fides tua te saluum fecit.'[103] While such statements might seem to suggest that God responds to individuals' faith, however (and as such appear dangerously close to Semi-Pelagianism), they do not actually indicate whence this faith comes.[104] What the *Homiliae* do make clear is that prior to conversion human beings have no capacity for good. Nurtured in vice, Gregory says, the unspiritual know nothing save the need to gratify their desires; everything they receive they turn into an opportunity for sin; they are, in short, darkness.[105] As a result, Gregory concludes: 'Hominis quippe meritum superna gratia non ut ueniat, inuenit, sed postquam uenerit, facit.'[106] Faith may be meritorious, but it is nonetheless due to grace.

Gregory's Theology of Free Will in Works Known to Anglo-Saxon Writers: Summary

In the texts available, then, to these five Anglo-Saxon writers, Gregory follows Augustine in asserting that humans are corrupted by fleshly desires. Like Augustine, Gregory portrays humanity's struggle as a result of the Fall. Likewise, Gregory teaches that God frees human wills to choose good. Where Augustine presents humanity's struggle as a battle of two wills, however, Gregory speaks of a throng of competing desires to which God brings order. Where Augustine views absolute corruption as human beings' state from conception, Gregory shows people becoming corrupt through their personal sin. Though Augustine believes that grace causes individuals inevitably to choose good, Gregory teaches that grace gives humans the freedom to cooperate with or reject God. Gregory suggests that even in their blindness, people can strain to see the light; like Augustine, however, he affirms that only God makes people see. Though he sometimes speaks of faith as meritorious, moreover, like the African Father, Gregory teaches that faith is due to grace.

Whereas for Augustine, therefore, God is absolutely responsible for human righteous achievements, for Gregory, human achievements are impossible without God's assistance. The difference is subtle but crucial, for while Gregory affirms that individuals must be helped by God at every step, he nonetheless carves out a clear place for their effort. Ultimately, however, Gregory stresses that from first to last, salvation comes from God. Like Job, he says, believers must acknowledge that 'Nudus egressus sum de utero matris meae et nudus reuertar illuc' – that is, 'Nudum me in fide prima gratia genuit, nudum eadem gratia in assumptione saluabit.'[107] It would be a third figure, arguably of comparable influence in Anglo-Saxon England, who would add to this affirmation of grace an emphasis on merit: the Venerable Bede.

CHAPTER THREE

Meriting Grace: The Venerable Bede

Between 673 and 674, the lands near the Northumbrian river Tyne saw two births that would prove of no minor import: that of a child named Bede and of the monastic community in which he would spend his days.[1] Entrusted to the monastery at Wearmouth at the age of seven and transferred to its twin foundation at Jarrow some years later, Bede lived in a world carefully circumscribed by the ritual, the walls of which, save for a few short trips, he would never leave. From those walls, however, and from the exceptional library which they contained, Bede engaged a vast array of subjects on which he left an indelible imprint. From his ordination as a priest around 703 to his death in 735, ranging from grammar to hagiography, *computus* to poetry, exegesis to history, Bede composed a collection of texts that would become standards of medieval study.

Bede's Works

Part of Bede's reputation in Anglo-Saxon England, as now, stemmed from his work as a historian: the *Historia abbatum*, examining the lives of the abbots of Wearmouth and Jarrow; the *Chronica maiora*, tracing biblical and extra-biblical events down through the Ages of the World; and that milestone of historiography most of all, the *Historia ecclesiastica gentis Anglorum*, a text propagated still further in Anglo-Saxon England by its translation by a scholar of Alfred's court in the ninth century. Sister to these works are his studies of time and space: *De temporibus*, discussing such measurements of time as the Ages of the World and chronicling highlights of biblical history; *De temporum ratione*, an expanded version of *De temporibus* that included the *Chronica maiora*;

and *De natura rerum,* an introduction to cosmology treating such subjects as the earth, planets, and stars. At least three works, moreover, focus on places mentioned in the Bible: *Liber de locis sanctis, Nomina locorum ex Beati Hieronimi,* and *Nomina regionum atque locorum de Actibus Apostolorum.* Bede also was interested in the craft of language: his *De arte metrica* examines Latin versification using commentaries on the grammarian Donatus; its accompanying *De schematibus et tropis* considers 'tropes' or figures or speech in scripture, including in particular a section on allegory; and *De orthographia* lists the meaning, correct use, and spelling of potentially troublesome Latin words.

Foremost among Bede's concerns, however, was scriptural exegesis: as George Brown notes, 'All his works relate to his exegetical profession and are affected by it.'[2] Bede himself, looking back on his career near the end of his life, says that 'Omnem meditandis scripturis operam dedi ... Haec in Scripturam sanctam meae meorumque necessitati ex opusculis uenerabilium patum breuiter adnotare, siue etiam ad formam sensus et interpretationis eorum superadicere curaui.'[3] The description is apt: while Bede's digestion of the Fathers is such that some mistakenly have viewed him simply as a compiler,[4] Bede also breaks new ground in treating scripture that had not been analysed extensively by his predecessors, as in *De templo Salomonis, De tabernaculo, In Ezram et Neemiam,* and studies of numerous pericopes not covered by Gregory's *Homiliae in Euangelia.*[5]

The Homilies

The last are particularly important for their impact not only on the northern English church of the early eighth century, but on late Anglo-Saxon England given their transmission through Paul the Deacon. As such, they warrant a word of caution, for they are potentially confusing in a variety of ways. To begin with, there are the discrepancies between the printed versions of Bede's homilies. A newcomer to the present standard edition, the *Homiliarum euangelii libri ii* edited by David Hurst (CCSL 122), might assume that Hurst's two volumes comprise the whole of Bede's sermonic output – especially as Bede's own overview of his works in the *Historia ecclesiastica* speaks of 'two books of homilies on the Gospels' (V.24). In fact, they do not: rather, they reproduce the first two books of *Homiliae genuinae* printed by Migne as PL 94.9–268, with certain notable differences. First, the order of homilies varies considerably between the two editions – a factor for which one must account when

examining older scholarship. Second, there is not a one-to-one correspondence between the editions: Hurst contains fifty homilies to
Migne's forty-nine and conflates certain texts in Migne. Third, Hurst
includes two texts – *Homiliae* III.31 and III.65 – from Migne's third
book of *Homiliae subdititiae* or 'Spurious Homilies.' The *Homiliae subdititiae* offer another potential source of confusion, particularly as
regards the question of which in fact are 'spurious.' According to
CCSL's *Clauis patrum latinorum*, of the 109 texts that make up the *Homiliae subdititiae*, only a quarter are likely not authentic – a patchwork
group of twenty-five texts collectively entitled *Sermones spurii e libro iii
homiliarum*.[6] The distinction should be treated with caution, however,
as not all the attributions are firm;[7] the *Sermones spurii* appear, moreover, not as a unit but sporadically throughout the *Homiliae subdititiae*.
Finally, then, there is the overlap between the homilies and Bede's
other exegetical work. The reason eighty-four of the *Homiliae subdititiae* are viewed as genuine, in fact, is because all but nine derive in
whole or in bulk (that is, with slight introductions and conclusions
added) from Bede's *In Lucae euangelium expositio* and *In Marci euangelium expositio*.[8] Twenty-two of Hurst's fifty homilies likewise reproduce portions of Bede's commentary on these two Gospels. While
appendices in Hurst's editions of Bede's homilies and commentaries,
combined with a review of Migne's edition and the *Clauis patrum latinorum*'s lists, do enable one to distinguish the relationship between
Hurst and Migne, the pericopes and liturgical occasions for the homilies, the textual parallels between the homilies and commentaries, and
the difference between genuine, spurious, or debatable Bedan works,
the newcomer to the field may be forgiven for not finding such dis-
tinctions intuitive. For such a one, Appendix II may perhaps prove of
some assistance.

Bede's Theology of Free Will: Overview

Given the central role of exegesis in Bede's work, it is remarkable that so
little scholarly attention has been paid to Bede's theology. In the 1930s
and 1940s, a few studies were published on Bede's use of numerology
and allegory, his treatment of the Eucharist and penance, and his teaching on the church, the sacraments, sin, and virtue.[9] The years following,
however, have not seen an abundance even of general studies of Bede. In
his preface to the reprint of Peter Blair's *World of Bede*, Michael Lapidge
states flatly that before the publication of Blair's work in 1970, 'there had

not been a monograph on Bede worthy of the name for over fifty years,' and that as late as 1990, George Brown's *Bede the Venerable* was 'the only general monograph on Bede which deserves comparison with [it].'[10] On the other hand, considerable progress has been made, particularly by David Hurst and C.W. Jones, on critical editions of Bede's writings, and such primary materials have paved the way for new generations of scholarship. In the 1990s, studies appeared on Bede's view of ecclesiology and the progressive stages of the Christian life, his approach to exegesis, and his teaching on prayer and contemplation.[11] PhD dissertations further considered Bede's commentaries in relation to his patristic sources and in comparison with other Anglo-Saxon writings.[12] Even so, with the exception of a brief analysis by Mary Carroll in 1946,[13] almost nothing has been said about Bede's view of free will and grace.

Some points have been made in regards to Bede's relation to Augustine and Gregory. On the one hand, Bede's respect for and debt to Augustine is clear. Carroll states, for example, that 'Bede had ... absorbed completely the spirit of the Doctor of Grace regarding the whole divine plan of salvation.'[14] On the other hand, like Ælfric, Bede feels a particular bond with Gregory, the former monk whose vision brought missionaries and the Benedictine Order to England. In his portrait of Gregory in the *Historia ecclesiastica*, for example, while noting that Gregory was humble, concerned for the poor, industrious despite physical affliction, and so forth, he stresses in his conclusion that 'Ad cuius pietatis et iustitiae opus pertinet etiam hoc, quod nostram gentem ... de dentibus antiqui hostis eripiens libertatis fecit esse participem.'[15] It is no wonder, then, that M.L.W. Laistner affirms 'that Gregory came first in Bede's affection and that, next to Gregory, Bede's deepest veneration was reserved for Augustine.'[16]

This subtle hierarchy of influences is directly reflected in Bede's understanding of the power of human will. Though Bede is far less concerned than Augustine to show the precise way in which volition and grace coexist, one passing comment by Carroll demonstrates a critical way in which Bede departs from the African Father. Though Bede follows Augustine in viewing grace as 'the source of all that was good in man's desire, thought, word, or deed,' Carroll notes that 'the functioning of grace is no merely passive process; it depends upon the cooperation of each individual. We can abuse the graces given.'[17] As we shall see, in saying that grace enables human beings to cooperate with or reject God's offer of further grace, Bede reveals a Gregorian rather than Augustinian perspective.

The Knowledge of Bede in Anglo-Saxon England

Perhaps uniquely among Anglo-Saxon writers, Bede serves as a bridge between the patristic and insular worlds. Himself viewed as a Church Father from the ninth century, Bede is both a conduit of patristic thought and an original influence on Anglo-Saxon England. Having surveyed in the chapters above to what extent he may have known works by Augustine and Gregory the Great, we may now turn to Bede's own impact on England before the Conquest. While this influence was no doubt greater than extant evidence suggests, as before, our four conservative points of consideration will be as follows: Bedan manuscripts surviving from centres associated with Bede himself, Alfred, Lantfred, Wulfstan, and Ælfric; Bedan manuscripts surviving from England as a whole during these periods; Bedan sources used by the four later authors; and continental collections of Bedan material known at least to Ælfric.

Manuscripts associated with our various centres, to begin with, are scant. Aside from a few early copies from Wearmouth-Jarrow,[18] only four works survive. One item remains from mid-tenth-century Winchester: predictably, it is the *Old English Bede*, a translation or adaptation of the *Historia ecclesiastica* made by Alfred's circle.[19] Three others may have formed part of Wulfstan's library at Worcester: *De arte metrica, De schematibus et tropis*, and the Latin *Historia ecclesiastica*.[20] While free will may not be a central focus of the first two works, both the Latin and vernacular versions of the *Historia* are noteworthy for their mention of Pelagianism.

Second, then, there are works surviving from England as a whole. Two texts in addition to the *Historia ecclesiastica* may be dated to Bede's lifetime: a study of Proverbs and *De temporum ratione*, the latter of which also warns against the dangers of Pelagian thought. A number of other works stem from the period up to Alfred's death: on language, there is *De orthographia*; for hagiography, there is the metrical Life of Cuthbert, saint and bishop of Lindisfarne (685–7); for history, there is *De temporum ratione* and the two versions of the *Historia*; for exegesis, there is Bede's treatise on Solomon's temple and his commentaries on Kings, Habakkuk, and Luke.[21] Prior to Wulfstan's death, still other works may be found: *De arte metrica* and *De schematibus et tropis* on language; the prose Life of Cuthbert; the *Historia abbatum*; *De natura rerum* on cosmology; *De die iudicii*, a poetic treatment of Last Things that served as the source for the Old English poem *Judgement Day II*; and a series of exegetical works – *De tabernaculo*, discussing the structure, vessels, and priestly garments worn therein; *Super epistulas catholicas expositio*; *Expositio Apocalypseos*; and the *Homiliarum euangelii libri ii.*[22]

A few of the above texts appear as sources for our later Anglo-Saxon authors, as well as other works no longer extant in Anglo-Saxon manuscripts. Alfred's translations of Augustine's *Soliloquia* and Boethius's *De consolatione Philosophiae* may draw on three Bedan works: the *Historia ecclesiastica*, *De natura rerum*, and *De temporum ratione.*[23] Translations commissioned by Alfred or produced at his court suggest other works he may have known: the *Liber de locis sanctis*, *Nomina locorum*, and *Nomina regionum* on places mentioned in the Bible; *De temporibus*, the precursor of *De temporum ratione*; and *In Lucae euangelium expositio*, the last being an important source for Bede's teaching on volition.[24] Lantfred, too, appears to have drawn on key works in this regard: in addition to the *Historia* and *De temporum ratione* with their comments on Pelagius, he had access to some version of Bede's homilies on the Gospels, works in which Bede would set forth his understanding of free will.[25] Wulfstan's knowledge of Bede, on the other hand, remains uncertain: while we have noted three texts which may have been in Wulfstan's library, as yet, to my knowledge, no Bedan source has been proposed for Wulfstan's works.

Ælfric's knowledge of Bede, by contrast, was considerable. As well as *De natura rerum* and the prose and verse Lives of Cuthbert, texts less concerned with the subject of free will,[26] Ælfric would have encountered the warnings against Pelagius in *De temporum ratione* and the original and Old English translation of the *Historia ecclesiastica*. More importantly, he also had exposure to exegetical teaching on a variety of biblical books – though with varying degrees of certainty. A few relevant passages, for example, are found in *In principium Genesis* and *Super Acta Apostolorum expositio*. Godden lists the first as a probable source for the *Sermones* but as a certain source for Ælfric's *Preface to Genesis*, *Interrogationes Sigewulfi in Genesin*, and *De temporibus anni.*[27] The three probable parallels to *Super Acta Apostolorum expositio* in the *Sermones*, however, are found side-by-side as extracts in Smaragdus, indicating that Ælfric may not have known the whole.[28] Considerably more comments on volition appear in *Super epistulas catholicas*, a set of seven disquisitions on the Epistles, on one of which (I Peter) Ælfric seems to draw in the *Sermones.*[29] None of the extant copies of *Super epistulas* suggest that it circulated other than as a unit, which might imply that Ælfric would have been unlikely to encounter the treatise on I Peter independent of *Super epistulas* as a whole;[30] the passages he cites, however, also appear side-by-side as extracts in Smaragdus.[31]

One tantalizing echo raises the possibility of Ælfric's knowledge of Bede's exposition of the *Cantica Canticorum* – a treatise of crucial importance for the subject of free will. As we shall see, however, aside from one extract preserved by Smaragdus, such knowledge remains at best doubtful. Finally, there are three works of particular significance for Bede's teaching on volition: *In Lucae euangelium expositio*, *In Marci euangelium expositio*, and the *Homiliarum euangelii libri ii*. Scholars have suggested cautiously that Ælfric may not have had direct access to the first two works;[32] at the very least, a number of passages from these texts are included in Paul the Deacon and Smaragdus (on which, more below). Above all, however, Ælfric drew on Bede's homilies on the Gospels, at least twenty-six of which he used for the *Sermones*.[33]

Lastly, then, in reconstructing the knowledge of Bede in Anglo-Saxon England, we come to the continental collections of material known to Ælfric. Bede is well represented, to begin with, in Paul the Deacon (Appendix I, Table I.5). In fact, with thirty-four of Bede's Gospel homilies and twenty excerpts from *In Lucae euangelium expositio* and *In Marci euangelium expositio* included as homilies, Bede supplies more readings in Paul the Deacon than any other author, comprising nearly a quarter of the total homiliary.[34] The expanded version of Paul the Deacon found in PL 95 omits the extracts from Luke and Mark, but includes thirteen additional (genuine) homilies from Migne's third book of *Homiliae subdititiae* (Table I.6).[35] It is not surprising, then, that the majority of Ælfric's borrowings from Bede come from these texts.[36] Smaragdus, on the other hand, is at once less comprehensive and more diverse (Table I.12). The florilegium includes extracts from between eight and thirty-nine homilies, between thirteen and twenty-two chapters of *In Lucam*, and between five and fourteen chapters of *In Marcum* – the precise numbers being difficult to determine because of the identical nature of many of these passages. While some of the extracts span several paragraphs rather than brief sentences, in general they do not treat the pericopes at as great a length as does Paul the Deacon. At the same time, Smaragdus draws on works not found in the other homiliary. In addition to the selections noted above from *Super Acta Apostolorum expositio* and *Super epistulas catholicas expositio*, which may have formed Ælfric's sole knowledge of these texts, he quotes from *Aliquot quaestionum liber*, the *Expositio Apocalypseos*, *Commentarius in Parabolas Salomonis*, and *De templo Salomonis*, works that are rare or otherwise unknown in Anglo-Saxon England. Finally, he includes one passage from *In Cantica Canticorum allegorica exposition*, which we shall treat below. All in all, despite some characteristic confusion from misattributed extracts (Table I.14), Smaragduṣ incorporates some important material not found in Paul the Deacon, and is on the whole a valuable source for Bedan references to free will.

Bede's Theology of Free Will as Known in Anglo-Saxon England

The breadth of Bede's corpus, though not as extensive as Augustine's, is nonetheless daunting to one seeking to summarize aspects of his theology. As with Augustine, however, two factors may provide boundaries to our investigation: not all of Bede's works address the issue of volition, and not all of his works were likely known to our later Anglo-Saxon authors. The known works that do deal with free will, moreover, form a substantial body of material in themselves, so that an examination of these works – along with a few notable exceptions perhaps not as well known to our later authors – may serve to illustrate Bede's overall teaching on the subject as received in both eighth-century and later Anglo-Saxon England. First, we have the *Historia ecclesiastica* and *De temporum ratione*, texts addressing in similar terms the dangers of Pelagianism: the latter was known to Lantfred, Ælfric, and possibly Alfred; the former known to Alfred, Ælfric, and possibly Wulfstan. Second, we have *In principium Genesis*, drawing on Augustine's *De Genesi ad litteram* and focusing in its exegesis of Genesis 3 on the consequences of humanity's Fall: the text was used in multiple works by Ælfric. Third, we have Bede's homilies on the Gospels and commentaries on the epistles: *In Lucae euangelium expositio* was possibly known to Alfred through his court; the *Homiliarum euangelii libri* were known to Lantfred in some form; and numerous selections from *In Lucam*, the *Homiliae*, and *In Marci euangelium expositio* were known to Ælfric, either directly or more likely through intermediate sources. As a representative sample, we may examine the Bedan texts found in Paul the Deacon and Smaragdus – texts taken primarily from the homilies on Luke, Mark, and the Gospels, but also including some important passages from *Super epistulas catholicas expositio*. Finally, there are texts not present in these collections that are of consequence to our discussion of free will: selections from the *Homiliae*, from *In Lucam*, and one key text perhaps unknown to any of our later authors – *In Cantica Canticorum allegorica expositio*. As we will see, in the case of Ælfric at least the omissions may be significant ones, for the works known to him may present him with an unbalanced view of Bede's teaching, emphasizing human merit at the expense of grace.

The Dangers of Pelagianism and the Reckoning of Easter
(Historia ecclesiastica gentis Anglorum and *De temporum ratione)*

By the time Bede came to write the *Historia ecclesiastica* and *De temporum ratione*, over three centuries had passed since Rome had condemned Pelagius's teachings; it had been nearly as long, furthermore, since Germanus of Auxerre squelched British proponents of 'contra auxilium gratiae supernae uenena suae perfidiae' (the poison of [Pelagius's] treachery against the assistance of heavenly grace).[37] For Bede, however, the heresy appears to have remained a dangerous if not living issue. He was not alone in his concern: as he records in the *Historia ecclesiastica*, as late as the seventh century the Roman see was admonishing Irish believers for what Rome perceived as a revival of Pelagian error. This anxiety appears to have stemmed, however, not from insular advocacy of heterodox theological arguments per se, but from what to modern eyes may appear an unexpected source: the dating of Easter.

Bede's *Historia* includes selections of a letter written in 640 by the pope-elect John IV (640–2) in response to correspondence received from northern Irish clergy during the brief tenure of John's predecessor, Pope Severinus (28 May–2 August 640). Considerable light on the letter has been cast by Dáibhí Ó Cróinín, who explains how the situation came to be charged with tension and urgency.[38] Some two hundred years before, Rome had commissioned one Victorius of Aquitaine to prepare a new set of tables calculating the date of Easter, intending thereby to insure conformity of observance in the church. Though the tables were published in 457 and made mandatory for all Gallican churches in 541, miscalculations in the tables only served to compound confusion for those seeking to follow Roman practice. Corrections were issued annually to major Western centres, but more distant provinces such as Ireland were not always so informed.

For Ireland, however, and sites such as Lindisfarne founded by Irish monks, the dating of Easter was a particularly charged issue. According to the Council of Nicea (325), Easter was to be dated to the first Sunday following both the Jewish Passover – the fourteenth day of the lunar month of Nisan – and the spring equinox, on which the length of day equals that of night. For the Roman church, this equation meant that Easter would fall between the fifteenth and twenty-first day of the month. A longstanding Irish system of computation, however, allowed Easter to fall on Passover itself.[39] Around 629, Severinus's predecessor, Honorius I (625–38), wrote to exhort the Irish church to follow Roman practice, and the subsequent debate led to division: prompted by figures such as Abbot Cummian,[40] the southern church submitted to the Roman system while northern Ireland and British monasteries founded by Columba appear to have resisted change. Ó Cróinín argues, however, that by 640 the northern church may have been using Victorian tables in addition to their own, and that their letter to Severinus was prompted by the fact that Easter 641 – but a few months away – was one of the dates Victorius miscalculated. Victorius provided two entries for each year: the Greek and Roman dates for Easter, the first of which did not take the equinox into account. For the year 641, he said that the Greeks would celebrate Easter on 1 April or the fifteenth day of the month, while for the Romans Easter would fall on 8 April or the twenty-second day of the month. As the latter was clearly false – Roman practice permitting Easter to fall no later than the twenty-first – the Irish wrote to alert Rome of their intention to use the Greek date, 1 April. Unfortunately for the Irish, however, 1 April was also a date which Victorius had gotten wrong, for the kalends of April 641 in fact would fall on the fourteenth day of the month – as the annual corrections circulated in Rome would have made clear. With maddening irony, therefore, though seeking to comply with a patently incorrect Roman formula, their letter may have merely solidified Roman suspicions of Irish intransigence: the northern church, it would seem, was again insisting that Easter could be celebrated on the Passover.[41]

What was the perceived danger of the traditional Irish position, and what did it have to do with free will? As presented by Bede, John IV's response of 640 treats the two issues in tandem, exhorting the Irish in one breath to revise their pascal computations and in the next to crush the poison of Pelagian heresy.[42] It is possible, of course, that the two concerns were unrelated, that Pelagius's teaching was apparently gaining a foothold. Ó Cróinín affirms, however, that though scholars have noted 'the surprising frequence with which medieval Irish writers referred to the heresiarch Pelagius and the extent to which they borrowed from his works ... all are agreed that they were not true Pelagians, in the sense that the famous theological arguments for which Pelagius was eventually condemned never found favor with Irish writers.'[43] By contrast, in both the *Historia* and *De temporum ratione* Bede draws a direct connection between the dating of Easter and the theology of volition. Since Christ is the Light by which people are saved (cf. John 1.9), *De temporum ratione* argues, celebrating people's redemption before light outweighs darkness – that is, before the spring equinox – is tantamount to saying that people can be saved apart from Christ's grace: 'Nam si qui plenilunium paschale ante aequinoctium fieri posse contenderit, ostendat uel ecclesiam sanctam priusquam saluator in carne ueniret extitisse perfectam, uel quemlibet fidelium ante praeuentum gratiae illius aliquid posse supernae lucis habere.'[44] Or as Ceolfrith, abbot of Wearmouth-Jarrow puts it in the *Historia*: 'Qui ergo plenitudinem lunae paschalis ante aequinoctium prouenire posse contenderit ... [concordat] eis qui sine praeueniente gratia Christi se saluari posse confidunt: quia etsi uera lux tenebras mundi moriendo ac resurgendo nunquam uicisset, perfectam se habere posse iustitiam dogmatizare praesumunt.'[45]

Though the Synod of Whitby in 663 or 664 would ultimately ensure that Northumbria and the English church as a whole would conform to Roman doctrine, Bede was thus still concerned that the theological implications of heterodox practice not be forgotten. It is ironic, therefore, that when Alfred's court sought to preserve the *Historia* in the vernacular for a new generation of Anglo-Saxons, the translation should omit Bede's conscientious warnings. Though headings in the *Old English Bede* note that Pelagius 'wið Godes gife geleafan unrihtlice lare onfeng' (wickedly espoused doctrine contrary to belief in God's grace) and that Germanus overcame the 'Pelagianiscan wol' (Pelagian pestilence),[46] the text itself makes no mention of Pelagius, Germanus, John IV's letter, or the significance of the equinox. It merely notes that Ceolfrith composed 'gewrit be gehealde rihtra Eastrana' (a letter about the more proper observance of Easter) – an observance potentially made the poorer for later Anglo-Saxons through lack of understanding of theological symbolism.[47]

The Impact of the Fall (In principium Genesis)

If Bede's studies of ecclesiastical history and the reckoning of time seek to build on established patristic material and adapt it for an insular audience, so too does his commentary on Genesis, a book long a subject of interest to the Fathers. *In principium Genesis* draws, for example, on Jerome as well as Isidore; primarily, however, it relies on works by Augustine, chief among these being *De Genesi ad litteram* – a work from which it departs by treating in its discussion of Genesis 3 the fall not of Satan and the demonic host but of human beings alone. Following hexameral exegesis on the days of creation, which Bede associates with the Ages of the World,[48] he turns to consider the Fall of humankind. The tree forbidden to Adam and Eve was not evil, Bede affirms; neither was God's command, the observance of which would have brought great good to human beings. Nor should God be condemned for allowing Adam and Eve to be tempted though he foreknew that they would fall: not only would they deserve scant praise for obedience were there no temptation to do otherwise, but their nature was able and their volition capable of resisting temptation ('in natura posse, et in potestate haberet uelle non consentire suadenti') with the help of him who gives grace to the humble.[49] Having in pride chosen disobedience, however, human-kind's good volitional freedom became 'malum noxiae libertatis' (the evil of pernicious liberty): the very will which humans exalted, seeking through it glorious autonomy, fell upon them with the weight of great devastation (*grandi ruinae pondere*).[50] The consequence of sin was not sim-ply the death of the body, but what Bede calls the death of the spirit, that perversion of desire lamented by Paul in Romans 7 that makes humans captive to the law of sin at work in their bodily members.[51] Obedient, they might have gained a form as blessed as the angels;[52] disobedient, they found their flesh the slave of sinful desires. Pure, they could have remained naked and unashamed; corrupted, they became subject to con-cupiscence and stripped inwardly of God's grace. Innocent, their eyes would not have known evil;[53] having transgressed, their understanding was opened not to good but to iniquity.[54] Adam and Eve, in shame and fear, may have hidden themselves from the face of God in the Garden, but it was God who inwardly turned his face from them. Given the enor-mity of this deprivation, Bede suggests, one has small cause to wonder at this result: human actions now resemble those of a madman (*dementiae*).[55]

The Corruption of the Will: Bondage and Blindness
(Homilies on the Gospels and Commentaries on the Epistles)

Turning from *In principium Genesis* to the Bedan homilies and commentar-ies transmitted by Paul the Deacon and Smaragdus, we find that Bede both follows and departs from his predecessors in his views of the Fall, the origin of faith, and the origin of good deeds. In terms of human cor-ruption, first of all, Bede draws on both Augustine and Gregory to show that because of humanity's transgression in Eden, individuals are sinful from conception and unable to save themselves.[56] 'Nisi dono Dei quisque uocatus,' Bede says, 'numquam reatum primae transgressionis numquam male blandentia augescentium cotidie peccatorum umbracula euadit numquam saluandus uenire meretur ad Christum.'[57] Like his precursors, one way in which he portrays this fallen state is through the image of bondage. Treating the Triumphal Entry, for example, Bede notes that just as the donkey on which Christ rides into Jerusalem had to be unbound, so humankind 'funibus peccatorum erat circumplexus et solutione diuina opus habebat' (was bound by the ropes of its sins, and needed to be set free by God).[58] Bede shows little concern, however, to explain the precise effects of this *solutio* on human will – either that grace 'frees' the will so that it necessarily chooses good (as Augustine would maintain), or that grace 'frees' the will so it can reject or cooperate with God's grace (as Gregory would suggest). Instead, Bede's focus is on the liberation of baptism. 'Liberi recte uocamur,' he says, 'quia per baptisma a peccatorum sumus nexibus absoluti, quia a daemoniaca seruitute redempti, quia filii Dei effecti.'[59] Such freedom is not necessarily permanent, however: Bede warns that if believers do not use their freedom to act as bondservants of God (I Pt. 2.16), 'mox libertate perdita servi efficimur peccati.'[60]

As with Augustine and Gregory, Bede describes fallen humanity not only as bound but blind. Again, part of this blindness is due to original sin. In the analogous example of Christ's healing of the deaf mute (Mark 7.32–5), Bede notes that humans became deaf after they listened to the serpent, and unable to declare God's praises from the time they spoke with Satan.[61] In addition, however, individuals are blinded by personal sin. The 'stulti et iniqui,' Bede says, 'ab humanae conditionis honore procul recedentes conparati sunt iumentis insipientibus et similes facti sunt illis atque ideo recte ueritatis luce priuantur.'[62] God has devised a means to save them, causing the invisible Light and Wisdom of God to put on flesh, so that human beings might be 'enlightened.'[63] When it comes to who is responsible for this enlightenment, however, we find a crucial dichotomy that runs throughout Bede's work: on the one hand, 'a Domino uos illustrari, non uestra prouisione, sed superna gratia uos praeueniente, contigit';[64] at the same time, however, Christ 'omnia quae inluminari *merentur* corda hominum ... inlustrat.'[65] Somehow, it would seem, humans must merit their enlightenment, even though they are enlightened by a grace that precedes any merits.

The Origin of Faith (Homilies on the Gospels and Commentaries on the Epistles)

One area in which this tension between merit and grace is apparent is that crucial element that precedes good deeds: faith. On the one hand, Bede refers repeatedly in his writings – nearly seventy times, in fact – to *gratiam fidei*, the grace of faith.[66] In Smaragdus, for example, Bede says that the evangelists convert the nations 'ad fidei euangelicae gratiam' (to the faith of Gospel grace); those who come from the nations are joined together 'per gratiam fidei' (through the grace of faith); and those who join themselves to the church 'fidei gratia' (by the grace of faith) may not exalt themselves 'de meritis gloriando' (by boasting about their merits).[67] On the other hand, Bede speaks of faith as being meritorious. A classic case is the centurion of whom Christ says, 'Non inueni tantam fidem in Israhel.'[68] In Paul the Deacon, Bede compares this centurion to the centurion Cornelius in Acts: the one, he notes, 'Fidem suam laudari a Domino ... promeruit,' while the other 'Magnae fidei ... merito spiritus sancti donum ... accepit.'[69] The precedents are all the more significant in that Bede views the centurions as types representing all gentile believers.[70] An even more intriguing figure identified with such believers, however, is Zaccheus, the diminutive tax collector who climbs above a crowd in order to see Christ. As we shall see, John Cassian views Zaccheus as a key example of the way in which human beings might sometimes seek God of their own desire, and Bede's account is ambiguous enough as to be understood in the same fashion. Zaccheus desires to see Jesus, Bede explains, 'Quia gratiae fidei quam mundo saluator attulit participare cupiebat'; that the crowd prevents him from doing so shows that 'Inolita uitiorum consuetudo ne ad uotum perueniret obstiterat.'[71] The latter is no surprise, as both Augustine and Gregory agree that people may be enslaved by sinful habits. What is unexpected, however, is that Zaccheus not only appears to desire grace for a faith that he has not yet received – implying a human initiative akin to that proposed by Cassian – but seems able to overcome his sinful habits as well: 'Suspiciens uidit illum quia per gratiam fidei a terrenis cupiditatibus eleuatum turbisque infidelibus praeminentem elegit.'[72] While Bede might be quick to say that it is God who enables Zaccheus to raise himself up, descriptions such as these do complicate the picture. Other passages, however, stress the primacy of grace. *Super epistulas catholicas*, for example, gives little impression that faith might be a meritorious initiative to which God responds. 'Non in nobis aliquid meriti boni pro quo saluaremur inuenit,' Bede says; 'quin potuis infirmos et inglorioso cernens sua nos uirtute recuperauit et gloria.'[73] And again: 'A domino uos illustrari non uestra prouisione sed superna gratia uos praeueniente contigit.'[74]

*The Origin of Good Works: Merit (Homilies on the Gospels
and Commentaries on the Epistles)*

When it comes to people's righteous deeds, however, the texts in Paul
the Deacon and Smaragdus in particular are swift to emphasize individuals' contribution. Indeed, if Gregory occasionally speaks of humans
'meriting' God's gifts, here it is a pounding refrain, covering everything
from individuals' initial liberation from bondage to their ultimate
reward in heaven. The deaf-mute whom Christ heals represents not
merely those freed by grace, but those who 'diuina *merentur* gratia liber-
ari' (*deserve* to be freed by divine grace).[75] Once freed, the believer 'pie et
sobrie conuersando ad perfectionem promissae nobis uitae mereatur
attingere' (by living righteously and solemnly should deserve to attain
to the perfection of the life promised to us).[76] Individuals are called to
follow Christ 'toto mentis nisu ... ut illo peruenire illius regni ianuam
mereamur' (with the whole striving of our mind ... so that we may
deserve to reach the gate of his kingdom thereby), recognizing that only
'qui uirtutum operibus insudant ... sunt digni' (those who sweat in
doing works of virtue are worthy [of reaching it]).[77] Those who are
aflame with pious zeal are 'maxime gratia Christi dignos' (especially
worthy of Christ's grace); when grace is received, 'gratias recte uiuendo
reddamus ut ad maiora percipienda digni existere mereamur' (we
should give thanks by living rightly, so that we may deserve to show
ourselves worthy to receive greater [gifts of grace]).[78] Right up to the
last days, Bede says, 'non sunt defuturi in mundo qui diuina mansione
et inhabitatione sint digni' (those worthy of God's abiding and indwell-
ing will not be lacking in the world); he who is received into heaven,
moreover, is one who by loving others 'portionem habere in terra
uiuentium meruit (deserved to have a part in the land of the living).'[79]

The very order of Bede's words at times can seem all too Pelagian. In
one homily, for example, he says: ·

> Oportet, fratres carissimi, ut ... a mundi nos inlecebris inmunes exhibea-
> mus quatenus ad percipiendam spiritus sancti gratiam quam mundus
> non potest accipere digni exsistere ualeamus. Diligamus Christum,
> eiusque mandata quae habemus incipiendo, seruemus perseuerando. Fit
> enim iusta mercede, ut illum diligendo diligi amplius mereamur a Patre.
>
> We must show, most beloved brothers, that ... we are free from the entice-
> ments of the world, that we may be able to become worthy to obtain the

grace of the Holy Spirit, which the world cannot receive [John 14.17]. We should love Christ, and by starting [to do] his commands which we have, we should serve him by persevering in them. For it happens by just reward that by loving him we may deserve to be loved more by the Father.[80]

Taken on its own, such language may seem to suggest that human efforts precede God's grace: only after humans resist the world can they receive the Spirit; only by loving God through obedience can they earn his love in turn. How, Augustine might object, can bound people live as though they were free? How can they obey if God does not first intervene?

The Origin of Good Works: Grace
(Homilies on the Gospels and Commentaries on the Epistles)

When one considers the source of human love, however – which, like Augustine and Gregory, Bede views as the 'fons omnium et origo uirtutum' (source and beginning of all the virtues)[81] – the counterpart to Bede's emphasis on merit becomes apparent. In Paul the Deacon, not only does Bede speak of the Spirit *accendens* (enkindling) people's hearts with the love of God and their neighbour,[82] but he affirms that only by such intercession do people come to love: 'Nemo uoluntate amplectitur nisi per gratiam spiritus sancti.'[83] Humans do not receive such grace because they are worthy of heavenly things; rather, Bede says, through the gift of this love 'digni efficiamini' (you may become worthy) of heaven.[84] Bede does note that Christ tells his disciples, 'Pater amat uos *quia* uos me amastis et credidistis quia ego a Deo exiui.'[85] In explaining the passage, however, Bede offers a largely Augustinian perspective.

Non ita intellegendum est quasi amor et credulitas discipulorum praecesserit amorem quo illos pater amaret meritumque humanum prius sit muneribus gratiae caelestis cum apertissime dicat apostolus: 'Aut quis prior dedit illi et retribuetur ei? Quoniam ex ipso et per ipsum et in ipso sunt omnia'; sed ita potius quia pater illos gratuito amore praeuenerit atque ad amandum credendumque filium amando sustulerit et quia ipsi agnitum filii dilectionem ac fidem pio et sollicito corde seruauerint maioribus eos donis paternae dilectionis esse remuneratos.

This must not be understood as if the love and belief of the disciples preceded the love with which the Father loved them, or that the merit of human beings may come before the gifts of heavenly grace, because the Apostle says quite clearly: 'Or who has first given to [God], and it will be repaid to him? For all things are from him and through him and in him' [Rom. 11.35–6]. Rather, it must be understood thus, that the Father preceded them with his gratuitous love and by loving them he supported their [subsequent] love and belief in the Son, and that they, having acknowledged him, themselves preserved their love for and faith in the Son with righteous and vigilant heart[s], and were rewarded with greater gifts of the Father's love.[86]

At first glance, this explanation seems at odds with Bede's earlier statement that 'illum diligendo diligi amplius mereamur a Patre' (by loving him we may deserve to be loved more by the Father). The context of that passage, however, is talking about God's response to the love of believers: when people love Christ by obeying him – thus demonstrating that they are *inmunis mundi* (free of the world) – God both sustains their faith and hope on earth, and allows them to see him face to face in heaven.[87] The present passage, by contrast, addresses the very beginnings of humankind's relationship with God. Here there is no question of human initiative, or even of virtues by which they 'merit' God's initiative. Rather, prevenient grace precipitates individuals' love and faith, so that 'ex ipso et per ipsum et in ipso sunt omnia.' With this divine intercession in view, Bede's earlier statement fits into place: as people love God now in response to God's intitiative, God helps them persevere in love and faith, rewarding these virtues afterward with the 'greater gifts' of heaven.

The fact that love is due to grace is also apparent in *Super epistulas catholicas*. As Bede says, 'Gratia quippe hominem preuenit ut diligat Deum qua dilectione operetur bona.'[88] The statement takes on new relevance, moreover, given Bede's concern in *Super epistulas* to condemn Pelagianism. If the love by which humans do good is a gift of God, then people cannot, as Pelagius would have it, be saved by their own efforts.[89] Bede states: 'Et ne quis sua uirtute mundi uel luxus uel labores se superare posse confideret ... "Haec est uictoria quae uincit mundum, fides nostra," illa nimirum fides ... qua eius humiliter auxilium flagitamus.'[90] By affirming that people overcome their corruption only through God's assistance, therefore, Bede opposes the Pelagians; by adding that victory comes also through individuals' faith and prayers, however, he preserves a role for human volition.

Bede and the Gregorian View of Volition
(Homilies on the Gospels and Commentaries on the Epistles)

If Bede's emphasis on human effort is not as Pelagian as it sometimes appears, it is nonetheless a significant departure from Augustine's view. In *Super epistulas*, for example, Bede states clearly that once grace has been extended to human beings, they have the power to accept or reject it: 'Gratia Christi eorum fit gratia qui hanc mundo corde suscipiunt, nam qui gratiam Dei spernit non ipsam gratiam minuit sed hanc suam non esse, id est sibi facit non prodesse.'[91] Such a statement, of course, would have been appalling to Augustine, for whom grace is not an offer of divine assistance but a manifestation of the divine will, which human beings in their weakness cannot deter. It is an apt reflection, however, of Gregory's view of the will.

A fascinating illustration of this perspective is found not far from the passage Ælfric quotes from *Super epistulas*, in which Bede speaks of the church as a house built of living stones. Normal or 'dead' stones, he notes, can do nothing to help the builder in any way, and indeed will fall if not continually supported. For Augustine, this would be an apt description of human beings, whose hearts invariably are pulled downward towards evil desires as by a *pondus* or weight. Bede, by contrast, exhorts people to act as living stones so that, 'sobrie et iuste et pie uiuendo *cooperemur* [Deo].'[92] What might seem a blatant Semi-Pelagian assertion of humans' power to 'cooperate' with God, however, is tempered by Bede's concomitant affirmation that people do this 'praeueniente se ac comitante Dei gratia' (with the grace of God preceding and accompanying them).[93] It is with this understanding, says Bede, that Paul is able to say, 'Abundantius illis omnibus laboraui' – and then, 'ne aliquid eiusdem pii laboris sibimet tribuisse uideretur' – 'Non ego autem sed gratia Dei mecum.'[94] Bede warns, however, that it is not only unbelievers, to whom grace has not been extended, who may be dead stones; those who have been reborn as members of God's house through baptism may grow hardened and dead again by rejecting the grace to work towards their salvation.[95]

In practical terms, then, what must people do to be living stones? At another point in *Super epistulas*, for example, Bede states, 'Qui habet spem in domino sanctificat se *quantum potest* ipse nitendo et eius per omnia gratiam flagitando qui ait: "Sine me nihil potestis facere."'[96] If the believer can do nothing without God's grace, however, what does it mean for him to strive *quantum potest* (as far as he can)? What precisely 'can' human beings do?

One thing the passage reveals is that people may *gratiam flagitare* – pray for further grace. As Bede says, 'Illius per omnia quaerendum est auxilium ut perficiamur a quo initium bonae actionis accepimus.'[97] When Christ looks up to heaven and groans before healing the deaf-mute, for example (Mark 7.34), Bede explains that this shows both 'ubi nobis speranda salus et qua conpunctionis uel lacrimarum sit deuotione quaerenda' (whence healing for us must be hoped for, and with what earnestness of remorse and tears it must be sought).[98] Granted, Bede is not always clear as to whether grace or prayer comes first. 'Eius continue flagitemus auxilium,' he says at one point, 'ut lucem scientiae quam contulit in nobis ipse conseruet et ad perfectum usque diem perducat. Et ut digni simus exaudiri precantes abiciamus ipsi opera tenebrarum.'[99] In other words, while it is God who initially illuminates individuals and helps them persevere until the end, God's grace seems to be dependent on people's prayers and efforts to deserve it. At other points, however, he paints a different picture: it is Christ who first stands at the door and knocks (Rev. 3.20), and human beings who respond 'quando illius ... ammonitionibus libenter assensum praebemus' (when we freely offer our assent to his directions).[100]

Given this context, it may be that Bede understands Christ's statement that 'Sine me nihil potestis facere' to mean that individuals can *accomplish* nothing without God, not that they can *do* nothing apart from him. The point is a crucial one: not only does it distinguish Bede from Augustine, for whom the verse means that the entirety of one's righteous choice is from God, but it informs how one understands Bede's own sweeping affirmations of human dependence: 'Ex ipso ... sunt omnia'; 'Quicquid boni agimus hoc Deo donante percepimus'; and 'Quicquid caeleste in terris agimus hoc profecto ut ageremus caelesti munere accepimus.'[101] This is not to miminize such statements; indeed, the fact that Bede repeats the point in his comments on James is particularly significant in that James is marked for its emphasis on the importance of good deeds.[102] Even so, Bede's focus seems to be on the fulfilment of such deeds: 'In bonis operibus perfector est Deus, non enim uolentis neque currentis sed Dei miserentis et adiuuantis est ut peruenire ualeamus ad calcem.'[103] In saying that God is ultimately rather than utterly responsible for people's righteous choices, therefore, Bede is able to affirm humankind's absolute need of grace for righteousness while preserving – like Gregory – a place for human will in the process.

Inward Inspiration and Congruent Vocation (Homilies on the Gospels)

By what means, then, does God bring humans to respond? In considering the way in which the Spirit changes human hearts, Augustine had
moved away from his early idea of congruent vocation, where God
might use carefully designed circumstances to influence individuals'
choices, to emphasize instead the Spirit's inward inspiration. Bede, by
contrast, seems content to acknowledge both. On the one hand, he
notes that 'Spiritus menti quam replet ... uim diuinae caritatis infundit
interius.'[104] This, for example, is how Matthew the tax collector comes
to abandon wealth to follow a teacher with few worldly goods: 'Ipse
dominus qui eum foris uerbo uocauit intus inuisibili instinctu ut
sequeretur edocuit infundens menti illius lumen gratiae spiritalis.'[105]
On the other hand, God's work in the elect is shown 'gratia piae *protec-
tionis* qua illos specialiter per praesentia dona uel flagella ... erudiendo
prouehit.'[106] For Augustine, the distinction is an important one: congruent vocation involves individuals' free (though predictable) choice,
whereas inspiration bypasses human volition and directly changes his
heart. In Bede's eyes, however, they are natural complements, showing
the Spirit's internal and external work. God, he says, 'electorum corda
per fidem et dilectionem suam *inhabitans* regit atque ad percipienda
supernae retributionis dona continua *protectione* gubernat.'[107]

The Emphasis on Grace in Material Omitted
from Later Bedan Collections

Despite Bede's acknowledgment of human dependence on divine
assistance, the texts in Paul the Deacon and Smaragdus still convey a
strong sense of the need for individual merit. The trend is ironic, for a
closer examination of the material omitted from these collections
reveals that in this regard the collections may give a misleading
impression of Bede's work. Some of the strongest statements of grace
in Bede's homilies, in fact, are found in passages from *In Lucae euangelium expositio* and the *Homiliarum euangelii libri* that Ælfric's immediate
sources happen to leave out. It could be argued, of course, that Ælfric
could have encountered these works independently, especially as
source studies have identified echoes in Ælfric of selections from *In
Lucam* or the *Homiliae* not found in Paul the Deacon and Smaragdus.[108]
We have already noted, however, that the various versions of Paul the
Deacon may account for all the homilies drawn upon by Ælfric, and

Godden comments that the putative parallels not in Paul the Deacon 'are slight or the material is found in similar form in Smaragdus or Haymo.'[109] Such parallels may thus indicate variations in Ælfric's version of Paul the Deacon more than the presence of complete copies of Bede's works at Ælfric's monastery of Cerne.[110] If so, Ælfric would have missed a number of key statements in Bede's homilies and commentary on Luke on the subject of grace. A number of references could be mentioned in this regard, but four will suffice for the present study: *Homiliae* II.14, two selections from *In Lucae euangelium expositio*, and *Homiliae* I.2.

In Lucae euangelium expositio and the Homiliarum
euangelii libri: Selections

Homiliae II.14 is particularly noteworthy for its discussion of faith and prayer in relation to grace. To describe faith, first of all, Bede uses the image of a fish immersed in water. Just as a fish is born, lives, and is nourished within water, Bede says, so faith is begotten, consecrated, and nourished by the Spirit. Thus sustained, faith 'inuisibilium praemiorum intuitu quaeque ualet bona operatur' (does all the good things of which it is capable with a view to invisible rewards).[111] Given this dependence, of what good things are humans capable? One thing, again, might seem to be prayer. Bede repeatedly exhorts people to ask for the Spirit's help, noting that 'Siue fidem spem caritatem siue alia quaelibet bona caelestia desideramus adipisci non aliter nobis haec quam per sancti spiritus donum tribuuntur.'[112] Whence then does the impetus for such prayer come? Using a florilegium of scriptural passages, Bede shows that the Spirit is known not only as the Spirit of wisdom, piety, love, and so forth, but 'spiritum gratiae et precum' (the Spirit of grace and prayers [Zec. 12.10]). He thus concludes: 'Nimirum quicquid boni ueraciter habemus quicquid bene agimus' – including the grace to pray, it would seem – 'hoc eodem spiritu largiente percipimus.'[113] While Bede asserts that people do *quaeque ualent* (all they can), therefore, ultimately he attributes their success to God.

   Two of the more striking passages from Bede's *In Lucae euangelium expositio* that are omitted in Paul the Deacon and Smaragdus deal with the thief on the cross (Luke 23.42–3) and Christ's parable of the Prodigal Son (Luke 15.11–32). In the first case, while Cassian may use the thief (as well as Zaccheus) to show that individuals may seek God of their own initiative, there are no such Semi-Pelagian sentiments here.

Though nails restrained the thief's limbs, Bede says, and nothing remained free from punishment save his heart and tongue, 'Inspirante deo totum illi obtulit quod in se liberum inuenit ut ... corde crederet ad iustitiam ore confiteretur ad salutem.'[114] Faith here stems not from individuals, but is inspired by God. A different image is found in Bede's exposition of the Prodigal Son, where Bede equates the son's rejection of his father with humankind's rejection of God. The son demands his inheritance from the father, Bede says, even as humanity, 'sua potestate delectatus per liberum sese arbitrium regere atque a dominio quaesiuit exuere conditoris.'[115] The father, in turn, 'divides' his property when God gives the unfaithful the natural ability for which they are eagerly striving, but not the support of his grace. The son leaves his father far behind just as individuals withdraw their hearts from grace through sin.[116] Though it seems good to the son to direct his own efforts and rely on his own powers, 'Quas uires tanto consumit citius quanto eum deserit a quo datae sunt.'[117] The image may not seem entirely Augustinian, in that human beings are implied to have lost their moral powers gradually rather than immediately upon Adam's transgression; in this sense, it is reminiscent of Gregory's portrait of humans 'becoming' rather than being born blind. As Bede clearly teaches that original sin has made people sinful from conception and unable to save themselves, however, it may be that the parallel need not be pressed so far. The moral of the story is orthodox enough: apart from God, Bede affirms, human beings are powerless.

Homiliae I.2, last of all, is remarkable for containing what is perhaps Bede's longest treatment of grace apart from his preface to *In Cantica Canticorum* (on which see below). If Bede's phraseology seems particularly Augustinian at points, it is hardly surprising, for one of the sources on which the text draws is *Tractatus in euangelium Ioannis*.[118] Among other things, Bede says that all have received whatever good they have from God; that no one can know or do anything if he has not received it from Christ;[119] that believing, loving, and doing good works are not attained by any preceding human merit; that it is only by grace that people attain eternal life as a result of their faith, love, and good works; that individuals always need God to lead them if they are not to turn aside; that the beginning of faith and good deeds is a gift of God; that in heaven God will reward those good works which he himself has enabled individuals to do; and that even though eternal life is bestowed for preceding merits, the merits themselves were first granted freely by the Saviour.[120] Such a testimony, augmented still further by images such as the fish encompassed by water and the son lost without his father, might well have been thought to balance any emphasis on meritorious deeds in Paul the Deacon or Smaragdus. Indeed, such passages make it clear that, however many times Bede may urge individuals to righteous efforts, humanity's part is minuscule compared to the ubiquity of grace.

In Cantica Canticorum allegorica expositio

One final text that is conspicuous by its absence in later Anglo-Saxon England is Bede's *In Cantica Canticorum allegorica expositio*. This exposition of the *Cantica* as a dialogue between Synagogue, Church, and Christ draws not only on Gregory, excerpts from whom form the final book of Bede's work, but, remarkably, on Julian of Eclanum, the Pelagian against whom Augustine directs his final writings. While Bede quotes from Julian 'without criticism' in the body of his work, however, a later recognition of Julian's heterodoxy leads Bede to refute the theology of Julian's own commentary on the *Cantica*.[121] This study of free will, which serves as the preface to *In Cantica Canticorum*, Bede writes 'pro defensione gratiae Dei quam ille impugnauit' (to defend the grace of God which [Julian] attacked).[122]

Grace indeed is at the heart of this treatise. Christ, Bede notes, 'non ait: "Sine me modicum quid potestis," sed: "Sine me," inquit, "nihil potestis facere."'[123] It is not, as Julian would have it, that God makes people self-sufficient through his gift of volition and the example of the Law. Rather, God both introduces virtue in human character and perfects it through discipline, 'ut diceret, gratia inchoet gratia consummet gratia coronet.'[124]

Marshalling a host of scriptural passages – many of them favourites of Augustine before him – Bede addresses Julian's heretical contentions point by point. When Julian denies that individuals are impelled towards evil by the vice of their nature, Bede recalls Paul's lament that 'Scio quia non habitat in me [bonum] ... non enim quod uolo bonum hoc facio.'[125] When he claims that human beings have equal freedom to do good or evil, Bede argues, 'Nec uiri est ut ... dirigat gressus suos' and 'Mente seruio legi Dei carne autem legi peccati.'[126] When he says that Jacob is distinguished from Esau not by grace but by the different merits of their wills, Bede reminds us that God loved the one and hated the other 'cum necdum nati fuissent aut aliquid egissent bonum aut malum.'[127] When he asserts that nothing stands in the way of people living well save long habits of sin, Bede notes, 'Graue iugum super filios Adam a die exitus de uentre matris eorum.'[128] When he maintains that God would not command what was impossible for humans to do, Bede retorts that the righteous voice calls upon God for help, saying 'Deduc me in semita mandatorum tuorum.' Those who trust in the strength of their own will, Bede concludes, are again refuted by Christ's statement, 'Sine me nihil potestis facere.'[129]

Despite the importance of *In Cantica Canticorum*, no copy remains from Anglo-Saxon England and no suggestion has been made that any of our authors may have known the work – save one. In his entry for Ælfric's second homily for Palm Sunday (*CH* II.14) in the *Fontes Anglo-Saxonici* database, Godden cites *In Cantica Canticorum* III.5 as a possible source for a passage discussing the saints who were resurrected at Christ's death (lines 298–301; Matt. 27.52–3). Having suggested that these figures did not die but ascended to heaven with Christ after his resurrrection, Ælfric characteristically defends his extra-biblical comment, saying that it is 'swa swa wise lareowas. geleaflice secgað.'[130] Bede's commentary does in fact offer a potential parallel at one point, stating, 'Qui resurgente Domino resurrexerunt a mortuis, etiam eo coelos ascendente, simul ascendisse credendi sunt.'[131] Even here, however, Godden presents *In Cantica Canticorum* more as an ultimate than an immediate source, for he notes that the passage also appears in Smaragdus.[132] It is, in fact, the only extract from the commentary reproduced by Smaragdus, suggesting still further that Ælfric would not have known the entire work. What is more, in his monumental printed commentary on the *Sermones*, released three years after his entry for *Fontes Anglo-Saxonici*, Godden makes no mention of *In Cantica Canticorum*. Rather, he notes that lines 298–301 repeat a point Ælfric makes twice earlier in the *Sermones*, on occasions when he was drawing on Paschasius Radbertus's *De Assumptione*.[133] Far from being familiar with the whole of Bede's commentary, therefore, Ælfric may not have known even the one sentence available to him.

The matter is of consequence. As with those texts omitted from Paul the Deacon and Smaragdus, Ælfric's ignorance of the preface to *In Cantica Canticorum* would have had a significant impact on the way in which he viewed Bede's teaching on free will, for the preface places far less emphasis on human merit and presents a stronger statement of grace than do those sources to which Ælfric certainly had access. It may be that this unbalanced perspective contributed to the emphasis on merit that we find – as we shall see – in the *Sermones catholici*.

Bede's Theology of Free Will as Known
in Anglo-Saxon England: Summary

Throughout Bede's works, then, there runs a tension between grace and merit. Bound and blind through the corruption of their desires, human beings paradoxically must merit God's gratuitous enlightenment. The examples of Zaccheus and the centurion suggest that faith is meritorious, while other references speak of *gratia fidei* (the grace of faith). Individuals must strive to deserve God's help in accomplishing good deeds, even though love, the source of righteous works, is the prevenient gift of God. Like Gregory, moreover, Bede teaches that God's initiative enables people to 'cooperate' with God. Like living stones, human beings should accept the grace they are given, and pray for further grace. Whereas *Homiliae* II.14 indicates that prayer too is from the Spirit, the works known to later Anglo-Saxon England are ambiguous as to whether God is responsible for human prayer. Despite these texts' disproportionate emphasis on merit, however, and Bede's subtle departures from Augustine, the overall impression our later authors would have received would likely have been one that would have pleased the African Father. Speaking of Peter, Bede states: 'Quicquid deuotae oboeditionis domini inpendit totum hoc nimirum praeueniente se gratia supernae pietatis ut habere posset accepit.'[134] While 'ut haec etiam nos intrare mereamur caelestem in terris exercere uitam contendimus,' therefore, the Church is at its most beautiful when 'nulla quae facimus ... bona nostris meritis adscribimus sed auctoris nostri per omnia gratiam respicimus.'[135] Ultimately, like his predecessors, Bede affirms the primacy of grace. Two hundred and fifty years later, however, a celebrated champion of the works of Augustine, Gregory, and Bede would provide another perspective altogether by adapting a Neoplatonic classical source for his discussion of free will.

CHAPTER FOUR

Alfred the Great and
the *Old English Boethius*

Around 855, at the age of six, the boy who would become known as Alfred the Great accompanied his father, Æthelwulf, king of the West Saxons, on his pilgrimage to Rome. At the time, few would have thought that Alfred was destined for the throne: four brothers, after all, preceded him by birth. When to the throne Alfred did come, however, the journey of his childhood seems to have had a lasting effect on his endeavours. One endeavour perhaps influenced both by his memory of Rome and by his struggles thereafter was a translation of what may have been the most influential study of free will in the Middle Ages: Boethius's *De consolatione Philosophiae*.[1]

The Martial and Literary Labours of Alfred

The trials that marked Alfred's youth and reign are of course well known.[2] The decade following the pilgrimage saw the death of Alfred's father and Alfred's two eldest brothers. Invasion also threatened: by the time Alfred's remaining brother took up office in 865, the Danes had moved from mere coastal raids to setting up permanent settlements. Between 867 and 870, they established control over a wide area of southern Northumbria, overran the Anglo-Saxon kingdoms of East Anglia and Mercia, and set their sights on Wessex. The results of the following battles were mixed: Æthelred and Alfred beat back the Danes at Ashdown in 871, but Æthelred died later that year following further skirmishes. Ascending the throne at the age of 21, Alfred first bought himself some five years' respite with a heavy payment of tribute. He used that time, however, to build up a fleet and assemble his forces; in consequence, when Viking attacks recommenced in 876–7, he was able to stop their advance and force them to swear peace. A surprise attack in 878, however, forced Alfred to flee to the fens of Somerset, where he organized guerrilla attacks on the invading forces. The following year, having regrouped, he defeated the Danes soundly at the battle of Edington; thereafter he confined them to that area called the Danelaw. Emerging improbably victorious from war, however, Alfred realized that more than walls needed to be rebuilt: character had to be strengthened through the restoration of learning.

Alfred's vision of education was remarkable in a number of ways. He recruited an international team of gifted scholars; he organized a court school after the example of Charlemagne; he had key works translated into English to promote literacy throughout his kingdom;[3] and he himself translated texts 'most necessary for all people to know.'[4] One feature shared by those texts is also striking, however: not a few date from the twilight of the Roman Empire in the face of Germanic invasion.[5] Augustine's *Soliloquia* was written in Italy in 386–7, eight years before the Empire's permanent division on Theodosius's death. Orosius's *Historia aduersos paganos* was written in 417 in response to the Visigothic sack of Rome. Gregory the Great's *Regula pastoralis* and *Dialogi* were written in the early 590s, as Gregory was making annual payments to the Lombards to keep Rome from being besieged. And then there was Boethius's *De consolatione Philosophiae*, written in 524 before his execution at the hands of Italy's Ostrogothic king.

Boethius in the Context of the Late Roman Empire

To understand the period of history of such interest to Alfred, as well as the possible appeal of *De consolatione* itself, one must review the political situation which led to Boethius's incarceration – a situation that was, as so typical of Roman affairs, not lacking in complexity.[6] Upon the death of Theodosius I in 395, the Roman Empire had been divided between his sons: one ruled from Constantinople, the seat of government since 330; the other governed the West first from Milan and then from his marsh-ringed (and thus naturally fortified) capital at Ravenna. Eighty years later, the line of Western emperors came to an end when the Germanic chief Odoacer deposed Romulus Augustus in 476; having successfully petitioned for recognition from the Eastern emperor Zeno, Odoacer ruled as king of Italy for seventeen years. Eventually, however, facing increasing pressure from his Ostrogoth allies for expansion and deteriorating relations with Odoacer, Zeno encouraged Theodoric, king of the Ostrogoths, to invade Italy and supplant the Germanic chief. This Theodoric did, capturing Ravenna and executing Odoacer in 493. To consolidate his power, however, Theodoric relied on more than Zeno's patronage; in addition, he courted Rome.

Rome had long been displaced as the centre of power in the West, with Milan having achieved preeminence in 286 during a previous division of the Empire under Diocletian. The sack of the city by Visigoths in 410 and Vandals in 455 did nothing to restore its former glory.[7] Nonetheless, two bodies – one still prestigious if curbed in power, the other growing in influence – remained players on the political scene: the senate and the episcopacy. Theodoric, an admirer of Roman culture since his exposure to the court of Constantinople in his youth, worked with the senate, allowed Roman citizens to live under Roman law, and kept key positions like that of consul – once the highest elected office of the Republic and still a prestigious appointment – in Roman aristocratic hands. Moreover, though an Arian, viewing Jesus as a created being rather than of the same essence as the Father, Theodoric avoided proselytizing to Catholics and was noted for his policy of religious tolerance.

By no means, however, were tensions absent. One area of friction with direct implications for Boethius was the relationship between the church at Rome and the Eastern Empire, which had been strained since Zeno's publication of the *Henotikon* or 'Act of Union' in 482. This document was an attempt to reconcile orthodox believers, who affirmed both the human and divine natures of Christ in accordance with the 451 Council of Chalcedon, with the Monophysites, who believed that Christ had but one nature. The situation was pressing: the provinces of Egypt, Syria, and Palestine were all marked by increasingly Monophysite leanings, and doctrinal differences were fuelling nationalistic, anti-imperial sentiment. Zeno's attempt at conciliation, however, satisfied few. Not only did the *Henotikon* fail to resolve the controversy by avoiding a pronouncement on Christ's nature, but Zeno alienated his own bishops by issuing the document without the approval of a synod. Felix III, pontiff or bishop of Rome from 483 to 492, condemned the *Henotikon* and excommunicated its alleged author, Patriarch Acacius of Constantinople, as well as the Monophysite bishops of Antioch and Alexandria. Felix's actions divided the East and West for some thirty-five years; the controversy over Monophysitism, however, aided Theodoric by diverting attention away from his equally heretical Arian beliefs. Thus matters stood in the early sixth century: an Ostrogoth ruled the former heart of the Western Roman Empire; one denying Jesus's eternality held power amid acute divisions over Christ's nature; an invader kept an uneasy peace between his Catholic, formerly imperial subjects and his Catholic, imperial overlord. And onto this political stage stepped Boethius.

Anicius Manlius Severinus Boethius was a son of two powerful Roman aristocratic houses: the Anicii, into which he was born, and the Symmachi, into which he was adopted by the former consul and influential senator Quintus Aurelius Memmius Symmachus. For many years, Boethius's political career was marked by singular success. He was named sole consul while still in his twenties, honoured by the joint investiture of his sons as consuls thereafter, and ultimately appointed Master of Offices at Ravenna, making him intermediary between Theodoric and all who sought audience with him. His literary endeavours were no less ambitious: his stated intent was to instruct citizens by providing translations of and commentaries on all of Aristotle's and Plato's works, and he made considerable progress in this regard, turning out works on mathematics and logic as well as original treatises on theology. These remarkable fortunes, however, were dramatically reversed when around 523–4 Boethius found himself charged with treason.

The problem started with the accession of Justin I as Eastern emperor in 518. Responding to ecclesiastical and diplomatic overtures guardedly sanctioned by Theodoric, Justin ended the schism between East and West by confirming Felix's excommunication of Acacius and becoming an active champion of orthodoxy – possibly even to the extent of persecuting Arians in the East. Facing an ever-increasing rapprochement between the Roman see and the Catholic emperor, who might be seen as an attractive alternative to a foreign heterodox king, Theodoric felt himself increasingly under threat, especially after the death of his son and intended heir. When in 523–4 the distinguished senator Albinus, who had played a key role in the ecclesiastical reconciliation, was accused of disparaging Theodoric to Justin's officials, Theodoric had him condemned without formal trial. In a move that would prove fatal, Boethius attempted to defend Albinus; swift accusations by political enemies of Boethius led to his imprisonment and execution. This incarceration proved the motive and the setting for the writing of *De consolatione*.

Why should these events of late-fifth and early-sixth-century Rome have brought Boethius to reflect so intensively on free will? Part of the reason must surely have been the sense of powerlessness Boethius felt at the end of his labours: for all his privileged origins, gifts, political success, and literary achievement, ultimately no effort on his part could prevail against the powers, political and ecclesiastical, that brought about his demise. Physical walls brought him to reflect on the confines of the human condition.[8] It would be small wonder if the plight of this figure, brought suddenly to ruin by a Germanic leader and asking hard questions about God's justice, should have resonated with a king with memories of treachery and the fens of Somerset. The strength of Alfred's reaction might be evidenced, in fact, by his description of the events surrounding Boethius's incarceration. Where *De consolatione* is cautious in its condemnation, presenting Boethius's senatorial colleagues rather than the king as the agents of his downfall, Alfred lays the blame squarely at Theodoric's feet: Theodoric is a tyrant, an invader, a heretic, an oathbreaker, a wreaker of manifold wrongs on the Christian faith, and the cruel oppressor of a chief most upright in learning and worldly affairs ('heretoha ... in boccræftum [ond] on woruldþeawum se rihtwisesta' [1.7.12–13]).[9] Such language may, of course, simply be literary, reflecting narratorial technique rather than Alfred's own perspective.[10] Nonetheless, by personally labouring to provide vernacular versions of Boethius's tale, Alfred presents us with another Anglo-Saxon perspective on free will – one that differs strikingly from the views of his original.

The Argument of *De consolatione Philosophiae*

To appreciate the extent to which Alfred departs from *De consolatione*, it may be helpful to review the overall argument of Boethius's work before examining specific ways in which it addresses the problem of free will. A thumbnail sketch might run as follows: While lamenting his arrest and confinement, Boethius is visited by Lady Philosophy, who dismisses the Muses of poetry to whom he has turned for comfort, upbraids him for neglecting her teachings, and responds to his complaint about the apparent injustice of Fortune by stating that Boethius is sick: he has forgotten the Providence that orders all events, the goal to which creation proceeds, and the nature of his immortal soul, which he must understand to attain a knowledge of God (Book I). Boethius does wrong, Philosophy says, to long for his lost wealth and position and to condemn Fortune's inconstancy: Fortune is fickle by nature, and her reversals must be expected; as her gifts last only to individuals' deaths, moreover, one cannot find true happiness in wealth, ambition, or fame (Book II). Again, nothing in this world of change – riches, public office, power, fame, or bodily pleasure – can provide lasting happiness, though true happiness or good subsumes the positive aspects of these false paths; rather, that which humans long for, even in their mistaken pursuit of such things, is the highest good, which is God, who is identical with happiness: in attaining happiness, human beings become divine (Book III). When Boethius questions how a good God could allow virtue to suffer and evil to flourish, Philosophy argues that since humans desire happiness or good, good people are rewarded with the fulfilment of their desires while the wickedness of the wicked is its own punishment; thus, while it may seem that God is unjust, humans simply lack the capacity to comprehend the overarching, beneficent ordering of Providence expressed through the daily unfolding of events called Fate (Book IV). Circumstances that appear to people as the product of chance are in fact conjunctions of causes arranged by Providence; neither this sovereignty, however, nor divine foreknowledge invalidates free will. While vice degrades the soul's capacity to make reasoned choices, people do make choices – choices that lead to actions which, along with naturally caused events (such as the sun's rising), God observes in his simultaneous apprehension of all things past, present, and future (Book V).

Free Will in *De consolatione*

The Problem of Providence

De consolatione addresses at least two major challenges to the concept of free will: divine sovereignty and foreknowledge. The first involves the extent to which God's omnipotence – not simply his authority or capability but his active ordering of events – impinges on human actions. Having spent Books I–II and most of Book III revealing the elusive and unsatisfying nature of worldly fortunes whose loss Boethius laments, in Book III Prose 10, Philosophy sets forth the goal that Boethius should seek: the highest good, the sum of all things worth pursuing, the perfection of happiness, God himself. This goal, she says, is the underlying aim of all humankind's misguided worldly pursuits, so that people rush towards the good with 'instinctive striving' (naturali intentione [III.pr12.17]). Philosophy's thesis has considerable implications for human freedom, for she concludes that all humans are willingly subject entirely to their Creator.

Nihil est igitur, quod naturam seruans deo contra ire conetur?
Nihil, inquam.
Quodsi conetur, ait, num tandem proficiet quicquam aduersus eum quem
iure beatitudinis potentissimum esse concessimus?
Prorsus, inquam, nihil ualeret.
Non est igitur aliquid quod summo huic bono uel uelit uel possit obsistere?
Non, inquam, arbitror. (III.pr12.19–21)

'There is nothing, therefore, that, acting according to nature, strives to go
against God?'
'Nothing,' I said.
'And if it thus strives,' she continued, 'would it make any progress
against him whom we have rightly granted as being supremely powerful
in happiness?'
'In a word,' I said, 'it could do nothing.'
'There is therefore nothing that would either desire or be able to resist this
highest good?'
'I think not,' I said.

Such apparent powerlessness to oppose God would seem to necessitate obedience and reduce people to automata; clearly, however, in this
world defiance of the divine Law abounds. Book IV begins, in fact,
with Boethius questioning how wickedness can exist given the absolute sovereignty of a God who wills only good. Philosophy in essence
suggests that God's sovereignty does not prevent people from choosing evil, but prevents their evil choices from going unpunished: human
volition cannot circumvent or otherwise thwart the divine rules by
which creation operates. Echoing an argument developed in Plato's
Gorgias, Philosophy states that since humans by nature long for happiness, the highest good, those who seek happiness by wicked means are
punished by their own wickedness: wretched and pitiable, they
deprive themselves of the very good which is their goal. For the righteous, by contrast, virtue is literally its own reward, for it is synony-
mous with the highest happiness. It is in this sense, therefore, that
Philosophy can maintain that of their own accord human beings direct
themselves 'according to the will of him who orders them' (uoluntaria
regantur seque ad disponentis nutum [III.pr12.17]).

For the incarcerated Boethius, however, Philosophy's logic is good in
theory but unsatisfying in practice: all too often, he notes pointedly, the

good are made to suffer while the wicked enjoy prosperity (IV.pr4.26 and IV.pr5.6). Philosophy's response is twofold: on the one hand, she says, the ways of Providence often seem inexplicable or unjust to human beings because humans are deceived by surface appearances while God sees the underlying reality. Like a heavenly physician, God treats individuals in accordance with their need, sparing the weak who would become depraved in time of hardship, sending trials to the righteous who will gain character thereby, or even allowing gross iniquity to flourish so that others, repulsed, would shun such evil ways. In addition, Philosophy explains, human confusion about the ways of Providence stems from the fundamental difference between divine and human nature. God's relationship to the created order, she says, may be thought of like an axis around which concentric circles revolve: in the centre, there is changeless simplicity; in the rings, there is ever-increasing motion and seeming disarray. The one is the permanence that moves all things; the other the wheel of unpredictable Fortune.[11] The one is the source of purity and happiness; the other the world of fleshliness and squalour. The more people focus on the one, the clearer is their judgment and the freer their will; the more they devote themselves to the other, the more clouded their reason and enfeebled their volition. Pursuing vice, people freely enslave themselves. Though human history may appear chaotic and unfair, therefore, that appearance results from human beings' distance from God and belies the divine righteousness that governs all events (IV.pr6 and V.pr2).

The Problem of Divine Foreknowledge

The second major challenge to the notion of free will which *De consolatione* addresses is that of God's foreknowledge. Boethius raises the issue, which dominates the final portion of the work, with a series of questions in Book V Prose 3. On the one hand, how can free will exist if necessity is antithetical to freedom, and that which is foreseen must necessarily come to pass (§§10–14 and 17)? On the other hand, if we say that God's foresight does not cause but follows from human choices, is it not incongruous to assert that the Axis and Mover of all things should be dependent for his knowledge on mutable temporal events (§§15–16)? If, by contrast, one should suggest that volitional freedom makes outcomes uncertain, in what way can God be said with certainty to know the future (§§18–26)? It would seem either that foreknowledge negates free will or that free will makes foreknowledge impossible.

Philosophy addresses the issue by redefining the notion of divine foreknowledge. She denies, first of all, that God's knowledge of future events compels those events to happen. If one sees a charioteer directing his horses, she asks, does one's observation influence the actions of the charioteer? Granted, said observation is of present rather than future events; God's omniscience is such, however, that to his eyes the whole of history is present: God apprehends simultaneously the past, present, and future. In his eternal present, therefore, God sees future events that proceed from the free choice of individuals – embracing at a glance, moreover, any volitional uncertainty or vacillation that may precede that choice.

As her exposition draws to a close, Philosophy asserts that her logical tour de force has also addressed Boethius's second objection, that it would be unworthy to suggest that human actions cause God's knowledge: rather, it is the latter, embracing everything in its gaze, that itself has fixed a limit to or appointed the bounds of all things ('rebus modum omnibus ipsa constituit' [V.pr6.43]). R.W. Sharples notes, however, that Philosophy's assertion is problematic, for her language may suggest that God orders or predetermines human events.[12] Even if one understands God's 'ordering' merely as his establishment of rules for human existence, which reward or deprive people of the good they seek according to their own behaviour, the statement fails to answer Boethius's objection. Either God is the first cause, the one ultimately responsible for human choices, or his foreknowledge follows from and is in some way subordinate to those choices. Nevertheless, *De consolatione*'s solution stands: in spite of God's providential and just orchestration of events, in the midst of his knowledge of all events in an eternal present, human beings as rational creatures possess freedom of the will – a freedom that becomes the more free as individuals focus their minds on the things of heaven.

De consolatione and Neoplatonism

Philosophy's defence of God's righteousness in the face of evil and her call for individuals to exercise their free will in seeking that righteousness held considerable appeal for Christian readers; indeed, a key reason *De consolatione* was so popular in the Middle Ages was the relative ease in which it could be interpreted along orthodox lines.[13] Boethius himself, moreover, was known to have produced conservative doctrinal work: Henry Chadwick describes Boethius's *De fide catholica*, for example, as a 'vibrant confession of faith in the biblical story of redemption as interpreted by Augustine.'[14] *De consolatione*, however, is a beast of an entirely different stripe altogether, for its perspective is rooted not in Christian doctrine but in Neoplatonism.

Neoplatonism was a new formulation of Plato's teachings initiated in third-century Rome by Plotinus (ca. 205–69). Plotinus's works were edited and built upon by his disciple Porphyry (ca. 232–305), whose work in turn was translated into Latin by the fourth-century Marius Victorinus. From its inception, Neoplatonism saw contact and overlap between its adherents and Christian figures. Plotinus's instructor Ammonius Saccas also taught Origen (ca. 185–254), head of the Christian catechetical school at Alexandria; Marius Victorinus, who converted to Christianity, served as a model for Augustine when attempting to reconcile Neoplatonic and Christian doctrine (*Confessiones* 8.2.3 and 8.5.10). Nevertheless, fundamental differences divide the two systems of thought. Describing the nature of God, for example, Plotinus spoke of the One or the Good from whom various levels of reality emanate. The first emanation he called the Mind, in which exist Forms or Ideas; from the Mind proceeds the World Soul. Out of the World Soul come human souls, which in turn are united with bodies as they descend into this corrupt and mutable world of matter, the antithesis of the One. Corollary to this process of emanation and descent is the soul's ascent through contemplation of the divine, which has implications both for the soul's present (increased righteousness) and future existence (union with the One).

Such Neoplatonic language features prominently in *De consolatione*. Philosophy speaks of Forms, the Mind, and the World Soul in her metaphor of the axis (IV.pr6.14–16). She asserts that while the wicked become bestial or subhuman through their evil choices (IV.pr3.16–21), those who pursue the Good or One ultimately become gods (III.pr10.24 and IV.pr3.10), their souls returning after death to the world of the Forms (IV.m1.23–6; cf. III.pr2.13). She speaks particularly of the various levels of reality and the transmigration of the soul in III Metre 9 – the section of *De consolatione* which, for this very reason, sparked the most controversy in the ninth and tenth centuries. As we have noted, this understanding of humanity's origin has direct implications for his will: as Philosophy explains, 'Humanas uero animas liberiores quidem esse necesse est cum se in mentis diuinae speculatione conseruant, minus uero cum dilabuntur ad corpora, minusque etiam cum terrenis artubus colligantur' (By necessity, human souls are more free when they keep themselves in the contemplation of the divine Mind, less so when they fall down into bodies, and less still when they are bound in earthly flesh [V.pr2.8]).[15] Chadwick summarizes the philosophy of the work thus: 'Boethius is not in quest of consolation from divine grace in the remission of sins and the promise of eternal life to those redeemed through Christ. His doctrine of salvation is humanist, a soteriology of the inward purification of the soul. The *Consolation* is a work written by a Platonist who is also a Christian, but is not a Christian work.'[16]

Christian Commentaries on a Neoplatonic Work

Despite the Neoplatonic framework of *De consolatione*, the bulk of the text lent itself well to interpretation from a Christian perspective: Philosophy calls people, after all, to renounce worldly pleasures, value the growth that comes from trials, and grow in righteousness by contemplating God. As a result, following its rediscovery during the Carolingian renaissance, the ninth and tenth centuries saw a number of influential Christian commentaries produced on Boethius's text. Not all viewed the Neoplatonic content therein as innocuous. Bovo of Corvey, for example, preparing a commentary for his monks in the early ninth century, found it astonishing that one who had composed such orthodox doctrine on the Trinity and on the person of Christ 'should have written such dangerous stuff.'[17] Nonetheless, the glosses established a tradition of Christian interpretation on *De consolatione* that provide an important context for Alfred's work – a tradition that is at present a subject of considerable confusion and debate. Unresolved questions include the precise number of strands of extant commentary (if such can even be distinguished), the dating and interrelationship of those strands, and the extent to which they influenced Alfred's composition. While the different bodies of commentary may be organized in various ways, for the present purpose we may group them into three broad categories: miscellaneous, St Gallen, and Remigian commentaries.

The first category includes a number of minor commentaries as well as one of potentially considerable importance. In his 1967 survey of the commentary tradition, Pierre Courcelle identified five minor sets of glosses on *De consolatione*: the early-ninth-century commentary of Bovo of Corvey; the Anonymous of Brussels 10066–77 (ca. s. x^1); the Anonymous of Einsiedeln 302 (s. x); the commentary of Adalbold d'Utrecht (d. 1026); and the Anonymous of Paris. lat. 10400 (s. x). All focus primarily if not exclusively on the problematic III Metre 9, save for the last, which glosses IV.m6 to V.pr3, a slightly larger area.[18] In addition, however, there is Vatican, Biblioteca Apostolica Vaticana, lat. 3363.[19] Written in the Tours region in the early ninth century, it contains Latin glosses in a variety of hands: one probably continental and contemporary with the text, two Welsh hands from the late ninth century (one being the primary glossator), and others from mid-tenth-century Glastonbury, including that of Dunstan (909–88).[20] The manuscript was thus in southern England by at least the middle of the tenth century, and earlier scholarship even suggested a connection between the Vatican glosses and Alfred's court. Courcelle offered such a link in his 1939 study of Boethian commentaries, and Fabio Troncarelli affirmed in 1981 that some of its glosses were written by Asser, Alfred's contemporary biographer. Joseph Wittig, however, responding to Troncarelli's argument two years later, discounted the hypothesis that Alfred used the manuscript for his translation.[21] A final verdict on the matter is hampered by the fact that no complete edition of the glosses exists: Troncarelli printed selections in 1973 and 1981, but concentrated on marginal comments rather than interlinear glosses and did not distinguish between the different hands. Compounding the issue (as we shall see) is the uncertain relationship between these glosses and other strands of Boethian commentary. Even so, the conclusion of conservative scholarship at present is that voiced by Malcolm Godden: 'Tempting though it is to think that the manuscript was brought to Alfred's court by one of his learned foreign advisers, it is more than the evidence will allow.'[22]

The second category of Boethian commentary comprises anonymous glosses composed at St Gallen either in the ninth or the first half of the tenth century. St Gallen was a likely setting for the reconciling of Boethius's thought with Christian doctrine: Jacqueline Beaumont notes that it was a noted centre of academic excellence, had a flourishing school, and housed a rich collection of Boethian manuscripts.[23] Analysis of the St Gallen Anonymous has been hindered by the absence of a critical edition;[24] nonetheless, depending on one's interpretation of the material, one may identify between two and four versions of the Anonymous that survive:

1) the earlier, shorter version: a body of marginal and interlinear glosses on the Boethian text, extant in two manuscripts, Naples, Biblioteca Nazionale, IV. G. 68 (text St Gallen or perhaps Tours,[25] s. ix[2/2]; glosses St Gallen s. x) and its later copy, St Gallen, Stiftsbibliothek, 844 (St Gallen, s. ix);[26] it shares a number of glosses in common with

Remigius (on whom more below), including the whole of his commentary on III Metre 9
2) the later, longer version: a continuous commentary on *De consolatione*
surviving in Einsiedeln, Stiftsbibliothek, 179 (St Gallen, s. x) and its
copy, St Gallen, Stiftsbibliothek, 845 (St Gallen, s. x);[27] it includes part
of its predecessor, including material found also in Remigius
3) the shorter continuous commentary: an abbreviated set of glosses in
continuous form found in Paris, Bibliothèque Nationale, lat. 13953
(s. x); it has no Remigian parallels but does include material not found
in the second version of the Anonymous (2). While Beaumont's 1981
study regards this commentary as a third version of the St Gallen
Anonymous, and Malcolm Godden in 2003 suggested that it might
represent an abridgement of the second version (2), the latest assessment by Petrus Tax shows that Paris 13953 represents a combination
of excerpts from the shorter (1) and longer (2) versions[28]
4) the diasporatic version: selected glosses from versions of the Anonymous found alongside Remigian commentary in other manuscripts.

Despite these multiple versions, the paucity of surviving manuscripts
may suggest that the influence of the Anonymous was limited. One reason may be found in the nature of the commentary itself: on the one
hand, the glosses are often so terse that they provide little insight into
Boethius's text; on the other, they provide inadequate explanations of
Boethius's classical allusions. In short, as Beaumont states, the St Gallen
Anonymous 'was not sufficiently full or clear to be a satisfactory starting
point for detailed study of the text.'[29]

Another continental commentary, however, was. Towards the end of
his life, a renowned teacher in Paris named Remigius (ca. 841–908)
composed what would prove the most influential of the Boethian commentaries.[30] In sharp contrast to the St Gallen Anonymous, Remigius
provides a wealth of knowledge of classical and patristic texts, drawing on his own extensive learning (and perhaps existing glosses from
his scholarly community)[31] to cite authors such as Virgil, Ovid, Cicero,
Jerome, and Augustine.[32] What is more, Remigius seeks to make such
material accessible, not simply copying sources but digesting them,
often conveying the sense rather than quoting verbatim. Remigius
wrote his work as an educational tool, and it was used as a school
commentary both in England and on the Continent. As Joseph Wittig
notes, 'Not only does it explain difficult words and proper names, but
it also uses the text as an occasion for instructing the reader in matters

grammatical, rhetorical, historical, mythological, philosophical and moral.'[33] First and foremost, moreover, Remigius seeks to interpret *De consolatione* in a manner reconcilable with Christian doctrine.

The extent to which Remigius was successful in his endeavour was sharply debated by subsequent students of Boethius, and a number produced commentaries that built on but modified his work. As with Vatican 3363 and the St Gallen Anonymous, analysis and even identification of these commentaries has been hampered by the lack of critical editions: no complete text of Remigius has been printed to use as a base for comparison, and scholars question whether the complexity of extant evidence will even allow the original work to be recovered.[34] Nonetheless, certain strands of Remigian commentary have been distinguished. In 1967, Courcelle spoke of one reviser on the Continent whose material differs from Remigius primarily in its discussion of *De consolatione* III Metre 9.[35] Ten years later, Diane Bolton demonstrated the extent to which Remigius was studied and revised in tenth-century England.[36] With one exception, she noted (Paris, Bibliothèque Nationale lat. 6401 [s. x^{ex}]), the fifteen surviving manuscripts of the *De consolatione* written in England all contain at least part of the Remigian commentary, some with 'distinctively English versions indicating an active process of grappling with the text.'[37] Bolton groups these reviser versions into three types, best represented by Cambridge, Trinity College O. 3. 7 (St Augustine's, Canterbury, s. x^2), Paris, Bibliothèque Nationale lat. 6401A (Christ Church, Canterbury, s. x^{ex}), and Cambridge, University Library, Kk. 3. 21 (s. x–xi). The first and earliest type is only slightly different from the text of Remigius himself. The second is more distinct, being the closest to the continental reviser. It is the third type, however, that provides the fullest and most independent glosses; Beaumont considers that it 'may well be purely English, since no parallels have been found in continental manuscripts.'[38]

Caution should be taken with Bolton's thesis: on the one hand, Bolton's tripartite classification of insular revisers may belie the complexity of manuscript evidence. As Malcolm Godden has recently stated, 'Preliminary comparisons and collations of other manuscripts ... suggest that there is an enormous amount of variation in commentary on the text, from one manuscript to another, and that we need to think of highly fluid collections or compilations of glosses and scholia rather than '"a commentary."'[39] On the other hand, the extent to which the versions of which Bolton speaks are exclusively English is difficult to determine. As she herself notes, as none of them show any internal evidence of authorship or nationality, it is possible that all the reviser versions originated on the continent.[40] It is not, moreover, as though the English versions are free of continental influence. Recent work by Godden has shown, for example, that there is 'a massive amount of agreement' between CUL Kk. 3. 21 and Vatican 3363, including glosses from Vatican 3363's early continental hand as well as its later Welsh and English ones.[41] The commentary offered by this continental hand, however, is not Remigian, but a separate, pre-existing set of glosses. Indeed, Godden states, the evidence of these manuscripts suggests that rather than continental Remigian revisers influencing British commentators, 'the relationship seems in fact to have been in the other direction. When the Remigian commentary came into use in England, it was enriched and expanded by compilers who drew heavily on the Vatican manuscript.'[42] Far from questioning the existence of an English commentary tradition, therefore, Godden's Alfredian Boethius Project uses CUL Kk. 3. 21 as a basis for collating other manuscripts with 'English' Remigian readings.[43]

Whatever the difficulty of recovering the 'original Remigius' or distinguishing between various strands of Remigian revisers, however, that such material was influential does not stand in doubt. Alfred's own *Boethius*, in fact, may stand in contrast to Remigius in this regard. While the linguistic accessibility of Alfred's work might have been welcome in the post-Viking Benedictine era,[44] the paucity of surviving manuscripts suggests that its impact was limited – though, as we will see, its life was prolonged through reuse by Ælfric. Bolton puts it bluntly: 'Alfred's version was probably too individual to have much influence ... the future of Boethius studies in England, as on the continent, lay with the Remigian commentaries.'[45] But would such commentaries have been known to Alfred?

The Dating of the Boethian Commentaries

Remigius's work has been described either as a synthesis and culmination of ninth-century studies of *De consolatione*, or as the base on which tenth-century studies were built. Gibson, for example, discusses and opposes the former, traditional view, arguing that it is the tenth century rather than the ninth that was the 'classic era' of Boethian study. She concludes: 'We should not postulate the existence of very much commentary on the *De consolatione Philosophiae* during the ninth century.'[46] Similarly, Lapidge remarks: 'It has yet to be demonstrated that the *De consolatione Philosophiae* was known in England before the late ninth century.'[47] Much depends on the dating of Remigius's commentary, which, like Alfred's *Boethius*, is traditionally viewed as a product of the last years of the author's life. The traditional dating of Alfred's death to 899 and Remigius's death to 908 makes the placement of Remigius's work all the more critical, for a couple of years either way might mean the difference as to whether Alfred could or could not have known Remigian material.

The traditional position may be that of Courcelle, who in 1967 dated Remigius's commentary to the years 902 x 908. Courcelle suggests that the work may be related to two other studies by Remigius; his commentary on Martianus Capella, which Courcelle dates to 901–2 and views as a source for the Boethian commentary, and a commentary on Boethius's *Opuscula*, which Courcelle also attributes to Remigius, dates to 902 x 908, and views as dependent on the Boethian commentary.[48] Little solid evidence exists either for these dates or the overall chronology of Remigius's work, however, and subsequent scholars have questioned Courcelle's view. Wittig finds Courcelle's argument 'informative but not compelling,' Gibson describes the case for so late a date as 'not irrefragable,' and John Marenbon has recently questioned whether Remigius composed the *Opuscula* commentary at all.[49] No one, however, has yet been able to establish that the work of Remigius (let alone his revisers) predates Alfred's demise.

Bound up with the question of Remigius's date is that of the St Gallen Anonymous: which came first, did one serve as a source for the other, and could either have influenced the composition of Alfred's *Boethius*? Earlier scholarship, to begin with, viewed the Anonymous as a ninth-century work. In 1980, for example, Bernhard Bischoff dated some of the glosses of the miscellaneous or 'diasporatic version' to the ninth century.[50] In 1981, Beaumont dated the first version of the Anonymous to the ninth century as well, stating that Remigius is dependent on the St Gallen commentary.[51] Bolton likewise argued in 1978 that the multiple layers of glosses contained even in the earliest versions of the Remigius commentary suggest its debt both to the Anonymous and to earlier commentaries now lost.[52] Tax, however, has recently suggested that the Anonymous may be a product of the tenth century, viewing the glosses in Remigius not as borrowings from an earlier tradition but as later interpolations. Noting that both the first and second versions of the Anonymous contain Remigian glosses in their main glossing hand, he argues that the St Gallen scribe was working at least a generation or so after Remigius – ca. 925 at the earliest. To corroborate his point, Tax points out that the second version contains late Old High German glosses that reflect the weakening of vowels that occurred after ca. 900–25. Tax concludes that in this very conservative dialect area such forms indicate a *terminus a quo* of ca. 950.[53] Following Tax, Godden has questioned the significance both of Bischoff's ninth-century dating of 'Anonymous' glosses and the parallels between the Remigian and Anonymous commentaries. On the one hand, Godden raises the question of whether the former belong to the St Gallen tradition at all, saying, 'whether [the correspondences] are sufficient to continue calling these ninth-century glosses witnesses to the St Gall commentary remains to be seen.' On the other hand, though he calls the parallels between Remigius and the Anonymous 'striking ... though perhaps of a limited kind,' he notes the difficulty of determining whether one borrows from the other or whether both draw on common, lost sources.[54] While the question remains open, therefore, the trend in scholarship seems to have shifted, positing a tenth- rather than a ninth-century date for the St Gallen Anonymous.

The debate over dating has obvious implications for the potential sources of Alfred's *Boethius*. One might accept that the St Gallen Anonymous was composed prior to Alfred's death, for example, if one dates the first version to the ninth century, understands the parallels between Remigius and the Anonymous as the former's dependence on the latter's work, and places weight on Bischoff's dating of certain glosses from the 'diasporatic version.' Similarly, one might allow that Remigius's work could have been known to Alfred if one discounts Courcelle's attribution of the *Opuscula* commentary to Remigius, his dating of Remigius's commentary on Martianus Capella to 901–2, or his assertion that the commentary on *De consolatione* postdates the other two. In neither case would one have demonstrated, however, that Alfred knew these other versions; simply that such knowledge was possible. Recent scholarship, indeed, seems to favour the converse postulation. John Brinegar has argued that Alfred relied extensively on sources other than Boethian commentaries.[55] Similarly, in her work for *Fontes Anglo-Saxonici*, Nicole Discenza identified limited parallels between Alfred's *Boethius* and Remigian material, and nearly none between Alfred and the St Gallen Anonymous.[56] Nonetheless, Godden has since affirmed Kurt Otten's contention that the parallels between Alfred and Remigius are 'often striking,' noting that whether or not Alfred knew Remigius directly, the latter might preserve material from a previous tradition available to the king. As a result, Godden suggests, 'Any manuscript [of Remigian commentary] of the tenth or eleventh century could in principle preserve comments that go back to the time of Alfred.'[57] What perspective, therefore, might these various commentary traditions have provided Alfred on free will?

Free Will in the Boethian Commentaries

Given the prominence of the issue to *De consolatione*, one might expect that Boethian glosses would pay particular attention to Philosophy's nuanced arguments on free will. Those which have been published from the Vatican commentary, the St Gallen Anonymous, and the Remigian commentaries, however, indicate that the opposite may well have been the case. In the first two, when treating passages that could provide an opportunity to discuss the Fall, glosses are of such brevity that they would have been of little use to Alfred even had he known them. One key passage where this trend may be seen is in Book V, where Philosophy confirms that '[Libertas arbitrii] est ... neque enim fuerit ulla rationalis natura quin eidem libertas adsit arbitrii' (Freedom of the will exists ... for there would have been no nature with reason without free will being present in it [V.pr2.3]). The insular glossing hand of Vatican 3363 makes two interlinear entries, explaining *inquit* as 'dixit' and *arbitrii* as 'proprius conatus' (personal effort). The Anonymous is of little more assistance, having no glosses in its shorter version and only three in its longer one, where it explains *rationalis natura* as 'humana' (human [nature]), *quin* as 'ut non' (that not), and *eidem* as either 'rationabili creature' or 'homini' (in the rational being or in man).[58] In regards to discussions of the will, at any rate, both Vatican 3363 and the Anonymous are more concerned to clarify vocabulary than to expound theological concepts.

Remigius's revisers similarly have been viewed as less than helpful. While further study of these commentaries may well alter our assessment of their significance, scholarship to date has drawn a sharp distinction between Remigius's approach and that of his followers. Beaumont, for example, states that whereas the former carefully selects and shows understanding of his sources, the latter 'appear simply to have scoured all available literature for anything which could be added and put it down haphazardly, without any attempt at critical evaluation or discrimination where sources were inconsistent.'[59] Certain material they include, moreover, would have been of little interest to Alfred. Wary of Boethius's references to pagan mythology, for example, Alfred disparages 'leasunga' (deceitful tales [35.99.4]) and incorporates biblical illustrations. The revisers, by contrast, are particularly interested in the mythological content of *De consolatione*, such as the stories of Orpheus (III Metre 12), Odysseus (IV Metre 3), and Hercules (IV Metre 7).

Remigius himself is a different story, however. Coming to Philosophy's affirmation of free will in V Prose 2, he seizes the chance to speak at length on the subject. In a passage reproduced (but not augmented) by the third English reviser, Remigius notes:

[1] Homo antequam peccaret liberum habuit arbitrium scilicet utrum in natura boni permaneret an ad malum rueret. Neque enim repugnabat caro legi mentis illius ad peccatum. [2] At postquam nullo cogente peccauit, arbitrium bene agendi penitus perdidit et ad malum tantum ad quod sponte lapsus est liberum habuit arbitrium. [3] Non solum igitur homo bonum per se non potest agere, sed nec cogitare sine solius Dei clementia. [4] Habet itaque homo liberum arbitrium, non tamen sanum sed corruptum et semper ad malum ruens.[60]

[1] Man had free will before he sinned both to remain good in nature or plunge into evil, for the flesh did not use to fight against the law of his mind towards sin. [2] After he voluntarily sinned, however, he inwardly lost the will to do good, and directed his free will only to evil, into which he fell of his own accord. [3] Not only was man unable to do good on his own, but he could not even think without the mercy of God alone. [4] Therefore man has free will, but not unimpaired; it is corrupt and always plunging into evil.

While Remigius is not quoting from Augustine, his perspective is clearly influenced by the African Father.[61] Remigius asserts, like Augustine, that God created humans with the capacity to persevere in righteousness, unhindered by the struggle of flesh and spirit ([1] above).[62] Like Augustine, Remigius affirms that through Adam's choice of evil human desires became wholly corrupt ([2]).[63] In consequence, he says, people can neither accomplish good nor even think rightly without God's help ([3]).[64] While individuals remain 'free' to choose good or evil, therefore, Remigius views human beings' desires as such that, apart from grace, evil will invariably be their choice ([4]). Does Alfred's version of *De consolatione* offer a similarly Augustinian perspective?

The Manuscript Evidence for the Two Versions of Alfred's *Boethius*

Before analysing the theological perspective of Alfred's *Boethius*, two clarifications are in order: first, there is more than one *Boethius*; second, the perspective of these texts may not necessarily be that of

Alfred.[65] Two versions of the *Old English Boethius* are extant: first of all, one alternating between prose and verse following the format of *De consolatione*; the other is written entirely in prose.[66] The prose version survives only in a twelfth-century manuscript, Oxford, Bodleian Library, Bodley 180; its preface identifies Alfred as the author and states that he composed the prose version before the prosimetric one. The later, prosimetric version survives (confusingly enough) in an earlier manuscript, the mid-tenth-century London, British Library, Cotton Otho A. vi. A number of issues complicate our understanding of Alfred's texts. First, there are the prefaces: the prose preface found in Bodley 180 (the prose version) actually appears to have been written for the prosimetric version, only later being incorporated into the twelfth-century copy. Two prefaces, however, seem to have been present in Otho A. vi: the prose preface, only slightly different from its counterpart in Bodley 180, and a brief verse preface telling how Alfred composed the work in verse; both prefaces appear to be by Alfred, their form perhaps reflecting the prosimetric nature of that version. Second, there is the structure of Alfred's versions: Bodley 180 divides the work into forty-two sections or chapters, following a table of contents apparently original to Alfred; in general, however, the divisions correspond neither with the five Books nor the transitions between prose and verse in *De consolatione*. Otho A. vi, furthermore, follows an entirely different plan, with sixty-three sections corresponding only intermittently with those in Bodley 180. Third, there is the damaged condition of Otho A. vi itself: the Cotton fire of 1731 destroyed the opening leaves with their prefaces, and charred the edges of the remainder of the work. Malcolm Godden has recently reconstructed the opening with the help of Oxford, Bodleian Library, Junius 12, Francis Junius's pre-conflagration transcript of Bodley 180 with collations and passages from Otho A. vi; nevertheless, he warns that Junius records spelling variants selectively, tends to emend or miscopy readings, and shows little interest in noting differences in layout.[67] Fourth, there are the various editions of Alfred's *Boethius*: these have either printed the verse sections of Otho A. vi as a seemingly independent work, or variously conflated the two versions into a new text – as in the case of the standard, nineteenth-century edition by Walter Sedgefield, quoted from below.[68] One can only welcome the work of the Alfredian Boethius Project and the forthcoming edition by Godden and Susan Irvine.

The Alfredian Voice

The various versions of Alfred's work are not the only obstacle to understanding Alfred's view of free will: there is the extent to which alterations in Alfred's account may be said to be Alfredian. While for convenience's sake we may speak of 'Alfred's thought' when highlighting areas where the *Old English Boethius* diverges from *De consolatione* – and departures we see even from Alfred's opening portrait of Theodoric – both Alfred's approach to translation in general and the ambiguity of narrative frames in *Boethius* itself make the term problematic. Godden has recently drawn attention to the 'deliberate and audacious' ways in which Alfred and his circle silently alter the works of authors whose authority they appropriate for their own views.[69] While Alfred's preface to Gregory's *Pastoral Care* sets forth what Godden calls 'a remarkably simple, perhaps even naive' description of Alfred's process of translation[70] – painstakingly rendering material even as he was taught, recording the sense of matter where not the exact word, and working consciously in that same tradition as Jerome and those others who translated Holy Scripture – that description seems far removed from Alfred's actual translation practice. One of the more egregious examples in this regard may be the Old English version of Augustine's *Soliloquia*, a dramatic dialogue between Augustine and (his) Reason on the nature of the self and of God. Among other things, the text inserts an entirely fictional passage in which (in stark contrast to the *Soliloquia*'s emphasis on logical deduction) Alfred-cum-Augustine cheekily affirms the importance of having faith in authoritative testimony.[71] What is more, having said up front that Augustine composed his work in two books, Alfred brazenly adds a third of his own invention, still set forth under Augustine's name. While some have posited that Alfred was simply unaware of the extent to which he differed from his originals,[72] and while others might be tempted to view such textual manipulation cynically, Godden suggests that Alfred's approach may rather be playful and literary: 'We might say that, however the Alfredian writers would have explained their activity to others, what they were engaged in was an imaginative fictionalising on themes suggested by their progenitors.'[73] If Alfred does permit himself a certain literary licence in his endeavour, it becomes harder to establish whether Alfred's additions express Alfred's personal view.

De consolatione, of course, like Augustine's *Soliloquia,* inherently involves 'imaginative fictionalising' inasmuch as its author purports to record a dialogue between himself and an allegorical character. This frame is only complicated by the extra layer of the Old English translator. Where Boethius can expect from his audience a familiarity with such rhetorical techniques and thus a willing suspension of disbelief, however, Alfred – if the testimony of his *Pastoral Care* preface is anything to go by – may not be able to expect literacy from his audience, let alone an understanding of the frames present in his work and thus a recognition of the dual nature of its authors. Anglo-Saxons may well have taken the author of *Boethius* to be Boethius. Even if one questions the preface's bleak portrait of education, moreover, the very fact that Alfred offers a translation of Boethius argues that knowledge of *De consolatione* in the original was not widespread. Not many who read Alfred's version, in other words, would have been so familiar with the Latin that they would readily have recognized Alfred's altered or added material. On the contrary, Alfred himself not only fails to draw attention to such additions, but goes out of his way to foreground Boethius as the source of the narrative.[74]

For two reasons, therefore, one may speak with caution of 'Alfred's thought': on the one hand, arguments introduced by Alfred through the mouths of characters in *Boethius* may not necessarily be his own. On the other, even statements that do appear 'authentically Alfredian' were not necessarily recognized by their Anglo-Saxon audience as such. While passages such as Mod's discussion of government (17.40.6–17.41.6) have been anthologized as expressive of Alfred's political views, therefore, and while in such passages speakers may challenge arguments present in *De consolatione,*[75] in no place does Alfred explicitly claim the views of his characters as his own.[76] Having granted, however, that 'Alfred's arguments' best describes original lines of reasoning in *Boethius* rather than ideas definitively espoused by Alfred, the cumulative thrust of that reasoning may nonetheless be significant. To what extent, in short, are Alfred's arguments in the *Boethius* in an Augustinian sense orthodox?

Free Will in Alfred's *Boethius*

Universal Submission and Unnatural Resistance

When Alfred comes to Philosophy's argument in Book III Prose 12 that since humans by their very nature long and seek for good, all submit

willingly to God's will – that is, to the highest good – he makes a crucial change in his version of the discussion.

[Ða] cwæð he: ... ealra gesceafta [agnum] willum God ricsað ofer hi ...
forðæmþe ealla [gesceafta] gecyndelice hiora agnum [willum fundiað] to
cumanne to Gode ... [Ða cwæð ic: Hwi ne] mæg [ic] þæs twiogan; [forþam
Godes anwe]ald nære full eadig[lic gif þa ge]sceafta hiora unwillum him
[herden] ... Ða [cwæð he]: Nis nan gesceaft þe tiohhie [þæt hio] scyle win-
nan wið hire scippen[des willa]n gif hio hire cynd healdan wille. [Ða
cwæð] ic: Nis nan gecynd þe wið hire scippen[des willa]n winne *buton
dys[ig mon, o]ððe eft þa wiðerweardan englas*. [Ða cwæð] he: Hwæt wenst
ðu? gif ænegu [gesceaft] tiohhode þ[æt] hio wið his willan [sceolde] win-
nan, hwæt hio meahte wið [swa mih]tigne swa we hine gereahtne [hab-
bað]? Ða cwæð ic: Ne magon hi nauht, þeah hi willon. (35.97.30–1,
35.98.2–3, 35.98.5–7, and 35.98.9–17, emphasis mine)

Then [Wisdom] said: '... God reigns over all creatures by their own will ...
for all creatures naturally and of their own will strive to come to God ...'
Then I said: 'I cannot doubt it, because God's power would not be com-
plete happiness if creatures obeyed him against their will ...'
Then he said: 'There is no creature who determines to fight against its
Creator's will, if it wishes to be true to its nature.'
Then I said: 'There is no creature who fights against its Creator's will save
foolish man or the rebellious angels.'
Then he said: 'What do you think? If any creature determined to fight
against his will, what could it do against one so mighty as we have shown
him to be?'
Then I said: 'They can do nothing, even if they wish to.'

Alfred's account anticipates the objection which Boethius will raise at
the start of Book IV: if no one opposes God, and all submit voluntarily
to his will, why is there rebellion and evil in the world? Alfred's
response is that such rebellion exists, but it is unnatural and ultimately
unsuccessful – an orthodox position that nonetheless departs significantly from the thrust of the original.
   In the Latin, when Philosophy states that nothing mindful of its own
nature opposes God ('Nihil ... naturam seruans deo contra ire conetur'),
her stress is on the impossibility of such resistance: all rush towards the
good, all submit to guidance, all direct themselves according to God's
will (III.pr12.17). As she will explain in Book IV, the wicked seek good

(happiness) in the very process of pursuing evil; by sinning, they deprive themselves of good, punishing themselves and upholding God's sovereign plan for justice. Even the rebellious, therefore, act in keeping with their nature insofar as they are seeking happiness, the highest good. For Alfred, however, the phrase 'naturam seruans' opens the door to another possibility: if none living according to their God-given nature rebel against him, then those who do rebel must be acting unnaturally. Such a position is not out of keeping with statements later in *De consolatione*. Echoing a theme found in Augustine as well as Plato,[77] Philosophy will maintain that through wickedness people not only become less like God but strip themselves of their own humanity, transforming themselves into beasts in the quality of their minds (IV.3pr.16 and IV.4pr.1). Here, however, Alfred appears to undercut this distinction between the righteous and the wicked by his definition of those who unnaturally disobey: no one wishes to resist God's will, he says, save the rebel angels and that other group of fallen sinners – 'dysig mon,' foolish humans.

Two examples which Alfred appends to this discussion may reinforce our understanding of 'dysig mon' as referring to humankind in general rather than a subcategory of unsaved or wicked souls. First, there is the mythological rebellion of the giants against Jove, to which Philosophy alludes in a couple of lines but which Alfred expands by way of explanation, condemning in the same breath such false tales or lies (*leasunga*): here the rebellion is not carried out by a few, but by an entire race against the gods. Second, there is the biblical tale of the tower of Babel, of which Alfred approves (Gen. 10.8–10 and 11.1–9): though Alfred focuses on Nimrod and the people of Babylon who actually construct the tower, it is not as though Alfred distinguishes this group from other, righteous people. On the contrary, the Vulgate emphasizes the universal implications of the episode, introducing and closing the account by saying 'Erat autem terra labii unius et sermonum eorundem ... Ibi confusum est labium universae terrae' (Now the earth had one language and the same speech ... There the language of the whole earth was thrown into disorder [11.1 and 9]). While Book IV may contrast good and evil individuals, therefore, here the focus is on humanity in general. For the Latin, the point is that people follow God's will insofar as they naturally seek good and live out God's justice; for the vernacular, the point is that individuals naturally desire good but live unnaturally in opposing God. For the former, humanity's rebellion is hypothetical; in the latter, it is actual and pervasive. In both cases, however, the result is the same: though people may determine to fight God, they cannot overcome him. Resistance is unnatural and without hope of success.

Will and Capacity

Between her discussion of sovereignty and submission in III Prose 12 and Boethius's objection in IV Prose 4 to the apparent suffering of the righteous and prosperity of the wicked, Philosophy introduces an argument completely counter to Augustinian thought regarding human desire and capacity for good. Philosophy begins by noting that both of these elements are needed for anything to be accomplished: no one will do what he does not desire, nor can he do something of which he is incapable. With this premise Augustine would have concurred, arguing that fallen beings, desiring only evil, will never do good without God changing their desire and empowering them to do so. Philosophy, however, having equated true good with happiness, reiterates that good is the whole aim of human will ('intentionem omnem uoluntatis humanae' [IV.pr2.10]), the end to which that virtually invincible aid, instinctive striving, not only leads but virtually forces them ('eos naturalis ducit ac paene compellit intentio ... paene inuicto [auxilio]' [IV.pr.2.26–7]). Philosophy's problem is not to explain how, given the condition of human beings, they can possibly do good, but how they end up doing evil. Her solution draws on a syllogism which she has offered in Book III: (A) if someone is omnipotent, there is nothing he cannot do; (B) God cannot commit evil; (C) therefore evil must be nothing (III.pr12.27–9). This conclusion, a key tenet of Neoplatonism, was not unknown to the Christian world: Augustine himself adopted it when addressing the problem of evil in the *Confessiones* (7.12.18). Here, however, the premise leads to radically non-Augustinian ends. First, Philosophy says, as the righteous attain the virtue they seek, clearly they have both the will and the capacity for good. That the wicked have the will but not the capacity for good, by contrast, is seen in the fact that they fail to accomplish good. The righteous therefore have power, whereas the wicked are powerless. How then are they able to accomplish evil things? Because evil is nothing – a nothing which God cannot perform and which the powerless can. What is more, by extension, the wicked themselves become nothing, for they have abandoned their nature: evil people are no more human than corpses are human. Therefore, in an absolute sense, the wicked do not exist.

Philosophy's line of argument presents a challenge for the conservative Alfred, one which in large part he fails to address. Most of his version of IV Prose 2, in fact, straightforwardly reproduces Philosophy's comments about the desire and capacity of the good and the wicked (36.106.1–36.110.31). At the end of this section, however, Alfred interjects a passage that undercuts one of Philosophy's most heterodox claims.[78] Having recounted Plato's assertion that only the righteous, not the wicked, can bring their desire for good to pass, Wisdom addresses an objection Boethius has not in fact raised:

> Ic nat nu ðeah ðu wille cweð[an þæt] þa goodan onginnen hwilum [þæt] hi ne magon forðbrengan; ac ic cweðe þ[æt] hi hit bringað symle forð. ðeah hi ðæt weorc ne mægen fullfremman, hi habbað ðeah fullne willan, [ond] se untweofealda willa bið to tellanne for fullfremed weorc. Forðæm he næfre ne forlist ðæm leanum oððe her oððe ðær oððe ægðer. Þeah willað ða yflan wircan þ[æt] þ[æt] hi lyst, ðeah hit nyt ne sie; ne forleosað hi eac ðone willan, ac habbaþ his wite oððe her oððe elleshwær oððe ægðer; se yfla willa to donne hiora welt. (36.110.32–36.111.7)

> Now, perhaps you will say that the righteous sometimes begin what they cannot accomplish; but I say that they always accomplish it. Although they may not be able to complete the deed, they nevertheless have the complete desire, and the sincere desire is to be accounted as the completed deed. Therefore it never loses its reward, either in this life or the next, or both. Though the wicked desire to carry out what they wish, yet it need not come to pass; they do not lose the desire, but are punished for it, either in this life or the next, or both. Their evil will directs them to act.

If the righteous are so powerful, Boethius may ask, why are they not able to accomplish the good that they desire? Wisdom answers the problem by redefining 'accomplishment': the desire for good, he says, is itself good; even though circumstances may prevent them from carrying out their good intention, therefore, the heart of the righteous attains that which it seeks – goodness itself. Fair enough – though Augustine, echoing the epistle of James, might underscore the importance of actions as well as intent. It is Wisdom's converse assertion, however, that throws the wrench into the preceding logic. Philosophy has maintained that the wicked cannot achieve good, a position posing no threat to orthodox doctrine. She also has affirmed the desire and capacity of the righteous for good, another tenable stance for the

Christian presupposing prevenient grace. In addition, however, she has argued that even the wicked desire good, and herein lies Alfred's problem. It is telling, therefore, that having set forth the heart's attitude as a basis by which the righteous will be judged, Wisdom asserts the same for the wicked: while in one sense they may desire the goodness of happiness, in another fundamental sense the wicked will evil, and for that they will be condemned.

Providence and Fate

If *De consolatione's* discussion of human will and capacity poses a challenge to Alfred, so does Philosophy's response in the remainder of Book IV to Boethius's concern over God's apparent injustice. As we have noted above, Philosophy adduces two metaphors to explain the ways of Providence. On the one hand, she describes God as the heavenly physician, bestowing ease or trials variously so as best to benefit human character; on the other, she uses the image of the axis. The first example need not have concerned Alfred, as such language was a Christian commonplace,[79] and to a large extent Alfred reproduces Philosophy's statements accordingly. Philosophy goes on, however, to call these heavenly ministrations Fate, and here Alfred's problems begin.

First, like his Latin counterpart, Alfred's Wisdom distinguishes between God's eternal, unchanging plan and the carrying out of that plan through history. God's singular plan he entitles Providence; the multifarious means by which God accomplishes that plan he calls Fate. When enumerating those forces by which Fate might be carried out, however, Philosophy had included an array of Platonic and Stoic concepts: the World Soul (that transcendent reality emanating from the Divine Mind, which in turn descends from the One), the whole of nature, the motions of the stars, angelic forces, and *daemones* or inferior deities (IV.pr6.13).[80] While the extent to which Alfred would have understood the pagan background of such terms is uncertain, similar concepts could be portrayed using more orthodox language. Indeed, in this case Alfred might even have looked to patristic precedent.

In *De ciuitate Dei*, a work on which Alfred probably drew for the *Old English Boethius* either directly or by means of Latin glosses to a Latin text of *De consolatione*,[81] Augustine discusses the concepts of Fate and free will set forth in Cicero's *De diuinatione* and *De fato*.[82] Augustine rejects out of hand the astrological concept of Fate as predetermination based on the position of the stars at one's conception or birth. He also takes issue with the Stoic notion of Fate as the chain of causes whereby history unfolds, all events being the inevitable result of antecedent factors – a chain which the Stoics seem to identify with divine Providence.[83] Augustine does not deny the existence of 'an order of causes in which God's will is most powerful' (ordinem causarum, ubi uoluntas Dei plurimum potest [5.9 (CCSL 47.138.83–4)]), but argues that one can only call this order 'Fate' in the sense of God's foreknowledge of events. If one understands *fatum*, 'that which is said,' to derive from *fari*, 'to speak,' says Augustine, then one may think of Fate as the unchangeable words of God. In an abrupt logical correlation, Augustine points to the Psalmist's statement that 'One time God has spoken' (Semel locutus est Deus [Psa. 61.12]) to equate this singular utterance with God's unalterable knowledge of that order of causes that results in human history – an order, he insists, that includes human beings' free exercise of their will. In contrast to *De consolatione*, therefore, which associates God's knowledge or plan with Providence, Augustine – to the extent that he accepts the term at all – calls such knowledge Fate. When he goes on to recount the various causes by which history unfolds, however, Augustine's list is remarkably similar to that used later by Philosophy when describing Fate, even though Philosophy is at pains to distinguish 'causes' from divine knowledge: events, Augustine says, are caused either directly by God, natural forces, angels, humans, animals, or 'those angels of the devil we call *daemones*' (angelos diaboli uel etiam daemones appellamus [V.9 (CCSL 47.139.119–20)]). Whether indebted to Augustine or not, Alfred follows a similar path, speaking not of the World Soul but of angels, human beings, creatures, the stars, and demons (*scuccan*). Only his reference to stars raises the question of orthodoxy, given Augustine's censure of astrology, and even this term may reflect the latter's reference to 'natural forces.'

A far more fundamental challenge, however, than the heterodoxy of such details is posed by the word for Fate itself: *fatum*, duly rendered by Alfred as *wyrd*.[84] Is he to endorse such a concept as one most needful for Christians to know? Nearly a century later, Ælfric would still feel the need to condemn such belief: 'Gewite þis gedwyld fram geleaf-fullum heortum. þæt æni gewyrd sy. buton se ælmihtiga scyppend se þe ælcum menn foresceawað. lif be his geearnungum' (Let this error depart from believing hearts, that there is any *wyrd* save the Almighty Creator, who preordains life for every man according to his merits [*CH* I.7.122 (Clemoes, *First Series* 236)]). Alfred too must have had concerns about how his audience would interpret the term, for in the midst of Wisdom's exposition he interjects this passage:

Sumc uðwiotan ... secgað þ[æt] sio wyrd wealde ægþer ge gesælða ge ungesælða ælces monnes. Ic þonne secge, swa swa ealle [cris]tene men secgað, þ[æt] [3] sio godcunde foretiohhung his walde, næs sio wyrd; [ond] ic wat þ[æt] hio demð eall þing swiðe rihte, þeah ungesceadwisum men [swa] ne þince. Hi wenað þ[æt] þa[ra] æl[c] sie go[d þe hiora will]an fulgæð; nis hit nan wundor, forðæm [1] hi beoð ablende mid ðæm þiostrum heora scylda. Ac [2] se godcunda foreþonc hit understent eall swiðe rihte, þeah us þince for urum dysige þ[æt] hit on woh fare; forðæm we ne cunnon þ[æt] riht understandan. (39.131.8–18)

Some philosophers ... say that *wyrd* governs both the joys and troubles of every individual. I say, however, as do all Christian people, that [3] divine predestination governs him, not *wyrd*, and I know that it judges all things most rightly, though it does not seem so to foolish people. They think that only that which fulfils their desire is good; it is no wonder, for [1] they are blinded by the darkness of their sins. But [2] divine Providence understands everything most rightly, though it seems to us in our folly that things go wrongly, for we cannot discern what is right.

At least two aspects of the interpolation are worthy of note. First, in contrast to the notion of *wyrd* as a deterministic force antithetical to volitional freedom, Alfred emphasizes human responsibility by means of a familiar metaphor: blindness ([1] above). This is not the only place where Alfred employs this kind of image. Following Philosophy, Wisdom has warned of the dangers of worldly pleasures that blind the eyes of the mind (e.g., 34.89.12–16; cf. II.pr1. III.m10.10). Where Philosophy disparages those who lack discernment because their eyes are accustomed to darkness, Wisdom explains that 'beoð ða synfullan mod ablend mid heora yflan willan' (sinful minds are blinded by their evil wills [38.121.12–13; cf. IV.pr4.27]). When Philosophy argues that individuals lose their freedom of will when they devote themselves to vices, Wisdom adds that 'ac sona swa hi hiora mod onwend[að] from gode, swa weorðað hi ablende mid unwisdome' (as soon as they turn their mind from God, they become blind with folly [40.141.5–6; cf. V.2.9]). Whereas for Augustine humans' fallen nature means that they are spiritually blind from birth, however, Alfred depicts human blindness as the result of a process of human choices: though individuals can increase their freedom – that is, their ability to make rational, righteous choices – by fixing their thoughts on godly things, they destroy their vision by turning from God and pursuing evil. In this sense, Alfred's thought seems closer to Gregory's than Augustine's. The source of Alfred's image, however, need not be patristic. In Book IV Prose 4, having cast scorn on those whose eyes are accustomed to darkness, Philosophy compares their state to that of a man who, having become wholly blind ('amisso penitus uisu'), forgets what sight is like and imagines himself to be unimpaired. Alfred, however, augments the image substantially: those lacking discernment, he says, are like 'sum cild sie full hal [ond] ful æltæwe geboren, [ond] swa fullice ðionde on eallum cystum [ond] cræftum þa hwile þe hit on cnihthade bið [ond] swa forð eallne giogoðhad, oð he wyrð ælces cræftes medeme, [ond] ðonne lytle ær his midferhðe weorðe bæm eagum blind' (a child who is born completely hale and healthy, and while still in childhood and throughout its youth so completely thrives in all virtues and excellence that he becomes perfect in excellence, and then a little before middle age becomes blind in both eyes [38.122.2–6; cf. IV.4.31]). If one comes to be enslaved by vice, Alfred stresses, he can blame neither *wyrd* nor God's Providence; his condition derives from his own free choices.

A second detail worth noting in our passage is Alfred's idiosyncratic use of two distinct but complementary terms: 'godcunda foreþonc' (divine Providence) and 'godcunde foretiohhung' (divine predestination; [2] and [3] above). Both are unique to the *Old English Boethius*. While variations of *foreþonc* appear in other texts, particularly in Alfred's translation of Gregory's *Cura pastoralis*, and while variations such as *Godes foreðanc* or *ðæm foreþonce þæs ælmehtigan Godes* also occur in the *Old English Boethius*, *godcunda foreþonc* appears a total of five times in extant Old English, and only in this text. Far more striking, however, is the fact that, having chosen a term with which to translate *De consolatione*'s *prouidentia*, Alfred should supplement it with another: *foretiohhung*, found again only here. Its Latin counterpart, *praedestinatio*, is conspicuously absent from *De consolatione*. Having prefaced the last section of the work by stating that the issue of how things are ordered in the world will involve the nature of Providence, Fate, chance, divine foreknowledge and predestination (*praedestinatione diuina*), and free will (IV.pr6.4), no other mention of the term does the text make save for one somewhat obscure reference which Alfred omits.[85] Alfred, by contrast, speaks of divine *foretiohhung* on eleven occasions. Some of these translate language from *De consolatione*: in Book IV Prose 6, for example, where Philosophy distinguishes the plan of Providence from the agency of Fate, Wisdom ascribes the accomplishment of events to

Fate but the plan for events to *Godes foreþanc* [*ond*] *his foretiohhung*, God's Providence and predestination (IV.pr6.12 and 39.129.2–3). Near the start of Book V, where Philosophy explains that someone's seemingly chance discovery of gold actually proceeded from a conjunction of causes – the chain of Fate, as decreed by Providence – Wisdom states that divine predestination (*godcunde foretiohhung*) instructed individuals where to bury the gold and find it (V.pr1.18–19 and 40.140.15–17). Other instances of the term appear in passages apparently original to Alfred. The character Boethius expresses concern about the implications of predestination on human freedom (41.142.25–8); Wisdom affirms that divine predestination made everything good and nothing evil (41.143.17–20); and Wisdom avers that all that predestination determines – including human capacity for free choice – comes to pass (41.144.3–5). On one occasion other than our passage above, moreover, Alfred uses his two terms in close proximity.

> Ac þ[æt] is openlice cuð þ[æt] sio *godcunde foretiohhung* is anfeald [ond] unandwendlic, [ond] welt ælces þinges endebyrdlice, [ond] eall þing gehiwað. Sumu þing þonne on þisse weorulde sint underðied þære wyrde, sume hire nanwuht underðied ne sint; ac sio wyrd [ond] eall ða þing þe hire underðied sint, sint underðied ðæm *godcundan foreþonce*. (39.129.7–12; emphasis mine)

> But it is clearly known that divine predestination is simple and unchangeable, and governs everything in an orderly manner, and shapes all things. Some things in this world, therefore, are subject to *wyrd*, and some are in no way subject; but *wyrd*, and all the things that are subject to it, are subject to divine Providence.

The immediate context is a theologically awkward one: Wisdom's reference to 'things not subject to Fate' reflects Philosophy's acknowledgment of things – possibly the Neoplatonic Forms, thoughts in the mind of God – so close to the First Divinity (*prima diuinitas*) that they are immobile, outside the realm of change ordered by Fate.[86] Setting aside the challenge of such language for a moment, however, we might note the analogous role played by the terms *foretiohhung* and *foreþonc*. As in the other examples of *foretiohhung* above, predestination and Providence seem not so much distinct as complementary, variant terms for the divine power responsible for the ordering of events through Fate. It may be argued, however, that Alfred's use of *forehiohhung* reinforces his point that human actions are not determined by an impersonal force such as the Germanic *wyrd*; rather, they are encompassed by God's personal plan. God, not *wyrd*, oversees human history.

The second metaphor, then, adduced by Philosophy to explain the ways of Providence is that of the divine axis – an illustration that in both the Latin and Old English follows immediately on the heels of the reference to 'things not subject to Fate.' Alfred expands substantially on *De consolatione*'s image of a series of concentric circles revolving around a pivot (*cardo*). In Wisdom's words, God is like the axis of a wagon (*wænes eax*), with human beings as the hub, spokes, or rim of the wagon wheel. Here the parts of the wheel are not various beings or levels of reality descending from the One into ever-increasing corporeality; rather, they represent the spiritual condition of human beings in this world. Those who are most righteous correspond to the hub; those who are inconstant in their thoughts, fixing one eye on heavenly things but the other on worldly matters, correspond to the spokes; and base people are like the rims, ever in contact with the dirt. Those closest to the axle exhibit the most stability; prizing God rather than earthly things, they remain secure, worrying little about the vicissitudes of Fate. Those on the rim, by contrast, are the most unsteady, being continually struck and tossed about by obstacles. The groups are in contact with one another, Wisdom notes, so that though the wicked may think themselves independent of God, their movement in the world depends ultimately upon him. The wagon itself, moreover – the world, one assumes? – will endure the longer the closer its proximity is to the axle ('se wæn bið micle leng gesund þe læs bið todæled f[rom] þære eaxe' [39.130.21–2]). The implications of some of these details are not entirely clear: read literally, for example, the metaphor might be taken to imply that God influences evildoers not directly, but through the intermediary levels of the righteous and moderately righteous.[87] What is clear, however, is that through this image Alfred manages to convey a central aspect of Philosophy's discourse – the contrast between unchanging Providence and the mutable world of Fate – while stripping it of heterodox Neoplatonic overtones. In both texts, the perversity of the wicked distances them from God; both texts likewise stress the difference between God's realm and the world inhabited by human beings. In *De consolatione*, however, the concentric circles represent a depiction of nature ultimately antithetical to Christian thought – various planes to which souls may ascend in successive lives depending on their merits.[88] In the *Old English Boethius*, the parts of the wheel merely illustrate the various conditions of humans, the extent to which they may be enslaved by fear or freed from worry by ignoring or focusing on God. As with Alfred's depiction of God as heavenly physician, caring for human souls through the agency of Fate, Alfred here emphasizes that it is God rather than some deterministic force that is at the heart of human history: 'Sio godcunde foretiohhung his walde, næs sio wyrd' (divine predestination governs him, not *wyrd*).

Foreknowledge and Free Will

Having addressed the apparent threat posed to free will by Providence, along with such concomitant questions as humans' power to resist God's will, their capacity for evil and good, and the precise nature of Fate, Alfred turns to Boethius's final major objection: the apparent incompatibility of free will and divine foreknowledge. As we have seen, starting in Book V Prose 3, Boethius sets forth his concerns in three main parts: First, how can free will exist if that which God foresees must necessarily come to pass? Second, is it not ludicrous to suggest that God depends on humans for his foreknowledge of events, inasmuch as human choices cause such events? Third, if outcomes are not certain, but subject to individuals' ability to change their minds, how can God have certain knowledge of the future? Either God's 'knowledge' is no better than human opinion, or people have no freedom in their decisions, making rewards, punishments, and prayers meaningless and making evil God's sole responsibility.

Alfred's alternations to this final section of *De consolatione* are considerable. To begin with, he ignores Boethius's nuanced questions, focusing instead on the suggestion that evil might be attributed to God – a notion regarding which Philosophy herself states 'nothing more monstrous might be conceived' (nihil sceleratius excogitari potest [V.pr4.32]). Alfred thus has Boethius ask: If God knows in advance that the wicked will do evil, why does he give them freedom to carry it out? Wisdom replies using a metaphor not found in *De consolatione*. Just as it would be unjust for a king to keep all his subjects as slaves, Wisdom says, so it would be improper (*uncynlic*) for God to have no free creatures in his kingdom. God therefore gave angels and humans 'micle gife freodomes, þ[æt] hi mosten don swa god swa yfel, swæðer swa hi wolden' (the great gift of freedom, so that they might do either good or evil – whichever they wished [41.142.9–10]). Where Philosophy has argued that all people desire good even though some do evil, therefore, Wisdom again links volition and deed, offering the orthodox premise that evil actions flow from blameworthy motives. Similarly, just as he has said that individuals' sincere will counts as righteousness performed, Wisdom reiterates that 'Gif men to godum weorce ne onhagie, hæbbe godne willan; þ[æt] is emngood' (If it is not possible for a man to do a good deed, let him have a good desire; that is equally good [41.142.19–20]). With such a statement Augustine would likely have agreed, though he would also have emphasized the importance of perseverance in good deeds for salvation.[89]

Next, Alfred's Boethius raises the issue of *Godes foretiohhunge* or predestination, which we have seen functions for Alfred in an analogous role to Providence. If all must come to pass as God from the first has purposed, he complains, then rewards are meaningless, punishment unjust, and prayers all in vain (41.142.25–41.143.3). Like Philosophy at the start of Book V Prose 4, Wisdom alludes to Cicero's treatment of the problem to show that the debate is a long-standing one. Whereas Philosophy goes on to argue that God's foreknowledge does not predestine future events, however, Wisdom tackles the issue in a manner reminiscent of Augustine's response to Cicero. Augustine, having grudgingly described Fate as God's unchangeable words, and equated this utterance with God's knowledge of the chain of causes that results in human history, stresses that 'ipsae nostrae uoluntates in causarum ordine sunt, qui certus est Deo eiusque praescientia continetur' (our wills themselves are included in that order of causes which is certain to God and included in his foreknowledge [5.9 (CCSL 47.138.96–8)]. In the same way, Wisdom, having recapped her argument that *godcunde foretiohhung* or predestination made all things good and set a system of rewards and punishment in place, concludes: 'God hæfde getiohhod freodom to sellanne monnum, [ond] swa dyde ... Hwæt magon men cweðan þ[æt] sio godcunde foretiohhung getiohhod hæfde þæs ðe hio ne þurhtuge?' (God determined to give freedom to human beings, and did so ... What can people say that divine predestination has determined and not carried out? [41.143.23–4 and 41.144.3–5]). Like Augustine, therefore, Wisdom suggests that by the very fact of ordaining all things predestination includes rather than precludes free will.

Having departed from *De consolatione* by focusing on the question of God's responsibility for evil and the implications of predestination for free will, Alfred echoes his source in discussing whether that which God foreknows necessarily comes to pass. Arguing that events foreseen by God will come about, though not as a result of that foresight, Philosophy here offers the example of people gazing on a charioteer:

just as people may observe a charioteer directing his horses without influencing the charioteer's choices, so God may see and know human history without necessarily causing events to occur (V.pr4.14–16). Alfred's Boethius, however, links the issue to his previous query regarding predestination: since God knows all things in advance, both good and evil, does that which God foreknows and has determined (*getiohhod*) negate free will by coming to pass unchangeably (*unanwendendlice* [41.144.14])? The apparently original explanation Wisdom puts forth is not without obscurity.

> [Ne] ðearf hit no eall geweorðan unanwendendlice; ac sum hit sceal geweorðan unanwendendlice; þ[æt] bið þ[æt]te ure nedþearf bið, [ond] his willa bið. Ac hit is sum swa gerad þ[æt] his nis nan nedþearf, [ond] þeah ne dereð no þeah hit geweorðe; ne nan hearm ne bið, þeah [hit] no [ne] geweorðe. Geþenc nu be ðe selfum hwæðer þu ænig þing swa fæst getiohhod hæbbe þæt þe þince þ[æt] hit næfre þinu[m] willu[m] onwend ne weorðe, ne þu butan bion ne mæge; oððe hwæðer þu eft on ængum geþeahte swa twioræde sie þ[æt] þe helpe hwæðer hit geweorðe, ðe hit no ne geweorðe. (41.144.15-24)

> It need not all inevitably come to pass, but some of it must inevitably come to pass – that is, that which is necessary for us and willed by him. But some things are of such a nature that there is no need for them, and yet they do not hurt should they come to pass; nor is there any harm if they do not come to pass. Now think about yourself: have you never resolved upon something so firmly that it seems that it by your will may never be changed, or that you cannot exist without it? Or again, have you ever been so irresolute in any plan that it is fine to you whether it comes to pass or not?

Like Philosophy, Wisdom draws an analogy between human and divine behaviour. On occasion, individuals resolve so strongly to do something that they will do it or die in the attempt; at other times, they are less concerned as to whether the event comes to pass or not. God's influence on history is similar, Wisdom suggests. Some things must and will take place, either brought about by 'our necessity' (such as the need to breathe or the eventuality of death, one assumes) or God's unthwartable will (such as his decision to send plagues on Egypt for Israel's deliverance or his Son to the cross for humankind's redemption). In other matters, however – so the reasoning seems to go

– God is less concerned as to how events transpire.[90] History may go one way or another, depending on human choices.

Alfred's Boethius, however, had spoken not only of God's knowledge of good, but of his foreknowledge of evil events, and to this issue Wisdom abruptly turns. 'Fela is þara þinga,' he says, 'þe God ær wat ær hit geweorðe, [ond] wat eac þ[æt] hit dereð his gesceaftum gif hit gewyrð. Nat he hit no forðyþe he wille þ[æt] hit geweorðe, ac forðy þe he wile forwernan þ[æt] hit ne geweorðe' (Many a thing God knows of before it should take place, and knows also that it will harm his creatures if it does take place. He knows it not because he desires that it should take place, but because he desires to prevent it so that it may not take place [41.144.25–8]). Wisdom's use of the subjunctive *geweorðe* reflects an intriguing shift. Having already addressed the question of why God allows humans to commit evil despite foreknowing their intent, Wisdom speaks not of certain but of potential ills – things that may happen and will be harmful if they come about. Wisdom uses the metaphor of a captain who senses from the elements that a storm is drawing nigh and commands his men in consequence to furl the sail and otherwise make the ship ready. Alfred's concern here again is the effect that God's foresight has on human decisions. His image is not one, unfortunately, that entirely clarifies the issue. Wisdom states, for example, that God desires to prevent troubles from befalling his people ('he wile forwernan þæt hit ne geweorðe'). In the portrait of the captain, therefore, we see a God-figure warning his people of danger and commanding them to act so as to prevent disaster. While obedience to the captain may minimize damage, however, troubles still transpire: no suggestion is given that the captain wills the storm away. Even as he seeks to deny that God brings about evil, Alfred thus runs the risk of presenting him as passive and weak. Both Boethius and Augustine, for example, would say that God brings about the storm, introducing hardships in order to punish the wicked and purify the righteous. Alfred might not disagree – he speaks at length of God's control of the elements in his expansion of Book III Metre 9, among other places (33.79.35–33.81.13) – but his depiction here stresses God's observation rather than ordination of future events. Some might also understand God's will as weak: God does not wish harmful events to come; he even wishes to prevent harmful events from coming, and yet (the implication is) they may come anyway. Seeking to explain the non-determinate nature of God's foreknowledge, Alfred raises the question of the efficacy of God's will. This said, Wisdom grants that metaphors fall short, inasmuch as individuals cannot conceive of God – or *se wisdom*, as the speaker paradoxically calls him – as he is. Nonetheless, Wisdom's overall point is clearly orthodox: just as God is not responsible for humanity's choice of evil, so he is blameless for various troubles that may come, having instructed humans as to how they might persevere in safety.

Following and expanding upon Philosophy, Wisdom makes two last major points to show the compatibility of foreknowledge and free will. Having stated that God's nature is ultimately beyond human understanding, Wisdom argues that the key to the problem of foreknowledge lies in understanding this divine nature. First, like Philosophy, Wisdom delineates the various ways in which creatures gain knowledge: immobile creatures have physical senses, moving creatures have feelings such as love and hate, humans have reason, and angels have definite understanding ('gewiss andgit or gearowito' [41.146.10 and 23]).[91] For Philosophy, of course, such abilities represent rungs which human beings should climb, seeking understanding in order to transcend the created world and gaze on the simple Form with the unclouded insight of the mind ('simplicem formam pura mentis acie' [V.pr4.30]). Alfred, as usual, speaks not of Neoplatonic Forms or Thoughts in the divine Mind; Wisdom even denies the possibility of transcendence, stating that humans were no more made to exalt themselves over angels than the angels were made to strive against God. Even if humans cannot equal the angels, however, they can still gain some measure of understanding, for Wisdom laments the tendency for people to act like beasts instead of seeking the 'gewis andget' possessed by angels 'ond wise men' (41.146.15–18, emphasis mine). Wisdom calls individuals, therefore, to raise their minds as high as possible, that they may return to the country whence they once came[92] and see clearly what now confuses them.

To this end, like Philosophy, Wisdom turns from the nature and knowledge of creatures to the nature and knowledge of God. Both begin with a discussion of eternity. Philosophy, on the one hand, defines one who is eternal as one who grasps simultaneously the entirety of life without end. In the same way, she says, the knowledge of one who is eternal must encompass in one moment the whole of human history. Such assertions lead her to the crowning argument of Book V: since all things are known to God in his eternal present, he may view events in the future in the same way that humans observe the present – observing without causing that which he beholds. Wisdom's conclusion, though similar, is nearly lost in a panegyric of praise. At the head of a list of virtues including God's omnipotence, absolute goodness, freedom from all constraint, and so forth, Wisdom notes that 'Him is eall andweard, ge þ[æt]te ær wæs, ge þ[æt]te nu is, ge þ[æt]te æfter us bið; eall þ[æt] is him andweard' (To him all is present, both that which previously was, and that which now is, and that which after us shall be; all is present to him [42.148.11–12]). Unlike Philosophy, Wisdom makes no explicit connection between this eternal knowledge and free will. The sense of crescendo in Alfred's conclusion does not showcase the seamlessness of his logic. Rather, the argument with which he closes his work is the argument of God to Job: 'Ubi eras quando ponebam fundamenta terrae?' (Where were you when I laid the foundations of the earth? [38.4]) Wisdom states: 'Ac hwæt ofermodie ge þonne, oððe hwy ahebbe ge eow wið swa heane anwald? forðæm ge nauht wið hine don ne magon' (But why should you then be proud, or why should you raise yourself up against so high a power? For you can do nothing against him [42.148.29–31]).

Wisdom thus appears to teach the following in this final section: though God foresees evil, he does not prevent it by denying individuals free will; both predestination and divine foreknowledge preserve a place for human choice; certain things (like death or the Judgment) do inevitably come to pass; God does not determine all things, but allows human decisions to shape some events; God gives commands that help his people guard against troubles in the world; humans should seek to draw nearer God through understanding; and God's knowledge encompasses all history in the present. None of these points has Alfred drawn entirely from *De consolatione*, even though Wisdom does follow the broad outline of Philosophy's argument. Most of the points are consonant, moreover, with an orthodox, Augustinian view, even though Augustine would balk at Wisdom's suggestion that God is not concerned as to how certain events transpire.[93] The image with which both Philosophy and Wisdom end, however, and that sounds so compatible with Christian theology – that of the Almighty seated on high, seeing all things and dispensing recompense in keeping with human deeds – is one which a later writer in Anglo-Saxon England will expand in a subtly heterodox treatise on free will.

CHAPTER FIVE

Lantfred of Winchester
and the *Carmen de libero arbitrio*

In responding to the need for learning in the late ninth century, Alfred had made a remarkable investment in providing vernacular translations for his people. To a certain extent, moreover, he had sought to address the Vikings' decimation of centres of learning, founding a monastery at Athelney and a nunnery at Shaftesbury, for example. It would be a few more decades, however, before widespread efforts would be made to revitalize English monastic communities – and with them, Latin education. When those efforts came, exchanges between the English reformers and their counterparts on the Continent would bring to Winchester a monk named Lantfred, whose work there would include perhaps the first Anglo-Latin study of free will since Bede.

Winchester and the Tenth-Century Benedictine Reform

As is well known, the impetus for what would become known as the tenth-century English Benedictine Reform came largely from three men: Dunstan, abbot of Glastonbury (ca. 940–56) and archbishop of Canterbury (960–88), Oswald, bishop of Worcester (961–92) and archbishop of York (971–92), and Æthelwold, abbot of Abingdon (ca. 954–63) and bishop of Winchester (963–84).[1] All three clerics had been influenced early in their careers by developments on the Continent, where leaders such as Odo of Cluny (abbot 926/7–942) and Gérard of Brogne (d. 959) reformed Benedictine houses such as those at Fleury and Ghent. Dunstan had been struck by monastic practice at Ghent when briefly exiled there around 956–7, Oswald had studied as a monk at Fleury before returning to England in 959, and Æthelwold was only prevented from such a trip by his appointment by King Eadred to

Abingdon around 954. Æthelwold's interest in continental customs was hardly dampened by insular responsibility, however, and on his elevation to the archbishopric he put his designs for reformation swiftly into practice. Assisted by King Edgar (957–75), who had been his former student and now lived close to him at Winchester, in 964 Æthelwold expelled the secular canons resident in Old and New Minster, replaced them with Benedictine monks from Abingdon, and began to turn Winchester into a centre of education.

Æthelwold's work at Winchester had national ramifications. Certain areas felt his influence directly, as he went on to found or refound monasteries beyond Winchester. More widespread may have been the effect of the *Regularis concordia*, compiled by Æthelwold following a council at Winchester between ca. 970 and 973 and designed to regularize English monastic observance. Still greater, moreover, may have been the impact of his educational vision. One of the foremost scholars and teachers of his day, Æthelwold translated Benedict's *Regula*, reformed the liturgy, oversaw a monastic school, promoted a standard body of English vocabulary, modelled clarity in vernacular writing and hermeneutic complexity in Latin, and instilled in at least one of his students – Ælfric of Eynsham – a respect for patristic authority and orthodox biblical exegesis.[2] While Æthelwold's actions may have provoked antimonastic sentiment among nobles or secular clerics who saw their influence over religious houses suffer,[3] reformed monasticism would remain a force until the Norman Conquest, and students of Æthelwold such as Ælfric would be read well into the twelfth century.

Lantfred of Winchester

One place in which Æthelwold's interest in the continental reformers may be seen is in his preface to the *Regularis concordia*, where he notes that the work was influenced by the counsel of monks from Ghent and Fleury.[4] The former centre may have been represented at Winchester by Womar, abbot of St Peter's in Ghent, who spent time at Old Minster probably while the *Regularis concordia* was being drafted in the early 970s.[5] From Fleury, on the other hand, perhaps invited by Æthelwold for the occasion and present at Winchester around the years 970–3, was likely a Frankish monk named Lantfred.[6]

Much of our understanding of Lantfred's history and literary output has come only recently with the publication of Michael Lapidge's monumental *The Cult of St Swithun*. Sketches based largely on passing comments in one of Lantfred's works, the *Translatio et miracula S. Swithuni*, appeared periodically in the sixteenth to eighteenth centuries,[7] but Lapidge himself states that 'nothing has been added to our knowledge of Lantfred during the ... centuries separating us from the antiquaries.'[8] From the *Translatio,* to begin with, rubricated in London, British Library, Royal 15. C. vii (Winchester, s. x[ex]) as 'epistola doctoris eximii Lantfredi uenerande sanctitatis, presbiteri et monachi' (the letter of the distinguished teacher Lantfred of reverential holiness, priest and monk), we may glean that Lantfred was a foreigner: he speaks, for example, of Old English as *lingua eorum* (their language) and refers to *mos Anglo-Saxonum* (Anglo-Saxon ways [cc. 7–8 and 31]). He also describes a miracle that he witnessed in *Gallia* and *prouincia Francorum* (c. 32), raising the possibility that he may have come from Francia. Furthermore, on occasion he employs 'Latinized French,' using words like *senior* (old man) in the sense of *seignor* (master or owner [cc. 25 and 38]), suggesting that he may have been a native speaker of Old French. Lapidge corroborates all these details from other sources: Ælfric, he notes, who was a contemporary of Lantfred's at Winchester, states that Lantfred *se ofersæwisca* (the foreigner) wrote of Swithun in Latin (*LS* I.22.402). Wulfstan of Winchester, another contemporary, says in his metrical version of Lantfred's work that the latter 'more cupit solito Gallorum uisere gentem' (sought in his usual way to visit the people of Gaul [*Narratio metrica de S. Swithuno* II.829–30]). Finally, Lapidge notes the significance of the form of the name itself: the spelling 'Lantfred' is attested in areas west of the Rhine in what was then Francia, whereas 'Lantfrid' appears east of the Rhine in Germany and Switzerland. That this seemingly Frankish monk was in Winchester by 971, however, is also apparent from the *Translatio,* for the author not only addresses the work to the monks of the Old Minster but describes himself as a witness of the miracles that followed the translation of Swithun's relics into the church of the Old Minster in July of that year.

According to Lapidge, Lantfred's known writings probably include six works besides the *Translatio,* all of which are marked by shared linguistic and stylistic features.[9] First of all, there are the mass-sets for the deposition and the translation of St Swithun, preserved in the eleventh-century Missal of the New Minster: both texts preserve Graecisms and unusual phrases contained in the *Translatio,* reflecting Lantfred's 'dazzling' hermeneutic style.[10] Next, there is a letter to Dunstan from one '.L.' found in London, British Library, Cotton Tiberius A. xv (s. xi[1]), fol. 168.[11] In it, '.L.' thanks '.D. archipresuli ... de bonis que ei contulistis paterno more quamplurimis ualde egenti in finibus uestris' (Archbishop D[unstan] ... for the many good things which you bestowed upon him in your fatherly way when he was in great need in your lands) and requests that certain books at Winchester be returned to him at Fleury, 'quo nunc degit' (where he now lives). Two details help to date the letter to the period 974 x 984: the author speaks of a fire which may be identified with one that damaged Fleury's library in 974, and asks for a volume to be returned by Osgar, abbot of Abingdon (963–84); the latter he may have encountered prior to 963 when Æthelwold sent Osgar to Fleury to study continental customs. The letter shares not only striking verbal similarities with the *Translatio*, but a rhyming prose which is extremely rare in tenth-century England, if not unique to Lantfred.[12] Finally, there are the three poems found in Cambridge, University Library, Kk. 5. 34 under a single rubric attributing them to one '.L.' The first two poems, the *Altercatio magistri et discipuli* and *Responsio discipuli*, comprise *flytings* or wars of words between a master and student which have been said to parody the daily fare of the Winchester classroom.[13] The last is a study of Providence and free will called by Lapidge the *Carmen de libero arbitrio*.

The Origin of the *Carmen de Libero Arbitrio*

The case for Lantfred's authorship of the *Carmen* is by no means closed to question: to say that a rubric attributes the poem to '.L.,' that a letter written by one '.L.' is linguistically similar to the *Translatio*, and that another rubric ascribes the *Translatio* to Lantfred may still leave room for doubt; as Lapidge says, 'probability is not proof.'[14] Nonetheless, further clues link the *Carmen* both to Winchester under Æthelwold and to other texts associated with Lantfred.

To begin with, there is the evidence of CUL Kk. 5. 34, the sole manuscript in which the poem is found. On the one hand, the ink used by the main hand is the black-brown ink associated with insular, as opposed to continental, scribes.[15] In addition, the foliation suggests some uncertainty with the method of like facing like: quires ix, x, and xiv follow the typical continental pattern of placing the flesh sides of folios together (HF'FH), while quires xi, xii, and xiii occasionally revert to the insular pattern of alternating between hair and flesh (HF'FH'FH'HF).[16] Such variation could well reflect the practice of an insular house of the later tenth century making the transition to the continental codicological practices introduced with Dunstan, Oswald, and Æthelwold.[17] Finally, the script is a form of Style I Anglo-Caroline, which is specifically associated with Abingdon and Winchester under Æthelwold.[18] Here the emphasis of the Reform is seen in attempts to emulate a pure Caroline minuscule with little insular influence.[19] While the principal examples of this script, such as the Benedictional of Æthelwold,[20] are lavish productions with large, rounded forms, David Dumville notes that at Winchester 'the script could be scaled down somewhat and elaborate decoration avoided, whether for hagiography or for Classical poetry.'[21] Dumville specifically cites CUL Kk. 5. 34 with its unornamented text as an illustration of his point.[22]

Second, there is the internal evidence of the poem itself. While scribal errors suggest that the text in CUL Kk. 5. 34 is a copy rather than an autograph,[23] references in the poem suggest that the original was composed at Winchester. Take, for example, the the *Carmen*'s conclusion, where the poet praises the patron (*praesul*) on whom he has previously called to supervise his work.

Pontificemque pium meritis et honore colendum   175
    insignemque humilem protege, Christe, libens,
quem deus omnipotens cathedra subuexit in alta,
    dogmate mellifluo uerteret ut scelera.
gentes Anglorum felices praesule tanto
    ritus qui prauos corrigit ut genitor,   180
extorresque superuenientes uosque beati:
    cunctis his tribuit quicquid opus fuerit.
quis numerare queat bona nobis quae bonus ille
    contulit hanc postquam uenimus ad patriam?

Be pleased, O Christ, to protect this bishop, godly, eminent, and humble, worthy to be honoured with rewards and respect, whom God Almighty lifted up to the high episcopal seat that he should change people's wicked ways by his sweet doctrine. [line 179:] The English people are fortunate with such a patron, who corrects depraved practices like a father. [line 181:] And you exiles who have arrived are blessed: to all these he has given whatever was needed. [line 183:] Who could count the good things that this good man has bestowed upon us since we came to this land? (lines 175–84)

On the one hand, the poet indicates that the subject is an English bishop who is known for his teaching (lines 175–9). While the portrait may be taken as a hyperbolic trope, one candidate arguably worthy of such praise was Æthelwold. The importance of pedagogy to Æthelwold's reforming vision is evident in his transmission of grammar and metrics to students such as Ælfric and Wulfstan Cantor, his efforts to promote standardized vocabulary, his collection and bequest of books, and his production of such texts as the *Regularis concordia*.[24] In addition, the poet describes his mentor as one who corrects corrupt practices in the church (line 180). As we have seen, Æthelwold was conspicuous in his zeal for establishing or reestablishing regular life in ecclesiastical communities: in addition to expelling the secular clerics at Winchester's Old and New Minsters, he may have followed a similar pattern in New Minster, Chertsey, Milton Abbas, and St Neots, which he went on to refound along with Peterborough, Ely, and Thorney.[25] Third, the bishop is said to welcome foreigners – including the poet himself – from abroad (lines 181–4). Æthelwold was known for importing monks from the Continent to ensure liturgical orthodoxy, such as from Corbie to teach the rules of psalmody and plain-chant to his monks at Abingdon, and (as we have noted) from Ghent and Fleury to advise in the preparation of the *Regularis concordia*.

In addition to such potential links to Æthelwold, the *Carmen* may be linked on linguistic grounds to texts associated with Lantfred. On the one hand, a connection has long been made between the *Translatio*, the *Altercatio magistri et discipuli*, and the *Carmen*, all of which share the extremely rare phrase 'caelica Tempe' (valley of heaven). The phrase occurs only once outside these three texts, and in both the *Altercatio* and the *Carmen* the quantity of 'Tempe' is false.[26] More recently, Lapidge also remarked on the rare nature of the compound 'cuncticreans' (all-creating), the term which opens the *Carmen* and which is also found in the *Translatio* and *Regularis concordia*.[27] In his *Cult of St Swithun*, moreover, Lapidge highlighted three parallels between the *Carmen* and the mass-set for the translation of St Swithun, a text which preserves Graecisms and unusual phrases contained in the *Translatio*. Just as the *Carmen* affirms that 'gentes Anglorum felices praesule tanto' (the English people are blessed with such a patron [line 179 above]), he notes, so the mass-set includes the apostrophe 'O felicem Anglorum gentem' (O blessed English people). Just as the *Carmen* includes the apostrophe 'O diuina Dei pietas quae cuncta gubernas' (O divine compassion of God, you who direct all things [line 29]), so the mass-set praises God's sovereign power which 'cuncta creata gubernat' (directs all creation). While the phrase may not be unusual in itself, the surrounding language is striking given both the liturgical context and its Boethian overtones: the mass-set addresses 'Cuius prouidentia diuino profecto omnia considerat, et cuius dispositio immota serie uniuersa ordinat, cuiusque maiestas sacro regimine cuncta creata gubernat' (You whose Providence regards all things by divine progress,[28] whose ordering arranges everything in a fixed chain, and whose sovereignty directs all creation with holy guidance).[29] Both palaeographic and internal evidence would suggest, therefore, that the *Carmen* may be dated to the term of Æthelwold's bishopric and perhaps specifically to Lantfred's residence at Winchester around the years 970–3.

Lantfredian Echoes of Boethius

Lantfred's reference in the mass-set above to Providence, sovereignty, the chain of being, and the divine vision of all things is not the only occasion on which his language reflects Boethian ideas; such ideas, in fact, recur throughout Lantfred's work. In his recent edition of the *Translatio*, for example, Lapidge identifies five echoes of *De consolatione Philosophiae*. At one point, he notes, a blind man calls upon God for help, using the rare phrase 'latere prouidentiam: Scio quia nihil tuam potest latere prouidentiam' (I know that nothing can be hidden from your Providence [300 n. 203]); similarly, discussing the effect of God's foreknowledge on free will, Providence notes, 'diuinam prouidentiam latere non posse' ([future events] cannot be hidden from divine Providence [V.pr3.8]). Earlier in its preface, the *Translatio* praises God for 'gerens pulchrum profunda mente empyrium' (holding the radiant firmament with his deep mind [254 n. 17]); so too, Boethius's text speaks of 'quisquis profunda mente uestigat uerum' (he who traces the truth with depth of mind [III.m11.1]). The phrase occurs rarely outside *De consolatione*, though the contrast here is striking: rather than extolling divine understanding, Philosophy points to the depths of the human soul, which can dimly recall truth from its previous existence among the Forms. Another parallel occurs when a paralytic, having been cured by Swithun, 'iter arripuit pedibus' (took to the road on foot [290 n. 180]); Philosophy uses the phrase to remark that 'quoniam uero manere non potuit infinitum temporis iter arripuit' (since indeed [the present] cannot endure, the endless march of time snatches it away [V.pr6.13]). Further movement in the *Translatio* comes when an earldorman sets off with a large retinue 'sicut mos est Anglosaxonicum' (as the custom is among the Anglo-Saxons): the author describes him as 'in caducis prepotens rebus' (very powerful in temporal affairs [318–20 n. 268]). Philosophy uses similar language when asking rhetorically whether 'aliquid in mortalibus caducisque rebus' (any of these mortal and transient things) can bestow happiness (III.pr9.29). Neither *iter arripuit* nor *in caducis rebus* are particularly uncommon in the Latin corpus, and the contexts in which they are used in the two texts differs considerably; nonetheless, the parallels may add to the overall evidence. Finally, there is the occasion on which Swithun instructs a sick man to keep vigil and pray: healing, the bishop says, will come as 'magnalia cuncticreantis Dei agnosces puroque intuitu mentis perspicies' (you shall acknowledge the mighty deeds of the all-creating God and regard them with the pure gaze of your mind [280 n. 140]). When Philosophy uses the phrase, it is God rather than humanity she has in view: 'suae mentis intuitu tam necessarie quam non necessarie uentura dinoscit' (with the gaze of his mind he distinguishes those future events that will necessarily occur from those which will not [V.pr6.22]). As we shall see, however, the term *intuitus* plays a key role in our understanding both of *De consolatione* and the *Carmen*.

As for the *Carmen* itself, the poem declares its association with *De consolatione* not simply by verbal parallels but by the theme it sets forth in its opening lines: calling on the Spirit's wisdom, the author seeks to know 'quid series fati, quid porrouidentia cosmi, / liber et effectus antesciens animus, / gratia quid regis, praedestiuenatio quid sit' (what might be the chain of Fate, the Providence of the universe, the unimpeded mind foreknowing future events, the grace of the king, and predestination [lines 5–8]). Such a statement is directly reminiscent of Philosophy's words as she turns in Book V to 'the greatest of all topics,' the relation of divine and human wills. To understand this issue, she says, one must inquire 'de prouidentiae simplicitate, de fati serie, de repentinis casibus, de cognitione ac praedestinatione diuina, de arbitrii libertate' (about the unity of Providence, the chain of Fate, unexpected chance, divine knowledge and predestination, and the freedom of the will (IV.pr6.4). In preserving the thought but not the precise language of *De consolatione*, the *Carmen*'s author signals from the start the nature of his work: rather than being simply a versified abridgment of Boethius, it is an original composition inspired by the Boethian text.

Lantfred and the Tenth-Century Study of Boethius

Lantfred's interest in *De consolatione* is hardly surprising given the attention received by the text both in England and on the Continent.

As we observed in the last chapter, the tenth century saw a number of commentaries disseminated on the continent and in England. To some of these Lantfred might conceivably have had access at Fleury: Orléans, Bibliothèque Municipale, 270 (Fleury, ix^{in}, glosses ix[1]), for example, is the earliest known manuscript with commentary on *De consolatione*; it contains interlinear and marginal 'miscellaneous' (i.e., non-Remigian or St Gallen) glosses. Bern, Bürgerbibliothek, Cod. 179 (Loire region, ix/x), is the earliest known manuscript containing Remigian commentary; it too includes interlinear and marginal glosses. Paris, Bibliothèque Nationale, lat. 16093 (Loire (?Fleury), xi^{med}) contains interlinear and marginal Remigian glosses as well; despite its late date, the manuscript could theoretically represent an earlier commentary tradition at Fleury.[30] While no copies of *De consolatione* with commentary are extant from Winchester, moreover, it is not beyond the realm of possibility that Lantfred could have encountered strands of commentary there: Vatican, Biblioteca Apostolica Vaticana, lat. 3363, for example, written in the Tours region (and thus close to Fleury) in the early ninth century, was in southern England by at least the middle of the tenth century and (as we have seen) has been associated by certain scholars with Alfred's court at Winchester.

In addition to the commentaries produced on *De consolatione*, the ninth and tenth centuries saw an increasing proliferation of copies of the text itself: we know of at least eight such manuscripts dating from the ninth century, five from the end of the ninth to the beginning of the tenth centuries, and seventy-one from the tenth to the eleventh centuries.[31] Diane Bolton notes that in England, moreover, it is not merely the number of manuscripts that survive, but their quality that bears witness to 'the unique position occupied by that work in late Anglo-Saxon England. The high quality of the parchment, the clarity of the script of text and glosses and the beauty of the illuminated initials ... [suggest that their] owners must have preserved them as treasures in the same category as the great Bibles.'[32] Given the fact that seven of the sixteen extant English manuscripts are from Canterbury and three are from Abingdon,[33] we may conclude not only that, as Bolton states, 'the commentaries were copied and read in Anglo-Saxon monasteries and many English monks must have been familiar with the contents of the *Consolation of Philosophy*,' but that 'Boethius studies were concentrated in the monasteries especially associated with the reforms of Dunstan, Æthelwold and Oswald.'[34] Even though no Winchester manuscripts of *De consolatione* are known, therefore, it is not surprising to find a

Frankish monk at Winchester drawing on this work. What is surprising is to find him drawing not on Christian commentaries but exclusively on Boethius's Neoplatonic text.

The Watchtower and the Race

Before arguing for Lantfred's independence of the commentary tradition, it is important to establish that the *Carmen*'s relationship to *De consolatione* is not limited to its opening invocation of Fate, Providence, and divine foreknowledge. One place where both Lantfred's debt to Boethius and Lantfred's originality can be seen is in a key metaphor he uses to describe the relationship between God's sovereignty and human free will. The passage is central to the poem, both in terms of its location and its importance to the poet's argument. It serves as the transition between an introductory, theological section (lines 9–54) and a subsequent section of commentary, which attempts to explain the metaphor in theological terms (lines 89–166). Lantfred himself highlights the passage by a two-part introduction: first, stating that 'Sermones nostri paucis paradigmata uerbis / ponimus in medium clarius ut resonent' (lines 55–6),[35] and then calling on Æthelwold to correct what he may present poorly (lines 57–68). In the manuscript, moreover, non-rubricated capitals mark the beginning and end of the section – a feature that otherwise occurs only at Lantfred's opening prayer and the beginning of his theological comments (lines 1 and 9). In this passage, then, Lantfred describes a king seated on a high watchtower who commands individuals to run in a race:

> Rex sapiens residet specula sublimis in alta
>   prouidus ac pugnax, praepete mente sagax,   70
> militibus multis circumdatus ac pretiosis,
>   bis seno procerum septus honore ducum,
> sarranis recubans ostris sericisque tapetis:
>   is iubet in stadio currere mille uiros.
> uestes purpureas centum totidemque coronas   75
>   imperat eximio ponere pro titulo
> ante suos uisus, ac tali uoce profatur:
>   'uelox miles erit qui meus esse cupit,
> qui celer optatam poterit contingere palmam
>   mox sertum capiat condicione mea,   80
> in numero satrapumque merebitur esse meorum
>   stemmate regali comptus et exuuiis;

qui piger et metam non quibit adire fugacem
   inmunis redeat et titulis careat.
hic caesus diris uibicibus atque flagellis   85
   nexus compedibus carceribus dabitur.
coetibus ille meis sociabitur atque cateruis;
   cleptibus iste feris, ridiculus populis.'

A wise king sits raised up on a high watchtower, provident and warlike, sagacious and swift of mind, surrounded with many valuable soldiers, hedged about with the eminence of twelve princely commanders, reclining in robes of Tyrian purple and on silken tapestries, and orders a thousand men to run in the stadium. [line 75:] He commands that a hundred purple garments and an equal number of crowns be placed before him as an exceptional award, and speaks as follows: 'Swift shall be that soldier who wishes to be mine. Let him who is quick and who can reach the coveted palm seize the wreath soon according to my compact, and he will deserve to be counted among my viceroys, adorned with a princely garland and clothes. [line 83:] Let him who is lazy and unable to attain the fleeting goal return empty-handed and lacking awards. [line 85:] Having been cut to pieces with fearsome blows and whips, bound with shackles, he shall be placed in prison. [line 87:] The one will be joined with my assembly and troop; the other with savage thieves, an object of ridicule to the multitudes.' (lines 69–88)

Several elements in this metaphor are drawn from *De consolatione*. The image of a provident king, first of all, seated on a high watchtower ('specula sublimis in alta / prouidus' [line 69]) who gazes upon the contest from his high throne ('a solio certamina conspicit alto' [line 93]), derives from a description of God that appears in various forms in Boethius's text. On one occasion, Philosophy describes God as the Great Physician, who knows what remedies will best help each individual, and treats people with gentleness or severity accordingly. God knows these things about humans, Philosophy says, because 'ex alta prouidentiae specula respexit' (he looks out from the high watchtower of Providence [IV.pr6.30]). The rare nature of this phrase makes it a striking verbal echo.[36] Even so, the parallel is seemingly undermined by the overall dissimilarity between the two portraits: in the *Carmen*, God is not a physician, but a judge, rewarding the swift and condemning the sluggish. On other occasions, however, Philosophy does present God as a judge overseeing worldly events. Earlier in Book IV, for example, she states that 'Sedet ... conditor altus / rerumque regens flectit habenas, / rex et dominus ... / lex et sapiens arbiter aequi.'[37] Similarly, in Book V, Philosophy describes God looking down on human beings and rewarding their actions: 'Manet spectator desuper cunctorum praescius deus ... bonis praemia malis supplicia dispensans.'[38] Again she states: 'Ab aeterno cuncta prospiciens prouidentiae cernit intuitus et suis quaeque meritis praedestinata disponit.'[39] Lantfred incorporates this imagery as well, identifying the king's promise to the runners as 'praedestiuenatio: caelo / promittit sanctis quae bona pro meritis, / inferni miseros et cogit adire tenebras / arbitrio proprio qui periere mali.'[40]

In addition to this portrait of the exalted judge, the *Carmen* draws on *De consolatione* for its description of royal trappings and the race itself. In presenting the king as arrayed in purple and surrounded by soldiers, first of all (lines 71–3), the *Carmen* parallels a reference by Philosophy to 'quos uides sedere celsos solii culmine reges, / purpura claros nitente, saeptos tristibus armis' (kings whom you see that sit high atop their thrones, resplendent in bright purple and hedged about by forbidding weapons [IV.m2.1–2]). Again, however, the context makes the parallel problematic: Philosophy here is lambasting proud and evil kings rather than praising a righteous one (IV.m2.3–10). While *De consolatione* makes several references to kings, however, this is one of the only descriptions it offers of royalty; it may be, therefore, that Lantfred simply drew on the imagery at hand, disregarding its original negative connotations. Second, then, there is the race itself. Humans are commanded to 'run in a stadium' (in stadio currere) with crowns (*coronas*) being promised to those who win the race (lines 74–6). Philosophy states: 'Currendi in stadio propter quam curritur iacet praemium *corona* ... quantumlibet igitur saeuiant mali, sapienti tamen corona non decidet, non arescet.'[41] Here the parallel is unmistakable, for these appear to be the only occasions on which the image of *currens in stadio* is combined with that of an onlooking judge.[42] Almost without exception, when medieval authors speak of running in an arena, they do so in the context of Paul's exhortation to the Corinthians: 'Nescitis quod hii qui in stadio currunt omnes quidem currunt, sed unus accipit bravium? Sic currite ut conprehendatis.'[43] Such an obvious association is not lost on Lantfred. As he himself notes, 'Currere nosque monent domini sintagmata Christi / militis ac Pauli currere nosque docent, / scamatis in specie nostros ubi significauit / actus humanos scamatis in specie.'[44]

The race in the stadium may not be the only aspect of Lantfred's metaphor that carries echoes of biblical texts. In closing the king's speech, Lantfred contrasts those who finish the race and are counted among the king's loyal subjects with those who neglect to run and are associated with thieves. It is an odd description of the wicked, for what has theft to do with the running of a race? Lantfred's portrait bears distinct similarities, however, to three scenes in the Gospels where God judges negligent servants. First of all, there is the parable of the Talents (Matt. 25.14–30), where servants are entrusted with money that they must invest wisely. When the day of reckoning comes, the master rewards those servants who have worked hard, but punishes the one who, by doing nothing, has 'robbed' his master of potential gain. Condemning this servant as lazy (*piger*) – the same term used by Lantfred (line 83) – the master has him thrown 'in tenebras exteriores, illic erit fletus et stridor dentium.'[45] The same phrase appears earlier in Matthew's account of Christ's parable of the Wedding Feast (Matt. 22.2–14). Here, those the king has invited to share in his celebration are adorned with special clothing for the occasion (cf. line 82); the one not marked by such clothes, conversely, is cast out of the Feast. Just as Lantfred's king states that the wrongdoer will be bound (line 86), so the king in the parable commands his servants: '*Ligatis* pedibus eius et manibus mittite eum in tenebras exteriores ibi erit fletus et stridor dentium.'[46] Finally, there is the parable of the Unmerciful Servant (Matt. 18.23–35); in it, a servant, having been forgiven an enormous debt by his king, goes out and imprisons another man who owes him a small sum. Outraged, the king hands the servant over to be tortured (*tradidit eum tortoribus*) – in prison, it would seem, given the parallelism of the parable – until the servant should repay his own debt. While the parable is not specific as to the nature of this torture, it does suggest that flogging and imprisonment, as Lantfred has it (lines 85–6), are appropriate punishments for 'theft.' While the parallels are rarely exact, therefore, such biblical scenes of judgment may well have shaped Lantfred's depiction of the king's decree. In blending such scriptural imagery with Boethian themes and language, however, Lantfred runs the risk of presenting a heterodox solution to the problem of free will. It is a risk compounded by the fact that Lantfred appears to fashion his text without relying on the Christian commentary tradition.

The *Carmen*'s Independence from the Commentary Tradition

Given Lantfred's association with two likely centres of Boethian study, it is difficult to imagine that he would have been unaware of the perceived need to approach *De consolatione* through the lens of Christian commentary: the very existence of the commentary traditition proclaimed the need for such mediation. Two sources on which this student of Boethius might have been expected to draw would have been the commentary of Remigius and the vernacular versions of Alfred the Great. At first glance, this pairing might seem somewhat of a mismatch: the number of surviving manuscripts alone suggests that Remigius's impact far exceeded that of Alfred. The extant copies of the *Old English Boethius* give no indication that it was present at Winchester or Fleury,[47] nor is it clear that Lantfred's contemporary Ælfric encountered the text at Winchester, though he draws on it in his writings some five to fifteen years later.[48] If Alfred's work were to be known anywhere, however, it might arguably have been studied in the city which was his capital and at the monastery where he was buried.

It is not easy, in fact, to establish that Lantfred did not use Alfred's work in addition to *De consolatione*, since Alfred generally follows Boethius's descriptions of the king on his tower. When Philosophy portrays God as a physician gazing out from the high watchtower of Providence who sends blessings and trials in accordance with human character (IV.pr6.27–30), Wisdom likewise speaks of the physician of the soul who 'wat hwæs ælc wyrðe bið ... forðæm he of þæm hean hrofe hit eall gesihð, [ond] þonan miscað [ond] metgað ælcum be his gewyrhtum.'[49] When Philosophy sings of the Creator sitting on high, ruling and guiding the reins of the world as its source, king, lord, law, and wise, just judge (IV.m6.34–7), Wisdom follows closely, saying 'sit se hehsta sceoppend on his heahsetle; þanon he welt þa[m] gewealdleðeru[m] ealle gesceaftu. Nis nan wundor, forþa[m]ðe he is cyning [ond] dryhten [ond] æwelm [ond] fruma [ond] æ [ond] wisdom [ond] rihtwis dema.'[50] Even in Alfred's largely original conclusion to the *Boethius*, he echoes Philosophy's statement that the gaze of Providence looks upon all things from its eternal perspective, judging and distributing predestined rewards according to individual merit (V.pr2.11). Wisdom states: 'Se ælmehtga sy[m]le sit on þæ[m] heahsetle his anwaldes; þonan he mæg eall gesion, [ond] gilt ælcu[m] [be þam] swiðe rihte æft[er] his gewyrhtu[m].'[51]

One departure in Alfred's translation, however, may confirm that his *Boethius* did not serve as Lantfred's source. In her reference to people running in the stadium, Philosophy reflects:

Perspicuum est numquam bonis praemia, numquam sua sceleribus deesse supplicia ... Uti currendi in stadio propter quam curritur iacet praemium [1] corona ... probos mores sua praemia non relinquunt. Quantumlibet igitur saeuiant mali, sapienti tamen corona [2] non decidet, non arescet.

It is clear that rewards are never lacking for good deeds, nor appropriate punishments for crimes ... Just as the prize for running in the stadium is the [1] crown for which the race is run ... upright conduct does not forfeit its appropriate reward. However much the wicked may rage, therefore, the crown of the wise [2] will not die and will not wither.[52]

Alfred paraphrases the passage as follows:

Þa goodan næfre ne beoð bedælde þara edlena heora goodes, ne ða yflan næfre þara wita ðe hi geearnigað ... Swa swa gio Romana þeaw wæs, and giet is on manegum þiodum, *þæt* mon hehð ænne [3] heofodbeag gyldenne æt sumes ærneweges ende; færð ðonne micel folc to, and yrnað ealle endemes, ða ðe hiora ærninge trewað. and swa hwelc swa ærest to þæm [4] beage cymð, þonne mot se hine habban him ... Forðæm is ælcu ðearf þæt he higie ealle mægene æft ðære mede; ðære mede ne wyrð næfre nan good man bedæled.

The righteous are never deprived of the rewards of their righteousness, nor the wicked of the punishments they earn ... Just as it was once the custom of the Romans – and still is in many countries – for people to hang a [3] golden crown at the end of a racecourse, many people who have confidence in their racing come there and run together, and whoever reaches the [4] crown first may have it for himself ... It is important for every man, therefore, to strive with all his strength after the reward, for [5] no righteous man will ever be deprived of it.[53]

Alfred, on the one hand, understands the *corona* that awaits the runners at the end of the course as a crown of metal, a *beag* or *heofodbeag gyldenne* ([1], [4] and [3] above). In saying that this crown will neither perish or wither, however (*non decidet, non arescet*), Philosophy indicates that she has a victor's garland in mind ([2] above). While Lantfred does speak of 100 *coronae* that are reserved for the winners of the race (line 75), these are not hung at the end of the course, as in Alfred's description. Rather, Lantfred depicts the runners as striving to reach a wreath – a *palma* or *sertum* (lines 79–80). While the evidence is limited, therefore, the probability is that the *Old English Boethius* was not a source for the *Carmen*.

If Lantfred does not draw on Alfred, might not his text show the influence of the Remigian tradition, that most prominent of Christian commentaries? It is not as though Remigius has nothing to say on the subject of free will. When in Book V Philosophy argues that while God knows all future events, some of those events proceed from individuals' free choice ('de libero proficiscuntur arbitrio' [V.pr6.32]), Remigius interposes Pauline language on the passage:

> Mala non solummodo libero fiunt arbitrio, quia postquam [1] primus homo sponte peccauit [2] ad bonum quidem liberum amisit arbitrium, [3] ad malum tantum retinuit. [4] Nisi ergo diuina inspiratio praeueniat, nullus aliquid valet agere boni. [5] Hinc Apostolus: Plus, inquit, omnibus laboraui, non autem ego sed gratia Dei mecum. Mirum uidetur quod dicit se laborasse et non laborasse, quod facile potest uideri, si simul et gratiam Dei quae illum praeuenit et liberum arbitrium consideremus.

> Free will is not the only reason evil things are done, because after [1] the first man voluntarily sinned [2] he lost the free will to do good [3] but retained the will to do great evil. [4] Therefore unless God's grace comes beforehand, he can do nothing good. [5] This is why the apostle says: "I have laboured more than all of them – yet not I, but the grace of God in me.' While it seems astonishing that he says he both laboured and did not labour, this can easily be understood if we consider both his free will and the grace of God which preceded it.[54]

The perspective Remigius interjects is strikingly Augustinian. Reiterating that human will turned wholly to evil through Adam's free choice ([1] – [3] above), Remigius spells out humanity's need for prevenient grace ([4]). The third English reviser, in fact, condenses the gloss to these bare essentials: 'Mala ex libero arbitrio proficiscuntur. Bona ex Dei gratia que preuenit liberoque demum arbitrio quod subsequitur uolendo.'[55] Not only is the emphasis on prevenient grace Augustinian, but so is the Pauline reference in this context: as Augustine repeatedly points out, 'Ne ipsa uoluntas sine gratia Dei putetur boni aliquid posse, continue cum dixisset ... "plus omnibus illis laboraui"; subiunxit atque ait, "Non ego autem, sed gratia Dei mecum."'[56]

Lantfred's work is remarkably free of such language. He does acknowledge that after Adam and Eve sinned, 'effectum libertatis habuere malignum, / corrupti uitiis criminibusque feris, / nec meritis uitam possent sperare beatam / adiuti domini ni pietate forent.'[57] He also asks that God's grace grant 'pellat ut a famulis arbitrium sceleris' (that he may drive away from his servants the will to do evil [line 160]) so that individuals may enter heaven. These statements are the closest Lantfred comes, however, to Remigius and his revisers' view of human beings' absolute corruption. Throughout his work, Lantfred depicts human volition not as a twisted force that inevitably drives men to evil, but as a free agent by which individals determine their destiny. Those runners who complete the race, for example, have not been carried to the finish-line by the king, but have run by their own power and by their own choice; Lantfred defines the racecourse, in fact, as human free will ('arbitrii libertatem ... scammata signant' [line 99; cf. lines 23–4 and 103–4]). Where Lantfred's departure from Augustine is perhaps most apparent, however, is in his depiction of God as a distant king who will not interfere with human self-determination.

The Distant King: Foreknowledge and Free Will

Reflecting on his metaphor of the watchtower, Lantfred explains the relationship between the king and the runners as follows:

> Intuitus regis certantibus haud nocet illis;   115
>   praesidium nulli ferre potest homini;
> rex etiam uastis interstitiis segregatus
>   nec solum uisu, sed neque uoce, manu.
> actus praeteritos, praesentes, necne futuros
>   auctor sic hominum prospicit intuitu,   120
> et quamuis ualeat mentes peruertere sontes
>   ad meliora, tamen nil nocet arbitrio.

> The king's gaze by no means harms those who are contending; nor can it offer help to any man. [line 117:] The king is isolated by immense spaces, not only from sight, but from voice and touch as well. [line 119:] Similarly, the maker of men watches with his gaze our past, present, and future deeds, and although he could completely change sinful minds to better things, nevertheless he does not harm individuals' will. (lines 115–22)

On the one hand, Lantfred is orthodox enough in stating that God does not 'harm' individuals' will (lines 115 and 122). Despite debate over passages such as God's 'hardening' of Pharaoh's heart (e.g., Ex. 7.3), the Fathers were consistent in affirming that God does not compel humans to evil.[58] The fact that the poet twice uses *nocet* instead of a word such as *cogit* or *compellit* ('force' or 'coerce'), moreover, might suggest that Lantfred has human beings' ultimate condition as well as their daily behaviour in mind: God's influence does not 'harm' people everlastingly by destining them to hell. This interpretation is consistent both with the immediate context of judgment and his statement just before that 'Praedestiuenatio ... / inferni miseros cogit adire tenebras / *arbitrio proprio* qui periere mali' – a statement that, as we have seen, echoes Philosophy's comment that 'Prouidentiae cernit intuitus et suis quaeque meritis praedestinata disponit' (cf. lines 115 and 120).[59] Again, such a point would be perfectly orthodox. Augustine argued against the proposition that God predestines humans to damnation,[60] as did Hrabanus Maurus and Hincmar of Reims in their ninth-century debate with Gottschalk.[61] Combined with the suggestion that God does not influence individuals' wills for good, however (line 121), this depiction of divine detachment becomes decidedly problematic.

First of all, Lantfred's suggestion seems to be in contrast with the descriptions of the king in *De consolatione* on which Lantfred draws for his metaphor. When Philosophy describes God as the Great Physician, for example, she portrays him not as a passive observer of human actions, but as the 'rector mentium' (the mind's guide) (IV.pr6.29). Similarly, when Philosophy depicts God as the exalted Judge, ruling and guiding the world, while her immediate emphasis is on God's control over creation, her statement follows on the heels of a discussion of how God deals with human beings: 'Naturarum omnium proditor deus idem ad bonum dirigens cuncta disponat.'[62] Both statements are opposed to the *Carmen*'s suggestion of divine non-interference.

Second, this suggestion seems to contradict Lantfred's affirmation of God's influence elsewhere in the poem. Just as here he indicates that God's gaze (*intuitus*) observes human beings' past, present, and future deeds (lines 119–20), so at the beginning of the *Carmen* he states that 'Mens diuina ... / uidet in praesens, praeteritumque, sequens, / cuius ab intuitu nequeunt res flectere cursus.'[63] God, in other words, 'ordinat omne quod est' (regulates everything that exists [line 12]). Similarly, following his comments here on the *intuitus regis*, Lantfred speaks of God not simply watching but showing individuals where they must go: God 'iter angustum raris comeantibus idem / signat' (draws the narrow path to the attention of those few who follow it [lines 125–6]).[64] At another point, he goes still further, saying that God 'destinat, amplificat [famulos], iustificatque coronat, / saluat, sanctificat, protegit

atque fouet.'[65] All three statements present God as active and control-
ling rather than distant and detached.

Third, the suggestion that God does not influence human minds is
completely at odds with Augustine's view of God's response to
human corruption. As we have seen, Augustine teaches that fallen
humanity's desires are such that, despite individuals' technical freedom to choose good, left to themselves people will always choose evil.
Through the Spirit's inward inspiration, therefore, God does exactly
what Lantfred here denies, turning minds fixed on evil towards righteousness ('mentes peruerte[ns] sontes / ad meliora') (lines 121–2).
The poet's portrait of a divine policy of laissez-faire, therefore, catches
him in a trifold quandary. To the extent that he uses specific phrases
from *De consolatione* in a way opposed to their context, he seems to be
unfaithful to his source. To the extent that he refers elsewhere to God's
assistance, he appears to contradict himself. To the extent that he
affirms humans' complete independence, he runs completely counter
to Remigius's Augustinian perspective. How then are we to understand this passage?

The answer lies in Boethius's solution to the tension between divine
foreknowledge and human volition, a solution that depends on Philosophy's definition of the divine gaze (*intuitus*). Boethius uses the term
fourteen times over the course of the text, at first merely in reference to
human sight. Half of those references, however, are clustered in Book
V, where Philosophy's comments have direct bearing on the poet's portrait of the *intuitus regis*. Immediately after Philosophy has said, for
example, that the *intuitus* of Providence judges and distributes predestined rewards (V.pr2.11), Boethius addresses the apparent contradiction between the boundlessness of God's gaze and the possibility for
human volition: if God sees in advance all that will happen, Boethius
asks, how can people do anything other than what God has foreknown
(V.pr.3.3–6)? Similarly, it is just after Lantfred has said that the king's
promise represents predestination, which gives rewards to individuals
based on their merits (lines 105–8), that he turns to the question of foreknowledge and the effect of the *intuitus regis* on those in the contest
(lines 109–10 and 115–22).[66]

Philosophy tackles the problem in this way:

Si praeuidentiam pensare uelis qua cuncta dinoscit, non esse praescientiam
quasi futuri sed scientiam numquam deficientis instantiae rectius aestima-
bis. Unde non praeuidentia sed prouidentia potius dicitur, quod porro a

rebus infimis constituta, quasi ab excelso rerum cacumine cuncta prospi-
ciat. Quid igitur postulas ut necessaria fiant quae diuino lumine lustrentur,
cum ne homines quidem necessaria faciant esse quae uideant? ... Ita igitur
cuncta dispiciens diuinus intuitus qualitatem rerum minime perturbat.
(V.pr6.16–18 and 23)

If you wish to consider the foreknowledge by which God discerns all
things, you will understand it more correctly not as foreknowledge of the
future, but as the knowledge of a never-ending presence. Therefore, it is
better described not as 'seeing beforehand' but 'looking forth,' because,
established far from things below, it may gaze out on all things as if from
a high summit. Why, then, do you insist that things which are observed
by the divine eye must necessarily come to pass? People certainly do not
make things which they see happen by necessity ... In the same way,
therefore, the divine gaze sees all things clearly but by no means disturbs
their nature.

Given this Boethian background, therefore, we understand the
Carmen's emphasis on the 'distance' between the king and those in
the race: Lantfred is affirming that the fact that God (fore)sees all
things does not mean that he causes them. Lantfred does not deny
that God supports those who have chosen to obey him, and emphasizes that God does not harm (nocet) individuals' will by destining
them to hell. Nevertheless, in saying that God will not turn human
minds towards righteousness, Lantfred directly opposes Augustine's
teaching on grace.

Unprompted Prayer: A Denial of Grace

Lantfred is thus caught in the tension between two ideologies. On the
one hand, his Christian training and heritage compels him to acknowledge humanity's fallen condition and dependence on God's help. On
the other hand, the Boethian perspective that so informs his analysis
acknowledges God's sovereignty but ardently defends individuals'
capacity for self-determination. His solution is to describe the 'work' of
human beings – their 'running' – in terms of prayer, thus affirming
both people's ability and responsibility to beseech God for his assistance. As the Carmen draws to a close, he prays:

O dee cunctipotens cosmi qui regmina flectis ...
te sine nil rectum nil iustum nilque pudicum

scire potest miser et praeuaricatus homo;   170
quapropter toto mentis conamine poscens
  deprecor, ac numen flagito teque tuum,
dirige sic actus hominum, rector, ualeant quo
  post finem uitae denarium capere.

Omnipotent God, you who direct the guidance of the universe ... without
you, wretched and sinful man can know nothing that is right or just or
virtuous. [line 171] For this reason, asking earnestly with the whole effort
of my mind, I entreat and beseech you and your divine will: so direct the
deeds of individuals, O Guide, that by this they may be able to gain the
denarius after the end of their life. (lines 167 and 169–74)

It is perhaps significant that Lantfred says that people cannot *know* anything good without God, rather than saying that people cannot *do* anything without him (line 170). Earlier, when he states that God draws the
narrow path to people's attention, Lantfred explains that God draws
individuals through the medium of his word: 'Nosque sequi dextrum
iubet ac uitare sinistrum ... / dogmatibus sanctis infit ubi populis.'[67] He
emphasizes the point twice thereafter by referring to what the decrees of
Christ teach ('demonstrent dogmata Christi' [line 137; *cf.* 143]). Once
God has pointed humans to the narrow way through 'dogmata sancta,'
however, whether this be direct reading of the scriptures or the preaching thereof, Lantfred suggests that individuals have the power to pursue it: 'Semita stricta polum poterit reserare supernum, / illam neruosus
siquis adire cupit.'[68] Here, then, in saying that people cannot know anything good without God, the poet is not suggesting, like Remigius, that
all righteous thought and action depends on God's prevenient grace,
but simply affirming once again people's need for godly instruction.
Having himself received this instruction, Lantfred then models how one
is to run the race or pursue the narrow way: wholeheartedly praying for
God to direct one's actions (lines 171–3). It is only after one has
responded freely to God's teaching, to the king's proclamation of the
race as it were, that God, through the invitation of prayer, becomes the
'rector mentium' (*cf.* line 173).
  One other passage in the *Carmen* reflects this pattern as well. Having
presented his illustrations of the race and the narrow path, Lantfred
draws his comments to a close by saying:

His patet exemplis quod contemplatio uiri
  haud uertat proprium iudicis arbitrium,   150

uota, preces domino nisi quis pro flagitioso
fuderit, omne scelus uertat ut in melius.

It is clear from these examples that the contemplation of man by no means
changes the Judge's own will, unless one has poured out prayers and
requests to the Lord for one's shameful deeds, that [God] would turn
every shame to something better. (lines 149–52)

In one sense, Lantfred's statement is somewhat problematic in that it
seems to contrast human 'contemplation' with divine judgment (lines
149–50). What is this *contemplatio* that does not change God's will? The
word is mentioned only one other time in the poem, when Lantfred
seeks to explain the twelve princely commanders who surround the
king (line 72); he states: 'Prospectusque ducum sit contemplatio rerum;
/ quod fuit, est, et erit haec uidet atque regit' (lines 95–6).[69] Who are
these sovereign and apparently omniscient figures? To a certain extent
one is tempted to think of the twelve apostles, who receive Christ's
promise that 'Qui secuti estis me, in regeneratione, cum sederit Filius
hominis in throno gloriae suae, sedebitis et uos super thronos duodecim, iudicantes duodecim tribus Israel.'[70] The absolute nature of the
qualities they possess, however, can only be divine: no mortal sees and
governs all things. If there had only been seven figures, we might have
taken this as an allusion to the sevenfold Spirit before God's throne (cf.
Rev. 1.4), especially as Lantfred has just said that 'Omne quod hic gerimus flamine deus [conspicit]' (By his Spirit God [observes] everything
we do here [line 94]). Whether the poet is referring directly to God or to
agents of his power such as the apostles, however, ultimately *contemplatio* must refer to the divine *intuitus* that is central to Lantfred's metaphor. This connection in turn may provide the key to Lantfred's later
reference to *contemplatio uiri*.

There are three possibilities, all of which lead to the same interpretation. Lapidge notes, first of all, that *uĭri* is metrically false, and could be a
dittographic error from *uiri* in the previous line.[71] His premise gains
even more strength when we consider that the line was accidentally
omitted from the text, and had to be written on top of the page with
signes-de-renvoi marking its proper place. The break in the scribe's concentration and need to relocate the line it was to follow would have
made the mistake an easy one. Given the poet's assumption that his
point about this *contemplatio* would be clear from his prior examples ('his
patet exemplis') (line 149), it may be that the original word hearkened

back to the other passage. While *contemplatio dĕi* or *contemplatio dūcum* does not scan properly, *contemplatio rērum*, the phrase used in line 95, does. If *rerum* were the original reading of line 149, then both lines would refer to God's contemplation of human beings, rather than humans' contemplation of God. Second, as the *Carmen* and its preceding poems contain a number of variations in spelling between *i* and *e*, it could be that line 149 originally read *contemplatio uēri*.[72] Assuming that the variations themselves were not scribal in orgin, the scribe may have retained Lantfred's spellings elsewhere, but altered the word here to *uiri*, lest it be confused with the dative of *uer* (spring). The simplest solution, however, especially given other cases of false quantity in the poem,[73] is to let the reading stand. In this case, *uiri*, like *ueri*, would be an objective genitive refering to God's vision of human beings. It is this vision, Lantfred says, like the omniscient *intuitus* of the king on his watchtower, that does not alter the will of the judge – that is, God's personal decision not to interfere with human minds: foreknowledge, Lantfred affirms, does not nullify free will. Rather, he asserts, it is only when individuals appeal to God through their prayers (lines 151–2) that God intervenes, driving from his servants the will to sin ('pella[ns] a famulis arbitrium sceleris'). While God will not turn guilty *minds* to better things, therefore ('[non] mentes peruerte[t] sontes ad meliora') (lines 121–2), he will turn their guilt to something better ('omne scelus uert[et] in melius') (line 152) – that is, righteousness.[74] Lantfred thus affirms both the sovereignty of human will and humanity's need to pursue God's help through prayer.

Lantfred's solution to the tension between Boethian and Augustinian perspectives is not an original one: Augustine, Gregory, and Bede, for example, all call on people to pray for God's assistance. Here again, however, Lantfred derives his position not from the Fathers, but from Boethius. In her closing exhortation in *De consolatione*, Philosophy states:

Nec frustra sunt in deo positae spes precesque, quae cum rectae sunt inefficaces esse non possunt. Auersamini igitur uitia, colite uirtutes, ad rectas spes animum subleuate, humiles preces in excelsa porrigite. Magna uobis est, si dissimulare non uultis, necessitas indicta probitatis cum ante oculos agitis iudicis cuncta cernentis. (V.pr6.46–8)

Hope placed in God and prayers are not in vain, for when they are righteous they cannot be ineffective. Turn from vice, therefore, cultivate virtue, lift up your mind to a righteous hope and offer up humble prayers on high. If you do not wish to hide [from God], you have a great and publicly proclaimed responsibility to be upright, for you live before the eyes of a judge who sees all things.

On one level, Philosophy's words are difficult to fault; indeed, this call to forsake temporal things in pursuit of eternal ones was one of the primary reasons *De consolatione* held such appeal for Christian scholars. It conceals, however, a subtle but crucial difference: in *De consolatione*, the initiative for human choice of good over evil comes not from God, but from individuals' own will. When the Fathers call on people to pray, they do so in the understanding that the very impulse to pray is a gift of God. Lantfred, by contrast, represents God as a distant king who responds to individuals' prayers but does not inspire them. Like Gregory and Bede, Lantfred attempts to preserve a role for human volition; unlike them, however, he does not acknowledge God's influence on the will. While he affirms that people must be helped by God's mercy, and speaks of God pointing people to the narrow path through the medium of his word, in terms of volition, Lantfred denies prevenient grace. In contrast to Alfred, whose revision of *De consolatione* presents a largely Augustinian perspective, Lantfred ultimately is caught by the implications of its philosophy. Asserting that human beings can choose good apart from God, he raises a Semi-Pelagian heresy at a leading centre of the Benedictine Reform. In doing so, however, Lantfred would not be alone. Some decades later, drawing on an entirely different tradition, a similar perspective would be offered by Wulfstan the Homilist.

CHAPTER SIX

Wulfstan the Homilist
and *De adiutorio Dei et libero arbitrio*

A few decades after the composition of the *Carmen de libero arbitrio*, a different study of free will was written or sponsored by another of Ælfric's contemporaries: the prolific author and influential statesman known variously as Wulfstan Lupus, Wulfstan of York, or Wulfstan the Homilist.[1] Like Lantfred and Ælfric, he was closely associated with a major centre of the Benedictine Reform. Like both these figures, his works were influential enough to be copied down through the eleventh century.[2] Where Lantfred draws on Boethius, and Ælfric on the Church Fathers, for their understanding of human volition, however, Wulfstan relies on a key Semi-Pelagian text that introduces another strain of heterodox theology into late Anglo-Saxon England.

Wulfstan the Homilist: Background

We know little for certain of Wulfstan's origins; later veneration at Peterborough and Ely, where he was buried, may suggest a connection with the east Midlands. From 996, however, he served as bishop of London where, playing on his name, he began to sign himself as *Lupus* or 'Wolf.' In 1002 he moved from London to take up the episcopacy of Worcester (1002–16) and the archbishopric of York (1002–23), holding both positions simultaneously as did his predecessor, archbishop Eadulf.[3] In 1016, the year of Cnut's ascension to the throne of England, Wulfstan either resigned his post at Worcester or appointed a suffragan (an official deputy) in his place. The move did not, however, mark a withdrawal from southern affairs: Wulfstan not only survived the transition to Danish authority, but served as advisor and author of legislation under Cnut even as he had under Æthelstan II before him.

A number of works have been attributed to Wulfstan. In the vernacular, on the one hand, his writings include treatises on ecclesiastical and political responsibility: *The Institutes of Polity*, discussing the duties of various classes in society; the *Canons of Edgar*, providing instruction for secular clergy; *Rectitudines* and *Gerefa*, advising on the management of large estates; a translation of Amalarius of Metz's *De regula canonicorum*, and so forth. Even better known, perhaps, are his homiletic writings: the thirty Old English homilies printed by Dorothy Bethurum that include Wulfstan's most famous work, the *Sermo Lupi ad Anglos* (Sermon of the Wolf to the English). Jonathan Wilcox has recently listed another twenty-two-odd 'undeveloped homiletic pieces' attributed since to Wulfstan.[4] The line between Wulfstan's 'legal' and homiletic works is somewhat fluid: his translation of Amalarius, for example, appears in Bethurum's homiletic collection (Homily Xa), and 'homiletic' emphasis on the urgent need for moral change appears in his legislation. Nonetheless, four factors help to associate Wulfstan with these vernacular works. First, a number of texts bear his pseudonym *Lupus* or were circulated under his name.[5] Second, his hand has been identified in at least ten manuscripts, including one on which we will focus in more detail.[6] Third, various manuscripts bear witness to a 'handbook' or 'commonplace book' compiled by Wulfstan containing material of interest to him.[7] Finally, Wulfstan is known for his distinctive prose style: his characteristic two-stress, alliterating, occasionally rhyming phrases; his habit of emphasis through repetition, intensifying adverbs, and energetic compounds; his habitual reuse of material and his love of sound-play.[8]

When one comes to Wulfstan's Latin writings, however, the known corpus is small, and fewer 'rules' have been posited for identifying Wulfstanian texts. In 1883, Arthur Napier edited four Latin sermons which he attributed to Wulfstan; in 1957, Dorothy Bethurum reedited these texts and added a fifth, a selection of passages from Ezekiel and Isaiah on the duty of priests to preach and warn their flock against sin.[9] In each case, the Latin texts bear close resemblance to Old English sermons reflecting Wulfstan's distinctive prose style.[10] Possibly prepared as pulpit notes for addressing educated clergy, and later used as the basis for sermons for the non-Latinate, these texts seem to have been linked to Wulfstan more by their correspondence to the vernacular versions than by any distinctively 'Wulfstanian' features of their own.

More recently, James Cross has tentatively identified ten additional sermons as belonging to Wulfstan or composed under his supervision;[11]

his analysis implicitly offers certain principles for identifying Wulfstan Latin texts. One sermon appears in at least seven manuscripts representing Wulfstan's 'Commonplace Book' or otherwise containing Wulfstan material[12] exhorts its audience to obedience and disciplined fasting in 'quintessentially Wulfstanian fashion,'[13] and employs a biblical exemplum found in another homily ascribed to Wulfstan.[14] Two more sermons are found in two of these 'Wulfstanian' manuscripts, one being an address to bishops presumably by someone of equal or higher standing.[15] One contains a passage that parallels a short text found in two 'Commonplace Book' manuscripts; the text also has a marginal correction in Wulfstan's hand.[16] One contains a passage that served as an immediate source for one of Wulfstan's vernacular homilies.[17] Four present 'firm rules of conduct in the manner of Wulfstan's Old English sermons on the Christian faith,'[18] while four others appear 'very much like the kind of preparatory compositions which Wulfstan habitually wrote in Latin before he undertook fuller sermons in Old English.'[19] One additional sermon, moreover, has recently been attributed to Wulfstan by Tom Hall.[20] Directed to bishops on the subject of episcopal responsibility, the text appears in three 'Commonplace Book' manuscripts, paraphrases a passage of scripture that recurs frequently in Wulfstan's sermons, and displays 'Wulfstan's penchant for defining basic theological or doctrinal terms by comparing synonyms in two languages' – a trait which, while not unique to Wulfstan, Hall describes as 'unmistakably characteristic of his own method of instruction in both his Latin and English sermons.'[21]

By their methodology, Napier, Bethurum, Cross, and Hall thus suggest that certain characteristics, especially found in combination, may constitute evidence for associating Latin semons with Wulfstan: (1) close textual parallels to works by Wulfstan in the vernacular, (2) a tone evocative of Wulfstan's didactic manner, (3) a voice appropriate to a clergyman of episcopal or archiepiscopal standing, (4) stylistic features characteristic of Wulfstan's vernacular writings, and (5) appearance in one or more manuscripts associated with Wulfstan by their origin, contents, or hand. This last feature is one which all ten sermons identified by Cross have in common, for all are present – six uniquely so – in a crucial collection of Wulfstanian material, Copenhagen 1595.

Wulfstan's Association with *De adiutorio Dei*

Copenhagen, Kongelige Bibliotek, Gamle Kongelige Sammlung 1595 (s. xi[1]) contains a set of twenty-four texts in seven 'sections' compiled at Worcester during Wulfstan's tenure there as bishop. Jennifer Tunberg argues that these sections were produced independently of one another, having been conceived as separate projects rather than a collection; her suggestion has been challenged effectively, however, by Johan Gerritsen, who views the manuscript as a complete work copied between 1020 and 1022 for Gerbrand, the new bishop of the Danish royal city of Roskild.[22] Tunberg shows that four of the seven sections may be firmly associated with Worcester on the basis of the hands contained therein: three of their scribes also contributed to London, British Library, Cotton Tiberius A.xiii, Part 1 (s. xi[1]), a cartulary originating from Worcester, as, Tunberg notes, 'the contents of the book indicate and the history of the book confirms.'[23] The hands in the remaining sections may also be linked to Worcester, but with less certainty.[24] A number of the texts, however, pertain not merely to a scriptorium associated with Wulfstan, but to Wulfstan himself. There are pieces commissioned by Wulfstan for clerical instruction, such as Ælfric's *First* and *Second Latin Letter for Wulfstan*.[25] There are works that have been recognized as Wulfstan's own compositions, such as sermons on the Antichrist, Isaiah's vision of Israel's sins, and instructions regarding baptism.[26] There are compilations of source material used by Wulfstan which Cross and Hall view as sermons in their own right, such as extracts from Augustine on the importance of not repeating baptism.[27] Most importantly, however, there are sixty-five annotations and at least one major set of insertions in what has plausibly been identified as Wulfstan's own hand.[28]

One portion of the manuscript in which these features are evident is Section VI. This group of material includes not only the sermon on Isaiah's vision and the extracts from Augustine above, but thirteen annotations as well as the set of insertions in Wulfstan's hand. To a certain extent, the presence of Wulfstanian notes in a collection of his work should come as no surprise: Wulfstan himself affirms that it is a bishop's daily duty to read and correct books,[29] and eleven other manuscripts contain annotations in his hand.[30] The presence of his notes here, however, evidence Wulfstan's investment in this manuscript and this section in particular; at the very least, therefore, we can say that texts therein were read and approved by him. As Tunberg concludes: 'The prevalence of Wulfstan's annotations throughout GKS 1595, the nature of his annotations, and the links which can be inferred between Wulfstan and the scribes whose work he does not annotate all suggest what is implied by the contents of the manuscript: Sections I–VII were copied at the behest of Wulfstan, and under his supervision.'[31] Reflecting the fifth 'rule' above for associating Latin texs with Wulfstan, moreover – their appearance in one or more manuscripts associated with Wulfstan by their origin, contents, or hand – Cross and Hall attribute three sermons in this section to Wulfstan himself, even where they contain no additions in Wulfstan's hand.[32] One of these sermons is a Latin treatise that addresses the question of free will: *De adiutorio Dei et libero arbitrio.*

De adiutorio Dei in the Context of Wulfstan's Other Sermons

In one sense, the question of human beings' power of moral choice would have been highly relevant to Wulfstan, since much of his work concerns the need for such choice in the face of national and eschatological crisis. Wulfstan's law codes, letters to clergy, and sermons all convey an earnest concern for proper conduct, and one need look no further than the thrice-revised *Sermo Lupi ad Anglos,* that urgent call for reform in the face of divine punishment through Danish raids, to see the connection in Wulfstan's mind between the need for righteous living and the perils of the times.[33] In the main, however, Wulfstan spends far more time in practical moral exhortation than subtle theological analysis. Throughout his sermons, rather than discussing the ultimate source of righteous decisions Wulfstan simply asserts as fact that human beings can and should obey God. Pointing to the Judgment to come, for example, he urges his audience: 'Utan don swa us mycel þearf is, habban æfre rihtne geleafan ... [ond] his willan a wyrcan swa we geornost magan.'[34] As in the other four sermons where the phrase occurs, *swa we geornost magan* underscores not the limitations of human depravity and dependence on grace – '[let us do good] as best we can' – but simply the importance of striving to one's utmost.[35] Similarly, he says, scripture exhorts people to turn from evil and forsake the devil because individuals always have the power to do so: '[Man gedo þæt] he wiðsace anrædlice deofles gemanan; þæt is, þæt he forsace [ond] forbuge his unlara, *þæs ðe he æfre mæge,* [ond] ðæt he geswutelige eac þæt *he hæbbe [ond] æfre habban wille anræde geðanc* [ond] anrædne geleafan on ænne soðne [ond] ealmihtigne Godd.'[36] Again, Wulfstan gives no hint that humans may be incapacitated by their sinful nature; his focus is not on the spiritual mechanics of volition but on the importance of choosing rightly. Wulfstan does acknowledge that people need God to defend them against the devil's deceptions, but also says that people should 'deserve' God's help: 'La, hwæt is se man on life buton hine God ælmihtig gehealde, [ond] he ær gewarnod þe bet sy, þæt he þonne ðurh deofol beswicen ne wyrðe? Utan warnian us georne [ond] geearnian to Gode þæt he us gescylde swa his willa sy.'[37] Indeed, people's ability to choose makes it incumbent upon them to 'repay' Christ's sacrifice by choosing good: 'We agan nu geweald hwæþer we geearnian willan þe ece lif & ece blisse, þe ecne deað [ond] endelease yrmðe. Witodlice witan we moton hu we Criste geleanian eal þæt he for us [ond] for ure lufan þafode [ond] ðolode.'[38] In this emphasis on merit, as we shall see, Wulfstan echoes Ælfric's own teaching in the *Sermones*. In his suggestion, however, that people can always reject evil and follow the precepts of scripture through the power of their will, Wulfstan appears not only to reject Augustine's teaching on human corruption, but to champion a Pelagian view. What is more, on occasion his emphasis on individuals' roles is such that God's grace appears to follow human effort: he says, for example, 'Ðonne is micel þearf þæt manna gehwylc ... his heortan geclænsige and mid godum þingum hine sylfne swa geglænge *þæt* þær Godes gast on him wunian wille.'[39] One might deny, of course, that Wulfstan's view is actually Pelagian, arguing that he focuses on the practical need for individuals to choose good rather than on the origin of their ability to do so. Where most of Wulfstan's sermons may lack the theological precision needed to clarify this impression, however, *De adiutorio Dei et libero arbitrio*, the one text on free will closely associated with Wulfstan, provides it. That a scion of the Benedictine Reform should have composed or authorized this study of free will is astonishing, however, for it draws heavily and exclusively on *Collatio* XIII by John Cassian.

Semi-Pelagianism and Cassian's *Collatio* XIII

Nearly a decade after the Councils of Milevis and Carthage officially condemned the views of Pelagius in 416, a new set of objections began to be raised concerning certain points of Augustine's teaching. In response to Pelagius's claim that through God's gifts of reason and the Law human beings have the resources to choose good and live righteously, Augustine had increasingly emphasized the importance of grace. Human will has been so corrupted by the Fall, he said, that without God's prevenient assistance, individuals will neither think nor do anything good. As we have noted, however, around 426 a delegation was sent by monks at Hadrumentum to ask how such a position

left room for free will. During the same time, opposition was foment-
ing among monks in southern Gaul to Augustine's denial of human
initiative in the process of salvation. This assertion, along with his doctrine of the predestination of the elect, seemed to them to leave no
room for human responsibility or effort.[40] In a monastic setting where
ascetic discipline was viewed as the pathway to spiritual perfection,
this was a particular concern. Nowhere was the concern felt more
acutely than in Marseilles, in the monasteries of John Cassian.

Cassian had spent roughly fifteen years exploring the monastic disci-
plines of Egypt, seeking out saintly figures who had withdrawn into the
isolation and austerity of the desert in their quest for spiritual purity.[41]
When he emerged at the beginning of the fifth century, he came increasingly to be recognized as an authority on monastic matters, gaining
prominence first through his association with and defence of John
Chrysostom, and, later, through his contacts with the monastic leaders of
southern Gaul. Settling here in the mid- to late-410s, he found a keen
interest in Egyptian monastic practice. Within a few years, he had written the *De institutis coenobiorum* to contrast what he saw as the poorly
organized and undisciplined regular life of the region with the earnest
pursuit of sanctity he had encountered in the desert.[42] This was followed
by the *Collationes*, in which he recorded twenty-four dialogues with desert Fathers on the process of spiritual perfection. The model they presented was decidedly one of self-denial and personal endeavour. Given
the lingering questions from the Pelagian debates, it was crucial to reas-
sure those undertaking such a quest that there was a legitimate role for
human volition and a responsibility to exercise it. The definitive statement of Cassian's thought on the issue was to be found in *Collatio* XIII.
Here, while denying that individuals could accomplish good without
God's help, he nevertheless affirmed that humans could desire good and
seek God's help in bringing it to pass.[43] This tenet was to be the corner-
stone of Semi-Pelagianism.

Cassian's role in the Semi-Pelagian debate left him with an ambiguous ecclesiastical status. Uncanonized in the West as a whole, vener-
ated as a saint in Marseilles and the East,[44] he was at once a dangerous
author of heresy and a treasured source for guidance. Cassiodorus may
have cautioned against Cassian's unorthodox teaching, but he also
drew on him freely in his work.[45] Caesarius of Arles may have engi-
neered Orange's condemnation of Semi-Pelagianism, but he also sent
his sister to be trained in one of Cassian's monasteries.[46] Gregory the
Great may have upheld the ruling of the Council, but he still referred

to its target as 'sanctus Cassianus.'[47] For monks, however, the admoni-
tion of Benedict's *Regula* assured his place among the orthodox: 'Ad
perfectionem conuersationis qui festinat', it states, 'sunt doctrinae
sanctorum patrum, quarum observatio perducat hominem ad celsitu-
dienem perfectionis ... Necnon collationes ... nisi bene uiuentium et
oboedientium monachorum instrumenta uirtutum?'[48]

In the wake of the Benedictine Reform in Anglo-Saxon England,
such words could not be without effect. It is not surprising, therefore,
that along with copies of the *Benedicti regula* and *Regularis concordia*,
there should be four of the *Collationes* – including one probably from
Worcester (Oxford, Bodleian Library, Hatton 23 [4115] [s. xi[2]]). The
manuscript is too late to be linked to Wulfstan, though it may attest
to an interest in Cassian in eleventh-century Worcester. Nor do copies
of Prosper's *Contra Collatorem* survive from Worcester to indicate that
Wulfstan would have known of the controversial nature of Cassian's
work. Nonetheless, before the Worcester copy of the *Collationes* was
produced, Wulfstan composed or commissioned an examination of
that section which Prosper had called into question, *Collatio* XIII. The
result was *De adiutorio Dei et libero arbitrio*.

The First Section: Conversion and the Call (Lines 1–12)

De adiutorio Dei develops in four sections, each being followed by a
passage of commentary. Two sections are direct quotations from *Collatio* XIII; two are summaries of key examples employed therein. The
first is taken from the centre of Cassian's work, recording two of a
series of paired scriptural quotations, each of which takes a key text
cited by Augustine in support of grace and matches it with a parallel
text on the responsibility of the will:[49]

> [1a] Audiuimus in euangelio, fratres karissimi, dominum nos uocantem ut
> ad eum per liberum arbitrium ueniamus. 'Venite,' inquid, 'ad me omnes qui
> laboratis et onerati estis, et ego reficiam uos.' [1b] Sed infirmitatem nostram
> idem dominus protestatur dicens: 'Nemo uenit ad me nisi pater qui misit me
> traxerit eum.' [2a] Et apostolus liberum arbitrium nostrum incitat dicens: 'Sic
> currite ut comprehendatis.' [2b] Sed infirmitatem nostram iohannes testatur
> cum ait: 'Non potest homo accipere quicquam nisi datum fuerit ei de caelo.'

> [1a] Most beloved brothers, in the Gospel we have heard the Lord calling us
> to come to him by our free will. He says: 'Come to me, all you who labour

and are burdened, and I will refresh you.' But the same Lord testifies against our weakness when he says: [1b] 'No one comes to me unless the Father who sent me shall have drawn him.' [2a] The apostle also urges on our free will, saying: 'Run in such a way as to gain [the prize].' [2b] But John testifies to our weakness when he says: 'A man can receive nothing unless it has been given to him from heaven.'[50]

Throughout the *Collatio*, Cassian juxtaposes verses that are at once logically disparate and semantically similar. His use of polyptoton, the use in close proximity of words based on the same root (indicated here and below by single underlines), emphasizes the connection between the two elements of each pair. As a result, they appear not as simple contradictions but flip sides of the same coin: 'Venite ad me ... Nemo uenit ad me.' By repeating phrases in the adjacent pairs, moreover (indicated by double underlining above), Cassian reinforces that his multiple examples have a single point in mind: the mutual existence and simultaneous validity of the roles of God and human beings.

The crucial question of the initiative of human righteousness comes into play in the very first sentence. To what extent does the fact that individuals are 'called' to faith in God mean that they depend on God for their belief? For Augustine, the divine call is a necessary prerequisite without which individuals cannot be saved; he says, for example: 'His modis quando deus agit cum anima rationali, ut ei credat – neque enim credere potest quodlibet libero arbitrio, si nulla sit suasio uel uocatio cui credat.'[51] As we have seen, moreover, when this call does come, the power of grace is such that it overrides all human resistance. These opening quotations in *De adiutorio Dei* might seem to reflect Augustine's perspective: humans may be told to come, but it is the Father who draws them; they may be told to pursue a prize, but only God bestows it. The redactor (that is, Wulfstan or Wulfstan's agent) even goes on to affirm, 'Sine adiutorio Dei nihil recte ualemus efficere.'[52]

Cassian, however, understands the verses in a different manner, and uses them elsewhere in the *Collatio* in ways that shed light on their juxtaposition here. Cassian presents Christ's call, first of all, not as Christ's individual work among the limited number of his chosen, but as his general invitation to all mankind: 'Praesto est ergo cotidie Christi gratia, quae ... cunctos absque ulla exceptione conuocat dicens: uenite ad me omnes qui laboratis et onerati estis, et ego reficiam uos' (cf. [1a] above).[53] In the same way, when Cassian refers here to God's role in 'drawing' individuals ([1b]), he pairs it with a verse that shows human initiative as well: 'Adpropiate Domino et adpropinquabit uobis.'[54] Certainly Cassian is at pains to stress the importance and universal possibility of this effort: as one of his later speakers states, renouncing the world for the monastery, 'Ad omnem sane aetatem omnemque sexum perfectionis magnificentiam pertinere et uniuersa ecclesiae membra ad conscendendam sublimium meritorum celsitudinem prouocari dicente apostolo: sic curite ut conprehendatis' (cf. [2a]).[55] In the midst of both God's general summons and his specific work in individuals, therefore, Cassian affirms the ability of human beings to respond to the call, run for the prize, and draw near to God.

This dualism in Cassian is partially explained by his belief that the initiative for salvation may come either from humans or from God: Paul and Matthew, he says, are drawn to God while blatantly sinning against him; Zaccheus and the thief on the cross seek him by their own desire.[56] Both Prosper and the Second Council of Orange specifically deny the point, attributing all these conversions to God's grace;[57] for Cassian, however, both possibilities are legitimate avenues to righteousness. As Cassian says:

> [Euidentissime poterimus aduertere] diuersis atque innumeris modis et inscrutabilibus uiis deum salutem humani generis procurare et quorundam quidem uolentium ac sitientium cursum ad maiorem incitare flagrantiam, quosdam uero etiam nolentes inuitosque conpellere, et nunc quidem ut inpleantur ea quae utiliter a nobis desiderata perspexerit adiuuare, nunc uero etiam ipsius sancti desiderii inspirare principia et uel initium boni operis uel perseuerantiam condonare.

> [We can very clearly perceive that] God brings salvation to mankind in diverse and innumerable ways and by inscrutable means, urging on the course of some, who are already wanting and thirsting for it, to greater zeal, and compelling others even without their consent and against their will. Sometimes he helps to fulfil those things which he sees we rightly desire; sometimes he even inspires the very beginnings of holy desires, bestowing either the start of a good work or perseverance in it.[58]

In affirming that humans have a certain capacity for righteous choice, Cassian does not go so far as to say – like the Pelagians – that people can accomplish good without God. He does not even deny that at times God unilaterally brings about the beginnings of good in individuals. He does assert, however, that not all good is the product of divine inspiration; rather, people can desire good and seek the help they need in bringing it to pass. In his conclusion to this section, the redactor reflects this view, saying: 'Per hoc ergo nobis intellegendum quia sine adiutorio Dei nihil recte ualemus efficere. Et rursum nobis liberi arbitrii uoluntas conceditur ut quaeramus dominum et eius mandata faciamus.'[59]

The Second Section: The Farmer and the Field (Lines 12–34)

In the second section, the redactor attempts to define this relationship of human will and divine grace further by summarizing a key example from the beginning of Cassian's text. A good farmer, he says, employs all his efforts to cultivate a field, scattering the seed, urging on his cattle, bearing the extremes of weather and physical hardship, and keeping birds from devouring the seed.[60] His labour is in vain, however,[61] if God does not provide rain and sunshine and defend against tempestuous weather.[62] So far the example is what we would expect from Cassian: human beings may desire and even pursue good, but they depend on God to bring it to fruition. At this point, however, Cassian offers what seems like a patently Augustinian formulation: 'Quibus manifeste colligitur,' he says, 'non solum actuum, uerum etiam cogitationum bonarum ex deo esse principium, qui nobis et initia sanctae uoluntatis inspirat et uirtutem atque oportunitatem eorum quae recte cupimus tribuit peragendi ... qui et incipit quae bona sunt et exsequitur et consummat in nobis.'[63] This is the one statement in the *Collatio* which Prosper unequivocally applauds, describing it as 'quod nos ualde amplectimur, catholicumque esse profitemur.'[64] It is also a golden opportunity for the redactor to present Cassian as orthodox in his teaching. Doing so, however, would be taking these words out of context. Cassian does not deny that God inspires good desires in human beings; his point is that God does not always do so. As he goes on to say, 'Qui cum in nobis ortum quendam bonae uoluntatis inspexerit, inluminat eam confestim atque confortat et incitat ad salutem, incrementum tribuens ei quam *uel* ipse plantauit uel nostro conatu uiderit emersisse.'[65] Such human initiative is possible in Cassian's view because he rejects Augustine's belief in the utter corruption of fallen humanity. As Cassian states:

> Nec talem deus hominem fecisse credendus est, qui nec uelit umquam nec possit bonum. alioquin nec liberum ei permisit arbitrium, si ei tantummodo malum ut uelit et possit, bonum uero a semet ipso nec uelle nec

posse concessit ... Cauendum nobis est, neita ad dominum omnia sanctorum merita referamus, ut nihil nisi id quod malum atque peruersum est
humanae adscribamus naturae.

We should not hold that God made man such that he can never will or be
capable of what is good; or else he has not granted him a free will, if he
has allowed him only to will or be capable of evil, but neither to will or be
capable of what is good of himself ... we must take care not to refer all the
merits of the saints to the Lord in such a way as to ascribe nothing but
what is evil and perverse to human nature.[66]

Remarkably, the conclusion the redactor substitutes reflects this larger
perspective. He depicts three stages in the growth of righteousnes, each
of which shows God responding to human initiative in seeking righteousness. First of all, he says, 'Nobis magno opere laborandum est ut
corda nostra preparentur ad suscipiendum semen uerbi Dei.'[67] Second,
'cum susceptum fuerit depraecandum est toto corde ut germinet et ad
fructum usque peruveniat.'[68] Third, 'Si domini adiuuante gratia in nobis
fructus bonorum operum excreuerit, magis ac magis depraecandus est
ut qui dedit ut germinet et crescat det etiam perseuerantiam una cum
uoluntate bona.'[69] Individuals prepare their hearts, and receive the seed
of the word; they pray, and it begins to grow; they continue their
prayers, and receive perseverance in willing good. Not only does the
redactor fail to attribute human ability to God when he has the clear
opportunity, but he reverses Augustine's teaching on prevenient grace,
maintaining that humans' labours 'prepare' the way for God.

Here again, however, the redactor seeks to keep a balance. Lest he
seem to downplay God's role in this process, he turns to Paul's assertion
that 'Deus autem qui operatur et uelle et perficere pro bona uoluntate.'[70]
For Augustine, of course, the passage is a crucial piece of evidence in his
argument that God is responsible for humans willing good: as he puts it,
'Ideo sic uelint, quia Deus operatur ut uelint.'[71] For Cassian, on the other
hand, the verse is a warning to humans not to assume that their will is
due to their endeavours alone, and he cites it three times in the *Collatio* to
this end.[72] Such a denial of human self-sufficiency, however, is far from
an assertion of their moral impotence, and it is this perspective which
the redactor reflects when he uses the verse to conclude rather than
introduce his description of righteousness. The process does not begin
with God bestowing a 'good will,' but with individuals' work of self-
preparation; they pray not for the inspiration to do good, but for God to

fulfil the inspiration that they (like the farmer) have already demonstrated in cultivating their field. God may produce the desire for good seen in human prayers ('Deus operatur uelle') and its realization in good fruit and perseverance ('et perficere'), but he does so through people's initial work of preparing their heart ('pro bona uoluntate'). This duality shows 'qualiter concors est adiutorium Dei nostrae bonae uoluntati arbitrio' (how God's assistance is in harmony with the power of our good will [lines 32–3]). The redactor's language echoes Cassian's own statement that 'Vel gratia Dei uel liberum arbitrium sibi quidem inuicem uidentur aduersa, sed utraque concordant ... nam cum uiderit nos deus ad bonum uelle deflectere, occurrit, dirigit atque confortat.'[73] Remaining true to his source, therefore, the redactor provides his readers with a clear statement of Semi-Pelagian theology.

The Third Section: The Six Quotation-Pairs (Lines 34–55)

Having thus affirmed the roles of both God and human beings, Cassian continues with six more pairs of quotations to illustrate the relationship between them. These passages comprise the next section of *De adiutorio Dei*. In the first set, the redactor uses polyptoton or verbal parallelism to emphasize the concept most central to Augustine's teaching on grace: prevenience.[74] '[1] Praeuenit ergo hominis uoluntatem gratia Dei qua dicitur: "Deus meus misericordia eius praeueniet me." [2a] Et nostra uoluntas praeuenit cum dicit: "Et mane oratio mea praeueniet te." [2b] Et iterum: "Praeuenerunt oculi mei ad te diluculo."'[75] On the one hand, then, God's grace is said to 'precede' human will. In Augustinian terms, the implication of the Psalm is clear: the initiative for righteousness depends upon God.[76] Cassian, however, interprets the verse earlier in the *Collatio* to mean that grace sometimes 'prevents' people from doing evil, saying, 'Nonnumquam perniciosas dispositiones nostras letalesque conatus ab effectu detestabili retardat ac reuocat, ac properantes ad mortem retrahit ad salutem.'[77] Such a statement does not attribute every impetus for good to God. It is soon after this passage, in fact, that Cassian distinguishes between the good will implanted by God and that which arises from human effort.[78] In a later *Collatio*, moreover, the same verses that here balance the reference to God's 'prevention' ([2a] and [2b] above) are used to stress the importance of self-discipline in 'preventing' corrupt thoughts. Having quoted the two Psalms, Cassian affirms: 'Omni nobis cautione curandum est, si tamen uim praedicti uersiculi opere uolumus adimplere, ut ita primos matutinarum cogitationum ortus sollers uigilantia tueatur, ne quid ex eis festina praesumptio liuentis adtaminet inimici.'[79] Here it is the devil's initiative in tempting people rather than God's intercession that serves as contrast to human self-discipline;[80] nonetheless, by such contrasts Cassian and his redactor affirm not only the possibility but the importance of human initiative in pursuing righteousness.

A converse formulation of the above passage – again emphasized by verbal parallelism – is found slightly ahead in the third set of quotations: 'Expectat nos cum dicit propheta: "Propterea expectat dominus ut misereatur uestri." Et expectamus eum cum dicimus: "Expectans expectaui dominum et intendit mihi."'[81] In one sense, waiting is the opposite of preceding, a show of restraint rather than intervention. Whereas sometimes God 'prevents' people's will, however, Cassian also says, 'Deum remorantem atque utiliter quodammodo subsistentem, ut nostrum experiatur arbitrium, uoluntas praeuenit nostra.'[82] In that situation, God's inaction makes room for humans to act. Here, on the other hand, waiting is presented as a proactive step: God's decision to wait is a conscious act of mercy; a human being's decision to wait is a conscious act of patience. Just as both parties were said to 'come before' the other, so here both show initiative by patiently focusing their attention on the other.

Looking back at the second pair of quotations, we find that while parallelism still emphasizes the similarity between its parts, its use of different verbs (shown by dotted underlining here) seems to present an ambiguous distinction: '[1] Admonet nos cum dicit: "Tota die expandi manus meas ad populum non credentem." [2] Et inuitatur a nobis cum diximus ei: 'Expandi manus ad te."'[83] While humans' insensitivity to God's outstretched hands is a rebuke to them, however, for both sides the gesture is an invitation. In this respect the passage is similar to the fifth set of quotations: 'Clamat Iesus cum dicit: "Si quis sitit ueniat et bibat." Clamemus etiam et nos cum propheta: "Clamaui ad te domine; dixi tu es spes mea."'[84] Both passages hearken back to the question of the divine call: does one's faith depend on God's initiative in holding out his hands and inviting people to drink? As with the opening lines of the text, however, the passages also emphasize individuals' ability to respond to the general call of Christ.[85] As Cassian makes clear in another reference to God's outstretched hands ([1] above), such an invitation does not preclude human initiative: 'Sicut liberi arbitrii facultas populi inoboedientia demonstratur, ita cotidiana circa eum prouisio Dei clamantis quodammodo et monentis ostenditur ... nos enim per haec quae protulimus non liberum arbitrium hominis uolumus submouere, sed huic adiutorium et gratiam Dei ... necessariam conprobare.'[86] Grace is necessary to free will, Cassian says – but necessary for the will to accomplish good, not to desire it.

The fourth set of quotations examines the source of human strength for righteous actions. In the example of the farmer, even though God's help was needed for the crop's fruition, humans alone seemed to be acknowledged for their efforts in cultivating the field.[87] In this passage, however, both parties are given credit for their contribution. '[1] Confortat nos cum dicit: "Et ego erudiui et confortaui brachia eorum." [2] Et ut nosmet ipsos confortemur hortatur cum dicit: "Confortate manus dissolutas et genua debilia roborate."'[88] In contrast with Augustine's emphasis on human beings' personal helplessness,[89] Cassian goes to considerable lengths to show that humans do have inherent strength that they may use to resist evil. One of his key examples is Job. On the one hand, Cassian acknowledges God's role in limiting the number of trials to which Satan could subject Job: as Paul tells the Corinthians, 'Fidelis autem Deus qui non patietur uos temptari super id quod potestis.'[90] At the same time, however, Cassian says: 'Sed utique nec temptari eos iustitia domini permisisset, nisi parem in eis resistendi scisset inesse uirtutem, qua possent aequitatis iudicio in utroque merito uel rei uel laudabiles iudicari.'[91] It is this power of resistance that Satan targets, asserts Cassian, when, pointing to God's protection and blessing of Job, Satan says: 'Sed aufer manum tuam, id est sine eum suis mecum uiribus decertare, nisi in faciem tuam benedixerit tibi.'[92] The fact that Satan does not return to gloat victoriously in the end shows Satan's recognition that he was vanquished by Job's strength rather than that of God.[93] Following Cassian in exhorting individuals to make themselves strong, therefore ([2] above), the redactor affirms humans' capacity for righteousness.

The last set of quotations looks at the beginning of righteousness in terms of those who seek it. '[1] Quaerit nos dominus cum dicit: "Quaesiui, et non erat uir, et non fuit qui responderet." [2a] Et rogat ut quaeramus cum dicit: "Quaerite faciem eius semper," et [2b] "Quaerite dominum dum inueniri potest."'[94] The first of these quotations is unusual for Cassian in that it departs significantly from the Vulgate – so much so, in fact, that its reference is doubtful.[95] Jacques-Paul Migne suggests that the passage comes from Isaiah: 'Vocaui et non erat qui responderet; locutus sum et non audierunt.'[96] There are other echoes of the passage in Isaiah as well, such as 'Vidit quia non est uir' (He saw that there is no one [59.16]) and 'Vidi et non erat' (I looked, and there was no one [41.28]). Michael Petschenig, on the other hand, in his edition of the *Collationes* notes a tempting parallel in *Canticum Canticorum*: 'Quaesiui et non inueni illum; uocaui et non respondit mihi.'[97] The parallel is unlikely, however, because the speaker here is the bride – in allegorical terms, the Church – whereas in Cassian it is the Lord, the bridegroom.[98] Indeed, in the original, Cassian contrasts God's seeking with this very verse from *Canticum Canticorum*: 'Quaeritur et ipse a sponsa flebiliter conquerente: in cubili meo in noctibus quaesiui quem dilexit anima mea: quaesiui eum et non inueni, uocaui eum et non respondit mihi.'[99] Whatever the source of the first quotation, however, the stark portrait it presents is tempered by the two shorter passages ([2a] and [2b]) with which the redactor replaces Cassian's reference to the bride. Far from leaving the impression that people are incapable of seeking God,[100] these exhortations twice affirm individuals' ability to do so. By pairing them with the first quotation, however, the redactor guards against an overemphasis on human independence,[101] presenting what appears to be a balanced perspective. Taken in context, however, this very balance is heterodox, for it affirms people's independent ability to seek after God.

Having presented his six pieces of evidence, the redactor has the chance to cite a passage that pointedly captures the teaching of *Collatio* XIII. Cassian concludes:

Et ita semper gratia Dei nostro [2] in bonam partem [1] cooperatur arbitrio atque in omnibus illud adiuuat, protegit ac defendit, ut nonnumquam etiam ab eo quosdam conatus bonae uoluntatis uel exigat uel expectet, ne penitus dormienti aut inerti otio dissoluto sua dona conferre uideatur, occasiones quodammodo quaerens quibus humanae segnitiei torpore discusso, non irrationabilis munificentiae suae largitas uideatur, dum eam sub colore cuiusdam desiderii ac laboris inpertit.

In this way, divine grace always [1] cooperates with our will [2] in great part, and in all things assists, protects, and defends it, in such a way as sometimes even to require and look for some efforts of good will from it that it may not appear to confer its gifts on one who is asleep or indolent in undisciplined idleness, as it seeks opportunities to show that as the languor of man's sluggishness is shaken off, the extent of its generosity is not unreasonable, when it bestows it under the pretext of some desire and efforts to gain it.[102]

After recording the first few words, however, the redactor completely reworks the passage – softening but not extirpating its Semi-Pelagian content. The result, unfortunately, is a somewhat obscure bit of Latin: 'Ita et huiusmodi gratia Dei nostro in bonam partem adiuuat arbitrio ut etiam quod bonum uolumus [3] adiuuet ut fiat[103] et suae gratiae consolationem[104] inmittit ut fiat.'[105] On the one hand, the redactor suggests that God 'helps' (*adiuuat*) rather than 'cooperates' with human will ([1] above). The choice of wording might be seen as an attempt to avoid portraying the two as equal partners. There is no possibility of that interpretation in Cassian, however, since he follows his example of the farmer by warning, 'Humana superbia nullatenus se gratiae Dei uel exaequare uel admiscere contendat participemque se in muneribus Dei per hoc conetur inserere.'[106] The redactor follows Cassian, moreover, in pointing out that grace assists 'in great part' or 'for the most part' ([2]). Rather than being theologically significant, then, the change may simply be another example of polyptoton, providing a parallel to the 'adiuuet' of the following line ([3] above).[107] The other alterations, however, are not so easily explained. The redactor says that God helps in two ostensibly separate ways: bringing about the good that individuals wish, and encouraging them so that it may come about. As the beginning of humans' desire for good and its fulfilment in reality are central focal points of the Pelagian debates, it is tempting to assume some similar distinction is being made here. The contrast in the manuscript between 'adiuuet ut fiet' and 'inmittit ut fiat' only heightens the sense of some theological subtlety: after all, if the redactor had meant to say that God helps individuals' very choice of good to come about, obviously this would be a radical inversion of Cassian's whole thesis. In the end, however, such conclusions cannot be drawn from the reading as it stands, and any contrast the redactor might have intended remains obscure. While he does not repeat Cassian's suggestion, then, that God may wait on human efforts before supplying his assistance – a suggestion perhaps, out of context, too susceptible to misinterpretation – he faithfully presents three basic tenets: people do will good; God's grace assists; and through this mutual effort (amply illustrated by the preceding quotations) God brings the desire of human beings to fruition.

The Fourth Section: The Choice of David (Lines 55–64)

The last section of the text confirms this relationship between volition and grace with an example that again derives from the *Collatio*: the sin and repentance of David.[108] The redactor introduces the section, first of all, with a personal interjection. Having noted that grace helps the will (lines 52–5), the redactor quickly adds that grace only helps individuals to do good; people fall into sin through their own evil choice ('malae uoluntatis arbitrium' [line 56]). This point is not a matter of debate: both Augustine and Cassian agree that sin is due to human choice rather than God's compulsion; they only differ on whether people can choose otherwise apart from grace.[109] The redactor continues, however, by presenting a view of repentance that is somewhat more contentious: 'Ad ueniam uero reuerti [1] per penitentiam post commissum et Dei misericordia et nostri est laboris intentio.'[110] The key question here is who is responsible for people's initial awareness and acknowledgment of sin – a point that becomes clear when the redactor turns to Cassian's example of David. Speaking of David's adultery with Bathsheba and murder of Uriah, the redactor states: 'Quod igitur crimen commissum libero fuit arbitrio; quod autem [2] arguitur per prophetam diuinae dignationis est gratia. Rursum quod peccatum suum [3] humiliatus [4] agnoscit suum est; quod breui temporis spatio [5] indulgentiam meruit domini misericordia est.'[111] Augustine does not deny the importance of penitence (cf. [1] above), and would agree both that chastisement and forgiveness are gifts of God (cf. [2] and [5]).[112] Augustine is adamant, however, that changing human hearts is the province of God alone: not just humbling people so that they themselves might come to recognize their failings (cf. [3]), but actually bringing people in their blindness to perceive their sin (cf. [4]).[113] In his own right, therefore, drawing on but supplementing his heterodox source, the redactor presents a Semi-Pelagian view of repentance: it is through individuals' own power, he says, that they see and turn from evil.

The Conclusion: Volition and Cooperating Grace (Lines 65–9)

To summarize all these points, the redactor turns to Cassian's own conclusion: 'Sic enim omnia in omnibus credendus est operari ut incitet protegat atque confirmet, non ut auferat quam semel concessit arbitrii libertatem' – adding to it a line of his own: 'sed cum ipsa nostra bonae uoluntatis operatione perficiatur in nobis uoluntas ipsius.'[114] As one might expect, in his later work Augustine understands this reference to God working 'all in all' to show the universal nature of divine assistance, so that the initiative for any kind of righteousness rests with God.[115] In Cassian's framework, however, even the statement that God 'incites' or 'inspires' (incitet) must be understood in a different manner. The point is clearly illustrated by the three other occasions in *Collatio*

XIII where he employs a series of three verbs to describe God's role. On the one hand, as we have seen, God is said to respond to individuals' good will by enlightening, strengthening, and urging it on to maturity: 'Qui cum in nobis ortum quendam bonae uoluntatis inspexerit, inluminat eam confestim atque confortat et incitat ad salutem, incrementum tribuens ei quam uel ipse plantauit uel nostro conatu uiderit emersisse.'[116] Similarly, when God sees someone's good desire, he meets, guides, and strengthens him: 'Cum uiderit nos deus ad bonum uelle deflectere, occurrit, dirigit atque confortat.'[117] Finally, as we have noted, God 'cooperates' with human beings by assisting, protecting, and defending their will: 'Ita semper gratia Dei nostro in bonam partem cooperatur arbitrio atque in omnibus illud adiuuat, protegit ac defendit, ut nonnumquam etiam ab eo quosdam conatus bonae uoluntatis uel exigat uel expectet.'[118] Whereas with Gregory and Bede, therefore, humans may 'cooperate' with God in response to his prevenient gift of grace, Cassian teaches that grace 'cooperates' with human beings' meritorious initiative in willing good (*ortum bonae uoluntatis*). The redactor's conclusion reflects this perspective. Hearkening back to his previous statement that individuals first work to receive the seed of God's word and then pray that God will allow it to grow, he portrays the harvest as the result of both parties' efforts: '[Deus operatur ut] cum ipsa nostra bonae uoluntatis operatione perficiatur in nobis uoluntas ipsius, quoniam sic orantes dicimus, ut fiat illius uoluntas in nobis.'[119]

The Unintentional Heterodoxy of *De adiutorio Dei*

Far from correcting the impression of Wulfstan's sermons, *De adiutorio Dei* underscores his emphasis on human beings' ability not only to pursue but even initiate righteousness. While he authorizes what is ultimately a heretical text, however, there is evidence that neither Wulfstan nor the redactor were being consciously unorthodox. The latter is at pains, in fact, to avoid drawing on material that had come under censure. To this end, he turns for his direction to Cassian's old rival, Prosper of Aquitaine. On the one hand, the redactor's example of the farmer draws on material that directly precedes the one statement in the *Collatio* which Prosper had applauded. Other material the redactor quotes comes from sections on which Prosper says nothing at all.[120] Most revealing, however, is one point at which Prosper draws a breath amid an extended critique of a series of passages. Coming to what he calls 'quaedam perplexa atque confusa' (a few ambiguous and confused [sentences]), Prosper decides not to spend his time on them. He says: 'Verum haec ut tolerabilia transeamus: quia et nos liberum arbitrium ideo dicimus, bonae uoluntatis affectum fideique principium, operante gratia concepisse.'[121] Despite the fact that the passage is surrounded by material Prosper condemns, and indeed continues the thought of that material, this is all the licence the redactor requires. The bulk of his quotations come from this section (see Figure 1 below).[122] This careful evasion of material that might be viewed as heretical is a clear indication not only that the redactor was aware of the controversial nature of his text, but that he had access to a hitherto unknown copy of the *Contra Collatorem* as well.[123] For all the redactor's efforts, however, *De adiutorio Dei* cannot escape the theological implications of its faithfulness to Cassian's text. In this respect, *De adiutorio Dei* bears a striking resemblance to the *Carmen de libero arbitrio*. Conceived in a different setting and drawing on a distinctly different source, it nonetheless brings Semi-Pelagian theology into an influential centre of the Benedictine Reform. In doing so, it contrasts markedly with the work of Lantfred's and Wulfstan's prolific contemporary, Ælfric of Eynsham.

FIGURE 1: Cassian's *Collatio* XIII as Quoted by *De adiutorio Dei et libero arbitrio* and Criticized by Prosper's *De gratia Dei et libero arbitrio contra Collatorem*

N.B.: This figure illustrates in broad terms how *De adiutorio Dei* avoids material censured by Prosper and quotes material condoned or passed over by Prosper; it does NOT aim to provide a legible text of *Collatio* XIII.

Cassian, *Collatio* XIII

uerba uerba uerba	Material approved or in some measure accepted in Prosper's *Contra Collatorem*
uerba uerba uerba	Material explicitly condemned by Prosper's *Contra Collatorem*
▶ uerba uerba uerba	Extracts from *Collatio* XIII quoted or summarized in *De adiutorio Dei et libero arbitrio*
▶ uerba uerba uerba	Extracts from *Collatio* XIII quoted or summarized in *De adiutorio Dei et libero arbitrio* and in some measure accepted in Prosper's *Contra Collatorem*

CHAPTER SEVEN

Ælfric of Eynsham
and the *Sermones catholici*

The Educational Mission of Ælfric of Eynsham

Around 987, some fourteen years after Lantfred's departure from England and fifteen years before Wulfstan would take up his duties at York and Worcester, a young monk and priest left the walls of Winchester to set out for his first post.[1] Behind him were decades of training at one of the finest centres of learning in the land. Before him was the humble abbey of Cerne Abbas, newly founded (or refounded) by Æthelmær, pious layman and later ealdorman of the Western Shires. Unknown to him, the years at Cerne and later at Æthelmær's abbey of Eynsham would see the foundation of an illustrious career, the patronage of bishops and archbishops, and keen interest in his works that would last through the early thirteenth century and surge again during England's Renaissance. For the present, however, he was conscious simply of the weight of an enormous responsibility. Perhaps even more than Alfred before him, he saw himself as one entrusted with staggering intellectual wealth in a land desolate with ignorance, living at the end of an age when knowledge meant salvation. The literary revival that would see its chief flowering in him was approaching its close; the Danish threat once put to flight by Alfred was even now making ready to topple the Anglo-Saxon royal line; the millennium, with all its ambiguous apocalyptic foreboding, was rapidly drawing nigh; sensationalist, apocryphal works were leading people astray into theological error; and the time of Antichrist, though its day no one might know, was nonetheless certain to come. As Paul the Apostle warned believers long before, the time was short. Unless humans were taught the tenets of the faith, doctrine set down in scripture and expounded by orthodox authorities, they would be lost. And he, who had been given much, would be held accountable for their blood.

Ælfric's view of the bleak peril of the times, the people's need, and his responsibility as their teacher comes through from the first pages of his early work at Cerne. For the next twenty years he would labour to make the riches of his learning accessible to the uneducated. He eschewed the fashion for arcane vocabulary and developed his own rhythmic, memorable style. He composed a grammar and pedagogical tools to teach students Latin. He translated and paraphrased books of the Old Testament. He wrote on behalf of bishops to instruct their clergy in ecclesiastical matters. He outlined proper liturgical practice for his own monastic community. He provided overviews of world history, treatises on calculating time and its theological implications, discussions about spiritual gifts, warnings against subtle and blatant vices, exhortations to sexual purity, models of saintly behaviour, and commentaries on scripture and on doctrine – all with the practical view of showing people what they needed to know and do for the salvation of their souls.

Of all his works, however, the crown of Ælfric's corpus is the two-volume set of homilies he composed in his first years as a monk of Cerne Abbas: the *Sermones catholici*. Here, through a complex process of editing and translation, Ælfric seeks to make orthodox doctrine – doctrine as expounded by such authorities as Augustine, Gregory, and Bede – accessible not only to clergy but, astonishingly, to laity as well.

The Importance of the *Sermones catholici*

The *Sermones* are remarkable, if not unique, in a number of ways. To begin with, in sharp contrast to most of Old English literature, where we do well to know the author's name, Ælfric is a self-conscious writer who provides insight into his concerns and struggles as an author. Reasons for concern he certainly has, not least because of the complex nature of his audience: not only does he address himself explicitly both to monks and laity – sometimes, as when teaching on sexuality, in practically the same breath – but he recognizes that the groups include a range of educational backgrounds. It is Ælfric's transparency in this regard that is striking, however. He agonizes over the extent to which he should convey complex material to his untutored audience, worries about their attention span, considers how they may react to expositions of the Old Testament, and apologizes to those with (some) learning for belabouring simple matters.[2] This sensitivity to the nature and limitations of his audience directly influences how Ælfric chooses to translate his sources. Second, Ælfric's work stands in sharp contrast to that of his contemporaries in its discriminating approach to source material. Peter Clemoes notes that the anonymous Blickling and Vercelli homilies, for example, are 'texts in which the distinction between orthodox dogma and popular theology is lost sight of behind a dazzling display of rhetoric.' Godden, moreover, observes that they often rely on 'narratives which were clearly fictitious and in some cases of dubious morality.'[3] Ælfric, by contrast, condemns the uncritical acceptance of apocrypha, relying instead on authoritative patristic authors. As he states regarding the Assumption of the Virgin Mary:

> Gif we mare secgað ... þonne we on ðam halgum bocum rædað þe ðurh godes dihte gesette wæron. ðonne beo we ðam dwolmannum gelice. þe be heora agenum dihte oððe be swefnum fela lease gesetnyssa awriton. ac ða geleaffullan lareowas Augustinus. Hieronimus. Gregorius. and gehwilce oðre þurh heora wisdom hi towurpon. (*CH* II.29.119–25)

> If we say more ... than we read in holy books which were composed by God's direction, then we shall be like those heretics who by their own direction or dreams have written many false narratives. Orthodox teachers, however – Augustine, Jerome, Gregory, and many others – in their wisdom have thrown them out.

Third, Ælfric's work is remarkable for the sheer scope of its endeavour. Paul the Deacon, fulfilling Charlemagne's wish for an authoritative homiletic compendium in the eighth century, may have brought together a number of patristic works; even he, however, did not weave them together to compose homilies of his own. Haymo of Auxerre may blend, edit, and augment numerous sources in his homiliary; even he, however, addresses his material to those who know Latin. Ælfric, however, composes multiple series of original homilies in Old English for alternating years, covering some sixty-two Sundays and feast days in his first two volumes alone. He does so, moreover, without any immediate precedent. As Milton Gatch observes, both in England and on the Continent 'no one before Ælfric or in the century after him produced or attempted to assemble in the vernaculars a coherent set of exegetical commentaries on the pericopes for the Christian year.'[4]

Fourth, there is the *Sermones'* exegetical and theological content. Exegesis, the methodological interpretation of scripture, is rare in Anglo-Saxon addresses to the laity; far more common is catechesis, or general moral instruction. Marcia Dalbey notes that while the Blickling homilies occasionally reveal 'disjointed and unclear' attempts at exegesis, they are primarily concerned with 'the immediate practical problem of convincing their hearers to live moral lives in this world ... the homilists seem uninterested or unable to explain points of dogma ... and to develop intricate exegetical arguments.'[5] Similarly, in his study of the Vercelli homilies, Lewis Nicholson affirms that only three sermons reflect the 'elaborate reasoning' of patristic exegesis.[6] The same trend is found among Ælfric's colleagues. Speaking of Wulfstan of Worcester, Dorothy Bethurum suggests that some of Wulfstan's sermons are carefully developed to 'constitute a central core of Christian teaching designed to instruct priest and laity alike in the essentials of their religion'; the rest are 'directed to a call to repentance on the part of a sinning people.' In neither case are the sermons exegetical.[7] In short, Gatch concludes: 'Most ... early medieval English and Latin writers of sermons for the laity contented themselves with general, catechetical addresses.'[8]

The *Sermones*, by contrast, are specifically concerned with expounding the Gospel readings of the liturgical year. This exposition goes far beyond mere moral instruction. As Cyril Smetana showed in his early study of the *Sermones'* immediate sources, of the eighty-five selections in the two volumes, while some recount saints' lives, and some simply expand a scriptural narrative, fifty-six are commentaries on the pericopes that 'are indebted either for matter or at least for inspiration to the homiletic and exegetical works of the Church Fathers.'[9] In the process, Ælfric grapples directly with issues that had occupied the greatest minds of the church – predestination, the Trinity, the dual nature of Christ, and so on – and tries to make them intelligible to a largely illiterate audience. It is here, more than anywhere else, drawing first and foremost on those Fathers we have examined, that Ælfric addresses as well the tension between free will and grace.

Ælfric's Relation to Augustine, Gregory, and Bede

In discussing free will or other theological matters, Ælfric seeks not simply to convey orthodox doctrine, but the importance of authoritative, orthodox sources for one's doctrine. As a result, at intervals throughout the *Sermones* Ælfric explicitly names his authorities, foregrounding the foundation on which his work is based. Ælfric's classic summary of his chief sources, in fact, is found in the Latin preface to his First Series of homilies, where he states: '[Hos] auctores in hoc explanatione sumus secuti. uidelicet Augustinum. ypponiensem. Hieronimum. Bedam. Gregorium. Smaragdum, et aliquando Hægmonem; Horum denique auctoritas ab omnibus catholicis. libentissime suscipitur.'[10] Others elsewhere have explained why Paul the Deacon does not appear in the list – Paul provides, in short, 'direct' access to patristic works rather than to extracts or amalgamations – or why Smaragdus and Haymo might figure so prominently here.[11] Others have also noted the numerous sources missing from this list.[12] For our purposes, however, it is the presence of three names that is of import, a triumvirate of Fathers considered in the first chapters of our study. As Godden concludes from his recent and nearly exhaustive analysis of the *Sermones*' sources, Ælfric's reliance on these three authors (unlike, perhaps, his use of Jerome) warrants their prominence here. He states:

> Augustine is mentioned first in Ælfric's list and was clearly the authority that he respected most (though also the one he differed from most) ... Jerome appears next in the list, though his influence is slight. It is not for his exegetical and theological work that he figures but for the works misattributed to him in the Middle Ages ... Bede comes next perhaps because of Ælfric's respect for him: the wise one or the teacher is how he refers to him (though the signs are that [Ælfric] had little enthusiasm for his style; there is seldom if ever the close imitation of Bede's wording that one can see so often with Augustine and Gregory). Gregory the Great was probably used more than any of these ... The distinction between him and Augustine is suggested by a remark in a CH II homily: 'Augustine the wise uncovered the deepness of this text, and the holy Gregory also wrote about it.'[13]

What is instantly apparent from Godden's remarks is not only the importance of these three authors to Ælfric, but Ælfric's complex relation to them. He differs from Augustine; he seldom imitates Bede's wording closely; he decides among the Fathers which one to use and when. No such complications are apparent in the statement of methodology that immediately precedes Ælfric's list of sources. Speaking in the third-person plural, he says, 'Nec ubique transtulimus uerbum ex uerbo. sed sensum ex sensu. cauendo tamen diligentissime deceptiuos errores. ne inueniremur aliqua heresi seducti seu fallacia fuscati.'[14] Ælfric presents his homilies, in other words, as mere translations: he might select, he might compile, but the ultimate product is a faithful rendition of authoritative teaching, made accessible in the vernacular to the unlearned. Even were Ælfric's editorial process no more than cutting and pasting, the issue of selection itself remains a fascinating one: when faced with multiple orthodox sources, differing interpretations of a passage, or divergent doctrinal understandings, which Father does he favour? Godden's analysis hints at a hierarchy in Ælfric's mind – Augustine, followed perhaps by Gregory, followed possibly by Bede – but was this in fact their ranking? If so, was Ælfric consistent in his favouritism, or did he follow Augustine as the source for one homily and Bede for another? How does Ælfric's juggling of multiple sources affect the consistency of his own theology, especially when he draws on two or even all three Fathers for a single homily? Careful analysis of the *Sermones* provides a unique opportunity to reconstruct this editorial process – a process, indeed, by which a man sincerely concerned to present orthodox thought does not merely select material but shapes it, silently adapting and adding his own words to sources to produce his own teaching in late Anglo-Saxon England.

If Ælfric and his contemporaries at Winchester and Worcester differ in the orthodoxy of their teaching on free will, our analysis below will nonetheless show that they are not entirely dissimilar. First of all, while the *Sermones, Carmen de libero arbitrio,* and *De adiutorio Dei et libero arbitrio* draw on different sources for their theology, they share a willingness to adapt these sources to produce original texts. Despite his respect for the Fathers, Ælfric does not hesitate to insert his own commentary, to moderate Augustine's teaching on corruption, to bring an Augustinian perspective to passages derived from Gregory, or to reinforce Bedan thought with material taken from another author. Ælfric demonstrates the same independence, moreover, in homilies which draw on more than one of of these Fathers. Second, the *Carmen* and *De adiutorio Dei* are not the only texts to rely on theologically suspect authors: at one point, we find Ælfric depending on the heterodox Pelagius, albeit unwittingly. Third, while Ælfric is no Semi-Pelagian and is a staunch believer in grace, he too places a conspicuous emphasis on the importance of human merit. Ultimately, however, for all these departures, Ælfric follows his patristic predecessors in identifying the source of human righteousness as grace.

Ælfric's Use of Augustine in the *Sermones catholici*

The Parable of the Friend at Midnight (CH I.18): The Origin of Faith and the Corruption of Human Nature

One text in which Ælfric draws on Augustine by name is his homily for Rogation (*CH* I.18).[15] Here, expositing the parable of the Friend at Midnight (Luke 11.5–8), Ælfric explores two areas of crucial interest to Augustine: the origin of faith and the corruption of human nature. In the parable, a man who has had a visitor arrive unexpectedly goes to his friend at midnight to borrow three loaves to feed his guest. The friend tells the man not to bother him, for he and his family have gone to bed; nonetheless, because of the man's persistence, the friend arises · and gives him as much as he needs. Following Augustine's homily on the same passage, Ælfric interprets night as human ignorance, the man in need of bread as mankind, the friend to whom he turns as Christ, and the three loaves for which he asks as understanding of and faith in the Trinity. Ælfric's explanation presents, first of all, a complex picture of the origin of human belief. He states:

> We sceolon clypian to criste. And biddan þæra þreora hlafa: þeah he us þærrihte ne getiðie. Ne sceole we for ði þære bene geswican ... Se hælend cwæð gif he þurhwunað cnuciende. þonne arist se hyredes ealdor for ðæs oðres onhrope. And him getiþað þæs þe he bit. Na for freondrædene. ac for his unstilnesse; Þy he cwæð na for freondrædene. for ðan þe nan mann nære wurðe ne ðæs geleafan. ne ðæs ecan lifes gif godes mildheortnys nære ðe mare. ofer mancynne. (*CH* I.18.82–4 and 87–92)

> We should call to Christ, and pray for the three loaves. Though he does not immediately grant them to us, we should not on that account desist from prayer ... The Saviour said, 'If he continues knocking, the master of the house will arise, because of the other's persistence, and grant him what he asks, not out of friendship, but because of his clamour.' He said, 'not out of friendship,' because no one would be worthy either of that faith, or of eternal life, if God's mercy were not the greater towards humankind.

Like Augustine, Ælfric teaches that faith comes from God. Having identified the loaves as faith, which Christ gives to human beings, Ælfric reinforces the point with Christ's portrait of a son making requests of his father (Luke 11.11–12 and Matt. 7.9–10). In Luke, the analogy follows immediately after the parable of the Friend at Midnight: just like a father would hardly give his son a snake if asked for a fish, or a scorpion if asked for an egg, or (in Matthew) a stone if asked for a loaf, so the Heavenly Father is sure to give the good gift of the Holy Spirit to those who ask him. Ælfric states that the fish, egg, and bread correspond to faith, hope, and love, which the good Father gladly gives to human beings.[16] Two factors, however, complicate this seemingly orthodox picture. On the one hand, both Augustine and Ælfric equate night with human ignorance of spiritual things; indeed, it is midnight, the depth of night, and (as Augustine says) 'saeculi huius ignorantia ualida est' (great is the ignorance of this world).[17] Given Augustine's belief in humanity's total depravity, and this apparent suggestion of individuals' complete lack of spiritual understanding, it is surprising that the man not only recognizes his lack, but desires, pursues, and obtains illumination.[18] In the same vein, there is Augustine's and Ælfric's insistence that people must pray for the loaves and ask for the fish. The fact that both understanding and faith are given in response to human initiative seems to suggest that God bestows grace as a reward for meritorious effort. Such a position, however, is antithetical to Augustine's understanding of grace as both prevenient and gratuitous.

Augustine's homily, at least, offers a solution to the discrepancy. Stepping outside the frame of the parable, Augustine notes that prevenient grace is present in the text in the very fact of Christ's presentation of the parable: it is Jesus who prompts people to ask God for understanding. As Augustine states, 'Hortanti credamus' (Let us believe him who exhorts us).[19] Ælfric, on the other hand, confines himself to the elements of the parable, and his homily emphasizes human initiative as a result.

One reason why Ælfric may not be alarmed by this emphasis is that his audience is composed of at least nominal 'believers,' for whom an emphasis on growth rather than conversion is appropriate. While he has no illusions that all the baptized will be saved,[20] Ælfric does suggest that at some level individuals' belief began at baptism – for most, *infant* baptism. In a later homily, in a section of apparently original commentary,[21] Ælfric notes that when the priest asks the newborn if it believes in God, it is the godfather who responds on its behalf. The child is then baptized 'mid þisum geleafan' (with this belief [*CH* II.3.285]). In this sense, the beginning of faith by no means stems from an individual's own volition. Since the child 'wexð and gæð forð. and ne cann þyses geleafan nan ðing', however, Ælfric recognizes that individuals' must make their belief personal: 'Is nu for ði micel neod gehwam þæt he leornige æt his lareowe hu he his cristendom healdan sceole. mid þam soðan geleafan.'[22] These then are the loaves that Ælfric wants people to seek: *additional* understanding of and faith in the one in whom they have 'professed' belief. Unlike the Pelagians, Ælfric does not suggest that such striving is sufficient for human salvation. Adding to his Augustinian source, Ælfric stresses that 'Nan mann nære wurðe ne ðæs geleafan. ne ðæs ecan lifes gif godes mildheortnys nære ðe mare. ofer mancynne.'[23] Nor does Ælfric suggest that even the desire for faith originates in human beings. Rather, in another interpolation reminiscent of Augustine, he says that 'Þa ðe on god belyfað. hi sind þurh þone halgan gast gewissode; Nis seo gecyrrednys to gode of us sylfum. ac of godes gife swa swa se apostol cwyð; Ðurh godes gife ge sind gehealdene on geleafan.'[24] Though Ælfric's treatment of the Friend at Midnight may emphasize individuals' contribution of prayer, elsewhere he is clear that God gives not only faith, but the 'turning' or conversion that enables human beings to ask for it.

A later passage in Ælfric's homily for Rogation finds Ælfric engaging with Augustine's view of human nature. Having discussed the son's requests for a fish, egg, and bread, Ælfric comes to Christ's assurance that 'Si uos cum sitis mali nostis bona data dare filiis uestris quanto magis Pater uester de caelo dabit spiritum bonum petentibus se.'[25] Ælfric comments:

> Us ís to smeagenne þæt word þe he cwæð ge ðe synd yfele; [1] Yfele we sind ac we habbað goodne fæder ... be þam þe is gecweden; Nís nan man góód buton gode anum; [2] Se ðe æfre ís góód: he [3] gebrincð us yfele to godum mannum: [4] Gif we bugað fram yfele and doð góód; [5] Good wæs se man gesceapen adám: Ac þurh hís agenne cyre and deofles tihtinge [6] he wearð yfel and eal his ofsprincg; [7] Se ðe synful bið he bið yfel; And [8] nan man nis on life buton sumere synne; Ac ure goda fæder us geclænsað and gehælð ... Se ðe god beon wyle: clypige to ðam þe æfre is gód. þæt he hine [9] godne gewyrce. (*CH* I.18.153–66)

> We have to consider the words which he said: 'You who are evil.' [1] We are evil, but we have a good Father ... of whom it is said, 'No one is good save God alone.' [2] He who ever is good will [3] bring us who are evil to be good people, [4] if we will shun evil and do good. [5] The man Adam was created good, but by his own choice and the instigation of the devil,

[6] he and all his offspring became evil. [7] He who is sinful is evil, and [8] there is no one in life without some sin. But our good Father will cleanse and heal us ... Let him who desires to be good call to him who ever is good, that he would [9] make him good.

On the whole, Ælfric keeps fairly close to Augustine's text. He follows Augustine, for example, in stating that God created human nature good ([5]) – an assertion important for Augustine both in terms of justifying God's righteousness and denying the Manichaeans' suggestion that human beings are derived from evil. The assertion also corresponds to Ælfric's statements elsewhere that God is 'good' in that no evil comes from him: God, Ælfric stresses, never compels people to sin.[26] In addition, Ælfric follows Augustine in saying both that fallen humanity is evil and that God 'brings' (*gebrincð*) or 'makes' (*gewyrcð*) human beings good ([1], [3], and [9]). Such statements reflect Augustine's view of human depravity and prevenient grace, respectively. Ælfric affirms elsewhere, moreover, that individuals are 'evil' in that they are born with sins through Adam's transgression,[27] even as he says that humans do nothing good without grace.[28] Even so, Ælfric inserts two revealing comments that mitigate the force of this dichotomy between God's goodness and human depravity. The first comes as Augustine is arguing for the totality of human weakness, saying: 'Qui semper est bonus, ipse facit ex malo bonum: quia ipse homo uoluntate sua se sanare non potuit.'[29] While Ælfric includes the first part of this statement ([2] and [3] above), he omits any reference to human incapacity. Instead, emphasizing individuals' responsibility, he says that God will make people good 'gif we bugað fram yfele and doð gód' (if we shun evil and do good) ([4]). In pedagogical terms, the point might seem like a reasonable and even necessary balance: Ælfric wants his audience to set about living righteous lives, not to abandon a task that seems out of their hands. By this change, however, Ælfric runs the risk of making grace appear to be conditional on human effort. Ælfric's second interpolation likewise mitigates Augustine's portrait of human corruption. Having acknowledged that mankind became 'evil' through the Fall ([6]), Ælfric does not say that people are utterly depraved; rather, he explains that humans are evil because of their personal misdeeds ([7]), recognizing that all are tarnished by at least 'sumere synne' (some sin) ([8]). Ælfric thus defines human corruption as guilt rather than a blemished nature, as a general tendency rather than an absolute state.

For all Ælfric's admiration for the African Father, the Rogation homily shows Ælfric departing from as well as affirming aspects of Augustine's thought: Ælfric may reflect Augustine's teaching on the origins
of human faith, but he modifies Augustine's view of human nature. As
the following section will show, moreover, Ælfric follows a similar pattern in his discussion of the effects of prevenient grace: while he is
faithful to Augustine's premise that grace is necessary and irresistible,
he follows Gregory in suggesting that people can reject the grace they
have been given.

Ælfric's use of Gregory in the *Sermones catholici*

The Vine and the Branches (CH II.35): Inward Inspiration

The complexity of Ælfric's patristic allegiance is evident in the use of his
Gregorian sources, for the material on which he draws not only reveals
characteristic Gregorian thought but provides the context for one of the
clearest examples of Augustinian teaching in the *Sermones*. The latter is
seen in Ælfric's homily for the Feast of One Apostle (*CH* II.35), where
Ælfric considers Christ's words to his disciples at the Last Supper.
Describing believers as branches that bear fruit by being rooted in him,
the Vine, Jesus states that 'Non uos me elegistis sed ego elegi uos et
posui uos ut eatis et fructum adferatis.'[30] Smetana originally suggested
that Ælfric's exposition of the passage was mostly a translation of Gregory's twenty-seventh homily, with the first fifty-odd lines drawing on
Augustine's *Tractatus in euangelium Ioannis*: 'There are no very close
translations,' Smetana says, 'but there are unmistakable turns of phrase
that remind one of Augustine's rhetoric.'[31] That Ælfric should rely on
these texts is not surprising, as they comprise the lections for this occasion in Paul the Deacon.[32] Godden's recent analysis, however, suggests
that the first part of Smetana's assessment is 'wide of the mark': '[Ælfric]
had clearly consulted Gregory the Great's homily on the text ... but used
it comparatively little.'[33] Gregory may provide 'a starting-point and a
basis' for Ælfric's discussion,[34] but it is an Augustinian perspective that
shows forth as Ælfric explains how Christ 'appoints' people to bear fruit.

Crist. cristenra manna heafod. ordfruma ælcere gife. dælð his gyfe his
limum. [1] be gehwilces mannes mæðe. be ðan þe he healdan mæg [2]
þurh his fultum. buton ðam ne deð nan man naht to gode; Næfð nan man
geleafan buton of cristes gife. Na nan man ne ðurhwunað on geleafan

buton þurh cristes gife. for ði sceal gehwa on his drihtne wuldrian. na on
him sylfum; [3] Crist gelogode his apostolas. and ealle his gecorenan ðurh
his gife. þæt hí ferdon sylfwilles and wæstm brohton. þurh góde weorc;
[4] Hi ferdon sylfwilles be godes hǽse. [5] and ðurh his fultum wæstm
brohton goddra weorca. swa swa god sylf cwæð. þurh ðone witegan Eze-
chiel; [6] Ic dó. þæt ge doð.' (*CH* II.35.81–91)[35]

Christ, the head of Christian people, source of every grace, distributes his   .
grace to his members, [1] according to each one's ability, according to that
which he may practise [2] through his support, without which no one
does anything good. No one has belief save by Christ's grace, and no one
perseveres in faith without Christ's grace; therefore everyone should
glory in his Lord, not in himself. [3] Christ arranged his apostles and all
his chosen through his grace, so that they should go voluntarily and bring
forth fruit through good work. [4] They went voluntarily, at his command, and [5] through his support brought forth fruit of good works, as
God himself said, through the prophet Ezekiel, [6] 'I do what you do.'

Ælfric takes considerable liberties with Gregory's text at this point. The
only clear parallel, in fact, is when Gregory paraphrases Christ's statement, 'Posui uos ut eatis' by saying that 'Plantaui ut eatis uolendo' (I
planted you to go willingly).[36] Similarly, Ælfric notes that the disciples
obey Christ's command 'sylfwilles' (voluntarily) ([4] above). Gregory's
innocuous explanation, however, is that people 'go willingly' because
'uelle aliquid facere, iam mente ire est' (to will to do something is already
to go in your mind).[37] Ælfric, on the other hand, is concerned to explain
the tension between grace and free will. Noting that humans have faith,
righteous deeds, and perseverance solely 'ðurh his fultum' (through
God's support) ([2] and [5]), Ælfric goes so far as to suggest that people obey God because Christ 'disposes' them thus – literally, 'arranges'
(*gelogað*) their will by his grace ([3]). This is not the wooing of congruent
vocation, but the direct intervention of inward inspiration. As Ælfric says
earlier in the homily, God places spiritual knowledge daily in believers'
hearts 'þurh orðunge ðæs halgan gastes' (through the inspiration of the
Holy Spirit).[38] Ælfric goes so far as to equate the process with what he
says are God's words in Ezekiel – ' Ic dó. þæt ge doð' (I do what you do
[6]) – implying that all righteousness is either directly or ultimately God's
doing. The quotation is remarkable for two reasons: not only does it
appear to be another interpolation by Ælfric, but in quoting, Ælfric
reverses Ezekiel's actual words. Commanded by God not to mourn his

wife's death as a sign to doomed Jerusalem, Ezekiel tells the Israelites that when the city falls and their loved ones die, 'Facietis sicut feci' (You will do as I have done).[39] Though Godden reasonably suggests that the Old English may simply reflect a variant Vulgate reading,[40] in practice Ælfric turns a prophecy of human actions into a statement of God's sovereignty.

Ælfric's comments are telling, for if they are indeed his own, not prompted by some unknown source, they reveal a personal perspective that is decidedly Augustinian. In short, Ælfric says, without grace 'ne deð nan man naht to gode' (no one does anything good [2]). This is not to suggest that Ælfric views humans as mere automata. People receive grace, he notes, according to their ability, that is, what they can do through God's support ([1]). The passage is not clear as to the extent of this ability: while it does not seem to suggest that human beings are capable of only evil, it does not say that people may cooperate with or reject God's grace. Given Ælfric's respect for both Augustine and Gregory, it may be that he would have been reluctant to judge either perspective heterodox; which one he chooses, however, remains to be seen.

The Healing of the Blind Man outside Jericho (CH I.10):
Enlightenment, the Tumult of Corruption, and the Rejection of Grace

If Ælfric's use of Gregory in the above passage seems more Augustinian than Gregorian, Ælfric's exposition of the healing of the blind man outside Jericho (Luke 18.35–43) in his homily for Quinquagesima Sunday conveys characteristic Gregorian thought. That it should do so is not surprising, for Ælfric's text is a fairly close translation of Gregory's second homily found in Paul the Deacon.[41] The text is instructive in three ways: its problematic depiction of the process of enlightenment, its concern with the mental tumult that is the result of fleshly corruption, and its suggestion that humans can reject grace.

Like Gregory, first of all, Ælfric explains the blind man as humankind, blinded by error and lack of faith as a result of Adam's sin. Jericho, interpreted by Jerome as the moon, represents mortality, for it waxes and wanes as do people's lives. Christ's coming to Jericho thus symbolizes his assumption of mortal nature, and it is through this that individuals are drawn from their errors and 'onlihte þurh geleafan' (enlightened by faith).[42]

[1] Se man þe nan ðing ne cann þæs ecan leohtes: He is blind; [2] Ac gif he gelyfð on þone hælend: þonne sit he wið þone weig; [3] Gif he nele

biddan þæs ecan leohtes: he sit þonne blind be ðam wege unbiddende ...
Swa hwa swa oncnæwð þa blindnysse his modes Clipige he mid
inweardre heortan: swa swa se blinda clypode: Hælend dauides bearn
gemiltsa min. (*CH* I.10.60–7)

[1] The one who knows nothing of the eternal light is blind; [2] if he
believes in Jesus, however, then he sits by the way. [3] If he will not pray
for the eternal light, then he sits blind by the way without prayer ... Who-
soever recognizes his mind's blindness, let him cry with inward heart, as
the blind man cried, 'Jesus, Son of David, have pity on me.'

As with Augustine, Gregory, and Bede, Ælfric associates sight with
both understanding and belief. The key question, then, is the same as it
is for faith: does sight originate in human beings or in God? Ælfric
begins with a seemingly Augustinian emphasis on the absolute nature
of human blindness: it is not simply that the blind cannot see the eternal light; rather, Ælfric suggests, they know nothing of it ([1] above).
Given this premise, one would expect people to have no awareness of
their spiritual condition, let alone desire for heavenly things. In Augustine's treatment of the man born blind, for example (John 9.1–7), the
man takes no initiative; it is Christ who sees him, puts clay on his eyes,
and sends him to be washed through baptism. In Gregory's terms,
however, while human beings lose the light of the invisible world
through sin, their blindness is not an absolute state from conception,
but a condition into which humans fall through their evil habits. Consequently, this blind man, though ostensibly knowing nothing of the
light, nonetheless is able to recognize his blindness, believe in Christ,
and actively pursue enlightenment. The first point is significant
because it implies that the man has some understanding of what he
lacks – understanding being something that comes, as both Augustine
and Gregory affirm, only through God's prevenient intervention. Ælfric's
depiction does not suggest otherwise. Though neither Ælfric nor Gregory make it explicit, prevenient grace is inherent in the fact of Christ's
coming, for it is through this that human beings are informed of their
blindness. As Ælfric says a few lines earlier, 'Nu synt we ute belocene
fram ðam heofonlican leohte: and ... ne we his na mare ne cunnon
buton swa micel swa we *þurh cristes lare* on bocum rædað.'[43] The second point, the blind man's belief, is somewhat more problematic.
Ælfric states that since Christ identifies himself as 'the way' (John 14.6),
when the blind man sits 'by the way' he demonstrates his belief

in Christ ([2]). On the one hand, it seems antithetical for the man to have faith, since Ælfric has said that he is 'ablend. mid geleafleaste' (blind with unbelief).[44] On the other hand, the fact that Christ tells the man that 'þin geleafa ðe gehælde' (your faith has healed you) makes it seem as though grace comes as a result of human merits.[45] The same problems are found in Ælfric's third point: the man who is 'ablend. mid ... gedwylde' (blind with ... error) is somehow able to pray rightly, and it is these prayers that cause Christ, who was 'ær eode' (previously going [on his way past]), to stop and heal him.[46] Ælfric further complicates the picture by saying that God wants people to pray 'for ðan þurh þa gebedu. bið ure heorte onbryrd: and gewend to gode.'[47] If one's heart has not already been inspired and turned to God, how will he even have the desire to pray?

The answer to all these questions is that, as with individuals' recognition of their blindness, Ælfric presupposes grace. It is grace that gives the man faith, it is grace that inspires him and teaches him how to pray, and it is to this grace that Christ responds when he hears the man and heals him. Understanding, Ælfric explains later in the homily, comes through the soul, and the life of the soul is God. Just as the body dies without the soul, Ælfric says, 'Swa eac seo sawul gif god hi forlæt. for synnum: ne deð heo nan ðing to gode ... gode adeadod sy: [ond] heo bið dead ælcere duguðe. and gesælðe.'[48] As a result, just as Ælfric notes in his comments on the Last Supper, 'Ne mæg nan man nan ðincg to gode gedon butan godes fultume.'[49] Once God has taken the initiative, coming as it were to Jericho, humans are able to pray and have their hearts further turned to God. Like Gregory, moreover, Ælfric recognizes that illumination is a process. Ælfric presents this text to his audience so they will pray and keep on praying, not so much for the initial enlightenment of conversion but for the ultimate enlightenment of heaven: 'Uton biddan þæs leohtes þe we magon mid englum ánum geseon. þæt ðe næfre nę bið geendad; To ðam leohte soðlice ure geleafa us sceal gebringan.'[50]

In addition to depicting the process of enlightenment, Ælfric's Quinquagesima homily reflects Gregory's concern with the mental tumult that is the result of fleshly corruption. Commenting on the crowds surrounding the blind man that tell him to be quiet, Ælfric states:

Seo meniu getacnað: ure unlustas and leahtras þe us hremmað. and ure heortan ofsittað þæt we ne magon us swa geornlice gebiddan swa we behofedon; Hit gelimpð gelomlice þonne se man wyle yfeles geswican: and his synna gebetan. and mid eallum mode to gode gecyrran: þonne cumað þa ealdan leahtras þe he ær geworhte. and hi gedrefað his mood and willað gestillan his stemne: þæt he to gode ne clypige; Ac hwæt dyde se blinda þa ða þæt folc hine wolde gestillan? He hrymde þæs þe swiðor: oð þæt se hælend his stemne gehyrde: and hine gehælde. (*CH* I.10.69–77)

> The multitude represents our evil desires and vices, which call to us and occupy our hearts, so that we cannot pray so fervently as we ought. It happens frequently when someone wants to withdraw from evil and atone for his sins, and with his whole mind turn to God, that his old misdeeds, which he had previously committed, will then come and afflict his mind and silence his voice, so that he may not cry out to God. But what did the blind man do when the people would keep him quiet? He called so much the louder, until Jesus heard his voice and healed him.

Ælfric's description draws on one of Gregory's images of the divided mind: that of a crowd of temptations and sordid memories that, as Gregory puts it, 'mentis nostrae aciem reuerberant, confundunt animum, et uocem nostrae deprecationis premunt' (obscure the vision of our mind, disturb our heart, and beat down the sound of our petition).[51] Augustine, on the one hand, views blind mankind as helpless before these desires: until people are illumined, they will not ask for light. Gregory and Ælfric, by contrast, say that blind persons can and should persevere in calling to God for help. In saying this, Ælfric attributes a measure of ability to the will that Augustine does not. Augustine agrees, of course, that God wants humans to desire and pray for his intercession, but he presents both prayer and desire as the product of the Spirit's prevenient inspiration: when people are illumined, they will necessarily ask for light. Gregory, on the other hand, does not deny that prayer is ultimately due to grace, but maintains like Bede that God empowers human beings to choose whether or not they will pray for further grace. This perspective is consistent with the picture in Ælfric's homily. Christ comes to Jericho, bringing prevenient grace to people who have become blind through their own sin (*gedwyld*); as a result, they may either call out for enlightenment or sit silently by the way ([3] above). Ælfric does not here suggest, as Gregory does elsewhere, that God ultimately brings order to human beings' mental tumult; nonetheless, Ælfric makes it clear that the crowd can be overcome.

Finally, then, Ælfric's Quinquagesima homily shows that humans can reject grace. In addition to Ælfric's earlier suggestion that people can sit silently by the way, Ælfric follows Gregory in saying that people enlightened by Christ may refuse to follow him. He states:

> Se blinda þa ða he geseon mihte: þa fylide he þam hælende; Se man gesi-
> hð and filið gode: se ðe can understandan gód: and god weorc wyrhð; [1]
> Se man gesihð. and nele gode fylian: se ðe understent góód: and nele
> good wyrcan; [2] Ac uton understandan gód: and god weorc wyrcean.
> (*CH* 1.10.136–41)

> The blind man, when he could see, followed Jesus. That man sees and fol-
> lows God, who can understand God, and does good works. [1] That man
> sees and will not follow God, who understands God, and will not do
> good works. [2] But let us understand God, and do good works.

It is possible, it should be said, to understand this potential disobedience in terms of Augustine's teaching on perseverance. Although the fact of human beings' sight represents a considerable infusion of grace – God having changed their *gedwyld* and *geleafleast* to understanding and faith – and though Augustine views grace as necessarily efficacious, Augus-tine also teaches that if people fail to do good thereafter, it is because God in his Providence has withdrawn his grace from them.[52] Or again, using the imagery of Aristotelian physics, if grace does not continually propel people towards righteousness, they will cease to move in that direction. Given the source of Ælfric's homily, however, it seems more reasonable to understand the passage in Gregorian terms. In this sense, when Ælfric says that people will not pray (nele biddan) or follow God (nele gode fylian) ([3], page 174, and [1] above), he means not that humans choose evil because, in the absence of grace, their corrupt nature demands it, but that grace makes it possible for people to accept or reject God's way. Ælfric certainly speaks as though he believes individuals have a legitimate choice before them: 'Uton understandan gód: and god weorc wyrcean,' he says ([2]), because 'gif we hi dóóð þonne mage we mid þam geswincum ðuruh godes fultum astigan þone sticolan weig. þe us gelæt to ðam ecan life.'[53] Human beings cooperate with God, there-fore, by striving with the help of grace.

The Star Over Bethlehem (CH I.7): Human Beings' Capacity to Reject Grace

The impression from the passage above that Ælfric understands human choice in Gregorian rather than Augustinian terms is reinforced by a striking passage on Fate and predestination in his first homily for Epiphany. Ælfric is discussing the star over Bethlehem at Christ's birth, following Gregory closely as he denies that the stars control human destiny, when he suddenly breaks off into an extensive section of what appear to be his own reflections. Speaking of God's creation of the angels, Ælfric states:

> His deope rihtwisnys nolde hi neadian to naþrum: ac forgeaf him agenne cyre: [1] for þan ðe þæt is rihtwisnyss þæt gehwylcum sy his agen geþafod; Ðonne wære seo rihtwisnys awæged gif he hi neadunge to his þeowte gebigde. oððe gif he hi to yfelnysse bescufe. (*CH* I.7.143–7)

> His great righteousness would not compel them to either [obedience or disobedience], but gave them their own choice; [1] for that is righteousness, that everyone should be allowed his own choice. For his righteousness would have been destroyed, if he had forcibly subjected them to his service, or if he had impelled them to evil.

Building on this passage, Ælfric goes on to suggest that what God did for the angels, he does for humans as well. Certainly this was true for Adam: Augustine, for one, teaches that Adam had a freedom of will unhindered by moral corruption, and Ælfric confirms that God 'forgeaf adame and euan agenne cyre.'[54] By presenting freedom of choice, however, as a defining characteristic of the righteousness of God ([1]), Ælfric argues that what mankind had at creation is still available to fallen people today: individuals may reject God 'þurh agenne cyre' (through their own choice) or decide wholeheartedly to obey his commands.[55] In his way, Augustine would have concurred, saying that God does not force individuals' decisions, but lets them choose what they desire: if people sin, it is because God has not checked their evil hearts; if they pursue righteousness, it is because God has changed their desires to good. Ælfric's whole point here, however, is to emphasize God's non-interference in human volition. Once Christ has redeemed (*alysde*) people from their guilt,[56] they can either obey his commands or 'þurh agenne cyre ... god forlætað' (forsake God through their own choice); if they choose the latter, however, 'God will abandon them also to eternal condemnation' (god forlæt hi eac to þam ecum forwyrde).[57] The order here is significant: Ælfric does not say that people forsake God because he has abandoned or withdrawn his grace from them, but that God withdraws his grace because people have rejected him.

As Ælfric says earlier in the homily, 'Se ðe fram gode bihð to deofle: he forlyst godes gife: þæt is his modes onlihtinge'; as with the blind man calling over the crowd, however, 'Gif he þonne eft þone deofol anrædlice forlæt þonne gemet he eft þæs halgan gastes gife þe his heortan onliht: and to criste gelæt.'[58] While at times Ælfric may use Gregorian material to present Augustinian thought, therefore, here the perspective is that of Gregory: having received grace, human beings have the ability to cooperate with or reject the grace they have been given. A similar perspective is reflected in Ælfric's use of material from Bede, especially as Ælfric focuses on Bede's depiction of human bondage.

Ælfric's Use of Bede in the Sermones catholici

The Triumphal Entry (CH I.14): Bondage and Liberation

Of the various facets of Bede's teaching on free will present in Ælfric's sources, one aspect that Ælfric takes up in the Sermones, in his first homily for Palm Sunday, is the extent to which people are bound by sin. The textual situation is somewhat complex. If in his homily for the Feast of One Apostle Ælfric introduces an Augustinian perspective to Gregorian material by interjecting his own comments, here Ælfric reinforces the perspective of Bedan material by incorporating comments from another source. The text at hand is Matt. 21.1–7, where the disciples prepare for Christ's Triumphal Entry into Jerusalem by untying the donkey and colt upon which Christ will ride. For his exposition, Ælfric relies largely on Bede's work for the same occasion (Homiliae II.3), which Smetana indeed cited as the sole source for the homily.[59] Ælfric's exposition is of interest not for its faithfulness to Bede, but for the crucial asides it makes regarding the bondage of humankind – asides which in turn reflect Bede's teaching on liberation.

Ælfric begins by following Bede point by point: the two disciples whom Christ sends represent preachers; the donkey and foal stand for Jews and Gentiles; they are tied because prior to Christ all humans were bound with sins. At this stage, however, Ælfric draws on another source: a second exposition of Matthew 21.1–7 in Paul the Deacon by Pseudo-Chrysostom.[60] After relating how the disciples untie the animals, telling the owner that Christ needs them and will send them back again, Ælfric states:

[1] We sint gemanode and geladode to godes rice ac we ne synd na genydde; [2] Þonne we sind geladode: þonne sind we untigede; And þonne we

beoð [3] forlætene to urum agenum cyre. Þonne bið hit swilce we beon
agean asende; [4] Godes mildheortnys is þæt we untigede syndon: [5] Ac
gif we rihtlice lybbað: þæt bið æigþer ge godes gyfu. Ge eac ure agen
geornfulnyss; [6] We sceolon symle biddan drihtnes fultum: for ðan þe [7]
ure agen cyre næfð nænne forðgang. buton he beo gefyrðrod þurh ðone
ælmihtigan. (*CH* I.14.77–85)

[1] We are exhorted and invited to God's kingdom, but we are not forced.
[2] When we are invited, then are we untied; and when we are [3] left to
our own choice, then it will be as if we are sent back again. [4] It is God's
mercy that we are untied; [5] but if we live rightly, that will be both God's
grace and our own zeal. [6] We should constantly pray for the Lord's support; because [7] our own choice has no success unless it is promoted by
the Almighty.

As in his homily for Epiphany, Ælfric denies that God compels people
to do good: God sends for human beings, but leaves them to choose
whether they will follow ([1] – [3]). Again, Augustine would have
agreed that God lets humans choose what they desire. He would also
note, however, that this invitation is not God's general call to humankind, but one by which individuals are set free ([2]); it is evidence of
the Spirit's inspiration, with which humans must necessarily comply.
Ælfric, however, emphasizes God's lack of interference: people, he
says, are 'left' (*forlæten*) to their own choice ([3]). The statement sounds
much more like Gregory and Bede's view that the will, freed by God, is
left to reject or to cooperate with grace. Similarly, Ælfric indicates that
humans' initial freedom comes from grace ([4]). While all three Fathers
would have concurred with such a sentiment, here Ælfric may be
drawing again on Bede's homily, which asserts that 'Non nostris ad
eum meritis sed sola ipsius gratia largiente peruenimus.'[61] Ælfric continues to reflect Bede and Gregory, moreover, by saying that righteous
deeds are the result of both grace and human effort ([5]). Augustine, of
course, would not deny that human efforts are important; nevertheless, he would hardly contrast human beings' initial freedom and subsequent deeds, attributing the one to grace and the other to grace *and*
effort ([4] and [5]). Furthermore, given Ælfric's emphasis on God's
non-interference and human efforts, we may understand Ælfric's reference to prayer in the same context. Rather than being solely the product of grace, as Augustine would maintain, prayer may be the response
of people left to their own choice ([3]) who recognize that, as Bede

would have it, 'Sine me nihil potestis facere' – that is, that humans cannot accomplish good without God ([7]).

Having said all this, however, what exactly does Ælfric mean by saying that humanity was bound? The answer lies in a remarkable metaphor, also drawn from Pseudo-Chrysostom, that depicts human bondage to the devil as that of a nation under a king. Ælfric states:

> We willað secgan eow sum byspel; Ne mæg nan man hine sylfne to cynge gedon [1] ac þæt folc hæfð cyre to ceosenne þone to cyninge þe him sylfum licað; Ac syððan he to cyninge gehalgod bið. þonne hæfð he [2] anweald ofer þam folce. and hi ne magon his geoc. of heora swyran asceacan; [3] Swa eac gehwylc mann: hæfð agenne cyre. ær þan þe he syngie: hwæðer he wille fylian deofles willan. oððe wiðsacan; þonne gif he mid deofles weorcum [4] hine sylfne bebint. þonne ne mæg he mid his agenre mihte. hine unbindan. [5] buton se ælmihtiga god. mid strangre handa his mildheortnysse hine unbinde; [6] agenes willan and agenre gymeleaste he bið gebunden. ac þurh godes mildheortnysse. he bið unbunden: gif he [7] ða alysednysse eft æt gode [8] gegearnað. (CH I.14.111–21)

> We will tell you a parable. No one may make himself king, for [1] the people have the option to choose him who pleases them to be their king. After he has been consecrated as king, however, he has [2] power over the people, and they may not shake his yoke from their necks. [3] In like manner everyone has his own choice, before he sins, as to whether he will follow the devil's will or withstand it. Thereafter, if he [4] binds himself with the works of the devil, he cannot unbind himself by his own power, [5] unless the Almighty God unbinds him with the strong hand of his mercy. [6] By his own will and his own heedlessness he is bound, but through God's mercy he will be unbound, if thereafter he [8] merits his [7] liberation from God.

In this passage, as Godden has demonstrated, Ælfric's point is to describe not a political but a theological reality: sin binds human beings so that they may no longer do good.[62] While Augustine would agree with this general principle,[63] the portrait Ælfric presents is by no means in keeping with Augustinian thought. First of all, Ælfric affirms that the devil or sin cannot rule people until they have chosen it ([1]). Augustine would concur insofar as humans did choose sin in their representative Adam, and thus bowed themselves under the yoke of original sin and a corrupted nature. While Ælfric agrees that individuals inherit guilt from Adam, however, here Ælfric says that despite the Fall human beings have a choice, unencumbered by any yoke of necessity, to submit to sin or to reject it ([3]). Ælfric's statement echoes the emphasis of his homily for Epiphany that God's righteousness by definition allows everyone his own choice. Ælfric may imply that the Fall has corrupted human nature in that – as he says in his Rogation homily – all people sin, but he does not present the Fall as the cause of human bondage. In a stance reminiscent of Gregory, Ælfric attributes bondage not so much to Adam's choice as to people's personal and habitual sin ([4] and [6]).

As a counterpart to people's bondage, Ælfric also discusses their liberation. Whereas humans bear the responsibility for the one, Ælfric says, only God can accomplish the other ([5]). Ælfric does not define liberation as a temporary reprieve from evil desires that causes people to choose good, as Augustine would have it. Rather, he depicts it as a restoration of the freedom to choose between good or evil, which people have to a certain extent before enslaving themselves with evil habits ([3]), even as Gregory would suggest. Once humans are unbound (*alysed* [7]), Ælfric implies, they again must decide whether they will have a demonic king over them.

Ælfric speaks of liberation in broader terms as well. Just as the king in this illustration has power (*anweald*) over individuals who have submitted to him ([2]), so after Adam's sin the devil had *anweald* over humankind as a whole. Again, in contrast to Augustine, Ælfric does not speak of this power as absolute; as he says elsewhere, it is 'on sumum maran on sumum læssan; On þam maran þe swiþor syngiað: on þam læssan ðe hwonlicor syngiað.'[64] Even so, Ælfric states here, Christ came for the *alysednysse* of all believers,[65] to *alysan* people by his death from Satan's *anweald* and eternal death.[66] Moreover, Ælfric says, Satan forfeits his power or jurisdiction over humankind when he seizes the bait of Christ's humanity,[67] so that thereafter people may be *alysede* from sins through baptism.[68] Ælfric thus describes a three-stage process: first, Christ frees humanity from Satan's control, which is not absolute but relative to individuals' own sinfulness; second, God frees humans from original and personal sin through baptism; third, God continues to free people from the bondage that results from their continuing choice of sin. Ælfric may be drawing on Pseudo-Chrysostom rather than Bede, but his comments reflect Bede's understanding of human liberation: all humans are bound by sins, from which they are freed by Christ through baptism; to this captivity they may return should they choose to sin again.

Finally, it is fitting that this passage should contain a reference to that aspect of Bede's teaching that, at least in Ælfric's sources, most distinguishes him from the other two Fathers: merit ([8]). Surprisingly, however, the reference comes not from Bede nor from Pseudo-Chrysostom, but from Ælfric himself. Where Pseudo-Chrysostom states that 'Nostra quidem uoluntate et negligentia alligamur, sed per Dei misericordiam absoluimur,' Ælfric adds this crucial corollary: 'Agenes willan and agenre gymeleaste he bið gebunden. ac þurh godes mildheortnysse. he bið unbunden: *gif he ða alysednysse eft æt gode gegearnað.'*[69] As we shall see, the example is typical of the *Sermones* as a whole: while references to merit abound in the *Sermones*, they do not appear, as we might expect, in passages drawn from Bede. Instead, by far the majority are found to be personal interjections by Ælfric.

Ælfric's Simultaneous Use of Augustine, Gregory, and Bede

It is one thing for homilies drawing predominantly on a single source to reflect that Father's perspective – a Rogation homily drawing on Augustine attributing human faith to grace, an Epiphany homily based on Gregory depicting humanity's capacity to reject grace, a Palm Sunday homily rooted in Bede showing a Bede-like emphasis on merit, and so on. The constraints of the liturgical cycle, the varying subject matter of the pericopes, the limited options in Ælfric's immediate sources, and Ælfric's high regard for the various Fathers all make variation in the homilies natural, as different authorities treat different topics in different ways. This said, if Ælfric seems content to permit slight differences of emphasis in his expositions, he also appears to blend patristic perspectives in a consistent fashion, setting forth his own dual vision of divine sovereignty and human ability. What, however, of those occasions when Ælfric finds himself with multiple patristic treatments of a passage? Rather than focusing on one to the exclusion of others, at times Ælfric draws on two or even all three of the above Fathers for discussions of free will. Such texts provide rare opportunities to observe how Ælfric discriminates between some of his most respected authorities, and thus reveal in a unique way his understanding of this issue. When Ælfric has to make a choice, whose theology does he choose?

The Labourers in the Vineyard (CH II.5): Pervasive Prevenient Grace

One text in which this process of selection may be seen is Ælfric's homily for Septuagesima Sunday (*CH* II.5), a homily that happens to contain one of Ælfric's most fundamental statements on free will. The passage under consideration is the parable of the Labourers in the Vineyard (Matt. 20.1–16). In the parable, a landowner seeks throughout the day to hire individuals to work in his vineyard. From early in the morning to nearly dusk (the eleventh hour) he goes out, finds men standing idle, and agrees to pay them a denarius for their work. At the end of the day he pays them their wages, starting with the latecomers and ending with those who worked all day. When the latter see that the landowner pays all the workers alike, they grumble at his apparent unfairness; the land-owner, however, defends his generous system of recompense, noting that the last shall be first, and the first last.

Ælfric's homily draws primarily on the one exposition of the peri-cope in Paul the Deacon: Gregory's *Homiliae* I.19. Ælfric observes that the vineyard represents God's people, to whom God sent patriarchs, prophets, and apostles from the first to the eleventh hours of the world. He refers, in a passage which Godden suggests is reminiscent of Bede, to the thief on the cross, who came at the eleventh hour but because of his faith rightly preceded the apostles to paradise.[70] Ælfric returns to Gregory for his comments on the last being first and the first last (Matt. 20.16). At this point, however, Ælfric breaks off from his sources for a concluding statement on God's mercy:

[1] Godes mildheortnys ús forestæpð. [2] and his mildheortnys ús fyligð; [3] Þa ða we wel noldon. [4] ða forhradode godes mildheortnys ús [5] þæt we wel woldon; [6] Nu we wel willað. [7] ús fyligð godes mildheortnys þæt ure willa ydel ne sy; [8] Hé gearcað urne godan willan to fultumi-genne and he fylst ðam willan gegearcodne. (*CH* II.5.226–32)

[1] God's mercy goes before us, [2] and his mercy follows us. [3] When our desire was wrong, [4] God's mercy prevented us, [5] so that we desired what was good; [6] now that we desire good, [7] God's mercy fol-lows us so that our choice will not be in vain. [8] He prepares our will to choose good, assisting it, and he fulfils the will that has been prepared.

The perspective of the passage is decidedly Augustinian; indeed, as we have noted above, Ælfric may be drawing on a section of the *Enchirid-ion* where Augustine states, 'Nolentem praeuenit, ut uelit; uolentem subsequitur, ne frustra uelit.'[71] Regardless, the passage is a remarkable portrait of prevenient grace. Ælfric says, first of all, that grace 'for-estæpð' human beings ([1]): both 'preventing' or 'forestalling' their evil will, and – as Ælfric uses *forestæppe* to gloss *praecaedo* in his *Grammar* –

'preceding' human will so that individuals come to desire good.[72] In this same dual sense, Ælfric asserts that grace 'forhradode' human beings ([4]) – a particularly apt word, which at least three copies of Benedict's *Regula* use to translate *praeuenire*.[73] The past tense suggests, moreover, that Ælfric may have not only believers' ongoing tendency to sin but their pre-Christian state in mind: when they had no good desire ('þa ða we wel noldon'), prevenient grace changed them so that now, while not perfect, they are characterized by the desire for good ('nu we wel willað') ([3] and [6]). Even so, Ælfric says, human beings' righteous desire will be useless or ineffectual (*ydel*) unless grace follows or fulfils it ([2] and [7]). Once the initial transformation has taken place, moreover, Ælfric affirms that the process continues: God helps believers by 'preparing' the will to desire good and 'supporting' the will that has been prepared ([8]). Ælfric's clear implication is that without this encompassing work of grace, humans can neither desire nor accomplish good.

Whether Ælfric here imports an extract from the *Enchiridion* or interjects his own comments, these condensed statements are a remarkable tribute to Augustine's influence, for they show an internalization of and commitment to Augustinian thought in the midst of Gregorian exegesis. The passage also echoes the Augustinian perspective of Ælfric's homily on the Vine and the Branches, where he depicts grace as the source for the whole of human righteousness, from the origin of his faith to his perseverance in good deeds. At the same time, Ælfric's exposition of the healing of the blind man outside Jericho and of the star over Bethlehem caution us against understanding the passage entirely in Augustinian terms. For Augustine, one implication of God's mercy going before and following human beings is that such grace is irresistible: if God prepares someone's will to do good ([8] above), that person's righteous action will surely follow. Ælfric's Quinquagesima and Epiphany homilies, however, present a Gregorian view of human beings' ability to respond to grace: some blind people are enlightened by God but refuse to do good works; God gives individuals the option of disobedience, for he will not compel their choice of good. Such a corollary governs (and explains) even Gregory's analogous statement in the *Moralia*, where he treats the classic Pauline query, 'Quid autem habes, quod non accepisti?' (What do you have that you did not receive? [I Cor. 4.7]). It is God, Gregory affirms, who 'et praeueniendo dedit eis bonum uelle quod noluerunt, et subsequendo concessit bonum posse quod uolunt.'[74] Here, as in Augustine's view, 'dedit' and 'conccssit' cannot mean that God 'granted' or 'allowed' individuals to will good; both words imply an active force whereby God 'gave' people the power to choose what they could not. Having affirmed, however, that God changes human hearts and enables them to do good, Gregory and Ælfric also assert that individuals have power to reject the grace they have been given.

Here, however, Ælfric's emphasis is on the source of righteousness, not humanity's capacity for evil as well as good. Driving home the point through repetition, Ælfric states that when God *forestæpð, forhradað*, and *gearcað* human will, this is the result: *we wel willað* ([1], [4], [8], and [6]). While Ælfric could be saying that a positive response to grace is inevitable, the context of the homily would suggest that Ælfric has believers in view, God's people who have agreed (rather than declined) to labour in the Vineyard. When grace prepared their will, they responded (and continue to respond) by choosing to desire good: 'Forhradode godes mildheortnys ús þæt we wel woldon' ([4] and [5]). Such a response is only possible, Ælfric insists, through God's pervasive, prevenient intervention.

In a homily drawing primarily on Gregory, Ælfric thus demonstrates his independence from his source by introducing an Augustinian perspective. If the decision does not reflect a hierarchy among the Fathers – Ælfric perceiving Augustine, for example, as more 'authoritative' than Gregory – it may at least reflect a hierarchy among doctrines. However much, drawing on Gregory, he may stress human beings' volitional freedom and responsibility for righteous choice, another goal for Ælfric is even more important: that his audience grasp the primacy of grace as set forth by the African Father.

Christ's Debate with the Jews (CH II.13):
Human Nature and the Origin of Corruption

One other text that shows Ælfric discriminating between his main patristic sources is his homily for the fifth Sunday in Quadragesima (*CH* II.13). Here, treating Christ's debate with the Jews in John 8.46–59, Ælfric explicitly says that he will be following both Augustine and Gregory.[75] Förster proposed a third source, Bede's *Homiliae* II.18, and Smetana agreed that Ælfric may have drawn on Bede towards the end of the homily.[76] Godden, however, deems this unlikely, suggesting that this concluding material also derives from Augustine.[77] In Godden's analysis, Ælfric begins by closely following Gregory and Augustine, and shifts smoothly between them thereafter, translating more freely as he goes along and interlacing his comments with passages from Haymo. Ælfric draws on both Fathers' exegesis of Christ's assertion that the Jews are not 'from God' (John 8.47), of the Jews' riposte that Jesus is a Samaritan and demon-possessed (8.48), of Christ's affirmation that those who obey will not see eternal death, that Abraham rejoiced to see Christ's day and that before Abraham was, 'I am' (8.51, 56, and 57–8), and of the Jews' attempt to stone Jesus for blasphemy (8.59).[78] It is from Augustine alone, however, that Ælfric draws his comments on the corruption of human nature. Ælfric states:

> Þa iudeiscan wæron fram gode. and hi næron fram gode; [1] Hi wæron fram gode gesceapene. [2] ac hi wæron geleahtrode þurh deofol. [3] and ðurh mandædum hi wæron deofles bearn ... [4] Ælc gesceaft is god on gecynde. [5] ac hit bið geleahtrod þurh yfelnysse; Þa iudeiscan wæron gode on gecynde. [6] and on gebyrde. for ðan ðe hi wæron abrahames ofspring. [7] ac hi wæron yfele and deofles bearn ðurh euenlæcunge. [8] na ðurh gecynde. (CH II.13.50–3 and 66–9)

> The Jews were from God, and they were not from God. [1] They were created from God [2] but they were corrupted by the devil, [3] and through deeds of wickedness they were children of the devil ... [4] Every creature is good in its nature, [5] but corrupted by evil. The Jews were good by nature [6] and by birth, because they were children of Abraham; [7] they were evil and children of the devil, however, through imitation of him, [8] not by nature.

Augustine, in his reaction to the Manichaeans, had been careful to deny that human beings derive their nature from an Evil Principle (the devil) opposed to the Principle of Good (God); rather, he affirmed that by their sin humans have corrupted what God made good. In his later *Tractatus in Euangelium Ioannis*, Augustine returns to this idea to explain what it means for humans to be 'from God': 'Natura ex Deo sunt,' he says; 'uitio non sunt ex Deo.'[79] Ælfric echoes the first part of this statement by arguing that since human beings are created by God, they are good *on gecynde* ([1] and [4] above) – good in 'origin' and 'nature,' though not necessarily in 'character,' since character is something that is determined by one's deeds. As Ælfric puts it earlier in the *Sermones*, if people are righteous, they are children of God both 'þurh gesceapenysse. and þurh godum geearnungum' (through their creation *and their meritorious efforts*).[80] In addition, Ælfric notes that the Jews were good *on gebyrde* ([6]). By this he means that they were descended from one who was good, not that they were good at birth themselves; Ælfric is not denying original sin.[81] Even so, he says, the Jews were 'not from God' in that they chose to imitate the devil ([3] and [7]). In this, they are not alone: 'Ælc gesceaft,' Ælfric says, 'bið geleahtrod þurh yfelnysse' ([4] and [5]). At first glance, this may seem to be simply a translation of Augustine's previous statement that 'Vitiata est hominis natura per uoluntatem malam' (Human nature was corrupted by an evil will).[82] In fact, however, Ælfric changes Augustine's formula in four interrelated ways. First, Ælfric says that it the character of human beings, not their nature, that is corrupted: people are evil 'na ðurh gecynde' ([8]). Earlier in the *Sermones*, he makes the same point, asserting that human beings are children of the devil 'na þurh gecynde. oððe þurh gesceapennysse. ac þurh ða geefenlæcunge. and yfelum geearnungum.'[83] Second, Ælfric does not say that humans *were* corrupted, alluding to the Fall; rather, he suggests that one is or will be corrupt – that is, one *becomes* corrupt – through one's own sinful ways (*bið geleahtrod þurh yfelnysse*). Ælfric's case in point is the sentence immediately preceding: that man is a murderer, Ælfric says, who perverts (*forpærð*) another's soul by tempting it to sin.[84] Corruption is thus an acquired rather than an intrinsic state. Third, Ælfric does not suggest that individuals are 'corrupted' in the Augustinian sense of retaining no desire for good; rather, Ælfric uses *geleahtrod* in the sense of 'blameworthy' or marked by sins (*leahtras*). In his prefaces to the *Sermones*, for example, referring to himself in the plural, Ælfric warns scribes to make accurate copies 'þy læs ðe we ... geleahtrode beon' (lest we ... be blamed [or considered blameworthy]).[85] The emphasis is reminiscent of Ælfric's Rogation homily, where he suggests that human beings are 'evil' not because they are utterly depraved, but because none are without sin. Fourth, Ælfric states that people become blameworthy through wickedness (*yfelnysse*), not through a wicked will. The point is the same: if one is 'not from God,' it is the result of one's own disobedience, not Adam's. As Ælfric concludes in his homily for Epiphany, 'Ne talige nan man his yfelan dæda to gode: ac talige ærest to þam deofle þe mancynn beswac. and to adames forgægednysse. ac þeah swiþost to him sylfum: þæt him yfel gelicað. and ne licað gód.'[86]

To make sure that his audience understands what he means by the above passage, at this point Ælfric inserts several lines of personal commentary. To begin, he reiterates that scripture calls people 'children of God' or 'children of the devil' depending on whom they imitate. Next, he recalls Christ's earlier statement that 'Omnis qui facit peccatum servus est peccati' (Everyone who sins is a servant of sin).[87] Should Ælfric wish to present clearly Augustine's view of human nature, this is a perfect opportunity. The Jews, questioning Christ's assertion that his truth would set them free, have just denied that they are enslaved (John 8.33). Ælfric could explain, as Augustine does, that individuals are enslaved first by Adam's sin, from which Christ's death frees them, and then by their own corruption, from which they will be freed only in heaven (*Tractatus* XLI.4–13). Instead, like Gregory and Bede, Ælfric reemphasizes that people are bound through their personal choices:

> [1] Ælc ðæra ðe synne wyrcð. he við þonne ðære synne ðeow; Witodlice se synfulla ðeowað þam wyrstum ðeowte. Þeah ðe he bruce brades rices; He is earm ðeowtling. Na anes hlafordes. ac swa manegum leahtrum swa he gehyrsumað. swa manega deofla him beoð to hlafordum gesette. (*CH* II.13.76–80)

> [1] Everyone who sins will then be the slave of that sin (cf. John 8.34). Now a sinful person is enslaved in the worst kind of slavery: though he rules over a wide kingdom, he is a wretched slave – not [just] to one master: rather, the more vices he obeys, the more devils are placed as masters over him.

The image is similar to Ælfric's description of a people enslaved by an evil king: it is only after one has chosen to sin, Ælfric says, that one becomes a slave to sinful habits ('he við þonne ðære synne ðeow' [1]). Such a one becomes like the Jews, unable to hear God's words gladly, unwilling to obey, with a heart of stone from which Christ may hide himself.[88] Returning to Augustine for his peroration, however, Ælfric holds out this hope: just as the Israelites who looked to the bronze serpent in the desert were healed, so those who look to Christ will be healed of their sins; though they are dead, nonetheless they will live.[89] Having shifted between his sources in the course of the homily, therefore, Ælfric's final interpolation reveals this intriguing perspective: while he is reluctant to present Augustine's view of human depravity, Ælfric is more than willing to echo Augustine's view of grace.

Ælfric's Use of Pelagius in the *Sermones catholici*

First Sunday in Advent (CH I.39):
Human Perfection and the Earning of Salvation

If the analysis above illustrates Ælfric's independence from and willingness to adapt his sources – a trait he shares in common with Alfred as well as his contemporaries Lantfred and Wulfstan – it should also underscore his commitment to present orthodox doctrine from authoritative sources. At one point, however, Ælfric parallels his fellow authors by the suspect nature of his source-material. In his homily for the First Sunday in Advent, having used the Gospel for the day – Matthew's account of Christ's entry into Jerusalem (Matt. 21.1–9) – aptly enough for Palm Sunday (*CH* I.14), Ælfric treats the epistle for the occasion, Rom. 13.11–14. The pericope addresses the need for believers to live virtuously in the face of Christ's approaching return – a traditional Advent theme – and Ælfric's homily in turn exhorts people to prepare for Christ's birth by renouncing sins and pursuing righteousness. Much of the text is Ælfric's own, and scripture is the only source that he reproduces verbatim. Nonetheless, what Godden describes as 'striking similarities' suggest that one source on which Ælfric drew was a version of the *Expositio in Romanos*, authored by none other than the heresiarch Pelagius.[90]

It is inconceivable that Ælfric would have done so knowingly. His stance in the *Sermones* against heretics is uncompromising: reporting on Arius's ignominious death, for example, in which Arius's entrails spill out as he goes to relieve himself, Ælfric concludes, 'Ða geswutelode god. þæt he wæs swa geæmtogod on his innoðe swa swa he wæs ær on his geleafan; He wolde don crist læssan þonne he is. and his godcundnysse wurðmynt wanian. þa wearð him swa bysmorlic deað geseald swa swa he wel wyrðe wæs.'[91] While Ælfric does not mention Pelagius in his works, and while Augustine typically refrains from referring to his adversary by name, Ælfric would almost certainly have known of him – from Bede's *De temporum ratione*, if nowhere else, where the entry for 4362 AM states that 'Pelagius Britto Dei gratiam inpugnatur.'[92] It is highly unlikely that Ælfric would have drawn on anything written by one who sought to diminish God's dignity by denying his grace.

By Ælfric's day, however, a number of versions of the *Expositio* were in circulation under different names than that of Pelagius. On the one hand, there was the sixth-century revision by Cassiodorus. Encountering Pelagius's commentaries on Paul's epistles without knowledge of their author, Cassiodorus had nonetheless been swift to excise Pelagian teaching therein, directly substituting passages of Augustine or otherwise rewriting along Augustinian lines. This, at any rate, was his intention: in fact, Cassiodorus himself only focused on the *Expositio in Romanos*, while leaving the other commentaries to be dealt with by his pupils. As a result, Cassiodorus's expositions of some of the epistles are little more than copies of Pelagius. While Cassiodorus's text was popular with such medieval compilers as Haymo of Auxerre, however, it is not the version closest to Ælfric's homily.[93] Next, there is Smaragdus's ninth-century *Collectiones in Euangelia et Epistolas*. Smaragdus may draw on as many as three versions of the *Expositio*: Cassiodorus's revision, a 'pure' copy of Pelagius, and a Pseudo-Jerome version as well (of which more in a moment). While Smaragdus's copies may have been anonymous, he apparently recognized their source, for he marks excerpts from these texts with a P for *ex Pelagio*. Given this explicit attribution, Ælfric would have been unlikely to have utilized such passages; that he did not do so is made certain by the fact that Smargdus does not include the Pelagian material on which Ælfric draws.[94] Third, there is the ninth-century *Homiliae in aliquot epistolas Pauli* of Haymo of Auxerre. While Haymo draws on both Cassiodorus and Smaragdus, he does not seem to use Pelagius directly; indeed, Haymo adapts his sources with such freedom that it is difficult to recognize Pelagius's text.[95] This text too is unlikely to be the source of Ælfric's comments in *Dominica I in Aduentu*. Finally, there is a version that went under the name of Jerome; it is distinguished by Pelagian interpolations that may date to the early fifth century. It, too, had multiple forms: a longer or 'Irish' set of commentaries that includes an exposition of Hebrews and is largely faithful to the Vulgate, and a shorter, 'Anglo-Saxon' set that omitted Hebrews and preserves old British readings of Scripture.[96] As Godden suggests, it is this 'pseudo-Jerome' version of Pelagius, and the Anglo-Saxon form in particular, that Ælfric may have used for his homily.[97] Had Ælfric been confident of the text's attribution, it would have made a considerable difference to his reception of it: Jerome is a trusted source for Ælfric, the one Father besides Augustine, Gregory, and Bede that he credits in his preface.[98] Ironically, therefore, it may be Jerome's orthodox reputation that leads Ælfric to draw on the work of a heretic.

Not all the material Ælfric employs, of course, is fraught with theological error. When Paul affirms that now is the time for people to waken from their sleep (Rom. 13.11), Ælfric follows Pelagius in defining sleep as sluggishness and disbelief.[99] When Paul says that night has passed and day is drawing near (Rom. 13.12), both Ælfric and Pelagius identify night as ignorance and day as knowledge.[100] When Paul exhorts people to behave properly, as in the day (Rom. 13.13), both agree that knowledge, like the light of day, restrains people from despising God's commands.[101] Taken on their own, the comments seem innocuous enough, though a

Pelagian would maintain that people rouse themselves from disbelief through knowledge of God's Law. Ælfric perhaps unwittingly guards himself against this charge by specifying that knowledge comes 'þurh onlihtinge his andwerdnysse' (through the illumination of Christ's presence [*CH* I.39.58]). On two other occasions, however, Ælfric seems actually to reinforce the Pelagian message.

In one instance, drawing on Pelagius's statement, 'Hora est ut [1] ad perfectiora tendatis: non enim debetis semper paruuli esse et lactantes,'[102] Ælfric appears to raise the possibility of human perfection: 'Witodlice ne gedafenað us þæt we symle hnesce beon on urum geleafan swa swa þas mearewan cild: ac we sceolon onettan [2] to fulfremedre geþincðe [3] þurh gehealdsumnysse godes beboda.'[103] Pelagius, on the one hand, urges individuals to strive towards 'perfectiora' (more perfect things) than the deeds of darkness which Paul here condemns (Rom. 13.12–13) ([1] above). Ælfric, however, with a subtle shift of expression, tells his audience to aim for 'fulfremedre geþincðe' (more perfect excellence) ([2]). It might be, of course, that Ælfric has heavenly 'excellence' or 'honour' in mind; as he says earlier in the *Sermones*, 'Godes gecorenan scinað on heofonlicum wuldre ælc be his geðingcðum.'[104] That heavenly honour, however, is directly linked to one's earthly deeds: God created humankind, in fact, 'to ðy. þæt hi scoldon mid gehyrsumnysse. and eaðmodnysse. þa heofonlican geþincðe geearnian. þe se deoful mid ofermettum forwyrhte.'[105] While Ælfric does not claim (as the Pelagian would) that perfection is actually possible on earth, the emphasis both of this passage and the homily as a whole is on the need for human effort rather than God's grace. Ælfric compounds this impression by adding that perfection should be sought through obeying God's commands ([3]). While Ælfric may mean no more than that people should do their best to obey God, ironically his language echoes Pelagius's contention that it is through obedience, not grace, that humans can and must live perfect lives on earth.

A few lines later, Ælfric appears to affirm another Pelagian premise: that through a knowledge of God's Law and a determination to follow it individuals are able to earn their salvation. Drawing on Paul's statement that 'Nunc propior est nostra salus quam cum credidimus' (Our salvation is nearer now than when we first believed [Rom. 13.11]), Pelagius asserts, 'Scientia proficiente propior est nostra salus quam cum [var.: quando primum] credidimus.'[106] The variant 'quando primum,' which does not appear in Weber's apparatus to the Vulgate, is found in the shorter, Anglo-Saxon form of Pseudo-Jerome's version of

Pelagius rather than the longer, Irish form. As the variant corresponds to Ælfric's own quotation ('þa ða ... æt fruman') ([4] below), it may suggest that this was the version of Pelagius's *Expositio* that Ælfric was using.[107] Ælfric suggests:

> [1] Đurh þeondum ingehide. and [2] godum willan: anum gehwylcum [3] is hæl gehendre þonne him wære. [4] þa ða he æt fruman gelyfde. and for þy [5] he sceal symle geþeon on dæighwomlicere gecnyrdnysse. swa swa se sealmscop cwæð be godes gecorenum [6] þa halgan farað fram mihte to mihte. (*CH* I.39.44–6)

> [1] Through increasing knowledge and [2] good will, [3] salvation is nearer to everyone than it was to him [4] when he at first believed, and therefore [5] one should always grow in daily zeal, as the Psalmist said about God's chosen: [6] 'The righteous go from strength to strength.'

Here, one might argue, there is no acknowledgment of grace, no suggestion that knowledge comes from Christ's illumination of human beings.[108] Ælfric does not call people to seek knowledge because the day of salvation is near. Rather, he says, believers' salvation is nearer because they are increasing in knowledge ([1] above). Nor is this all. Ælfric inexplicably adds that salvation is closer because of human beings' 'godum willan' ([2]), a phrase that occurs nowhere in this section of Pelagius's text. Pelagius himself would certainly agree: while God's grace provides people with the knowledge of his requirements and the ability to carry them out, it is individuals' use of that knowledge and their righteous choices that bring them to the reward of heaven. Granted, Ælfric may presuppose grace in the fact of speaking to 'godes gecorenum' (God's chosen); nonetheless, he suggests that it is through their own persistent diligence ('dæighwomlicere gecnyrdnysse') that these chosen ones increase their righteousness ('farað fram mihte to mihte') and bring heaven nearer to them ([5] and [6]; cf. [3]).

Far from editing out questionable material from his source, therefore, Ælfric reinforces Pelagian ideas that, had he been aware of them, he would doubtless have condemned. In the end, however, the material that he incorporates contains no overt heresy. While these passages do emphasize human effort rather than God's grace, ultimately they show only that Ælfric, for all his pains, does not quite escape the taint of suspect source material.

Ælfric's Emphasis on Merit in the *Sermones catholici*

Ælfric's homily for Advent is by no means the only place in which he stresses the importance of human effort. Indeed, given the disproportionate emphasis on merit in his Bedan sources, one might even expect passages derived from Bede to hint that humans should 'earn' their salvation – Ælfric's belief in grace notwithstanding. What even a cursory reading of the *Sermones* reveals, however, is that merit is in fact one of Ælfric's preeminent concerns. In addition to numerous general exhortations to righteous living, some ninety-five statements in over half of Ælfric's homilies specifically use forms of *geearnian* ('to earn' or 'merit') and *geearnung* ('merit' or 'reward').[109] True, the terms can also simply mean 'to labour for' or 'labour': Ælfric notes, for example, that people must repay their teachers 'þurh godum geearnungum' – through good deeds, putting instruction into practice.[110] Throughout, however, Ælfric makes it clear that this labour is a meritorious act through which the believer gains entry into heaven. Though this notion seems to fly in the face of his affirmations elsewhere that salvation is gratuitous, Ælfric suggests that the labour of human beings 'earns' their eternal reward.

The number of these references alone is striking, for it rivals even the number of times that Ælfric mentions grace. While the latter is difficult to determine precisely (through electronic means, at least) given the similarity of the ubiquitous conjunction *gif* to the nominative form of *gif* ('grace'), Ælfric does have a penchant for using the dative form *gife*, and phrases such as 'ðurh godes gife' (through God's grace) appear some 102 times in the *Sermones*.[111] Even more striking, however, is the fact that so few of these references stem from Bede or any other of Ælfric's sources.

Of the ninety-five passages that mention 'earnings,' Godden's analysis suggests that only twenty-three may derive from our three Fathers: four from Augustine, twelve from Gregory, and seven from Bede. Even these figures, moreover, present an inflated picture. First of all, eight of the passages have little to do with the subject of 'earning' one's salvation. Ælfric follows Augustine, for example, in affirming that the efficacy of baptism depends on the merits of Christ rather than the priest,[112] Gregory in asserting that cherubim are near God because of their merits,[113] and Bede in condemning those whose supposed merits lead to pride.[114] These usages can all be discounted for our present study.

Second, on at least six occasions Ælfric follows his source in general, but interjects the phrase involving merit. Two of the more noteworthy examples derive in part from Bede.[115] On the one hand, Ælfric seems to draw on Bede's statement that 'Spiritus sancti septiformis est gratia' (grace comes from the sevenfold Holy Spirit) when he says that '[Se halga gast] onbryrd ure mod mid seofonfealdre gife.'[116] Ælfric immediately goes on, however, to speak of 'se ðe þurh godum geearnungum becymð to ðisum seofonfealdum gifum.'[117] In another case, Bede turns to Christ's statements that only he ascends to heaven (John 3.13) and yet his followers are with him (John 12.26). Following his source closely, Ælfric states:

> Witodlice [1] cristes ðenas ... becomon to heofenan rice swa swa he sylf cwæð. [2] and ealle ða þe ðurh clænre drohtnunge and godum geearnungum criste ðeniað. becumað untwylice to his rice; [3] He is ealra geleaffulra manna heafod. and we sind his lyma. (*CH* II.24.119–24)

> Now [1] the servants of Christ ... attain to the kingdom of heaven, as he himself said; [2] and all those who through a pure life and good merits serve Christ undoubtedly attain to his kingdom. [3] He is the head of all believing people, and we are his limbs.

Ælfric explains that since Christians are members of Christ's body, they are with him even though he has gone before them into heaven ([3] above). Where Bede is content to describe those who are assured of entering heaven as the elect, however ('electi se ueraciter confidant ascensuros in caelum'), Ælfric makes it clear that these 'cristes ðenas' ([1]) are apostles, martyrs, saints and all others who arrive there as a direct result of their purity and 'godum geearnungum' (meritorious labours [2]).[118]

Third, in at least three of the passages derived from the Fathers, Ælfric appears to be following his source, but in fact adapts the text to make his own point about merit. Early in the *Sermones*, on the one hand, Ælfric discusses the reasons for God's injunction against eating of the tree of knowledge of good and evil (Gen. 2.17). Augustine, in a statement later repeated verbatim by Bede, had said, 'Oportebat autem, ut homo sub domino deo positus alicunde prohiberetur, ut ei promerendi dominum suum uirtus esset ipsa oboedientia.'[119] While one might understand *promerere dominum* to mean that individuals should 'merit' God, that is, merit spending eternity with God in heaven, a more straightforward reading might simply be that people should please him.[120] Ælfric, however, chooses to emphasize the former sense. 'Hwi wolde god swa lytles þinges him forwyrnan ... [ac] hu mihte adam tocnawan hwæt he wære. buton he wære gehyrsum on sumum þincge his hlaforde; Swilce god cwæde to him ... mid þære eaðelican gehyrsumnysse. þu *geearnast* heofenan rices myrhðe. and þone stede þe se deofol of afeoll þurh ungehyrsumnesse.'[121] The result is hardly an accident of translation. On at least four other occasions, two within this very homily, Ælfric reiterates that human beings were made to merit through humility the heavenly place which the devil lost through pride.[122] The statements may well be Ælfric's own, since for none of them have sources been identified to my knowledge. The implication is that Ælfric here is reflecting his own theory of merit rather than that of Augustine. A similar case is found in Gregory's assertion that people must repay with interest the spiritual knowledge they receive from preaching: 'Quod auditis,' he says, 'etiam alia studeatis intelligere quae non auditis.'[123] Whereas Gregory focuses on the importance of increasing understanding, however, Ælfric stresses the need to put instruction into practice: 'Ge gehyrað godes beboda æt lareowa muðum. and ge agyfað hí eft gode mid ðam gafole. gif hi beoð þurh eower gecnyrdnysse gemenigfylde ... and ge sylfe him gegað *þurh gódum geearnungum.*'[124] It is possible that Bede may contribute to this emphasis on action, for an analogous statement which Godden cites as an alternate possible states, 'Qui uerbi pecuniam a doctore ... eam cum usuris soluat operando ut quod auditu didicit exsequatur et actu.'[125] 'Þurh godum geearnungum,' however, is a phrase that Ælfric uses six other times in the *Sermones*, and on each occasion the statement appears to be an Ælfrician interpolation.[126] The language itself is particular to Ælfric: of the seventeen known references to *godum geearnungum* in Old English, Ælfric is responsible for thirteen, with twelve of the references coming from the *Sermones*.[127] Even if Ælfric does draw on Bede, therefore, the impression is that here Ælfric introduces a characteristic expression to convey an idea of personal importance – an idea not found in his main Gregorian source.

Finally, Ælfric follows Gregory again for his treatment of Fate in his homily for Epiphany (*CH*. I.7). Both note that Jacob grasped Esau's heel at birth, so that the two were born at practically the same moment. Nevertheless, Gregory says, though 'uno tempore, eodemque momento utrumque mater fuderit, non una utriusque uitae qualitas fuit'.[128] Gregory's point is that the time of individuals' birth – and thus the stars under which they are born – does not determine the outcome of

their lives. Ælfric concurs, but specifically interprets *qualitas* as 'character': 'Hi næron þeah gelice on þeawum ne on lifes geearnungum; Witodlice þæt halige gewrit cwyð þæt god lufode iacob. and he hatode esau.
na for gewyrde: ac for mislicum geearnungum.'[129] Setting aside the fact
that Ælfric's statement seems to be a remarkable rejection of both
Augustine's and Gregory's teaching on election – namely that Jacob is
chosen based on no merit of his own[130] – it is clear that Ælfric goes
beyond his source in asserting the importance of human 'earnings.'

Of our initial twenty-three references, then, five remain which associate merit and heaven and may actually derive from their patristic
sources. Even these sources, however, do not directly state that humans
must earn their salvation. Ælfric follows Gregory, for example, in
affirming that people will have different levels of authority in heaven
based on their different merits – though he neglects to mention that
these are 'acceptae uirtutes,' virtues that have been received from
God.[131] In the same homily, Ælfric suggests that Christians with different 'merits' – wisdom, miraculous powers, authority over spirits, and
so forth – will be associated with the different types of angelic hosts in
heaven.[132] While he recognizes that such virtues are gifts of the Spirit
(cf. I Cor. 12.8–10), Ælfric explains, 'Nabbað ealle men gelice gife æt
gode: for þan ðe he forgifð þa gastlican geþincþu. ælcum be his gec-
nyrdnyssum' – again emphasizing the importance of effort rather than
the gratuity of grace.[133] The same priority is found in a double reference in a later homily, where Ælfric discusses grace and the Feast of
heaven in the context of the Last Supper. Gregory, having described
those who will attend the heavenly banquet as those who strive
towards perfection and transcend earthly things, explains that 'Quae
uidelicet cena hoc ultimo conuiuio exprimitur, cui septem discipuli
adesse memorantur, quia illos ... tunc interna refectio reparat, qui pleni
nunc septiformi gratia in amore spiritus anhelant.'[134] Though Gregory
implies that only those filled with God's grace (*pleni gratia*) have this
righteous desire, nonetheless he directly links it with attendance at the
banquet: the one seems to be dependent on the other. Ælfric takes the
principle a step further, saying, 'He gereordode hine æfter his æriste
mid seofon leorningcnihtum. for ðan ðe he geswutelode mid þære
dæde. þæt ða men becumað to his ecan gereorde þe on andwerdum
life ðurh geearnungum becumað to seofonfealdre gife þæs halgan
gastes ... Þurh ðas seofon mægenu. bið þæt ece lif geearnod.'[135] It is
through merit, Ælfric affirms, that people gain the sevenfold virtues of
grace, and it is through this augmented merit that they earn eternal

life. Finally, then, there is a quotation from Bede. Appropriately, given Bede's emphasis on merit, it is this quotation that comes closest to suggesting that individuals earn their salvation. Bede states: 'Si moyses et omnes prophetae christum locuti sunt et hunc per angustiam passionis in gloriam suam intraturum, qua ratione se gloriantur esse christianos qui ... neque ad gloriam quam cum christo habere cupiunt per passiones tribulationum desiderant attingere?'[136] Through this last word Bede suggests that people are only Christians if they 'attain' heaven through their labour on earth. Yet for Ælfric the statement does not go far enough. Reproducing Bede's statement nearly word for word, Ælfric translates *attingere* not as *geræcan*, the synonym he uses in his *Grammar*,[137] but *geearnian*.[138] Humans, Ælfric affirms, must *merit* their eternal glory through hardship.

If this is how Ælfric treats passages derived from the Fathers, what of references to merit drawn from other sources? The same trends are apparent here as well. On the one hand, we find Ælfric inserting crucial phrases. At one point, for example, Ælfric follows Haymo in interpreting Nebuchadnezzar as the devil, Babylon as hell, and Jerusalem as the heavenly city; he adds, however, 'We ðider cumað untwylice gif we hit on andweardan life geearniað.'[139] On other occasions, we see him adapting passages to his own purpose. A fine example occurs during a discussion of the name of John the Apostle. Hericus of Auxerre states that 'Conuenienter etiam Joannes nominari potest, si per iustitiam mandata Creatoris adimplens, nil sibi deputat, sed cuncta bonorum omnium largitori assignat.'[140] Ælfric paraphrases: 'Iohannes is gecweden godes gyfu: se bið gelimplice godes gyfu geciged. þe ðurh godum geearnungum godes gife begyt. to þy þæt he his beboda geornlice gefylle.'[141] While the texts share many similarities, their point is not the same: according to Hericus, when fulfilling God's commands, one should ascribe everything to grace; according to Ælfric, one should endeavour to merit grace, that one might fulfil God's commands. Lastly, the passages on merit that Ælfric does reproduce do not suggest that humans earn their salvation. One of these presents a paradox, nevertheless, that does much to explain Ælfric's confusing stance. Following Paschasius Radbertus in praising virgins and the Virgin Mary, Ælfric says, 'Ða þe on mæigðhade wuniað. blission hi. for þan ðe hi geearnodon þæt beon þæt hi heriað. habbon hi hoge ... Ða ðe on clænan wydewan hade sind herion hi. and arwurþion. for þan ðe swutol is þæt hi ne magon beon clæne buton þurh cristes gife.'[142] Virtue, Ælfric says, is obtained through meritorious labour; even this merit, however, is dependent on God's grace.

Despite the disproportionate emphasis on merit in Ælfric's Bedan and even Gregorian sources, therefore, the surprising fact is that most of the numerous references to merit in the *Sermones* derive not from Ælfric's sources but from Ælfric himself. We have seen Ælfric's hand at work in the twenty-three passages from the Fathers; we have alluded to his influence on passages gleaned from other sources. For nearly half of the ninety-five references, moreover – forty-seven – Godden lists no known source.[143] While future scholarship may discover potential sources for some, at present these statements seem to be original to Ælfric. They share, for one thing, a common theme: fully twenty-seven concern the need for people to merit eternal life through good deserts.[144] Five times Ælfric opens his homily by speaking of this need; eleven times it forms his closing exhortation.[145] The call to merit is present in the preface to the first series, present at the first series' conclusion, and present at the *Sermones*' end.[146] Present in the preface too, however, is this call's crucial corollary: despite the crucial need to labour, labour itself is due to grace. Ælfric says: 'He wyrcð his weorc þurh his gecorenan. na swylce he behofige ures fultumes. ac þæt we geearnion þæt ece lif þurh his weorces fremminge; Paulus se apostol cwæð; We sind godes gefylstan. and swa ðeah ne do we nan ðing to gode. buton godes fultume.'[147]

This fundamental stance is seen in one final passage, the last of the twenty-three references drawn from the Fathers. Ironically, the source is Bede. Ælfric states: 'Ða synfullan he gebigð to dædbote. and ða rihtwisan he geeacnað mid maran rihtwisnysse ... Eal mennisc wæs synfull. ac drihten gerihtwisode buton geearnungum ðurh his gife ða ða he geceas.'[148] Like Bede, Ælfric does not suggest that it is the preeminent in virtue who are chosen by God; rather, it is sinners, those without merit, whom God makes virtuous. As a pastor, Ælfric is deeply concerned that people strive their utmost to be righteous. Even so, he affirms that ultimate success is due to God alone.

Ælfric's Treatment of Free Will Apart from the *Sermones catholici*

Given the attempt in previous chapters to present the theology of Augustine, Gregory, and Bede as found in the corpus of their writings as a whole, it may seem strange that here our focus should be on two sets of homilies from the beginning of Ælfric's career: Alfred, Lantfred, and Wulfstan may have produced only one major treatise on free will, but surely Ælfric was more prolific? A survey of Ælfric's work on the subject, however, reveals that the bulk of his comments are in fact concentrated in the *Sermones*, and that his teaching thereafter adds little to his initial views.

First, then, while the issues of free will and grace are of distinct importance in the *Sermones*, they seem to decrease in prominence over the course of Ælfric's career (Table 1). To begin with, we might examine forms of *agen willa* or *agen cyre* ('[one's] own will' or '[one's] own choice'), expressions favoured by Ælfric when discussing free will. While by no means unique to Ælfric, the phrases may almost be called characteristic to his vocabulary: forms of *agen willa* in Ælfrician works account for almost half of the total instances of the expression in extant Old English (30 of 67), while forms of *agen cyre* account for nearly two thirds (21 of 35). Most of these references concentrated, however, in the First Series of *Sermones*, where forms of *agen willa* and *agen cyre* appear 18 and 10 times respectively. Thereafter, the phrases appear sporadically throughout Ælfric's corpus, and no more than three times in any one text. Next, there are the forms of *(ge)earnian* ('to earn/merit') and *(ge)earnung* ('merit'), a concept on which (as we have seen) Ælfric lays particular stress. Again, just under half of Ælfric's references to the terms occur in the *Sermones*. A number of references are found in the *Lives of Saints*, a series of hagiographic sermons written in the decade after the *Sermones*, but otherwise the terms are spread through twenty-four texts composed over Ælfric's twenty-odd-year career. Finally, there is the dative form of *gif* ('grace'), a form which (as we have noted) Ælfric uses often and which may easily be distinguished from the conjunction *gif*. If merit is a theme on which Ælfric touches repeatedly in his writings, grace is a subject even more on Ælfric's mind, appearing in thirty-three texts besides the *Sermones* and *Lives of Saints*. The lasting importance of grace to Ælfric does not mean, however, that he continues to treat the matter in depth: rather, nearly two thirds of these references occur in Ælfric's homilies.

This concentration may itself explain the pattern of diminishing references in later work: having spent the beginning of his career expounding key issues, it may be that Ælfric felt that he had covered them sufficiently. We see this trend explicitly in the case of the *Pater noster* and Creed, fundamental texts which Ælfric wanted laymen to know and which he treated in detail in the First Series (*CH* I.19–20). Some years later, in a treatise for Lent, Ælfric refers his audience back to his previous work: 'Be ðisum we habbað on oðre stowe awriten, ræde þæt se ðe wylle.'[149] Even later, in his *Letter to Sigeweard* surveying the Old and New Testaments, he directs the reader to his *Lives of Saints* for fuller discussions of the passions of the apostles: 'Ealra þissera apostola geendunge ic hæbbe awriten buton Mathian anes, þe ic ofacsian [ne] mihte: ða ge mihton rædan & eow aræman on þam, gif ge holde wæron eowrum agenum sawlum.'[150] The same may well be true of his teaching on volition, merit, and grace.

Table 1
References to Will, Merit, and Grace in Ælfric's Corpus

Work	Date[a]	Forms of agen willa / agen cyre [one's] own will or choice	Forms of (ge)earnian / (ge)earnung [to] merit	gife / gyfe grace [dative][b]
ca. 989 x ca. 995				
Sermones catholici I	989 x 991[c] or 990 x 994[d]	28	54	66
Sermones catholici II	992[e] or 995[f]	2	41	49
Brotanek 1	Perhaps shortly after 992[g]		2	1
Letter for Wulfsige	993 x ca 995[h]		2[i]	
Supplementary Homilies I.2	Early in the period 992 x 998			2
Supplementary Homilies I.3	Early in the period 992 x 998	2		
Supplementary Homilies I.5	Early in the period 992 x 998			3
Supplementary Homilies I.6	Early in the period 992 x 998			1
Supplementary Homilies II.21	Early in the period 992 x 998[j]		1	
Supplementary Homilies II.30	Early in the period 992 x 998			1
Bidding Prayers	Early in the period 992 x 1002		3	
Grammar	Early in the period 993 x 1002		9	1
De temporibus anni	Early in the period 992 x 1002			2
Total number of references in the Sermones:		30	95	115
Total excluding the Sermones:		2	17	11
ca. 995 x ca. 1005				
Interrogationes Sigeuulfi in Genesin	993 x 1002	3	2	
Lives of Saints I (22 sermons)[k]	Late in the period 993 x 1002	4	24	9

Table 1
References to Will, Merit, and Grace in Ælfric's Corpus (*continued*)

Work	Date[a]	Forms of agen willa / agen cyre [one's] own will or choice	Forms of (ge)earnian / (ge)earnung [to] merit	gife / gyfe grace [dative][b]
Lives of Saints II (11 sermons)	Late in the period 993 x 1002	1	14	4
Hexameron	Late in the period 993 x 1002		2	1
Supplementary Homilies I.7	998 x 1005			1
Supplementary Homilies I.8	998 x 1005			
Supplementary Homilies I.9	998 x 1005			2
Supplementary Homilies I.10	998 x 1005			5
Supplementary Homilies I.12	998 x 1005			2
Supplementary Homilies II.19	998 x 1005			1
Supplementary Homilies II.20	998 x 1005		2	1
Supplementary Homilies I.11	Somewhat late in the period 998 x 1005		7	2
Supplementary Homilies II.18	Somewhat late in the period 998 x 1005		1	
Assmann 8	Early in the period 1002 x 1005			1
Assmann 9	Early in the period 1002 x 1005	1		
Belfour 7	Probably 1002 x 1005		1	
Belfour 9	1002 x 1005	3		
Admonitio ad filium spiritualem	1002 x 1005	2		2
De septiformi Spiritu	1002 x 1005		1	1
Napier 8	1002 x 1005			
Total number of references in the *Lives of Saints*:		4	38	13
Total excluding the *Lives of Saints*:		10	16	20

Table 1
References to Will, Merit, and Grace in Ælfric's Corpus (continued)

Work	Date[a]	Forms of agen willa / agen cyre [one's] own will or choice	Forms of (ge)earnian / (ge)earnung [to] merit	gife / gyfe grace [dative][b]
ca. 1005 x ca. 1010				
Assmann 3	1005 x 1006	2	7	5
Letter to Sigefyrth [Assmann 2]	1005 x 1006		2	1
Letter to Sigeweard	1005 x 1006			3
Letter to Wulfgeat [Assmann 1]	1005 x 1006	1	4	1
First Old English Letter for Wulfstan [Fehr II]	1006			2
Second Old English Letter for Wulfstan [Fehr III]	1006		2	
De creatore et creatura	1006	1	2	1
The Old English Ely Privilege	ca 1006[l]			2
Supplementary Homilies I.11a	Late in the period 992 x ca 1010		2	2
Supplementary Homilies II.27	Late in the period 992 x ca 1010		3	
Supplementary Homilies II.14	1005 x 1010			1
Supplementary Homilies II.15	1005 x 1010			1
Supplementary Homilies II.16	1005 x 1010		2	1
Supplementary Homilies II.17	1005 x 1010		1	2
Supplementary Homilies II.17	Late in the period 1005 x 1010		3	5
Belfour 3	1006 x ca 1010		1	2

Table 1
References to Will, Merit, and Grace in Ælfric's Corpus (*concluded*)

Work	Date[a]	Forms of agen willa / agen cyre [one's] own will or choice	Forms of (ge)earnian / (ge)earnung [to] merit	gife / gyfe grace [dative][b]
Assman 4	1006 x ca 1013[m]	1	2	29
Total number of references:		5	31	
Total number of references in Ælfric's corpus:		51	197	188

a Unless otherwise stated, dates are taken from Clemoes, 'Chronology.'

b As noted above, Ælfric's use of the dative form of *gif* ('grace') is instructive given his penchant for using the word in phrases such as 'ðurh godes gife' (through God's grace); it is also easier to track than the nominative form given its similarity to the ubiquitous conjunction *gif*.

c Clemoes, 'Chronology,' 56, and Eliason and Clemoes, *Royal 7 C. XII*, 35. Here and below, the form '[date] x [date]' is used to designate the inclusive period in which a text may have been composed.

d Godden, *Introduction, Commentary, and Glossary*, xxxv.

e Clemoes, 'Chronology,' 56, and Pope, *Homilies*, 1:146.

f Godden, *Introduction, Commentary, and Glossary*, xxxv.

g Pope, *Homilies*, 1:141n1.

h That is, perhaps early in Wulfsige's episcopacy (Whitelock et al., *Councils*, 193, and Clemoes, "Supplement" cxliv–cxlv).

i Two forms appear in the version of the *Letter for Wulfsige* found in Cambridge, Corpus Christi College 190; only one form appears in the version found in Oxford, Bodleian Library, Junius 121.

j For the dates of individual Supplementary Homilies, see Pope, *Homilies*, 1:148–50.

k Four sermons published in Skeat's edition of the *Lives* are not by Ælfric: *LS* I.23, II.23b, II.30, and II.33.

l McIntosh, 'Wulfstan's Prose,' 129, and Pope, 'Ely Privilege,' 111.

m That is, the approximate tenure of Æthelwold II, bishop of Winchester, to whom the sermon is dedicated (Whitelock et al. *Councils*, 260).

Second, when one does consider Ælfric's later comments on free will, one sees little that Ælfric has not discussed in the *Sermones*. God made humans sinless, Ælfric says, with reason and a will by which they could submit themselves to good or evil.[151] Since they corrupted themselves by their own free choice, human nature is now torn by temptations so that it is only with great effort that they hold onto virtues.[152] God still lets individuals have power over their choices, for he will not force them to do good, and desires that they obey him voluntarily.[153] If God were not to give people this power, they could have neither reward for good works nor punishment for evil; they would be brute beasts.[154] Nevertheless, people's abilities are not sufficient to save them. They will be delivered through God's grace, as long as they obey.[155] Many of these points may be seen in one of the most extensive treatments of free will apart from the *Sermones*, the concluding section of a sermon in Ælfric's *Lives of Saints* entitled *De auguriis* ('On Auguries').

De auguriis (LS I.17.222–71): Ælfric's Use of Alfred on Free Will

As its name suggests, *De auguriis* in large part addresses the evils of idolatry, witchcraft, and sorcery, and as such has generated debate as to whether Ælfric has in view contemporary pagan practice.[156] Towards the end of the text, however, having exhorted his audience to turn from sinful ways, he encourages them by saying that a transformation of lifestyle is indeed possible. The basis for his encouragement is one source of surprise, for the bulk of his comments emphasize not humans' need of grace but the effectiveness of their capacity for free choice. Another surprise comes, moreover, in the source of Ælfric's remarks. Rather than drawing on his own teaching in the *Sermones* or on patristic exposition, Ælfric turns to Alfred's version of *De consolatione Philosophiae* – or more specifically, to comments inserted by Alfred into his version of Boethius's work.

As we have noted, Alfred makes a number of original points in the penultimate chapter of the *Old English Boethius*. To begin with, Wisdom introduces a metaphor to defend God's decision to give evil people free will: just as it would be unjust for an earthly king to be served only by slaves, Wisdom says, so it would be improper (*uncynlic*) for God to have no free creatures in his kingdom.[157] God thus created two creatures with reason, angels and human beings, giving them the *micle gife freodomes* (great gift of freedom), the *swiðe fæste gife* (exceedingly firm gift) of being able to do good or evil as they chose. With it came the *swiðe fæste æ* (exceedingly firm law) by which God's creatures will be judged.[158] Though Boethius objects that divine predetermination may render God's recompense meaningless and individuals' righteous efforts vain, Wisdom insists that God neither constrains people to do good nor hinders them from doing evil: he has given them freedom.[159]

In typical fashion, Ælfric rearranges and subtilely adapts this material. He leads off with Boethius's comments regarding predestination, using the objection to affirm that individuals can in fact turn from their evil deeds: if people did not have such power, Ælfric argues, their labour would be futile and both rewards and punishments unjust.[160] Noting that God made humans and angels with reason and freedom of choice, he then echoes Alfred's final point that God neither constrains people to do good nor hinders them from doing evil. To a certain extent, Ælfric here may be merely stating the obvious – that people in this world do choose both good and evil – without depicting the precise mechanics of human choice. At the same time, the statement is in keeping with the *Sermones'* teaching that God gives individuals the power either to pursue good or to reject it – a Gregorian rather than Augustinian view of the will. Ælfric's subsequent use of the Alfredian phrase *swiðe fæste gife* reinforces this possibility. While the phrase could simply mean that God will not revoke his 'gift' of volition even in the face of human disobedience, it may also carry resonances of the lasting effects of 'grace.' As Ælfric states immediately after, 'Þæt is seo gifu þæt se man mot don þæt he wile' (This is the gift: that one may do what he will [*LS* I.17.253]). Grace does not bring people inevitably to obey, but enables their free choices. This said, it is individuals' dependence on God, not their volitional power, that is, characteristically, Ælfric's last word on the matter. Adding to his Alfredian source, he states: 'Behofað ure freo-dom æfre godes fultumes. forþan ðe we ne doð nan god butan godes fultume.'[161] Here, as in the *Sermones*, though Ælfric is earnestly concerned that his audience pursue good, it is in grace that Ælfric puts his hope for their success.

Ælfric's Treatment of Free Will: Summary

Ælfric's works reveal a complex relationship between him and his various sources. Perhaps more than any other author we have considered, Ælfric shows painstaking concern to present his audience with authoritative, orthodox doctrine. Like Gregory and Bede before him, he is heavily influenced by and respectful of Augustinian thought, insisting first and foremost on the primacy of grace: it is grace, he says, that enables righteousness, from the very beginnings of human faith. At the same time, his work reflects Gregorian and Bedan teaching regarding volitional capacity and human corruption. Concerned with motivating his audience to righteous efforts, Ælfric describes people as sinful but not incapacitated, as dependent on God but, made able to choose or reject him. Moreover, like his Northumbrian forebear, Ælfric persistently speaks of the importance of earning heavenly rewards through meritorious deeds. Though he relies on all three Fathers, as his preface states, his resulting teaching reflects different emphases in their theology. Ælfric's view of volition may thus be said to be founded on Augustine, modified by Gregory, and supplemented by Bede.

While he might like to set himself apart from comtemporary *gedwyld* or error, however, his work does share similarities with that of Lantfred and Wulfstan. Like these writers, Ælfric attaches great importance to human merit. Like them, he draws (albeit unwittingly) on heretical source material. Like them, moreover, he adapts this material to form an original text, demonstrating both respect for and independence from his authorities. In the end, however, where their sources lead them to Semi-Pelagian conclusions, Ælfric consistently attributes the whole of human righteousness to grace.

Conclusion

Our exploration of views of free will in Anglo-Saxon England has revealed a picture that is far from straightforward. To begin with, we examined the teaching of Augustine of Hippo, setting it as a benchmark against which later perspectives might be measured. While his works before his episcopate suggest that humans have the unhindered ability to choose either good or evil, Augustine's mature view emphasizes the corrupting effects of the Fall and humanity's consequent dependence on grace. Adam's disobedience, Augustine says, has marred human nature, so that while they still have the capacity to choose good or evil, their desires lead them inevitably – and voluntarily – to choose evil. If people are to desire righteousness, to believe, to accomplish good, and to persevere in doing it, God's prevenient grace must first intervene, inspiring faith and changing human desires to good.

Particularly in light of the shift in Augustine's thought, we next sought to reconstruct which Augustinian works might have been known to the Anglo-Saxon authors under consideration. We looked for Augustinian manuscripts surviving from the relevant centres, manuscripts surviving from England as a whole during these time periods, Augustinian sources used by the various authors, and continental collections of Augustinian material known in late Anglo-Saxon England. While the evidence is of course incomplete, collectively it offers the remarkable conclusion that Augustine's major works on free will, written towards the close of his career, may have been known neither to our authors nor to Anglo-Saxon England as a whole. An examination of those works likely known to or used by these authors suggests, however, that the gap was irrelevant for their understanding of basic doctrine: texts such as the

Confessiones, De ciuitate Dei, and the material transmitted by Paul the Deacon and Smaragdus clearly convey Augustine's view of man's nature, volition, and need for grace.

Chapter 2 turned to another Father with a profound influence on Anglo-Saxon England, Gregory the Great. Written for the most part over a brief period, Gregory's works present a consistent perspective rather than major shifts in thought, and an analysis of the evidence suggests that his views were amply conveyed to Anglo-Saxon England. Gregory both affirms and departs from the teachings of the Doctor of Grace. Like Augustine, he portrays humans as corrupted by fleshly desires. Indeed, he speaks of people struggling against a throng of competing desires, to which God ultimately brings order in the lives of the righteous. Where Augustine views human beings as corrupt from conception, however, Gregory depicts people as becoming corrupt through their own sin. As a result, while Gregory agrees that fallen humans are blind to righteousness, he does not present this blindness as absolute: even in their blindness, he says, people can strain to see the light. At the same time, Gregory acknowledges that only God makes people see; the illumination of faith, therefore, is due to grace. Though Gregory departs from Augustine in his depiction of corruption and blindness as a process, however, even more distinctive is his stance on the notion of irresistible grace. For Gregory, God's intervention does not inevitably produce obedience: individuals indeed require grace if they are to will good, Gregory affirms, but having received it, they can choose either good or evil, cooperating with or rejecting God's grace. While he rejects the Semi-Pelagian assertion that humans may independently initiate good, therefore, and affirms Augustine's belief in human beings' dependence on God, Gregory nonetheless introduces the possibility of meritorious human choice.

In chapter 3, we examined a further bridge between the patristic and Anglo-Saxon worlds: the teaching of the Venerable Bede. Gregory and Augustine stand first and second in Bede's hierarchy of authorities, and their theology impacts his teaching accordingly. Though Bede is less concerned with the precise way in which grace and volition interact, like Gregory he both insists on the Augustinian primacy of grace and states that individuals may reject the grace received. In his works known to later Anglo-Saxon England, he warns against the Pelagian danger inherent in the miscalculation of Easter, teaches that humans are bound and blind due to original and personal sin, and emphasizes human responsibility both for belief and right action. One of Bede's most significant contributions to later understandings of free will, in fact, may be his repeated emphasis on the need for individuals to merit their heavenly reward. Bede teaches that God frees people through baptism from bondage and blindness, but suggests that they must somehow merit their enlightenment. On numerous occasions he refers to the 'grace of faith,' while suggesting through the examples of Zaccheus and the centurion that faith is meritorious. Bede calls people to earn God's help in doing good deeds, even though he says that love, the source of righteous works, is the prevenient gift of God.

Behind this seeming paradox, however, lies Bede's Gregorian view that prevenient grace enables individuals to cooperate with God. Like living stones, he says, people should accept the grace they are given and pray for further grace. This foundational counteremphasis to merit – that grace precedes and makes possible people's faith, love, and righteous deeds – is a key theme in Bede's work. It is particularly evident, however, in a few texts apparently unknown to our later authors, such as his commentary on the *Cantica Canticorum*. While it is impossible to say for certain, it may be that this omission may have impacted their view of free will, reinforcing – particularly for his fellow monk Ælfric – Bede's stress on the need for meritorious choices. Even so, Bede is no Pelagian: however human beings may labour, he says, and whatever they may accomplish, people are to attribute their efforts and success to God.

Alfred the Great's version of Boethius's *De consolatione Philosophiae* forms the subject of chapter 4. Boethius's justification of God's righteous sovereignty in the face of worldly evils, we noted, discusses at least two key issues related to free will. On the one hand, it treats the problem of Providence. Though God's absolute control of history might seem to reduce human beings to automata, Philosophy argues that God's sovereignty neither prevents people from choosing evil nor prevents their evil choices from going unpunished: human volition cannot thwart God's just rules by which creation operates. In addition, *De consolatione* addresses the conundrum of divine foreknowledge. How can free will exist, one might ask, if the future which God foresees must necessarily come to pass? For Philosophy, the key is to understand the all-encompassing nature of God's knowledge: in his eternal present, God sees future events that proceed from human beings' free choice and embraces at a glance any uncertainty or vacillation that may precede that choice.

When we examined the philosophical roots of Boethius's work, however, we found that the Neoplatonic framework in which his comments are set is fundamentally antithetical to a Christian world view; his teaching on free will, moreover, is not without heterodox implications for theological discourse. At the same time, we saw that *De consolatione* was widely read in the Middle Ages and that numerous commentaries were composed both in England and on the Continent seeking to interpret Boethius's text in a way consonant with Christian doctrine. Alfred, on the other hand, attempted to 'Christianize' the work not by glossing it but by radically transforming it in the vernacular. Where Philosophy says that humans by their very nature submit to God's will, inasmuch as by sinning they enforce God's justice by depriving themselves of the happiness they seek, Alfred's Wisdom states that people oppose God by living unnaturally. Where Philosophy argues that the wicked desire good (or happiness) but fail to attain it in their pursuit of evil, Wisdom states that the wicked desire evil, attain it, and are judged by God accordingly. Where Philosophy describes Fate as the multifarious means by which God accomplishes his providential plan, Wisdom affirms that divine predestination rather than *wyrd* orchestrates all things. Where Philosophy speaks of the all-encompassing nature of God's vision, Wisdom teaches that God does not determine all things, but allows human decisions to shape some events; divine foreknowledge thus preserves a place for human choice. The result is a view that, with certain exceptions, conveys an Augustinian perspective in spite of its heterodox source material.

Coming to the late tenth and early eleventh centuries, our final chapters examined works influenced by and produced under Anglo-Saxon England's Benedictine Reform. Chapter 5 treats another text drawing on *De consolatione Philosophiae*: Lantfred of Winchester's *Carmen de libero arbitrio*. Having set forth the evidence for Lantfred's authorship of the poem, as well as its close linguistic and conceptual ties to *De consolatione*, we considered his potential access to Christian commentaries on Boethius's work. Rather than following such commentaries, however, like that of Remigius with his Augustinian perspective, Lantfred appears to rely exclusively on *De consolatione*, drawing on Boethian imagery to produce a striking portrait of God's relationship to human beings and their volitional power. In keeping with Philosophy's explanation that divine foreknowledge does not negate free will, the *Carmen* depicts a king gazing upon people running a race without interfering with the outcome. Though Lantfred urges individuals to seek God's help in running, his contention that God does not influence human minds directly opposes orthodox thought, for it denies that grace inspires and enables individuals to pursue good. Lantfred's attempts to preserve a role for human volition thus bring Semi-Pelagian thought to the Benedictine training ground of Winchester.

Chapter 6 considered yet another work drawing on suspect source material, one commissioned and approved, if not composed, by Wulfstan the Homilist: *De adiutorio Dei et libero arbitrio*. Having discussed its manuscript context, a collection of material compiled by Wulfstan for a Danish bishop, and having set the work in context of Wulfstan's other remarks on free will, we examined *De adiutorio Dei*'s surprising source: John Cassian's *Collatio* XIII. Drawing closely on this central treatise of Semi-Pelagianism, *De adiutorio Dei* affirms that though humans need God's help to accomplish good, people can desire good and seek the help they need in bringing it to pass. Using the example of the farmer and his field, the redactor repeatedly portrays God as responding to human labour, whether it be in preparing their hearts to receive the seed of God's word, praying that it would sprout and grow, or persevering in prayer that they might continue in righteousness. A similar pattern is revealed in the redactors' paired quotations, where grace is balanced against human effort. The redactor speaks of grace preceding human will even as he speaks of the will preceding grace; he speaks of God stretching out his hands to humans even as humans stretch out their hands to God; he speaks of God seeking people, even as he calls on people to seek God. Whereas with Gregory and Bede, therefore, individuals may cooperate with God in response to his prevenient gift of grace, *De adiutorio Dei* teaches that grace cooperates with human beings' meritorious initiative. Remarkably, however, even while basing itself on *Collatio* XIII, *De adiutorio Dei* appears to be guided by Prosper of Aquitaine's Augustinian critique of the work, for it reproduces only passages that Prosper does not condemn. Like Alfred and Lantfred before him, therefore, Wulfstan seems to show concern for theological correctness despite drawing on dubious material; like them too, however, ultimately he cannot escape the heterodox implications of his source. In supervising and authorizing this study of free will, Wulfstan not only brings Semi-Pelagian theology to another influential centre of the Benedictine Reform, but exports it as well to the Danish episcopate of Roskilde.

Finally, chapter 7 examined the work of the Anglo-Saxon writer who perhaps more than any other sought to set forth orthodox doctrine: Ælfric of Eynsham. Having outlined Ælfric's vision for educating laymen and clergy in the fundamentals of the faith, and described the unique nature of the *Sermones catholici* that followed as a result, we discussed the particular importance to Ælfric of Augustine, Gregory, and Bede. We then sought to clarify Ælfric's complex debt to these Fathers – the ways in which he used, adapted, blended, supplemented, and selected among their works. Treating the parable of the Friend at Midnight, for example, Ælfric draws primarily on Augustine to address the origin of faith and the corruption of human nature. In the first case, though the parable shows God bestowing faith in response to those who ask him – a potentially Semi-Pelagian scenario – Ælfric follows Augustine in attributing human belief to God. On the other hand, Ælfric mitigates the Father's view of corruption by describing humans not as depraved, but sinful: people are 'evil,' Ælfric explains, to the extent that all have committed at least some sin – a position that leaves open the possibility of righteous effort.

Ælfric also departs from Augustinian doctrine in homilies drawing on either Gregory or Bede. In his Gregory-based exposition of Christ's healing of the blind man outside Jericho, for example, Ælfric presents humans as blind not through Adam's sin but through their own evil habits. As a result, he says, people may still be able to recognize their spiritual need and call to God for help, despite the crowd of fleshly desires that hinder their prayers. Prevenient grace may be implied in the very fact of Christ's coming, but Ælfric does not suggest that such grace is irresistible. On the contrary, like Gregory, Ælfric teaches that individuals can reject grace, refusing to follow Christ even after he has enlightened them. Ælfric reinforces this message in his discussion of the Star over Bethlehem, where he presents human freedom of choice as an intrinsic part of God's righteousness: for humans not to have the one would violate the other. Like Gregory, therefore, Ælfric argues that God gives people the ability to cooperate with or reject his grace. A similar perspective is evident in Ælfric's discussion of the Triumphal Entry, drawing on Bede. Just as Christ has the disciples untie the donkey and foal, Ælfric says, so God frees individuals, leaving them to choose whether they will follow him. Incorporating a metaphor from Pseudo-Chrysostom, Ælfric depicts individuals' bondage to the devil as that of a nation under a king: sin binds people, Ælfric says, so that they may no longer do good. In a stance reminiscent of Gregory as well as Bede, Ælfric depicts this bondage as a process, affirming that sin does not rule people until they have chosen it. In his portrayals both of humans' volitional capacity and the corruption of their nature, therefore, Ælfric presents a perspective removed from Augustine's thought.

The implications of Ælfric's view of human will and nature are seen both in his unexpected (and unintentional) use of Pelagius and in his repeated (and largely original) stress on the importance of merit. Drawing on a Pelagian work likely circulating under the name of Jerome, Ælfric urges people to seek perfection by obeying God's commands and says that humans draw near to salvation through their righteous knowledge and good deeds. Throughout the *Sermones*, moreover, Ælfric inserts numerous statements calling people to earn heavenly rewards through meritorious belief and action. Despite such emphasis – influenced, perhaps, by Bede as well as by his own practical pastoral concerns – Ælfric takes pains to prevent his audience from thinking too highly of their abilities. In homilies drawing on individual and multiple Fathers, in both the *Sermones* and in later works, Ælfric insists with Augustinian force that humans ultimately must rely on grace: no one, he says, does anything good without God.

The writings of Anglo-Saxon England reveal a multiplicity of perspectives on the subject of free will. Drawing on disparate sources, showing varying concern for orthodoxy, through wide-ranging means they seek to explain the enigmatic relationship between divine sovereignty and human choice. All depart to some extent from Augustinian doctrine; all offer unique if often complementary approaches to the question. In the face of troubled times, however, all underscore humanity's need of God's aid even as they labour to affirm the legitimacy of human effort. However important it may be for human beings to strive, they say, humans will only succeed if they strive with grace.

APPENDIX I

Patristic Texts in Paul the Deacon and Smaragdus

Table I.1
Augustinian Texts in Paul the Deacon's Homiliary

Augustinian Work	PD Location	Use in Ælfric's *Sermones*
De ciuitate Dei 20.5.3	PD 55, Summer	–
De ciuitate Dei 22.8	PD 29, Winter	*CH* II.2 (certain antecedent source)
De diuersis quaestionibus lxxxiii 59.1–4	PD 121, Summer	–
De sermone Domini in monte 1.9	PD 58, Summer	–
Enchiridion XXIII.84–93	PD 132, Summer	–[1]
Enchiridion XXIX.109–11	PD 131, Summer	–
Sermo 31	PD 113, Summer	–
Sermo 82	PD 93, Summer	–
Sermo 370 (excerpt)	PD 65, Winter	*CH* I.9 (probable source)
Tractatus in Euangelium Ioannis 24	PD 1, Winter	*CH* I.12
Tractatus 51.13	PD 68, Summer	–[2]
Tractatus 67–71	PD 23, Summer	–
Tractatus 80–2	PD 100, Summer	–
Tractatus 83	PD 102, Summer	–
Tractatus 87	PD 103, Summer	–
Tractatus 105.1–107.4	PD 25, Summer	*CH* II.22 (*Tract.* 105, 106 [probable], and 107 [possible source])
Tractatus 121.4–5	PD 14, Summer	–

1. *Tractatus* 51.13 appears in two of Ælfric's later works, *SH* II.25a.15–19, and Irvine 4.340–7.
2. Ælfric may possibly have used *Enchiridion* 98–104 in *CH* II.5.227–32.

Table I.2
Augustinian Texts in Later Versions of Paul the Deacon's Homiliary

Augustinian Work	PDM[1] Location	Use in Ælfric's *Sermones*
De ciuitate Dei 22.8.10	PDM 34, Temporale	*CH* II.2 (certain antecedent source)
Enarrationes in psalmos 21.2.3	PDM 112, Temporale	–
Enarrationes in psalmos 63.2	PDM 117, Temporale	–
Enarrationes in psalmos 63.6	PDM 119, Temporale	–
Enarrationes in psalmos 63.13	PDM 121, Temporale	–

Table I.2

Augustinian Texts in Later Versions of Paul the Deacon's Homiliary (*continued*)

Augustinian Work	PDM[1] Location	Use in Ælfric's *Sermones*
Sermo 40	PDM 67, Temporale	–
Sermo 62	PDM 68, Temporale	–
Sermo 67	PDM 58, Temporale	–
Sermo 70	PDM 3, Sanctorale	–
Sermo 76	PD 33, Sanctorale	*CH* II.24
Sermo 83	PDM 191, Temporale	*CH* I.31[2]
Sermo 93	PDM 94, Sanctorale	*CH* II.39
Sermo 99	PDM 35, Sanctorale	–
Sermones 103–4	PDM 47, Sanctorale	*CH* II.29
Sermo 115	PDM 170, Temporale	*CH* II.28 (possible source)
Sermo 115	PDM 170, Temporale	*CH* II.28 (possible source)
Sermo 172	PDM 65, Sanctorale	–
Sermo 186	PDM 27, Temporale	*CH* I.2 (possible source)
Sermo 279	PDM 6, Sanctorale	*CH* I.27 (possible source)
Sermo 105	Durham PD[3]	*CH* I.18 (probable source)
Sermo 292	PDM 20, Sanctorale	–
De sermone Domini in monte 1.1.2–3 (?)	PDM 81, Sanctorale	–
De sermone Domini in monte 2.6.16	PDM 92, Sanctorale	–
De sermone Domini in monte 2.7.19	PDM 165, Temporale	–
De sermone Domini in monte 2.23.77	PDM 167, Temporale	–
De sermone Domini in monte 12.40	PDM 66, Temporale	–
Tractatus in Euangelium Ioannis 11.3	PDM 16, Sanctorale	–
Tractatus 12	PDM 150, Temporale	*CH* II.13[4]
Tractatus 26	PDM 152, Temporale	*CH* II.15 (probable source; certain antecedent source)
Tractatus 45	PDM 151, Temporale	–
Tractatus 49	PDM 67, Sanctorale	–[5]
Tractatus 51.3	PDM 42, Sanctorale	–
Tractatus 67–8	PDM 15, Sanctorale	–
Tractatus 80	PDM 69, Sanctorale	–

Table I.2
Augustinian Texts in Later Versions of Paul the Deacon's Homiliary (*concluded*)

Augustinian Work	PDM[1] Location	Use in Ælfric's *Sermones*
Tractatus 80–1	PDM 18, Sanctorale	–
Tractatus 87–8	PDM 71, Sanctorale	–
Tractatus 104.1	PDM 142, Temporale	*CH* II.22 (probable source)
Tractatus 124.1	PDM 35, Temporale	–

1. PDM is the later medieval form of the homiliary, expanded and considerably revised, printed as PL 95.1159–1566.
2. *Sermo* 83 also serves as a source for Ælfric's later homily Irvine 2.
3. Augustine's *Sermo* 105 appears in the version of Paul the Deacon found in Durham Cathedral Library A 3.29 (s. xi[ex], Durham).
4. *Tractatus* 12.5.20–2 also serves as a source for Ælfric's later *SH* I.12.156–7.
5. Portions of *Tractatus* 49 serve as sources for two of Ælfric's later works, *SH* I.6 and Assmann 5.

Table I.3
Gregorian Texts in Paul the Deacon's Homiliary

Gregorian Work	PD Location	Use in Ælfric's *Sermones*
Homiliae in Euangelia I.1	PD 3, Winter	*CH* I.40
Homiliae in Euangelia I.6	PD 5, Winter	*CH* I.32 (probable)
Homiliae in Euangelia I.7	PD 8, Winter	*CH* I.25 (possible)
Homiliae in Euangelia I.20	PD 13, Winter	*CH* I.25 (probable) and II.3 (probable)
Homiliae in Euangelia I.8	PD 24, Winter	*CH* I.2
Homiliae in Euangelia I.10	PD 48, Winter	*CH* I.7 and I.15
Homiliae in Euangelia I.19	PD 69, Winter	*CH* I.35 (probable) and II.5 (probable)
Homiliae in Euangelia I.15	PD 71, Winter	*CH* II.6
Homiliae in Euangelia I.2	PD 73, Winter	*CH* I.10 (probable)
Homiliae in Euangelia I.16	PD 76, Winter	*CH* I.11 (probable) and II.7 (probable)
Homiliae in Euangelia I.18	PD 94, Winter	*CH* II.13
Homiliae in Euangelia II.21	PD 5, Summer	*CH* I.15 and II.12 (probable)
Homiliae in Euangelia II.23	PD 9, Summer	*CH* II.16
Homiliae in Euangelia II.24	PD 11, Summer	*CH* II.16
Homiliae in Euangelia II.25	PD 12, Summer	*CH* I.14 (possible)

Table I.3
Gregorian Texts in Paul the Deacon's Homiliary

Gregorian Work	PD Location	Use in Ælfric's *Sermones*
Homiliae in Euangelia II.26	PD 15, Summer	*CH* I.16 and I.22 (probable)
Homiliae in Euangelia I.14	PD 20, Summer	*CH* I.17
Homiliae in Euangelia II.29	PD 28, Summer	*CH* I.3 and I.21
Homiliae in Euangelia II.30	PD 33, Summer	*CH* I.22, II.3, II.5, and II.19
Homiliae in Euangelia II.36	PD 38, Summer	*CH* II.23
Homiliae in Euangelia I.34	PD 39, Summer	*CH* I.2, I, 24, and II.5
Homiliae in Euangelia II.31	PD 86, Summer	*CH* II.26 (possible source)
Homiliae in Euangelia I.5	PD 98, Summer	*CH* I.38
Homiliae in Euangelia II.27	PD 101, Summer	*CH* I.35 (possible), I.36, II.19 (probable), and II.35
Homiliae in Euangelia I.9	PD 104, Summer	*CH* II.38
Homiliae in Euangelia I.13	PD 109, Summer	–[1]
Homiliae in Euangelia II.37	PD 112, Summer	–
Homiliae in Euangelia II.35	PD 116, Summer	*CH* II.37
Homiliae in Euangelia II.32	PD 118, Summer	–
Homiliae in Euangelia I.12	PD 122, Summer	*CH* I.28 and II.39
Homiliae in Euangelia I.11	PD 123, Summer	–
Homiliae in Euangelia I.3	PD 124, Summer	–

Homiliae in Euangelia not included in PD: I.4, I.17, II.22, II.28, II.33, II.38, II.39, and II.40

1. Ælfric does not appear to use this homily in the *Sermones*, but does rely on it as an ultimate source for Assmann 4; see Clayton, 'Records for Source Title *Hom.Euang.* 13.'

Table I.4
Gregorian Texts in a Later Version of Paul the Deacon's Homiliary

Gregorian Work	PDM[1] Location	Use in Ælfric's *Sermones*
Homiliae in Euangelia I.1	PDM 3, Temporale	*CH* I.40
Homiliae in Euangelia I.6	PDM 5, Temporale	*CH* I.32 (probable)
Homiliae in Euangelia I.20	PDM 9, Temporale	*CH* I.25 (prob) and II.3 (prob)
Homiliae in Euangelia I.7	PDM 13, Temporale	*CH* I.25 (possible)
Homiliae in Euangelia I.8	PDM 18, Temporale	*CH* I.2 (probable)
Homiliae in Euangelia I.10	PDM 48, Temporale	*CH* I.7 and I.15

Table I.4

Gregorian Texts in a Later Version of Paul the Deacon's Homiliary (*continued*)

Gregorian Work	PDM[1] Location	Use in Ælfric's *Sermones*
Homiliae in Euangelia I.19	PDM 59, Temporale	*CH* I.35 (prob) and II.5 (prob)
Homiliae in Euangelia I.15	PDM 61, Temporale	*CH* II.6
Homiliae in Euangelia I.2	PDM 64, Temporale	*CH* I.10
Homiliae in Euangelia I.16	PDM 72, Temporale	*CH* I.11 (prob) and II.7 (prob)
Homiliae in Euangelia I.18	PDM 105, Temporale	*CH* II.13
Homiliae in Euangelia II.21	PDM 123, Temporale	*CH* I.15 and II.12 (probable)
Homiliae in Euangelia II.23	PDM 125, Temporale	*CH* II.16
Homiliae in Euangelia II.24	PDM 129, Temporale	*CH* II.16
Homiliae in Euangelia II.25	PDM 131, Temporale	*CH* I.14 (possible)
Homiliae in Euangelia II.22	PDM 133, Temporale	*CH* II.15
Homiliae in Euangelia II.26	PDM 134, Temporale	*CH* I.16 and I.22 (probable)
Homiliae in Euangelia I.14	PDM 137, Temporale	*CH* I.17
Homiliae in Euangelia II.29	PDM 143, Temporale	*CH* I.3 and I.21
Homiliae in Euangelia II.30	PDM 147, Temporale	*CH* I.22, II.3, II.5, and II.19
Homiliae in Euangelia II.40	PDM 159, Temporale	*CH* I.23 and II.37
Homiliae in Euangelia II.36	PDM 160, Temporale	*CH* II.23
Homiliae in Euangelia II.34	PDM 161, Temporale	*CH* I.2, I.24, and II.5
Homiliae in Euangelia II.39	PDM 169, Temporale	*CH* I.23 and I.28
Homiliae in Euangelia II.31	PDM 184, Temporale	*CH* II.26 (possible source)
Homiliae in Euangelia II.38	PDM 188, Temporale	*CH* I.17 and I.35
Homiliae in Euangelia II.28	PDM 189, Temporale	*CH* I.8 (prob) and I.40 (poss)
Homiliae in Euangelia I.5	PDM 2, Sanctorale	*CH* I.38
Homiliae in Euangelia I.3	PDM 34, Sanctorale	–
Homiliae in Euangelia II.33	PDM 36, Sanctorale	–
Homiliae in Euangelia I.17	PDM 60, Sanctorale	*CH* II.36 and II.38
Homiliae in Euangelia I.4	PDM 70, Sanctorale	–
Homiliae in Euangelia II.27	PDM 72, Sanctorale	*CH* I.35 (poss), I.36, II.19 (prob), & II.35
Homiliae in Euangelia II.37	PDM 75, Sanctorale	–
Homiliae in Euangelia II.32	PDM 77, Sanctorale	–

Table I.4
Gregorian Texts in a Later Version of Paul the Deacon's Homiliary (*concluded*)

Gregorian Work	PDM[1] Location	Use in Ælfric's *Sermones*
Homiliae in Euangelia II.35	PDM 80, Sanctorale	*CH* II.37
Homiliae in Euangelia I.9	PDM 85, Sanctorale	*CH* II.38
Homiliae in Euangelia I.13	PDM 88, Sanctorale	–[2]
Homiliae in Euangelia I.12	PDM 95, Sanctorale	*CH* I.28 and II.39

Homiliae in Euangelia not included in PDM: I.11

1. PDM is the later medieval form of the homiliary, expanded and considerably revised, printed as PL 95.1159–1566.
2. Ælfric does not appear to use this homily in the *Sermones*, but does rely on it as an ultimate source for Assmann 4; see Clayton, 'Records for Source Title *Hom. Euang.* 13.'

Table I.5
Bedan Texts in Paul the Deacon's Homiliary

Bedan Work (whole/extracts)	PD Location	Use in Ælfric's *Sermones*
Homiliae I.3[1]	PD 11, Winter	*CH* I.13
Homiliae I.4	PD 12, Winter	*CH* I.13
Homiliae I.7	PD 25, Winter	*CH* I.2 (probable)
Homiliae I.8	PD 26, Winter	–
Homiliae I.9	PD 33, Winter	*CH* I.4 and I.37
Homiliae I.11	PD 36, Winter	*CH* I.6 (probable)
Homiliae I.11	PD 40, Winter	*CH* I.6 (probable)
Homiliae I.15	PD 49, Winter	–
Homiliae I.12	PD 58, Winter	*CH* II.3 (probable)
Homiliae I.19	PD 59, Winter	–
Homiliae I.14	PD 60, Winter	*CH* II.4
Homiliae I.18	PD 67, Winter	*CH* I.9 (probable)
Homiliae I.24	PD 87, Winter	–
In Lucam V.*inuocatio*	PD 90, Winter	–
Homiliae II.2	PD 92, Winter	*CH* I.12 (probable)
Homiliae II.3	PD 97, Winter	*CH* I.14
Homiliae II.4	PD 99, Winter	–
Homiliae II.5	PD 105, Winter	*CH* II.15 (doubtful)
Homiliae II.7	PD 2, Summer	*CH* I.15 (probable)
Homiliae II.9	PD 10, Summer	*CH* I.21 (probable)
Homiliae II.8	PD 13, Summer	–

Table I.5
Bedan Texts in Paul the Deacon's Homiliary (*continued*)

Bedan Work (whole/extracts)	PD Location	Use in Ælfric's *Sermones*
Homiliae II.18	PD 16, Summer	*CH* II.24
In Lucam III.11	PD 19, Summer	–
Homiliae II.13	PD 21, Summer	–
Homiliae II.11	PD 22, Summer	–
Homiliae II.12	PD 24, Summer	–
Homiliae II.16	PD 29, Summer	*CH* I.22 (possible)
Homiliae II.17	PD 30, Summer	*CH* I.22 (very doubtful)
In Lucam II.6 (cf. PD 114)	PD 37, Summer	–
Homiliae II.19	PD 40, Summer	*CH* I.25 (possible)
Homiliae II.20	PD 44, Summer	*CH* I.25 (probable)
Homiliae II.22	PD 45, Summer	–
Homiliae I.20	PD 52, Summer	*CH* I.25 (probable)
In Lucam II.5 (cf. PD 84)	PD 57, Summer	–
In Marcum II.8	PD 60, Summer	*CH* II.25
In Lucam III.10 (cf. PD 63)	PD 63, Summer	–
In Lucam V.18	PD 64, Summer	*CH* II.28 (probable)
Homiliae II.6	PD 69, Summer	–
In Lucam III.10 (cf. PD 63)	PD 70, Summer	–
In Lucam V.17	PD 74, Summer	–
In Lucam V.16	PD 75, Summer	*CH* II.31
In Lucam II.7 and *Homiliae* I.4 (cf. PD 12)	PD 76, Summer	*CH* I.33 (possible, drawing on *Luc.*)
In Lucam IV.14	PD 80, Summer	–
In Marcum III.8	PD 82, Summer	–
In Lucam II.5 (cf. PD 57)	PD 84, Summer	–
In Marcum III.13	PD 87, Summer	–
In Lucam V.20	PD 95, Summer	–
In Lucam III.8	PD 96, Summer	*CH* I.33 (possible)
Homiliae I.16	PD 97, Summer	–
Homiliae I.21	PD 99, Summer	*CH* II.32
In Lucam IV.11	PD 107, Summer	–
In Lucam II.6 (cf. PD 37)	PD 114, Summer	–
Homiliae II.25	PD 125, Summer	–
Homiliae II.24	PD 126, Summer	*CH* II.40 (probable)

Table I.5
Bedan Texts in Paul the Deacon's Homiliary (*concluded*)

Bedan Work (whole/extracts)	PD Location	Use in Ælfric's *Sermones*
In Lucam V.19	PD 129, Summer	–

Book I and II *Homiliae* not included in PD: I.1, I.2, I.5, I.6, I.10, I.13, I.17, I.22, I.23, I.25, II.1, II.10, II.14, II.15, II.21, and II.23

Book I and II *Homiliae* not in PD but used by Ælfric: I.6 (probably), I.13 (possibly), II.21 (probably), and II.23

1. Bedan homilies are numbered according to Hurst's edition in CCSL 122; for the considerably-different numeration found in PL 94, see Appendix II, Tables II.1–2 below.

Table I.6
Bedan Texts in a Later Version of Paul the Deacon's Homiliary

Bedan Work	PDM[1] Location	Use in Ælfric's *Sermones*
Homiliae I.3[2]	PDM 7, Temporale	*CH* I.13
Homiliae I.4	PDM 9, Temporale	*CH* I.13
Homiliae II.7 (cf. PDM 122, Temporale)	PDM 16, Temporale	*CH* I.15 (probable)
Homiliae I.6	PDM 19, Temporale	*CH* I.2 (probable)
Homiliae I.7	PDM 20, Temporale	*CH* I.2 (probable)
Homiliae I.8	PDM 21, Temporale	–
Homiliae I.9	PDM 36, Temporale	*CH* I.4 and I.37
Homiliae I.10	PDM 37, Temporale	*CH* I.5 (possible)
Homiliae I.11	PDM 45, Temporale	*CH* I.6 (probable)
Homiliae I.15	PDM 50, Temporale	–
Homiliae I.12	PDM 51, Temporale	*CH* II.3 (probable)
Homiliae I.19	PDM 52, Temporale	–
Homiliae I.14	PDM 53, Temporale	*CH* II.4
Homiliae II.18 (cf. PDM 157, Temporale)	PDM 70, Temporale	*CH* I.9 (possible)
Homiliae III.43	PDM 75, Temporale	–
Homiliae I.22	PDM 80, Temporale	–
Homiliae III.49	PDM 89, Temporale	–
Homiliae III.58	PDM 90, Temporale	–
Homiliae III.50	PDM 91, Temporale	–
Homiliae II.2	PDM 97, Temporale	*CH* I.12 (probable)
Homiliae II.3	PDM 113, Temporale	*CH* I.14
Homiliae II.5	PDM 118, Temporale	*CH* II.15 (doubtful)

Table I.6
Bedan Texts in a Later Version of Paul the Deacon's Homiliary (*continued*)

Bedan Work	PDM[1] Location	Use in Ælfric's *Sermones*
Homiliae II.7 (cf. PDM 16, Temporale)	PDM 122, Temporale	*CH* I.15 (probable)
Homiliae II.9	PDM 127, Temporale	*CH* I.21 (probable)
Homiliae II.8	PDM 132, Temporale	–
Homiliae II.13	PDM 138, Temporale	–
Homiliae II.11	PDM 139, Temporale	–
Homiliae II.12 (part)	PDM 140, Temporale	–
Homiliae III.82 (part)	PDM 141, Temporale	–
Homiliae II.16	PDM 145, Temporale	*CH* I.22 (possible)
Homiliae II.17	PDM 146, Temporale	*CH* I.22 (very doubtful)
Homiliae II.18 (cf. PDM 70, Temporale)	PDM 157, Temporale	*CH* II.24
Homiliae II.6	PDM 172, Temporale	–
Homiliae III.16 (part)	PDM 180, Temporale	–
Homiliae III.21	PDM 182, Temporale	–
Homiliae III.54 (not by Bede)	PDM 196, Temporale	–
Homiliae II.25 [= III.65]	PDM 200, Temporale	–
Homiliae II.24	PDM 201, Temporale	*CH* II.40 (probable)
Homiliae I.16	PDM 1, Sanctorale	–
Homiliae I.18	PDM 9, Sanctorale	*CH* I.9 (probable)
Homiliae I.20	PDM 11, Sanctorale	*CH* I.26
Homiliae II.19	PDM 19, Sanctorale	*CH* I.25 (possible)
Homiliae II.20	PDM 22, Sanctorale	*CH* I.25 (probable)
Homiliae II.21	PDM 37, Sanctorale	*CH* II.27 (probable) and II.37 (possible)
Homiliae III.60	PDM 49, Sanctorale	–
Homiliae II.23	PDM 51, Sanctorale	*CH* I.32
(not by Bede?)	PDM 53, Sanctorale	–
Homiliae III.56	PDM 54, Sanctorale	–
Homiliae III.53 (part)	PDM 61, Sanctorale	–
Homiliae III.70	PDM 62, Sanctorale	–
Homiliae III.87 (part; not by Bede)	PDM 82, Sanctorale	–
Homiliae III.82	PDM 87, Sanctorale	–
Homiliae III.77	PDM 90, Sanctorale	–

Table I.6

Bedan Texts in a Later Version of Paul the Deacon's Homiliary (*concluded*)

Bedan Work	PDM[1] Location	Use in Ælfric's *Sermones*
(not by Bede?; cf. PL 92.465B)	PDM 91, Sanctorale	–

Book I and II *Homiliae* included in PDM but not in PD: I.6, I.10, II.21, and II.23
Book I and II *Homiliae* included in PD but not in PDM: I.21, I.24, II.4, and II.22
Book I and II *Homiliae* not included in PDM: I.1, I.2, I.5, I.13, I.17, I.21, I.23, I.24, I.25 II.1, II.4, II.10, II.14, II.15, and II.22
Book I and II *Homiliae* not included in PD or PDM: I.1, I.2, I.5, I.13, I.17, I.23, I.25 II.1, II.10, II.14, and II.15
Book I and II *Homiliae* not in PD or PDM but used by Ælfric: I.13 (possibly)

1. PDM is the later medieval form of the homiliary, expanded and considerably revised, printed as PL 95.1159–1566.
2. References to homilies from Book I and II are according to Hurst's edition in CCSL 122, whereas references to Book III homilies are to the *Homiliae subditiciae* in PL 94; for the latter, and for the considerably different numeration of Bedan homilies in PL 94, see Appendix II, Tables II.1–2.

Table I.7

Texts Correctly Attributed to Augustine in (at least one manuscript of) Smaragdus's *Collectiones in Euangelia et Epistolas*[1]

Citations	Source of Extract(s)
PL 102.56B	*De ciuitate Dei* 10.1.3
PL 102.148C	*De ciuitate Dei* 15.2; *cf.* 18.54
PL 102.149A	*De ciuitate Dei* 17.7.4 (attributed in some MSS to Ambrose)
PL 102.398A	*De ciuitate Dei* 20.5.3
PL 102.65D	*De ciuitate Dei* 20.6.1 (attributed in some MSS to Ambrose)
PL 102.41A	*De consensu euangelistarum* 2.75.145
PL 102.223B	*De consensu euangelistarum* 3.24.65
PL 102.233D	*De consensu euangelistarum* 3.25.73
PL 102.237A	*De consensu euangelistarum* 3.25.74
PL 102.311B	*De consensu euangelistarum* 3.25.76
PL 102.126A	*De diuersis quaestionibus* 57.2
PL 102.549B	*De diuersis quaestionibus* 59.3 (attributed to 'A' in one MS)
PL 102.549D	*De diuersis quaestionibus* 59.3
PL 102.550A	*De diuersis quaestionibus* 59.3 (attributed to 'A' in one MS)
PL 102.550B	*De diuersis quaestionibus* 59.3
PL 102.550B	*De diuersis quaestionibus* 59.3
PL 102.551A	*De diuersis quaestionibus* 59.3
PL 102.551C	*De diuersis quaestionibus* 59.3

Table I.7

Texts Correctly Attributed to Augustine in (at least one manuscript of) Smaragdus's *Collectiones in Euangelia et Epistolas* (*continued*)

Citations	Source of Extract(s)
PL 102.551C	*De diuersis quaestionibus* 59.3
PL 102.551D	*De diuersis quaestionibus* 59.3 (attributed to 'A' in one MS)
PL 102.552B	*De diuersis quaestionibus* 59.3
PL 102.552D	*De diuersis quaestionibus* 59.3
PL 102.200D	*De diuersis quaestionibus* 73.1
PL 102.200B	*De diuersis quaestionibus* 73.2
PL 102.200C	*De diuersis quaestionibus* 73.2 and *De trinitate* 1.7.14
PL 102.473D	*De doctrina Christiana* 5.27.59–60
PL 102.505C	*Enarrationes in psalmos* 4.8 (attributed in some MSS to Bede)
PL 102.520D	*Enarrationes in psalmos* 147.13
PL 102.413C	*Enarrationes in psalmos* 149.2
PL 102.463B	*Epistula* 140.26.63 (attributed in some MSS to Ambrose)
PL 102.344D	*Epistula* 147.9.22
PL 102.66B	*Epistula* 149.3.33
PL 102.66C	*Epistula* 149.3.33
PL 102.202A	*Epistula* 187.13.40 [*De praesentia Dei*]
PL 102.72A	*Contra Faustum* 2.5
PL 102.491A	*Contra Faustum* 13.16
PL 102.354B	*In Ioannis epistulam ad Parthos tractatus x* 5.10
PL 102.491A	*Contra litteras Petiliani* 2.45.106
PL 102.529C	*De moribus ecclesiae catholicae et de moribus Manichaeorum* 1.11.19
PL 102.367A	*Ad Orosium contra Priscilliantista et Origenistas* 8.11
PL 102.498B	*Quaestiones Euangeliorum* 1.25
PL 102.375D	*Quaestiones Euangeliorum* 2.2 (joined silently to Bede, In Lucae euangelium expositio 2.5)
PL 102.350B	*Quaestiones Euangeliorum* 2.38
PL 102.128A	*Quaestiones in Heptateuchum* 1.63
PL 102.50A	*De sancta uirginitate* 27.27
PL 102.492A	*Sermo* 67.3.5
PL 102.498D	*Sermo* 83.2.2–6.7
PL 102.500D	*Sermo* 83.6.7 (attributed to 'A' in one MS)
PL 102.485C	*Sermo* 167.2.3
PL 102.58B	*Sermo* 169.2.3
PL 102.247C	*Sermo* 251.1.1–8.7
PL 102.472C	*Sermo* 350.2

Table I.7
Texts Correctly Attributed to Augustine in (at least one manuscript of) Smaragdus's
Collectiones in Euangelia et Epistolas (concluded)

Citations	Source of Extract(s)
PL 102.234D	*Sermo* 352.1.3
PL 102.545A	*De sermone Domini in monte* 1.1.2
PL 102.403C	*De sermone Domini in monte* 1.9.21
PL 102.404A	*De sermone Domini in monte* 1.9.24
PL 102.404B	*De sermone Domini in monte* 1.9.22
PL 102.405B	*De sermone Domini in monte* 1.10.27
PL 102.460A	*De sermone Domini in monte* 2.14.47
PL 102.460B	*De sermone Domini in monte* 2.14.47
PL 102.89B	*Sermones quatuor* 3
PL 102.17C	*De praedestinatione sanctorum* 15.31–16.32
PL 102.32A	*Tractatus in Euangelium Ioannis* 1.13
PL 102.32C	*Tractatus* 1.16–19
PL 102.33A	*Tractatus* 2.5
PL 102.33C	*Tractatus* 2.10–11
PL 102.34C	*Tractatus* 2.13; cf. *Contra duas epistulas Pelagianorum* 1.3 and *Contra Iulianum opus imperfectum* 1.94
PL 102.35A	*Tractatus* 2.16
PL 102.31C	*Tractatus* 3.4 (?)
PL 102.85D	*Tractatus* 8.12 (but drawing mainly on Bede, *Commentarius in Ioannem* 1.3.2.3–4)
PL 102.86C	*Tractatus* 9.7
PL 102.156C	*Tractatus* 10.9 and 12.3; cf. 11.2–4
PL 102.160C	*Tractatus* 44.1–2
PL 102.235C	*Tractatus* 120.1
PL 102.259A	*Tractatus* 121.3
PL 102.45C	*Tractatus* 124.4–5; see also 124.8
PL 102.235A	*De trinitate* 2.5.9
PL 102.372D	*De trinitate* 8.6.9
PL 102.527B	*De trinitate* 15.18.24

1. As noted above, the various Smaragdus manuscripts differ widely in the number of passages they attribute to Augustine; the material here follows and expands Souter's reconstruction of passages cited as Augustinian in at least one manuscript.

Table I.8

Augustinian Texts Attributed to Other Writers in Smaragdus's *Collectiones in Euangelia et Epistolas*

Citations	Source of Extract(s)
PL 102.115B	*De ciuitate Dei* 22.29.2 (attributed here to Ambrose)
PL 102.121D	*Enarrationes in psalmos* 2.5 (attributed here to Ambrose)
PL 102.138B	*Epistula* 217.3.11 (attributed here to Bede)
PL 102.125B	*Sermo* 263.4 (attributed here to Ambrose)
PL 102.120D	*Sermo* 350.2–3 (attributed here to Ambrose)

Table I.9

Texts Falsely Attributed to Augustine in (at least one manuscript of) Smaragdus's *Collectiones in Euangelia et Epistolas*

Citations	Source of Extract(s)
PL 102.257B	Alcuin, *In Iohannis euangelium* 7.41.20.11
PL 102.246A	Alcuin, *In Iohannis euangelium* 7.43.21.11
PL 102.61B	Ambrose, *Expositio euangelii secundum Lucam* 2
PL 102.408A	Pseudo-Augustine, *Sermo* 81.1 (attributed in other MSS to Bede)
PL 102.274D	Pseudo-Augustine, *Sermo* 125.3
PL 102.326C	Bede, *Super Acta Apostolorum expositio* 2
PL 102.277A	Bede, *Super epistulas catholicas expositio* I John 5
PL 102.302C	Bede, *Homiliae euangelii* 2.7
PL 102.384C	Bede, *In Lucae euangelium expositio* 1.1
PL 102.376D	Bede, *In Lucae euangelium expositio* 2.5
PL 102.137D	Bede, *In Lucae euangelium expositio* 5.inuocatio and *Homiliae subdititiae* 3.49 (both quoting from Jerome, *Commentarii in euangelium Matthaei* 2.12.28)
PL 102.417D	Bede, *In Lucae euangelium expositio* 5.16
PL 102.543B	Bede, *In Lucae euangelium expositio* 5.19 and *Homiliae euangelii* 3.82
PL 102.189D	Bede, *In Lucae euangelium expositio* 6.23, *Homiliae subdititiae* 3.53, and Pseudo-Bede, *In Matthaei euangelium expositio* (quoting briefly from Augustine, *Tractatus* 118.4)
PL 102.237B	Bede, *In Lucae euangelium expositio* 6.24; *cf.* Augustine, *De consensus euangelistarum* 3.25.74
PL 102.192B	Bede, *In Marci euangelium expositio* 4.15 and *Homiliae subdititiae* 3.53
PL 102.530B	Pseudo-Bede, *In Ioannis euangelium expositio* 15
PL 102.55C	Cassiodorus, *Expositio psalmorum* 2.10
PL 102.417A	Pseudo-Jerome, *Commentarius in epistulas Paulinas*, I Cor. 10
PL 102.114D	Pseudo-Jerome *Commentarius in epistulas Paulinas*, I. Cor. 13

Table I.9

Texts Falsely Attributed to Augustine in (at least one manuscript of) Smaragdus's
Collectiones in Euangelia et Epistolas (*concluded*)

Citations	Source of Extract(s)		
PL 102.63D	Pseudo-Jerome *Commentarius in epistulas Paulinas*, Gal. 4		
PL 102.502A	Pseudo-Jerome *Commentarius in epistulas Paulinas*, Phil. 3		
PL 102.147C	PL 102.263B	PL 102.474D	source unidentified
PL 102.229A	PL 102.263D	PL 102.528D	(original to Smaragdus [?])[1]
PL 102.229B	PL 102.439C	PL 102.546D	

1. Godden notes, however, that Smaragdus 'scarcely wrote a line in his exegetic collection that was not taken verbatim from another source' (*Introduction, Commentary, and Glossary*, xxxix).

Table I.10

Texts Correctly Attributed to Gregory in (at least one manuscript of) Smaragdus's
Collectiones in Euangelia et Epistolas

Citations	Source of Extract(s)
PL 102.107C	*Dialogorum libri iv* II.3 ['Numquid iam ... campum quaesiuit']
PL 102.518D	*Homiliae in Euangelia* I.1.2–3
PL 102.116C	*Homiliae in Euangelia* I.2.1
PL 102.117B	*Homiliae in Euangelia* I.2.1
PL 102.117D	*Homiliae in Euangelia* I.2.3–4 ['Quid isti ... amissa reparatur'] and I.2.7–8 ['Nunquid qui ... laudem Deo']
PL 102.433A	*Homiliae in Euangelia* I.3.2
PL 102.522B	*Homiliae in Euangelia* I.6.1
PL 102.524B	*Homiliae in Euangelia* I.7.1 ['Joannes igitur ... responderet']
PL 102.525B	*Homiliae in Euangelia* I.7.3
PL 102.24B	*Homiliae in Euangelia* I.8.1
PL 102.25C	*Homiliae in Euangelia* I.8.1
PL 102.72D	*Homiliae in Euangelia* I.10.1
PL 102.73B	*Homiliae in Euangelia* I.10.1
PL 102.74B	*Homiliae in Euangelia* I.10.6
PL 102.549A	*Homiliae in Euangelia* I.12.1
PL 102.550A	*Homiliae in Euangelia* I.12.1 ['Per oleum ... regis intus']
PL 102.550B	*Homiliae in Euangelia* I.12.1
PL 102.550C	*Homiliae in Euangelia* I.12.2
PL 102.550C (second citation)	*Homiliae in Euangelia* I.12.3

Table I.10

Texts Correctly Attributed to Gregory in (at least one manuscript of) Smaragdus's
Collectiones in Euangelia et Epistolas (*continued*)

Citations	Source of Extract(s)
PL 102.550C (third citation)	*Homiliae in Euangelia* I.12.3
PL 102.550D	*Homiliae in Euangelia* I.12.3 (attributed in at least one MS to Augustine)
PL 102.551A	*Homiliae in Euangelia* I.12.3
PL 102.551C	*Homiliae in Euangelia* I.12.3
PL 102.551C (second citation)	*Homiliae in Euangelia* I.12.3
PL 102.552A	*Homiliae in Euangelia* I.12.4 ['O si sapere ... tempus perdit']
PL 102.552B	*Homiliae in Euangelia* I.12.5
PL 102.552C	*Homiliae in Euangelia* I.12.5–6
PL 102.286A	*Homiliae in Euangelia* I.14.2–3 ['Non pastor ... diligit amittat']
PL 102.111B	*Homiliae in Euangelia* I.15.1 ['et tamen ... uirtutibus faciunt'[1]] and I.15.3 ['Notandum uero ... emolliunt']
PL 102.122C	*Homiliae in Euangelia* I.16.1
PL 102.167C	*Homiliae in Euangelia* I.18.1
PL 102.103A	*Homiliae in Euangelia* I.19.1
PL 102.102C	*Homiliae in Euangelia* I.19.1–2
PL 102.226B	*Homiliae in Euangelia* II.21.2 ['Illae autem ... amplexabitur me']
PL 102.236A	*Homiliae in Euangelia* II.21.5 ['Galilaea namque ... interpretatur']
PL 102.276A	*Homiliae in Euangelia* II.22.3
PL 102.376B	*Homiliae in Euangelia* II.24.3
PL 102.245A	*Homiliae in Euangelia* II.24.4
PL 102.257B	*Homiliae in Euangelia* II.25.1 (attributed in some MSS to Augustine)
PL 102.257C	*Homiliae in Euangelia* II.25.3
PL 102.257D	*Homiliae in Euangelia* II.25.3
PL 102.259A	*Homiliae in Euangelia* II.25.5–6
PL 102.281B	*Homiliae in Euangelia* II.26.2–3 ['Pater filium misit ... amorem Dei']
PL 102.282A	*Homiliae in Euangelia* II.26.7
PL 102.282C	*Homiliae in Euangelia* II.26.7 [quoted in Alcuin, *In Iohannis euangelium* 7.42.20.29]
PL 102.311C	*Homiliae in Euangelia* II.29.2
PL 102.312D	*Homiliae in Euangelia* II.29.8 ['Quid in his ... secuta sunt']
PL 102.328B	*Homiliae in Euangelia* II.30.1 ['Probatio ergo ... uoluptatibus coarctamur']
PL 102.360C	*Homiliae in Euangelia* II.34.2–3 ['non solum ad colloquendum ... quaerebatur in terra']

Table I.10
Texts Correctly Attributed to Gregory in (at least one manuscript of) Smaragdus's
Collectiones in Euangelia et Epistolas (*concluded*)

Citations	Source of Extract(s)
PL 102.355D	*Homiliae in Euangelia* II.36.2 (attributed in some MSS to Jerome)
PL 102.532C	*Homiliae in Euangelia* II.37.2, quoted in Bede, *In Lucae euangelium expositio* 4.14 and *Homiliae subdititiae* 3.76 (attributed in some MSS to Bede)
PL 102.487D	*Homiliae in Euangelia* II.38.2
PL 102.488A	*Homiliae in Euangelia* II.38.3
PL 102.488C	*Homiliae in Euangelia* II.38.4
PL 102.489B	*Homiliae in Euangelia* II.38.5
PL 102.489C	*Homiliae in Euangelia* II.38.7
PL 102.490C	*Homiliae in Euangelia* II.38.12
PL 102.491A	*Homiliae in Euangelia* II.38.14
PL 102.76D	*Homiliae in Ezechielem* II.1.18 ['Dum enim ... discutimus, aberremus': entry omitted in some MSS]
PL 102.121A	*Homiliae in Ezechielem* II.7.15
PL 102.478A	*Moralia in Iob* VI.37.57
PL 102.486A	*Moralia* V.39.70
PL 102.191B	*Moralia* XVIII.40.64 ['In corde ... praedicauit']

1. As against Souter, 'Contributions,' 589, who suggests that the quotation begins at *Mirum quomodo* in the line before.

Table I.11
Gregorian Texts Attributed to Other Writers in Smaragdus's *Collectiones in Euangelia et Epistolas*

Citations	Source of Extract(s)
PL 102.550C	Jerome, *Commentarii in Euangelium Matthaei* 5.25.5 ['Consequenter ... suscitandae sunt']
PL 102.550D	Jerome, *Commentarii in Euangelium Matthaei* 5.25.5 ['Per angelorum ... aduentum Christi']

Table I.12
Texts Falsely Attributed to Gregory in (at least one manuscript of) Smaragdus's
Collectiones in Euangelia et Epistolas

Citations	Source of Extract(s)
PL 102.237A	Alcuin, *In Iohannis euangelium* 7.42.20.19

Table I.12

Texts Falsely Attributed to Gregory in (at least one manuscript of) Smaragdus's
Collectiones in Euangelia et Epistolas (*concluded*)

Citations	Source of Extract(s)
PL 102.280B	Alcuin, *In Iohannis euangelium* 7.42.20.19
PL 102.274C	Ambrose, *Expositio Euangelii secundum Lucam* 10.156, quoted in Bede, *In Lucae euangelium expositio* 6.24 (attributed in some MSS to Augustine or Bede)
PL 102.551D	Augustine, *De diuersis quaestionibus lxxxiii* 59.3 (attributed in other MSS to Augustine)
PL 102.142C	Augustine, *Tractatus in Euangelium Ioannis* 15.7
PL 102.438A	Augustine, *Tractatus* 51.9–10 ['Amen amen ... amando']
PL 102.523D	Pseudo-Bede, *In Ioannis euangelium expositio* 1, quoted in Alcuin, *In Iohannis euangelium* 1.2.1.19 ['His uerbis ...usurparet']
PL 102.495B	Pseudo-Bede, *In Ioannis euangelium expositio* 4 ['Regulus diminutivum ... habuit fidem']
PL 102.285D	Pseudo-Bede, *In Ioannis euangelium expositio* 10, quoted in Alcuin, *In Iohannis euangelium* 5.25.10.11–12
PL 102.538C	Bede, *In Lucae euangelium expositio* 4.12 and *Homiliae subdititiae* 3.78
PL 102.349A	Bede, *In Lucae euangelium expositio* 5.16 and *Homiliae subdititiae* 3.1 ['Nonnulli autem ... fuerat, non peruenit']
PL 102.350C	Bede, *In Lucae euangelium expositio* 5.16 and *Homiliae subdititiae* 3.1 ['Nonnulli autem ... fuerat, non peruenit']
PL 102.418C	Bede, *In Lucae euangelium expositio* 5.16 and *Homiliae subdititiae* 3.8 ['Cadus Graece ... retributionis erigi']
PL 102.421D	Bede, *In Lucae euangelium expositio* 5.19 and *Homiliae subdititiae* 3.9
PL 102.233A	Bede, *In Lucae euangelium expositio* 6.24 and *Homiliae subdititiae* 3.62
PL 102.237D	Bede, *In Lucae euangelium expositio* 6.24 ['Resurrectionem suam certam ... post resurrectionem']
PL 102.408C	Bede, *In Marci euangelium expositio* 2.7 and *Homiliae subdititiae* 3.6 ['Turba ergo ... esse cibariis']
PL 102.325D	Bede, *Super Acta Apostolorum expositio* 2 ['Hoc est in cenaculo ... eorum adhaeserint iuri']
PL 102.193A	Source unidentified (original to Smaragdus [?])[1] ['Lignum aduersus ... infirmitatis nostrae']

1. Godden notes, however, that Smaragdus 'scarcely wrote a line in his exegetic collection that was not taken verbatim from another source' (*Introduction, Commentary, and Glossary*, xxxix).

Table I.13
Texts Correctly Attributed to Bede in (at least one manuscript of) Smaragdus's *Collectiones in Euangelia et Epistolas*

Citations	Source of Extract(s)
PL 102.308B	*Super Acta Apostolorum expositio* 1
PL 102.325D	*Super Acta Apostolorum expositio* 2
PL 102.37A	*Super Acta Apostolorum expositio* 7 ['Cum Dominus ... adiutorem habuit'][1]
PL 102.37C	*Super Acta Apostolorum expositio* 7
PL 102.38A	*Super Acta Apostolorum expositio* 7
PL 102.251A	*Super Acta Apostolorum expositio* 8
PL 102.251D	*Super Acta Apostolorum expositio* 8 ['In corde ... rarissimus est']
PL 102.252A	*Super Acta Apostolorum expositio* 8 ['Non solum ... rarissimus est']
PL 102.252B	*Super Acta Apostolorum expositio* 8
PL 102.253B	*Super Acta Apostolorum expositio* 8, *In Lucae euangelium expositio* II.6, and *In Marci euangelium expositio* I.3 ['Philippus ...fuisse baptizatum']; cf. Pseudo-Bede, *In Matthaei euangelium expositio* II.10[2] (attributed in some MSS to Primas [Hugh of Orléans])
PL 102.396C	*Super Acta Apostolorum expositio* 9
PL 102.229A	*Super Acta Apostolorum expositio* 10 ['Id est, Pater ... cadere uideamur']
PL 102.317B	*Super Acta Apostolorum expositio* 10
PL 102.389D	*Super Acta Apostolorum expositio* 12 ['Hunc Herodem ... percussum'] (attributed in some MSS to Josephus)
PL 102.389D	*Super Acta Apostolorum expositio* 12
PL 102.72D	*Aliquot quaestionum liber* 1
PL 102.105C	*Aliquot quaestionum liber* 2
PL 102.194B	*In Cantica Canticorum allegorica expositio* IV.4
PL 102.475C	*Expositio Apocalypseos* I.1
PL 102.48D	*Expositio Apocalypseos* II.14 ['Magna uox ... psallere']
PL 102.49B	*Expositio Apocalypseos* II.14 [Smaragdus: 'Concitharistae ... ierit'; Bede: 'Cum citharistae ... uadit']
PL 102.50A	*Expositio Apocalypseos* II.14 ['Singulariter canticum ... uestigia eius']
PL 102.50C	*Expositio Apocalypseos* II.14 ['de illo sancto ... eliguntur']
PL 102.292D	*Super epistulas catholicas expositio* Iac 1
PL 102.293B	*Super epistulas catholicas expositio* Iac 1 ['Et de antiquo ... permittunt']
PL 102.300A	*Super epistulas catholicas expositio* Iac 1 ['Non auditores ... scripta sunt']; cf. *In Lucae euangelium expositio* VI.24 and *Homiliae* III.62
PL 102.303C	*Super epistulas catholicas expositio* Iac 5
PL 102.353D	*Super epistulas catholicas expositio* 1 John 3
PL 102.343D	*Super epistulas catholicas expositio* 1 John 4 ['Quomodo ipse ... uiuifica me']

Table I.13

Texts Correctly Attributed to Bede in (at least one manuscript of) Smaragdus's *Collectiones in Euangelia et Epistolas* (*continued*)

Citations	Source of Extract(s)
PL 102.287D	*Super epistulas catholicas expositio* 1 Pt. 1
PL 102.534D	*Super epistulas catholicas expositio* 1 Pt. 1
PL 102.266C	*Super epistulas catholicas expositio* 1 Pt. 2
PL 102.284D	*Super epistulas catholicas expositio* 1 Pt. 2
PL 102.260B	*Super epistulas catholicas expositio* 1 Pt. 3
PL 102.358C	*Super epistulas catholicas expositio* 1 Pt. 5 ['Hanc ergo ... non posse']
PL 102.371B	*Super epistulas catholicas expositio* 1 Pt. 3
PL 102.19D	*Homiliarum euangelii libri ii* I.5 ['Antequam conuenirent ... deprehendit intuitu']
PL 102.31D	*Homiliae* I.7
PL 102.33B	*Homiliae* I.7
PL 102.33D	*Homiliae* I.7
PL 102.34C	*Homiliae* I.7 ['Carnalis quippe ... spiritus est']
PL 102.35A	*Homiliae* I.7
PL 102.35B	*Homiliae* I.7
PL 102.45A	*Homiliae* I.8 ['Non inquit ... inuenitur alienus']
PL 102.51D	*Homiliae* I.9 ['Possumus quoque ... committi']
PL 102.52A	*Homiliae* I.9 ['usque ad obitum ... insinuat']
PL 102.52C	*Homiliae* I.9 ['morte ... coronandam]
PL 102.53C	*Homiliae* I.9 ['Rachel ... gregem']
PL 102.53D	*Homiliae* I.9 ['Rachel ... coronandi ad Christum']
PL 102.54C	*Homiliae* I.9
PL 102.58C	*Homiliae* I.10
PL 102.59A	*Homiliae* I.10
PL 102.84D	*Homiliae* I.13
PL 102.85C	*Homiliae* I.13
PL 102.87A	*Homiliae* I.13
PL 102.151D	*Homiliae* I.21
PL 102.413D	*Homiliae* III.7
PL 102.413D	*Homiliae* III.7 ['Spinas reor ... non potest']
PL 102.40B	*Homiliae* III.83 ['Hierusalem ... fleuerit'] (attributed in some MSS to Jerome)
PL 102.379D	*In Lucae euangelium expositio* I.1 ['Plerumque justitia ... vitat']
PL 102.379B	*In Lucae euangelium expositio* I.1
PL 102.380C	*In Lucae euangelium expositio* I.1

Table I.13
Texts Correctly Attributed to Bede in (at least one manuscript of) Smaragdus's *Collectiones in Euangelia et Epistolas* (*continued*)

Citations	Source of Extract(s)
PL 102.381A	*In Lucae euangelium expositio* I.1
PL 102.384B	*In Lucae euangelium expositio* I.1
PL 102.23B	*In Lucae euangelium expositio* I.2
PL 102.24A	*In Lucae euangelium expositio* I.2 ['prospera mundi ... offerre']; cf. *Homiliae* II.11 ['prospera mundi simul et aduersa contemnere']
PL 102.24C	*In Lucae euangelium expositio* I.2
PL 102.25A	*In Lucae euangelium expositio* I.2 and *Homiliae* III.31
PL 102.26A	*In Lucae euangelium expositio* I.2 and *Homiliae* III.31
PL 102.26B	*In Lucae euangelium expositio* I.2
PL 102.49B	*In Lucae euangelium expositio* I.2
PL 102.60C	*In Lucae euangelium expositio* I.2
PL 102.61C	*In Lucae euangelium expositio* I.2
PL 102.65A	*In Lucae euangelium expositio* I.2
PL 102.65D	*In Lucae euangelium expositio* I.2
PL 102.66A	*In Lucae euangelium expositio* I.2 ['Signum ... contradicitur'] (attributed in some MSS to Jerome)
PL 102.66C	*In Lucae euangelium expositio* I.2 ['et usque hodie ... pertractat'] and *Homiliae* III.32 (attributed in some MSS to Augustine)
PL 102.66C	*In Lucae euangelium expositio* I.2 and *Homiliae* III.32
PL 102.66D	*In Lucae euangelium expositio* I.2 and *Homiliae* III.32
PL 102.67B	*In Lucae euangelium expositio* I.2 and *Homiliae* III.32
PL 102.67D	*In Lucae euangelium expositio* I.2 and *Homiliae* III.32
PL 102.78A	*In Lucae euangelium expositio* I.2
PL 102.414B	*In Lucae euangelium expositio* I.3
PL 102.525A	*In Lucae euangelium expositio* I.3 and *Homiliae* III.30
PL 102.126C	*In Lucae euangelium expositio* I.4 and *Homiliae* III.41
PL 102.126D	*In Lucae euangelium expositio* I.4 and *Homiliae* III.41
PL 102.128C	*In Lucae euangelium expositio* I.4 and *Homiliae* III.41 ['Dicens diabolus ... Graeco λατρευωντες']
PL 102.94A	*In Lucae euangelium expositio* II.5, *In Marci euangelium expositio* I.1, and *Homiliae* III.33
PL 102.94B	*In Lucae euangelium expositio* II.5, *In Marci euangelium expositio* I.1, and *Homiliae* III.33
PL 102.375A	*In Lucae euangelium expositio* II.5 and *Homiliae* III.5
PL 102.483B	*In Lucae euangelium expositio* II.5 ['Curatio paralytici ... appellant']
PL 102.368C	*In Lucae euangelium expositio* II.6

Table I.13

Texts Correctly Attributed to Bede in (at least one manuscript of) Smaragdus's *Collectiones in Euangelia et Epistolas* (*continued*)

Citations	Source of Extract(s)
PL 102.305A	*In Lucae euangelium expositio* II.6 (?)
PL 102.95B	*In Lucae euangelium expositio* II.7 and *Homiliae* III.38
PL 102.464D	*In Lucae euangelium expositio* II.7 and *Homiliae* III.15 ['Naim ciuitas ... meridiem']
PL 102.521C	*In Lucae euangelium expositio* II.7 and *Homiliae* III.26 ['Non ait ... missurus es']
PL 102.98B	*In Lucae euangelium expositio* III.8, *In Marci euangelium expositio* II.4, and *Homiliae* III.34
PL 102.99C	*In Lucae euangelium expositio* III.8, *In Marci euangelium expositio* II.4, and *Homiliae* III.34
PL 102.432B	*In Lucae euangelium expositio* III.8 and *In Marci euangelium expositio* I.3
PL 102.433A	*In Lucae euangelium expositio* III.8
PL 102.506D	*In Lucae euangelium expositio* III.8 ['Princeps itaque ... illuminatur'] (attributed in some MSS to Primas [Hugh of Orléans])
PL 102.446A	*In Lucae euangelium expositio* III.10 and *Homiliae* III.12 and III.106
PL 102.306A	*In Lucae euangelium expositio* III.11 ['Rogatus ... fonte emanant']
PL 102.136B	*In Lucae euangelium expositio* IV.*inuocatio* and *Homiliae* III.49
PL 102.136D	*In Lucae euangelium expositio* IV.*inuocatio*, *In Marci euangelium expositio* II.8, and *Homiliae* III.49
PL 102.538B	*In Lucae euangelium expositio* IV.12 and *Homiliae* III.78
PL 102.468D	*In Lucae euangelium expositio* IV.14 and *Homiliae* III.16
PL 102.532C	*In Lucae euangelium expositio* IV.14 and *Homiliae* III.76
PL 102.38D	*In Lucae euangelium expositio* V.*inuocatio*
PL 102.40D	*In Lucae euangelium expositio* V.13 and *Homiliae* III.83
PL 102.348D	*In Lucae euangelium expositio* V.16 and *Homiliae* III.1
PL 102.478C	*In Lucae euangelium expositio* V.17, *In Marci euangelium expositio* III.9, and *Homiliae* III.67
PL 102.116C	*In Lucae euangelium expositio* V.18 and *Homiliae* III.36
PL 102.398D	*In Lucae euangelium expositio* V.18
PL 102.435C	*In Lucae euangelium expositio* V.18 and *Homiliae* III.10
PL 102.421D	*In Lucae euangelium expositio* V.19 and *Homiliae* III.9, quoting Gregory, *Homiliae* II.39 (attributed in some MSS to Gregory)
PL 102.514A	*In Lucae euangelium expositio* V.19, *In Marci euangelium expositio* III.11, and *Homiliae* III.24
PL 102.540D	*In Lucae euangelium expositio* V.19 and *Homiliae* III.82 ['Homo nobilis ... ostenduntur']

Table I.13

Texts Correctly Attributed to Bede in (at least one manuscript of) Smaragdus's *Collectiones in Euangelia et Epistolas* (*continued*)

Citations	Source of Extract(s)
PL 102.473A	*In Lucae euangelium expositio* V.20
PL 102.505C	*In Lucae euangelium expositio* V.20, *In Marci euangelium expositio* III.12, and *Homiliae* III.19 ['Caesarem non ... faciens uoluntatem']
PL 102.505C	*In Lucae euangelium expositio* V.20, *In Marci euangelium expositio* III.12, and *Homiliae* III.19; cf. Pseudo-Bede, *In Matthaei euangelium expositio* III.22
PL 102.518B	*In Lucae euangelium expositio* VI.21 and *Homiliae* III.25 ['Quod uero ... exspectant euentum']
PL 102.519B	*In Lucae euangelium expositio* VI.21 and *Homiliae* III.25
PL 102.180A	*In Lucae euangelium expositio* VI.22 ['Cum uero Satanas ... confortare memento']
PL 102.181B	*In Lucae euangelium expositio* VI.22 ['In documento ... fine saeculorum']
PL 102.184C	*In Lucae euangelium expositio* VI.22, *In Marci euangelium expositio* IV.14, and *Homiliae* III.53 ['Velauerunt ... sanctorum arcana']
PL 102.185D	*In Lucae euangelium expositio* VI.23 ['Hoc est quod ... damnaret inuenit']
PL 102.188B	*In Lucae euangelium expositio* VI.23
PL 102.191B	*In Lucae euangelium expositio* VI.23
PL 102.195B	*In Lucae euangelium expositio* VI.23; cf. Pseudo-Bede, *In Matthaei euangelium expositio* IV.27
PL 102.196A	*In Lucae euangelium expositio* VI.23, *In Marci euangelium expositio* IV.15, and *Homiliae* III.53 ['Decurio uocatur ... resurgere promisisti']
PL 102.231B	*In Lucae euangelium expositio* VI.24 and *Homiliae* III.62
PL 102.238B	*In Lucae euangelium expositio* VI.24 ['Aliter namque ... esse donatum']
PL 102.240B	*In Lucae euangelium expositio* VI.24 ['Vide quomodo ... esse donatum']
PL 102.274C	*In Lucae euangelium expositio* VI.24 ['Sicut in principio ... et gratiam'] (attributed in some MSS to Augustine or to Gregory)
PL 102.280D	*In Lucae euangelium expositio* VI.24
PL 102.282B	*In Lucae euangelium expositio* VI.24 ['Quod autem dicit ... appareret']
PL 102.282C	*In Lucae euangelium expositio* VI.24
PL 102.125A	*In Marci euangelium expositio* I.1
PL 102.483D	*In Marci euangelium expositio* I.2 and *Homiliae* III.18
PL 102.484B	*In Marci euangelium expositio* I.2 and *Homiliae* III.18
PL 102.132B	*In Marci euangelium expositio* II.7
PL 102.440D	*In Marci euangelium expositio* II.7
PL 102.408A	*In Marci euangelium expositio* II.8 and *Homiliae* III.6 (attributed in some MSS to Augustine or Ambrose)
PL 102.479B	*In Marci euangelium expositio* III.9 and *Homiliae* III.67

Table I.13

Texts Correctly Attributed to Bede in (at least one manuscript of) Smaragdus's *Collectiones in Euangelia et Epistolas* (*concluded*)

Citations	Source of Extract(s)
PL 102.472A	*In Marci euangelium expositio* III.12 and *Homiliae* III.17
PL 102.175B	*In Marci euangelium expositio* IV.14 and *Homiliae* III.53 ['Mulier ista ... pauperum curam']
PL 102.176D	*In Marci euangelium expositio* IV.14 and *Homiliae* III.53 ['Multi hodie ... charitas est']; cf. Pseudo-Bede, *In Matthaei euangelium expositio* IV.26
PL 102.178A	*In Marci euangelium expositio* IV.14 and *Homiliae* III.53 ['Non ideo ... sanguine dedicatum']; cf. Pseudo-Bede, *In Matthaei euangelium expositio* IV.26
PL 102.178C	*In Marci euangelium expositio* IV.14 and *Homiliae* III.53 ['Frangit autem ... sanguine dedicatum']; cf. Pseudo-Bede, *In Matthaei euangelium expositio* IV.26
PL 102.179C	*In Marci euangelium expositio* IV.14 and *Homiliae* III.53 ['Potest autem ... conscendere debere']
PL 102.181A	*In Marci euangelium expositio* IV.14 and *Homiliae* III.53 ['Quod autem ... ipse inuocat']
PL 102.184A	*In Marci euangelium expositio* IV.14 and *Homiliae* III.53 ['Altiori autem ... castitas']
PL 102.186D	*In Marci euangelium expositio* IV.15 and *Homiliae* III.53 ['Pro regia ... martyrum gloriatur']
PL 102.190D	*In Marci euangelium expositio* IV.15 and *Homiliae* III.53 ['Etiam nolentes ... non crederetis']
PL 102.193B	*In Marci euangelium expositio* IV.15 and *Homiliae* III.53; cf. Pseudo-Bede, *In Matthaei euangelium expositio* IV.27
PL 102.196D	*In Marci euangelium expositio* IV.15 and *Homiliae* III.53; cf. Pseudo-Bede, *In Matthaei euangelium expositio* IV.27 ['De monumento ... permistus']
PL 102.225A	*In Marci euangelium expositio* IV.16 and *Homiliae* III.61 ['In euangelio ... mentis uidetur'] (attributed in one MS to Gregory the Great)
PL 102.424D	*Commentarius in Parabolas Salomonis* III.31; cf. Pseudo-Bede, *De muliere forti libellus* Aleph
PL 102.521C	*De templo Salomonis* 5 ['id est, quem prophetae uenturum praedicarunt']

1. Where Bedan extracts are not marked in PL 102 (with 'Ex Beda,' for example), I have indicated the relevant passage from Smaragdus. Note that wording may differ somewhat from the printed text of the Bedan source in question.

2. On Ælfric's (non-)use of this Pseudo-Bedan text, see Pope, *Homilies of Ælfric*, 1:168; see also Godden, *Introduction, Commentary, and Glossary*, 474.

Table I.14

Texts Falsely Attributed to Bede in (at least one manuscript of) Smaragdus' *Collectiones in Euangelia et Epistolas*

Citations	Source of Extract(s)
PL 102.44A	Alcuin, *In Iohannis euangelium* 7.46
PL 102.46D	Alcuin, *In Iohannis euangelium* 7.46 ['Hic manifeste ... quae promisit']
PL 102.138B	Augustine, *Epistulae* 217.3
PL 102.339C	Pseudo-Bede, *In Ioannis euangelium expositio* 3 ['Princeps scilicet ... ostendere saluatorem']
PL 102.301C	Pseudo-Bede, *In Ioannis euangelium expositio* 16
PL 102.281D	Pseudo-Bede, *In Ioannis euangelium expositio* 20
PL 102.193A	Pseudo-Bede, *In Matthaei euangelium expositio* IV.27
PL 102.24A	Pseudo-Bede, *De Psalmorum libro exegesis* 80 ['Ioseph ... interpretatur']
PL 102.135B	Jerome, *Commentariorum in epistolam ad Ephesios libri tres* III.5.8 ['Eratis enim aliquando ... rerumque cognoscit']
PL 102.193C	Jerome, *De quaestionibus xii* 8.2 ['Quaerendum est ... scire non possumus'] (attributed in some MSS to Jerome)
PL 102.474C	Jerome, *Commentariorum in euangelium Matthaei* V.23.6 ['arguuntur ... magister dicitur']
PL 102.478C	Jerome, *Commentariorum in euangelium Matthaei* III.18.6 and Cassian, *De institutis coenobiorum* IX.8 ['Nota quod ... non recipiunt']

Source Unidentified (original to Smaragdus [?])[1]

PL 102.21B	PL 102.37D ['Videte ... a te suscipiatur']
PL 102.39B	PL 102.47D ['In hoc istarum ... elegit nos']
PL 102.235D	PL 102.50C ['redempti pretioso ... corpore uestro']
PL 102.332A	PL 102.104D ['Id est, illos ... exhauriunt']
PL 102.510D	PL 102.241B ['Notandum quod ... provocat uerbum']

1. Godden notes, however, that Smaragdus 'scarcely wrote a line in his exegetic collection that was not taken verbatim from another source' (*Introduction, Commentary, and Glossary*, xxxix).

APPENDIX II

Bede's *Homiliae* – Editions and Parallels
to *In Lucae* and *In Marci euangelium expositio*

Table II.1
Bede's *Homiliae*, Book I

Pericope	Occasion	Hurst	CcsI 122	Migne	PL 94	*In Lucam* / *In Marcum* (CCSL·120)
Mark 1.4–8	*In Aduentu*	I.1	1–6	I.3	22–6	I.1.7–19 = *Luc.* I.2223–32; *Marc.* I.126–35; I.1.85–112 = *Marc.* I.162–71; I.1.127–43 = *Luc.* I.2407–76; *Marc.* I.174–93 and I.2407–28
John 1.15–18	*In Aduentu*	I.2	7–13	I.4	26–31	
Luke 1.26–38	*In Aduentu*	I.3	14–20	I.1	9–14	
Luke 1.39–55	*In Aduentu*	I.4	21–31	I.2	15–22	I.4.208–29 = *Luc.* II.2272–6, III.542–6, IV.254–60
Matt. 1.18–25	*In uigilia natiuitatis domini*	I.5	32–6	I.5	31–4	I.5.103–34 = *Luc.* I.1177–99
Luke 2.1–14	*In natiuitate domini ad primam missam*	I.6	37–45	III.31	334–9	I.6.220–4 = *Luc.* I.1270–4
Luke 2.15–20	*In nat. domini ad secundam missam*	I.7	46–51	I.6	34–8	I.7.134–54 = *Luc.* I.1417–31; I.7.147–9 = *Luc.* I.1234–7
John 1.1–14	*In nat. domini ad tertiam missam*	I.8	52–9	I.7	38–44	
John 21.19–24	*Sancti Iohannis Euangelistae*	I.9	60–7	I.8	44–9	I.125.130– = *Marc.* III.915–23
Matt. 2.13–23	*Sanctorum Innocentium*	I.10	68–72	I.9	50–3	
Luke 2.21	*In octaua natiuitatis domini*	I.11	73–9	I.10	53–8	I.11.40–221 = *Luc.* I.1464–1640
Matt. 3.13–17	*In Theophania seu Epiphania domini*	I.12	80–7	I.11	58–63	I.12.80–106 = *Marc.* I.252–61; I.12.117–29 = *Marc.* I.272–9; I.12.135–8 = *Marc.* I.225–31; I.12.219–21 = *Luc.* I.1779–94

Table II.1
Bede's Homiliae, Book I (concluded)

Pericope	Occasion	Hurst	CCSL 122	Migne	PL 94	In Lucam / In Marcum (CCSL 120)
Matt. 19.27–9	Sancti Benedicti episcopi	I.13; cf. I.20	88–94	II.17	224–8	
John 2.1–11	Post Epiphaniam	I.14	95–104	I.13	68–74	
John 1.29–34	Post Epiphaniam	I.15	105–10	I.14	74–9	
John 1.35–42	Post Epiphaniam	I.16	111–18	II.23	256–61	
John 1.43–51	Post Epiphaniam	I.17	119–27	I.17 and II.24	89–95, 261–8	
Luke 2.22–35	In purificatione sancti Mariae	I.18	128–33	I.15	79–83	I.18.58–80 = Luc. I.1779–94 I.18.173–96 = Luc. I.1745–76
Luke 2.42–52	Post Epiphaniam	I.19	134–40	I.12	63–8	
Matt. 16.13–19	In cathedra sancti Petri	I.20; cf. I.13	141–7	II.16 and II.17 (part)	219–22, 225–6	
Matt. 9.9–13	In Quadragesima	I.21	148–55	II.22	249–56	I.21.1 = Marc. I.800
Matt. 15.21–8	In Quadragesima	I.22	156–60	I.19	102–5	
John 5.1–18	In Quadragesima	I.23	161–9	I.16	83–9	I.23.81–100 = Luc. II.863–76; Marc. I.774–85 and I.1864–7 I.23.156–201 = Marc. I.731–65
Matt. 16.27–17.9	In Quadragesima	I.24	170–7	I.18	96–101	I.24.82–259 = Luc. III.1491–1637; Marc. III.6–155
John 8.1–12	In Quadragesima	I.25 cf. II.2	178–83	I.20	106–10	

Table II.2
Bede's *Homiliae*, Book II

Pericope	Occasion	Hurst	CCSL 122	Migne	PL 94	In Lucam / In Marcum (CCSL 120)
John 2.12–22	*In Quadragesima*	II.1	184–92	I.22	114–20	II.1.4–21 = *Marc.* II.529–37; II.1.34–141 = *Marc.* III.1430–56
John 6.1–14	*In Quadragesima*	II.2	193–9	I.21	110–14	I.2.112–201 = *Luc.* III.1295–1353; *Marc.* II.938–1011
Matt. 21.1–9	*Dominica in Palmis*	II.3	200–6	I.23	121–5	II.3.131–40 = *Marc.* III.1225–37
John 11.55–12.11	*Maioris Hebdomadae*	II.4	207–13	I.24	125–9	
John 13.1–17	*In caena domini*	II.5	214–19	I.25	130–4	
Mark 7.31–7	*Sabbato sancto*	II.6; cf. III.11	220–4	II.19	234–7	II.6.220–4 = *Marc.* II.1434–1511
Matt. 28.1–10	*Sabbato sancto*	II.7	225–32	II.1	133–9	
Matt. 28.16–20	*Dominica Resurrectionis*	II.8	233–8	II.3	144–9	
Luke 24.36–47	*Post Pascha*	II.9	239–45	II.2	139–44	II.9.102–89 = *Luc.* VI.2250–2306
Luke 24.1–9	*Post Pascha*	II.10	246–52	II.4	149–54	II.10.24–36 = *Luc.* VI.1903–9; II.10.184–97 = *Marc.* IV.1680–90
John 16.5–15	*Post Pascha*	II.11	253–9	II.6	158–63	
John 16.23–30	*Post Pascha*	II.12	163–266	II.7	163–8	
John 16.16–22	*Post Pascha*	II.13	267–71	II.5	154–8	
Luke 11.9–13	*In litaniis maioribus*	II.14	272–9	II.8	168–74	
Luke 24.44–53	*In Ascensione domini*	II.15	280–9	II.9	174–81	
John 15.26–16.4	*Post Ascensionem domini*	II.16	290–300	II.10	181–9	

Table II.2
Bede's *Homiliae*, Book II (*concluded*)

Pericope	Occasion	Hurst	CCSL 122	Migne	PL 94	*In Lucam / In Marcum* (CCSL 120)
John 14.15–21	Dominica Pentecostes	II.17	301–10	II.11	189–97	
John 3.1–16	Octaua Pentecostes	II.18	311–17	II.12	197–202	
Luke 1.5–17	In uigilia natiuitatis sancti Iohannis Baptistae	II.19	318–27	II.13	202–10	II.19.17–334 = *Luc.* I.75–305
Luke 1.57–68	In natiuitate sancti Iohannis Baptistae	II.20	328–34	II.14	210–14	II.20.18–29 = *Luc.* I.239–43 II.20.61–73 = *Marc.* II.791–807 II.20.61–78 = *Luc.* III.1225–32
Matt. 20.20–3	Sanctorum Iohannis et Pauli	II.21	335–41	II.18	228–33	II.21.28–216 = *Marc.* III.895–939
John 21.15–19	Sanctorum Petri et Pauli	II.22	342–8	II.15	214–19	
Matt. 14.1–12	In decollatione sancti Iohannis Baptistae	II.23	348–57	II.20	237–43	II.23.32–68 = *Marc.* II.729–43 II.23.37–41 = *Luc.* I.283–84 II.23.48–59 = *Luc.* I.2172–9 II.23.189–208 = *Luc.* III.1225–32 II.23.224–8 = *Marc.* II.809–11
John 10.22–30	In dedicatione ecclesiae	II.24	358–67	II.21	243–50	
Luke 6.43–8	In dedicatione ecclesiae	II.25	368–78	III.65	433–9	

Table II.3
Bede's *Homiliae*, Book III [PL 94.264–516]

Pericope	Occasion	Homiliae	PL 94	In Lucam / In Marcum	PL 92 (columns)	CCSL 120 (pages.lines)	Duplication and Authorship
Luke 6.19–31	*Dom. I post Trinitatem*	III.1	267–72	*Luc.* V.16.19–31	533C–538B	302.241–307.460	
Luke 14.16–24	*Dom. II post Trinitatem*	III.2	272–4	*Luc.* IV.14.16–24	514A–516C	278.1901–281.2023	
Luke 15.1–10	*Dom. III post Trinitatem*	III.3	274–6	*Luc.* IV.15.1–10	519C–522A	284.2163–287.2276	
Luke 6.37–42	*Dom. IV post Trinitatem*	III.4	276–8	*Luc.* II.6.37–42	408C–410C	146.1826–149.1932	
Luke 5.1–11	*Dom. V post Trinitatem*	III.5	278–80	*Luc.* II.5.1–11	381D–384B	113.518–116.650	*Luc.* II.642–50 = *Marc.* I.372–82
Mark 8.1–9	*Dom. VII post Trinitatem*	III.6	280–3	*Marc.* II.8.1–9	205B–208C	527.1512–531.1680	*Marc.* II.1595–1626 = *Luc.* III.504–35
Luke 6.43–6	*Dom. VIII post Trinitatem*	III.7	283–4	*Luc.* II.6.43–6	410C–412B	149.1933–151.2017	
Luke 16.1–12	*Dom. IX post Trinitatem*	III.8	284–6	*Luc.* V.16.1–12	529B–531D	296.29–299.153	
Luke 19.41–8	*Dom. X post Trinitatem*	III.9	286–9	*Luc.* V.19.41–8	570C–574A	346.2021–350.2194	*Luc.* V.2065–70 = *Marc.* III.1481–6; *Luc.* V.2143–50 = *Marc.* III.1486–1493 [see *Homiliae* III.43]
Luke 18.9–14	*Dom. XI post Trinitatem*	III.10	289–90	*Luc.* V.18.9–14	551D–553B	323.1118–325.1192	
Mark 7.31–7	*Dom. XII post Trinitatem*	III.11	290–3	*Hom.* II.6	CCSL 122. 220–224		

Table II.3
Bede's *Homiliae*, Book III [PL 94.264–516] *(continued)*

Pericope	Occasion	Homiliae	PL 94	In Lucam / In Marcum	PL 92 (columns)	CCSL 120 (pages.lines)	Duplication and Authorship
Luke 10.23–37	*Dom. XIII post Trinitatem*	III.12 [= III.106]	293–6	*Luc.* III.10.23–37	467B–470D	221.2152–225.2310	
Luke 17.11–19	*Dom. XIV post Trinitatem*	III.13	296–8	*Luc.* V.17.11–19	542B–544D	312.657–315.777	
Luke 16.13–15	*Dom. XV post Trinitatem*	III.14	298	*Luc.* V.16.13–15	531D–532C	299.154–300.193	
Luke 7.11–16	*Dom. XVI post Trinitatem*	III.15	299–300	*Luc.* II.7.11–16	417B–419A	157.2260–159.2339	*Luc.* II.2267–71 = *Marc.* II.468–74
Luke 14.1–15	*Dom. XVII post Trinitatem*	III.16	300–2	*Luc.* IV.14.1–15	510D–514A	274.1741–278.1896	
Mark 12.13–37	*Dom. XVIII post Trinitatem*	III.17	302–4	*Marc.* III.12.18–37	254A–257A	588.1823–592.1967	*Marc.* III.1944–67 = *Luc.* V.2574–95
Mark 2.1–12	*Dom. XIX post Trinitatem*	III.18	304–7	*Marc.* I.2.1–12 *Marc.* I.660–84 = *Luc.* II.790–812; *Marc.* I.686–700 = *Luc.* II.814–26; *Marc.* I.703–15 = *Luc.* II.829–41;	146A–149C	452.613–457.792	*Marc.* I.646–58 = *Luc.* II.775–88; *Marc.* I.719–27 = *Luc.* II.845–53; *Marc.* I.768–92 = *Luc.* II.855–82
Luke 20.20–6	*Dom. XXIII post Trinitatem*	III.19	307–8	*Luc.* V.20.20–26	578D–579D	356.2417–357.2476	*Luc.* V.2201–2565 = *Marc.* III.1567–1889
Mark 5.21–43	*Dom. XXIV post Trinitatem*	III.20	308–12	*Marc.* II.5.22–43 *Marc.* II.380–404 = *Luc.* III.982–1005; *Marc.* II.415–30 = *Luc.* III.1021–33;	179B–184C	495.261–501.509	*Marc.* II.262–366 = *Luc.* III.866–971; *Marc.* II.437–40, 445–8 = *Luc.* III.1037–42; *Marc.* II.450–509 = *Luc.* III.1044–1101

Table II.3
Bede's *Homiliae*, Book III [PL 94.264–516] *(continued)*

Pericope	Occasion	Homiliae	PL 94	In Lucam / In Marcum	PL 92 (columns)	CCSL 120 (pages.lines)	Duplication and Authorship
Mark 9.13–49	*In Septembris feria IV quatuor temporum*	III.21	312–14	*Marc.* III.9.14–29	220D–223D	546.191–550.344[1]	*Marc.* III.206–54 = *Luc.* III.1641–85; *Marc.* III.300–4 = *Luc.* III.1687–90
Luke 18.1–8	*In feria VI quatuor temporum*	III.22	314–15	*Luc.* V.18.1–8	550C–551D	322.1047–323.1117	
Luke 13.6–17	*In Septembri sabbato quatuor temporum*	III.23	315–18	*Luc.* IV.13.6–17	503C–506C	265.1379–269.1532	*Luc.* IV.1400–6 = *Marc.* III.1400–9
Luke 19.29–38	*Dom. I Aduentus*	III.24	318–20	*Luc.* V.19.29–38	566D–570A	342.1839–346.1998	*Luc.* V.1842–1922 = *Marc.* III.1127–1205; *Luc.* V.1904–13 = *Marc.* II.1290–3 [see *Homiliae* III.52]; *Luc.* V.1924–41 = *Marc.* III.1206–22
Luke 21.25–33	*Dom. II Aduentus*	III.25	320–2	*Luc.* VI.21.25–33	588D–591B	368.225–371.344	*Luc.* VI.237–70 = *Marc.* IV.211–35
Luke 7.19–27	*Dom. III Aduentus*	III.26	322–4	*Luc.* II.7.19–27	419A–421A	160.2351–162.2434	*Luc.* II.2412–15 = *Marc.* I.159–62
Luke 1.26–38	*In feria IV quatuor temporum*	III.27	324–7	*Luc.* I.1.26–38	315D–320A	30.425–35.631	
Luke 1.39–55	*In feria VI quat-uor temporum*	III.28	327–30	*Luc.* I.1.38–55	320A–323B	35.632–39.795	
Luke 3.1–6	*In sabbato quat-uor temporum*	III.29	330–2	*Luc.* I.3.1–6	351A–353A	74.2169–77.2276	*Luc.* I.2222–32 = *Marc.* I.125–35

Table II.3
Bede's *Homiliae*, Book III [PL 94.264–516] (*continued*)

Pericope	Occasion	Homiliae	PL 94	In Lucam / In Marcum	PL 92 (columns)	CCSL 120 (pages.lines)	Duplication and Authorship
Luke 3.15–18	*Dom. IV Aduentus*	III.30	332–4	*Luc.* I.3.15–18	355B–357C	79.2387–82.2509	*Luc.* I.2407–28 = *Marc.* I.174–93
Luke 2.1–14	*In Galli cantu natalis domini*	III.31	334–9	*Hom.* I.6	CCSL 122.37–45		
Luke 2.33–41	*Dom. infra octauam nat. dom.*	III.32	339–41	*Luc.* I.2.33–41	345D–348C	67.1904–71.2051	
Luke 5.12–16	*Dom. III post Epiphaniam*	III.33	342–3	*Luc.* II.5.12–15	384C–386B	116.651–118.741	*Luc.* II.656–85= *Marc.* I.524–54;
				Luc. II.686–97= *Marc.* I.558–68; *Luc.* II.697–717= *Marc.* I.568–89; *Luc.* II.720–41= *Marc.* I.592–612 *Luc.* V.1378–82 = *Marc.* III.883–6;	*Luc.* V.1389–92 = *Marc.* III.887–90; *Luc.* V.1420–7 = *Marc.* III.985–90; *Luc.* V.1453–4 = *Marc.* III.1069–70; *Luc.* V.1459–81 = *Marc.* III.1094–1115		
Luke 8.22–6	*Dom. IV post Epiphaniam*	III.34	343–5	*Luc.* III.8.22–5	434C–436D	180.547–192.661	*Luc.* III.549–58= *Marc.* II.3–12; *Luc.* III.563–627= *Marc.* II.28–91
Luke 8.4–15	*Dom. sexagesimae*	III.35	345–7	*Luc.* III.8.4–15	429D–432D	173.307–177.450	*Luc.* III.323–33= *Marc.* I.1704–16;
				Luc. III.358–60= *Marc.* I.1748–51; *Luc.* III.384–404= *Marc.* I.1776–89; *Luc.* III.410–13= *Marc.* I.1818–21;	*Luc.* III.422–5= *Marc.* I.1828–32; *Luc.* III.447–50= *Marc.* I.1833–9		
Luke 18.31–43	*Dom. quinquagesimae*	III.36	347–9	*Luc.* V.18.31–43	557A–559C	330.1374–333.1494	
Luke 12.33–4	*In die cinerum*	III.37	349–50	*Luc.* IV.12.33–4	494D–495B	255.959–86	

Table II.3
Bede's *Homiliae*, Book III [PL 94.264–516] *(continued)*

Pericope	Occasion	Homiliae	PL 94	In Lucam / In Marcum	PL 92 (columns)	CCSL 120 (pages.lines)	Duplication and Authorship
Luke 7.1–10	*In feria V post diem cinerum*	III.38	350–2	*Luc.* II.7.1–10	414B–417B	153.2113–157.2263	*Luc.* II.2250–2 = *Marc.* I.1839–42
Luke 6.27–34	*In feria VI post diem cinerum*	III.39	352–4	*Luc.* II.6.27–34	404D–407C	142.1651–145.1784	
Mark 6.47–56	*Sabbato post cinerum diem*	III.40	354–6	*Marc.* II.6.47–56	196B–198C	516.1081–519.1194	
Luke 4.1–13	*Dom. I quadragesimae*	III.41	356–60	*Luc.* I.4.1–13	366A–372A	93.2914–99.3169	*Luc.* I.2921–7 = *Marc.* I.284–90
Matt. 21.10–17	*In feria III primae hebdomadis quadragesimae*	III.42	360–3	*Incipit:* 'Dominus et Deus, auctor et reparator ...'			Not by Bede
Mark 11.15–17	*In eadem feria*	III.43	363–4	*Marc.* III.11.15–19	245D–247B	578.1416–580.1493	*Marc.* III.1481–6 = *Luc.* V.2065–70; *Marc.* III.1486–93 = *Luc.* V.2143–50 [see *Homiliae* III.9]
Matt. 12.39–50	*In feria IV primae hebdomadis quadragesimae*	III.44	364–8	*Incipit:* 'Narratur in superioribus quomodo ...'			Not by Bede
Luke 9.28–36	*In sabbato I hebdomadis quadragesimae*	III.45	369–71	*Luc.* III.9.28–	453D–456D	204.1490–205.1521[2]	*Luc.* III.1411–1637 = *Marc.* II.1961–III.155
Luke 20.45–7	*In feria III post dom. reminiscere*	III.46	371–2	*Luc.* V.20.45–7	582B–583A	360.2596–361.2632	*Luc.* V.2574–672 = *Marc.* III.1944–2061

Table II.3
Bede's *Homiliae*, Book III [PL 94.264–516] (*continued*)

Pericope	Occasion	Homiliae	PL 94	In Lucam / In Marcum	PL 92 (columns)	CCSL 120 (pages.lines)	Duplication and Authorship
Luke 20.9–19	*In feria VI post dom. reminiscere*	III.47	372–5	*Luc.* V.20.9–19	575A–578D	351.2236–356.2416	*Luc.* V.2201–2565 = *Marc.* III.1567–1889
Luke 15.11–32	*In sabbato post dom. reminiscere* [cf. III.107]	III.48	375–80	*Luc.* IV.15.11–32	522A–528C	287.2277–295.2583	
Luke 11.15–26	*Dom. III quadragesimae* [cf. III.109]	III.49	380–2	*Luc.* IV.11.14–26	475D–479C	231.31–236.212	*Luc.* IV.44–54 = *Marc.* I.1482–92;
				Luc. IV.55–62 = *Marc.* II.1687–96; *Luc.* IV.77–83 = *Marc.* I.1508–15; *Luc.* IV.104–10 = *Marc.* II.1447–55;		*Luc.* IV.118–21 = *Marc.* I.1517–21; *Luc.* IV.127–9 = *Marc.* I.1531–3	
Luke 4.23–30	*In feria II post dom. oculi*	III.50	383–6	*Luc.* II.4.22–30	375A–378D	104.193–109.374	*Luc.* II.193–257 = *Marc.* II.515–61
Luke 17.4–10	*In feria III post dom. oculi*	III.51	386	*Luc.* V.17.3–4	539A–539D	308.497–309.541	
Mark 7.1–23	*In feria IV post dom. oculi*	III.52	387–9	*Marc.* II.7.1–23	198C–201C	519.1195–523.1339	*Marc.* II.1290–93 = *Luc.* V.1904–13 [see *Homiliae* III.24]
Mark 14–15	*In feria III post dom. palmarum*	III.53	389–410	*Marc.* IV.14.1–15.47	266D–294C	604.367–639.1705	*Marc.* IV.367–410 = *Luc.* VI.403–41;
	Marc. IV.518–79 = *Luc.* VI.453–525; *Marc.* IV.621–32 = *Luc.* VI.595–605; *Marc.* IV.651–70 = *Luc.* VI.622–50; *Marc.* IV.582–7 = *Luc.* VI.653–8; *Marc.* IV.605–15 = *Luc.* VI.659–68; *Marc.* IV.589–92 = *Luc.* VI.675–8; *Marc.* IV.868–76 = *Luc.* VI.888–96;			*Marc.* IV.919–22 = *Luc.* VI.978–81; *Marc.* IV.925–8 = *Luc.* VI.995–8; *Marc.* IV.937–42 = *Luc.* VI.1067–72; *Marc.* IV.999–1027 = *Luc.* VI.1076–1104; *Marc.* IV.1126–31 = *Luc.* VI.1106–11; *Marc.* IV.1139–71 = *Luc.* VI.1125–52; *Marc.* IV.1173–9 = *Luc.* VI.1161–6;			*Marc.* IV.1101–21 = *Luc.* VI.1168–83; *Marc.* IV.1066–76 = *Luc.* VI.1212–20; *Marc.* IV.1206–13 = *Luc.* VI.1377–85; *Marc.* IV.1315–35 = *Luc.* VI.1436–55; *Marc.* IV.1337–43 = *Luc.* VI.1526–33; *Marc.* IV.1385–98 = *Luc.* VI.1546–68; *Marc.* IV.1443–57 = *Luc.* VI.1569–82;

Table II.3
Bede's *Homiliae*, Book III [PL 94.264–516] *(continued)*

Pericope	Occasion	*Homiliae*	PL 94	*In Lucam* / *In Marcum*	PL 92 (columns)	CCSL 120 (pages.lines)	Duplication and Authorship
							Marc. IV.1361–76 = *Luc.* VI.1601–16; *Marc.* IV.1460–2 = *Luc.* VI.1618–21; *Marc.* IV.1558–9 = *Luc.* VI.1629–31; *Marc.* IV.1436–41 = *Luc.* VI.1641–7; *Marc.* IV.1468–77 = *Luc.* VI.1663–76; *Marc.* IV.1506–21 = *Luc.* VI.1717–32; *Marc.* IV.1586–93 = *Luc.* VI.1737–44; *Marc.* IV.1601–5 = *Luc.* VI.1763–6; *Marc.* IV.1631–4 = *Luc.* VI.1788–93; *Marc.* IV.1659–73 = *Luc.* VI.1794–1806; *Marc.* IV.1635–56 = *Luc.* VI.1824–47; *Marc.* IV.1674–8 = *Luc.* VI.1896–1903; *Marc.* IV.1694–1720 = *Luc.* VI.1854–76
Matt. 8.23-7		III.54	411–13	*Incipit:* 'Ingrediente domino in nauiculam ...'			Possibly by Pseudo-Origen?; see CCSL 122.382 n. 26
Matt. 1.1–16	*In natali diuae Mariae uirginis*	III.55	413–19	*Incipit:* 'Beatus Matthaeus euangelista, dilectissimi ...'			Not by Bede (PL 92.413–418D = Pseudo-Alcuin, *Interpretatione nominum* [PL 100.725–33])
Luke 5.27–32	*In uigiliis diui Matthaei apostoli*	III.56	419–20	*Luc.* II.5.26-32	389A–390B	122.883–124.951	*Luc.* II.884–904= *Marc.* I.810–35;
Luke 10.38–42	*In die assumptionis Mariae*	III.57	420–1	*Luc.* II.905–14= *Luc.* II.925–30= *Luc.* III.10.38-42	*Marc.* I.840–50; *Marc.* I.863–70; 470D–472A	*Luc.* II.933–42= *Luc.* II.945–51= 225.2311–226.2378	*Marc.* I.873–82; *Marc.* I.855–60
Luke 11.27–8	*In commemoratione diuinae uirginis Mariae*	III.58	421–2	*Luc.* IV.11.27	479C–480C	236.213–237.263[3]	*Luc.* IV.254–60 = *Marc.* I.1637–9

Table II.3
Bede's *Homiliae*, Book III [PL 94.264–516] *(continued)*

Pericope	Occasion	Homiliae	PL 94	*In Lucam / In Marcum*	PL 92 (columns)	CCSL 120 (pages.lines)	Duplication and Authorship
	De sancta Maria uirgine	III.59	422–3	*Incipit:* 'Hodie, fratres carissimi, celebramus festiuitatem sanctae Mariae ...'			Not by Bede
Luke 22.24–30	*In natale diui Bartholomaei apostoli*	III.60	423–5	*Luc.* VI.22.24–30	598A–600A	380.681–382.782	
Mark 16.1–7	*In Die sancto Paschae*	III.61	425–7	*Marc.* IV.16.1–7	294C–297A	639.1706–642.1827	*Marc.* IV.1694–1720 = *Luc.* VI.1854–76; *Marc.* IV.1722–47 = *Luc.* VI.1886–1915
Luke 24.13–35	*In feria II Paschae*	III.62	427–9	*Luc.* VI.24.13–35	625B–628C	413.2011–417.2167	
Mark 16.14–20	*In die ascensionis domini*	III.63	429–32	*Marc.* IV.16.14–20	298D–302C	644.1918–648.2077	
Mark 10.35–45	*In festo diui Ioannis euangelistae ante portam latinam*	III.64	432–3	*Marc.* III.10.35–45	235A–236B	564.891–566.962	
Luke 6.43–8	*In dedicatione ecclesiae*	III.65	433–9	*Hom.* II.25	CCSL 122.368–78		
Luke 19.2–10	*In dedicatione ecclesiae*	III.66	439–41	*Luc.* V.19.1–10	559D–562B	333.1495–336.1620	

Table II.3
Bede's *Homiliae*, Book III [PL 94.264–516] *(continued)*

Pericope	Occasion	Homiliae	PL 94	In Lucam / In Marcum	PL 92 (columns)	CCSL 120 (pages.lines)	Duplication and Authorship
Mark 9.34–47	In festo diui Michaelis	III.67	441–3	Marc. III.9.35–48	224C–225A, 226A–227C	551.373–552.398, 553.443–555.518	Marc. III.353–422 = Luc. III.1703–68; Marc. III.453–69 = Luc. V.480–96
Luke 10.1–20	In festo sancti Lucae	III.68	443–7	Luc. III.10.1–20	461C–466B	213.1871–219.2103	Marc. III.1922–6= Marc. II.604–8; Luc. III.1930–7 = Marc. II.659–67
Luke 6.17–23	In solemnitate omnium sanctorum	III.69	447–50	Luc. II.6.17–23	399D–403D	136.1415–141.1600	
	In eodem solem-nitate omnium sanctorum	III.70	450–2	Incipit: 'Hodie, dilec-tissimi, omnium sanctorum ...'.			Possibly spurious? See *CPL* §1369 and cf. PL 39.2135, PL 90.33, and PL 112.1319
	In eodem solem-nitate omnium sanctorum	III.71	452–5	Incipit: 'Legimus in ecclesiasticis historiis ...'.			Possibly by Ambro-sius Autpertus?; see CCSL 122.383 n. 32.
Luke 9.1–6	In Die sancto unius apostoli	III.72	455–7	Luc. III.9.1–6	445D–447D	194.1102–196.1198	Luc. III.1106–13 = Marc. I.1299–1307; Luc. III.1116–58 = Marc. II.608–53; Luc. III.1158–62 = Marc. II.653–7; Luc. III.1164–76 = Marc. II.671–82; Luc. III.1187–92 = Marc. II.685–90
Luke 12.1–10	In festo martyrum	III.73	457–60	Luc. IV.12.1–10	487B–490D	245.594–250.765	Luc. IV.595–8 = Marc. II.1758–61; Luc. IV.713–29 = Marc. I.1549–65

Table II.3
Bede's *Homiliae*, Book III [PL 94.264–516] (*continued*)

Pericope	Occasion	Homiliae	PL 94	*In Lucam / In Marcum*	PL 92 (columns)	CCSL 120 (pages.lines)	Duplication and Authorship
Luke 21.9–19	*In festo martyrum*	III.74	460–1	*Luc.* VI.21.9–19	585D–587D	365.82–367.1:73	*Luc.* VI.54–100 = *Marc.* III.13–76
Luke 9.23–7	*In festo unius martyris*	III.75	461–3	*Luc.* III.9.23–7	452A–453D	202.1408–204.1489	*Luc.* III.1411–1637= *Marc.* II.1961–III.155
Luke 14.26–33	*In festo unius martyris*	III.76	463–4	*Luc.* IV.14.25–33	516D–518D	281.2024–284.2129	
Luke 11.33–6	*In festo confessorum prima*	III.77	465	*Luc.* IV.11.33–6	481D–482D	239.321–240.371	
Luke 12.35–48	*In festo confessorum secunda*	III.78	465–9	*Luc.* IV.12.35–48	495B–499C	255.987–261.1187	
Luke 18.24–30	*In festo confessorum tertia*	III.79	469–70	*Luc.* V.18.25–30	555B–557A	328.1283–330.1373[4]	*Luc.* V.1197–1373 = *Marc.* III.672–856
Mark 13.33–7	*In festo confessorum quarta*	III.80	470–1	*Marc.* IV.13.33–7	265D–266C	603.331–604.366	
Mark 1.16–21	*In die festo sancti Andreae*	III.81	471	*Marc.* I.1.16–17	140D–141B	446.355–382	
Luke 19.11–27	*In die festo sancti Nicolai*	III.82	471–5	*Luc.* V.19.11–27	562C–566D	336.1629–341.1833	
Luke 13.34–5	*In die festo sancti Stephani protomartyris*	III.83	475	*Luc.* IV.13.34–5	510A–510D	273.1704–274.1740	
Mark 8.27–33	*In die festo sancti cathedrae sancti Petri*	III.84	475–7	*Marc.* II.8.27–33	212C–214B	536.1863–538.1949	*Marc.* II.1876–1905 = *Luc.* III.1367–93; *Marc.* II.1908–14 = *Luc.* III.1395–1402

Bede's *Homiliae*

Table II.3
Bede's *Homiliae*, Book III [PL 94.264–516] (*continued*)

Pericope	Occasion	Homiliae	PL 94	In Lucam / In Marcum	PL 92 (columns)	CCSL 120 (pages.lines)	Duplication and Authorship
	In die festo sancti Wigberthi	III.85	477–9	*Incipit*: 'Laudate et exultate in domino, dilectissimi ...'			Not by Bede
	In die festo sancti Wigberthi secunda	III.86	479–80	*Incipit*: 'Restat igitur adhuc aliquid de beato Wigbertho ...'			Not by Bede
Matt. 13.44–7	*In die festo sanctae scholasticae uirginis*	III.87	480–9	*Incipit*: 'Lectio sancti euangelii, fratres carissimi, quam modo uestra caritas audiuit ...'			Possibly by Bertarius of Monte Cassino?; see CCSL 122.383 n. 36.
	De Simone et Iuda	III.88	489–90	*Incipit*: 'Simon et Iudas apostoli ...'			Not by Bede (*Homiliae* 88–103 perhaps by the author of 85–6?; see CCSL 122.383 n. 37)
	De sancto Bartholomaeo	III.89	490	*Incipit*: 'Ezechiel propheta uidit quondam arborem ...'			Not by Bede
	De sancto Laurentio	III.90	490–1	*Incipit*: 'Cum uenisset beatus Bartholomaeus ...'			Not by Bede
		III.91	491–4	*Incipit*: 'Venite, filii, audite me ...'			Not by Bede

Table II.3
Bede's *Homiliae*, Book III [PL 94.264–516] (*continued*)

Pericope	Occasion	Homiliae	PL 94	In Lucam / In Marcum	PL 92 (columns)	CCSL 120 (pages.lines)	Duplication and Authorship
	De sancto Ioanne Euangelista	III.92	494	*Incipit*: 'Hodie, fratres carissimi, celebramus festum sancti Iohannis euangelistae ...'			Not by Bede
	De inuentione sanctae crucis	III.93	494–5	*Incipit*: 'Quomodo inuenta fuit sancta crux ...'			Not by Bede
	De sancto Petro et Paulo	III.94	495–8	*Incipit*: 'Felix per omnes festum mundi cardines apostolorum Petri et Pauli ...'			Not by Bede
	De natiuitate Domini	III.95	498	*Incipit*: 'Apparuit benignitas et humanitas ...'			Not by Bede
	De uinculis sancti Petri	III.96	498–9	*Incipit*: 'Notandum est, fratres carissimi, qua de causa celebretur festiuitas S. Petri a uinculis ...'			Not by Bede
	De maiori litania	III.97	499	*Incipit*: 'Fratres carissimi, dignum est ut audiatis qua de causa litaniae rogationum fuerant inuentae ...'			Not by Bede

Table II.3
Bede's *Homiliae*, Book III [PL 94.264–516] *(continued)*

Pericope	Occasion	Homiliae	PL 94	In Lucam / In Marcum	PL 92 (columns)	CCSL 120 (pages.lines)	Duplication and Authorship
	Ad populum	III.98	499–500	*Incipit:* 'Homo natus de muliere ...'			Not by Bede
	In die cinerum	III.99	500–1	*Incipit:* 'Hodie, fratres carissimi, in pugnam ...'			Not by Bede
		III.100	501–2	*Incipit:* 'Dies dominicus dies electus est ...'			Not by Bede
	In reuelatione sancti Michaelis	III.101	502–3	*Incipit:* 'Deus uolens angelos honorari ...'			
	Ad quamlibet diem	III.102	503–4	*Incipit:* 'Pius et misericors dominus ...'			
	Ad quamlibet diem	III.103	504–5	*Incipit:* 'Fratres carissimi, tempus est transeundi ...'			
	Ad quamlibet diem	III.104	505–7	*Incipit:* 'Misericordia et ueritas ...'			
	In die palmarum	III.105	507	*Incipit:* 'Cum appropinquasset Iesus ....'			
Luke 10.23–37	*Dom. XIII post trinitatem*	III.106 [= III.12]	507–10	*Luc.* III.10.23–37	467B–470D	221.2152–225.2310	

Table II.3
Bede's *Homiliae*, Book III [PL 94.264–516] *(concluded)*

Pericope	Occasion	*Homiliae*	PL 94	*In Lucam / In Marcum*	PL 92 (columns)	CCSL 120 (pages.lines)	Duplication and Authorship
Luke 15.11–32		III.107 [cf. III.48]	510–12	*Incipit:* 'Euang. lect., fratres carissimi, audistis duorum filiorum parabolam ...'			Not by Bede Cf. *In Lucam* IV.15.11–18 (CCSL 120.2277–367);
John 2.13–22		III.108	512–13	Hom. II.1	CCSL 122.184–92		Not by Bede Cf. Pseudo-Bede, *In Ioh.* 2 (PL 92.663A–666A)
Luke 11.14–26		III.109 [*cf.* III.49]	513–16	*Incipit:* 'Virtutes quidem domini nostri ...'			Cf. *In Lucam* IV.11.14–17 (CCSL 120.31–74)

Book III *Homiliae* not by Bede: III.42, III.44, III.55, III.59, III.85–6, III.88–104, and III.107–8.

1. The opening to III.21, 'Narratur in praecedenti ... salutabant eum,' is not in *In Marcum*.
2. The last two-thirds of III.45, 'Et transfiguratus est ... crux scandalum faceret,' are not found in *In Marcum*.
3. The conclusion of III.58, 'Unde et recte dicitur: Beati ... per omnia saecula saeculorum. Amen,' is not found in *In Lucam*.
4. The conclusion to III.79, 'Verum quia multi uirtutum studia ... carne consummare,' does not appear in *In Lucam*.

APPENDIX III

Primary Texts

Edition, *De adiutorio Dei et libero arbitrio*, Copenhagen, Kongelige Bibliotek, Gamle Kongelige Sammlung 1595 (s. xi[1]), fols 59r–60v

Audiuimus in euangelio, fratres karissimi, dominum nos uocantem
ut ad eum per liberum arbitrium ueniamus. 'Venite,' inquid, 'ad me
omnes qui laboratis et onerati estis, et ego reficiam uos' (Matt. 11.28).
Sed infirmitatem nostram idem dominus protestatur dicens:
'Nemo uenit ad me nisi pater qui misit me traxerit eum' (John 6.44).[1]   5
Et apostolus liberum arbitrium nostrum incitat dicens: 'Sic currite
ut comprehendatis' (I Cor. 9.24). Sed infirmitatem nostram Iohannes
testatur cum ait: 'Non potest homo accipere quicquam nisi datum fuerit ei
de caelo' (John 3.27).[2] Per hoc ergo[3] nobis intellegendum
quia sine adiutorio Dei nihil recte ualemus efficere. Et rursum   10
nobis liberi arbitrii uoluntas conceditur ut quaeramus
dominum et eius mandata faciamus. Exemplum igitur
agricolae bene operantis ponimus cum omnes labores suos
in agri cultura exercet ad proscindendam terram uel exarandam,
semen[4] etiam iacientis et pecorum labores ac   15
sui sudoris frigorisue famis ac sitis iniuria sustinentis[5]
omnique ingenio agrum custodiendum ut aues semen[6] non comedant
uel ferarum incursio deuastet. Et cum haec omnia suo labore
uiderit,[7] omnis eius labor in uanum consumitur nisi dominus
desuper pluuiam miserit ad crescendam messem, uel calorem solis,   20
ut ad maturitatem perueniat. Sed nec ista quidem proficiunt si
aut grandine aut tempestate aut nimietate pluuiarum ad nihilum
redigantur. Proinde nobis magno opere laborandum est ut corda nostra
praeparentur ad suscipiendum semen uerbi Dei.
Et cum susceptum fuerit depraecandum est toto corde ut[8]   25
germinet et ad fructum usque perueniat. Et si domini adiuuante gratia
in nobis fructus bonorum operum excreuerit, magis ac magis depraecandus
est ut qui dedit ut germinet et crescat det etiam perseuerantiam una
cum uoluntate bona, dicente apostolo: 'Deus autem qui operatur
et uelle et perficere pro bona uoluntate' (Phil. 2.13).[9]   30
Vt ergo de multis aliqua exempla dicamus sanctarum
scripturarum qualiter concors est adiutorium Dei nostrae bonae uoluntatis
arbitrio, intendat Caritas uestra[10] ex diuinis scripturis
testimonia. Praeuenit ergo hominis uoluntatem gratia Dei qua
dicitur: 'Deus meus misericordia eius praeueniet me' (Psa. 58.11).[11] Et   35
nostra uoluntas praeuenit cum dicit: 'Et mane oratio mea praeueniet
te' (Psa. 87.14). Et iterum: 'Praeuenerunt oculi mei ad te diluculo' (Psa.
118.148).[12] Admonet nos cum dicit: "Tota die expandi

**Translation, *De adiutorio Dei et libero arbitrio*, Copenhagen, Konge-
lige Bibliotek, Gamle Kongelige Sammlung 1595 (s. xi[1]), fols 59r–60v**

On Divine Assistance and Free Will

Most beloved brothers, in the Gospel we have heard the Lord calling us
to come to him through free will. He says: 'Come to me,
all you who labour and are burdened, and I will refresh you' (Matt. 11.28).
But the same Lord testifies against our weakness when he says:
'No one comes to me unless the Father who sent me has called him' (John   5
6.44). The apostle also urges on our free will, saying: 'Run in such a way
as to gain the prize' (I Cor. 9.24). But John testifies to our weakness
when he says: 'One can receive nothing unless it has been given to him
from heaven' (John 3.27). By this, therefore, we should understand (on the
one hand) that without God's help we can do nothing right, and (on   10
the other) that he allows us the power of free choice that we may seek
the Lord and obey his commands. Therefore we may take the example
of a farmer working well, when he employs all his efforts
in the cultivation of the field to break up or plough the soil,
and also scattering the seed and sustaining the efforts of his cattle and   15
himself by the hardships of sweat and chill, hunger and thirst,
and with all his ability caring for the field, so that birds do not eat up the
seed or a raid of wild beasts lay it waste, and when by his effort he has
seen to all these things, all his labour is spent in vain unless the Lord
should have sent rain from above to make the crop grow, or the sun's heat   20
to bring it to maturity. But indeed, those things do not help if
they are reduced to nothing either by hail or a storm or excessive rain.
Therefore, we must strive with great labour so that our hearts
may be prepared to receive the seed of the word of God,
and when it has been received, we must pray wholeheartedly that   25
it may sprout and mature to ripeness. And if by the Lord's assisting grace
the fruit of good deeds should grow in us, we must pray all the more
that he who granted it to sprout and grow may also give perseverance
together with a good will, as the apostle says: 'Now it is God who works
both to will and to accomplish through a good will' (Phil. II.13).[1]   30
Therefore, in order that we may quote some examples among many of holy
Scripture [to show] how God's assistance is in harmony with the power of
our good will, let your Love turn his attention to these testimonies of
divine Scripture. Therefore, God's grace comes before human will where
it is said: 'O my God, his mercy will precede me' (Psa. 58.11),[2] and   35
our will precedes when it says: 'In the morning my prayer will come before
you' (Psa. 87.14), and again: 'My eyes came before you at dawn' (Psa.
118.148).[3] He admonishes us when he says: 'All day long I have held out

manus meas ad populum non credentem' (Rom. 10.21).[13] Et inuitatur
a nobis cum diximus ei: 'Expandi manus ad te' (Psa.   40
142.6).[14] Expectat nos cum dicit propheta: 'Propterea expectat dominus
ut misereatur uestri' (Isa. 30.18). Et expectamus eum cum
dicimus: 'Expectans expectaui dominum et intendit mihi' (Psa.
39.2). Confortat nos cum dicit: 'Et ego erudiui et confortaui
brachia eorum' (Hos. 7.15). Et ut nosmet ipsos confortemur hortatur cum   45
dicit: 'Confortate manus dissolutas et genua debilia roborate' (Isa. 35.3).
Clamat Iesus cum dicit: 'Si quis sitit ueniat et bibat'
(John 7.37). Clamemus etiam et nos cum propheta: 'Clamaui ad te domine;
dixi tu es spes mea' (Psa. 141.6). Quaerit nos dominus cum dicit:
'Quaesiui, et non erat uir, et non fuit qui responderet.'[15]   50
Et rogat ut quaeramus cum dicit: 'Quaerite faciem eius semper' (Psa.
104.4),[16] et 'Quaerite dominum dum inueniri potest' (Isa. 55.6). Ita et
huiusmodi gratia Dei nostro in bonam partem adiuuat arbitrio ut etiam
quod bonum uolumus adiuuet ut fiat[17] et suae gratiae
consolationem[18] inmittit ut fiat. Cadere namque in peccato   55
malae uoluntatis[19] est arbitrium; ad ueniam uero reuerti per penitentiam
post commissum et Dei misericordia et nostri est laboris intentio.
Sicut Dauid qui libero corruit arbitrio, et duo tam grauia commisit
scelera, homicidium scilicet et[20] adulterium, per Dei clementiam peccatum
illius dimissum legitur. Quod igitur crimen commissum   60
libero fuit arbitrio; quod autem arguitur per prophetam
diuinae dignationis est gratia. Rursum quod peccatum suum humiliatus
agnoscit suum est; quod breui temporis spatio
indulgentiam meruit domini misericordia est.
Sic enim omnia in omnibus credendus est operari[21] ut incitet protegat   65
atque confirmet, non ut auferat quam semel concessit arbitrii libertatem,
sed cum ipsa nostra bonae uoluntatis operatione perficiatur in nobis
uoluntas ipsius, quoniam sic orantes dicimus, ut fiat illius uoluntas
in nobis.[22] AMEN.

my hands to an unbelieving people' (Rom. 10.21),[4] and he is invited
by us when we have said to him: 'I have held out my hands to you' (Psa. 40
142.6).[5] He waits for us when the prophet says: 'Therefore the Lord waits
so that he may have pity on you' (Isa. 30.18), and we wait for him when
we say: 'I waited expectantly for the Lord, and he turned towards me' (Psa.
39.2). He strengthens us when he says: 'I have trained and strengthened
their arms' (Hos. 7.15), and he encourages us to strengthen ourselves when 45
he says: 'Strengthen weak hands and make firm feeble knees' (Isa. 35.3).
Jesus cries out when he says: 'If anyone is thirsty, let him come and drink'
(John 7.37); we may also cry out with the prophet: 'I cried to you, O Lord;
I said, "You are my hope"' (Psa. 141.6). The Lord seeks us when he says:
'I sought, and there was no one; there was none who would respond,'[6] 50
and he asks us to seek when it says: 'Seek his face always' (Psa.
104.4)[7] and 'Seek the Lord while he may be found' (Isa. 55.6). In this way
this kind of divine grace helps our will in great part, so that it both
assists the good we wish so that it may come about, and instils the
encouragement of his grace that it may come about. For indeed, to fall in sin 55
is the choice of an evil will, but to return to grace through penitence
once sin has been committed is both God's mercy and our concerted effort.
David, for instance, fell by his own free will, and committed two very grave
sins, namely murder and adultery; yet we read of his sins being forgiven
through God's mercy. Therefore, the fact that the sin was committed was 60
by free will; the fact that he was reproved by the prophet, however, is the
grace of divine favour. Again, the fact that, having been humbled,
he recognizes his sin is his own doing; the fact that in a brief space of time
he merited forgiveness is the mercy of the Lord.
For so he must be believed to work 'all in all':[8] so as to urge on, protect, 65
and support, not to take away the freedom of will he once granted,
but to bring his will about in us with our work of good will,
since when praying we say as follows: 'May his will be done
in us.'[9] Amen.

Edition, *Carmen de libero arbitrio*, Cambridge, University Library, Kk. 5. 34 (s. x^2), fols 75v–80r. Ed. Michael Lapidge, 'Three Latin Poems from Æthelwold's School at Winchester', *ASE* 1 (1972), 85–137, at 126–37 [Repr. in his *Anglo-Latin Literature, 900–1066* (London, 1993), 25–77, at 266–77]; used by permission and with gratitude.

Carmen de libero arbitrio[1]
Cuncta creans, natura triplex in usiade[2] simpla,
   est natura deus, quicquid et ipse creat.[3]
mentes insipidas sancto qui pneumate purgas
   me modo ueridica, posco, doce sophia
quid series fati, quid porrouidentia[4] cosmi,   5
   liber et effectus antiesciens animus,
gratia quid regis, praedestiuenatio[5] quid sit,
   omnia qui uerbo condidit ex nihilo.
mens diuina cubum tria tempora nectit in unum;
   haec uidet in praesens, praeteritumque, sequens, 10
cuius ab intuitu nequeunt res flectere cursus.
   fatalis series ordinat omne quod est:
omnipotentis heri quicquid prouincia cernit
   actus per uarios digerit haec series.
dicimus haud aliud fatum uarios nisi rerum   15
   successus. taceat, flagito, stultiloquax![6]
notio, credo, quod est rerum qua prescius auctor
   quos nouit iustos conuocat ad superos,
uerbis quod sanctis exponit apostolus. Inquit:
   'praesciuit famulos omnipotens proprios,   20
destinat, amplificat hos, iustificatque coronat,
   saluat, sanctificat, protegit atque fouet.'[7]
arbitrii quoque libertas est priua uoluntas;
   haec mortem miseris praebet et astra probis.
partes in geminas dirimit genuine potestas: 25
   his reserat caelum, pandit et his herebum.
cognitio domini nec[8] uult abolere superni
   arbitrium per quod comprobat ipsa suos
o diuina dei pietas quae cuncta gubernas,
   legibus aeternis cosmica nexa ligas;[9]   30
pande tuis rigidum famulis rimantibus aequum:
   hoc genus humanum cur habet arbitrium
quod uehit a! poenas miseras barathrique ruinas,

Translation, *Carmen de libero arbitrio*, Cambridge, University Library, Kk. 5. 34 (s. x^2), fols 75v–80r. Trans. Michael Lapidge, 'Three Latin Poems from Æthelwold's School at Winchester', *ASE* 1 (1972), 85–137, at 126–37 [Repr. in his *Anglo-Latin Literature, 900–1066* (London, 1993), 225–77, at 266–77]; used by permission and with gratitude.

Carmen de libero arbitrio

All-creating, threefold nature in uniform substance, God is nature and whatsoever he creates. You who purify our feeble minds through the agency of the Holy Ghost, teach me now with true wisdom, I pray, what be the series of fate, what the Providence of the cosmos, what the unrestricted mind foreknowing [future] events, what the grace of the [heavenly] king, who created all things out of nothing by means of the Word, [and] what be predestination.

[Line 9:] The divine mind binds the three times together into one cube; it sees into the present, the past, and the future, from whose inspection created things may not bend their course. The fatal series ordains everything which exists: whatsoever the office of the omnipotent Lord regards, this series orders through various acts. I say that fate is nothing other than the various successive occurrences of things. Let any foolish objector be silent, I earnestly request! [Line 17:] I think that it is a conception of the world whereby the prescient creator summons those whom he knows to be just to him on high, which the apostle [Paul] expounds in holy words. He says: 'The omnipotent Father knew his own servants beforehand, he destines and strengthens these, vindicates and crowns, saves, sanctifies, protects, and cherishes them.' Also, freedom of will is a personal choice; it grants death to the miserable and [life beyond the] stars to the good. This inborn power divides [mankind] into two halves: to these it opens heaven, to others it throws open hell. [Line 27:] The understanding of our heavenly Lord does not wish to do away with this free will through which it proves who are its own [i.e., God's own]. O divine mercy of God which governs all things, tying together cosmic bonds with eternal laws: explain your stern justice to your inquiring servants – why does the human race have this free will which brings about (alas!) miserable punishments and the catastrophe of hell,

pro dolor! unde nefas promeruere iuge?
fraudibus anguinus postquam periere perempti   35
  ah! patria pulsi primigenae miseri
a quibus omne scelus uastum defluxit in orbem
  (quot natura creat sors hominisque[10] necat!)
effectum libertatis habuere malignum,
  corrupti uitiis criminibusque feris,   40
nec meritis uitam possent sperare beatam
  adiuti domini ni pietate forent
sanguine qui geniti lauit contagia mundi.
  felix culpa fuit talia quae meruit![11]
nam nesciret homo quantum se diligit auctor   45
  ni factura pius fieret ille deus,
qui nobis cupiens praebere suam deitatem
  artus humanos horruit haud fragiles.
hinc tamen effectus sileat, rogo, seditiosus:
  nullam uim patitur cognitione dei.   50
hoc propter poenis reprobi cruciantur amaris
  atque diem nequeunt cernere luciferum;
caelica Tempe[12] probos facitis[13] penetrare cluentes
  ut capiti Christo membra uenusta iugent.[14]
sermones nostri paucis paradigmata uerbis   55
  ponimus in medium clarius ut resonent.[15]
praesul et insigni clarissime dignus honore,
  uates clariuidens, doctor et egregie,
augustam regi sedem qui corde parasti
expertem neui, criminis ac uitii,   60
rex quia quem celsi nequeunt concludere[16] caeli,
  mentibus in sanctis is manet ac nitidis.
dogmate quodque mones claris prius actibus imples,
  solamen, uirtus, pastor et exulibus.
claret hoc a domino quod celsa[17] talenta benigno   65
  sint tibi, summe pater: te decus omne decet.
mente meos sensus stolidos tu conspice, rector,
  quod male dico loquens, corrige, posco cliens.
rex sapiens residet specula sublimis in alta
  prouidus ac pugnax, praepete[18] mente sagax,   70
militibus multis circumdatus ac pretiosis,
  bis seno[19] procerum septus honore ducum,
sarranis[20] recubans ostris sericisque tapetis:
is iubet in stadio currere mille uiros.

from whence (how sad!) they deserved this perpetual wretchedness?

[Line 35:] After the wretched first men [Adam and Eve] perished, brought to ruin by the deceptions of the serpent and expelled (alas!) from their first home, from whom all sin poured into the vast world (how many things nature creates and the fate of man destroys!), they possessed the wicked effect of [their] free will, corrupt in vice and bestial sins, nor could they by their own merits hope for the blessed [eternal] life unless they had been assisted by the mercy of the Lord who, with the blood of his only-begotten Son washed away the sins of the world. [Line 44:] A happy guilt it was which merited such [a redemption]! For man would not know how much his creator loves him unless that merciful God had become a creature himself, who, desiring to offer his godhead to us, did not scorn fragile human limbs. Hence let the quarrel-some creature be silent, I pray: it suffers no violence through the understand-ing of God's ways. For this reason sinners are tormented with bitter pains and cannot see the light-bringing day; but you [God] make your virtuous followers penetrate to the vales of heaven that they may join their beautiful limbs to the head, Christ.

[Line 55:] That our doctrine may resound more clearly, we put forward in a few words some examples. [Line 57:] Most distinguished bishop, worthy of extraordinary esteem, far-seeing poet, excellent man of learning, who prepared a mighty seat for the king with your heart free of blemish, sin, and vice, a king who, since the high heavens cannot contain him, yet remains in our holy and shining minds. Whatsoever you preach, you first practise in noble deeds; you are a solace, [a source of] virtue, and a good shepherd to exiles. It is clear from the beneficent Lord that heavenly rewards are to be yours, greatest father: all glory is appropriate for you. Supervise with your mind my stolid faculties, master; what I express poorly correct, I your follower beseech you.

[Line 69:] A wise king sits elevated on a high watch-tower, provident and militant, sagacious because of his alert mind, surrounded by many splendidly arrayed soldiers, enclosed by the dignity of twelve great leaders, reclining in purple garments on silk coverlets: this king commands a thousand men to run a race in the stadium.

uestes purpureas centum totidemque coronas   75
   imperat eximio ponere pro titulo
ante suos uisus, ac tali uoce profatur:
   'uelox miles erit qui meus esse cupit,
qui celer optatam poterit contingere palmam
   mox sertum capiat condicione mea,   80
in numero satrapumque merebitur esse meorum
   stemmate regali comptus et exuuiis;
qui piger et metam non quibit adire fugacem
   inmunis redeat et titulis careat.
hic caesus diris[21] uibicibus atque flagellis   85
   nexus compedibus carceribus dabitur.
coetibus ille meis sociabitur atque cateruis;
   cleptibus[22] iste feris, ridiculus populis.'
rex deus est genitor, cuius sapientia proles,
   spiritus et sanctus splendida[23] sit specula;   90
pallade[24] ceu proprios sapiens rex ordinat actus,
   sic pater omnipotens omnia per sobolem;
sicut hic a solio certamina conspicit alto,
   omne quod hic gerimus flamine[25] sicque deus.
prospectusque ducum sit contemplatio rerum;   95
   quod fuit, est, et erit haec uidet atque regit.
gratia sit domini pietas regisue uoluntas
   militibus dignis praemia quae tribuit.
arbitrii libertatem nam scammata signant;
   praesens uita gerit sic spatium stadii   100
ut cursus alios dampnant aliosque coronant:[26]
   uictus supplicium, uictor adit pretium.
liber hic effectus nostros sic dirigit actus;
   hunc uehit ad caelum, destinat hunc barathro.
sponsio sic regis praedestiuenatio: caelo   105
   promittit sanctis quae bona pro meritis,
inferni miseros et cogit adire tenebras
   arbitrio proprio qui periere mali.
rebus in humanis reor antescientia non sit;
   cunctisator[27] rerum possidet hoc proprium.   110
in quantum fragilis hominum natura creantem
   aequiperare potest? esse quid hoc specimen
dicere nemo ualet; sed quantum res periturae
   distant[28] a stablili simplicitate dei!

He orders a hundred purple robes and as many crowns to be placed before him as the highest possible reward, and speaks as follows: [Line 78:] 'That soldier who wishes to be mine shall be swift; [he] who can attain to the desired victor's palm, let him capture the wreath according to my conditions, and he will deserve to be among the number of my viceroys, adorned with regal garlands and clothing; he who is sluggish and cannot attain the elusive goal, let him return unrewarded and lack recognition. Carved up with weals and lashes, and bound with shackles, he shall be committed to prison. The one will be associated with my followers and flock; the other with savage thieves, a laughing-stock to the people.'

[Line 89:] The king represents God the Creator, whose wisdom is his Son, and let the splendid watch-tower be the Holy Ghost; as the king ordains his particular actions providently, so the omnipotent Father ordains everything through the agency of the Son; as the king observes the competition from his lofty throne, so God [observes] everything we do on earth through the agency of the Holy Ghost. Let the inspection of the leaders represent the [cosmic] contemplation of things; this [contemplation] sees and governs everything that was, is, and shall be. Let the mercy or will of the king which grants rewards to worthy soldiers be the grace of the Lord. [Line 99:] For the racecourse signifies free will; as the length of the racecourse represents this present life, so the racecourse damns some and crowns others: the conquered gets punishment, the conqueror reward. Here on earth free action thus directs our deeds: it takes one man to heaven, destines another to hell. Similarly the promise of the king [represents] predestination, which promises bounties to the saints in heaven according to their merits, and compels those miserable wretches to go to the shadows of hell who perished by their own will. [Line 109:] I reckon that there is no foreknowledge in the human condition; the all-creator alone possesses this. In what way may the fragile nature of men equal [their] creator? What the difference is, no one is able to say; but how greatly do ephemeral things differ from the stable simplicity of God!

intuitus regis certantibus haud nocet illis;   115
    praesidium nulli ferre potest homini;
rex etiam uastis interstitiis segregatus
    nec solum uisu, sed neque[29] uoce, manu.
actus praeteritos, praesentes, necne futuros
    auctor[30] sic hominum prospicit intuitu,   120
et quamuis ualeat mentes peruertere sontes
    ad meliora, tamen nil nocet arbitrio;
sed pandit geminos mortalibus utique calles:
    sentosus dexter, leuus ubique patet.[31]
uix iter angustum raris comeantibus idem   125
    signat, et is uitam ducit ad aetheriam;
alter adest spatio diffusus denique uasto:
    omne uehit barathrum pene genus hominum.
nosque sequi dextrum iubet ac uitare sinistrum
    cunctorum dominus lucifer atque salus   130
Christus cunctipotens qui cum patre[32] regnat ubique,
    dogmatibus sanctis infit ubi populis.
Semita stricta polum poterit reserare supernum,
    illam neruosus[33] siquis adire cupit;
perniciemque parant sinuosi competa callis.   135
    mentis nunc oculis cernite uos, socii.
credo quod hoc domini demonstrent dogmata Christi:
    nemo labore carens percipiet requiem.
quapropter uitam si uultis habere perhennem
    ut sitis, fratres, uos moneo, celeres,   140
ne torpore graui perdatis praemia caeli
    miles ut ille piger brauia[34] tripudii.[35]
currere nosque monent domini sintagmata Christi
    militis ac Pauli currere nosque docent,[36]
scamatis in specie nostros ubi significauit   145
    actus humanos scamatis in specie.
pergite, posco, uiri, capiatis ut astra tonantis
    atque[37] superna poli: pergite, posco, uiri.[38]
his patet exemplis quod contemplatio uiri
    haud uertat proprium iudicis arbitrium,   150
uota, preces domino nisi quis pro flagitioso
    fuderit, omne scelus uertat ut in melius.
proles at[39] aetherii splendorque sophia parentis
    laxat dira suis crimina tortoribus.

The inspection of the king does not harm those who are in the contest; it may offer no assistance to any man. The king is even separated by vast distances, cut off not only by sight, but by voice and touch as well. [Line 119:] Likewise the creator of men observes with his understanding our past, present, and future deeds, and although he could turn our minds to better things yet he does not interfere with our will; but he does provide as it were two paths for mortals: the one on the right is thorny, the one on the left is completely open. He scarcely draws the narrow path to the attention of those few who follow it, and it leads to eternal life. The other is spread out over a wide space: it takes nearly the whole human race to hell. [Line 129:] The Lord of all things, the light-bringer and salvation, admonishes us to follow the right and avoid the left [path], Christ the all-powerful who reigns everywhere with his Father, in those places where he speaks to the peoples through his holy teaching. The straight and narrow path will open [the way to] the skies above, if anyone is energetic enough to follow it. The crossways of the winding path prepare destruction. Now, my friends, look with the eyes of your spirit. [Line 137:] I believe that the teachings of Christ the Lord demonstrate this: [that] no one who fails to work will receive rest. Wherefore, if you wish to have eternal life, brothers, I advise you to be swift, lest you lose the rewards of heaven through heavy-footed sluggishness, as that lazy runner lost the prize of the race.

[Line 143:] The teachings of Christ the Lord advise us to run, and those of Paul his soldier advise us to run [as well], where he signified our human actions with the likeness of the arena. Press on, men, I beseech you, that you may acquire the stars of the thunderer [i.e., God] and the lofty realms of the heavens: press on, men, I beseech you.

[Line 149:] It is clear from these examples that the contemplation of man does not alter the will of the judge, unless one will have poured prayers and supplications to the Lord for one's sins, in order that one may turn all one's sins into something better. But the Son, the splendour and wisdom of the aetherial parent, forgives the dire sins of his tormentors.

plures inde polum meruerunt scandere clarum   155
    consortes facti coetibus angelicis.
hac Stephanus Leuita pius uirtute coactus,[40]
    illustrem Paulum fecit adire deum.
sic quoque nos caeli dominum rogitemus, adhelphi,
    pellat ut a famulis arbitrium sceleris,   160
quatinus a uitiis et neui crimine mundi
    conciues Petri simus in arce poli,
clauibus inmensi reserat qui limen Olimphi,
    cui mandauit oues altitonans niueas.
omnibus hoc nobis concedat gratia Christi   165
    sanguine quos proprio traxit ab hoste fero.
o dee cunctipotens cosmi qui regmina[41] flectis,
    parce meo fluxit quicquid ab ore nequam.
te sine nil rectum nil iustum nilque pudicum
    scire potest miser et praeuaricatus homo;   170
quapropter toto mentis conamine poscens
    deprecor, ac numen flagito teque tuum,
dirige[42] sic actus hominum, rector, ualeant quo
    post finem uitae denarium capere,[43]
pontificemque pium meritis et honore colendum   175
    insignemque humilem protege, Christi, libens,
quem deus omnipotens cathedra subuexit in alta,
    dogmate mellifluo uerteret ut scelera.
gentes Anglorum felices praesule tanto
    ritus qui prauos corrigit ut genitor,   180
extorresque superuenientes uosque[44] beati:
    cunctis his tribuit quicquid opus fuerit.
quis numerare queat bona nobis quae bonus ille
    contulit hanc postquam uenimus ad patriam?
idcirco dominum rogitemus corde fideli   185
    praebeat ut famulo gaudia pro merito.

Therefore many have deserved to ascend the bright heaven, made consorts to the angelic hosts. [Line 157:] The pious Stephen the Levite, moved by this virtue, made the illustrious Paul proceed to God. Thus let us too beseech the lord of heaven, brothers, that he may drive away from his servants the will to sin, so that, clean from sin and the evil of stain, we may be compatriots of Peter in the summit of heaven, Peter who unlocks the threshold of Olympus with huge keys, to whom God the thunderer entrusted his snowy-white flocks. Let the grace of Christ grant this to all of us whom he drew away from the savage fiend with his own blood.

[Line 167:] O God omnipotent, you who control the governance of the cosmos, have mercy on whatever worthless proceeds from my mouth. Without your assistance miserable and sinful man may not know anything that is right or just or modest. Wherefore, striving with the total effort of my spirit I beseech you, and entreat you and your divinity: so direct the deeds of men, master, that they may be able to get the *denarius* after the end of their life. And willingly protect, Christ, the merciful, renowned, and humble bishop, who is to be respected for his merits and his honour, whom the omnipotent God elevated to the lofty *cathedra* so that he would alter our sins by his mellifluous doctrine. [Line 179:] Happy the English with such a bishop, who corrects the depraved practices of the church like a father; and you foreigners lately arriving are blessed as well: to all these he has granted whatsoever was necessary. Who could count all the bounties which that good man has conferred on us since we came to this land? For that reason let us beseech the Lord with faithful heart that he grant happiness to his servant as he [i.e., the servant or bishop] well deserves.

Notes

Introduction

1 Grundy, *Books and Grace*, 7. Grundy does describe Ælfric as a 'developer, nourisher and disseminator of [Augustine's] ideas, as Gregory the Great, Bede ... Haymo and Smaragdus had been before him'; nevertheless, she maintains that 'it is generally true to say that his teaching fits into the Augustinian tradition' (7–8).

1. A Doctrine Defined: The Influence of Augustine

1 Ninety-nine of these manuscripts contain material actually written by Augustine, out of some 1240 manuscripts listed in Gneuss, *Handlist of Anglo-Saxon Manuscripts*.
2 As will be seen, the notion of 'orthodoxy' becomes problematized through consideration of influential conservative figures other than Augustine: Gregory the Great's doctrine, for example, by its papal nature cannot be counted heterodox, and yet it departs significantly if subtly from that of the African Father. Ælfric, indeed, though committed to providing 'orthodox' teaching – canonical, conservative, sanctioned under-standing – identified such teaching by its origin in recognized ecclesiastical authorities, authorities that included but were not limited to Augustine; as a result, the doctrine he presents reflects different theologi-cal emphases. This said, however, Augustine's impact on Christian understanding of free will is indisputable. Frederick Van Fleteren, for example, summarizes the foundational nature of Augustine's achieve-ment thus: 'Several Christian writers before Augustine: Tertullian, Ambrose, and Cyprian to be specific, mention free choice ... None of

these thinkers develops a comprehensive doctrine of free will – it is left to Augustine' ('Principles of Augustine's Hermeneutic,' 3).

3 For general background to Augustine, see, for example, Trapè, 'Augustine of Hippo'; Markus, 'Life, Culture, and Controversies'; Rist, 'Augustine of Hippo'; and the seminal biography by Peter Brown, *Augustine of Hippo*. Particularly valuable for navigating the immense range of secondary studies of Augustine are the annual bibliographies furnished by the Institut des Études Augustiniennes in Paris and published in the *Revue des études augustiniennes*; bibliographical information prior to the last decade has been compiled from this source and published on CD-ROM as the *Corpus Augustinianum Gissense*, ed. C. Mayer (Basel, 1996). One landmark reference on Augustinian matters is the *Augustinus-Lexikon*, the first volume of which, edited by Cornelius Mayer, appeared in fascicles from 1986–94; when complete, it should provide an authoritative staple of Augustinian scholarship.

4 For studies of Augustine's engagement with the Manichaeans, see for example Lee, *Augustine, Manichaeism, and the Good*; Martin, *Augustine's Interpretation of Romans*, 8–14; Teske, 'Augustine, the Manichees and the Bible'; and Ries, 'Le jugement porté sur le Manichéisme.'

5 On Augustine and the Donatists, see further Harrison, *Christian Truth and Fractured Humanity*, 145–57; Paas, *Conflict on Authority*; Crespin, *Ministère et sainteté*; and Kaufman, 'Augustine, Evil, and Donatism.'

6 For a historical survey of the Pelagian controversy, see Brown, *Augustine of Hippo*, 340–64, 'Pelagius and his Supporters,' and 'The Patrons of Pelagius.' For an overview of Pelagian theology, see Pelikan, *Christian Tradition*, 315–17. For a portrait of Pelagianism as a holiness movement reacting against the corruption of the late Roman Empire, see Bonner, *Life and Controversies*, 353, and Brown, *Augustine of Hippo*, 340–3.

7 Portalié, *Guide*, 188. For these aspects of Pelagian thought, see, for example, *De bono uiduitatis* 21–2, *De gratia Christi* I.22.24, *De gestis Pelagii* X.22, *De gratia Christi* I.6.8, *Contra duas epistulas* IV.4.6, *Contra secundam Iuliani responsionem* IV.103, and *De gratia et libero arbitrio* V.10–11.

8 Brown, *Augustine of Hippo*, 381.

9 As James Wetzel puts it, 'At the very least, it must be conceded that Augustine's provocative way of reading Paul disrupts the delicate *pas de deux* of western theism, between ethical self-assertion and religious self-surrender' ('Snares of Truth,' 124–5). At the same time, Augustine was anything but an advocate of spiritual complacency or inertia: as Aaron Stalnaker states, 'It would not be overstating the case to say that Augustine regards the Christian life – in lay, clerical, and monastic forms – as consisting essentially of the practice of spiritual exercises ... such as sexual restraint or renunciation,

voluntary poverty, almsgiving, communal pownership of property, fasting, self-examination, private and public confession, various kinds of prayer ... and various forms of penance' ('Spiritual Exercises,' 138). For a careful study of the concerns of the monks of Hadrumentum and Marseille, Augustine's response thereto, and the theological nuances thereof, see Ogliari, *Gratia et certamen*, 26–183.

10 Again, Wetzel writes: 'He handed human will, root and branch, over to God ... Still, Augustine writes as if being wholly subject to God changes nothing about the urgency of moral striving' ('Snares of Truth,' 125).

11 More than simply disagreement with Augustine likely prompted the *Collatio*'s composition: as Conrad Leyser states, 'It is now largely agreed that Cassian was quite as concerned as Augustine and his disciples by the persistence of Pelagian error, and wrote *Conference* 13 to contribute to a papally-sponsored campaign to affirm orthodoxy in sourthen Gaul' (*Authority and Asceticism*, 40). Wetzel puts it thus: 'Cassian's thirteenth *Collatio*, though not expressly aimed at Augustine, offers an irenic and elegant alternative to Augustine's numbing emphasis on God's intiative' ('Snares of Truth,' 127). For discussions of Cassian's knowledge of Augustine, see Markus, *The End of Ancient Christianity*, 177–9; Ramsey, 'John Cassian: Student of Augustine'; and de Vogüé, 'Les Sources des Quarters Premiers Livres des Institutions de Jean Cassien.' For a reexamination of Cassian's (potentially favourable) estimation of the African Father, see Casiday, 'Cassian, Augustine, and *De Incarnatione*.'

12 For the scholarly divide on the dating of *Collatio* XIII, see Stewart, *Cassian*, 153 n. 161 and Weaver, *Divine Grace*, 93–7.

13 While such monastic communities may have seen in Cassian's view a welcome moderation of Augustine's more 'extreme' position, Marianne Djuth points out in fact that both Augustine and Cassian present their perspective as a cautious middle way between the error that human beings can live without sin (Pelagius) and the error that human beings cannot rid themselves of sin – either because of spiritual/material dualism (Manichaeans) or corrupted desire (Augustine) ('The Royal Way,' 135–9).

14 'All diligence is eliminated and virtue abolished if God's decision precedes human will' (Prosper, *Pro Augustino responsiones* 3 [CSEL LVII, p. 458, lines 9–11]). Here and below, all translations are my own.

15 Hilary, *Epistula ad Augustinum*. For a comparative study of Prosper and Hilary's letters to Augustine, see Chéné, 'Le Semipélagianisme.'

16 'What do you have that you did not receive?' (Augustine, *De praedestinatione* III.7 [PL 44.964]; I Cor. 4.7).

17 Nestorius objected to references to Mary as the 'Mother of God,' which he felt implied a beginning to the eternal Divinity; he preferred 'Mother of Christ.' His arguments were taken as a denial of Christ's divinity. Nestorius was suspected of Pelagian sympathies at least in part because in writing to announce his views to Pope Celestine, he noted his uncertainty on how to judge the case of bishops who refused to accept Rome's condemnation of Pelagius and were seeking refuge with him. On this subject, see Chadwick, *Cassian*, 131 and 138–47.

18 On Celestine's response, see Cappuyns, 'Le premier représentant,' 319 n. 26.

19 For a study of the *Contra Collatorem*, see Weaver, *Divine Grace*, 121–31.

20 Faustus, abbot of Lérins (422–57) and bishop of Riez (457–90/5) set out the Gallic position in detail in his *De gratia*, ca. 472, and was instrumental in guiding the Synod of Arles held ca. 473. Reflecting on the latter, he affirmed that 'adnisum hominis et conatum gratiae semper adiungam et libertatem uoluntatis humanae non exstinctam, sed attenuatam et infirmatam esse pronuntiem' (I should always join human effort and endeavour to God's grace, and proclaim that human freedom of will is not utterly destroyed, but just weak and feeble) (*Epistula ad Lucidum* [PL 53.684]). For Cassian's influence on Lérins and Faustus in particular, as well as the factors contributing to this lull in the debate, see Stewart, *Cassian*, 18 and 24; Weaver, *Divine Grace*, 155–6 and 162–80; and Markus, 'Legacy,' respectively.

21 'Through the sin of the first human, free will was so bent and weakened that from that point no one has been able to love God as he should, or believe in God, or do good for God, unless the grace of God's mercy precedes him' (CCSL 148A, p. 62, lines 178–82). While the Council affirmed that the corruption of human nature makes prevenient grace necessary for the whole of one's righteousness, including both faith and good deeds – all subjects we will treat in detail hereafter – it did condemn the belief that God predestines humans to damnation, a conclusion some might draw from Augustine's teaching on irresistible grace (CCSL 148A, p. 63, lines 209–12; cf. the teaching on 'double predestination' by the ninth-century monk Gottschalk, whose views were condemned by the Synod of Quiercy in 849). Though linked to Augustine's teaching on grace, however, the subject of predestination is beyond the scope of our present inquiry – though see the necessary discussion of Providence and Fate in Alfred's *Boethius*, below.

22 For Boniface's decree, see CCSL 148A, pp. 66–9.

23 It is not simply the extensive nature of his corpus that makes identifing with precision Augustine's theological position on an issue a challenge. Van Fleteren, speaking of Augustine's interpretation of scripture, notes that

the corpus is characterized by a diverse range of audiences, contexts, and methodological approaches. He states: 'Because Augustine's treatment of Scripture is so extensive, study of his techniques can lead us into an intellectual quagmire. His hermeneutical principles are not found in one place ... Augustine's axioms of biblical interpretation are scattered throughout his works ... [and his] exegetical technique varies according to purpose and audience' ('Principles of Augustine's Hermeneutic,' 2–3).

24 See Portalié, *Guide*, 177; Pelikan, *Christian Tradition*, 281; and Dougherty, 'The Role of the Will,' 93 and 107 n. 20; cf. Justin Martyr, *Apologia* XLIII and XLIV.11; Tertullian, *De idololatria* IX.1; Origen, *De oratione* VI.3–4, *De principiis* III.1.4, and *Contra Celsum* V.21.

25 Portalié, *Guide*, 197; cf. 222–3 and 178. Portalié himself objects to this view, saying that 'the texts are absolutely against this accusation.'

26 Bonner, *God's Decree*, xii.

27 'What do you have that you did not receive?' (I Cor. 4.7); *Retractationes* II.1.

28 See Portalié, *Guide*, 82–3; Bonner, *Modern Research*, 16, and 'Augustine, the Bible, and the Pelagians,' 231 and 238; and Kaye and Thomson, *On Augustine*, 21. Such is not to suggest a complete cessation of theological development. Thomas Martin's extensive study, *Augustine's Interpretation of Romans 7:24–25a*, for example, leads him to conclude that Augustine matures in his view of humanity's struggle against concupiscence: he finds that whereas in *Ad Simplicianum* Augustine understands the war with the flesh depicted in Romans 7 as the condition of the unbeliever, much later Augustine begins to believe that Paul may be describing his believing state (*Retractationes* II.1.1; Martin, *Augustine's Interpretation of Romans*, especially p. 37; see also Fredricksen, 'Paul and Augustine,' 25; Bonner, 'Augustine, the Bible, and the Pelagians,' 237; and Rydstrøm-Poulsen, *Gratia in Augustine*, 61–6). Such development reflects not a fundamental shift, however, as much as a fuller application of the principle of the letter to Simplicianus, that the whole of human virtue must be attributed to God. Likewise, J.Patout Burns, who argues for a change in Augustine's understanding of the mechanics of grace ('A Change'), states that 'Augustine's culminating explanation of Romans IX was in *Ad Simplicianum*' ('Grace,' 345; cf. Wetzel, 'Pelagius,' 122, and 'Recovery,' 109). One notable exception to the scholarly consensus is offered by Carol Harrison, who, while acknowledging that 'the theory of a revolution in Augustine's thought in the 390s in working out a doctrine of original sin and grace is now almost universally accepted' – indeed, 'almost canonical in Augustine scholarship' – nonetheless examines Augustine's writings between 388 and 396 to argue for 'a clear continuity between Augustine the new convert and Augustine the new bishop': these works

insist, Harrison says, 'that human beings, subject to the ignorance and difficulty of original sin, can merit nothing, but that all is of grace' (*Rethinking
Augustine's Early Theology,* 14, vi, and 237). Augustine himself, looking back
on his career, repeatedly appeals to this work as evidence of the continuity
of his anti-Pelagian views (*Retractationes* II.1, *De praedestinatione sanctorum*
IV.8, and *De dono perseuerantiae* XX.52). At the same time, as Wetzel notes,
'In *De praedestinatione sanctorum* [IV.8], Augustine tells the monks that they
will find there [in *Ad Simplicianum*] ... a radical change of view. He cites the
judgement of his *Retractationes* [II.1]: "In resolving the question, I really
worked for the free choice of human will, but the grace of God won out"
[In cuius quaestionis solutione laboratum est quidem pro libero arbitrio
uoluntatis humanae, sed uicit dei gratia (CCSL 57, pp. 89–90)]' ('Snares
of Truth,' 128).

29 Augustine, *De libero arbitrio,* I.13.29, cited in Babcock, 'Sin,' 229. When
Augustine later says that the theology of *De libero arbitrio* is compatible with
his anti-Pelagian writings (*cf. De dono perseuerantiae* XX.52–3 and *Retractationes* I.9.6), he is not referring to this notion of the will's ability to do good,
for he explicitly condemns it in *De praedestinatione* III.7. Rather, he sees continuity 'not because he never changes his mind in regard to the will's natural capacity for goodness, but because he never ceases to affirm the reality
of the will' – that is, human beings' technical capacity for moral choice
(Djuth, 'Human Freedom,' 395). Bonner notes, moreover, that the passages
from *De libero arbitrio* that Augustine quotes in the *Retractationes* are all
from the later parts of the work (*St Augustine,* 384).

30 Gal. 5.17; Rom. 7.23–5; and Eph. 2.3.

31 This admission 'contains the germ of all Augustine's later understanding of
man's helplessness' (Alflatt, 'Responsibility,' 171). For the shift in Augustine's
thought from Book I to Book III, see for example Powers, 'St. Augustine's
Transformation,' 118, and O'Connell, 'Involuntary Sin.' Harrison, again, is an
exception to this view: she argues for the unity of *De libero arbitrio,* affirming
that Augustine 'was fully persuaded from the beginning that, if we do not
acknowledge our complete and absolute dependence upon God's grace we
will be overcome' (*Rethinking Augustine's Early Theology,* 223).

32 *Liberum arbitrium,* human beings' technical capacity for moral choice, should
be distinguished from *uoluntas.* Though Augustine initially conceives of this
too as a neutral instrument, capable of being used for good or evil (*De libero
arbitrio* II.18.50–19.53, cited in O'Daly, 'Predestination,' 88), he comes to view
it as either good or evil (cf. the 'two wills' in *Confessiones* VIII.5.10). People 'of
good will' (*bonae uoluntatis*) are by definition good (cf. *De trinitate* XIII.13.17).
As Rist puts it, '*uoluntas* is not a decision-making faculty of the individual ...

but the individual himself'; it is not 'part of the human psyche; rather it is the human psyche in its role as a moral agent ... Hence it can be good or bad' ('Free Will,' 421–2).

33 When in later works Augustine says that humans lost freedom of choice through the Fall, he is referring not to individuals' technical capacity to choose evil or good (which they still have), but the original perfection of the will when it was free from the overwhelming influence of evil desires (concupiscence). See, for example, *De correptione et gratia* XII.37 and *Contra secundam Iuliani responsionem* I.47. On Augustine's treatment of Romans in *Ad Simplicianum*, see Martin, *Augustine's Interpretation of Romans*, 37 and 40; TeSelle, 'Exploring the Inner Conflict,' 313, 321, 324–5; and Fredriksen, 'Augustine and Israel,' 93–4 and 106 n. 6.

34 For this distinction, see *Enchiridion* 32 and *Contra secundam Iuliani responsionem* VI.11. Cf. Gilson, *Christian Philosophy*, 157 and 161: 'A will which acts like a will thereby bears witness to its free choice ... Even when God enables the will to will, and bestows on it the assistance it needs to do what He orders, it is still the will which wills and does what He commands.' Or, as Lancel says simply: 'The true debate ... was not between free will and grace, it was between liberty and grace' (*Saint Augustine*, 192). See also Burnaby, *Amor Dei*, 227; Djuth, 'Hermeneutics,' 286–7; Rist, *Augustine*, 132; and Weismann, 'The Problematic of Freedom,' 104–7.

35 See *Ad Simplicianum* I.1.2 and I.1.7, cited in Djuth, 'Human Freedom,' 387; cf. *Retractationes* I.9.6, and *De spiritu et littera* XXVIII.48. Portalié observes that as the key difference in Augustine's works before *Ad Simplicianum* is his lack of understanding that the beginning of salvation comes from God, such material leaves an opening for Semi-Pelagianism, but not Pelagianism (*Guide*, 181–2).

36 *Expositio quarumdam propositionum* 55 and 60–2 [versus *Retractationes* I.23.1–2]; *De diuersis quaestionibus lxxxiii* LXVIII.4–5 [versus *Retractationes* I.26]; cf. Wetzel, 'Recovery,' 108–9; Babcock, 'Augustine and Paul,' 477; and Portalié, *Guide*, 181–2.

37 Sage lists some fifty occasions on which Augustine uses the phrase 'Voluntas praeparatur a Deo' (the will is prepared by God); see 'Praeparatur uoluntas,' 19–20. For the shift in Augustine's thinking from *Expositio quarundam propositionum* to *Ad Simplicianum*, see also Scott, *Thought in Context*, 178–81. For a discussion of Augustine's doctrine of irresistible grace, see Wetzel, *Limits of Virtue*, 197–206.

38 Again, the absolute effect of motivations – in fallen humanity, stemming from evil desire or concupiscence – does not mitigate human beings' technical capacity for moral choice. As Gilson states, 'Voluntary choice is never

without motives, and some motives can ever bear upon it with irresistible force, but free choice is precisely a choice exercised on the strength of motives' (*Christian Philosophy*, 157; cf. 162).

39 On congruent vocation, see *Ad Simplicianum* I.2.13; Portalié, *Guide*, 199–204 and 215; Wetzel, 'Pelagius,' 125, and 'Recovery,' 110–11; Oroz Reta, 'Vocation divine,' 305–6; and Babcock, 'Augustine and Paul,' 478. Eugene TeSelle points to Book VIII of the *Confessiones*, written shortly after *Ad Simplicianum* between 397 and 401, as an example of congruent vocation in Augustine's own life: 'Augustine emphasizes that Antony, then he himself, then his friend Alypius were converted by hearing or reading ... exactly the [biblical] passages that each needed to hear' (*Augustine*, 43). As regards the irresistibility of this vocation, Portalié argues that when Augustine states that humans cannot resist the will of God [e.g., *De correptione* XIV.45], he means that 'freedom of choice cannot hinder God from choosing among his graces that one which will in fact meet with acceptance' (*Guide*, 227; see likewise Wetzel, 'Snares of Truth,' 128–9).

40 For the following, see Burns, 'A Change,' and *The Development of Augustine's Doctrine of Operative Grace*. Hubertus Drobner, in his 'Overview of Recent Research' on Augustine, notes the lasting influence of Burns's conclusions – or at least the lack of major challenges thereto. Citing works for example by Dodaro ('Augustine on the Christology of Pelagius') and Hombert (*Gloria gratiae*), he states: 'Following J. Patout Burns' research, scholars have continued for the most part to examine Augustine's theology of grace in relation to both the developing accounts of the role of Christ in his thought' – that is, the extent to which Augustine views the transmission of grace as rooted in the sanctifying work of Christ – 'and the increasingly historical investigations concerning the Pelagian controversy' (29).

41 Burns, 'A Change,' 491–2.

42 *Epistulae* 194.3.15.

43 Burns, 'A Change,' 493–5. Burns suggests that subsequent texts continue to reflect his view, thus contradicting Portalié's earlier study, which goes through *Ad Simplicianum*, *De spiritu et littera*, *De dono perseuerantiae*, *De praedestinatione*, and *Contra secundam Iuliani responsionem* to argue an ongoing belief in congruent vocation (*Guide*, 199–204). Burns is supported, however, in a recent study by Wetzel, who notes two other scholars who have identified this shift: Lebourlier, 'Essai,' 299, and de Broglie, 'Meilleure Intelligence,' 332. Wetzel argues that these three 'were quite right ... to note that Augustine does not dwell on the deeply transformative effects of grace until late in the Pelagian controversy, 418. The anti-Pelagian emphasis on inwardly working grace is conspicuously absent from *Ad Simplicianum*.

Nevertheless, I suspect that when Augustine moves the locus of grace's operation to deeper recesses within the human personality, he does so in a way that maintains an essential continuity with the framework of *Ad Simplicianum*' (Wetzel, 'Pelagius,' 122).

44 Augustine states that to be compelled to will is a contradiction in terms (*Contra secundam Iuliani responsionem* I.101): volition is by definition voluntary (*De libero arbitrio* III.3.7). Augustine insists that humans consent to the divine work within them (*Ad Simplicianum* I.2.10). Wetzel notes, however, that 'After *Ad Simplicianum* this consent is never understood by Augustine to be a veto power exercised from outside the redemptive process. In his mature theology of grace, consent emerges as the delicate task of self-integration faced by all those who discover themselves changed by the grace of God. God can guarantee this consent, but he cannot do it for us' ('Pelagius,' 130; cf. Clark, *Augustine*, 45–6).

45 See Gilson, *Christian Philosophy*, 162, and Gowans, *The Identity of the True Believer*, 133–6 and 158–9.

46 *Sermones* CXXXI.1.1 – 2.2; cf. Harrison, 'Delectatio Victrix,' 302; Rydstrøm-Poulsen, *Gratia in Augustine*, 56; and Oroz Reta, 'Divine Attraction,' 155–67. The image of humans being drawn to the sweetness of righteousness may be compared to Augustine's description of love as a gravitational mass (*pondus*); see below, p. 24.

47 Oroz Reta thus speaks of two vocations: 'L'une qui est efficace et l'autre qui se perd' ('Vocation divine,' 304).

48 Gilson notes that in this way grace is 'irresistible without being constraining, because it is either suited to the free choice of those it has decided to save, or by transforming from within the will to which it is applied, it causes it to delight freely in things which it would otherwise find repugnant' (*Christian Philosophy*, 155–6). On Augustine's teaching on irrestistible grace, see also Rist, 'Free Will,' 236–9.

49 *De nuptiis* I.31.35 and Rom. 7; cf. Alflatt, 'Responsibility,' 176 and 183. While Augustine had originally seen this struggle as characteristic of unbelievers, he comes to view it as part of the Christian experience as well (*Contra duas epistulas* I.10.22; cf. Alflatt, 'Development,' 130).

50 'Or more accurately,' as Wetzel puts it, Augustine finds himself divided 'between the two contrary inclinations of a wounded will, neither of which has the power to transform and incorporate the other' ('Snares of Truth,' 130). For a contrast of Augustine's developing position to Manichaean dualism, see Fredriksen and Stroumsa, 'Two Souls and the Divided Will,' 209–17.

51 *Confessiones* VIII.5.10, 9.21, and 10.24. See the fine study by Saarinen, *Weakness of the Will*, 26–43. Cf. Stark, 'Dynamics of the Will,' 53, and 'Pauline

Influence'; Wetzel, *Limits of Virtue*, 126–38; and Djuth, 'The Problem of Free Choice of Will,' 36–41. Although here Augustine is actually examining his inward division prior to conversion, as Bonner notes, the passage provides an apt portrait of his later understanding of the believer's condition as well (*Life and Controversies*, 357).

52 Gneuss, *Handlist*, §320.

53 Ibid., §27.

54 No copies from any of these centres survive of Pseudo-Augustinian works; as noted below, however, an examination of doctrines of free will in works falsely attributed to Augustine is beyond the scope of the present study.

55 Gneuss, *Handlist*, §516.

56 Ibid., §§27, 67, 137, 168, 188, 255, 283, 475, 506, 512, 559, 581, 583, 692, 716, 722, 751, 752, 794.5, 799.5, 801, 808, 918, 919.3, and 944.5.

57 Ibid., §§67, 795, and 801.

58 One other copy of these six works survives from Anglo-Saxon England before ca. 1100: Brussels, Bibliothèque Royale 444–52 (1103) (s. xi/xii, Canterbury, St Augustine's [Gneuss, *Handlist*, §805.5]), which contains Augustine's *De perfectione iustitiae hominis, De natura et gratia, De gratia et libero arbitrio, De correptione et gratia, De praedestinatione sanctorum, De dono perseuerantiae*, and *Contra duas epistulas Pelagianos*; Prosper's *Pro Augustino responsiones ad capitula obiectionum Gallorum*; Hilary's *Epistola ad Augustinum de querela Gallorum*; Pseudo-Augustine's *Hypomnesticon*, a refutation of Pelagianism and Semi-Pelagianism that draws on all the Augustinian works above (see Chisholm, *Hypomnesticon*, 77–129 and 184–6); and Jerome, *Contra Jouinianum*, arguing that people can only accomplish good if God gives them help – a basic tenet of Augustine's against the Pelagians, whom Jerome would later call Jovinian's heirs (*Dialogi contra Pelagianos* II.24). The collection is a fascinating one that evinces a strong interest in the issue of free will in post-Conquest Canterbury; it is too late, however, to be considered for our present purposes.

59 Gneuss, *Handlist*, §722.

60 Personal correspondence, 10 and 16 February 1999. On the founding of Salisbury and early acquisition of manuscripts there, see Webber, *Scribes and Scholars*.

61 For studies of Bede's Augustinian sources, see Lapidge, *The Anglo-Saxon Library*, 196–204; Love, '*Commentarius in Genesim* [*In principium Genesis*],' '*Explanátio Apocalypsis* [*Expositio Apocalypseos*],' 'Letter to John,' 'Martyrologium,' 'Passio S. Anastasii,' '*Vita S. Cuthberti* (prose),' and '*Vita S. Felicis*'; Orchard, '*De die iudicii*'; Orchard and Love, '*Vita metrica S. Cuthberti*'; Scarfe Beckett, '*Historia ecclesiastica gentis Anglorum*'); and Laistner, 'Library

of the Venerable Bede,' 263.

62 See Godden, '*Augustine, Soliloquies*'; Discenza, '*Boethius, The Consolation of Philosophy*'; and Joan Hart, '*Gregory the Great, The Pastoral Care.*' Rohini Jayatilaka also suggests that *De ciuitate Dei, In Ioannis epistulam ad Parthos tractatus x*, and *Tractatus in Euangelium Ioannis* may have been possible sources for the *Old English Orosius*, commissioned by Alfred, and thus known at least to Alfred's circle (see '*Gregory the Great, Dialogues*' and '*Orosius, History Against the Pagans*').

63 Namely, *De ciuitate Dei, Enarrationes in psalmos, Quaestiones in Heptateuchum*, (probably) *De trinitate*, and *Tractatus in Euangelium Ioannis*. For a discussion of works known to Lantfred, particularly as manifested by the sources of his *Translatio et miracula S. Swithuni* (on which, see below), see Lapidge, *The Anglo-Saxon Library*, 240, and *Cult of St Swithun*, 234–35.

64 Further studies of Wulfstan are needed to determine fully his patristic debt, but at present connections between the archbishop and African Father are scarce: Tom Hall and Dorothy Bethurum suggest Augustine's *De baptismo contra Donatistas* VI.1.1–2.4 and *Tractatus in Euangelium Ioannis* XI.6–11 as sources for Wulfstan's *Sermo sancti Augustini de baptismo non iterando*, and *In Ioannis epistulam ad Parthos tractatus x* 3.4 as a source for his *Sermo* Ib (see Hall, 'Wulfstan's Latin Sermons,' 100 and 106; and Bethurum, *Homilies of Wulfstan*, 283).

65 Godden, 'Source Summary for Anglo-Saxon Text *Catholic Homilies*' and *Introduction, Commentary, and Glossary*, xlvii–xlix.

66 'The wise Augustine ... whom we well trust for such great depth' (*CH* II.22.21–2).

67 *CH* I.praef.15; see Godden, 'Source Summary for Anglo-Saxon Text *Catholic Homilies*' and *Introduction, Commentary, and Glossary*, xlvii–xlix and liii–liv.

68 *Introduction, Commentary, and Glossary*, xlviii. A number of the Tractates were also available to Ælfric in the homiliary of Paul the Deacon, on which, see below.

69 Godden, 'Source Details: C.B.9.4.001.01.'

70 Smetana, 'Early Medieval Homiliary' and 'Haymo'; Joyce Hill, 'Smaragdus' and 'Sources Reconsidered.'

71 Smetana, 'Paul the Deacon,' 75.

72 Hill, 'Smaragdus,' 205–8. For Smaragdus's life and works, see Rädle, *Studien*, and Leclercq, 'Smaragdus.'

73 Hill, 'Smaragdus,' 205; cf. 'Sources Reconsidered,' 363.

74 Godden, *Introduction, Commentary, and Glossary*, xli.

75 Smaragdus, *Expositio in Regulam Sancti Benedicti* and *Diadema monachorum*;

see Godden, *Introduction, Commentary, and Glossary*, xxxix and lx. For seminal studies arguing for increased recognition of Smaragdus's importance for Ælfric, see Joyce Hill, 'Authority and Intertextuality' and 'Smaragdus.'

76 See Souter, 'Contributions,' 'Further Contributions,' and 'A Further Contribution.'

77 Gneuss, 'Liturgical Books in Anglo-Saxon England,' 123. See now, however, Joyce Hill, 'Paul the Deacon, Homiliary.'

78 On which text, see Brown, *Augustine of Hippo*, 151–75, at 159.

79 *Confessiones* IV.15.26 (CCSL 27, p. 53, line 50).

80 Ibid. X.29.40 (CCSL 27, p. 176, line 9)

81 *Confessiones* XIII.9.10 (CCSL 27, p. 247, line 17).

82 Brown, *Augustine of Hippo*, 64.

83 Godden lists *Enarrationes in psalmos* as a 'probable source' for *CH* II.40 in 'Record C.B.1.2.49.009.02 for Source Title *Enarr.psalm.*,' but calls it a 'faint parallel' in *Introduction, Commentary, and Glossary*, xlviii.

84 *Enarrationes* 118.19.7 (CCSL 40, p. 1729, lines 13–14).

85 Ibid. (CCSL 40, p. 1729, lines 22–4).

86 Ibid. 118.23.8 (CCSL 40, p. 1744, line 5).

87 Ibid. 118.26.7 (CCSL 40, p. 1755, lines 21–2).

88 Ibid. 78.12 (CCSL 39, p. 1106, lines 6–7).

89 'We have free will; but how much can we do with our free will in this regard [keeping God's commands], unless he who commands helps us?' (Ibid. 138.13 [CCSL 40, p. 1999, lines 21–3]).

90 Fiedrowicz, Introduction, p. 155. On Augustine's exegetical principles in *De Genesi ad litteram*, see Greene-McCreight, *Ad litteram*, 32–94, at 35–40; and Van Fleteren, 'Principles of Augustine's Hermeneutic,' 17–20. For overviews of Augustine's treatment of creation in works not primarily dedicated to the subject, see also Fiedrowicz, General Introduction, p. 14, and TeSelle, 'Nature and Grace.'

91 Specifically, it was used as a source for Ælfric's *Preface to Genesis* (Griffith, 'Ælfric's *Preface to Genesis*' and 'Ælfric's Use of His Sources'); a probable source for *CH* I.1 and a possible source for *CH* II.12 (Godden, *Introduction, Commentary, and Glossary*, l); a probable source for Assmann 4 (Cross, 'The Elephant,' 367–73; Pope, *Homilies of Ælfric*, I:394–5; and Clayton, 'Of Mice and Men'); a source for the *Interrogationes Sigewulfi in Genesin* (Bedingfield, '*Interrrogationes*,' and Wilcox, *Ælfric's Prefaces*, 118; see also MacLean, 'Ælfric's Version' [1883, p. 471 and 1884, fourth-tier apparatus]); and a source for *De temporibus anni* (Atherton, '*De temporibus anni*,' and Henel, Ælfric's *De Temporibus Anni*, liv). Ælfric may have drawn on *De Genesi ad litteram* directly for *CH* I.1, but the passage is one he may also

have encountered in Bede's *In principium Genesis*; see Godden, *Introduction, Commentary, and Glossary*, xlviii.

92 I am grateful to my first anonymous external reader for suggesting that I incorporate a discussion of this work; I agree with said reader, moreover, that sustained commentary throughout this volume on the first free choices of the will, as seen in the fall of both wicked angels and human beings, would address a key aspect of the subject at hand, historical understandings of volition. It is my sincere regret that, as with the associated question of predestination, I cannot within the bounds of this study do justice to these issues. For the relationship of human volition not only to predestation and the angelic and human fall, but also to the further complicating question of the origin of the soul, see Burns, 'From Persuasion to Predestination.'

93 As in *De ciuitate Dei* XI.29, Augustine's point is not to suggest the seeming omniscience of the angels, but the omniscient source of their knowledge. Indeed, he says, just as Genesis states, that 'Appellauitque lucem diem et tenebras noctem' (And he called the light 'day' and the darkness 'night' [I.5]), so the difference between knowledge gained through the Word and knowledge gained by individuals' own power is literally the difference between day and night (*De Genesi ad litteram* IV.23).

94 See also 1 John 3.8: 'Ab initio diabolus peccat' (From the beginning, the devil sins).

95 *De Genesi ad litteram* CSEL 28.1, p. 292, lines 20–2 and 25-6. Much of the above also appears in Book XI of *De ciuitate Dei*. There Augustine notes that God gave angels a 'day-like knowledge' (*cognitio diurna*) of himself and creation through direct exposure to the Word (XI.29). The righteous angels were blessed not only through this enjoyment of the unchangeable good – God himself – but by the foreknowledge that they would eternally remain in that enjoyment: their blessedness was not marred, in other words, by the knowledge that it would one day be lost (X.13). Satan was not so blessed: though he could have remained in righteousness, he was a murderer from the beginning and did not stand firm in the truth (XI.13 and 15; John 8.44). The evil angels, likewise, though made light (XI.11), became darkness and were separated by God from the light ('diuisit lucem ac tenebras' [XI.19 and 33; Gen. 1.4]). In both cases, however, God both foreknew their evil choices and foresaw the good which he would bring about as a result (XI.17–18).

96 On the circumstances surrounding the composition of *De ciuitate Dei*, see Brown, *Augustine of Hippo*, 297–311; for Augustine's teaching on volition therein, see Dougherty, 'The Role of the Will.'

97 'Indeed, our wills themselves are included in that order of causes which is certain to God and which is encompassed by his foreknowledge'

(*De ciuitate Dei* V.9 [CCSL 47, p. 138, lines 97–8]). For Augustine's discussion of foreknowledge and volition in *De ciuitate Dei*, see for example Matthews, *Augustine*, 96–104.

98 God 'helps those willing good, judges those willing evil, orchestrates everyone, giving power to some and not to others' (*De ciuitate Dei* V.9 [CCSL 47, p. 139, lines 128–30]).

99 Ibid. XI.21 (CCSL 48, p. 339, lines 18–22).

100 Ibid. XII.22 (CCSL 48, p. 380, line 19).

101 'The chain of this disaster ... with its concatenation of griefs which leads the human race from its depraved origin, as from a corrupted root, right to the ruin of the second death which has no end, excepting only those who are freed by the grace of God' (ibid. XIII.14 [CCSL 48, p. 396, lines 11–15]).

102 Ibid. XIV.11 (CCSL 48, p. 432, lines 43–4).

103 For a clear discussion of this image and the the Aristotelian physics behind it, see Gilson, *Christian Philosophy*, 134–6, and Dougherty, 'The Role of the Will,' 98–9; for Augustine's comparison of the will to the gravity of a stone in *De libero arbitrio* 3.1, see Wetzel, *Limits of Virtue*, 77–85. Cf. Augustine's image of humans being drawn to the sweetness of righteousness, above.

104 Love, 'Records for Source Title *Ench*[*iridion*].'

105 'What good can a ruined person do, save to the extent that he has been freed from ruin? Can he do anything by the free power of his will? May this never be!' (*Enchiridion* CCSL 46, p. 65, lines 35–7).

106 Ibid. CCSL 46, p. 67, lines 103–4.

107 Ibid. CCSL 46, p. 107, lines 44–5.

108 Gneuss lists two copies of *De haeresibus* surviving from after this date: Cambridge, Trinity College, B.3.25 (104) (s. xi/xii; provenance Canterbury, Christ Church [§163]) and London, British Library, Harley 3859 (s. xi/xii, England or Continent? [§439]).

109 Godden, 'The Translations of Alfred and His Circle,' 2.

110 *Soliloquia* I.15.30 (CSEL 89, p. 44, lines 12–13).

111 Ibid. II.1.1 (CSEL 89, p. 45, lines 6–8).

112 'Command, I beg you, and order what you wish, but ... heal and open my eyes, through which I may see your will ... and I hope that I will do all that you command' (*Soliloquia* I.1.5 [CSEL 89, p. 8, lines 10–12 and 14–15]).

113 *Soliloquia* I.1.4 (CSEL 89, p. 8, lines 10–12); cf. Plotinus, *Enneads* III.7.11 as noted by Watson, 'Commentary: Soliloquies,' 168.

114 Ibid. I.1.4 (CSEL 89, p. 8, lines 13–15).

115 Godden, 'Records for Source Title *Retract*[*ationes*]'.

116 'Those who think that free will is denied when God's grace is defended, so defend free will so as to deny God's grace, affirming that it is given according to our merits' (*Retractationes* §66 [CCSL 57, p. 141, lines 3–5]).

117 'Diffuses through all things and uses all things according to the unchangeable judgment of his purpose ... whether for good through his grace or for
evil through a person's own will' (*De Trinitate* III.4.9 [CCSL 50, p. 135,
lines 11–12 and 14–15]).

118 See Ex. 7.3.

119 'That a person should be impelled here or there by his evil nature ... that
such impulses should exist or not exist – this is not in a person's control;
but such impulses come from secret Providence, manifestly most just and
wise' (*Quaestiones in Heptateuchum* II.18 [CCSL 33, p. 76, lines 226–31]).

120 Ibid. II.18 (CCSL 33, p. 77, line 248).

121 Ibid. V.15.4 (CCSL 33, p. 286, lines 403–4). Contrast this position with
Cassian's view of human 'cooperation' below.

122 *De baptismo* IV.24.31 (CSEL 51, p. 260, line 1).

123 Augustine's version differs slightly from the Vulgate, which reads 'sanctificat se sicut et ille sanctus est.'

124 *In Ioannis epistulam* IV.7 (PL 35.2009). Immediately before this passage,
Augustine does state that God does not purify the unwilling ('*Deus te
nolentem non castificat*'), but in context of his other work we understand
that God first makes human beings willing through his grace.

125 *De praedestinatione* 15.31 (PL 44.982).

126 Ibid. 16.32 (PL 44.983).

127 Godden, *Introduction, Commentary, and Glossary,* 58, and 'Record
C.B.1.1.8.020.01 for Source Title *Corr.grat.*'

128 *De correptione* PL 44.933.

129 Ibid. PL 44.940.

130 Goden, *Introduction, Commentary, and Glossary,* 58.

131 'You are from your father, the devil' (John 8.44).

132 *Tractatus* XLII.10. Cf. XII.12: 'Quod audis homo, Deus fecit; quod audis
peccator, ipse homo fecit' [That you are called human is God's doing; that
you are called a sinner is humanity's own doing] (CCSL XXXVI, pp. 128,
lines 24–5).

133 *Tractatus* XLII.15. Cf. XLII.16: 'A natura uitium secernatur' (Let human vice
be distinguished from human nature) (CCSL XXXVI, p. 373, lines 3–4).

134 *Sermones* LVII.8.8, citing Rom. 7.23–5 and Gal. 5.17; cf. *De sermone Domini
in monte* II.11.38.

135 'No one has anything of his own except falsehood and sin' (*Tractatus* V.1
[CCSL XXXVI, p. 40, lines 6–9]).

136 'You will unquestionably be beaten if you do not have [God] to help you'
(*Sermones* LVII.9.9 [PL 38.391B]).

137 'Potestatis suae fortioribus uinculis, sic eripit uasa eius, quaecunque
praedestinauit eripere, ab ejus liberans potestate, ut illo non impediente,

credant in istum libera uoluntate' (*Epistulae* 217 [CSEL 57, p. 411, line 10]; this is mislabelled as *Ex Beda* in PL).

138 *De correptione* XIII.42 (PL 44.942), a passage not among Ælfric's sources.

139 'It takes when it is taken' (*Tractatus* XLII.1 [CCSL XXXVI, p. 366, lines 19–20]).

140 *Sermones* LXXVI.3.5. It might be objected, however, that this is faith in God's willingness and power to save in daily life rather than faith in his willingness and power to save at the Judgment [i.e., the faith of conversion].

141 The devil is equated to the serpent in the parable, which the good Father does not give in contrast to the fish ['quis autem ex uobis patrem petet ... piscem numquid pro pisce serpentem dabit illi'] (*Sermones* CV.4.6 [PL 38.620–1]; Luke 11.11).

142 'To the one who does not work, but believes in him who justifies the ungodly, his faith is counted as righteousness' (Rom. 4.5).

143 'Even our very faith in Christ is the work of Christ. He works this in us, though certainly not without us' (*Tractatus* LXXII.2 [CCSL XXXVI, p. 508, lines 21–3]).

144 'He is drawn by what he runs to, drawn by loving it, drawn without hurt to the body, drawn by a cord of the heart ... For what does the soul more strongly desire than the truth?' (*Tractatus* XXVI.5 [CCSL XXXVI, p. 262, lines 27–8 and 31–2]).

145 'What they understand is given them within, flashes within, is revealed within' (*Tractatus* XXVI.7 [CCSL XXXVI, p. 263, lines 5–6]).

146 'Everyone who has heard and learned from the Father comes to me' (Ibid.; John 6.45).

147 *Collectiones in Euangelia et Epistolas* (PL 102.160C), quoting *Tractatus* XLIV.1–6. Cf. Gregory's treatement of the blind man outside Jericho.

148 'Illumination is faith' (*Collectiones* [PL 102.160CD], quoting *Tractatus* XLIV.1–2).

149 'To those who received him, to those who believed in his name, to them he gave power to become sons of God.'

150 'Therefore the power is given that they who believe on him should become the sons of God, since this very thing is given, that they believe on him' (*Collectiones* [PL 102.34C], quoting *Tractatus* II.13; cf. *Contra duas epistulas* I.3.6).

151 'Grace ... precedes us so that from servants we may be [made] friends. For this reason, let not pride creep up on us, as if we received anything for our own merits while we were children of wrath. But now we have been made sons of God through grace, without which we can do nothing' (*Collectiones* [PL 102.531AB]).

152 'Embrace the truth, *so that* you may gain freedom'; 'Blot out what you have done, *so that* God may save what he has done' (*Tractatus* XLII.13 and XII.12 [CCSL XXXVI, p. 371, lines 26–7 and p. 128, lines 22 and 25–6]; emphasis mine).

153 'For your sin would not have displeased you if God did not shine into you and reveal it to you by his truth' (*Tractatus* XII.13 [CCSL XXXVI, p. 128, lines 35–6]).

154 *Tractatus* LXXX.2 and LXXXI.1.

155 'By the grace of God I am what I am' (I Cor. 15.10).

156 '[This] sounds as if you have begun to give yourself credit for what a short while ago you had been attributing to God. Admit it, and continue, "Not I, though, but the grace of God with me"' (*Sermones* LXXVI.5.7 [PL 38.482A]).

157 'Work out your own salvation with fear and trembling'; 'It is God who works in you both to will and to do' (Phil. 2.12–13; *Tractatus* LXXII.3).

158 *Tractatus* LXXII.3 (CCSL XXXVI, pp. 508–9).

159 *Sermones* LXXI.19; cf. Rom. 5.5 and *Tractatus* XXVI.1.

160 'Therefore let no one say, "Who can do that?" Strive to accomplish these things in your hearts. Persevere that you may love. Struggle and you shall overcome' (*Sermones* V.3 [CCSL XLI, p. 52, lines 75–7]).

161 'Christ conquers there [in your hearts]' (*Sermones* V.3 [CCSL XLI, p. 52, line 77]).

162 'He himself slipped this desire into [men's hearts]' (*Sermones* LVI.3.4 [PL 38.379A]).

163 'Unless the Lord keeps watch over the city, the watchman labours in vain.'

164 'Labour, by all means, guard it'; 'but it is good for you that you are being guarded. Because you are not up to guarding yourself' (*Sermones* CCX–CVII.7 [PL 38.1362C]).

165 'I have fought the good fight; I have finished the course' (II Tim. 4.7).

166 'You have completed the course – but with whose leading, whose direction, whose help? ... This is due not to him who wills or him who runs, but to God who has mercy' (*Sermones* CCXCVII.6 [PL 38.1362B]; cf. Rom. 9.16).

167 'Nothing is ever done by you which God himself does not do in you' (*Sermones* LVI.7 [PL 38.280B]).

168 Cf. Saarinen's statement that 'although the modern research is convinced that Augustine's philosophy of freedom underwent significant changes between *De libero arbitrio* and his anti-Pelagian writings, the medieval scholars did not pay any attention to the shifts that occurred over the years in Augustine's thought' (*Weakness of the Will*, 21), as well as Johnson's comment that 'the difficulty with appealing to Orange II as the conciliar triumph of Augustinianism is that during most of the Middle Ages it was either not understood or not known at all ... Accordingly, the knowledge that there was a Semi-Pelagian controversy was by and large lost to the Middle Ages' ('Augustinian Synthesis,' 158–9). One factor that would have made such a recognition more likely is if Alfred or others like him had access to the *Retractationes* (one pre-eleventh-century copy of which survives in Cambridge, Clare College 19 [England?, s. x^2].

2. Cooperating with Grace: Gregory the Great, Apostle to the English

1 Cf. McEniery, 'Infallibility,' 265.
2 For biographical studies of Gregory, see Dudden, *Gregory* (still 'the standard work on Gregory's pontificate' [Richards, *Consul of God*, 2]); Henry Chadwick, *The Church in Ancient Society*, 658–74; Scharer, 'The Gregorian Tradition in Early England' (for the tribute paid in medieval England to Gregory as teacher and instigator of English conversion); and Kannengiesser, 'Gregory the Great,' 30–6. See also Ælfric's account of Gregory in *CH* II.9.12–42. On the Augustinian mission, see Gameson, 'Augustine of Canterbury'; Markus, 'Augustine and Gregory the Great'; and Stancliffe, 'The British Church and the Mission of Augustine.'
3 *CH* II.9.1 – the term having been introduced long before by the early eighth-century bishop of Sherborne, Aldhelm, and his contemporary, the anonymous Whitby-based author of the *Liber beati Gregorii* (Hall, 'The Early English Manuscripts of Gregory,' 115; see also Lendinara, 'Gregory and Damasus,' 138–9).
4 See Godden, '*Catholic Homilies*.' On Ælfric's Life of Gregory, see Gretsch, 'Ælfric and Gregory the Great.'
5 *Dialogorum libri iv*, Book II.
6 For the biographical overview and survey of works that follows, see Recchia, 'Gregory the Great'; Rush and Hester, 'Gregory (the Great)'; Zinn, 'Gregory I the Great'; Barnish, 'Gregory I'; and Cross and Livingstone, *ODCC*, 706–7; see also Peterson, '"Homo omnino Latinus"?'
7 *Epistula* 5.6 and 42.
8 Deleeuw, 'Gregory the Great's "Homilies on the Gospels,"' 868; see also perhaps the overview by von Hagel, 'The Forty Gospel Homilies of Gregory the Great.'
9 Zinn, 'Gregory I the Great,' 490.
10 Rush and Hester, 'Gregory (the Great),' 482.
11 See for example Evans's review of Ricci, *Mysterium Dispensationis*, and Wilken, 'Interpreting Job Allegorically.'
12 On Gregory's contributions to the liturgy, see for example Jungmann, *Mass of the Roman Rite*, 1: 63.
13 Reccia, 'Gregory the Great,' 367, and Rush and Hester, 'Gregory (the Great),' 483.
14 See Meyvaert, 'Bede's Text of the *Libellus Responsionum*.' For the potential purpose of its positioning in Book III of the *Old English Bede*, see Rowley, 'Reading Gregory the Great's *Libellus Responsionum*.' On the *Libellus* and the Augustinian mission, see Gameson, 'Augustine of Canterbury'; Markus,

'Augustine and Gregory the Great'; and Stancliffe, 'The British Church and the Mission of Augustine.'

15 For an examination of the influence of the *Dialogi* on early medieval England, Ireland, Spain, and Gaul, see Kuzdale, 'The "Dialogues" of Pope Gregory the Great'; for its influence on Bede in particular, see pp. 231–60. An intriguing study of the influence of the *Dialogi* (specifically, of Jewish apocryphal accounts of the Fall preserved therein) on *Genesis B* by way of the Old Saxon *Genesis* is found in Cole, 'The *Dialogi* of Gregory the Great and the Old Saxon *Genesis*.'

16 Seeberg, *Lehrbuch*, III.45, quoted by Atwell, 'Augustine to Gregory,' 173.

17 Straw, *Perfection in Imperfection*, 13. Evans posits that one reason for this is that whereas Augustine's work is both theoretical and explorative, pioneering the expression of Christian doctrine, Gregory's mind is practical, focused on the needs of pastoral instruction. Teaching with the confidence that church councils have ruled on the issues of the faith, he is concerned to show how they are relevant to the daily life of the believer. In doing so, he struck such a note with his audience that his work had an enormous impact on the medieval world (*The Thought of Gregory*; cf. Atwell, 'Augustine to Gregory,' 176–7).

18 Not that such exhortation is not a key component of Augustine's work: as he says in *De dono perseverantiae* when questioned on the relationship of preaching and predestination, 'Numquid quia dixit, *Deus est qui operatur in uobis et uelle et operari, pro bona uoluntate* [Phil. 2.13]; ideo non ipse, et ut uelimus quae Deo placeant, et ut operemur, hortatus est?' (Because he said, 'It is God who works in you both to will and to do according to [his] good will,' therefore did he not exhort us both to will and to do what pleases God?' [14.34 (PL 45.1013)]).

19 Pelikan, *Christian Tradition*, 330.

20 Semi-Pelagianism takes the view that God may bestow grace in response to individuals' meritorious initiative of faith; on which, see below.

21 Dudden, *Gregory*, 2:393; cf. 382–3, 395–6, and 398–9.

22 The point is not an uncontested one. On the one hand, scholars have repeatedly argued for texts such as the *Moralia* as being sources for Anglo-Saxon literature, whether for *Genesis B* (Dando, 'The *Moralia in Job*'; Hill, 'Satan's Injured Innocence'); the Old English *Exodus* (Green, 'Gregory the Great as Inspirational Source'); or even *Beowulf* (Goldsmith, *The Mode and Meaning of 'Beowulf'*; Allen, 'Gregory and the Poet of *Beowulf*, and now Johnson, 'The Gregorian Grendel'). Similarly, the *Homiliae in Euangelia* have been cited as sources for texts as wide-ranging as *Christ II* (noted early by Dietrich,

'Cynevulfs Crist,' 204); Alfred's *Soliloquia* (Gatch, 'King Alfred's Version of Augustine's *Soliloquia*,' 35–6); Byrhtferth's *Enchiridion* (Baker and Lapidge, *Byrhtferth's Enchiridion*, 126–8 and 316–17); and the *Old English Martyrology* (Cross, 'On the Library of the Old English Martyrologist,' 232–3, and 'The Use of Patristic Homilies in the Old English Martyrology,' 107); to say nothing of Old English homilies, whether anonymous (Förster, 'Zu den Blickling Homilies,' 180–2; Gatch, 'Eschatology in the Anonymous Old English Homilies,' 120; and Scragg, *Vercelli Homilies*, 108–9, 116–21, 139, 143, 266, and 269–70) or Ælfrician (as discussed hereafter). Mechthild Gretsch, assessing the availability of Gregory's works in Anglo-Saxon England, affirms that the paucity of early surviving Gregorian material should not lead us to discount the presence of these influential texts: 'there is a similarly low survival rate of pre-Conquest in proportion to post-Conquest manuscripts [of the popular patristic homiliary of Paul the Deacon] as for Gregory's collections of homilies or his *Moralia*. This situation, in turn, may permit us to think not too pessimistically about the availability of these Gregorian texts in a great library such as that of the Old Minster [at Winchester]' ('Ælfric and Gregory the Great,' 37–8). Michael Lapidge notes, moreover, that both the *Moralia in Iob* and the *Homiliae in Euangelia* appear repeatedly in the recorded contents of Old English libraries ('Surviving Booklists from Anglo Saxon England,' 51, 59, 63, 66, 70, and 77; see Hall, 'The Early English Manuscripts of Gregory,' 115–16), recently going so far as to include the *Dialogi, Regula pastoralis, Homiliae in Euangelia*, and *Moralia* among the staple texts 'which were almost certainly to be found in any Anglo-Saxon library, whether large or small' (Lapidge, *The Anglo-Saxon Library*, 127–8; see also 304–7). Given such evidence, as well as that adduced below, it seems reasonably safe to conclude along with Kees Dekker that 'the *Moralia in Iob* and the *Homiliae in Evangelia* were well-known in Anglo-Saxon England' ('King Alfred's Translation,' 29 n.12, pointing specifically to the work of Johnson and Hall ['The Gregorian Grendel' and 'The Early English Manuscripts of Gregory']). At the same time, however, I have repeatedly encountered senior scholars who have expressed doubts, off the record, as to the consistent and widespread knowledge of Gregory's works through the Anglo-Saxon period. One of my clearly erudite anonymous external readers, for example, registers concern about this claim, noting that the *Moralia*, for example, might have been known not in its entirety but through epitomes or abbreviations such as that of Paterius (bishop of Brescia, d. 606; notary for and abstractor of Gregory's works). The point is well taken, even if Paterius's *Liber de expositione uetus ac noui testamenti* refrains, in fact, from including extracts from Gregory's complex work on Job – Paterius himself apologizing for this fact (PL 79.685A) – and if certain of our authors may have been shown to be independent of

Paterius altogether (Laistner states categorically, for example, that 'it may be said at once that Bede did not use Paterius' ['Bede as a Classical and a Patristic Scholar,' 87]). For the present, therefore, my argument as to the early English knowledge of Gregory with confidence is set forth here with confidence tempered with a degree of caution.

23 Gneuss, *Handlist*, §§858, 865.5, and 937.3.

24 Ibid., §§375 and 626.

25 Ibid., §§37 and 626.

26 Ibid., §§261, 359, 565, 632, 667, 767, and 771.

27 On which manuscript, see Clemoes, *Ælfric's Catholic Homilies*, 1.

28 Ibid., §§42, 255, 346, 375, 626, 771, 804.5, 831.6, 833, 840.5, 856.1, 894, 898.5, 911, 930.5 [on which, see Hall, 'Early English Manuscripts', p. 122 (§6)], 943.8, 944.5, and 946.5.

29 Ibid., §§37, 70, 90, 180, 207, 208, 261, 353, 359, 510, 564, 565, 583.3, 590, 632, 667, 684, 668.5, 715, 767, 804.5, and 924.

30 For Bede's Gregorian sources, see Lapidge, *The Anglo-Saxon Library*, 128 and 209–12; Colgrave and Mynors, *Bede's Ecclesiastical History*, 3 n. 3, 129 n. 3, 157 n. 2, 266 n. 2, 446 n. 1, 502 n. 1, and 592 (index); Plummer, *Venerabilis Baedae Opera Historica*, 43–4, 62–3, 65–7, 74, 78, and 214; Wallace-Hadrill, *Bede's Ecclesiastical History*, 39; Kitson, 'Lapidary Traditions,' 89; Quentin, *Les Martyrologes Historiques*, 102; Love, '*Commentarius in Genesim* [*In principium Genesis*],' '*Explanatio Apocalypsis* [*Expositio Apocalypseos*],' '*Letter to John*,' '*Martyrologium*,' '*Passio S. Anastasii*,' '*Vita S. Cuthberti* (prose),' and '*Vita S. Felicis*'; Orchard, '*De die iudicii*'; Orchard and Love, '*Vita metrica S. Cuthberti*'; and Scarfe Beckett, '*Historia ecclesiastica gentis Anglorum*.' On the knowledge of and particular reverence for Gregory in another early eighth-century Northumbrian centre of learning, Whitby (on which, see Blair, 'Whitby'), see also Rambridge, 'The Northumbrians and Pope Gregory'; and Dekker, 'King's Alfred's Translation,' 33–5.

31 For Alfred's Gregorian sources, see Carnicelli, *Soliloquies*, 104–5; Jost, 'Zur Textkritik,' 262–4; Discenza, 'Alfred's Cræft,' 319–21; Otten, *König Alfreds Boethius*, 48; Godden, '*Augustine, Soliloquies*'; Discenza, '*Boethius, The Consolation of Philosophy*'; Joan Hart, '*Gregory the Great, The Pastoral Care*'; Gatch, 'King Alfred's Version of Augustine's *Soliloquia*,' 35–6; Hall, 'The Early English Manuscripts of Gregory the Great's *Homilies on the Gospel*,' 115–16; and see Gretsch, 'Ælfric and Gregory the Great,' 22–5. Gregorian texts that influenced works by Alfred's circle are noted by Bately, *The Old English Orosius*, 326; and Jayatilaka, '*Gregory the Great, Dialogues*' and '*Orosius, History Against the Pagans*.' For the view that the *Regula pastoralis* particularly shaped Alfred's notion of society, articulating 'his understanding of how

the community is structured and how each part of it functions', see Discenza, 'The Influence of Gregory the Great on the Alfredian Social Imaginary' (67).

32 For a discussion of works known to Lantfred, particularly as manifested by the sources of his *Translatio et miracula S. Swithuni* (on which, see below), see Lapidge, *The Anglo-Saxon Library,* 241, and *Cult of St Swithun,* 234–5. Again, however, note that not all are convinced that knowledge of the *Moralia* in Anglo-Saxon England was widespread: one of my anonymous external readers notes that Lantfred's use of the text 'seems to be limited to the odd pair of words here and there,' and that figures such as Lantfred may well have accessed the *Moralia* indirectly through epitomes or abbreviations of Gregory's work.

33 Wulfstan, *De Anticristo et eius signis* (Bethurum Ia). Bethurum comments that one explanation in the homily 'is found in several places in the writings of Gregory, though the wording is not taken exactly from any of them' (*Homilies,* 23); see also Hall, 'Wulfstan's Latin Sermons,' 95. Bethurum notes that material in *De septiformi spiritu* (Bethurum IX) may be dependent on Gregory, but only indirectly so, as Wulfstan's immediate source was Ælfric's discussion of the subject (Napier VIII [Bethurum, *Homilies,* 305]).

34 On Gregorian sources for Ælfric's *Sermones catholici,* see Godden, *Introduction, Commentary, and Glossary,* liii–liv, and 'Catholic Homilies'; see also Oetgen, 'Ælfric's Use of Gregory the Great's *Homiliae in Euangelia.*'

35 For the possibility that the section of Book IV of the *Dialogi* adapted in Vercelli XIV may have been drawn from a complete tenth-century translation of the *Dialogi,* now lost – a translation to which Ælfric may refer as well (*CH* II.21.176–80) – see Szarmach, 'Another Old English Translation.'

36 See Godden, *Introduction, Commentary, and Glossary,* liv.

37 Godden, *Introduction, Commentary, and Glossary,* 592.

38 Besserman, 'A Note'; see also Förster, 'Der Inhalt,' 57 n. 1, as noted in Godden, *Introduction, Commentary, and Glossary,* 593.

39 Gabrielson, 'Guischart de Beauliu.'

40 *SH* I.1.10–16 and I.18.347–65.

41 'God's mercy goes before us, and his mercy follows us. When our desire was wrong, God's mercy prevented us, so that we desired what was good; now that we desire good, God's mercy follows us so that our choice will not be in vain' (*CH* II.5.227–30).

42 'Both by going before enabled them to will the good that they did not desire, and by following after enabled them to be able to do the good which they do desire' (*Moralia* IV.22.9.20 [CCSL 143A, p. 1108]).

43 '[God's mercy] precedes the unwilling to make him willing; it follows the willing so that he may not will in vain' (*Enchiridion* IX.32 [CCSL 46,

p. 67, lines 103–4; cf. the expanded treatment of this theme in *De natura et gratia* 31.35]).

44 Godden, *Introduction, Commentary, and Glossary,* p. 593. One should note that not all share this confidence in Ælfric's direct knowledge of the *Moralia*: my first anonymous reader, for example, finds Godden's assertion here 'highly unlikely.'

45 Another reason may be the sheer influence of the *Homiliae in Euangelium* compared with other homiletic collections, including other homilies by Gregory: see Deleeuw, 'Gregory the Great's "Homilies on the Gospels."'

46 For full listings, see Appendix I, Tables I.3 and I.4, respectively. *Homiliae in Euangelia* I.11 is the exception, and it appears as part of the 'original' homiliary (PD 123, Summer; see Appendix I, Table I.3).

47 Nonetheless, references where appropriate are supplied in the footnotes below.

48 The *Moralia* are a signfiicant exception, having their roots in conversations with his monks at Constantinople from ca. 579; even this work, however, saw its final revisions completed in the years leading to and immediately following Augustine's mission in 596.

49 See Adriaen, 'Prolegomena,' v; Martin, Introduction in *Acts of the Apostles,* i; and Cross and Livingstone, *Oxford Dictionary,* 706–7. Leyser notes, however, that 'the possibility that Gregory could have encompassed contradictions as a thinker and a writer is, perhaps, too rarely admitted (in contrast to the ample room for complexity and development afforded Augustine of Hippo)' (*Authority and Asceticism,* 135).

50 Note, however, that it is uncertain whether Ælfric knew the *Confessiones,* whence this image comes, since it is not among the recorded sources for the *Sermones.*

51 *Moralia* VIII.6.8.

52 *Moralia* II.8.32.54, VIII.32.53, and VIII.10.19.

53 *Homiliae* I.2.2, and Jerome, *Liber interpretationis hebraicorum nominum* Matth. I–O (CCSL 72, p. 137, line 9); cf. *Regula pastoralis* II.10 and III.12.

54 He also compares such distractions to a crowd of anxieties which block any view of individuals' hearts (*Moralia* XXIV.11.30). Here, too, Gregory's view of human mutability appears, being opposed to discipline and thus any hope of righteousness.

55 *Homiliae* I.2.3–4.

56 *Moralia* XXVI.44.79 (CCSL 143B, p. 1325, lines 9–13).

57 *Moralia* XXV.6.10 (CCSL 143B, p. 1236, lines 42–3); holy people 'are assuredly never subject to the pressure of any tumults in their breast ... for their desires are fixed upon the eternal country alone, and loving none of the

things of this world, they enjoy a perfect tranquillity of mind' (IV.30.58 [CCSL 143, p. 203, lines 67 and 71–3]).

58 *Moralia* VI.28.22.46 and VI.28.19.43.

59 *Moralia* IV.20.5.12.

60 *Homiliae* III.3 (PL 76.1087D; also noted in Straw, 'Purity and Death,' 24); cf. *Dialogi* III.20.

61 *Moralia* XXVIII.19.43 (CCSL 143B, p. 1430, lines 13–16 and 20–4).

62 *Moralia* IX.57.86 (CCSL 143, pp. 517–18).

63 *Homiliae* II.26.4 (PL 76.1199).

64 *Moralia* XXIV.11.26 (CCSL 143B, p. 1206).

65 *Moralia* XVII.16.22 (CCSL 143A, p. 865).

66 He actually notes a fourth, the first terror of judgment, but this in fact precedes conversion (*Moralia* XXVII.17.33).

67 *Moralia* IV.34.68 (CCSL 143, p. 212), and XXIV.11.28–9; cf. above, p. 17.

68 *Moralia* IV.35.71 (CCSL 143, p. 215; emphasis mine).

69 'Unshackles the bands of the heart, that our mind may raise itself to the freedom which comes through repentance, and loosed from the fetters of the flesh, may freely direct the steps of its love towards its creator' (*Moralia* IX.62.94 [CCSL 143, p. 523]). Again, this is not to imply that humans are completely freed from concupisence; Gregory immediately goes on to say, 'Iustitiam nos spiritus erigit, ad consuetudinem caro restringit' (The spirit lifts us up to righteousness; the flesh holds us back in our old habits') (ibid.).

70 Dudden, *Gregory*, 2:395–6.

71 'Heavenly pity first works something in ourselves without our help, so that with our own free will following it as well, it may do the good which we now desire with us' (*Moralia* XVI.25.30 [CCSL 143A, p. 816]).

72 'By the grace of God I am what I am' (I Cor. 15.10, quoted in *Moralia* XV.25.30).

73 'His grace bestowed upon me was not in vain, but I laboured more than all of them' (ibid.).

74 'Yet not I, but the grace of God [with me]' (ibid).

75 'That he might neither be unthankful for the divine gift, nor remain a stranger to the merit of free will' (*Moralia* XXIV.10.24 [CCSL 143B, p. 1204]).

76 'I have said these things so that no one now occupied in good works may attribute the strength with which he does them to himself' (*Homiliae* II.38.15 [PL 76.1291]).

77 *Moralia* V.29.52, and *Homiliae* I.2.

78 *Moralia* V.34.61 (CCSL 143, p. 261).

79 A point also noted by Baasten, *Pride*, 60 and 72.

80 *Moralia* IV.13.25 (CCSL 143, p. 180). Gregory's image is somewhat confused

by his concurrent assertion that humans are conceived in the darkness of night, i.e., that the concupiscence inherent in intercourse passes on their fleshly corruption. Gregory does not deny the original sin of infants, or Augustine's view that apart from grace they will do nothing good, but he does seem to view corruption as a process: the infant's sins may be inevitable, but they have yet to be realized. ·

81 *Regula pastoralis* I.11 (PL 77.25).
82 *Moralia* XXVII.25.48 (CCSL 143B, p. 1367); cf. *Homiliae* II.31.3, and Dudden, *Gregory*, 2:383; cf. p. 386.
83 McCready, *Signs of Sanctity*, 213; cf. *Moralia* XX.14.37.
84 'Has placed itself, as it were, in the middle of the way as we were passing along it, in order [namely] that we should strike against that which we are unwilling to look for' (*Moralia* XXV.12.30 [CCSL 143B, p. 1255]; cf. III.14.55.70).
85 'This very evil that it [the soul] commits inserts itself to the soul as a bar before the eye of reason. Whence it comes to pass that [i.e., as a result,] the soul, being first encompassed by voluntary darkness, afterwards does not any longer even know the good it should seek' (*Moralia* XX.14.37 [CCSL 143A, p. 1029]; cf. I.4.13.25, and *Homiliae* II.38.13).
86 *Moralia* V.34.61 (CCSL 143, p. 261).
87 *Moralia* VII.25.31 (CCSL 143A, p. 355).
88 *Moralia* VII.28.34 (CCSL 143A, p. 358).
89 *Homiliae* I.2.2 (PL 76.1083).
90 'If anyone recognizes the darkness of his blindness ... let him cry from the bottom of his heart ... saying, "Jesus, son of David, have mercy on me!"' (*Homiliae* I.2.4 [PL 76.1083]).
91 'The mind slumbers of itself, overcome by the love of this present world ... unless it is aroused by the breath of divine grace'; 'If we are roused suddenly by the hand of divine favour, we open at once those eyes, which have been long closed, to the light of truth' (*Moralia* XXVII.16.32 and XXVII.17.33 [CCSL 143B, p. 1355]).
92 'Prevenient grace, which if it never arose of free gift in our heart, assuredly our mind would remain dim in the darkness of its sins' (*Moralia* XVII.14.20 [CCSL 143A, p. 863]).
93 E.g., *Moralia* XX.4.11, XXIX.22.46, and XVIII.26.43, respectively.
94 *Homiliae* II.30.8 (PL 76.1226A), and *Moralia* IV.27.52; see John 11.43.
95 *Moralia* XI.10.15 (CCSL 143A, p. 594; cf. XI.10.16, and Acts 9.1–20).
96 Cf. above, p. 21.
97 *Homiliae* I.2; cf. John 14.6.
98 *Homiliae* II.36.9. Gregory also identifies a third group, those who understand

and are 'forced' (*compulsi*) by trials to do good, even as the master in the parable finally commands his servants to 'conpelle intrare' (compel [men] to come in). Even here, however, adverse circumstances merely give people pressing reasons to heed God's invitation; throughout, humans retain the power of resistance.

99 *Homiliae* II.38.5, quoted in Smaragdus, *Collectiones* (PL 102.488D–489A); cf. Matt. 22.5–6.

100 'Where were you when I was laying the foundation of the earth?' (Job 38.4).

101 *Moralia* XXVIII.9.20; cf. XVIII.40.65.

102 *Homiliae* II.26.3.

103 *Homiliae* II.26.1 (PL 76.1197); 'Your faith has healed you' (*Homiliae* I.2.7, quoting Mark 10.52; II.33.4, quoting Matt. 9.22).

104 Smaragdus does attribute to Gregory the statement that grace is something the believer 'consequi meruit per fidem' (deserved to obtain through faith); it is not explicit, however, that this faith originates in human beings (PL 102.77A). The attribution, in any case, is false, for the quotation comes from Sedulius Scotus, *Collectanea in Pauli epistulas*, Ad Romanos (PL 103.111).

105 *Homiliae* II.32.1, II.35.1, and II.21.3, quoting Eph. 5.8.

106 'Heavenly grace does not find human merit, in order to make it [grace] come, but after it [grace] has come, causes the same [i.e., merit]' (*Moralia* XVIII.40.63 [CCSL 143A, p. 929]).

107 'Naked I came from my mother's womb, and naked shall I return to it' (Job 1.21); 'Naked I was by grace first brought forth in the faith, and naked I shall be saved by that the same grace when taken up to heaven' (*Moralia* II.53.85 [CCSL 143, p. 111]).

3. Meriting Grace: The Venerable Bede

1 For a discussion of Bede's life and works, see George Hardin Brown, *Bede the Venerable*, v–vi, and 'Bede the Venerable (ca. 673–735)'; Grégoire, 'Bede, the Venerable'; Donahue, 'Bede, St.'; and Ward, 'Bede the Theologian.'

2 Brown, *Bede*, 42.

3 'I have devoted my whole effort to the study of the scriptures ... To meet my own need and that of my brothers, I have taken pains either to briefly remark on these things in holy Scripture from the writings of the worthy Fathers, or add to them in keeping with the Fathers' meaning and interpretation' (*Historia ecclesiastica* V.24, p. 566, also noted by Brown, *Bede*, 42]).

4 As noted by Martin, Introduction in *Acts*, xxvii–xxviii.

5 Meyvaert, 'Bede the Scholar,' 45, and Martin, Introduction in *Homilies*, xvi.
6 *Sermones spurii* III.42, III.44, III.55, III.59, III.85–6, III.88–104, and III.107–8 (Dekkers, *Clauis patrum latinorum*, 451, §1368; cf. p. 875).
7 See for example III.54, III.70–1, and III.87.
8 The exceptions are *Homiliae subdititiae* III.11 (= *Homiliae* II.6), III.31 (= *Homiliae* I.6), III.54, III.65 (= *Homiliae* II.25), III.70, III.71, III.87, III.105, and III.109, on all of which see Appendix II, Table II.3 below.
9 Jenkins, 'Bede as Exegete'; Capelle, 'Le rôle théologique'; and Carroll, *The Venerable Bede*, respectively.
10 Lapidge, Forward to Blair, *World of Bede*, vii–viii
11 See Holder, 'Mysteries of Our Salvation'; Robinson, 'Bede as Exegete'; and DeGregorio, 'Bede on Prayer and Contemplation,' respectively.
12 Houghton, 'Bede's Exegetical Theology'; Fox, 'Augustinian Hexameral Exegesis in Anglo-Saxon England'; and DeGregorio, 'Explorations of Spirituality.'
13 Carroll, *The Venerable Bede*, 140–4.
14 Ibid., 140.
15 'This also is part of his work of godliness and virtue: snatching our nation from the teeth of the ancient foe, he made it a shareholder of [eternal] freedom' (*Historia ecclesiastica* II.1 [Colgrave and Mynors, *Bede's Ecclesiastical History*, 130]). On the knowledge of and particular reverence for Gregory in early eighth-century Northumbria, see Rambridge, 'The Northumbrians and Pope Gregory'; cf. Tugene, 'L'histoire ecclésiastique de Bède le Vénérable,' 260–1.
16 See Meyvaert, 'Bede and Gregory,' 122; see also Laistner, 'The Library,' 248–9; Martin, Introduction in *Homilies*, xv–xvi; and Robinson, 'Bede as Exegete,' 217.
17 Carroll, *The Venerable Bede*, 143.
18 Namely, copies of the *Historia ecclesiastica* [Gneuss, *Handbook*, §846], *In Prouerbia Salomonis* [ibid., §604], and *De temporum ratione* [ibid., §818 and possibly §856].
19 A Mercian scholar of Alfred's court appears to have been responsible for the work; see Wormald, 'Alfred,' and Gneuss, *Handlist* §357.
20 Ibid., §§765 and 487.
21 For works by Bede written or owned in England from ca. 735 to ca. 899 (Alfred's Death), see ibid., §§25, 81, 133, 330, 367, 377, 744, 791,9, 809.9, 821.2, 835, 856.2, 863, and p. 117 regarding Arras, Bibliothèque Municipale (Médiathèque) 1079 (235), fols 28–73 and 75–80; see also §791.6.
22 For works by Bede written or owned in England from ca. 900 to ca. 1022 (Wulfstan's Death), see ibid., §§39, 56, 65, 69, 181, 190, 274, 280, 326, 357, 384, 401, 410.5, 418.8, 427, 433, 438, 489, 492, 506, 521.7, 546, 555, 557, 607,

630, 668, 673, 681, 690, 759, 784, 882, and 913; see also §459.

23 For Alfred's Bedan sources, see Brinegar, '"Books Most Necessary,"'
31–2, 37, 39, 42, 51–2, and 55; Otten, *König Alfreds Boethius*, 244; Godden,
'*Augustine, Soliloquies*'; and Discenza, 'Source Summary for Anglo-Saxon
Text *Boethius, The Consolation of Philosophy.*'

24 See Bately, *The Old English Orosius*, 161, 163, 212–14, 226, 237, 265, 268, 314,
316, 319, 334, and 339; and Jayatilaka, '*Gregory the Great, Dialogues*' and
'*Orosius, History Against the Pagans.*'

25 Lantfred also appears to have known Bede's *Expositio Apocalypseos* (Lapidge,
The Anglo-Saxon Library, 240). For a discussion of works known to Lantfred,
as manifested by the sources of his *Translatio et miracula S. Swithuni*, see
Lapidge, ibid., and *Cult of St Swithun*, 234.

26 Godden lists *De natura rerum* as a probable source for the *Sermones catholici*
but as a certain source for Ælfric's *Interrogationes Sigewulfi in Genesin* and *De
temporibus anni*; see 'Source Summary for Anglo-Saxon Text *Catholic Homilies*' and *Introduction, Commentary, and Glossary*, l–li.

27 See Godden, 'Source Summary for Anglo-Saxon Text *Catholic Homilies* and
Introduction, Commentary, and Glossary, l–li; see also Griffith, 'Source Summary
for Anglo-Saxon Text *Ælfric, Preface to Genesis*'; Bedingfield, '*Interrogationes
Sigewulfi*'; and Atherton, '*Interrogationes Sigewulfi.*'

28 See Godden, *Introduction, Commentary, and Glossary*, 165, 480, and 559; idem,
'Source Summary for Anglo-Saxon Text *Catholic Homilies*'; and Pope, *Homilies
of Ælfric*, 1:394–5 n.3.

29 *CH* II.40.125–31, quoting *Super epistulas catholicas* I Pt. II.5.61–7; see also *CH*
II.40.108–17, perhaps drawing on I Pt. II.5.93–8.

30 See Gneuss, *Handlist* §§11.5, 49, 160, 607, and 681.

31 *Super epistulas catholicas* I Pt. II.5.61–7 appears as PL 102.268A, while I Pt.
II.5.93–8 immediately precedes it at PL 102.267D–268A; see Appendix I,
Table I.13 below.

32 Godden, *Introduction, Commentary, and Glossary*, l, but cf. Pope, *Homilies of
Ælfric*, 1:167.

33 See Godden, 'Source Summary for Anglo-Saxon Text *Catholic Homilies*,' and
Introduction, Commentary, and Glossary, l–li.

34 Martin, Introduction in *Homilies*, xiv.

35 Given Ælfric's use of passages from *In Lucae euangelium expositio* and *In
Marci euangelium expositio*, if the version in PL 95 more closely resembles the
collection known to Ælfric, such could provide evidence that Ælfric knew
In Lucam and *In Marcum* independently; at present, however, the question
remains an open one.

36 Between them, the early and later versions of Paul the Deacon include all
but one of the homilies drawn upon by Ælfric, and Godden notes that 'the

exception (I.13) is a very doubtful source anyway' (*Introduction, Commentary, and Glossary*, l).

37 *Historia ecclesiastica* I.10 (Plummer, *Opera Historica*, 23); see also I.17 and 21.
38 Ó Cróinín, '"New Heresy for Old."'
39 See, for example, McCarthy and Ó Cróinín, 'The Lost Irish 84-Year Easter Table Rediscovered.'
40 On whom, see Walsh and Ó Cróinín, *Cummian's Letter De controversia paschali*.
41 Ó Cróinín, '"New Heresy for Old,"' 510–12.
42 *Historia ecclesiastica* II.19.
43 Ó Cróinín, '"New Heresy for Old,"' 505.
44 'If anyone were to assert that the full moon at Easter can come before the equinox, it would appear either that the holy Church was perfect before the Saviour came in the flesh, or that one of the faithful can have some of the eternal light prior to the prevenient gift of Christ's grace' (Bede, *De temporum ratione* 6. 46–50, p. 292). Ælfric in turn will teach that Easter is never to be observed *ær oferswiðdum þeostrum*, before the overcoming of darkness (*De temporibus anni* 6. 4, p. 46; see Kleist, 'The Influence of Bede's *De temporum ratione*,' 83).
45 'He, therefore, who should claim that the full Paschal moon can occur before the equinox ... [agrees] with those who are assured that they can be saved without the prevenient grace of Christ: because they presume to assert that they can have perfect righteousness even if the true Light had never conquered the world's darkness by dying and rising again' (*Historia* V.21 [Plummer, *Opera Historica*, 340]).
46 Anonymous, *Old English Version of Bede's Ecclesiastical History*, vol. I, p. 6, lines 23–4 and p. 8, line 27, respectively.
47 Ibid., vol. I, p. 468, line 31 – p. 470, line 1.
48 For Bede's teaching on which, particularly as related to that of Augustine, see Kleist, "The Influence of Bede's *De temporum ratione*,' 84–92 and 94–6.
49 *In Genesim* I.3.1 (CCSL 118A, p. 59, lines 1890–1, and James 4.6; cf. Augustine, *De Genesi ad litteram* XI.4).
50 *In Genesim* I.2.16–17 (CCSL 118A, p. 52, line 1639; cf. Augustine, *De Genesi* VIII.14. Immediately after, in material not reproduced by Bede, Augustine goes on to discuss the relation of human nature to divine goodness in terms evocative of Boethius's *De consolatione Philosophiae*: our nature is good, but mutable, increasing in goodness as it adheres to God, the unchangeable good; on depriving ourselves of the good which we ought to have loved, we experience evil, the loss of the good.
51 *In Genesim* I.2.17 and Rom. 7.23; cf. *De Genesi* VIII.10. On the same subject, see also *In Genesim* I.2.25 (*De Genesi* XI.1).
52 A point reiterated, for example, at I.2.18 and I.3.22–3; cf. *De Genesi* IX.6 and XI.40, respectively.

312 Notes to pages 69–70

53 Indeed, Bede says, God placed mankind in Eden so that 'praesente gratia sui conditoris malorum omnium liber ac nescius frueretur' (free and ignorant of all evils, [mankind] might enjoy the grace of his Creator immediately at hand [CCSL 118A, p. 36, lines 1099–1100]). My thanks to my first anonymous reader for drawing this line to my attention.

54 *In Genesim* I.3.6–7, and Gen. 3.7; cf. *De Genesi* XI.31.

55 *In Genesim* I.3.8 (CCSL 118A, p. 63, line 2014), and Gen. 3.8; cf. *De Genesi* XI.33.

56 *Homiliae* I.11.53–6 and I.3.159–63; cf. Augustine, *De ciuitate Dei* XVI.27, and Gregory, *Moralia* XVIII.52.84, respectively; parallels noted by Martin and Hurst, *Homilies*, 1:105 n. 11 and 1:25 n. 19.

57 'Unless one is called by the gift of God, he never escapes the condemnation of original sin; he never escapes the wickedly alluring cover of daily increasing sins; he never deserves to come to Christ to be saved' (*Homiliae* I.17 [CCSL 122, p. 125, lines 222–5]).

58 Literally, needed 'a divine loosing' (*Homiliae* II.3 [CCSL 122, p. 202, lines 64–5]; cf. Matt. 21.1–7 and Augustine, *Tractatus* LI.5.

59 'We are rightly called free, because through baptism we are unfettered from the bonds of our sins, redeemed from slavery to the devil, and made sons of God' (Smaragdus, *Collectiones* [PL 102.289C; cf. 102.320D], quoting *Super epistulas* I Pt. II.16–17.293–5).

60 'Soon, having lost our liberty, we are made slaves of sin' (ibid.). Similarly, when discussing the blindness of human beings (see below), Bede says that if a believer does not take care to put into practice what he has understood, he may well be blinded 'grauioribus peccatorum nebulis' (by the burdensome clouds of his sins) (*Homiliae* I.18 [CCSL 122, p. 131, lines 121–2]).

61 *Homiliae* II.6.4–7.

62 The 'foolish and wicked ... when they remove themselves far from the dignity of the human condition [*i.e.*, through sins], are compared to ignorant beasts of burden and have become like them, and thus are rightly deprived of the light of truth' (*Homiliae* I.8 [CCSL 122, pp. 54–5, lines 101 and 94–7]; cf. Psa. 48.13).

63 Ibid.

64 'It comes about that you are enlightened by the Lord, not by your own vision coming first, but by heavenly grace preceding you' (Smaragdus, *Collectiones* [PL 102.293C], quoting *Super epistulas* Iac. I.18.257–9). Ælfric may not have recognized this passage as Bede's, as only one copy of the *Collectiones* identifies it as such [Souter, 'Contributions,' 75], but similar statements may be found in *Homiliae* I.8.142–7 and I.3.172–4, and *In Lucam* II.6.46.

65 'Enlightens ... all the hearts of people which are *worthy* to be enlightened' (*Homiliae* I.8 [CCSL 122, p. 55, lines 99–101]; emphasis mine).
66 Based on a search in *Cetedoc* for *grati* fidei* in five words' proximity. This is not to say that Bede alone uses this phrase; it is, however, particularly prominent in his works. Augustine refers to *gratia fidei* some fifty times, but does so over a corpus that is seven times larger than Bede's: *Cetedoc* lists nearly 250,000 *sententiae* for Augustine, compared with 36,000 for Bede. Gregory, by contrast, in a corpus twice as big as Bede's (about 60,000 *sententiae*), only uses the phrase about twenty times. Only three other authors speak of *gratia fidei* to this extent: Ambrosius Mediolanensis (nearly 40,000 *sententiae*), Fulgentius Ruspensis (about 10,000 *sententiae*), and Paschasius Radbertus (nearly 35,000 *sententiae*), all of whom use the phrase some thirty times.
67 *Collectiones* (PL 102.542A, 270BC, and 469D–470A, respectively).
68 'Nowhere in Israel have I found such faith' (Matt. 8.10).
69 '[The centurion] deserved ... to be praised by the Lord for his faith'; '[Cornelius] received ... the gift of the Holy Spirit ... by merit of his great faith' (*In Lucam* II.7.6).
70 Ibid.
71 'Because he longed to share in the grace of faith which the Saviour brought to the world'; 'The ingrained habit of sins stood in his way so that he could not come to his desire' (*In Lucam* V.19.1–4 [CCSL 120, p. 333, lines 1514–16]).
72 'Looking upwards, [Jesus] saw [Zacchaeus], because through the grace of faith [Jesus] chose the one lifted above earthly lusts, and superior to the unfaithful crowds' (*In Lucam* V.19.5 [CCSL 120, p. 334, lines 1542–4]).
73 'He did not find any good merits in us for which we might be saved; rather, it was when he saw us to be weak and inglorious that he restored us by his own power and glory' (*Super epistulas* II Pt. I.3 [CCSL 121, p. 262, lines 54–6]).
74 'By the Lord it comes about that you are enlightened, not by your own effort but by grace from on high anticipating you [i.e., preceding your will]' (*Super epistulas* Iac. I.19 [CCSL 121, p. 190, lines 257–9]).
75 *Homiliae* II.6 (CCSL 122, p. 220, lines 3–4); emphasis mine.
76 Smaragdus, *Collectiones* (PL 102.343A), quoting *Homiliae* II.18.217–18.
77 *Homiliae* II.11 and I.7 (CCSL 122, p. 258, lines 201–2, and p. 48, lines 89–91).
78 *Homiliae* I.14 and I.3 (CCSL 122, p. 96, lines 55–6, and p. 20, lines 236–8).
79 *Homiliae* II.8 (CCSL 122, p. 236, lines 104–5), and Smaragdus, *Collectiones* (PL 102.354A), quoting *Super epistulas* I John 3.14.212–13.
80 *Homiliae* II.17 (CCSL 122, p. 310, lines 352–8).
81 *Super epistulas* I John 2.15 (CCSL 121, p. 293, lines 160–1); cf. Augustine, *Sermones* LXXI.19, and Gregory, *Moralia* X.6.8–10 and V.27.29.53.
82 See, for example, *Homiliae* I.15.126–8, II.18.249–50, and II.17.220–2 [*succendens*].

83 'No one loves by his free will save through the grace of the Holy Spirit' (*In Lucam* II.6.46 [CCSL 120, p. 151, lines 2016–17]; cf. *Homiliae* II.22.15–16).

84 *Homiliae* II.11 (CCSL 122, p. 257, lines 136–7).

85 'The Father loves you *because* you loved me and believed that I came from God' (John 16.27; emphasis mine).

86 *Homiliae* II.12 (CCSL 122, p. 264, lines 140–9); cf. Augustine, *Tractatus* CII.5.

87 *Homiliae* II.17 (CCSL 122, p. 310, lines 353 and 360–402; cf. I Cor. 13.12.

88 'Grace precedes a person so that he might love God with that love by which he may do good' (*Super epistulas* I John 4.10 [p. 313, lines 118–19], cited in Smaragdus, *Collectiones* [PL 102.344A]).

89 *Super epistulas* I John 3.1.12–15.

90 'And lest anyone is confident that he in his own strength is able to overcome either the dissipations or doings of the world ... "This is the victory that overcomes the world, our faith" [I John 5.4], that faith undoubtedly ... by which we humbly request his help' (*Super epistulas* I John 5.4 [CCSL 121, p. 320, lines 50–4]).

91 'The grace of Christ becomes the grace of those who accept it with a pure heart, for the person who rejects the grace of Christ does not diminish this grace but causes it not to be his, that is, he causes it to be of no benefit to him' (*Super epistulas* I Pt. V.12 [CCSL 121, p. 259, lines 115–18]).

92 'By living solemnly and justly and righteously [Tit. 2.12], we may *work together* [with God]' (*Super epistulas* I Pt. II.5 [CCSL 121, p. 234, lines 77–8]; emphasis mine).

93 Ibid., line 70.

94 'I worked more than all those [apostles]' (I Cor. 15.10a); 'Lest he should seem to have ascribed anything of this same conscientious labour to himself' (*Super epistulas* I Pt. II.5 [CCSL 121, p. 234, line 82]); 'It was not I, however, but the grace of God with me' (I Cor. 15.10b).

95 *Super epistulas* I Pt. II.5.85–8.

96 'He who hopes in the Lord makes himself holy, *as far as he can*, by himself striving and in everything seeking the grace of him who says, "Without me you can do nothing" [John 15.5]' (*Super epistulas* I John 3.3 [CCSL 121, p. 303, lines 86–9]; emphasis mine).

97 'In everything we must seek the help of him from whom we received the beginning of the good action so that we may complete it' (*Super epistulas* I Pt. I.5 [CCSL 121, p. 227, lines 94–5]).

98 *Homiliae* II.6 (CCSL 122, p. 222, lines 71–2).

99 'Let us constantly ask for his help, so that he may preserve the light of knowledge which he has bestowed upon us and bring us all the way to full day. That we may be worthy to be heard when we pray, moreover, let us cast off the works of darkness' (*Homiliae* II.20 [CCSL 122, p. 334, lines 209–13]).

100 *Homiliae* I.21 (CCSL 122, p. 151, lines 118–19).
101 'From [God] are all things'; 'Whatever good we do we have received as a gift from God'; 'Undoubtedly, whatever heavenly thing we do on earth, we have truly received help from heaven to do it' (*Homiliae* II.12, and *Super epistulas*. Iac. I.17 [CCSL 121, p. 189, line 231] and III.6 [p. 205, lines 129–30]).
102 For example, Iac. II.26b: 'Fides sine operibus mortua est' (Faith without works is dead).
103 'The perfecter of good works is God, for it is not by willing or running but by God having mercy [Rom. 9.16] and helping that we are able to reach the goal' (*Super epistulas* Iac. I.14 [CCSL 121, p. 188, lines 181–3], quoting Jerome, *Aduersus Iouinianum* II.3).
104 'The Spirit inwardly pours the power of divine love into the mind which it fills' (*Homiliae* II.11 [CCSL 122, p. 255, lines 60–1]).
105 'The Lord himself, who called him outwardly with a word, taught him inwardly with invisible inspiration so that he followed. He poured into his mind the light of spiritual grace' (*Homiliae* I.21 [CCSL 122, p. 150, lines 72–4]).
106 'By the grace of the compassionate *protection* by which he carries them forward, teaching them individually through present circumstances, whether blessings or scourges' (*Homiliae* II.8 [CCSL 122, p. 236, lines 113–15]; emphasis mine).
107 [God] 'rules the hearts of the elect as he *inhabits* them through faith and his love, and he governs them by his constant *protection* so that they may obtain the gifts of heavenly reward' (*Homiliae* I.3 [CCSL 122, p.17, lines 121–3]; emphasis mine).
108 See for example Godden, *Introduction, Commentary, and Glossary*, l–li.
109 *Introduction, Commentary, and Glossary*, l.
110 Alternatively, one might argue that Ælfric encountered full texts of *In Lucam* or the *Homiliae* during his study at Winchester, occasionally recalling particular select passages thereafter. Unfortunately, the extant evidence does not suggest that Winchester may have housed these works: the two copies of *In Lucam* (Oxford, Bodleian Library, Bodley 218 [Tours, s. ix[1]; provenance England by s. x?], and Hanover, Kestner-Museum, Cul.I.71/72 (fragment) [England or Germany, s. viii/ix]) are of general provenance, and the one copy of the *Homiliae* (Lincoln, Cathedral Library, 182 (C.2.8) [Abingdon, s. x/xi; provenance Lincoln]) is probably too late for Ælfric to have encountered it at Abingdon.
111 *Homiliae* II.14 (CCSL 122, p. 276, lines 171–2).
112 'Whether we want to obtain faith, hope, love or any other good things of heaven, they are not given to us other than by the gift of the Holy Spirit' (ibid. [p. 278, lines 242–4]).

113 'Undoubtedly whatever good we truly have, whatever we do well, this we
    receive by the same Spirit lavishing it upon us' (ibid. [p. 279, lines 248–50]).
114 'When inspired by God [the thief] offered to [God] all that he found free in
    himself, so that ... he believed with his heart to righteousness (and) con-
    fessed with (his) mouth to salvation [cf. Rom. 10.10]' (*In Lucam* VI.23.40–2
    [CCSL 120, p. 405, lines 1685–7], quoting Gregory, *Moralia* XVIII.40.64; cf.
    Augustine, *Enarrationes in psalmos* XXXIX.15). As Appendix I, Table I.13
    indicates, Smaragdus does include a number of passages from *In Lucam*
    VI.23 ('Hoc est quod ... damnaret inuenit' [PL 102.610A–610B], 'Viride lig-
    num ... non timent?' [PL 102.615A–615B], 'Extra urbem ... praecellit
    omnem intellectum' [PL 102.615C–616B], 'Semper enim ... accepere
    privantur' [PL 102.619A–619B], 'Non solus ... coeleste promissum' [PL
    102.620A–620C], and 'Hoc est, quod ... resurgere promisisti' [PL 102.620D–
    621C]), but he omits this exposition of the thief's response.
115 'Delighting in his own power, sought to rule himself through his free will
    and divest himself of the dominion of his Creator' (*In Lucam* IV.15.11–12
    [CCSL 120, p. 288, lines 2293–5]).
116 Carroll uses this passage to show that grace depends upon humans' 'coop-
    eration,' and can be rejected by them – again, a Gregorian rather than
    Augustinian understanding of the will (*The Venerable Bede*, 143).
117 'He used up these powers the more quickly, the more he abandoned him
    by which they were given' (*In Lucam*, IV.15.13 [CCSL 120, p. 288, lines
    2309–10]).
118 Cf. Augustine, *Tractatus* III.9 and XCII.1; parallels noted by Martin and
    Hurst, *Homilies*, 1:11 n. 13.
119 Here again quoting II Cor. 2.5 ('Non quod sufficientes simus cogitare
    aliquid a nobis ...' ['Not that we are sufficient of ourselves to thinking any-
    thing by ourselves ...']) and I Cor. 15.10 ('Non ego autem sed gratia Dei
    mecum' [Not I, however, but the grace of God in me]).
120 *Homiliae* I.2.28–106 (CCSL 122, pp. 8–10).
121 Meyvaert, 'Bede the Scholar,' 64 n. 20, and Carroll, *The Venerable Bede*, 141.
    Julian's commentary, *De amore*, survives only in those extracts quoted
    by Bede.
122 *In Cantica Canticorum* VI (CCSL 119B, p. 359, lines 2–3); cf. prol. (CCSL 119B,
    p. 180, lines 503–4). The relation of preface to text is not unproblematic:
    while scholars have viewed the preface as a later apology for an already
    completed work (e.g., Ward, *The Venerable Bede*, 76), Arthur Holder points
    out that 'Bede begins the preface by saying that he was about to write (*scrip-
    turus*) a commentary on the Song of Songs, not that it had already been writ-
    ten' ('The Patristic Sources of Bede's Commentary,' 317 n. 7).

123 '[Christ] does not say, "Without me you are able [to do] little," but "without me," he says, "you can do nothing"' (*In Cantica Canticorum* prol. [CCSL 119B, p. 167, lines 25–6]; John 15.5).

124 'So that one might say that grace begins, grace perfects, grace crowns' (ibid. [p. 172, lines 226–7]).

125 'I know that nothing good lives in me ... for I do not do the good I wish [to do]' (ibid. [p. 178, lines 448 and 450], quoting Rom. 7.18–19).

126 'It is not in a person ... to direct his steps'; 'With my mind I serve the Law of God, but with my flesh I serve the law of sin' (ibid. [p. 178, lines 453–6], quoting Jer. 10.23 and Rom. 7.25).

127 'When they had not yet been born or done anything good or bad' (ibid. [p. 179, lines 465–6, quoting Rom. 9.11]).

128 'There is a heavy yoke on the sons of Adam from the day they leave their mother's womb' (ibid. [p. 179, lines 471–2, quoting Sir. 40.1]).

129 'Lead me in the way of your commands'; 'Without me you can do nothing' (ibid. [p. 179, lines 475 and 477, quoting Psa. 118.35 and John 15.5]).

130 'Just as wise teachers credibly say' (*CH* II.14.301).

131 'Those who rose up from the dead at the Lord's resurrection must also be believed to have ascended together on his ascension to heaven' (III.5 [CCSL 119B, p. 274, lines 101–3]).

132 Godden, 'Record C.B.1.2.16.047.02 for Source Title *Comm.Cant.*' and '*Catholic Homilies*' 2.14.

133 *CH* I.30.76–80 and *CH* I.15.133–9; see *Introduction, Commentary, and Glossary*, 485.

134 'However he applied himself to earnestly obeying the Lord, it was undoubtedly through the prevenient grace of heavenly compassion that he received the ability to have it' (*Homiliae* I.16 [CCSL 122, pp. 115–16, lines 166–70]).

135 'We strive to practise a heavenly life on earth so that we also may deserve to enter these [joys of heaven]'; 'We attribute no good deeds we do ... to our own merits, but in everything we see the grace of our Creator' (*Homiliae* II.19 [CCSL 122, p. 327, lines 337–40]).

4. Alfred the Great and the *Old English Boethius*

1 For the striking but controversial tradition that in an earlier visit by Alfred to the city around 853 Pope Leo made Alfred consul of Rome – a title borne by Boethius himself – see Whitelock, *English Historical Documents*, no. 219 and pp. 879–80; Wormald, 'Alfred (848/9–899),' who accepts the tradition; and Nelson, 'The Problem of King Alfred's Royal Anointing.'

2 For recent biographical overviews of Alfred, see for example Wormald, 'Alfred (848/9-899)'; Nelson and Bately, 'Alfred the Great'; and Smyth, *Alfred the Great.*

3 On the translation of Gregory's *Dialogi* commisssioned by Alfred, see in particular Dekker, 'King's Alfred's Translation,' and Godden, 'Wærferth and King Alfred'; recent studies of the *Old English Orosius*, also commissioned by Alfred, include Godden, 'The Anglo-Saxons and the Goths' and 'The Translations of Alfred and His Circle'; Mengato, 'The Old English Translations; and Harris, 'The Alfredian World History.'

4 'Niedbeðearfosta sien eallum monnum to wiotonne' (Sweet, *King Alfred's West-Saxon Version of Gregory's Pastoral Care,* 7). For recent studies of Alfred's translation of Gregory's *Regula pastoralis,* see Discenza, 'Alfred's Verse Preface'; Atherton, 'King Alfred's Approach to the Study of Latin'; and Davis, 'King Alfred's "Pastoral Care."' Recent studies of Alfred's translation of Augustine's *Soliloquia* include Godden's 'Translations of Alfred and His Circle,' 'Identification and Self-Representation,' and 'Text and Eschatology'; Zanna, *Alfredo il grande re e filosofo*; and Green, 'Speech Acts and the Question of Self.'

5 A similarity noted by Godden, 'The Translations of Alfred and His Circle,' 2.

6 For accounts of Boethius's historical background, see Chadwick, *Boethius*; Matthews, 'Anicius Manlius Severinus Boethius'; Marenbon, *Boethius,* 7–16; and Kannengiesser, 'Boethius,' 24–7.

7 For the significance and depiction of the events of 410 in Anglo-Saxon England, see Godden, 'The Anglo-Saxons and the Goths.'

8 A parallel noted by Payne, *King Alfred and Boethius,* 11.

9 An alternative reading is offered by Payne, who notes that Alfred, unlike Boethius, makes the prisoner guilty of Theodoric's charge that he has plotted Theodoric's overthrow (*King Alfred and Boethius,* 12). Despite himself being a royal ruler, however, Alfred clearly aligns the reader's sympathies with the treacherous party: Boethius wonders 'hu he þ[æt] rice þam unrihtwisan cyninge aferran mihte, [ond] on ryhtgeleaffulra [ond] on rihtwisra anwealde gebringan' (how he might take power away from the unrighteous king and offer command to people of right belief and upright lives [that is, the Roman people] [1.7.17–19]); see also Godden, 'Identification and Self-Representation,' 140. For the arguably deliberate contrast in *De consolatione* between Theodoric's tyranny and God's just rule, see Lopez, 'Reading the *Consolation of Philosophy.*'

10 See 'The Alfredian Voice,' below.

11 Robert McMahon notes that this metaphor in fact transforms the image of Fortune's Wheel seen earlier in *De consolatione* into 'the cosmic revolutions

entailing Fate in time' – that is, the daily unfolding of events (Fate) by which Providence is expressed (*Understanding the Medieval Meditative Ascent*, 232).

12 Sharples, *Cicero*, 231.

13 Here and below, one might caution against applying theological terminology to a philosophical work: technically, therefore, we should understand Boethius's treatment of free will not to be heterodox in and of itself, but heterodox when brought into the context of theological discourse. Thanks are due to my second anonymous reader for drawing my attention to this distinction.

14 Chadwick, *Boethius*, 175.

15 On the Neoplatonic philosophy of *De consolatione*, see Chadwick, *Boethius*, 228–51 and LaChance, 'Theology in Boethius.'

16 Chadwick, *Boethius*, 249.

17 Gibson, 'Boethius in the Tenth Century,' 122; for the text of Bovo, see Huygens, 'Kommentare,' 383–4.

18 For a description of these texts, see Courcelle, *La Consolation*, 290–9. While Paris lat. 10400 is unpublished, the text of the others may be found respectively in Huygens, 'Kommentare,' 383–98, 400–4, and 409–26, and Silvestre, 'Jean Scot Érigène.'

19 Selections of this badly damaged manuscript have been published by Troncarelli, 'Per una ricerca' and *Tradizioni perdute*, 152–96. Omissions in the latter have been criticized by Frakes, 'Latin Commentaries on Boethius' *Consolatio*,' 24 n. 5, a critique to which Troncarelli responds with corrections and additions to his glosses in 'Le più antiche gloss carolinge,' 239 n. 41. For a helpful survey of scholarship on the *Consolatio* commentary traditions and an important study of the glosses in Vatican 3363, see Godden, 'Alfred, Asser, and Boethius.'

20 See Godden, 'Latin Commentary Tradition and the Old English Boethius,' 9 and 11, and 'Alfred, Asser, and Boethius,' 343; Parkes, 'A Note,' 426; and Hunt, *Saint Dunstan's Classbook*. For Vatican 3363's influence on the third English Remigian revisor tradition, see below.

21 Courcelle, 'Étude critique sur les commentaires de la Consolation de Boèce,' 45–6; Troncarelli, *Tradizioni perdute*, 204; and Wittig, 'King Alfred's *Boethius*,' 161.

22 Godden, 'Alfred, Asser, and Boethius,' 343.

23 Beaumont, 'The Latin Tradition,' 282.

24 Book I of the Anonymous glosses has been edited by Grant Roti based on St Gall, Stiftsbibliothek, 845 ('Anonymus in Boetii Consolationem Philosophiae Commentarius'); a complete edition is in preparation by Petrus Tax, who has published portions of the gloss in Einsiedeln 179 in 'Die althochdeutschen "Consolatio"-Glossen.'

25 For the postulation of a French origin for Naples IV. G. 68, see Wittig, 'Mss and Sigles,' 3.
26 For the dating of these manuscripts, see Passalacqua and Smith, *Codices Boethiani*, 3:254–6, and 2:207–8. For a full listing of manuscripts containing the St Gallen commentary, see Wittig, 'King Alfred's *Boethius*,' 188–9.
27 Neither manuscript is listed in Passalacqua and Smith's *Codices Boethiani*, but Godden describes both as 'of the late tenth century or early eleventh century' ('Latin Commentary Tradition,' 7). On the St Gallen *De consolatione* commentary tradition in general, see now Hehle, *Boethius in St. Gallen*; on Einsiedeln 179, see Hoffmann, *Schreibschulen*, 1:67, 121, 132, and especially 96. Where Hoffmann views the manuscript as originating in Einsiedeln, however, Tax suggests that dating the small glossing hands is complex enough to warrant consideration of other nearby scriptoria, such as at St Gallen, as possible centres of origin (personal correspondence, 6 May 2007).
28 Beaumont, 'The Latin Tradition,' 283; Godden, 'Latin Commentary Tradition,' 7; and Tax, personal correspondence, 9 September 1998 and 6 May 2007. Tax dates the Latin and Old High German glosses in Paris 13953 to ca. 1000, and notes that they excerpt glosses from 1) Naples IV. G. 68 and St Gallen 844, and 2) mainly Einsiedeln 179; he therefore assumes that Paris 13953 drew on these manuscripts 'or very recent predecessors of them' (personal correspondence, 6 May 2007). I am indebted to Professor Tax for the insights above from his long study of the commentary tradition on *De consolatione*.
29 Beaumont, 'The Latin Tradition,' 284.
30 For a full list of continental manuscripts containing Remigius's commentary, see Wittig, 'King Alfred's *Boethius*,' 187–8. For continental and insular Remigian manuscripts from the tenth and eleventh century, see Jeudy, 'Remigii autissiodorensis opera.'
31 Wittig wonders, for example, 'whether Remi did more than give his particular stamp to glosses which originated as the common teaching of a whole school, for instance at Rheims or at Paris, much of which material antedated a specific course of lectures given by Remi or a commentary written down under his direction' ('King Alfred's *Boethius*,' 160). ·
32 See Bolton, 'Remigian Commentaries,' 389.
33 Wittig, 'King Alfred's *Boethius*,' 161; see also Wittig, 'Boethius,' 79; and Gibson, 'Boethius in the Carolingian Schools.' Not all, it should be said, are impressed with Remigius's achievement. Courcelle, for example, calls him a 'vieux savant, médiocrement intelligent, qui se préoccupe moins de comprendre, interpréter et juger le text de Boèce, que de le garnir de notes historiques, philologiques et mythologiques où il pourra faire étalage d'érudition' (*La Consolation*, 278; opposed by Beaumont, 'The Latin

Tradition,' 286).

34 Quotations from the 'original' or at least continental version of Remigius have been printed by H.F. Stewart, 'A Commentary by Remigius,' and Silk, *Saeculi noni auctoris in Boetii Consolationem Philosophiae commentarius*. Other extracts appear in Naumann, *Notkers Boethius*; Schepss, 'Zu König Alfreds Boethius'; Otten, *König Alfreds Boethius*; Donaghey, 'Boethius's *De consolatione Philosophiae*'; and Wittig, 'King Alfred's Boethius.' Godden warns, however, that the wide variation in extant witnesses considerably problematizes the task of recovering the 'original' Remigius: 'Whether it is possible to identify ... a manuscript or a corpus of scholia which can be attributed to Remigius must at present be doubtful; as must the very notion of a single commentary composed *ab initio* by a single author at one time' ('Latin Commentary Tradition,' 6). Analysis of the various forms of commentary from the ninth to the eleventh centuries will be immeasurably assisted by the Boethius Commentary Project, a new endeavour by Godden and Rosalind Love: see http://www.english.ox.ac.uk/boethius.

35 Courcelle, *La Consolation*, 290–9.

36 Bolton, 'The Study of the *Consolation*.' Lapidge, moreover, in a study of the learned writer Byrhtferth of Ramsey, demonstrates Byrhtferth's knowledge and use of Remigius in the early eleventh century ('Byrhtferth at Work,' 29–34).

37 Bolton, 'The Study of the *Consolation*,' 78; Lapidge lists only eleven Anglo-Saxon manuscripts with Remigian commentary ('Byrhtferth at Work,' 31–2).

38 Beaumont, 'The Latin Tradition,' 290.

39 Godden, 'Latin Commentary Tradition,' 6. Wittig, moreover, observes that scholars' failure to identify the manuscript of *De consolatione* used by Alfred, plus the migration of other manuscripts from England, suggests that 'other copies of the *Consolatio* owned or made in Anglo-Saxon England' – and thus insular commentaries on Boethius's work – 'have not survived' ('Boethius,' 79).

40 Bolton, 'The Study of the *Consolation*,' 38–9 and 49.

41 See above, and Godden, 'Alfred, Asser, and Boethius,' 337–9, at p. 337. Godden also notes the possible influence of Vatican 3363 on Paris 6401A, representing the second English Remigian reviser tradition (ibid., 340).

42 Ibid., 342.

43 Godden, 'Latin Commentary Tradition,' 6. For details of the Project and the forthcoming edition of the *Old English Boethius by Godden and Irvine*, see http://www.english.ox.ac.uk/boethius/AlfredianBoethiusIndex.html.

44 Ælfric notes in his preface to the *Sermones*, for example, that few works of doctrine were available in the vernacular save 'þam bocum ðe ælfred

cyning snoterlice awende of ledene on englisc. ða synd to hæbbene' (those works that may be obtained [of those] which king Alfred wisely translated into English from Latin) (*CH* I.*praef*.55–7).

45 Bolton, 'The Study of the *Consolation*,' 38.
46 Gibson, 'Boethius in the Tenth Century,' 121–3.
47 Lapidge, 'Surviving Booklists,' 47.
48 Courcelle, *La Consolation*, 254–9.
49 Wittig, 'King Alfred's *Boethius*,' 159 n. 12; Gibson, in Beaumont, 'The Latin Tradition,' 302 n. 28; Marenbon, *Boethius*, 171.
50 Bischoff, *Die südostdeutschen Schreibschulen* 2:227–8; see Courcelle, *La Consolation*, 405, and Godden, 'Latin Commentary Tradition,' 8.
51 Beaumont, 'The Latin Tradition,' 283.
52 Bolton, 'The Study of the *Consolation*,' 38–9.
53 Personal correspondence with Tax, 9 September 1998; see also Das Längezeichen e im Fränkischen und Alemannischen schon um 1000?
54 Godden, 'Latin Commentary Tradition,' 8.
55 Brinegar suggests that the texts Alfred 'most probably used' were Bede's *De natura rerum*, Ambrose's *Hexameron*, Virgil's *Aeneid* and *Georgics* along with Servius's commentary on them, Ovid's *Metamorphoses*, Eutropius's *Breuiarium ab urbe condita*, Orosius's *Historiarum aduersus paganos*, Gregory's *Homilia XXXIV in Euangelia*, and biblical wisdom literature ('"Books most necessary,"' iii; see also Pratt, 'The Political Thought of Alfred,' 249–62).
56 Of Discenza's 742 records identifying potential sources for Alfred's *Boethius*, only 25 or 3.4 per cent of the total refer to Remigian commentaries; only one record, moreover, indicates a possible parallel with the St Gallen Anonymous ('Records for Anglo-Saxon Text *Boethius, The Consolation of Philosophy*'). Discenza's conclusions about Alfred's use of the Anonymous echo those of Wittig ('King Alfred's *Boethius*') and Bately ('The Literary Prose of King Alfred's Reign').
57 Godden, 'Latin Commentary Tradition,' 5–6; see also Otten, *König Alfreds Boethius*, 119–57. Discenza, by contrast, summarizes her own conclusions and the general scholarly consensus thus: 'Alfred used a commentary or commentaries, but only very selectively; or ... Alfred need not have used a commentary at all but could garner the same information elsewhere' (*The King's English*, 132).
58 I am grateful to Professor Tax for supplying these readings from his inspection of the St Gallen Anonymous manuscripts.
59 Beaumont, 'The Latin Tradition,' 289; *cf.* Bolton, 'The Study of the *Consolation*,' 47.
60 Passage edited by H.F. Stewart, 'Commentary,' 39–40. Here and below, numbers in brackets are inserted into quotations to serve as points of reference.
61 While a distinctive case, it is not an isolated one: Bolton notes that Remigius

quotes six times from Augustine, mostly in allusions to Fate and free will ('Remigian Commentaries,' 385).

62 Cf. *De correptione* X.28–9, where Augustine notes 1) that Adam would have been rewarded 'in quo statu recto ac sine uitio, si per ipsum liberum arbitrium manere voluisset' [if he had chosen by his own free will to continue in this state, upright and free from sin], and 2) that 'Ille non opus habebat eo adiutorio, quod implorant isti cum dicunt: "Video aliam legem in membris meis, repugnantem legi mentis meae" ... [sed] in illo beatitudinis loco sua secum pace fruebatur' [He had no need of that assistance which they beg for when they say, "I see another law in my flesh warring against the law of my mind" [Rom. 7.23] ... [but] in that blessed situation enjoyed peace] (PL 44.933–4).

63 Cf. *De gratia Christi* I.50.55: 'Ipsa est enim per peccatum primi hominis, quod ex libero eius uenit arbitrio, uitiata et damnata natura, cui sola ... diuina subuenit gratia' [For through the sin of this first man, which came from his free will, human nature became corrupted and condemned, and nothing but God's grace ... supports it] (CSEL 42, p.165, lines 22–6).

64 Cf. *De natura et gratia* XXIII.25 and *De gratia Christi* I.25.26: 'Necesse est mortua opera faciat, donec Christi gratia reuiuescat' [[The soul] must produce dead works until it lives again by the grace of Christ] (CSEL 60, p. 252, lines 2–4); '"Quod possumus bene cogitare, Dei est"' ['The fact that we can think rightly is due to God'] (CSEL 42, p. 147, line 2, citing II Cor. 3.5).

65 The question of Alfred's authorship, which has come to be accepted for both the prose and prosimetric *Boethius*, has most recently been addressed by Anlezark, 'Three Notes on the Old English Meters of Boethius.'

66 For discussions of the two versions and the challenges posed by both the manuscipts and their editors, see Godden, 'Editing Old English,' and Szarmach, 'Meter 20: Context Bereft.'

67 Godden, 'Editing Old English,' 170–1; for the reconstructed text and challenges thereof, see 164–6 and 172–6.

68 *King Alfred's Old English Version of Boethius*, ed. Sedgefield. Sedgefield's pace as well as methodology are subject to question: anyone who has laboured to recover readings from damaged Cotton manuscripts can only shudder at the satisfied statement in the preface to his translation that 'individual pages of this MS. have received as much as an hour's scrutiny' (Preface, vii).

69 Godden, 'Misappropriation of the Past,' 26; see also Discenza, 'Alfred's Cræft' and *The King's English* for detailed analysis of Alfred's approach to translation.

70 Godden, 'Misappropriation of the Past,' 2; cf. Sweet, *King Alfred's West-Saxon Version of Gregory's Pastoral Care*, 2–8.

71 For the passage in question, see Carnicelli, *King Alfred's Version of St Augustine's Soliloquies*, 87.18–89.15; on Alfred's adaptation of the *Soliloquia*, see Godden,

'Misappropriation of the Past,' 16–26.

72 For which perspective regarding the *Old English Boethius*, see for example Otten, *König Alfreds Boethius*, and W. F. Bolton, 'How Boethian is Alfred's *Boethius*?'

73 Godden, 'Misappropriation of the Past,' 28.

74 See for example Godden, 'The Player-King,' 138–9.

75 For anthologies, see Keynes and Lapidge, *Alfred the Great*, 132–3; Whitelock, *English Historical Documents*, 919–20; and Whitelock, *Sweet's Anglo-Saxon Reader*, 15–16; see also Godden, 'Misappropriation of the Past,' 14–15.

76 Not that even such a claim would constitute incontrovertible proof, as the Retractions of the *Canterbury Tales* attest.

77 See for example Augustine, *Tractatus in euangelium Ioannis* 18.7: 'Si uiuit homo secundum carnem, pecoribus comparatur: si uiuit secundum spiritum, Angelis sociatur' (If a person lives according to the flesh, he is on a level with the beasts; if he lives according to the Spirit, he is united with the angels [CCSL 36.184.21–3]), and Plato, *Timaeus* 42B–C: 'ο μεν ευ τον προσνκοντα χρονον βιους ... βιον ευδαιμονα και συνηθη εξοι . . . . μη παυομενος τε εν τουτοις ετι κακιας τροπον ον κακυνοιτο, κατα την ομοιοτητα της του τροπου γενεσεως εις τινα τιοαυτην αει μεταβαλοι θηριον' (he that has lived his appointed time well ... shall gain a life that is blessed and congenial; .... [but] if, in that shape, he still refraineth not from wickedness, he shall be changed every time, according to the nature of his wickedness, into some bestial form after the similitude of his own nature [Bury, *Plato: Timaeus*, 90 and 92, trans. Cornford, *Plato's Cosmology*, 144]); on the difference between the two perspectives, however, see O'Daly, *Augustine's Philosophy of Mind*, 72–5. In Philosophy's Neoplatonic perspective, of course, the bestiality of the wicked can become literal after death, with degenerate souls being reborn as animals; see for example P.G. Walsh's note to III.m9.18–19 (his lines 25–6) in *Boethius: The Consolation of Philosophy*, 139.

78 Again, here and below, one speaks of Boethian concepts as more or less 'orthodox' when using (as Alfred does here) a theological lens.

79 Christ applies the image to himself by extension in Luke 5.31–2, saying 'Non egent qui sani sunt medico sed qui male habent; non ueni uocare iustos sed peccatores in paenitentiam' (Those who are well do not need need a physician, but the sick; I have not come to call the righteous, but sinners to repentance); Augustine is only one of those who makes the connection explicit, saying 'Iesum Christum medicum [est] nostrae salutis aeternae' (Jesus Christ [is] the Physician of our eternal health [*Sermones* 88.1 (PL 38.539)]).

80 On the Stoic and Platonic association of such forces with Fate, see Sharples,

Cicero, 204–5 (§13), and Walsh, Boethius, 153 (§13).

81 See Discenza, 'Ciuit.Dei Records,' and 'Anglo-Saxon Text Title Details: Boethius.

82 For a study of Cicero's De fato and Augustine's De ciuitate Dei, see Djuth, 'The Problem of Free Choice of Will,' 10–18; on the relationship in Augustine between foreknowledge and predestination, see also Ogliari, Gratia et certamen, 330–4.

83 De ciuitate Dei V.9; Cicero, De diuinatione 1.125–6. On the Stoic identification of Fate and Providence, see Sharples, Cicero, 8 (§3.1.6) and 29–30 (§§8.1.–2), and Courcelle, La Consolation, 203–4.

84 For Alfred's use of wyrd to translate fortuna and casus (event) as well as fatum, see Frakes, The Fate of Fortune in the Early Middle Ages, 83–100, and Payne, King Alfred and Boethius, 78–108.

85 At the end of Book V prose 2, Philosophy refers to the distribution by Providence of predestined rewards (praedestinata) based on human merit (on which see below); Alfred states simply that God 'gilt ælcum æfter his gewyrhtum' (gives to each in keeping with his deeds [40.141.9]). For the use of this passage (IV.pr6.4) in Lantfred's Carmen de libero arbitrio, see below.

86 IV.pr6.14; see Walsh, Boethius, 153 (§14), and Sharples, Cicero, 205 (§14), who describes the phrase prima diuinitas as 'scarcely Christian.'

87 Alfred's distinction, after all, is between God's transcendent plan and those factors governed by Fate by which his plan is carried out – factors which would include human agencies. In fact, however, the image need not be pressed so far: Alfred's emphasis seems to be on God's connection to all humankind and the mixture of people in the world, not on the precise way in which God influences the wicked.

88 On the Neoplatonic sources of Philosophy's image of the encircled axis, which may include both Plotinus and Proclus, see Sharples, Cicero, 205 (§15); Courcelle, Late Latin Writers and Their Greek Sources, 305–6; de Vogel, 'Boethiana I,' 56; and Scheible, Die Gedichte in der Consolatio Philosophiae des Boethius, 185–8 n. 8.

89 See for example De sermone Domini in monte 2.13.46: 'Non ergo quid quisque faciat, sed quo animo faciat, considerandum est' (It is not what one does that must be considered, therefore, but the intention with which he does it [CCSL 345.137.1004–5]).

90 Referring to this passage in passing, Payne states that Alfred here suggests that God 'does not always choose to foreknow' (King Alfred and Boethius, 21). The issue here is not God's foreknowledge, however – Wisdom implicitly accepts Boethius's statement that God knows everything beforehand – but whether God's knowledge precludes or includes free will.

91 41.146.10 – 41.147.2 draw on Bodley 180, the corresponding folio in Otho A. vi being lost.

92 *Þe ðu ær come*, a surprisingly Neoplatonic phrase corresponding to Philosophy's suggestion in Book V metre 4 that the mind combines knowledge gained from the senses with that recalled from its former existence in the world of the Forms: '[mentis uigor] introrsumque reconditis / formis miscet imagines' ([the mind's energy] mingles its thoughts with the forms hidden within [V.m4.39–40]).

93 See Augustine's teaching on prevenience and irresistible grace above. William Rowe suggests that Augustine's understanding of volition – that necessity does not invalidate freedom of the will – informs his solution to the question of divine foreknowledge: neither God's certain knowledge of the future nor fallen human beings' inevitable choice of evil apart from grace mean that people do not choose what they desire; what they will choose is simply obvious and foreknown (Augustine on Foreknowledge and Free Will, 210–12). See also T.D.J. Chappell, who notes Augustine's insistence that God foreknows but does not compel human beings' choice of evil (*Augustine on Freedom*, 127–8).

5. Lantfred of Winchester and the *Carmen de libero arbitrio*

1 For general studies of the Benedictine Reform, see Gretsch, *The Intellectual Foundations*; Yorke, *Bishop Æthelwold*; Ramsay, *St Dunstan*; and Brooks and Cubitt, *St Oswald*; and for a synthesis of the last three volumes, Cubitt, 'Benedictine Reform.'

2 On Æthelwold, see for example Lapidge, 'Æthelwold as Scholar'; Gneuss, 'Origin of Standard Old English'; and Gretsch, 'Benedictine Rule.'

3 See for example Fisher, 'Anti-Monastic Reaction.'

4 Æthelwold, *Regularis concordia*, 3, §5.

5 Lapidge, *St Swithun*, 222. On the date of the *Regularis concordia*, see Lapidge and Winterbottom, *Wulfstan of Winchester*, lx, and Symons, *Regularis concordia*, xxiv.

6 Lapidge argues that Lantfred remained at Winchester 'perhaps a year or two at most' following the translation of Swithun's relics in 971 and that he composed the *Translatio et miracula S. Swithuni* during that time (*St Swithun*, 23); when later dating the *Translatio*, however, he concludes that it was written between 972 and 974, and in any case not later than ca. 975 (ibid. 235–7); the period here suggested (970–93) reflects Lapidge's earlier estimate, during which time the whole or the bulk of the *Translatio* was likely completed.

7 Bale, *Catalogus*, 139; Pits, *Relationum*, 178; and Leland, *Commentarii*, 1:173.

8 Lapidge, *St Swithun*, 218. Other studies of Lantfred, contributing palaeographical and textual if not biographical detail, include Carley, 'Two Pre-Conquest Manuscripts from Glastonbury Abbey,' 204–12, examining Cambridge, University Library, Kk. 5. 34; and O'Keeffe, 'Body and Law in Late Anglo-Saxon England,' 218–27, regarding the treatment of law and corporal punishment in Lantfred's *Translatio*. For the following account of Lantfred, see Lapidge, *St Swithun*, 216–24.

9 For the following, see Lapidge, *St Swithun*, 22–3 and 77–80; idem, 'Three Latin Poems,' 85–107; and Lapidge and Winterbottom, *Wulfstan of Winchester*, xciv n. 192. Lapidge edits all seven texts as follows: the mass-set for Swithun's deposition is found in *St Swithun* 76–7; the mass-set for Swithun's translation, ibid., 78–9; the letter from .L. to Dunstan, ibid., 220–1; the *Altercatio magistri et discipuli*, 'Three Latin Poems,' 108–20; the 'Responsio discipuli,' 'Three Latin Poems,' 122–6; and the *Carmen de libero arbitrio*, 'Three Latin Poems,' 126–36.

10 On which style, see Lapidge *St Swithun*, 224–32 and 'The Hermeneutic Style.' Lapidge also suggests that Lantfred may have authored a third mass-set from the Missal, that for the vigil of Swithun's deposition, even though the text is not marked by distinctively 'Lantfredian' vocabulary (Lapidge, *St Swithun*, 78).

11 The early-eleventh-century manuscript preserves a collection of correspondence compiled between 990 and 1000; it is in this collection that the Lantfred letter is found (Lapidge, *St Swithun*, 220 and 241–2).

12 Lapidge, *St Swithun*, 222.

13 Lapidge, 'Lantfred,' 410.

14 Lapidge, *St Swithun*, 223. Lapidge had in fact originally leaned away from attributing the *Carmen* to Lantfred, noting that while both the *Carmen* and the preceding *Altercatio magistri et discipuli* share rare vocabulary with the *Translatio*, the stark difference in tone between the *Carmen* and *Altercatio* made him doubt that they were products of the same author ('Three Latin Poems,' 106–7); the evidence amassed in the three decades following that publication, however, has brought a shift in his position. For ease of reference, the whole of Lapidge's edition and translation of the *Carmen de libero arbitrio* appears by permission below in Appendix III.

15 See Bischoff, *Latin Palaeography*, 16.

16 I am grateful to Timothy Graham for calling my attention to this point.

17 See Brown, *Western Historical Scripts*, 59.

18 Bischoff, *Latin Paleography*, 124; Brown, *Western Historical Scripts*, 59; and Dumville, *English Caroline Script*, 145. The Cambridge University Library

Catalogue of Manuscripts is of little help on this point, suggesting it is 'a very early half-Saxon hand ... which may perhaps be assigned to the ninth or tenth century' (3:705).

19 Catherine Cubitt notes that 'all the Reformers turned to continental styles for inspiration but Æthelwold's circle was the most extreme in this respect: Style One Caroline Minuscule, associated with his houses, was particularly pure and free from native forms' ('Benedictine Reform,' 88; see also Bishop, *English Caroline Minuscule*, xxi–xxiii, and Dumville, *English Caroline Script*, 1–6).

20 See Bishop, *English Caroline Minuscule*, plate X.

21 Dumville, *English Caroline Script*, 145.

22 Ibid., 145 n. 26. Gneuss likewise identifies the origin of the manuscript as Winchester (Gneuss, *Handlist*, §27).

23 See, e.g., the unintelligible 'Tes qua' of line 148 and dittography of 'uiri' in line 149.

24 See Lapidge, 'Æthelwold as Scholar'; Gneuss, 'Æthelwold's School'; and Hofstetter, 'The Standardization of Old English'; Lapidge, 'Surviving Booklists,' 52–5; and Lapidge and Winterbottom, *Wulfstan of Winchester*, lxxxvi–xcix, respectively.

25 See Wulfstan of Winchester's *Vita Sancti Æthelwoldi*, ch. 16, and Lapidge and Winterbottom, *Wulfstan of Winchester*, xlvii–xlix.

26 Lapidge, 'Three Latin Poems,' 89, 106, 114, and 128.

27 Lapidge, 'Æthelwold as Scholar,' 100 n. 75.

28 This providential regard perhaps refers, in Boethian terms, to God's experience of history as previously discussed, his 'eternal present' by which he views or knows all things.

29 Lapidge, *St Swithun*, 78–9; see also the evidence adduced on 223. One might also note the comparable use of the terms *praesul* and *archipresuli* in the *Carmen* and the letter of '.L.' to Dunstan.

30 On these manuscripts, see Wittig, 'Mss and Sigles,' 1–4.

31 Bieler, 'Praefatio,' xxvii. More manuscripts may well come to light as a result of the ongoing *Codices Boethiani* project , three volumes of which have been edited thus far by Gibson et al., Passalacqua and Smith, and Smith.

32 Bolton, 'Study,' 3.

33 The sixteen manuscripts are listed by Wittig, 'Boethius,' 77–8; fourteen of them are described in Bolton, 'The Study of the *Consolation*,' 51–60. See also Gibson et al., *Codices Boethiani*.

34 Bolton, 'Study,' 50.

35 'We place these examples in the middle [of the poem] in a few words that our discussion may sound forth more clearly'; though plural, *paradigmata* seems to refer specifically to this metaphor of the race.

36 A search for variations of *alta* and *specula* in a proximity of five words in *Cetedoc, Patrologia Latina,* and Schumann, *Lateinisches Hexameter-Lexicon,* whose work is also relevant for the hexametrical portion of this elegiac verse, reveals that though writers do speak of gazing out from high towers, in few cases is God the subject, and in none is there any reference to 'providence' or foresight. This said, one of my anonymous external readers helpfully points out that the phrase may not be original to Boethius but stem ultimately from classical verse. Using *Poetria Nova,* a comprehensive database of Latin poetry up to the thirteenth century (see, for example, Lapidge, *The Anglo-Saxon Library,* 107 n. 74), he notes that Virgil's *Aeneid,* for example, depicts Misenus sounding an alarm 'specula ab alta' (from a high lookout [III.239]) and Turnus like a lion seeing his prey 'specula ab alta' (from a high vantage point [X.454]); the first-century Silius Italicus in his *Punica* even depicts one of his characters using the precise phrase here ('specula sublimis ab alta' [VII.521]). Even if Boethius was influenced by such precedent, however, the strong contextual correspondence between *De consolatione* and the *Carmen* argues for the latter's debt to Boethius himself rather than to Boethius's classical precursors.

37 'The Creator sits on high, ruling and guiding the reins of the world. King and Lord ... he is its law and wise, just Judge' (IV.m6.34–7).

38 'The prescient God remains an observer on high of all things ... dispensing rewards to the good and punishments to the wicked' (V.pr6.45).

39 'Looking forth on all things from eternity, the gaze of Providence judges and distributes predestined [rewards] according to each person's merits' (V.pr2.11).

40 'Predestination, which promises good things in heaven to the saints according to their merits, and compels those wretches who perished by their free choice of evil to go to the shadows of hell' (lines 105–8).

41 'The prize for running in the stadium is the crown for which the race is run ... however much the wicked may rage, the crown of the wise will never perish or wither away' (IV.3.2 and 5).

42 This observation is based on a search for forms of *currere* with *in stadio* in any order within five words' proximity in *Cetedoc* and *Patrologia Latina;* Schumann contains no entry for this phrase.

43 'Do you not know that in the stadium all the runners run, but only one gets the prize? Run in such a way that you may capture it' (I Cor. 9.24).

44 'The teachings of Christ the Lord advise us to run, and those of Paul his soldier advise us to run [as well], where he signified our human actions with the likeness of the arena' (143–6).

45 'Into the outer darkness, where there will be weeping and gnashing of teeth' (Matt. 25.30).

46 'Having *bound* his feet and hands, cast him outside into the darkness, where there will be weeping and gnashing of teeth' (Matt. 22.13; emphasis mine).

47 See above, and Sedgefield, Introduction, xi–xvi.

48 Again, dating Ælfric's appointment to Cerne to 987, and the *LS* to 992 x 1002 (Clemoes, 'Chronology,' 34).

49 '[God] knows what is appropriate for each ... since he sees everything from the high roof, and thence apportions and measures out to each according to his deserts' (*OEBoeth.* 39.132.17–19).

50 'The supreme Creator sits on his high throne; thence he directs the reins of all creatures. This is no wonder, for he is the king and lord and source and beginning and law and wisdom and just judge' (ibid., 39.136.22–3).

51 'The Almighty sits continually on the high throne of his power; thence he can see all, and in his great justice he renders to each according to his deeds' (ibid., 42.148.31–3).

52 *De consolatione* IV.3.1–2 and 4–5.

53 *OEBoeth.* XXXVII.2.112.16–18, 20–5 and 30–1.

54 Passage edited by H.F. Stewart, 'Commentary,' 42. Again, compare this with the other commentaries: neither Vatican 3363 nor the shorter version of the St Gallen Anonymous have any glosses for this passage, and the in-line and interlinear glosses in the longer St Gallen version focus on the verb *proficiscor* rather than on free will: '*de libero proficiscuntur arbitrio*. oriuntur ['they proceed'] ambulatio ['a walk']'.

55 'Evil things arise from free will; good things come from the grace of God which comes before and [men's] free will which follows by willing thereafter' (CUL Kk. 3. 21, 101v).

56 'Lest it should be thought that the will can do anything good without God's grace, he follows his statement that "I have laboured more than all of them" by saying "Yet not I, but the grace of God in me" [I Cor. 15.9–10]' (*De gratia et libero arbitrio* 12 [PL 44.889]).

57 'They retained the malignant effect of freedom, corrupted by vices and bestial crimes. Nor could they hope for the blessed life on the basis of merit, unless they were helped by the mercy of the Lord' (lines 39–42).

58 See, for example, Ireneus (*Aduersus haereses* IV.29.1), Clement of Alexandria (*Paedagogus* I.9), Origen (*De Principiis* III.1.8), Jerome (*Epistulae* LXXXV.2), and Augustine (*De gratia et libero arbitrio* XX.41 and XXIII.45). Similarly, Alfred, in one of his expansions of *De consolatione*, notes that 'He gesihð (*eall*) ure weorc ge good ge yfel, ær hi gewordene sien, oððe furðum geþoht; ac he us ne ned no þy hraðor to þæm þæt we nede scylen good don, ne us ne wernð þæt we yfel don, forðæmþe he us sealde freodom' ('He sees all our deeds, both good and evil, before they come about or are even conceived. He never compels us

to do good, however, nor does he prevent us from doing evil, for he has given
us freedom,' *OEBoeth.* XLI.4.145.13–16, a passage quoted by Ælfric in *LS*
I.17.248–50).

59 'Predestination ... compels those wretches who perished *by their free choice*
of evil to go to the shadows of hell' (105 and 107–8; emphasis mine); 'The
gaze of Providence judges and distributes predestined [rewards]'
(V.pr2.11).

60 Augustine, *De dono perseuerantiae* IX.21.

61 Gottschalk (d. ca. 868), originally a monk at Fulda under Hrabanus
Maurus, had fomented considerable controversy through his contention that
– as Hrabanus himself would later put it – 'sicuti qui per praescientiam Dei
ac praedestinationem uocati sunt ad percipiendam gloriam aeternae uitae,
non possunt non saluari, ita et illi qui ad aeternum interitum uadunt, praedestinatione Dei coguntur, et non possunt euadere interitum' (just as those
called to gain the glory of eternal life through the foreknowledge and predestination of God are unable not to be saved, so also those who rush to eternal
destruction are compelled by the predestination of God and are unable to
escape destruction [PL 112.1531B]). For Gottschalk as for his opponents, such
teaching had practical implications: to the latter, it suggested that abstaining
from sin and submitting to ecclesiastical authority were inconsequential in
determining one's eternal state; to the former, it argued the urgent need for
missionaries to reach those waiting to hear and believe (Otten, 'Carolingian
Theology,' 77). To this end, after fleeing from Fulda and being transferred to
the monastery of Orbais, Gottschalk left to spread his teachings throughout
northern Italy. Hrabanus Maurus, having been elevated to the archbishopric
of Mainz in 845, censured the peripatetic monk in stern letters to Gottschalk's
Italian patrons, to which Gottschalk responded in 848 with a defence of his
views to the synod of Mainz. Here he was officially condemned and handed
over to Hincmar, archbishop of Reims, who returned him to Orbais.
Gottschalk's doctrines would be condemned again in councils at Quierzy
(849 and 853), Valence (855), and Langres and Savonnières (859), but were
also in the interim the subject of intense debate. Hincmar wrote *De praedestinatione Dei et libero arbitrio* (PL 125.65B–474B), solicited the help of Johannes
Scotus Erigena (whose *De diuina praedestinatione* obscured the issue by arguing that God's singularity of nature made a 'double' predestination impossible); Ratramnus of Corbie considered the issue at the request of Charles
the Bald, only to defend Gottschalk's position in *De praedestinatione Dei*
(PL 121.11C–80C); and Prudentius, bishop of Troyes, similarly supported
Gottschalk's views in his *Epistola ad Hincmarum* (PL 115.971D–1010B),
as did other writers such as Loup de Ferrières and Florus of Lyon. Though

most of Gottschalk's writings have now been lost, it may be that ambiguity in Gottschalk's formulation of his ideas, to say nothing of the complexity of the ideas themselves, may have played a role in furthering the controversy. Regardless, ultimately his views were condemned both as fallacious and as a misrepresentation of Augustinian doctrine. Lapidge suggests that Lantfred was familiar with the debate, perhaps through the work of Ratramnus ('Three Latin Poems,' 245), a suggestion all the more plausible given the proximity of Fleury to Orbais, Troyes, and Reims, where much of the debate was centred.

62 'God, the author of all natures, orders all things and directs them towards goodness' (ibid., IV.pr6.56).

63 'The divine mind ... sees into the present, past, and future; from his gaze things may not change their course' (lines 9–11; emphasis mine).

64 On the straight and narrow paths, see Matt. 7.13–14. While Lantfred's point here is actually that God 'scarcely' (uix) draws the narrow path to peoples' attention, and does so only to those who are (already?) following it, nonetheless he attributes an activity to God that seems at odds with his suggestion immediately before of God's passivity.

65 'Destines and strengthens, justifies and crowns, saves, sanctifies, guards and supports [his servants]' (lines 20–2, paraphrasing Rom. 8.29–30).

66 'Rebus in humanis reor antescientia non sit; / cunctisator rerum possidet hoc proprium' (I believe that there is no foreknowledge in the human condition; the creator of all possesses this exclusively lines 109–10).

67 'He commands us to follow the right [path] and avoid the left ... where he speaks to people through his holy decrees' (lines 129 and 132).

68 'The strict, narrow way will be able to open high heaven if any vigorous person desires to undertake it' (lines 133–4).

69 'Let the observation of the commanders represent the contemplation of events; this contemplation sees and governs everything that was, is, and shall be.'

70 'At the resurrection, when the Son of Man sits enthroned in his glory, you who have followed me will also sit on twelve thrones, judging the twelve tribes of Israel' (Matt. 19.28).

71 Lapidge, 'Three Latin Poems,' note for p. 274, line 149, on p. 486.

72 I am grateful to Andy Orchard for bringing this possibility to my attention. On this variation of spelling in the Carmen, see Lapidge, ibid., p. 268.

73 E.g., Tempe in line 53 and denarium in line 174.

74 Lapidge takes the subject of uertat to be the same as that of fuderit (lines 150 and 152), saying that a person prays in order that he, not God, may turn his shame into something better. If Lapidge's translation is correct, the line

would echo Lantfred's previous exhortations for human effort (e.g., 'Pergite, posco, uiri' [line 148]), and attribute to human beings the capacity to sanctify themselves; in consequence, the line would highlight yet further Lantfred's departure from Augustine. The semantic parallel of this passage to Lantfred's comments on the *intuitus regis*, however (lines 121–2), would suggest rather that God is the one responsible for individuals' change.

6. Wulfstan the Homilist and *De adiutorio Dei et libero arbitrio*

1 For general background to Wulfstan, see Bethurum, 'Wulfstan'; Orchard, 'Wulfstan the Homilist'; and Mary Richards, 'Wulfstan of York.' On the corpus of Wulfstan's works, see Wilcox, 'The Dissemination of Wulfstan's Homilies'; Wormald, 'Wulfstan'; and Cross and Hamer, *Wulfstan's Canon Law Collection*. For studies of Wulfstan's theology and homiletic style, see Gatch, *Preaching and Theology*; Orchard, 'Crying Wolf'; and Jost, *Wulfstanstudien*.
2 On the popularity and influence of Wulfstan's works as evidenced by their recopying, see Wilcox, 'The Dissemination of Wulfstan's Homilies.' Wilcox contrasts the eleventh-century interest in Wulfstan's sermons with the paucity of manuscripts from the period that followed in 'Wulfstan and the Twelfth Century,' concluding that the very 'rhetoric of historical specificity' which contributed to their earlier popularity 'made them of limited value a century or two later' (96).
3 Wulfstan the Homilist should not be confused with Wulfstan, archbishop of York (931–56), St Wulfstan, bishop of Worcester (1062–95), or Wulfstan Cantor, monk and priest of Winchester and Anglo-Latin poet (fl. 996).
4 Bethurum, *Homilies*; Wilcox, 'The Dissemination of Wulfstan's Homilies,' 200–1. The extent to which all thirty texts printed by Bethurum may be counted as homilies has been debated: Wormald, for example, draws a distinction between (a) the three versions of the *Sermo Lupi* included by Bethurum and six texts consisting of what he calls 'little more than preparatory matter,' and (b) the other twenty-two 'mainline homilies' – that is, Bethurum Ib, II–VII, VIIIb, VIIIc, IX, Xc, XI–XV, XVIb, XVII–XXI ('Wulfstan'). Orchard, by contrast, views the three versions of the *Sermo Lupi* as distinct texts worthy of individual consideration (see, for example, 'Crying Wolf').
5 See the penitential letters printed by Bethurum as Appendix 2 (*Homilies*, 374–7); the rubric preceding Bethurum VI–VII, XX, and XXI in certain manuscripts (*Homilies*, 144, 261, 266, and 276, apparatus); the rubric to Napier LIX (*Wulfstan*, ed. Napier, 307); and (for explicit attribution to Wulfstan) the opening of one version of Bethurum XIII (*Homilies* 225, apparatus); see Wilcox, 'The Dissemination of Wulfstan's Homilies,' 200.

6 See Ker, 'The Handwriting of Archbishop Wulfstan'; and Tunberg, 'Scribal Habits,' 47–9.
7 See Bethurum, 'Archbishop Wulfstan's Commonplace Book'; and Sauer, 'Transmission and Structure.'
8 See in particular Orchard, 'Crying Wolf.' Wilcox argues that Wulfstan's style is shaped by his sense of responsibility for preaching effectively: Wulfstan's concern to craft memorable language, he says, 'is precisely the point of all Wulfstan's writings' ('The Wolf on Shepherds,' 412).
9 Napier Ia, VIIIa, Xb, and XI (*Wulfstan*, 76–8, 29–32, 60–5, and 41–4); Bethurum Ia, VIIIa, Xb, XI, and XVIa (*Homelies* 113–15, 169–71, 194–9, 211–14, and 239).
10 Bethurum Ia serves as the basis for Ib, a vernacular translation with some omissions and a new conclusion; VIIIa appears as the Old English VIIIb and VIIIc; Xb provides the rough model for the Old English Xc; XI, comprising a series of passages from Isaiah and Jeremiah, offers the Latin first and Old English translations immediately after; and XVIa is translated closely as XVIb.
11 The sermons are listed and discussed by Hall, 'Wulfstan's Latin Sermons,' 96–100, on which the following draws. I use Hall's numbering for the sermons. See also Cross, 'A Newly-Identified Manuscript,' 65–6, 'Contents of the Manuscript,' and 'Wulfstan's *De Anticristo*,' 208–9 and 217–20.
12 *De ieiunio quattuor temporum* (Hall, 'Wulfstan's Latin Sermons,' 97) is found in five witnesses to the 'Commonplace Book': Cambridge, Corpus Christi College 190 (s. xi[1]; provenance s. xi[1], Exeter); Copenhagen, Kongelige Bibliotek, Gamle Kongelige Sammlung 1595 (1002 × 1023); London, British Library, Cotton Nero A. i (s. xi[3/4] and 1003 × 1023); Rouen, Bibliothèque Municipale 1382 (s. s. xi[1]); and Oxford, Bodleian Library, Barlow 37 (s. xii[ex] or xiii[in], ?Worcester). It also appears in Cambridge, St John's College 42 (s. xii) and London, British Library, Cotton Vespasian D. ii (s. xi/xii, ?Normandy), manuscripts containing other texts associated with Wulfstan (see Cross, 'Wulfstan's *De Anticristo*'), as well as in one manuscript not as closely identified with Wulfstan, Châlons-sur-Marne, Bibliothèque Municipale 31 (33) (s. xi2, Saint-Pierre-aux-Monts).
13 Hall, 'Wulfstan's Latin Sermons,' 99.
14 Napier XXXVI, cautiously attributed to Wulfstan by Wilcox, 'The Dissemination of Wulfstan's Homilies,' 200.
15 *De decimis dandis* and *Contra iniquos iudices et falsos testes* (Hall 7 and 8), found in St John's 42 and Copenhagen 1595; on the latter text, found also in Vespasian D.ii and Châlons-sur-Marne 31, see Cross, 'Contents of the Manuscript,' 19.
16 *Sermo ad coniugatos et filios* (Hall 9), paralleled in Barlow 37 and Cambridge, Corpus Christi College 265 (s. xi[med] – xi[2], Worcester).

17 *Sermo sancti Augustini de baptismo non iterando* (Hall 15), which serves as a source for Bethurum VIIIc.

18 Hall, 'Wulfstan's Latin Sermons,' 100; namely, *Contra iniquos iudices, Sermo ad coniugatos, De dominis et seruis,* and *Sermo ad uiduas* (Hall 8 and 11).

19 Hall, 'Wulfstan's Latin Sermons,' 100; namely, *De conuersione et penitentia et communione, De resurrectione mortuorum,* our *De adiutorio Dei et libero arbitrio,* and the *Sermo sancti Augustini de baptismo non iterando* (Hall 12–15).

20 *Admonitio episcoporum utilis* (Hall Appendix I), discussed, edited, and translated in Hall, 'Wulfstan's Latin Sermons,' 101–9, 110–13, and 113–14.

21 Hall, 'Wulfstan's Latin Sermons,' 107, The *Admonitio* appears in Barlow 37, Corpus 190, and Corpus 265.

22 See Tunberg, 'Physical Description,' 27–8; and Gerritsen, 'The Copenhagen Wulfstan Manuscript.' The late date for this manuscript closely associated with Wulfstan suggests that his activity at Worcester did not cease with his resignation of the episcopacy or appointment of a suffragan at Worcester in 1016.

23 Tunberg, 'Physical Description,' 29; cf. 36 and Ker, 'Hemming's Cartulary,' 51 and 65–7.

24 Tunberg, 'Physical Description,' 29.

25 Fehr, 2 and 3 (Copenhagen 1595, Section VII, 67r–74r and 74r–77r). Fehr's numbers refer to edited texts in his edition.

26 *De Anticristo et eius signis* (Section V, 51r–52r), *De uisione* (Section VI, 65v–66v; Bethurum XII), and *De baptismo* (Section VII, 78r–79r; Bethurum VIIIa); other works attributed to Wulfstan include (possibly) the untitled work on chrism (Section VII, fol. 79r) and certain letters (Section III, 41r–42r). On the authorship of these texts, see Bethurum, 'Wulfstan,' 24–8, 29, 31, and 32; Cross, 'Contents of the Manuscript,' 13 and 18 (regarding the letters); Jost, *Wulfstanstudien,* 17, 116, and 183–268; Jost, 'Einige Wulfstantexte,' 301–5 (regarding Bethurum XIIIa); and Wilcox, 'The Dissemination of Wulfstan's Homilies,' 200–1.

27 *Sermo sancti Augustini de baptismo non iterando* (Section VI, 60v–62r; Hall 15 ['Wulfstan's Latin Sermons,' 136-7]), drawing on Augustine's *De baptismo contra Donatistas* and *Tractatus in Euangelium Ioannis,* which includes a passage used in Wulfstan's second Old English sermon on baptism (Bethurum VIIIc; see Hall, 'Wulfstan's Latin Sermons,' 100).

28 The latter being printed by Ker, 'The Handwriting of Archbishop Wulfstan,' 320; cf. 315–6 and 319, as well as Ker, *Catalogue,* §99. Jost discusses the passage (*Wulfstanstudien,* 268–70), but Cross notes that he was mislead by a reading in the Holthausen's transcription of the manuscript ('Contents of the Manuscript,' 22). Arguments against the objections to Ker's view are presented by Cross and Brown, 'Wulfstan and Abbo,' 73–5, and by Tunberg, 'Scribal Habits,' 44–7.

29 'Bisceopes dægweorc, ðæt bið mid rihte / his gebedu ærest *and* ðonne his bocweorc, / ræding oððon rihting, lar oððon leorning' (The daily work of a bishop is properly to pray, first of all, and then do his book-work: reading or writing, teaching or learning) (Jost, *Institutes of Polity* VII.77, p. 75); cf. VI.58: 'Bisceopas sculan bocu*m and* gebedum fyligean' (Bishops must attend to books and prayers) (ibid., 67).

30 1) London, British Library, Addit. 38651 (s. xi^{in}), fols 57 and 58; 2) London, British Library, Cotton Claudius A iii (s. x/xi–xi^1), fols 31–86 and 106–50; 3) London, British Library, Cotton Nero A i (York or Worcester, s. xi^{in}), fols 70–177; 4) London, British Library, Cotton Tiberius A xiii, fols 1–118 (Worcester, s. xi^1–xi^{ex}); 5) London, British Library, Cotton Vespasian A xiv (Worcester or York, s. xi^1), fols 114–79; 6) London, British Library, Harley 55 (s. xi^1), fols 1–4; 7) Oxford, Bodleian Library, Hatton 20 (SC. 4113) (890–7 A.D.); 8) Oxford, Bodleian Library, Hatton 42 (SC. 4117) (composed of three manuscripts: Brittany, s. ix^2; France, s. x; France, s. x); 9) York, Minster Library Addit. 1. (s. xi^1–s. xi^2); 10) Cambridge, Corpus Christi College 190, part 1, pp. iii–xii, 1–294 (s. xi^1); 11) Rouen, Bibliothèque Municipale 1382 (U109), 173r–198v.

31 Tunberg, 'Scribal Habits,' 49; cf. Whitelock, 'Archbishop Wulfstan,' 31.

32 *De adiutorio Dei*, fols 59v–60v; *De baptismo non iterando*, fols 60v–62r; and *De uisione*, fols 65v–66v (Cross, 'Contents of the Manuscript,' 21–2; and Hall, 'Wulfstan's Latin Sermons,' 95 and 98).

33 See, for example, Gatch, *Preaching and Theology*, 105–16; Lainé, 'Les homélies eschatologiques'; and Godden, 'Apocalypse and Invasion,' 142–61.

34 'Let us do what there is pressing need for us to do, ever to believe rightly ... and always do God's will as zealously as we can' (Bethurum VIIa.44–7).

35 See also Bethurum III.78, VIIa.47, VIIIc.178, and XX.3.175.

36 '[Man should act in such a way that] he strives resolutely against the devil's company; that is, in such a way that he rejects and turns away from his false teaching, *since he may always do so*, and shows that *he has and ever shall have a resolute will* and faith in the one true and almighty God' (Bethurum VIIIc.11–3, emphasis mine; cf. Xb.45–50).

37 'Look, what is a person in this life unless God Almighty should uphold him and unless he previously should be admonished [to be] the better so that he should not be deceived by the devil? Let us earnestly guard ourselves and deserve for God to protect us according to his will' (Bethurum IV.83–7; cf. IX.51).

38 'We now have the ability either to choose to earn eternal life and eternal joy or eternal death and endless anguish. Clearly, we must know how we [are] to repay Christ all that he endured and suffered for us and for our love' (Bethurum VII.74–78).

39 'There is great need that every person ... should cleanse his heart and adorn himself with good deeds *so that* the Spirit of God will live in him' (Bethurum XVIII.82; emphasis mine).

40 See again Djuth, 'Augustine's Freedom of the Will and the Monastic Tradition,' 135–9.

41 For the chronology followed here, see Stewart, *Cassian*, 8–19; see also the discussion in Driver, *John Cassian*, 12–19, and Ogliari, *Gratia et certamen*, 118–24.

42 Indeed, Conrad Leyser speaks of the region not simply as disunified but as 'fissiparous [and] polemically charged,' tracing the tensions between northern and southern Gallic monasticism, between the monastic centres of Tours and Lérins, and between monastic rivals within Marseilles (*Authority and Asceticism*, 41–4).

43 In taking such a stance, Cassian reveals more a reservation with Augustinian theology than any identification with Pelagius, whose views he explicitly condemns. (Cf. *Collatio* XIII.16: 'Nemo autem aestimet haec a nobis ob hoc fuisse prolata, ut nitamur adstruere summam salutis in nostrae fidei dicione consistere secundum quorundam profanam opinionem, qui totum libero arbitrio deputantes gratiam Dei dispensari secundum meritum uniuscuiusque definiunt' (Let no one imagine that we have brought forward these instances to try to make out that the chief share in our salvation rests with our faith, according to the profane notion of some who attribute everything to free will and maintain that the grace of God is bestowed according to each person's merit [CSEL 13, p. 391, lines 1–5]). Given this perspective (as has often been noted), his views would be better described as Semi-Augustinian rather than 'Semi-Pelagian,' a label attached late to the movement in the seventeenth century (Wetzel, 'Snares of Truth,' 126; see also Ogliari, *Gratia et certamen*, 7–9). Indeed, in her recent dissertation, Lauren Pristas goes so far as to deny that Cassian's belief in the 'gradual rehabilitation in grace of the faculty of free choice' amounts to Semi-Pelagian theology ('The Theological Anthropology of John Cassian,' abstract). See, however, the discussion below of Cassian's theology in *Collatio* XIII, as well as the overview in Djuth, 'The Problem of Free Choice of Will,' 112–47.

44 His saint's days are on July 23 and February 29, respectively. Loorits posits that the latter was fixed during a time of tension between East and West, and thus as a 'Roman' Cassian was suspect – as he puts it, robbed of 'three-quarters of his saintliness' (*Kassian*, noted in Stewart, *Cassian*, 156 n. 196).

45 See Cassiodorus, *De institutis diuinarum litterarum*, 29; and Vogüé, 'Les Mentiones,' 280–2, respectively.

46 See Stewart, *Cassian*, 21; cf. 25. This traditional view of Caesarius as the champion at Orange of Augustine's theology of grace is likewise noted by

Leyser, who speaks of Caesarius's 'special affiliation with Augustine' – the effect of the African Father, that is, on Caesarius's theological views – as 'an accepted [scholarly] point of reference' (*Authority and Asceticism*, 82–3).

47 Gregory, *Epistolae* VII.12 (PL 77.866–7); cf. Stewart, *Cassian*, 156 n. 196.

48 'For those who are eager for a perfect way of life, there are the writings of the holy Fathers, the observance of which will lead a person to the heights of perfection … What else but examples of the virtue of right-living, obedient monks are the *Collationes*?' (LXXIII.5 [CSEL 75, p. 164, lines 2 and 5 – p. 165, line 6], cf. XLII.3 and 5). Cf. Vogüé, 'Les Mentiones,' 217–21; and Kardong, 'Cassianic Formulae,' 233–52.

49 There are sixteen pairs total in *Collatio* XIII, eight occurring in XIII.9, eight in XIII.10; these are the thirteenth and fourteenth pairs in the series. Chadwick notes that Cassian here addresses all but one of the main texts cited by Augustine in support of grace in *De correptione* (*Cassian*, 122).

50 Lines 1–9. Here and below, line numbers taken from my edition of *De adiutorio Dei* in this volume, Appendix III. The edition may serve to supplement the transcription in Hall, 'Wulfstan's Latin Sermons,' 133–4, printed 'with minimal editorial intervention' (115).

51 'God acts in such ways upon the rational soul that it may believe in him – and indeed there is no ability whatsoever in free will to believe if there is no persuasion or call to the one in whom he should believe' (*De spiritu et littera* XXXIV.60 [CSEL 60, p. 220, lines 15–17]); see also *De praedestinatione* III.7: 'Neque uelle possumus, nisi uocemur' (We are not able to will unless we are called [PL 44.965]).

52 'Without the help of God we can do nothing right' (line 10).

53 'The grace of Christ is thus at hand every day, which … calls all without any exception, saying, "Come to me, all you who labour and are burdened, and I will refresh you"' (*Collatio* XIII.7 [CSEL 13, p. 369, line 24 – p. 370, line 1]).

54 'Draw near to God, and he will draw near to you' (*Collatio* XIII.9 [CSEL 13, p. 372, lines 24–5]; James 4.8).

55 'The splendour of perfection truly is open to any age and either sex, and all the members of the church are urged to ascend the heights of sublime virtues when the apostle says, "Run in such a way that you may gain the prize"' (*Collatio* XXI.9 [CSEL 13, p. 582, lines 7–10]). Some caution must be taken with this example, as it may be a case of a believer seeking further purity rather than an unbeliever coming to Christ. Even so, however, its emphasis is on individuals' personal contrbutions to righteousness. Cassian does not have another example of the last verse ([2b] above).

56 Cassian, *Collatio* XIII.11.

57 See Prosper, *Contra Collatorem* VII.3 and XIX.1 (PL 51.231–3 and 267) and the Second Council of Orange (CCSL 148A, p. 63, lines 218–23).

58 *Collatio* XIII.17 (CSEL 13, p. 392, line 27 – p. 393, line 7).
59 'By this, therefore, we should understand (on the one hand) that without God's help we can do nothing right, and (on the other) that he allows us the power of free choice that we may seek the Lord and obey his commands' (lines 9–12).
60 This image is evocative of Christ's warning in the Parable of the Sower that 'Omnis qui audit uerbum regni et non intellegit, uenit malus et rapit quod seminatum est in corde eius' (When anyone hears the word of the kingdom, and does not understand it, the evil one comes and snatches away what has been sown in his heart), just as birds come and snatch away the seed scattered beside the road: 'Et dum seminat, quaedam ceciderunt secus uiam, et uenerunt uolucres et comederunt ea' (Matt. 13.19 and 4).
61 The wording here ['omnis eius labor in uanum consumitur' (line 19)] is reminiscent of the Psalmist's statement that 'nisi Dominus aedificauerit domum in uanum laborauerunt qui aedificant eum' (Psa. 126.1).
62 Lines 12–23, drawing on *Collatio* XIII.3.
63 'From this we clearly infer that the initiative not only of our actions but also of good thoughts comes from God, who inspires us with a good will to begin with, and supplies us with the opportunity of carrying out what we rightly desire ... He both begins what is good, and continues it and completes it in us' (*Collatio* XIII.3 [CSEL 13, p. 364, lines 15–19 and 21–2]).
64 'This statement we welcome greatly and acknowledge to be orthodox' (*Contra Collatorem* XIX.1 [PL 51.266B]; see also II.2 [PL 51.218C–219A]).
65 'When he sees in us some beginnings of a good will, he at once enlightens it and strengthens it and urges it on to salvation, increasing that which he himself implanted *or* which he sees to have arisen from our own efforts' (*Collatio* XIII.8 [CSEL 13, p. 371, lines 23–6], emphasis mine; Prosper objects to this point in *Contra Collatorem* II.3 and XIX.1 [PL 51.219–20 and 266]). The sixteen pairs of quotations, from which the first section is drawn, immediately follow in *Collatio* XIII as illustrations of this statement.
66 *Collatio* XII.12 (CSEL 13, p. 378, lines 3–6 and p. 378, line 25 – p. 379, line 1; Prosper objects to this notion in *Contra Collatorem* XI.2 and XIX.1). Again, in allowing for human initiative Cassian does stress the importance of God's help in fulfilling it: 'Per naturae bonum, quod beneficio creatoris indultum est,' he says, 'nonnumquam bonarum uoluntatum prodire principia, quae tamen nisi a domino dirigantur ad consummationem uirtutum peruenire non possunt' [Through the excellence of nature which is granted by the goodness of the Creator, sometimes first beginnings of a good will arise; this, however, cannot attain to the complete performance of what is good unless it is guided by the Lord] (*Collatio* XII.9 [CSEL 13, p. 374, lines 5–8]; Prosper objects to Cassian's statement, however, in *Contra Collatorem* IV.2 and XIX.1).

67 'We must strive with great labour so that our hearts may be prepared to receive the seed of the word of God' (lines 23–4).

68 'When it has been received, we must pray wholeheartedly that it may sprout and mature to ripeness' (lines 25–6). One is reminded of the conclusion to Boethius's *De consolatione* and Lantfred's 'solution' to the issue of free will; see above.

69 'If by the Lord's assisting grace the fruit of good deeds should grow in us, we must pray all the more that he who granted it to sprout and grow may also give perseverance together with a good will' (lines 26–9).

70 'It is God who works both to will and to accomplish through a good will' (lines 29–30; Phil. 2.13).

71 'For this reason they will thus: because God works so that they will' (Augustine, *De correptione* XII.38 [PL 44.939]); see also *De gratia et libero arbitrio* IX.21.

72 *Collatio* XIII.9, 10 and 12 (CSEL 13, p. 372, lines 20–2; p. 375, lines 21–2; and p. 381, line 7).

73 'The grace of God and free will seem opposed to each other, but really are in harmony ... for when God sees us inclined to will what is good, he meets, guides, and strengthens us' (*Collatio* XIII.11 [CSEL 13, p. 377, lines 15–17 and 20–1]).

74 Cf. Augustine, *De gratia et libero arbitrio* XVIII.38: 'Quia electi sunt,' he affirms, 'elegerunt ... Eligentium hominum meritum nullum esset, nisi eos eligentis gratia Dei praeueniret' [It was because they were chosen that they chose him ... There could be no merit in human choice, if God's grace was not prevenient in choosing them] (PL 44.904).

75 '[1] Therefore God's grace precedes human will where it is said, "My God, his mercy will precede me" [Psa. 58.11], [2a] and our will precedes when it says, "In the morning my prayer will precede you" [Psa. 87.14], [2b] and again: "My eyes preceded you at break of day" [Psa. 118.148]' (lines 34–7).

76 As he says, 'misericordia et gratia Dei conuertit hominem, de qua Psalmus dicit, "Deus meus, misericordia eius praeueniet me"' (the mercy and grace of God converts a person, of which the Psalmist says, "My God, his mercy will precede me" [*Epistulae* 214.4 (CSEL 57, p. 384, lines 3–5)]).

77 'Sometimes he delays and hinders our injurious purposes and deadly attempts from having their horrible effects, and, while we are rushing headlong towards death, draws us back to salvation' (*Collatio* XIII.7 [CSEL 13, p. 370, lines 14–17]). The comment here prefaces his citation of Psa. 58.11 in *Collatio* XIII.8.

78 *Collatio* XIII.8 (CSEL 13, p. 371, lines 23–6).

79 'If we want to fulfil the point of the aforementioned verse, we must take the
greatest care that an agile alertness should guard the first beginnings of our
morning thoughts, that the preemptive haste of our envious enemy should
not defile any of them' (*Collatio* XXI.26 [CSEL 13, p. 602, lines 7–11]).
80 'Qui si praeuentus a nobis peruigili mentis circumspectione non fuerit, antici-
pationis nequissimae consuetudinem non deponens cotidie nos fraudibus
suis praeuenire non desinet' [If he is not prevented by us with constant vigi-
lance of mind, he will not set aside his habit of most wicked anticipation nor
cease to prevent us daily with his deceits] (ibid. [CSEL 13, p. 602, lines 12–15]).
81 'He waits for us when the prophet says: "Therefore the Lord waits so that
he may have pity on you," and we wait for him when we say, "I waited
expectantly for the Lord, and he inclined towards me"' (lines 38–40).
82 'When God waits and delays for our good, that he might put our desires
to the test, our will precedes' (*Collatio* XIII.12 [CSEL 13, p. 381, lines 24–6
[p. 381, line 24 – p. 382, line 1]). The redactor omits this phrase from the first
set of quotations, both perhaps to tighten the semantic parallel of the
quotations and to avoid confusion with the point of the quotations here.
83 '[1] He admonishes us when he says, "All day long I have held out my hand
to an unbelieving people" [Rom. 10.21, paraphrasing Isa. 65.2], [2] and he is
invited by us when we have said to him: "I have held out my hand to you"
[Psa. 142.6]' (lines 38–40). In this the redactor surprisingly departs from Cassian's text, using 'admonet' for his first verb instead of 'aduocat nos et inuitat.' It is conceivable that *admonet* is a scribal corruption of *aduocat*, or that
that the redactor wanted to distinguish it from 'clamat' (line 47), since the
main verbs of the six sets of quotations are otherwise conceptually distinct
[*praeuenire, admonere/inuitare, expectare, confortare, clamare* and *quaerere*]. If this
were so, however, the problem would have been easily overcome by keeping
Cassian's 'inuitat'; such an approach would also have provided the semantic
repetition that is such a distinguishing characteristic of these quotations.
Admonet does, however, more precisely reflect the force of this verse in both
Romans and Isaiah. For the prophet, this is a people 'qui graditur in via non
bona post cogitationes suas, populus qui ad iracundiam prouocat me ante
faciem meam semper ... Non tacebo sed reddam et retribuam in sinu eorum'
[who walk in evil ways, pursuing their own imaginations – a people who
continually provoke me to my very face ... I will not keep silent but will pay
back in full (Isa. 65.2–3 and 6).
84 'Jesus cries out when he says: "If anyone is thirsty, let him come and drink";
[John 7.37] we may also cry out with the prophet: "I cried out to you, O
Lord; I said, 'You are my hope'"' [Psa. 141.6]' (lines 47–9). Again, note the
use of polyptoton.

85 The redactor actually replaces Cassian's verse at this point to emphasize the call of humans to God. Cassian states: 'Clamat etiam ad eum propheta: laboraui clamans, raucae factae sunt fauces meae: defecerunt oculi mei, dum spero in deum meum' [The prophet also cries to him: 'I have laboured with my crying; my jaws have become hoarse; my eyes have failed, while I hope in God'] (*Collatio* XIII.12 [CSEL 13, p. 382, lines 15–18]; Psa. 68.3). The substitution retains the Psalmist's hope in God while nicely changing his tears into an evocation, thus strengthening the parallel of the quotations.

86 'Just as the power of free will is evidenced by the disobedience of the people, so the daily foresight of God who declares and admonishes him is shown ... For we have no wish to do away with a person's free will by what we have said, but only to establish the fact that the assistance and grace of God are ... necessary to it' (*Collatio* III.22 [CSEL 13, p. 94, lines 9–11 and 26–8]).

87 In this respect, Cassian's version does more to emphasize both sides: 'Ne ipsos quidem conatus ... suis uiribus inpendere potuisset, nisi eum ad exercendum omne opus ruris protectio domini ac misericordia roborasset' [He could not by his own strength apply those very efforts ... unless the Lord's protection and pity had given him strength for the performance of all agricultural labours] (*Collatio* XIII.3 [CSEL 13, p. 364, lines 1–4; cf. p. 363, line 28 – p. 364, line 1]).

88 '[1] He strengthens us when he says: "I have trained and greatly strengthened their arms," [2] and he encourages us to strengthen ourselves when he says: "Strengthen weak hands and make firm feeble knees"' (lines 44–6). Again, note the use of polyptoton.

89 Cf. Augustine, *De praedestinatione* III.7: 'Non sufficit uoluntas nostra, et cursus noster, nisi Deus et uires currentibus praebeat' [Our willing is not sufficient, nor our running, unless God gives strength to run] (PL 44.965).

90 'God is faithful; he will not let you be tempted beyond what you can bear' (I Cor. 10.13; *Collatio* XIII.14 [CSEL 13, p. 387, lines 5–7]).

91 'Certainly the Divine righteousness would not have permitted them [him] to be tempted, unless it knew that there was within them [him] an equal power of resistance, by which they [he] could be an equitable judgment be found ... either guilty or worthy of praise' (*Collatio* XIII.14 [CSEL 13, p. 386, line 28 – p. 387, line 3]).

92 'Take away your hand,' i.e., allow him to fight with me in his own strength, 'and he will curse you to your face' (ibid. [CSEL 13, p. 385, lines 1–3]; Job 2.5).

93 *Collatio* XIII.14 (CSEL 13, p. 385, line 5). Prosper objects to this notion in *Contra Collatorem* XIV.1 and XIX.1.

94 '[1] The Lord seeks us when he says: "I sought, and there was not one; there was none who would respond," [2a] and he asks us to seek him when it

says: "Seek his face always" and [2b] "Seek the Lord while he may be found"' (lines 49–52). Again, note the use of polyptoton.

95 Our modern edition of Cassian differs slightly from the redactor's version, reading: 'Quaerit nos dominus *dicens*: quaesiui, et non erat uir: *uocaui*, et non *erat* qui responderet' (*Collatio* XIII.12 [CSEL 13, p. 382, lines 18–19], emphasis mine).

96 'I called, but no one answered; I spoke, but they did not listen' (Isa. 66.4); see PL 49.932.

97 'I sought and did not find him; I called, and he did not answer me' (Song of Songs 5.6; see CSEL 13, p. 382).

98 On Christ as the bridegroom, see for example John 3.28 and Matt. 25.1–13.

99 'He himself is sought by the bride as she tearfully laments: "On my bed in the night I looked for the one whom my soul loved: I looked for him, and did not find him; I called him, and he did not respond"' (*Collatio* XIII.12 [CSEL 13, p. 382, lines 20–3]). Cassian, too, departs from the original by adding the phrase 'uocaui ... mihi.' The Vulgate reads: 'In lectulo meo per noctes quaesiui quem diligit anima mea; quaesiui illum, et non inueni' [All night long on my bed I looked for the one my soul loves; I looked for him but did not find him] (Song of Songs 3.1).

100 Cf. Psa. 13.2–3 and 53.3–4: 'Dominus de caelo prospexit super filios hominum ut uideat si est ... requirens Deum. Omnes declinauerunt' [The Lord has looked down from heaven on the sons of men to see if there are any ... who seek after God. All have turned aside].

101 As the Pelagians would have it: 'Meritum nostrum in eo esse, quod quaerimus eum; et secundum hoc meritum dari eius gratiam, ut inueniamus eum' [Our merit lies in the fact of seeking God, and then his grace is given according to this merit, in order that we may find him] (*De gratia et libero arbitrio* V.11 [PL 44.888]).

102 *Collatio* XIII.13 (CSEL 13, p. 382, line 24 – p. 383, line 6).

103 MS *fiet*.

104 MS *consolationis*.

105 'In this way this kind of divine grace helps our will in great part, so that it both assists the good we wish so that it may come about, and instils the encouragement of his grace that it may come about' (lines 52–5).

106 'Man should never arrogantly aim to equal or join himself to the grace of God, attempting by this to introduce himself as a partner in the work of God' (*Collatio* XIII.3 [CSEL 13, p. 363, lines 22–4]).

107 Indeed, if it were not for the appropriate change in mood between the two verbs, this use of *adiuuat* might be considered a dittographic scribal error.

108 The six quotation-sets, summary statement, and discussion of David flow consecutively in *Collatio* XIII.12–13. Though the redactor does not reproduce the last verbatim, his fidelity to the overall plan again draws attention to his changes in the central section.

109 Again, on this point Cassian is clear: 'Nec liberum ei permisit arbitrium, si ei tantummodo malum ut uelit et possit, bonum uero a semet ipso nec uelle nec posse concessit' [God has not granted him a free will, if he has allowed him only to will and be capable of evil, but not to will or be capable in himself of what is good] (*Collatio* XIII.12 [CSEL 13, p. 378, lines 4–6]; cf. XIII.14 and Augustine, *De correptione* XII.37).

110 'Returning to favour through penitence once sin has been committed is both God's mercy and our concerted effort' (lines 56–7).

111 'Therefore, the fact that the sin was committed was by free will; the fact that he was reproved by the prophet, however, is the grace of divine favour. Again, the fact that, having been humbled, he recognizes his sin is his own doing; the fact that in a brief space of time he merited forgiveness is the mercy of the Lord' (lines 60–4; cf. II Sam. 11.4–17).

112 Cf. Augustine, *Epistulae* 104.3.9, *De correptione* XIV.45, and *Enarrationes in psalmos* CIII.2, respectively.

113 Cf. Augustine, *De dono perseuerantiae* VI.12: 'Nihil enim fit, nisi quod aut ipse facit, aut fieri ipse permittit. Potens ergo est, et a malo in bonum flectere uoluntates, et in lapsum pronas conuertere, ac dirigere in sibi placitum gressum' [Nothing comes to pass except what either he himself does or allows to be done. He has the power both to turn wills from evil to good, and to change those prone to fall and direct them in a way pleasing to himself] (PL 45.1000); cf. also *De gratia et libero arbitrio* XX.41.

114 'For so he must be believed to work "all in all": so as to urge on, protect and support, not to take away the freedom of will he once granted, but to bring his will about in us with our work of good will' (lines 65–8). The reference to God working 'all in all' comes from a Pauline discussion of the various gifts of the Spirit: 'Diuisiones uero gratiarum sunt, idem autem Spiritus. Et diuisiones ministrationum sunt, idem autem Dominus. Et diuisiones operationum sunt, idem uero Deus qui operatur omnia in omnibus' [Now there are differences of gifts, but the same Spirit. There are differences of ministries, but the same Lord. There are differences of works, but the same God who works all things in all [people]] (I Cor. 12.4–6).

115 While Augustine had taken the passage to say that God is responsible for individuals' works, not their faith – a position akin to that of the Semi-Pelagians – by the end of his career he attributes the whole of human righteousness to God, saying that 'ipsam fidem inter Dei munera reperiri,

quae dantur in eodem Spiritu' [faith itself is also found among those gifts of God which are given by the same Spirit] (*De praedestinatione* III.7 [PL 44.964–5].

116 'When he sees in us some beginnings of a good will, he at once enlightens, strengthens, and urges it on towards salvation, increasing that which he himself planted or which he sees to have arisen from our own efforts' (*Collatio* XIII.8 [CSEL 13, p. 371, lines 23–6].

117 'When God sees us inclined to will what is good, he meets, guides, and strengthens us' (*Collatio* XIII.11 [CSEL 13, p. 377, lines 20–1]).

118 'The grace of God always cooperates with our will in large part, and in all things assists, protects, and defends it, in such a way as sometimes even to require and look for some efforts of good will from it' (*Collatio* XIII.13 [CSEL 13, p. 382, line 24 – p. 383, line 2].

119 '[God works so that] his will is brought about in us with our work of good will, since when praying we say as follows: "May his will be done in us"' (lines 67–9; cf. lines 17–22).

120 Lines 1–9.

121 'Let us pass over these things as tolerable, since we also say that free will *with the help of grace* conceives a desire of what is good and a beginning of faith' (emphasis mine; *Contra Collatorem* XIV.1 [PL 60.252–3]).

122 Lines 34–52 and 58–64.

123 Given the richness of its library and clear interest in Cassian, it would not be implausible for this copy also to have been at Worcester; see for example Elaine N. Treharne, 'The Role of Worcester in the Production and Dissemination of Old English Homiliaries' (forthcoming).

7. Ælfric of Eynsham and the *Sermones catholici*

1 Substantial work has been done on Ælfric's career and the corpus of his writings. For overviews of his life, see Clemoes, 'Ælfric'; Hurt, *Ælfric*; and Wilcox's introduction to his *Ælfric's Prefaces*, as well as the entries by Godden, 'Ælfric of Eynsham,' in *The Blackwell Encyclopedia of Anglo-Saxon England*, and 'Ælfric of Eynsham,' in the *Oxford Dictionary of National Biography*; Leinbaugh, 'Ælfric'; Chaney, 'Ælfric Grammaticus'; and the collection edited by Magennis and Swan, *A Companion to Ælfric* (Leiden, forthcoming). On Ælfric's works, see Clemoes, 'Chronology'; Pope, *Homilies of Ælfric*, 136–45; and Kleist, 'Ælfric's Corpus.'

2 On which, see for example *CH* II.30.4–6, *CH* II.34. *Excusatio*.2–4; *CH* I.6.49 and II.11.413–15; and *CH* II.30.227–30, respectively.

3 Clemoes, 'Ælfric,' 184; Godden, 'Ælfric and the Vernacular,' 102.

4 Gatch, 'The Achievement of Ælfric,' 60.
5 Dalbey, 'Themes and Techniques,' 221.
6 Namely, Vercelli V, XVI, and XVII; see Nicholson, *The Vercelli Book*, 2, 5, and 9.
7 Bethurum, 'Wulfstan,' 216.
8 Gatch, 'The Achievement of Ælfric,' 44.
9 Smetana, 'Early Medieval Homiliary,' 181.
10 'We have followed [these] authors in this exposition, namely, Augustine of Hippo, Jerome, Bede, Gregory, Smaragdus, and sometimes Haymo; their authority, in short, is most freely recognized by all the orthodox' (*CH* I.*praef*.14–16).
11 See for example Hill, 'Smaragdus,' 203–6, and Godden, *Introduction, Commentary, and Glossary*, xli–xlii, liv, and lx.
12 See in particular Godden, *Introduction, Commentary, and Glossary*, xlvi–lxii, for a list of sources for the *Catholic Homilies*, as well as Lapidge, *The Anglo-Saxon Library*, 250–66, for a list of Latin sources quoted or alluded to in Ælfric's works as a whole.
13 Godden, *Introduction, Commentary, and Glossary*, xxxviii–xxxix, quoting *CH* II.39.25–6.
14 'We have not translated everywhere word for word, but sense for sense, nonetheless guarding most carefully against deceptive fallacies, lest we should be found to have been led astray by any heresy or darkened by deceit' (*CH* I.*praef*.11–14).
15 As Ælfric says when introducing his exposition, 'Se halga augustinus trahtnode þis godspel' [Saint Augustine treated this Gospel passage] (*CH* I.18.61).
16 *CH* I.18.100–1; cf. I Cor. 13.13. We may note in passing, moreover, that as Ælfric concurs with the Fathers that love is 'fulfremednys. godes .æ' (the perfection of God's Law [*CH* II.35.25–6]), he views good deeds, too, as gifts of God.
17 Augustine, *Sermones* CV.2.3 (PL 38.619D).
18 The pattern is remarkably similar to the healing of the blind man outside Jericho, which Gregory, however, treats in a distinctly different manner, as discussed above.
19 Augustine, *Sermones* CV.2.2 (PL 38.619A).
20 Cf. *SH* II.15.153–5: Even among 'eall Cristen folc þe on God nu gelyfað' he says, 'on ðam syndon ægðer ge yfele ge gode, and hy sume misfarað' [[among] all Christians who now believe in God, there are both evil and good, and some of them go astray].
21 That is, a section for which no sources have been identified either by myself or by Godden in his entries for *Fontes Anglo-Saxonici* and in his *Introduction, Commentary, and Glossary*.

22 '[The child] grows up, and goes forth, and knows nothing of this belief. It is now vital, therefore, for everyone to learn from his teacher how he must practise his Christianity with true belief' (*CH* II.3.285–8).

23 'No one would be worthy either of that faith, or of eternal life, if God's mercy were not the greater towards humankind.'

24 'Those who believe in God are directed by the Holy Spirit. Turning to God is not of ourselves, but by God's grace, as the apostle says, "Through God's grace we are held in faith"' (*CH* I.7.179–81; cf. I Pet. 1.5).

25 'If you, though you are evil, know how to give good gifts to your children, how much more will your Father in heaven give a good spirit to those who ask him' (Luke 11.13).

26 E.g., *CH* I.7.172–3: 'Se rihtwisa god nænne mann ne neadað to syngienne'; cf. I.7.186–9 and I.1.155–7; all these comments appear to be original to Ælfric.

27 E.g., *CH* II.1.110–11: 'Ælc man bið mid synnum gestryned and geboren ðurh adames forgægednysse'; cf. II.13.126–7, drawing on Augustine, *Tractatus* XLIII.9.25–39; and *CH* I.13.137–8, drawing on Bede, *Homiliae* I.3.

28 See ([2]) below, pp. 176–7.

29 'It is he who is ever good, who makes good people out of evil ones; for man by his own will had no power to heal himself' (Augustine, *Sermones* LXI.2 [PL 38.419D]).

30 'You did not choose me, but I chose you and appointed you to go and bear fruit' (John 15.16a).

31 Smetana, 'Ælfric,' 201.

32 Ibid., 178.

33 Godden, *Introduction, Commentary, and Glossary*, 635, n. 1, and 634.

34 Ibid., 636, in regards particularly to *CH* II.35.87–108; see below for a discussion of lines 81–91.

35 Again, here and below, numbers in brackets are inserted to serve as points of reference for the discussion to follow.

36 Gregory, *Homiliae* II.27.5 (PL 76.1207C), 'planting' referring still to Christ's image of the vine branches.

37 Ibid.

38 'Which he also daily fixes in the hearts of his faithful, through inspiration of the Holy Spirit' (*CH* II.35.53–4, drawing on Gregory, *Homiliae* II.27).

39 Eze. 24.22; cf. Gregory, *Homiliae* II.27.5 (PL 76.1207–8).

40 Godden, *Introduction, Commentary, and Glossary*, 637.

41 Godden notes that Ælfric seems also to have used Haymo's expansion of Gregory's homily, which he 'occasionally found helpful,' and knew both Smaragdus's and Bede's treatment of the passage; the latter two, however,

'are heavily indebted to Gregory and offered [Ælfric] nothing new' (ibid., 77). Gregory's homily remains Ælfric's primary source for this exposition.

42   *CH* I.10.38–9 and 46–59.

43   'Now we are shut out from the heavenly light, and ... we do not know more about it than what, *through Christ's teaching*, we read in books' (*CH* I.10.41–4; emphasis mine).

44   *CH* I.10.46–7.

45   *CH* I.10.116; Luke 18.42.

46   *CH* I.10.46–7 and 82. It is intriguing to note that Ælfric suggests that people may sit by the way, that is, believe in Christ, but refuse to pray ([1b]), and to this point we will return.

47   'Because by prayers our heart is stimulated and turned to God' (*CH* I.10.104).

48   'So also the soul, if God forsakes it for its sins, will do nothing good ... it will be deadened to good [and] dead to every excellence and happiness' (*CH* I.10.128–9 and 131–2).

49   'No one may do anything good without God's support' (*CH* I.10.129–30).

50   'Let us pray for that light which we can see with angels only, which shall never be ended. To that light our faith shall bring us' (*CH* I.10.113–15).

51   Gregory, *Homiliae* I.2.3 (PL 76.1083B).

52   Cf. Augustine, *Sermones* LVII.9.9, quoting Rom. 1.24: 'Tradidit illos Deus in desideria cordis eorum' (God gave them over to the [evil] desires of their heart).

53   'If we do them, then may we with those labours, through God's support, ascend the steep way which leads us to eternal life' (*CH* 1.10.175–7).

54   God, 'Gave to Adam and Eve their own choice' (*CH* I.7.151). For a more detailed study of Ælfric's teaching on the angelic fall than space permits here, see in particular Fox, 'Ælfric on the Creation.'

55   *CH* I.7.159–61.

56   Here, as elsewhere, Ælfric says that through the Fall humans became mortal and guilty – not that they became utterly corrupt.

57   *CH* I.7.160–1.

58   'He who turns from God to the devil loses God's grace, that is, the enlightening of his understanding ... But if he afterwards resolutely forsakes the devil, then he will have found the grace of the Holy Spirit again, which enlightens his heart and leads to Christ' (*CH* I.7.110–15).

59   Aside from a few lines from Haymo; see Smetana, 'Ælfric,' 188–9. Godden, by contrast, also identified Ælfric's use of the homily by Pseudo-Chrysostom discussed below, as well as details from Bede's commentaries on Luke and Mark and from Gregory the Great; see *Introduction, Commentary, and Glossary*, 110.

60 See Godden, *Introduction, Commentary, and Glossary*, 110, and 'Anglo-Saxon Kingship,' 912.

61 'We come to him not by our own merits, but by the granting of his grace alone' (Bede, *Homiliae* II.3 [CCSL 122, p. 201, lines 42–3]).

62 Godden, 'Anglo-Saxon Kingship.'

63 It is unfortunate for what follows that when Augustine treats this passage, he does not comment on the untying of the animals, and thus we do not have a direct point of comparison; see his *Tractatus* LI.5.

64 'More in some, less in others: more in those who sin more, less in those who sin less' (*CH* I.31.100–2).

65 *CH* I.14.150 and 166.

66 *CH* I.14.163–4 and 170–1; cf. I.12.142–4.

67 *CH* I.14.167–78; cf. Gregory, *Homiliae* II.25.

68 *CH* I.14.52–3.

69 'We are bound indeed by our own choice and heedlessness, but freed through the mercy of God' (Alfred, *Opus imperfectum* XXXVII [PG LVI.835]); 'By his own choice and his own heedlessness [man] is bound, but through God's mercy he will be unbound, *if thereafter he merits his liberation from God*' (*CH* I.14.119–21; emphasis mine).

70 *CH* II.5.140–2; Godden, *Introduction, Commentary, and Glossary*, 384, where Godden also offers another of Gregory's *Homiliae* as an alternate source. Cf. Luke 23.43, Bede, *In Lucam* VI.23.40–2 (CCSL 120, p. 405, lines 1697–9), and Gregory, *Homiliae* II.30 (PL 76.1225).

71 '[God's mercy] precedes the unwilling to make him willing; it follows the willing so that he may not will in vain' (Augustine, *Enchiridion* IX.32 [CCSL 46, p. 67, lines 103–4]); see Godden, *Introduction, Commentary, and Glossary*, 387.

72 Ælfric, *Grammar*, p. 171, line 9.

73 Logeman, *The Rule of St Benet*, 22.54.17, and 37.68.15; Schröer, *Die angelsächsischen Prosabearbeitungen*, 37.61.14; and Schröer, *Die Winteney-version*, 37.81.24.

74 'Both by going before enabled them to will the good that they did not desire, and by following after enabled them to be able to do the good which they do desire' (Gregory, *Moralia* IV.22.9.20 [CCSL 143A, p. 1108]).

75 *CH* II.13.42–3.

76 Förster, 'Die Quellen,' 15, and Smetana, 'Haymo,' 458.

77 Augustine, *Tractatus* 12. For the attributions here and below, see Godden, *Introduction, Commentary, and Glossary*, 466–72.

78 *CH* II.13.50–69 [Augustine] and 81–94 [Gregory]; 99–107 [Augustine] and 107–17 [Gregory]; 145–9 [Gregory] and 152–68 [Augustine]; 185–90 [Gregory] and 190–204 [Augustine]; 208–20 [both]; and 224–8 [both].

79 'In nature, they are from God; in sin, they are not from God' (Augustine, *Tractatus* XLII.15 (CCSL 26, p. 372, line 12).

80 *CH* I.19.37–8; emphasis mine. Confusingly, Ælfric here denies that people are children of God 'gecyndelice' (naturally); this is only to distinguish them, however, from the Son of God, who is truly good by nature. In saying that humans are good 'þurh gesceapenysse,' Ælfric still affirms that God created human beings good.

81 As he goes on to say, 'We menn beoð mid synnum acennede' [We humans are born with sins] (*CH* II.13.126–7).

82 Augustine, *Tractatus* XLII.10 (CCSL 26, p. 369, lines 13–14).

83 'Not through their nature or creation, but through their imitation [of the devil] and evil merits' (*CH* I.19.34–6).

84 *CH* II.13.64–6.

85 *CH* I.*praef*.131 and II.*praef*.45–6.

86 'Let no one ascribe his evil deeds to God, but let him ascribe them first to the devil, who deceived humankind, and to Adam's transgression, but most of all to himself, because evil pleases him and good does not' (*CH* I.7.186–9).

87 John 8.34; *CH* II.13.70–6.

88 *CH* II.13.91–4, 221–3 and 229–31.

89 Augustine, *Tractatus* XII.11.22–46, Num. 21.9, and John 11.25.

90 Godden, *Introduction, Commentary, and Glossary*, 330.

91 'Thus God manifested that Arius was as void in his insides as he had before been in his belief. He wanted to make Christ less than he is, and diminish the dignity of his Godhead; then a death was given him as ignominious as that which he well deserved' (*CH* I.20.227–31).

92 'The grace of God was attacked by Pelagius the Briton' (LXVI.4362 [CCSL 123B, p. 513, line 1538;] cf. LXVI.4410).

93 Souter, *Earliest Latin Commentaries*, 210, and *Pelagius's Expositions*, 1:60 and 323.

94 Souter, *Pelagius's Expositions*, 1:63 and 335, and *Earliest Latin Commentaries*, 212; see PL 102.512.

95 Souter, *Pelagius's Expositions*, 1:340–1.

96 Ibid., 1:266 and 268–9, and Souter, *Earliest Latin Commentaries*, 208. Souter also mentions a third type found in a single manuscript, Göttweig Abbey, MS 23 (36) (s. xii), but it is not germane to the present study (ibid., 208–9).

97 Godden, *Introduction, Commentary, and Glossary*, 330.

98 *CH* I.*praef*.15. It is odd that Smaragdus should have been able to recognize Pelagius's work while Ælfric does not, but this may well reflect the state of their respective sources, as well as Ælfric's limited exposure to Pelagian material in general.

99 'Se apostol us awrehte þæt we of slæpe ure asolcennysse and ungeleafful-
nysse æt sumum sæle arisan' [The apostle has excited us to arise at some
time from the sleep of our sluggishness and disbelief] (*CH* I.39.34–5); '[*De
somno surgere.*] De somno inertiae et ignorantiae' [[*To arise from sleep.*] From
the sleep of idleness and ignorance] (Pelagius, *Expositiones epistularum
Pauli* Rom. 13.11 [Souter, *Pelagius's Expositions*, 2:104.12]).

100 'Her asette se apostol niht for þære ealdan nytennysse þe rixode geond
ealne middaneard ær cristes tocyme: ac he toscoc þa dwollican nytennysse
þurh onlihtinge his andwerdnysse: swa swa se beorhta dæig todræfð þa
dymlican þeostru þære sweartan nihte' [Here the apostle has placed night
for the old ignorance, which reigned through all the world before Christ's
advent; but he scattered the erroneous ignorance by the illumination of his
presence, as the bright day drives away the dim darkness of the dark
night] (*CH* I.39.56–9); '[*Nox praecessit, dies autem adpropinquabit.*] Comparat
diei scientiam et ignorantiam nocti' [[The night has passed, but the day
will draw near.] He likens knowledge to day and ignorance to night]
(Pelagius, *Expositiones epistularum Pauli* Rom. 13.12 [Souter, *Pelagius's
Expositions*, 2:104.16–17]).

101 'Swa swa dæges leoht forwyrnð gehwylcne to gefremmenne. þæt þæt
seo niht geþafað: swa eac soðfæstnysse ingehid. Þæt is geþoht ures drihtnes willan: us ne geþafað mandæde to gefremmenne; Symle we beoð
fram gode gesewene æigðer ge wiðutan ge wiðinnan. ði sceal eac gehwa
se þe fordemed beon nele eallunga warnian þæt he godes beboda ne
forgæge' [As the light of day forbids everyone to perpetrate that which
the night allows, so also the knowledge of truth, that is, the thought of
our Lord's will, does not permit us to perpetrate deeds of wickedness.
We are ever seen by God, both without and within; therefore everyone
who does not wish to be condemned should especially take care that he
does not transgress God's commandments] (*CH* I.39.70–5); '[*Sicut in die
honeste ambulemus.*] Sicut lux diei prohibet unum quemque agere quod
nocte libere committebat, ita et scientia nos prohibet legis mandata con-
temnere. Siue: Quo[d] sciamus nos a deo semper uideri' [Just as the light
of day forbids everyone to do that which by night he will perpetrate
freely, so also knowledge forbids us to despise the commands of the
Law. Or: because we know that we are always seen by God] (Pelagius,
Expositiones epistularum Pauli Rom. 13.13 [Souter, *Pelagius's Expositions*,
2:105.2–5] [S2]).

102 'It is time for you to strive towards more perfect things, for you ought not
to be always little children and suckling babes' (Pelagius, *Expositiones epistularum Pauli* Rom. 13.11 [Souter, *Pelagius's Expositions*, 2:104.8–10]).

103 'It is not fitting that we should always be weak in our faith, like a tender child, but we should hasten to perfect excellence by obeying God's commandments' (*CH* I.39.37–9).

104 'God's chosen [will] shine in heavenly glory, each according to his status' (*CH* I.30.149–50).

105 'That they might with obedience and humility merit those heavenly honours which the devil had forfeited through pride' (*CH* I.13.5–8).

106 'With advancing knowledge our salvation is nearer than when [var.: when first] we believed' (Pelagius, *Expositiones epistularum Pauli* Rom. 13.11 [Souter, *Pelagius's Expositions*, 2:104.14–15]).

107 The primary manuscript that Souter cites as an example of this Anglo-Saxon version of the *Expositio* is Paris, Bibliothèque Nationale 9525 (s. xii-i[ex]; provenance Echternach abbey); see *Pelagius's Expositions*, apparatus for line 15, as well as 1:268 and 272.

108 An assumption present, for example, in Ælfric's treatment of the blind man outside Jericho above.

109 Ælfric almost invariably uses the *ge-* prefix with these terms; the only exceptions among his works are two instances of *earnode* and *earnung* in Belfour 3.98 and *SH* II.16.106, respectively.

110 *CH* II.38.128–9.

111 The nominative plural form, by contrast (*gifu*), only appears twelve times.

112 *CH* II.3.222 and Augustine, *Tractatus* VI.8.8–13 (CCSL 36, p. 57). For the attributions here and below, see Godden, 'Source Summary for Anglo-Saxon Text *Catholic Homilies*,' and *Introduction, Commentary, and Glossary.*

113 *CH* I.24.96 and Gregory, *Homiliae* II.34 (PL 76.1252AB). Cf. *CH* I.22.111, 126, and 127, where Ælfric probably draws on Gregory to say that at Pentecost the apostles merited the understanding of languages which the people of Babel had lost.

114 *CH* II.28.27 and Bede, *In Lucam* V.18.11 (CCSL 120, p. 324, lines 1143–8). Cf. *CH* I.32.138 and II.10.333, which draw on Bede when mentioning the saintly merits of John the Baptist and Cuthbert.

115 Cf. also *CH* II.15.203 and II.24.184 (drawing on Augustine) and I.10.163 and I.7.122 (drawing on Gregory).

116 '[The Holy Spirit] inspires our mind with his sevenfold grace' (*CH* I.22.229); Bede, *Hom.* II.16 (CCSL 122, p. 299, lines 317–19).

117 'The one who through good deserts attains to this sevenfold gift' (*CH* I.22.231–2).

118 *CH* II.24.119–20; cf. Bede, *Hom.* II.18 (CCSL 122, p. 294, line140). Study of the rest of the ninety-five references to merit, those not attributed to the Fathers, reveals that such interjections are common for Ælfric. While space

prevents us from illustrating this at length, suffice it to point out the intriguing gaps in the *Fontes* database at *CH* I.19.87 (between passages possibly from Augustine); I.24.192, II.6.163, and II.11.576–7 (between passages certainly from Gregory); and II.40.124–5 (between passages probably from Bede). While sources may eventually be found for these lacunae, at present they seem to be original to Ælfric.

119 'It was fitting that humanity, having been placed under the Lord by God, should be forbidden something, so that he should have the virtue of pleasing his lord by that obedience' (Augustine, *De Genesi ad litteram* VIII.6 [CSEL 28.1, p. 239, lines 23–5]; Bede, *In principium Genesis* 1.1485–7).

120 Lewis and Short cite Heb. 13.6 as an example of this sense: 'Talibus enim hostiis promeretur Deus' [With such sacrifices God is pleased] (*Latin Dictionary*, 1464).

121 'Why would God forbid him so little a thing ... [but] how could Adam know what he was [i.e., God's servant], unless he were obedient to his Lord in something? It is as if God had said to him, "... with that easy obedience you shall *merit* the joys of heaven and the place from which the devil fell through disobedience"' (*CH* I.1.74–7 and 80–1; emphasis mine).

122 *CH* I.1.64, I.1.126, I.13.7, and II.31.79–80; cf. I.25.183.

123 'Because you hear you should also strive to understand other things which you do not hear' (Gregory, *Homiliae* 9 [PL 76.1108B]).

124 'You hear God's commands from teachers' lips and return them to God with interest if through your diligence they are multiplied ... and you yourselves put them into practice *through meritorious efforts*' (*CH* II.38.125–9; emphasis mine).

125 'He who receives the money of the word from a teacher ... should repay this money with interest by working so that what he learned by listening he should carry out also in action' (Bede, *In Lucam* V.19.22–3 [CCSL 120, p. 340, lines 1780–3]); Godden, *Introduction, Commentary, and Glossary*, 652.

126 *CH* I.19.37–8, I.20.276, I.22.231–2, I.30.90, II.19.56–7, and II.24.122–3.

127 Similarly, if we expand our search to include variations of the phrase *god* geearnung** within five words' proximity, we find twenty-six examples in Old English, seventeen by Ælfric, fourteen coming from the *Sermones*.

128 'Though at one time and in the same moment their mother bore both, there was not one kind of life for both' (Gregory, *Homiliae* I.10 [PL 76.1112B]).

129 'They were not alike in character, nor in the merits of their life. Scripture indeed says that God loved Jacob and hated Esau [Rom. 9.13], not because of Fate, but because of their differing merits' (*CH* I.7.130–3).

130 See, for example, *De praedestinatione* III.7 and *Moralia* XI.9.13.

131 'Sunt nonnulli qui acceptis uirtutibus etiam electorum hominum merita transcendunt; cum que et bonis meliores sunt, electis quoque fratribus principantur' [There are many who having received virtues also surpass the merits of elect people; and because they are also better in righteousness, they also rule over their elect brothers] (Gregory, *Homiliae* II.34 [PL 76.1253A]); 'Ða gecorenan þe ðurh healicum geearnungum þa læssan gebroþru oferstigað mid ealdorscipe: þa habbað eac heora dæl betwux þam heafonlicum ealderdomum' [Those chosen ones, who through great merits excel their humbler brothers in authority, will have their portion also among the heavenly princes] (*CH* I.24.121–3).

132 'Quia enim tanta illuc ascensura creditur multitudo hominum, quanta multitudo remansit angelorum, superest ut ipsi quoque homines qui ad caelestem patriam redeunt ex eis agminibus aliquid illuc reuertentes imitentur' [Because it is believed that as large a host of humans is about to ascend to heaven as the host of angels that remained, it follows that those people who come to the heavenly country may reflect something of those hosts when they arrive there] (Gregory, *Homiliae* II.34 [PL 76.1252BC]); 'Nu bið eft seo micelnyss geþungenra manna swa micel swa ðæra staþolfæstra engla wæs. and we beoð geendebyrde to heora werodum. æfter urum *geearnungum*' [Now the host of righteous people will be as great as was that of the steadfast angels; and we shall be arranged according to their hosts, in keeping with our *merits*] (*CH* I.24.107–9; emphasis mine).

133 'All people do not have the same grace from God, for God gives spiritual honours to everyone according to his endeavours' (*CH* I.24.151–2).

134 'This dinner [i.e., the heavenly Feast] is portrayed by this last supper, at which the seven disciples are mentioned as being present, because ... internal refreshment then will renew those who now, filled with the sevenfold grace, desire [this refreshment] eagerly in the love of [their] spirit' (Gregory, *Homiliae* II.24 [PL 76.1187C]).

135 'He feasted after his Resurrection with seven disciples, because he wished to reveal thereby that those people come to his eternal feast who in the present life through merits come to the sevenfold grace of the Holy Spirit ... Through these seven virtues everlasting life is earned' (*CH* II.16.200–3 and 205–6).

136 'For if Moses and all the prophets said that this Christ through the anguish of his suffering would enter into his glory, why do those pride themselves on being Christians who ... do not wish to attain the glory which they want to have with Christ by suffering hardships?' (Bede, *In Lucam* VI.24.25–7 [CCSL 120, p. 415, lines 2086–96]).

137 Page 180, line 17.

138 'Gif moyses and ealle witegan witogoden þæt crist sceolde ðurh nearuny-
sse his ðrowunge into his heofonlican wuldre faran. humeta mæg ðonne
se beon cristen geteald. se ðe nele ... ðurh nanre earfoðnysse. þæt ece wul-
dor mid cristè geearnian?' [If Moses and all the prophets prophesied that
Christ, through the anguish of his suffering, should pass into his heavenly
glory, how then can he be accounted a Christian who will not ... through
any difficulty merit eternal glory with Christ?] (CH II.16.58–63).
139 'We shall undoubtedly come there if we merit it in this present life'
   (CH II.4.239; Haymo, Homiliae de tempore 18 [PL 118.134CD]).
140 'One can aptly be called John if when fulfilling the Creator's commands
through righteousness one attributes nothing to oneself but ascribes
everything to the Giver of all good things' (Hericus of Auxerre, In octaua
sancti Andraea [PL 95.1460CD]).
141 'John is interpreted "God's grace." He is aptly called God's grace, who
obtains the grace of God through good deserts, to the end that he may
zealously fulfil his commandments' (CH I.38.166–8).
142 'Let those who continue in virginity rejoice, for they have deserved to be
that which they praise [i.e., virgins like Mary] ... Let those who are in
chaste widowhood praise and honour her [Mary], for it is clear that they
cannot be chaste but through Christ's grace' (CH I.30.175–9); cf. Paschasius
Radbertus: 'Quod si uirgo es, gaude quia meruisti esse et tu, quod laudas
... Quod si continens et casta, uenerare et lauda, quia non aliunde constat,
ut possis esse casta, quam ex gratia Christi' [Now if you are a virgin,
rejoice that you have deserved to be what you praise ... Now if you are
self-disciplined and chaste, honour and praise her, because it does not
depend on anything else that you should be able to be chaste than on
Christ's grace] (De assumptione VI.35 [CCCM 56C, p. 124, lines 281–5).
143 CH I.praef.126; I.1.64, 124, 126, and 295; I.6.97; I.7.133 and 194; I.10.170;
I.13.7; I.17.AppB.3.105 and 225; I.19.36, 37–8, 87, 174, and 176; I.20.268, 273,
275 (two) and 276; I.24.189 and 192; I.25.160; I.32.203; I.37.5; I.40.186;
II.2.94; II.3.284 and 289; II.6.163; II.10.1–2; II.11.3 and 576–7; II.16.224;
II.19.55, 56–7 and 298; II.22.162; II.30.38; II.31.79–80; II.35.12; II.38.209;
II.39.188; II.40.124–5 and 292.
144 CH I.praef.126; I.1.64, 126 and 295; I.6.97; I.10.170; I.13.7; I.17.AppB.3.105;
I.19.87 and 174; I.20.268 and 275; I.24.192; I.25.160; I.32.203; I.40.186;
II.3.284 and 289; II.11.3; II.16.224; II.19.298; II.22.162; II.31.79–80; II.38.209;
II.39.188; II.40.124–5 and 292.
145 Incipits: CH I.13.7, I.37.5, II.10.1–2, II.11.3, II.35.12; Explicits: CH I.1.295;
I.20.273, 275 (two) and 276; I.40.186, II.10.333, II.16.224, II.19.298, II.20.267,
II.32.223.

146 *CH* I.praef.126, I.40.186 and II.40.292.
147 '[God] works his work through his chosen, not because he has need of our aid, but that we may earn eternal life by the performance of his work. Paul the apostle said, "We are God's assistants," and yet we do nothing for God without the assistance of God' (*CH* I.praef.125–8).
148 'God inclines the sinful to repentance, and the righteous he increases with more righteousness ... All humankind was sinful, but the Lord justified, without merits, through his grace, those whom he chose' (*CH* II.32.68–70 and 72–4). Cf. Bede, *Hom.* I.21: 'Vocat peccatores ut per paenitentiam corrigantur uocat iustos ut magis magis que iustificentur. Quamuis et ita recte intellegi possit quod ait, non ueni uocare iustos sed peccatores, quia non illos uocauerit qui suam iustitiam uolentes constituere iustitiae Dei non sunt subiecti sed eos potius qui fragilitatis suae conscii non erubescunt profiteri quia in multis offendimus omnes' [He calls sinners so that they should be corrected through discipline; he calls the righteous so that they may be made more and more just. Although it may also rightly be understood that he says "I did not come to call the righteous, but sinners" [Matt. 9.13] because he did not call those who, wishing to establish their own righteousness, did not submit themselves to the righteousness of God [Rom. 10.3], but rather those who, being conscious of their own weakness, were not ashamed to confess that "We all offend in many ways" [James 3.2]'] (CCSL 122, p. 153, lines 204–10).
149 'We have written elsewhere about this; let him read it who will' (Ælfric, *In xl de penitentia*, II.604.20–1).
150 'Of the death of all these apostles I have written save Mattias alone, about whom I could not find out; those [works] you may read and edify yourself in them, if you have taken care to guard your own souls' (Ælfric, *Letter to Sigeweard*, p. 60, lines 1006–9; see also p. 18, lines 48–9).
151 *Hexameron* lines 420–2, *Interrogationes* 27.176–7 and 5.36–7, and *LS* I.1.94–6 and 171–2.
152 *LS* I.1.172–3, *Hexameron* lines 465–73, and *De creatore et creatura* lines 217–25.
153 *LS* I.1.172–3, *SH* I.3.108–10, and Assmann 3.233–7.
154 *Interrogationes* 5.38–40.
155 *LS* I.1.175.
156 See for example Meaney, 'Ælfric's Use of his Sources in his Homily on Auguries,' and 'Ælfric and Idolatry.'
157 Alfred, *OEBoeth.* 41.141.28–41.142.8.
158 Ibid. 41.142.8–15.
159 Ibid. 41.142.28–41.143.3, and 41.145.14–16.

160 Ælfric's stance against predestination suggests a potential departure from Augustine that regrettably remains beyond the purview of the present study.

161 'Our freedom always needs God's assistance, because we can do nothing good without God's help' (*LS* I.17.266–7).

Appendix III: Primary Texts

Edition of De adutorio Dei et libero arbitrio

1 Vulg.: 'Nemo potest uenire [MS *Nemo uenit*] ad me nisi Pater qui misit me traxerit eum.'

2 Vulg.: 'Non potest homo accipere quicquam nisi fuerit ei datum [MS *datum fuerit ei*] de caelo.'

3 MS *Per ergo hoc*, with reversal marks.

4 MS *seminis*.

5 MS *sustinenti*.

6 MS *sementem*.

7 MS *euiderit*.

8 MS *et*.

9 Vulg.: 'Deus est enim [MS *Deus autem*] qui operatur in uobis [MS *in uobis* omitted] et uelle et perficere pro bona uoluntate.'

10 A form of direct address often used by Augustine; cf. *Sermones* LXXX-VIII.14 and *Enarrationes in psalmos* XLIX.2.7.

11 Vulg.: 'Deus meus uoluntas [MS *misericordia* (a Vulgate variant)] eius praeueniet me.'

12 Vulg.: 'Praeuenerunt oculi mei ad diluculum [MS *ad te diluculo*].'

13 Cf. Isa. 65.2 and and Psa. 87.10: 'Expandi manus meas tota die ad populum incredulum'; 'Tota die expandi ad te manus meas.'

14 Vulg.: 'Expandi manus meas [MS *meas* omitted] ad te.'

15 Cf. Isa. 59.16 and 41.28: 'Vidit quia non est uir'; 'Vidi et non erat.'

16 Cf. I Chr. 16.11.

17 MS *fiet*.

18 MS *consolationis*.

19 MS *uolutatis*.

20 MS *et* omitted.

21 Cf. I Cor. 12.6: 'Deus qui operatur omnia in omnibus'; cf. also 15.28.

22 Cf. Matt. 6.10: 'Fiat uoluntas tua sicut in caelo et in terra' – an allusion here, not a quotation.

Translation of De adutorio Dei et libero arbitrio

1 Vulg.: 'For it is God [MS *Now* [*it is*] *God*] who works in you [MS *in you* omit-
   ted] both to will and to accomplish through a good will.'
2 Vulg.: 'O my God, his will [MS *mercy* (a Vulgate variant)] shall precede me.'
3 Vulg.: 'My eyes came before the dawn [MS *before you at dawn*].'
4 Cf. Isa. 65.2 and Psa. 87.10: 'All day long I held out my hands to an unbelieving people'; 'All day long I held out my hands to you.'
5 Vulg.: 'I have held out my [MS my omitted] hands to you.'
6 Cf. Isa. 59.16 and 41.28: 'He saw that there was no one'; 'I looked and there
   was no one.'
7 Cf. I Chr. 56.11.
8 Cf. I Cor. 12.6: '[It is] God who works all things in all'; cf. also 15.28.
9 Cf. Matt. 6.10: 'May your will be done on earth as it is in heaven.'

Edition and Translation of Carmen de libero arbitrio (Notes taken from Lapidge,
'Three Latin Poems'; additions by Kleist in square brackets)

1 This poem is written in elegiac couplets.
2 *Usiade.* I have not found this form elsewhere. One wonders whether the
   poet (or his source) had misunderstood Greek ου?σία δέ or ου?σία δή. Or perhaps the –*de* is added to satisfy the metrical requirement, as –*or* is added to
   prouidentia in line 5.
3 *Est, creat.* The translation to *purgas* in line 3 would be less abrupt if one were
   to read *es* and *creas* in line 2, though the transmitted text makes some sense.
4 *Porrouidentia.* The poet clearly means *prouidentia*, but that word would not satisfy
   the exigencies of metre (*prōuĭdentĭa*). So the poet added an extra syllable, after the
   manner of Ennius, *induperator* (*Ann.* 1.27) and Lucretius, *indugredi* (1.82).
5 *Praedestiuenatio.* Neither would *praedestīnātĭo* scan. The enclitic –*ue* is
   inserted in the stem of the word to provide an extra syllable; this by a
   respectable practice called tmesis.
6 *Taceat ... stultiloquax.* The outburst against the imagined interlocutor is a
   device found frequently in Anglo-Latin poetry.
7 Cf. Rom. 8.29.
8 MS *ne.*
9 MS *legas.* It will be noticed that the variation of *i* and *e* is frequent in this manuscript; cf. *Altercatio* [*magistri et discipuli*] 14 (*atqui* for *atque*), 31 (*metuet* for
   metuit), 49 (*quesquiliarum*), 71 (*inqui* for *inque*), 72 (*infi* for *infe*), as well as *de libero
   arbitrio* 38 and 181. Thus *legas* for *legis* is to be considered rather as a variant
   spelling than as a scribal error. [Here and below, citations from the *Altercatio*

magistri et discipuli refer to Lapidge's edition in 'Three Latin Poems,' 105–21.]

10 MS *hominesque.* See note 9.

11 This line is from the Blessing of the Paschal Candle (*The Gregorian Sacramentary,* ed. H.A. Wilson. Henry Bradshaw Society [London, 1915]): 'o felix culpa quae talem ac tantum meruit habere Redemptorem.'

12 *Tempe.* Here, as in *Altercatio* 45, the quantity of *Tempe* is false.

13 *Facitis* is apparently a 'majestic' plural and addresses God.

14 MS *et, iugat.* It is not easy to see what MS *iugat* might refer to here. I conjecture *ut ... iugent*: 'that they may join their beautiful members to Christ, the head.' The line is thus a conflation of two Pauline passages: I Cor. 12.12 – 'sicut enim corpus unum est, et membra habet multa, omnia autem membra corporis cum sint multa, unum tamen corpus sunt: ita et Christus' (cf. I Cor. 15.15) together with Eph. 4.15–16 – 'per omnia, qui est caput Christus: ex quo totum corpus compactum, et connexum per omnem iuncturam subministrationis' (cf. Eph. 1.22–3).

15 The syntax [in lines 55–6] is difficult: 'ut sermons nostri resonent clarius, ponimus paucis uerbis paradigmata in medium.'

16 MS *uel circumdare* written above *concludere* in main hand. The alternative reading which the scribe has added here in superscript (*circumdare*), as he has done at lines 85 and 101, presents some problem, for in each case the proposed alternatives cannot be construed simply as glosses, and in each case there seems to be little reason for deciding in favour of either reading. One is inclined to assume that the scribe was copying from the poet's working manuscript, and that the alternative readings were jotted down by the poet himself.

17 MS *cessa.*

18 MS *praepote.*

19 *Bis seno.* The use of singular distributives is not common in Latin poetry of any period. This line is possibly modelled on Juvencus 2.430–1: 'haec fatus populo ex omni delecta seorsum/fortia conglomerat bisseno pectora coetu.'

20 *Sarranis.* This word is found nowhere else. It is perhaps a corrupt form of either *saracis* ('a sort of tunic,' see Du Cange [*Glossarium ad scriptores mediae et infimae Latinitatis,* 3: 781] s.v. *sarica*) or perhaps *sarapis,* a Latinized form of Greek σάραπις, 'a Persian robe with purple stripes.'

21 MS *uel multis* written above *diris* in main hand.

22 *Cleptibus. Cleptes* is a common glossary word from Greek κλέπτης; see *CGL* [Goetz, *Corpus Glossariorum Latinorum*] II, 74.36, 350.28, 507.18, and 556.42 and III, 5.17, 14.7, 86.76, 147.47, 179.32, 251.41, 406.61, and 449.49; in each of these instances it is glossed as *fur.*

23 MS *spendida*.

24 *Pallade*. This word is unknown elsewhere and would seem to mean 'wisely' or something of the sort. It is perhaps a coinage from Pallas the goddess of wisdom, meaning 'after the manner of Pallas,' that is, 'wisely.'

25 *Flamine* 'through the agency of the Holy Ghost.' *Flamen* in this sense (translating πνευμα) is frequently found in Anglo-Latin. E.g., Lantfridus, *Translatio et miracula S. Swithuni* (ed. E.P. Sauvage, *Analecta Bollandiana* 4 [1885], 400 [now ed. Lapidge, *The Cult of St Swithun*, 252–332, at 322):

> Alme Deus atque clemens,
> qui coelum, terram ac mare
> sancto gubernas flamine ...

Also Frithegodus, *Breuiloquium* 491: 'in Patris et Nati, necnon et Flaminis Almi.'

26 MS *uel [dampn]e[nt] uel [coron]e[nt]* written in main hand above *dampnant* and *coronant*.

27 *Cunctisator*. This word is not attested anywhere in Latin, to my knowledge, and is perhaps a neologism here. Anglo-Latin authors are particularly fond of compound words in *cuncti-*, such as *cunctipotens* and *cunctitonans*.

28 MS *distent*.

29 *Neque* after *nec* is slightly awkward. A small change to *quoque* would afford a more elegant expression.

30 MS *autor*.

31 The image of the *bivium* is common in medieval literature of all periods; see the recent study by Harms, *Homo Viator in Bivio*.

32 MS *patere*.

33 MS *neuosis*. This emendation was suggested to me by Dr D.B. Gain of the University of Witwatersrand. I am very grateful to Dr Gain for reading the text of these poems.carefully and for making many helpful suggestions.

34 *Brauium*. A biblical word from Greek βραβειον meaning 'prize' or 'reward'; cf. I Cor. 9.24 and Phil. 3.14.

35 *Tripudii*. A word of biblical origin meaning 'joy' (Esther 8.16), but known from the glossaries to mean specifically the joy of winning (*CGL* [Goetz, *Corpus Glossariorum Latinorum*] IV, 425.10 and V, 487.5 and 541.38).

36 I Cor. 9.24.

37 MS *tes qua*.

38 These lines [143–8] are epanaleptic. Epanaleptic verses seem to have been popular at Winchester at this time. There are three hymns to St Swithun in a manuscript at Rouen (formerly at Jumièges but written at Winchester) which are both epanaleptic and abecedarii (ed. E.P. Sauvage, *Analecta Bollandiana* 5 [1886], 53–8), as well as a hymn to St Æthewold and one to St Birin (ed. C. Blume, *Sitzungsberichte der Akademie der Wissenschaften in Wien* 146.3 [1903] 3–12) which are also both epanaleptic and abecedarii.

As Blume has shown (14 ff.), these hymns are to be attributed to Wulfstan.

39 MS *ut*. There are two possibilities here: either the transmitted *ut* may be retained, in which case *laxat* of line 154 must be emended to *laxeat* and the full stop after line 152 removed. The reading *at* in line 153 allows *laxat* in line 154 to stand.

40 Acts 6.5 and 7.55.

41 *Regmina*. A syncopated form of *regimina*, it would seem, *metri gratia*.

42 MS *dirie*.

43 Matt. 20.10: 'uenientes autem et primi arbitrati sunt quod plus essent accepturi: accepterunt autem et ipsi singulos denarios.' Cf. Augustine, *De Genesi ad litteram* IX.6 (PL 34, col. 396 [now CSEL 28.1, p. 274, lines 9–10]): 'erunt sancti, quando peracto operis die denarium partier accepturi sunt.' Note that the quantity of *dēnārĭum* here is false; this, with *uenīmus* in line 184, is one of the very few examples of false quantity in this poem that cannot be paralleled elsewhere in Anglo-Latin verse.

44 MS *uos qui*, with *e* written above the *i* of *qui*.

Select Bibliography.

Primary Sources

Ælfric. *Admonitio ad filium spiritualem*, ed. H.W. Norman. In *The Anglo-Saxon version of the Hexameron of St. Basil, or, Be Godes six daga weorcum: And the Saxon Remains of St. Basil's Admonitio ad filium spiritualem*. London, 1848. Rev. 1849.

– 'Ælfric's Version of *Alcuini Interrogationes Sigeuulfi in Genesin*,' *Anglia* 7 (1884), 1–59.

– 'Bidding Prayers' or *Gebedu on English* (Prayers in English), ed. B. Thorpe. In *The Homilies of the Anglo-Saxon Church: The First Part, Containing the <u>Sermones catholici</u> or Homilies of Ælfric*, 2:598–600. London, 1844–6.

– *De creatore et creatura*, unpublished text in London, British Library, MS. Cotton Otho C.I, vol. 2 (Worcester?, s. xi^{in} and xi^{med}; provenance Worcester), quotations from Dictionary of Old English's electronic edition [edition forthcoming by Kleist].

– *De temporibus anni*, ed. H. Henel, 2–82. In *Ælfric's De Temporibus Anni, Edited From All the Known MSS. and Fragments, with an Introduction, sources, Parallels, and Notes*. EETS os 213. London, 1942. Repr. 1970.

– *Grammar*, ed. J. Zupitza. In *Ælfrics Grammatik und Glossar*. Berlin, 1880.

– *Hexameron*, ed. S.J. Crawford. In *Exameron Anglice, or the OE Hexameron*. BaP 10. Hamburg, 1932.

– *Interrogationes Sigeuulfi in Genesin*, ed. George E. Maclean. *Anglia* 6 (1883), 425–73.

– *In xl de penitentia*, ed. B. Thorpe. In *The Homilies of the Anglo-Saxon Church: The First Part, Containing the <u>Sermones catholici</u> or Homilies of Ælfric*, 2:602–8. London, 1844–6.

– *Letter for Wulfsige*, ed. D. Whitelock, M. Brett, and C.N.L. Brooke. In *Councils and Synods with Other Documents Relating to the English Church*, vol. 1, *AD 871–1204*, ed. D. Whitelock. Oxford, 1981.

– *Letter to Sigeweard*, ed. S.J. Crawford. In *The Old English Version of The Heptateuch: Aelfric's Treatise on the Old and New Testament and his Preface to Genesis.* EETS 160, 15–75. London, 1922.

– *The Old English Ely Privilege*, ed. John C. Pope. 'Ælfric and the Old English Version of the Ely Privilege.' In *England Before the Conquest: Studies in Primary Sources Presented to Dorothy Whitelock*, ed. Peter Clemoes and Kathleen Hughes, 85–113. Cambridge, 1971.

– *Preface to Genesis*, ed. S.J. Crawford. *The Old English Version of The Heptateuch: Aelfric's Treatise on the Old and New Testament and his Preface to Genesis.* EETS 160, 76–80. London, 1922.

– *Sermones catholici.* See *CH* I and *CH* II under Abbreviations.

– *Vita S. Æthelwoldi*, ed. M. Lapidge and M. Winterbottom. In *Wulfstan of Winchester*. App. A., 70–80. Oxford, 1991.

Æthelwold. *Regularis concordia*, ed. T. Symons. New York, 1953.

Alcuin. *In Iohannis euangelium*, ed. Jacques-Paul Migne. PL 100, cols 737–1008. Paris, 1851.

Pseudo-Alcuin. *Interpretatione nominum hebraicorum progenitorum domini nostri Iesu Christi*, ed. Jacques-Paul Migne. PL 100, cols 723–34. Paris, 1851.

Ambrose. *Expositio euangelii secundum Lucam*, ed. M. Adrianen. CCSL 14, 1–400. Turnhout, 1957.

Augustine. *Ad Orosium contra Priscilliantista et Origenistas*, ed. Klaus-D. Daur. CCSL 49, 168–78. Turnhout, 1985.

– *Confessiones*, ed. L. Verheijen. CCSL 27. Turnhout, 1981.

– *Contra Adimantum Manichei discipulum liber unus*, ed. J. Zycha. CSEL 25.1, 115–90. Vienna, 1891.

– *Contra aduersarium legis et prophetarum*, ed. Klaus-D. Daur. CCSL 49, 35–131. Turnhout, 1985.

– *Contra duas epistulas Pelagianorum*, ed. K. Urba and J. Zycha. CSEL 60, 421–570. Vienna, 1913.

– *Contra epistulam Parmeniani libri iii*, ed. Michael Petschenig. CSEL 51, 17–141. Vienna, 1908.

– *Contra Faustum Manichaeum*, ed. J. Zycha. CSEL 25.1, 249–797. Vienna, 1891.

– *Contra Fortunatum Manichaeum*, ed. J. Zycha. CSEL 25.1, 81–112. Vienna, 1891.

– *Contra Gaudentium Donatistam episcopum libri ii*, ed. Michael Petschenig. CSEL 53, 201–74. Vienna, 1910.

– *Contra Iulianum haeresis Pelagianae defensorem libri vi*, ed. Jacques-Paul Migne. PL 44, cols 641–874. Paris, 1845.

– *Contra litteras Petiliani*, ed. M. Petschenig. CSEL 52, 1–227. Vienna, 1909.
– *Contra litteras Petiliani libri iii*, ed. Michael Petschenig. CSEL 51, 1–227. Vienna, 1909.
– *Contra Maximinum haereticum Arrianorum episcopum libri ii*, ed. Jacques-Paul Migne. PL 42, cols 743–814. Paris, 1841.
– *Contra secundam Iuliani responsionem opus imperfectum*, ed. M. Zelzer [*libri* i–iii]. CSEL 85. Vienna, 1974.
– *Contra secundam Iuliani responsionem opus imperfectum*, ed. Jacques-Paul Migne [*libri* iv–vi]. PL 45, cols 1337–1608. Paris, 1845.
– *Contra Secundinum Manichaeum liber*, ed. J. Zycha. CSEL 25.2, 903–47. Vienna, 1892.
– *De adulterinis coniugiis*, ed. J. Zycha. CSEL 41, 347–410. Vienna, 1900.
– *De agone christiano*, ed. J. Zycha. CSEL 41, 101–38. Vienna, 1900.
– *De anima et eius origine*, ed. K. Urba and J. Zycha. CSEL 60, 303–419. Vienna, 1913.
– *De baptismo contra Donatistas libri vii*, ed. Michael Petschenig. CSEL 51, 143–375. Vienna, 1908.
– *De bono coniugali*, ed. J. Zycha, CSEL 41, 187–231. Vienna, 1900.
– *De bono uiduitatis*, ed. J. Zycha. CSEL 41, 305–43. Vienna, 1900.
– *De catechizandis rudibus*, ed. J.B. Bauer. CCSL 46, 121–78. Turnhout, 1969.
– *De ciuitate Dei*, ed. B. Dombart and A. Kalb. 2 vols. CCSL 47–8. Turnhout, 1955.
– *De consensu euangelistarum libri iv*, ed. F. Weihrich. CSEL 43. Vienna, 1904.
– *De correptione et gratia*, ed. Jacques-Paul Migne. PL 44, cols 915–46. Paris, 1845.
– *De diuersis quaestionibus ad Simplicianum*, ed. A. Mutzenbecher. CCSL 44. Turnhout, 1970.
– *De diuersis quaestionibus lxxxiii*, ed. A. Mutzenbecher. CCSL 44A, 1–249. Turnhout, 1975.
– *De diuinatione daemonum*, ed. J. Zycha. CSEL 41, 599–618. Vienna, 1900.
– *De doctrina Christiana*, ed. J. Martin. CCSL 32, 1–167. Turnhout, 1962.
– *De dono perseuerantiae*, ed. Jacques-Paul Migne. PL 45, cols 993–1034. Paris, 1845.
– *De Genesi ad litteram imperfectus liber*, ed. J. Zycha. CSEL 28.1, 459–503. Vienna, 1894.
– *De Genesi ad litteram libri xii*, ed. J. Zycha. CSEL 28.1, 1–435. Vienna, 1894.
– *De Genesi contra Manichaeos*, ed. Dorothea Weber. CSEL 91. Vienna, 1998.
– *De gestis Pelagii*, ed. K. Urba and J. Zycha. CSEL 42, 49–122. Vienna, 1902.
– *De gratia Christi et de peccato originali*, ed. K. Urba and J. Zycha. CSEL 42, 123–206. Vienna, 1902.
– *De gratia et libero arbitrio*, ed. Jacques-Paul Migne. PL 44, cols 881–912. Paris, 1845.

– *De haeresibus*, ed. R. Vander Plaetse and C. Beukers. CCSL 46, 286–345. Turnhout, 1969.
– *De libero arbitrio*, ed. W.M. Green. CCSL 29, 205–321. Turnhout, 1970.
– *De mendacio*, ed. J. Zycha. CSEL 41, 413–66. Vienna, 1900.
– *De moribus Ecclesiae catholicae et de moribus Manichaeorum*, ed. J.B. Bauer. CSEL 90. Vienna, 1992.
– *De natura boni*, ed. J. Zycha. CSEL 25.2, 853–89. Vienna, 1892.
– *De natura et gratia*, ed. K. Urba and J. Zycha. CSEL 60, 231–99. Vienna, 1913.
– *De natura et origine animae* [see *De anima et eius origine* above].
– *De nuptiis et concupiscentia*, ed. K. Urba and J. Zycha. CSEL 42, 209–319. Vienna, 1902.
– *De opera monachorum*, ed. J. Zycha. CSEL 41, 531–95. Vienna, 1900.
– *De patientia*, ed. J. Zycha. CSEL 41, 661–91. Vienna, 1900.
– *De peccatorum meritis et remissione et de baptismo paruulorum*, ed. K. Urba and J. Zycha. CSEL 60, 1–151. Vienna, 1913.
– *De perfectione iustitiae hominis*, ed. K. Urba and J. Zycha. CSEL 42, 1–48. Vienna, 1902.
– *De praedestinatione sanctorum*, ed. Jacques-Paul Migne. PL 44, cols 959–92. Paris, 1845.
– *De sancta uirginitate*, ed. J. Zycha. CSEL 41, 235–302. Vienna, 1900.
– *De schematibus et tropis*, ed. C.B. Kendall. CCSL 123A, 142–71. Turnhout, 1975.
– *De sermone Domini in monte libri ii*, ed. A. Mutzenbecher. CCSL 35. Turnhout, 1967.
– *De spiritu et littera*, ed. K. Urba and J. Zycha. CSEL 60, 153–229. Vienna, 1913.
– *De trinitate*, ed. W.J. Mountain and F. Glorie. 2 vols. CCSL 50–50A. Turnhout, 1968.
– *De uera religione*, ed. Klaus-D. Daur. CCSL 32. Turnhout, 1962.
– *Enarrationes in psalmos*, ed. E. Dekkers and J. Fraipont. 3 vols. CCSL 38-40. Turnhout, 1956; rev. ed. 1990.
– *Enchiridion ad Laurentium, seu de fide, spe et caritate*, ed. E. Evans. CCSL 46, 49–114. Turnhout, 1969.
– *Epistulae*, ed. A. Goldbacher. 4 vols in 5. CSEL 34.1–2, 44, 57, and 58. Vienna, 1895, 1989, 1904, and 1923.
– *Epistulae ad Galatas expositio*, J. Divjak. CSEL 84, 53–141. Turnhout, 1971.
– *Epistulae ad Romanos expositio inchoata*, ed. J. Divjak. CSEL 84, 143–81. Turnhout, 1971.
– *Expositio quarumdam propositionum ex epistula ad Romanos*, ed. J. Divjak. CSEL 84, 1–52. Vienna, 1971.
– *In Ioannis epistulam ad Parthos tractatus x*, ed. Jacques-Paul Migne. PL 44, cols 1977–2062. Paris, 1845.

– *Quaestiones Euangeliorum*, ed. A. Mutzenbecher. CCSL 44B. Turnhout, 1980.
– *Quaestiones in Heptateuchum*, ed. J. Fraipont. CCSL 33, 1–377. Turnhout, 1958.
– *Retractationes*, ed. A. Mutzenbecher. CCSL 57. Turnhout, 1974.
– *Sancti Augustini sermones quatuor nunc primum ab illustrissimo cardinali Maio editi*, ed. Jacques-Paul Migne. PL 47, cols 139–1148. Paris, 1849.
– *Sermones*, ed. C. Lambot [*serm.* 1–50]. CCSL 41. Turnhout, 1961.
– *Sermones* [*Sermonum classes quatuor*], ed. Jacques-Paul Migne. PL 38 and 39, cols 332–1638. Paris, 1845.
– *Sermones inediti*, ed. Jacques-Paul Migne. PL 46, cols 817–940. Paris, 1845.
– *Soliloquiorum libri duo*, ed. Wolfgang Hörmann. CSEL 89. Vienna, 1986.
– *Tractatus in Euangelium Ioannis*, ed. R. Willems. CCSL 36. Turnhout, 1954.
Bede. *Aliquot quaestionum liber*, ed. Jacques-Paul Migne. PL 93, cols 455–62. Paris, 1840 [*quaestiones* 1–8 genuine].
– *Chronica maiora*, ed. C.W. Jones. CCSL 123B, 463–544. Turnhout, 1977.
– *Collectio Bedae presbiteri ex opusculis sancti Augustini in epistulas Pauli Apostoli*, ed. David Hurst, I. Fransen, and R. Demeulenaere (forthcoming) [described in detail by Fransen, 'Description de la Collection de Bède le Vénérable sur l'Apôtre,' *Revue Bénédictine* 71 (1961): 22–70].
– *Commentarius in Genesim* [see *Libri iv in principium Genesis* below].
– *Commentarius in Parabolas Salomonis*, ed. David Hurst. CCSL 119B, 1–19. Turnhout, 1983.
– *De arte metrica*, ed. C.B. Kendall. CCSL 123A, 81–141. Turnhout, 1975.
– *De die iudicii*, ed. J. Fraipont. CCSL 122, 439–44. Turnhout, 1955.
– *De natura rerum*, ed. C.W. Jones. CCSL 123A, 189–234. Turnhout, 1975.
– *De orthographia*, ed. C.W. Jones. CCSL 123A, 7–57. Turnhout, 1975.
– *De schematibus et tropis*, ed. C.B. Kendall. CCSL 123A, 142–71. Turnhout, 1975.
– *De tabernaculo*, ed. David Hurst. CCSL 119A, 1–139. Turnhout, 1969.
– *De templo Salomonis*, ed. David Hurst. CCSL 119A, 143–234. Turnhout, 1969.
– *De temporibus*, ed. C.W. Jones. CCSL 123C, 585–611. Turnhout, 1980.
– *De temporum ratione*, ed. C.W. Jones. CCSL 123B, 263–460. Turnhout, 1977.
– *Expositio Actuum Apostolorum et Retractatio* [see *Super Acta Apostolorum expositio*].
– *Expositio Apocalypseos*, ed. Roger Gryson. CCSL 121A. Turnhout, 2001.
– *Historia abbatum*, ed. C. Plummer. In *Venerabilis Baedae Opera Historica*, 1:364–87. Oxford, 1946 [originally printed as two vols 1896].
– *Historia ecclesiastica gentis Anglorum*, ed. C. Plummer. In *Venerabilis Baedae Opera Historica*. Oxford, 1946 [originally printed as two vols 1896].
– *Homiliae subdititiae*, ed. Jacques-Paul Migne. PL 94, cols 267–360, 363–4, 369–413, 419–22, 423–77, 480–9, 507–10, and 513–16. Paris, 1850.
– *Homiliarum euangelii libri ii*, ed. David Hurst. CCSL 122, 1–378. Turnhout, 1955.

– *In Cantica Canticorum allegorica expositio*, ed. David Hurst. CCSL 119B, 165–375. Turnhout, 1983.

– *In Ezram et Neemiam prophetas allegorica expositio*, ed. David Hurst. CCSL 119A, 235–392. Turnhout, 1969.

– *In librum beati patris Tobiae allegorica expositio*, ed. David Hurst. CCSL 119B, 1–19. Turnhout, 1983.

– *In Lucae euangelium expositio*, ed. David Hurst. CCSL 120, 1–425. Turnhout, 1960.

– *In Marci euangelium expositio*, ed. David Hurst. CCSL 120, 427–648. Turnhout, 1960.

– *In Prouerbia Salomonis libri iii*, ed. David Hurst. CCSL 119B, 23–163. Turnhout, 1983.

– *In Regum librum xxx quaestiones*, ed. David Hurst. CCSL 119, 293–322. Turnhout, 1962.

– *In Samuelem prophetam allegorica expositio*, ed. David Hurst. CCSL 119, 1–272. Turnhout, 1962.

– *Liber de locis sanctis*, ed. J. Fraipont. CCSL 175, 251–80. Turnhout, 1965.

– *Libri iv in principium Genesis* [= *Hexaemeron*], ed. C.W. Jones. CCSL 118A. Turnhout, 1967.

– *Martyrologium*, ed. J. Dubois and G. Renaud. In *Édition pratique des martyrologes de Bède, de l'anonyme Lyonnais et de Florus*. Paris, 1976.

– *Nomina locorum ex Beati Hieronimi et Flaui Iosephi collecta opusculis*, ed. David Hurst. CCSL 119, 273–87. Turnhout, 1962.

– *Nomina regionum atque locorum de Actibus Apostolorum*, ed. M.L.W. Laistner. CCSL 121, 167–78. Turnhout, 1983.

– *The Old English Version of Bede's Ecclesiastical History of the English People* [= *Old English Bede*], ed. and trans. Thomas Miller. EETS os 95, 96, 110, and 111, printed as two vols. London, 1890 and 1898.

– *Super Acta Apostolorum expositio*, ed. M.L.W. Laistner. CCSL 121, 1–99. Turnhout, 1983.

– *Super Canticum Abacuc allegorica expositio*, ed. J.E. Hudson. CCSL 119B, 381–409. Turnhout, 1983.

– *Super epistulas catholicas expositio*, ed. David Hurst. CCSL 121, 179–342. Turnhout, 1983.

– *Vita Cuthberti metrica*, ed. W. Jaager. Leipzig, 1935.

– *Vita et miracula Cuthberti*, ed. B. Colgrave. In *Two Lives of St Cuthbert*, 141–307. Cambridge, 1940.

Pseudo-Bede. *Sermones spurii e libro iii homiliarum*, ed. Jacques-Paul Migne. PL 94, cols 360–3, 364–8, 413–19, 422–3, 477–80, 489–507, and 510–13. Paris, 1850.

Benedict of Monte Cassino. *Die angelsachsischen Prosabearbeitungen der Benedik-tinerregel*, ed. A. Schröer. BAP 2. Kassel, 1885-8. Repr. with an Appendix by H. Gneuss, Darmstadt, 1964.

– *Regula*, ed. R. Hanslik. CSEL 75. 2nd ed. Vienna, 1977.

– *The Rule of St Benet: Latin and Anglo-Saxon Interlinear Version*, ed. H. Logeman. EETS 90, 1–118. London, 1888. Repr. 1973.

– *Die Winteney-version der Regula Benedicti*, ed. A. Schröer, 3–147. Halle, 1888. Repr. with an appendix by M. Gretsch, Tübingen, 1978.

Biblia Sacra: Iuxta Vulgatam uersionem, ed. R. Weber. Stuttgart, 1969.

Boethius. *Boethii Philosophiae Consolatio*, ed. L. Bieler. CCSL 94. Turnhout, 1957.

Boniface II. *Epistula ad Caesarium*, ed. C. de Clercq. CCSL 148A, 66–9. Turnhout, 1963.

Cassian. *Collationes*, ed. Michael Petschenig. CSEL 13. Vienna, 1886.

– *De incarnatione domini contra Nestorium*, ed. Michael Petschenig. CSEL 17, 235–391. Vienna, 1888.

– *De institutis coenobiorum*, ed. Michael Petschenig. CSEL 17, 3–231. Vienna, 1888.

Cassiodorus. *Expositio psalmorum*, ed. M. Adriaen. CCSL 97–8. Turnhout, 1958.

– *De institutis diuinarum litterarum*, ed. R.A.B. Mynors. Oxford, 1937.

Celestine I. *Epistula xxi ad episcopos Gallicorum*, ed. Jacques-Paul Migne. PL 50, cols 528–37. Paris, 1846.

Chrysostom. *Ioannis Chrysostomi interpretatio omnium epistularum Paulinarum*, ed. F. Field. 7 vols. Oxford, 1861.

Pseudo-Chrysostom. *Opus imperfectum*, ed. Jacques-Paul Migne. PG 56, cols 834–8. Paris, 1857.

Cicero. *De diuinatione*, ed. W.A. Falconer. Cambridge, MA, 1923.

Clement I. *Homiliae*, ed. Jacques-Paul Migne. PG 2, cols 279–82. Paris, 1857.

Clement of Alexandria. *Paedagogus*, ed. Jacques-Paul Migne. PG 8, cols 247–684. Paris, 1857.

Concilium Arausicanum. 529 AD. Ed. C. de Clercq. CCSL 148A, 55–76. Turnhout, 1963.

Faustus of Riez. *De gratia*, ed. A. Engelbrecht. CSEL 21, 3–96. Vienna, 1891.

– *Epistula ad Lucidum*, ed. Jacques-Paul Migne. PL 53, cols 683D–685B. Paris, 1847.

Gottschalk. *De praedestinatione*. In *Oeuvres Théologiques et Grammaticales de Godescalc d'Orbais*, ed. D.C. Lambot, 180–258. Louvain, 1945.

Gregory the Great. *Dialogorum libri iv*, ed. A. de Vogüé. 3 vols. In *Sources Chrétiennes* 252–3 and 257. Paris, 1978–9.

– *Epistularum libri xiv*, ed. Jacques-Paul Migne. PL 77, cols 431–1328. Paris, 1849.

– *Homiliae in Ezechielem*, ed. M. Adriaen. CCSL 142. Turnhout, 1971.

– *Homiliae ii in Canticum Canticorum*, ed. P. Verbraken. CCSL 144, 3–46. Turnhout, 1963.

– *Homiliae xl in Euangelia*, ed. Jacques-Paul Migne. PL 76, cols 1075–1312. Paris, 1849.

– *In librum primum Regum expositionum libri vi*, ed. P. Verbraken. CCSL 144, 49–614. Turnhout, 1963.

– *Moralia siue Expositio in Iob*, ed. M. Adriaen. 3 vols. CCSL 143, 143A, and 143B. Turnhout, 1979–85.

– *Regula pastoralis*, ed. Jacques-Paul Migne. PL 77, cols 13–128. Paris, 1849.

Gregory of Nyssa. *Oratio catechetica magna*, ed. J.H. Srawley. In *The Catechetical Oration of Gregory of Nyssa*, 113–14. Cambridge, 1903.

Haymo of Auxerre. *Homiliae de tempore*, ed. Jacques-Paul Migne. PL 118, cols 11–746. Paris, 1852.

– *Homiliae in aliquot epistolas Pauli*, ed. Jacques-Paul Migne. PL 118, cols 803–16. Paris, 1852.

Hericus of Auxerre. *In octaua Sancti Andraea*, ed. Jacques-Paul Migne. PL 95, cols 1458–61. Paris, 1851.

Hilary. *Epistula ad Augustinum de querela Gallorum* [= Augustine, *Epistulae* 226], ed. A. Goldbacher. CSEL 57, 468–81. Vienna, 1911.

Hincmar. *De praedestinatione Dei et libero arbitrio*, ed. Jacques-Paul Migne. PL 125, cols 65–474. Paris, 1852.

Irenaeus. *Aduersus haereses*, ed. Jacques-Paul Migne. PG 7, cols 433–1224. Paris, 1857.

– *Aduersus Iouinianum*, ed. Jacques-Paul Migne. PL 23, colls 211–338. Paris, 1845.

– *Commentarii in Euangelium Matthaei*, ed. David Hurst and M. Adriaen. CCSL 77. Turnhout, 1969.

Jerome. *Dialogi contra Pelagianos*, ed. C. Moreschini, CCSL 80 (Turnhout, 1990).

– *Epistulae*, ed. I. Hilberg. 3 vols. CSEL 54–6. Vienna, 1910–18.

– *Liber interpretationis hebraicorum nominum*, ed. P. de Lagarde. CCSL 72, 59–161. Turnhout, 1959.

Pseudo-Jerome. *Commentarius in epistulas Paulinas*, ed. H.J. Frede. In *Ein neuer Paulustext und Kommentar*, i–ii. Freiburg, 1973–4.

John of Damascus. *Expositio fidei orthodoxae*, ed. Jacques-Paul Migne. PG 94, cols 790–1228. Paris, 1860.

Justin Martyr. *Apologia*, ed. E.J. Goodspeed. In *Die ältesten Apologeten*, 26–89. Göttingen, 1915.

Lantfred of Winchester. *Carmen de libero arbitrio*, ed. Michael Lapidge, 'Three Latin Poems from Æthelwold's School at Winchester,' *ASE* 1 (1972): 85–137. Repr. in his *Anglo-Latin Literature, 900–1066*, 225–77. London, 1993.

– *Translatio et miracula S. Swithuni*, ed. Michael Lapidge. In *The Cult of St Swithun*, 252–332. Oxford, 2003.

Maximus of Turin. *Sermones*, ed. A. Mutzenbecher. CCSL 23. Turnhout, 1962.

Origen. *Contra Celsum*, ed. P. Koetschau. In *Origenes Werke* I and II. Die grieschis-chen christlichen Schriftsteller 2 and 3, 49–374, and 1–293. Leipzig, 1899.

– *De oratione*, ed. P. Koetschau. In *Origenes Werke* II. Die griechischen christli-chen Schriftsteller 3, 297–403. Leipzig, 1899.

– *De principiis*, ed. P. Koetschau. In *Origenes Werke* V. Die grieschischen christli-chen Schriftsteller 22. Leipzig, 1913.

Paschasius Radbertus. *De assumptione sanctae Mariae uirginis*, ed. A. Ripberger. CCCM 56C. Turnhout, 1985.

Paulus Deaconus. *Homiliarius*, ed. Jacques-Paul Migne. PL 95, cols 1159–1584. Paris, 1851.

Pelagius. *Expositiones xiii epistularum Pauli*, ed. A. Souter. In *Pelagius's Exposi-tions of Thirteen Epistles of St Paul*. 3 vols. Cambridge, 1922–31.

Prosper of Aquitaine. *Epistula ad Rufinum de gratia et libero arbitrio*, ed. Jacques-Paul Migne. PL 51, cols 77–90. Paris, 1846.

– *De gratia Dei et libero arbitrio contra Collatorem*, ed. Jacques-Paul Migne. PL 51, cols 213–76. Paris, 1846.

– *Pro Augustino responsiones ad capitula obiectionum Gallorum calumniantium* [= *Epistulae* 225], ed. A. Goldbacher. CSEL 57, 454–68. Vienna, 1911.

Ratramnus. *De praedestinatione Dei*, ed. Jacques-Paul Migne. PL 121, cols 11–80. Paris, 1852.

Second Council of Orange. See *Concilium Arausicanum*.

Sedulius Scotus. *Collectanea in omnes beati Pauli epistulas*, ed. Jacques-Paul Migne. PL 103, cols 9–270. Paris, 1851.

Smaragdus. *Collectiones in Euangelia et Epistolas* [=*Expositio libri comitis*], ed. Jacques-Paul Migne. PL 102, cols 15–552. Paris, 1851.

– *Diadema monachorum*, ed. Jacques-Paul Migne. PL 102, cols 593–690. Paris, 1851.

– *Expositio in Regulam Sancti Benedicti*, ed. A. Spannagel and P. Engelbert. Corpus Consuetudinum Monasticarum 8. Siegburg, 1974.

Tertullian. *Aduersus Marcionem*, ed. R. Braun. Sources Chrétiennes, 365, 368, and 399. Paris, 1990–1 and 1994.

– *De idololatria*, ed. A. Gerlo. CCSL 2, 1101–24. Turnhout, 1954.

Wulfstan the Homilist. *Homilies*, ed. D. Bethurum. In *The Homilies of Wulfstan*. Oxford, 1957.

– *Homilies*, ed. Arthur Napier. In *Wulfstan: Sammlung der ihm zugeschriebenen Homilien nebst Untersuchungen über ihre Echtheit*. Berlin, 1967. Repr. Berlin, 1883.

Wulfstan of Winchester. *Vita Sancti Æthelwoldi*. In *Wulfstan of Winchester: The Life of St Æthelwold*, ed. M. Lapidge and M. Winterbottom, 2–69. Oxford, 1991.

Secondary References

Adriaen, M. 'Prolegomena.' In *Moralia in Iob: Libri I–X*, ed. Adriaen. CCSL 143, v–xxix. Turnhout, 1979.

Alflatt, M. 'The Development of the Idea of Involuntary Sin in St Augustine.' *Revue des Études Augustiniennes* 20 (1974): 113–34.

– 'The Responsibility for Involuntary Sin in St Augustine.' *Recherches Augustiniennes* 10 (1975): 172–86.

Allen, J.B. 'God's Society and Grendel's Shoulder Joint: Gregory and the Poet of *Beowulf.*' *Neuphilologische Mitteilungen* 78 (1977): 239–40.

Anlezark, Daniel. 'Three Notes on the Old English Meters of Boethius.' *Notes and Queries* 51 (2004): 10–15.

Atherton, Mark. 'King Alfred's Approach to the Study of Latin.' In *History of Linguistics 1996: From Classical to Contemporary Linguistics*, ed. David Cram, Andrew Linn, and Elke Nowak, 15–22. Amsterdam, 1999.

– 'Source Summary for Anglo-Saxon Text Ælfric, Interrogationes Sigewulfi in Genesin.' 1996. In *Fontes Anglo-Saxonici*, accessed October 2004.

– 'Source Summary for Anglo-Saxon Text Ælfric, De temporibus anni.' 1996. In *Fontes Anglo-Saxonici*, accessed November 2006.

Atwell, R.R. 'From Augustine to Gregory the Great: An Evaluation of the Emergence of the Doctrine of Purgatory.' *Journal of Ecclesiastical History* 38 (1987): 173–86.

Baasten, M. *Pride According to Gregory the Great: A Study of the Moralia.* Lewiston, 1986.

Babcock, W.S. 'Augustine and Paul: The Case of Romans IX.' In *Papers Presented at the Seventh International Conference*, 473–9. Berlin, 1985.

– 'Sin, Penalty and the Responsibility of the Soul: A Problem in Augustine's *De libero arbitrio*, III.' In *Papers Presented at the Eleventh International Conference*, 225–30. 1993.

Baker, P.S. and Michael Lapidge. *Byrhtferth's Enchiridion.* EETS ss 15. Oxford, 1995.

Bale, John. *Scriptorum illustrium maioris Brytannie, quam nune Angliam & Scotiam uocant: Catalogus.* Basel, 1557–9.

Balk, Catherine Batten. 'Augustine and the Donatists.' *Chicago Theological Seminary Register* 86 (1996): 12–24.

Barnish, Samuel James Beeching. 'Gregory I.' In *Oxford Classical Dictionary*, 3rd rev. ed., ed. Simon Hornblower and Antony Spawforth. Oxford, 2003.

Barré, H. *Les homélaires carolingiens de l'école d'Auxerre.* Vatican City, 1962.

Bately, Janet M., ed. *The Old English Orosius.* EETS ss 6. London, 1980.

– 'The Literary Prose of King Alfred's Reign: Translation or Transformation?' Inaugural Lecture of the Chair of English Language and Medieval Literature, King's College, University of London, 4 March 1980. Repr. as *Old English Subsidia* 10 (1984).

Beaumont, J. 'The Latin Tradition of *De consolatione Philosophiae*.' In *Boethius: His Life, Thought and Influence*, ed. M. Gibson, 278–305. Oxford, 1981.

Bedingfield, M.B. 'Source Summary for Anglo-Saxon Text *Ælfric, Interrogationes Sigewulfi in Genesin*.' 2000. In *Fontes Anglo-Saxonici*, accessed November 2006.

Besserman, L.L. 'A Note on the Source of Ælfric's Homily on the Book of Job.' *English Language Notes* 10 (1973): 248–52.

Bethurum, Dorothy. 'Archbishop Wulfstan's Commonplace Book.' *Publications of the Modern Language Association of America* 57 (1942): 916–29.

– ed. *The Homilies of Wulfstan*. Oxford, 1957.

– 'Wulfstan.' In *Continuations and Beginnings*, ed. E.G. Stanley, 210–46. London, 1966.

Bieler, L., ed. 'Praefatio.' In *Boethii Philosophiae Consolatio*, vii–xxviii. CCSL 94. Turnhout, 1957.

Bischoff, Bernhard. *Die südostdeutschen Schreibschulen und Bibliotheken in der Karolingerzeit*. 2 vols. Wiesbaden, 1940 (vol. 1, 2nd ed., 1960) and 1980.

– *Latin Palaeography: Antiquity and the Middle Ages*, trans. Dáibhí Ó Cróinín and David Ganz. Cambridge, 1990.

Bishop, T.A.M. *English Caroline Minuscule*. Oxford, 1971.

Blair, Peter Hunter. 'Whitby as a Centre of Learning in the Seventh Century.' In *Learning and Literature in Anglo-Saxon England: Studies Presented to Peter Clemoes on the Occasion of His Sixty-Fifth Birthday*, ed. Michael Lapidge and Helmut Gneuss, 3–32. Cambridge, 1985.

– *The World of Bede*, rev. M. Lapidge. Cambridge, 1990.

Bolton, D.K. 'Remigian Commentaries on the *Consolation of Philosophy* and Their Sources.' *Traditio* 33 (1977): 380–94.

– 'The Study of the *Consolation of Philosophy* in Anglo-Saxon England.' *Archives d'Histoire Doctrinale et Littéraire du Moyen Age* 44 (1977): 33–78.

Bolton, W.F. 'How Boethian Is Alfred's *Boethius*?' In *Studies in Earlier Old English Prose*, ed. Paul E. Szarmach, 153–68. Albany, NY, 1986.

Bonner, Gerald. *St Augustine of Hippo: Life and Controversies*. London, 1963.

– *Augustine and Modern Research on Pelagianism*. Villanova, 1972.

– *God's Decree and Man's Destiny: Studies on the Thought of Augustine of Hippo*. London, 1987.

– 'Pelagianism Reconsidered.' In *Papers Presented at the Eleventh International Conference*, 237–41. 1993.

– 'Saint Bede in the Western Tradition of Apocalyptic Commentary.' In *Bede and His World: Jarrow Lectures, 1958–1993*, 153–83. Aldershot, 1994.

– *Church and Faith in the Patristic Tradition: Augustine, Pelagianism, and Early Christian Northumbria*. Brookfield, VT, 1996.

– 'Augustine, the Bible, and the Pelagians.' In *Augustine and the Bible*, ed. Pamela Bright, 227–42. Notre Dame, 1999.

Brinegar, John H. '"Books Most Necessary": The Literary and Cultural Contexts of Alfred's Boethius.' PhD dissertation, University of North Carolina at Chapel Hill, 2000.

de Broglie, G. 'Pour une Meilleure Intelligence du *De correptione et gratia*.' *Augustinus Magister* 3 (1954): 317–37.

Brooks, N., and C. Cubitt, eds. *St Oswald of Worcester: Life and Influence*. London, 1996.

Brown, George Hardin. *Bede the Venerable*. Boston, 1987.

– 'Bede the Venerable (ca. 673–735).' In *Medieval England: An Encyclopedia*, ed. Paul E. Szarmach, M. Teresa Tavormina, and Joel Thomas Rosenthal, 114–17. New York, 1998.

Brown, M.P. *A Guide to Western Historical Scripts from Antiquity to 1600*. Toronto, 1990.

Brown, Peter. *Augustine of Hippo*. 2nd ed. London, 2000.

– 'The Patrons of Pelagius: The Roman Aristocracy Between East and West.' *Journal of Theological Studies* 21 (1970): 56–72. Repr. in his *Religion and Society in the Age of Saint Augustine*, 208–26. London, 1972.

– 'Pelagius and His Supporters: Aims and Environment.' *Journal of Theological Studies* 19 (1968): 93–114. Repr. in his *Religion and Society in the Age of Saint Augustine*, 183–207. London, 1972.

Bullough, D.A. 'The Continental Background of the Reform.' In *Tenth-Century Studies: Essays in Commemoration of the Millennium of the Council of Winchester and Regularis Concordia*, ed. D. Parsons, 20–36. London, 1975. Repr. in his *Carolingian Renewal: Sources and Heritage*, 272–96. Manchester, 1991.

Burnaby, J. *Amor Dei: A Study of the Religion of St Augustine*. London, 1938.

Burns, J. Patout. *The Development of Augustine's Doctrine of Operative Grace*. Paris, 1980.

– 'A Change in Augustine's Doctrine of Operative Grace in 418.' In *Papers Presented at the Seventh International Conference*, 491–6.

– 'Grace: The Augustinian Foundation.' In *Christian Spirituality: Origins to the Twelfth Century*, ed. B. McGinn and J. Meyendorff, 331–49. London, 1986.

– 'From Persuasion to Predestination: Augustine on Freedom in Rational Creatures.' In *In Dominico Eloquio, In Lordly Eloquence: Essays in Patristic Exegesis in Honor of Robert L. Wilken*, ed. Paul M. Blowers et al., 294–316. Cambridge, 2002.

Bury, R.G., ed. *Plato: Timaeus*. Cambridge, MA, 1966.

Cambridge University Library Catalogue of Manuscripts, 6 vols. Cambridge, 1856–8.

Campbell, J. 'Bede (673/4–735).' 2004. In *Oxford Dictionary of National Biography*. Oxford University Press, http://www.oxforddnb.com/view/article/1922, accessed September 2004.

Capelle, Bernard. 'Le rôle théologique de Bède le Vénérable.' *Studia Anselmiana* 6 (1936): 1–40.

Cappuyns, M. 'Cassien.' In *Dictionnaire d'Histoire et de Géographie Ecclésiastique*, ed. A. Baudrillart et al., 11:1319–48. Paris, 1912.

– 'Le premier représentant de l'Augustinisme médiéval, Prosper d'Aquitaine.' *Recherches de Théologie Ancienne et Médiévale* 1 (1929): 309–37.

Carley, James P. 'Two Pre-Conquest Manuscripts from Glastonbury Abbey.' *ASE* 16 (1987): 197–212.

Carnicelli, T.A., ed. and trans. *King Alfred's Version of St. Augustine's Soliloquies*. Cambridge, MA, 1969.

Carroll, Mary T.A. *The Venerable Bede: His Spiritual Teachings*. Washington, 1946.

Casiday, A.M.C. 'Cassian, Augustine, and *De Incarnatione*.' In *Papers Presented at the Thirteenth International Conference*, 41–7.

Catalogue of Manuscripts in Salisbury Cathedral Library. London, 1880.

Chadwick, Henry. *Boethius: The Consolations of Music, Logic, Theology and Philosophy*. Oxford, 1981. Repr. 1998.

– *The Church in Ancient Society: From Galilee to Gregory the Great*. Oxford, 2001.

Chadwick, O. 'Cassianus.' In *Theologische Realenzyklopädie*, ed. H.R. Balz et al., 7:650–7. Berlin, 1977.

– *John Cassian*. 2nd ed. Cambridge, 1968.

Chaney, W.A. 'Ælfric Grammaticus.' In *New Catholic Encyclopedia*, ed. Thomas Carson and Joann Cerrito. 2nd ed., 1:136. London, 2003.

Chappell, T.D.J. *Aristotle and Augustine on Freedom : Two Theories of Freedom, Voluntary Action, and Akrasia*. New York, 1995.

Chéné, J. 'Le Semipélagianisme du midi de la Gaule d'après les lettres de Prosper d'Aquitaine et d'Hilaire à saint Augustin.' *Recherches de Science Religieuse* 43 (1955): 321–41.

Chisholm, John Edward. *The Pseudo-Augustinian Hypomnesticon against the Pelagians and Celestians*. Volume 1,: *Introduction*. Fribourg, 1967.

Clark, Mary T. *Augustine*. London, 1994. Repr. 2000.

Clayton, Mary. 'Of Mice and Men: Ælfric's Second Homily for the Feast of a Confessor.' *Leeds Studies in English* 24 (1993): 1–26.

– 'Records for Source Title *Hom*[iliae in].*Euang*[elia]. 13.' 1991. In *Fontes Anglo-Saxonici*, accessed September 2004.

Clement, Richard W. 'King Alfred and the Latin Manuscripts of Gregory's *Regula Pastoralis*.' *Journal of the Rocky Mountain Medieval and Renaissance Association* 6 (1985): 1–13.

Clemoes, P.A.M. 'Ælfric.' In *Continuations and Beginnings*, ed. E.G. Stanley, 176–209. London, 1966.
– 'Supplement to the Introduction.' In *Die Hirtenbriefe Ælfrics in altenglischer und lateinischer Fassung*, ed. B. Fehr, lxxvii-lxlviii. BAP 9. Darmstadt, 1966.
– 'The Chronology of Ælfric's Works.' In *The Anglo-Saxons: Studies in Aspects of Their History and Culture presented to Bruce Dickins*, ed. Clemoes, 212–47. London, 1959. Repr. in *Old English Newsletter Subsidia* 5 (1980): 1–37.
– Introduction to *Ælfric's Catholic Homilies: The First Series, Text*, ed. Clemoes, 1–171. EETS ss 17. Oxford, 1997.
Cole, Andrew. 'Jewish Apocrypha and Christian Epistemology of the Fall: The *Dialogi* of Gregory the Great and the Old Saxon *Genesis*.' In *Rome and the North: The Early Reception of Gregory the Great in Germanic Europe*, ed. Rolf H. Bremmer, Jr, Kees Dekker, and David F. Johnson, 157–88. Louvain, 2001.
Colgrave, B., and R.A.B. Mynors, eds. *Bede's Ecclesiastical History of the English People*. Oxford, 1969.
Cornford, Francis, trans. *Plato's Cosmology: The Timaeus of Plato*. London, 1937. Repr. 2000.
Courcelle, Pierre. 'Étude critique sur les commentaires de la Consolation de Boèce (IXe – XVe) siècles.' *Archives d'histoire doctrinale et littéraire du Moyen Âge* 14 (1939): 5–140.
– *La Consolation de Philosophie dans la tradition littéraire: Antécédents et postérité de Boèce*, Paris, 1967.
– *Late Latin Writers and Their Greek Sources*, trans. Harry E. Wedeck. Cambridge, MA, 1969.
Crespin, Rémi. *Ministère et sainteté: Pastorale du clergé et solution de la crise Donatiste dans la vie et la doctrine de saint Augustin*. Paris, 1965.
Cross, F.L., and Elizabeth A. Livingstone, eds. *Oxford Dictionary of the Christian Church*. 3rd ed. Oxford, 1997.
Cross, James E. 'The Elephant to Alfred, Ælfric, Aldhelm and Others.' *Studia Neophilologica* 37 (1965): 367–73.
– 'On the Library of the Old English Martyrologist.' In *Learning and Literature in Anglo-Saxon England: Studies Presented to Peter Clemoes on the Occasion of His Sixty-Fifth Birthday*, ed. Michael Lapidge and Helmut Gneuss, 227–49. Cambridge, 1985.
– 'The Use of Patristic Homilies in the Old English Martyrology.' *ASE* 14 (1985): 107–28.
– 'Wulfstan's *De Anticristo* in a Twelfth-Century Worcester Manuscript.' *Anglo-Saxon England* 20 (1991): 203–20.
– 'A Newly-Identified Manuscript of Wulfstan's "Commonplace Book", Rouen, Bibliothèque Municipale 1382 (U. 109), fols 173^r–198^v.' *Journal of Medieval Latin* 2 (1992): 63–83.

– 'Contents of the Manuscript.' In *The Copenhagen Wulfstan Collection: Copenhagen Kongelige Bibliotek Gl. Kgl. Sam. 1595*, ed. James E. Cross and Jennifer Morrish Tunberg, 14–23. Early English Manuscripts in Facsimile 25. Copenhagen, 1993. 14–23.

Cross, James E., and A. Brown. 'Wulfstan and Abbo of Saint Germain-des-Prés.' *Mediaevalia* 15 (1993 for 1989): 71–91.

Cross, James E., and A. Hamer, eds. *Wulfstan's Canon Law Collection.* Cambridge, 1999.

Cross, James E., and Jennifer Morrish Tunberg. *The Copenhagen Wulfstan Collection: Copenhagen Kongelige Bibliotek Gl. Kgl. Sam. 1595.* Early English Manuscripts in Facsimile 25. Copenhagen, 1993.

Cubitt, Catherine, 'The Tenth-Century Benedictine Reform in England.' *Early Medieval Europe* 6 (1997): 77–94.

Dalbey, Marcia A. 'Themes and Techniques in the Blickling Lenten Homilies.' In *The Old English Homily and Its Backgrounds*, ed. P.E. Szarmach and B.F. Huppé, 221–39. Albany, NY, 1978.

Dando, M. 'The *Moralia in Job* of Gregory the Great as a Source for the Old Saxon *Genesis B.*' *Classica et Mediaevalia* 30 (1969): 420–39.

Davis, B.J. 'The Art of Translation in the Age Of Æthelwold: A Legacy of King Alfred.' PhD dissertation, Arizona State University, 2002.

Davis, Kathleen M. 'King Alfred's "Pastoral Care": Translation and Production of the Lord's Subject.' PhD dissertation, Rutgers University, 1997.

DeGregorio, Scott. 'Explorations of Spirituality in the Writings of the Venerable Bede, King Alfred and Abbot Ælfric of Eynsham.' PhD dissertation, University of Toronto, 1999.

– 'The Venerable Bede on Prayer and Contemplation.' *Traditio* 54 (1999): 1–39.

Dekker, Kees, 'King Alfred's Translation of Gregory's *Dialogi*: Tales for the Unlearned?' In *Rome and the North: The Early Reception of Gregory the Great in Germanic Europe*, ed. Rolf H. Bremmer, Jr, Kees Dekker, and David F. Johnson, 27–50. Louvain, 2001.

Dekkers, E. *Clauis patrum latinorum.* 3rd ed. Turnhout, 1995.

Deleeuw, Patricia Allwin. 'Gregory the Great's "Homilies on the Gospels" in the Early Middle Ages.' *Studi Medievali* 26 (1985): 855–69.

Dennison, James T., Jr. 'Augustine and Grace.' *Kerux* 18 (2003): 38–52.

Dien, Stephanie. 'Sermo Lupi ad Anglos: The Order and Date of the Three Versions.' *Neuphilologische Mitteilungen* 76 (1975): 561–70.

Dietrich, F.E. 'Cynevulfs Crist.' *Zeitschrift für deutsches Altertum und deutsche Literatur* 9 (1853): 193–214.

Discenza, Nicole G. 'Alfred's Cræft of Translation: The Old English Boethius.' PhD dissertation, University of Notre Dame, 1996.

- 'Alfred's Verse Preface to the Pastoral Care and the Chain of Authority.' *Neophilologus* 85 (2001): 625–33.
- 'Anglo-Saxon Text Title Details: *Boethius, The Consolation of Philosophy.*' 2001. In *Fontes Anglo-Saxonici*, accessed September 2004.
- 'Ciuit.Dei Records Used in Anglo-Saxon Text *Boethius, The Consolation of Philosophy.*' 2001. In *Fontes Anglo-Saxonici*, accessed September 2004.
- 'The Influence of Gregory the Great on the Alfredian Social Imaginary.' In *Rome and the North: The Early Reception of Gregory the Great in Germanic Europe*, ed. Rolf H. Bremmer, Jr, Kees Dekker, and David F. Johnson, 67–81. Louvain, 2001.
- 'Records for Anglo-Saxon Text *Boethius, The Consolation of Philosophy.*' 2001. In *Fontes Anglo-Saxonici*, accessed September 2004.
- 'Source Summary for Anglo-Saxon Text *Boethius, The Consolation of Philosophy.*' 2001. In *Fontes Anglo-Saxonici*, accessed September 2004.
- *The King's English: Strategies of Translation in the Old English 'Boethius.'* Albany, NY, 2005.
Dixon, Sandra Lee. *Augustine: The Scattered and Gathered Self.* St Louis, 1999.
Djuth, Marianne. 'The Problem of Free Choice of Will in the Thought of Augustine, John Cassian, and Faustus of Riez.' PhD dissertation, University of Toronto, 1988.
- 'The Hermeneutics of *De libero arbitrio*, III: Are There Two Augustines?' In *Papers Presented at the Eleventh International Conference*, 281–9.
- 'Where There's a Will, There's a Way: Augustine on the Good Will's Origin and the *Recta uia* before 396.' *University of Dayton Review* 22.3 (1994): 237–50.
- 'Stoicism and Augustine's Doctrine of Human Freedom after 396.' In *Augustine: Second Founder of the Faith*, ed. Frederick Van Fleteren and Joseph C. Schnaubelt, 387–401. New York, 2000.
- 'The royal way: Augustine's freedom of the will and the monastic tradition.' In *Augustine: Biblical Exegete*, ed. Frederick Van Fleteren and Joseph C. Schnaubelt, 129–45. New York, 2001.
Dodaro, Robert. '*Sacramentum Christi*: Augustine on the Christology of Pelagius.' In *Papers Presented at the Eleventh International Conference*, 274–80.
Donaghey, B.S. 'The Sources of King Alfred's Translation of Boethius's *De consolatione Philosophiae.*' *Anglia* 82 (1964); 23–57.
Donahue, C.J. 'Bede, St.' In *New Catholic Encyclopedia*, ed. Thomas Carson and Joann Cerrito, 2:195–7. 2nd ed. 15 vols. London, 2003.
Dougherty, Richard J. 'Creation, the Fall, and the Role of the Will in St. Augustine's *De civitate Dei*, Books XI–XIV.' *University of Dayton Review* 22.3 (1994): 89–115.

Driver, Steven D. *John Cassian and the Reading of Egyptian Monastic Culture*. New York and London, 2002.

Drobner, Hubertus R. 'Studying Augustine: An Overview of Recent Research.' In *Augustine and His Critics: Essays in Honour of Gerald Bonner*, ed. Robert Dodaro and George Lawless, 18–34. New York, 2000.

Du Cange, Charles du Fresne. *Glossarium ad scriptores mediae et infimae Latinitatis*. Frankfurt, 1710. First ed. Paris, 1678 (3 vols); enlarged by Benedictines of Paris, 1733–6 (6 vols); Dom Carpentier, Paris, 1766 (10 volumes); G.A.L. Henschel, Paris, 1840–50 (7 vols); L. Faure, Niort, 1883–7 (10 vols).

Dudden, F.H. *Gregory the Great: His Place in History and Thought*. 2 vols. London, 1905.

Dumville, D.N. 'King Alfred and the Tenth-Century Reform of the English Church.' In his *Wessex and England from Alfred to Edgar: Six Essays on Political, Cultural, and Ecclesiastical Revival*, 185–205. Woodbridge and Rochester, 1992.

– *English Caroline Script and Monastic History: Studies in Benedictinism, A.D. 950–1030*. Woodbridge, 1993.

Eliason, Norman, and Peter Clemoes. *Ælfric's First Series of Catholic Homilies: British Museum, Royal 7 C. XII, fols 4–218*. Early English Manuscripts in Facsimile 13. Copenhagen, 1966.

Evans, G.R. *The Thought of Gregory the Great*. Cambridge, 1986.

– 'Review of Cristina Ricci: *Mysterium Dispensationis. Tracce di una teologia della storia in Gegorio Magno* [Rome: Centro Studi S. Anselmo, 2002].' *Journal of Theological Studies* 54 (2002): 809–10.

Fiedrowicz, M. General Introduction in *On Genesis: On Genesis – A Refutation of the Manichees; Unfinished Literal Commentary on Genesis*; [and] *The Literal Meaning of Genesis*, ed. John E. Rotelle, trans. Edmund Hill and Matthew O'Connell, 155–66. Hyde Park, NY, 2002.

– Introduction [to *The Literal Meaning of Genesis*], in *On Genesis*, ed. John E. Rotelle, trans. Edmund Hill and Matthew O'Connell, 13–22. Hyde Park, NY, 2002.

Fisher, D.J.V. 'The Anti-Monastic Reaction in the Reign of Edward the Martyr.' *Cambridge Historical Journal* 10 (1950–2): 247–70.

Fontes Anglo-Saxonici: A Register of Written Sources Used by Anglo-Saxon Authors. http://fontes.english.ox.ac.uk.

Förster, M. 'Zu den Blickling Homilies.' *Archiv* 91 (1893): 179–206.

– 'Über die Quellen von Aelfrics exegetischen Homiliae Catholicae.' *Anglia* 16 (1894): 1–61.

– 'Der Inhalt der altenglischen Handschrift Vespasianus D. XIV.' *Englische Studien* 54 (1920): 46–68.

Fox, Michael A.E. 'Augustinian Hexameral Exegesis in Anglo-Saxon England: Bede, Alcuin, Aelfric and Old English Biblical Verse.' PhD dissertation, University of Cambridge, 1997.
– 'Ælfric on the Creation and Fall of the Angels.' *ASE* 31 (2002): 175–200.
Frakes, Jerold C. 'The Knowledge of Greek in the Early Middle Ages: The Latin Commentaries on Boethius' *Consolatio.' Studi Medievali* 3.27 (1986): 23–43.
– *The Fate of Fortune in the Early Middle Ages: The Boethian Tradition.* Leiden and New York, 1988.
Fredriksen, Paula. 'Paul and Augustine: Conversion Narratives, Orthodox Traditions, and the Retrospective Self.' *Journal of Theological Studies* 37 (1986): 3–34.
– 'Beyond the Body/Soul Dichotomy: Augustine on Paul against the Manichees and the Pelagians.' *Recherches augustiniennes* 23 (1988): 87–114.
– 'Augustine.' In *Antiquity: A Guide to the Late Antique World*, ed. G.W. Bowersock, Peter Brown, and Oleg Grabar, 323–4. Cambridge, MA, 1999.
– 'Augustine and Israel: *Interpretatio ad litteram*, Jews, and Judaism in Augustine's Theology of History.' In *Papers Presented at the Thirteenth International Conference*, 119–35. Repr. in *Engaging Augustine on Romans: Self, Context, and Theology in Interpretation*, ed. Daniel Patte and Eugene TeSelle, 91–110. Harrisburg, 2002.
Fredricksen, Paula, and Guy G. Stroumsa. 'Two Souls and the Divided Will.' In *Self, Soul and Body in Religions Experience*, ed. A Baumgarten, 198–217. Leiden, 1988.
Gabrielson, A. 'Guischart de Beaulieu's Debt to Religious Learning and Literature in England.' *Archiv* 128 (1912): 309–28.
Gameson, Richard. 'Augustine of Canturbury: Context and Achievement.' In his *St Augustine and the Conversion of England*, 1–40. Phoenix Mill, Gloucestershire, 1999.
– *The Manuscripts of Early Norman England (c. 1066–1130).* Oxford, 1999.
Gatch, M. McC., 'Eschatology in the Anonymous Old English Homilies.' *Traditio* 21 (1965): 117–65.
– *Preaching and Theology in Anglo-Saxon England: Ælfric and Wulfstan.* Toronto, 1977.
– 'The Achievement of Ælfric and His Colleagues in European Perspective.' In *The Old English Homily and Its Backgrounds*, ed. P.E. Szarmach and B.F. Huppé, 43–73. Albany, NY, 1978.
– 'King Alfred's Version of Augustine's *Soliloquia*: Some Suggestions on Its Rationale and Unity.' In *Studies on Earlier Old English Prose*, ed. Paul E. Szarmach, 17–45. Albany, NY, 1986.
Gerritsen, J. 'The Copenhagen Wulfstan Manuscript: A Codicological Study.' *English Studies* 79 (1998): 501–11.
Gibson, Margaret T. 'Boethius in the Carolingian Schools.' *Transactions of the Royal Historical Society*, 5th series, 32 (1982): 43–56.

- 'Boethius in the Tenth Century.' *Mittellateinisches Jahrbuch* 24/5 (1989/90): 117–24.
Gibson, Margaret T., Lesley Smith, and Joseph Ziegler. *Codices Boethiani: A Conspectus of Manuscripts of the Works of Boethius* 1. *Great Britain and the Republic of Ireland*. London, 1995.
Gilson, E. *The Christian Philosophy of Saint Augustine*, trans. L. Lynch. London, 1961.
Gneuss, Helmut. 'The Origin of Standard Old English and Æthelwold's School at Winchester.' *ASE* 1 (1972): 63–83.
- 'Manuscripts Written or Owned in England up to 1100: A Preliminary List.' *ASE* 9 (1981): 1–60.
- 'Liturgical Books in Anglo-Saxon England and Their Old English Terminology.' In *Learning and Literature in Anglo-Saxon England*, ed. Michael Lapidge and Helmut Gneuss, 91–141. Cambridge, 1985.
- *Handlist of Anglo-Saxon Manuscripts: A List of Manuscripts and Manuscript Fragments Written or Owned in England up to 1100*. Tempe, AZ, 2001.
Godden, Malcolm R. Introduction in *Ælfric's Catholic Homilies: The Second Series, Text*, ed. Godden, xix–xcvi. EETS ss 5. London, 1979.
- 'Ælfric and the Vernacular Prose Tradition.' In *The Old English Homily and Its Backgrounds*, ed. P.E. Szarmach and B.F. Huppé, 99–117. Albany, NY, 1978.
- 'Ælfric and Anglo-Saxon Kingship.' *English Historical Review* 102 (1987): 911–15.
- 'Editing Old English and the Problem of Alfred's *Boethius*.' In *The Editing of Old English: Papers from the 1990 Manchester Conference*, ed. D.G. Scragg and Paul E. Szarmach, 162–76. Woodbridge, 1994.
- 'Apocalypse and Invasion in Late Anglo-Saxon England.' In *From Anglo-Saxon to Early Middle English: Studies Presented to E.G. Stanley*, ed. Malcolm Godden, Douglas Gray, and Terry Hoad, 130–62. Oxford, 1995.
- 'Wærferth and King Alfred: The Fate of the Old English *Dialogues*.' In *Alfred the Wise: Studies in Honour of Janet Bately on the Occasion of Her Sixty-Fifth Birthday*, ed. J. Roberts, J.L. Nelson, and Malcolm Godden, 35–51. Cambridge, 1997.
- 'Record C.B.1.1.8.020.01 for Source Title *Corr.grat.*' 1997. In *Fontes Anglo-Saxonici*, accessed September 2004.
- 'Record C.B.1.2.16.047.02 for Source Title *Comm.Cant.*' 1997. In *Fontes Anglo-Saxonici*, accessed October 2004.
- 'Source Summary for Anglo-Saxon Text *Catholic Homilies*' 1.praefatio – 2.40. 1997–2000. In *Fontes Anglo-Saxonici*, accessed September 2004.
- 'Record C.B.1.2.49.009.02 for Source Title *Enarr.psalm.*' 1998. In *Fontes Anglo-Saxonici*, accessed September 2004.

– 'Ælfric of Eynsham (*c.* 950 – *c.* 1010).' In *The Blackwell Encyclopedia of Anglo-Saxon England*, ed. Michael Lapidge, 8–9, Oxford, 1999.
– *Ælfric's Catholic Homilies: Introduction, Commentary, and Glossary.* EETS ss 18. Oxford, 2000.
– 'Records for Source Title *Retract*[*ationes*].' 2001. In *Fontes Anglo-Saxonici*, ed. Joyce Hill, accessed September 2004.
– 'Source Details: C.B.9.4.001.01.' 2001. In *Fontes Anglo-Saxonici*, accessed September 2004.
– 'Source Summary for Anglo-Saxon Text *Augustine, Soliloquies.*' 2001. In *Fontes Anglo-Saxonici*, accessed September 2004.
– 'The Anglo-Saxons and the Goths: Rewriting the Sack of Rome' The Anglo-Saxons and the Goths: Rewriting the Sack of Rome.' *Anglo-Saxon England* 31 (2002): 47–68.
– 'Text and Eschatology in Book III of the Old English *Soliloquies.*' *Anglia* 121 (2003): 177–209.
– 'Latin Commentary Tradition and the Old English Boethius: The Present State of the Question.' Paper delivered at the first annual symposium of The Alfredian Boethius Project, University of Oxford, July 2003 (http://www.english.ox.ac.uk/boethius/Symposium2003.html).
– 'The Player King: Identification and Self-Representation in King Alfred's Writings.' In *Alfred the Great: Papers from the Eleventh-Centenary Conferences*, ed. Timothy Reuter, 137–50. Aldershot and Burlington, VT, 2003.
– 'Ælfric of Eynsham (c.950–c.1010).' 2004. *Oxford Dictionary of National Biography.* Oxford University Press, http://www.oxforddnb.com/view/article/187, accessed September 2004.
– 'The Translations of Alfred and His Circle, and the Misappropriation of the Past.' H.M. Chadwick Memorial Lectures 14. Cambridge, 2004.
– 'Alfred, Asser, and Boethius.' In *Latin Learning and Old English Lore: Studies in Anglo-Saxon Literature for Michael Lapidge*, ed. Katherine O'Brien O'Keeffe and Andy Orchard, 1:326–48. Toronto, 2005.
Godden, Malcolm, and Susan Irvine. *The Old English Boethius: An Edition of the Old English Versions of Boethius's* De·consolatio Philosophiae. Oxford, forthcoming.
Goetz, G. *Corpus Glossariorum Latinorum.* 7 vols. Leipzig, 1888-1923.
Goldsmith, Margaret. *The Mode and Meaning of 'Beowulf.'* London, 1970.
Gowans, Coleen Hoffman. *The Identity of the True Believer in the Sermons of Augustine of Hippo: A Dimension of his Christian Anthropology.* Lewiston, NY, 1998.
Gransden, A. 'Traditionalism and Continuity during the Last Century of Anglo-Saxon Monasticism.' *Journal of Ecclesiastical History* 40 (1989): 159–207. Repr. in her *Legends, Traditions and History in Medieval England*, 31–79. London, 1992.

Green, Brian. 'Gregory the Great as Inspirational Source to *Exodus.*' *Classica et Mediaevalia* 32 (1971–80): 251–62.

Green, Eugene. 'Speech Acts and the Question of Self in Alfred's *Soliloquies.*' In *Interdigitations: Essays for Irmengard Rauch*, ed. Gerald F. Carr, Wayne Harbert, and Lihua Zhang, 211–18. Frankfurt am Main, Bern, and New York, 1998.

Greene-McCreight, Kathryn. *Ad litteram: How Augustine, Calvin, and Barth read the 'Plain Sense' of Genesis 1–3.* New York, 1999.

Grégoire, Reginald. 'Bede, the Venerable.' In *Encyclopedia of the Early Church*, ed. Angelo Di Berardino, 1:117–18. Oxford, 1992.

Gretsch, Mechthild. 'Æthelwold's Translation of the *Regula Sancti Benedicti* and Its Latin Exemplar.' *ASE* 3 (1974): 125–51.

– 'The Benedictine Rule in Old English: A Document of Bishop Æthelwold's Reform Politics.' In *Words, Texts, and Manuscripts: Studies in Anglo-Saxon Culture Presented to Helmut Gneuss*, ed. Michael Korhammer et al., 131–58. Woodbridge, 1992.

– *The Intellectual Foundations of the English Benedictine Reform.* Cambridge, 1999.

– 'Ælfric and Gregory the Great.' In *Ælfric's Lives of Canonised Popes*, ed. Donald Scragg, 11–54. Kalamazoo, 2001.

Griffe, É. *La Gaule Chrétienne à l'Époque Romaine.* 2nd ed., 3 vols. Paris, 1957 and 1965.

Griffith, Mark S. 'Source Summary for Anglo-Saxon Text *Ælfric, Preface to Genesis.*' 2000. In *Fontes Anglo-Saxonici*, accessed October 2004.

– 'Ælfric's *Preface to Genesis*: Genre, Rhetoric and the Origins of the *ars dictaminis.*' *ASE* 29 (2000): 215–34.

– 'Ælfric's Use of His Sources in the *Preface to Genesis*, together with a Conspectus of Biblical and Patristic Sources and Analogues.' *Florilegium* 17 (2002 for 2000): 127–54.

Grundy, Lynne. *Books and Grace: Ælfric's Theology.* London, 1991.

Hall, Thomas N. 'The Early English Manuscripts of Gregory the Great's *Homiliae in Evangelia* and *Homiliae in Hiezechihelem*: A Preliminary Survey.' In *Rome and the North: The Early Reception of Gregory the Great in Germanic Europe*, ed. Rolf H. Bremmer, Jr, Kees Dekker, and David F. Johnson, 115–36. Louvain, 2001.

– 'Wulfstan's Latin Sermons.' in *Wulfstan, Archbishop of York: The Proceedings of the Second Alcuin Conference*, ed. Matthew Townend, 93–139. Studies in the Early Middle Ages 10. Turnhout, 2004.

Harms, W. *Homo Viator in Bivio: Studien zur Bildlichkeit des Weges.* Medium Aevum, Philologische Studien 21. Munich, 1970.

Harris, Stephen. 'The Alfredian World History and Anglo-Saxon Identity.' *Journal of English and Germanic Philology* 100 (2001): 482–510.

Harrison, Carol. 'Delectatio Victrix: Grace and Freedom in Saint Augustine.' In *Papers Presented at the Eleventh International Conference*, 298–302.

– *Augustine: Christian Truth and Fractured Humanity.* Oxford, 2000.

– *Rethinking Augustine's Early Theology.* Oxford, 2006.

Hart, C.R. *The Early Charters of Northern England and the North Midlands.* Leicester, 1975.

Hart, Joan. 'Source Summary for Anglo-Saxon Text *Gregory the Great, The Pastoral Care*.' 1992. In *Fontes Anglo-Saxonici*, accessed September 2004.

Hehle, Christine. *Boethius in St. Gallen: die bearbeitung der 'Consolatio Philosophiae' durch Notker Teutonicus zwischen Tradition und Innovation.* Tübingen, 2002.

Henel, H., ed. *Ælfric's De Temporibus Anni.* EETS 213. London, 1942.

Hill, Joyce. 'Ælfric and Smaragdus.' *ASE* 21 (1992): 203–37.

– 'Ælfric's Sources Reconsidered: Some Case Studies from the Catholic Homilies.' In *Studies in English Language and Literature*, ed. M.J. Toswell and E.M. Tyler, 362–86. London, 1996.

– 'Authority and Intertextuality in the Works of Ælfric.' *Proceedings of the British Academy* 131 (2005): 157–81.

– 'Ælfric's Manuscript of Paul the Deacon's Homiliary: A Provisional Analysis.' In *The Old English Homily: Precedent, Practice, and Appropriation*, ed. Aaron J Kleist, 67–96. Turnhout, 2007.

Hill, Thomas D. 'Satan's Injured Innocence in Genesis B, 360–62: A Gregorian Source.' *English Studies* 65 (1984): 289–90.

Hoffmann, Hartmut. *Schreibschulen des 10. und des 11. Jahrhunderts im Südwesten des Deutschen Reiches, mit einem Beitrag von Elmar Hochholzer.* 2 vols. MGH Schriften 53. Hanover, 2004.

Hofstetter, W. 'Winchester and the Standardization of Old English Vocabulary.' *ASE* 17 (1988): 139–61.

Holder, Arthur G. 'The Venerable Bede on the Mysteries of Our Salvation.' *American Benedictine Review* 42 (1991): 140–62.

– 'The Patristic Sources of Bede's Commentary on the Song of Songs.' In *Papers Presented at The Thirteenth International Conference*, 370–5.

Hombert, Pierre-Marie. *Gloria gratiae: Se Glorifier en Dieu, Principe et Fin de la Théologie Augustinienne de la Grâce.* Paris, 1996.

Houghton, John William. 'Bede's Exegetical Theology: Ideas of the Church in the Acts Commentaries of St. Bede the Venerable.' PhD dissertation, University of Notre Dame, 1994.

Hunt, R.W. *Saint Dunstan's Classbook from Glastonbury.* Amsterdam, 1961.

Hurst, D. 'Praefatio' in *In Marci euangelium expositio* and *In Lucae euangelium expositio*, ed. David Hurst, v–vii. CCSL 120. Turnholt, 1960.

– 'Praefatio' in *Homeliarum euangelii libri ii*, ed. David Hurst, vii–viii. CCSL 122. Turnholt, 1960.

– 'Praefatio' in *In Tobiam, In Prouerbia* and *In Cantica Canticorum*, ed. David Hurst, i. CCSL 119B. Turnholt, 1983.

Hurt, J. *Ælfric.* New York, 1972.

Huygens, R.B.C. 'Mittelalterliche Kommentare zum *O qui perpetua.*' *Sacris Eruditi* 6 (1954): 373–427.

Irvine, Susan. *Old English Homilies from MS Bodley 343.* EETS os 302. Oxford, 1993.

Jayatilaka, Rohini. 'Source Summary for Anglo-Saxon Text *Gregory the Great, Dialogues.* 1997. In *Fontes Anglo-Saxonici*, accessed October 2004.

– 'Source Summary for Anglo-Saxon Text *Orosius, History Against the Pagans.*' 2001, updated 2002. In *Fontes Anglo-Saxonici*, accessed October 2004.

Jenkins, Claude. 'Bede as Exegete and Theologian.' In *Bede: His Life, Times, and Writings; Essays in Commemoration of the Twelfth Centenary of His Death*, ed. A.H. Thompson, 152–200. Oxford, 1935.

Jeudy, C. 'Remigii autissiodorensis opera (Clavis).' In *L'École carolingienne d'Auxerre: de Murethach à Remi 830–908*, ed. D. Iogna-Prat, C. Jeudy, and G. Lobrichon, 457–500. Paris, 1991.

Johnson, David F. 'The Gregorian Grendel: *Beowulf* 705B–09 and the Limits of the Demonic.' In *Rome and the North: The Early Reception of Gregory the Great in Germanic Europe*, ed. Rolf H. Bremmer, Jr, Kees Dekker, and David F. Johnson, 51–65. Louvain, 2001.

Johnson, David W. 'The Myth of the Augustinian Synthesis.' *Lutheran Quarterly* 5 (1991): 157–69.

Jones, C.A. *Ælfric's Letter to the Monks of Eynsham.* Cambridge, 1998.

Jones, C.W. Introduction in *Libri quatuor in prinicpium Genesis*, ed. Jones, i–x. CCSL 118A. Turnholt, 1967.

– 'Some Introductory Remarks on Bede's Commentary on Genesis.' *Sacris Eruditi* 19 (1969–70): 115–98.

– Introduction in *De temporum ratione liber*, ed. Jones, 241–61. CCSL 123B. Turnholt, 1977.

Jost, K. 'Zur Textkritik der altenglischen Soliloquienbearbeitung.' *Beiblatt zur Anglia* 31 (1920): 259–72 and 280–90; 32 (1921): 8–16.

– 'Wulfstan und die Angelsächsische Chronik.' *Anglia* 47 (1923): 105–23.

– 'Einige Wulfstantexte und ihre Quellen.' *Anglia* 56 (1932): 265–315.

– *Wulfstanstudien.* Bern, 1950.

– *Die 'Institutes of Polity, Civil and Ecclesiastical.'* Bern, 1959.

Jungmann, Josef A. *The Mass of the Roman Rite.* 2 vols. New York, 1951 and 1955.

Kannengiesser, Charles. 'Boethius, Cassiodorus, Gregory the Great.' In *The Medieval Theologians*, ed. G.R. Evans, 24–36. Oxford, 2001.

Kardong, T. 'Benedict's Use of Cassianic Formulae for Spiritual Progress.' *Studia Monastica* 24 (1992): 233–52.

Kaufman, Peter Iver. 'Augustine, Evil, and Donatism: Sin and Sanctity before the Pelagian Controversy.' *Theological Studies* 51 (1990): 115–26.

Kaye, Sharon M., and Paul Thompson. *On Augustine*. Belmont, CA, 2001.

Ker, N.K. 'Hemming's Cartulary: A Description of the Two Worcester Cartularies in Cotton Tiberius A.xiii.' In *Studies in Medieval History Presented to Frederick Maurice Powicke*, ed. R.W. Hunt, et al, 49–75. Oxford, 1948.

Ker, N.R. *Catalogue of Manuscripts Containing Anglo-Saxon*. Oxford, 1957.

– 'The Handwriting of Archbishop Wulfstan.' In *England Before the Conquest: Studies in Primary Sources Presented to Dorothy Whitelock*, ed. P. Clemoes and K. Hughes, 315–31. Cambridge, 1971.

Kermit, Scott T. *Augustine: His Thought in Context*. New York, 1995.

Keynes, Simon, and Michael Lapidge, trans. *Alfred the Great: Asser's Life of King Alfred and Other Contemporary Sources*. London, 1983.

Kitson, Peter. 'Lapidary Traditions in Anglo-Saxon England: Part II, Bede's "Explanatio Apocalypsis" and related works.' *ASE* 12 (1983): 73–123.

– 'Geographical Variation in Old English Prepositions and the Location of Ælfric's and Other Literary Dialects.' *English Studies* 74 (1993): 1–50.

Kleist, Aaron J. 'An Annotated Ælfrician Bibliography, 1983–1996.' In *Basic Readings on Old English Prose*, ed. P.E. Szarmach et al., 503–52. New York, 2000.

– 'The Influence of Bede's *De temporum ratione* on Ælfric's Understanding of Time.' In *Time and Eternity: The Medieval Discourse*, ed. Gerhard Jaritz and Gerson Moreno-Riano, 81–97. Turnhout, 2003.

– 'Ælfric's Corpus: A Conspectus.' *Florilegium* 18 (2001 [published 2002]): 113–64.

Knowles, D. *The Monastic Order in England*. 2nd ed. Cambridge, 1963.

Kuzdale, Ann Elizabeth. 'The "Dialogues" of Pope Gregory the Great in the Literary and Religious Culture of Seventh- and Eighth-Century Europe.' PhD dissertation, University of Toronto, 1995.

LaChance, Paul Joseph. 'Theology in Boethius.' PhD dissertation, Boston College, 2003.

Ladner, G.B. 'Gregory the Great and Gregory VII: A Comparison of their Concepts of Renewal.' *Viator* 4 (1973): 1–26.

Lainé, Ariane. 'L'Antéchrist dans les homélies eschatologiques de Wulfstan: un mal du siècle.' *Historical Reflections* 26 (2000): 173–87.

Laistner, M.L.W. 'Bede as a Classical and a Patristic Scholar.' *Transactions of the Royal Historical Society* 16 (1933): 69–93.

– 'The Library of the Venerable Bede.' In *Bede: His Life, Times, and Writings; Essays in Commemoration of the Twelfth Centenary of His Death*, ed. A.H. Thompson, 237–62. Oxford, 1935.

– Praefatio in *Expositio Actuum Apostolorum et Retractatio*, ed. Laistner, i. CCSL 121. Turnholt, 1983. Originally printed Cambridge, MA, 1939.

Lancel, Serge. *Saint Augustine*, trans. Antonia Nevill. London, 2002.

Lapidge, Michael. 'Æthelwold as Scholar and Teacher.' In *Bishop Æthelwold: His Career and Influence*, ed. B. Yorke, 87–117. Woodbridge, 1988. Repr. in his *Anglo-Latin Literature*, 183–211.

– 'Three Latin Poems from Æthelwold's School at Winchester.' *ASE* 1 (1972): 85–137. Repr. in his *Anglo-Latin Literature*, 225–77, 484–6.

– 'The Hermeneutic Style in Tenth-Century Anglo-Latin Literature.' *ASE* 4 (1974): 67–111. Repr. in his *Anglo-Latin Literature*, 105–49.

– 'Surviving Booklists from Anglo-Saxon England.' In *Learning and Literature in Anglo-Saxon England: Studies Presented to Peter Clemoes on the Occasion of His Sixty-Fifth Birthday*, ed. Michael Lapidge and Helmut Gneuss, 33–89. Cambridge, 1985.

– Forward to *The World of Bede*, ed. Peter Hunter Blair, vii–x. 2nd ed. Cambridge, 1990.

– 'Schools, Learning and Literature in Tenth-Century England.' *Settimane di Studio del Centro Italiano di Studi sull'Alto Medioevo* 38 (1991): 951–1005. Repr. in his *Anglo-Latin Literature 900–1066*, 1–48. London, 1993.

– *Anglo-Latin Literature, 900–1066*. London, 1993.

– 'Lantfred.' In *Medieval England: An Encyclopedia*, ed. Paul E. Szarmach, M. Teresa Tavormina, and Joel Thomas Rosenthal, 410. New York, 1998.

– 'Byrhtferth at Work.' In *Words and Works: Studies in Medieval English Language and Literature in Honour of Fred C. Robinson*, ed. P.S. Baker and N. Howe, 25–43. Toronto, 1998.

– with contributions by John Crook, Robert Deshman, and Susan Rankin. *The Cult of St Swithun*. Oxford, 2003.

– 'Lantfred (fl. 974–984).' 2004. *Oxford Dictionary of National Biography*. Oxford University Press, accessed September 2004.

– *The Anglo-Saxon Library*. Oxford, 2006.

Lapidge, Michael, and Michael Winterbottom. *Wulfstan of Winchester*. Oxford, 1991.

Lebourlier, J. 'Essai sur la responsabilité du pécheur dans la réflexion de saint Augustin.' *Augustinus Magister* 3 (1954): 287–307.

Leclercq, J. 'The Tenth Century Benedictine Reform Seen from the Continent.' *Ampleforth Review* 84 (1980): 8–23.

– 'Smaragdus.' In *An Introduction to the Medieval Mystics of Europe*, ed. P. Szarmach, 37–51. Albany, NY, 1984.

Lee, Kam-lun Edwin. *Augustine, Manichaeism, and the Good*. New York, 1999.

Leinbaugh, Theodore. 'Ælfric (ca. 945 – ca. 1015).' In *Medieval England: An Encyclopedia*, ed. Paul E. Szarmach, M. Teresa Tavormina, and Joel Thomas Rosenthal, 4–7. New York, 1998.

Leland, John. *Commentarii de scriptoribus Britannicis*, ed. Anthony Hall. 2 vols. Oxford, 1709.

Lendinara, Patrizia. 'Gregory and Damasus: Two Popes and Anglo-Saxon England.' In *Rome and the North: The Early Reception of Gregory the Great in Germanic Europe*, ed. Rolf H. Bremmer, Jr, Kees Dekker, and David F. Johnson, 137–56. Louvain, 2001.

Lewis, C.T., and C. Short. *A Latin Dictionary*. Oxford, 1879.

Leyser, Conrad. *Authority and Asceticism from Augustine to Gregory the Great*. Oxford, 2000.

Logeman, H. See above under *Benedict of Monte Cassino*.

Loorits, O. *Der Heilige Kassian und die Schaltjahrlegende*. Helsinki, 1954.

Lopez, David. 'Translation and Tradition: Reading the *Consolation of Philosophy* through King Alfred's *Boethius*.' In *The Politics of Translation in the Middle Ages and the Renaissance*, ed. Renate Blumenfeld-Kosinski et al, 69–84. Ottawa, 2001.

Love, Rosalind C. 'Source Summary for Anglo-Saxon Text *Vita S. Cuthberti* (prose).' 1997. In *Fontes Anglo-Saxonici*, accessed September 2004.

– 'Source Summary for Anglo-Saxon Text *Vita S. Felicis*.' 1997. In *Fontes Anglo-Saxonici*, accessed September 2004.

– 'Records for Source Title *Ench[iridion]*.' 1998. In *Fontes Anglo-Saxonici*, accessed September 2004.

– 'Source Summary for Anglo-Saxon Text *Letter to John*, prefatory to *Vita metrica S. Cuthberti*. 1998. In *Fontes Anglo-Saxonici*, accessed September 2004.

– 'Source Summary for Anglo-Saxon Text *Commentarius in Genesim* [*In principium Genesis*] (Libri I et II).' 2000. In *Fontes Anglo-Saxonici*, accessed September 2004.

– 'Source Summary for Anglo-Saxon Text *Explanatio Apocalypsis* [*Expositio Apocalypseos*].' 2000. In *Fontes Anglo-Saxonici*, accessed September 2004.

– 'Source Summary for Anglo-Saxon Text *Martyrologium*.' 2000. In *Fontes Anglo-Saxonici*, accessed September 2004.

– 'Source Summary for Anglo-Saxon Text *Passio S. Anastasii*.' 2000. In *Fontes Anglo-Saxonici*, accessed September 2004.

Maclean, G.E. 'Ælfric's Version of *Alcuini Interrogationes Sigeuulfi in Genesin*.' *Anglia* 6 (1883): 425–73.

– 'Ælfric's Version of *Alcuini Interrogationes Sigeuulfi in Genesin*.' *Anglia* 7 (1884): 1–59.

Magennis, Hugh, and Mary Swan, eds. *A Companion to Ælfric*. Leiden, forthcoming.

Marenbon, John. *Boethius*. Oxford, 2003.

Markus, Robert A. 'Chronicle and Theology: Prosper of Aquitaine.' In *The Inheritance of Historiography*, ed. C. Holdsworth and T.P. Wiseman, 31–43.

Exeter, 1986. Repr. in his *Sacred and Secular: Studies on Augustine and Latin Christianity*. Aldershot, 1994.
- 'The Legacy of Pelagius: Orthodoxy, Heresy and Conciliation.' In *The Making of Orthodoxy*, ed. R.D. Williams, 214–34. Cambridge, 1989. Repr. in his *Sacred and Secular: Studies on Augustine and Latin Christianity*. Aldershot, 1994.
- *The End of Ancient Christianity*. Cambridge, 1990.
- *Gregory the Great and His World*. Cambridge, 1997.
- 'Augustine and Gregory the Great.' In *St Augustine and the Conversion of England*, ed. Richard Gameson, 41–9. Phoenix Mill, Gloucestershire, 1999.
- 'Life, Culture, and Controversies of Augustine.' In *Augustine Through the Ages: An Encyclopedia*, ed. Allan Fitzgerald and John C. Cavadini, 498–504. Grand Rapids, MI, 1999.
Martin, Lawrence T. Introduction in *Commentary on the Acts of the Apostles*, trans. Lawrence T. Martin, i–xxxv. Kalamazoo, 1989.
- Introduction in *Homilies on the Gospels*, trans. Lawrence T. Martin and David Hurst, 1:1–4. 2 vols. Kalamazoo, 1991.
Martin, Lawrence T., and David Hurst. *Homilies on the Gospels*. 2 vols. Kalamazoo, 1991.
Martin, Thomas F. *Rhetoric and Exegesis in Augustine's Interpretation of Romans 7:24–25a*. Lewiston, 2001.
Mastandrea, Paolo, and Luigi Tessarolo, eds. *Poetria Nova: Latin Medieval Poetry (650–1250 A.D.), with a Gateway to Classical and Late Antiquity Texts; A CD-ROM*. Società Internatzionale per lo Studio del Medioevo Latino, 2001.
Matthews, Gareth B. *Augustine*. Oxford, 2005.
Matthews, John. 'Anicius Manlius Severinus Boethius.' In *Boethius: His Life, Thought and Influence*, ed. Margaret Gibson, 15–43. Oxford, 1981.
Matthews, John F. 'Augustine, St (Aurelius Augustinus).' In *Oxford Classical Dictionary*. 3rd rev. ed., ed. Simon Hornblower and Antony Spawforth, 215–16. Oxford, 2003.
McCarthy, Daniel P., and Dáibhí Ó Cróinín. 'The Lost Irish 84-Year Easter Table Rediscovered.' *Peritia* 6–7 (1987–8): 227–42.
McCready, W.D. *Signs of Sanctity: Miracles in the Thought of Gregory the Great*. Toronto, 1989.
McEniery, P. 'Pope Gregory the Great and Infallibility.' *Journal of Ecumenical Studies* 11 (1974): 263–80.
McGinn, B. *The Growth of Mysticism: From Gregory the Great through the Twelfth Century*. London, 1995.
McHugh, Michael P. 'Bede (ca. 673–735).' In *Encyclopedia of Early Christianity*, ed. Everett Ferguson, Michael P. McHugh, and Frederick W. Norris, 1:78–9. 2nd ed. 2 vols. New York, 1998.

McIntosh, Angus. 'Wulfstan's Prose.' *Proceedings of the British Academy* 35 (1949): 109–42.

McMahon, Robert. *Understanding the Medieval Meditative Ascent: Augustine, Anselm, Boethius, and Dante.* Washington, 2006.

Meaney, Audrey L. 'Ælfric and Idolatry.' *Journal of Religious History* 13 (1984): 119–35.

– 'Ælfric's Use of his Sources in his Homily on Auguries.' *English Studies* 66 (1985): 477–95.

Mengato, Simonetta. 'The Old English Translations of Bede's *Historia Ecclesiastica* and Orosius's *Historiuarum* [sic] *Adversus Paganos*: A Comparison.' *Linguistica e filologia* 16 (2003): 191–213.

Menner, R.J. 'Anglian and Saxon Elements in Wulfstan's Vocabulary.' *Modern Language Notes* 63 (1948): 1–9.

Meyvaert, Paul. 'Bede's Text of the *Libellus Responsionum* of Gregory the Great to Augustine of Canterbury.' in *England Before the Conquest: Studies in Primary Sources Presented to Dorothy Whitelock*, ed. Peter Clemoes and Kathleen Hughes, 15–33. Cambridge, 1971. Repr. in Meyvaert, *Benedict, Gregory, Bede, and Others*, no. X. London, 1977.

– 'Bede the Scholar.' In *Famulus Christi: Essays in Commemoration of the Thirteenth Centenary of the Birth of the Venerable Bede*, ed. G. Bonner, 40–69. London, 1976.

– 'Bede and Gregory the Great.' In *Bede and His World: Jarrow Lectures, 1958–1993*, 103–32. Aldershot, 1994.

Miles, Margaret R. 'Augustine.' In *Encyclopedia of Early Christianity*, ed. Everett Ferguson, Michael P. McHugh, and Frederick W. Norris, 1:148–53. 2nd ed. New York, 1998.

Moye, Roy Ray, Jr. 'Alfred's Method of Translation in the Old English "Pastoral Care."' PhD dissertation, University of North Carolina, Chapel Hill, 1993.

Naumann, H. *Notkers Boethius: Untersuchungen über Quellen und Stil.* Strasbourg, 1913.

Nelson, Janet L. 'The Problem of King Alfred's Royal Anointing.' *Journal of Ecclesiastical History* 18 (1967): 145–63.

Nelson, Janet L., and Janet M. Bately. 'Alfred the Great (849–899; r. 871–99).' In *Medieval England: An Encyclopedia*, ed. Paul E. Szarmach, M. Teresa Tavormina, and Joel Thomas Rosenthal, 18–22. New York, 1998.

Nicholson, Lewis E., ed. *The Vercelli Book Homilies: Translations from the Anglo-Saxon.* Lanham, 1991.

O'Connell, Robert J. 'Involuntary Sin in the *De libero arbitio*.' *Revue des Etudes Augustiniennes* 37 (1991): 23–6.

Ó Cróinín, Dáibhí. '"New Heresy for Old": Pelagianism in Ireland and the Papal Letter of 640.' *Speculum* 60 (1985): 505–16.

O'Daly, G. *Augustine's Philosophy of Mind*. London, 1987.
- 'Predestination and Freedom in Augustine's Ethics.' In *The Philosophy in Christianity*, ed. G. Vesey, 85–97. Cambridge, 1989.
O'Donnell, James J. *Augustine: A New Biography*. New York, 2005.
Oetgen, Jerome John. 'Ælfric's Use of Gregory the Great's *Homiliae in Euangelia* in the Catholic Homilies, First and Second Series.' PhD dissertation, University of Toronto, 1977.
Ogliari, Donato. *Gratia et certamen: The Relationship Between Grace and Free Will in the Discussion of Augustine with the So-Called Semipelagians*. Dudley, MA, 2004.
O'Keeffe, Katherine O'Brien. 'Body and Law in Late Anglo-Saxon England.' *ASE* 27 (1998): 209–32.
Orchard, Andy. 'Crying Wolf: Oral Style and the *Sermones Lupi*.' *ASE* 21 (1992): 239–64.
- 'Source Summary for Anglo-Saxon Text *De die iudicii*.' 1995. In *Fontes Anglo-Saxonici*, accessed September 2004.
- 'Wulfstan the Homilist.' In *The Blackwell Encyclopedia of Anglo-Saxon England*, ed. Michael Lapidge, 494–5. Oxford, 1999.
Orchard, Andy, and Rosalind C. Love. 'Source Summary for Anglo-Saxon Text *Vita metrica S. Cuthberti*.' 1995. In *Fontes Anglo-Saxonici*, accessed September 2004.
Oroz Reta, J. 'Vocation divine et conversion humaine d'après saint Augustin.' In *Papers presented to the Tenth International Conference*, 300–8.
- 'The Role of Divine Attraction in Conversion According to St Augustine.' In *From Augustine to Eriugena*, ed. F.X. Martin and J.A. Richmond, 155–67. Washington, 1991.
Otten, Kurt. *König Alfreds Boethius*. Tübingen, 1964.
Otten, Willemien. 'Carolingian Theology.' In *The Medieval Theologians*, ed. G.R. Evans, 65–82. Oxford, 2001.
Paas, Steven. *A Conflict on Authority in the Early African Church: Augustine of Hippo and the Donatists*. Zomba, Malawi, 2005.
Papers Presented at the Seventh International Conference on Patristic Studies Held in Oxford 1975: Monastica et ascetica, Orientalia, e saeculo secundo, Origen, Athanasius, Cappadocian Fathers, Chrysostom, Augustine. Ed. Elizabeth A. Livingstone. Studia Patristica 16.2. Berlin, 1985.
Papers Presented to the Tenth International Conference on Patristic Studies Held in Oxford 1987. Ed. Elizabeth A. Livingstone. Studia Patristica 22. Louvain, 1989.
Papers Presented at the Eleventh International Conference on Patristic Studies Held in Oxford 1991: Cappadocian Fathers, Greek Authors after Nicaea, Augustine, Donatism, and Pelagianism. Ed. Elizabeth A. Livingstone. Studia Patristica 27. Louvain, 1993.

Papers Presented at the Thirteenth International Conference on Patristic Studies Held in Oxford 1999: St Augustine and His Opponents; Other Latin Writers. Ed. Maurice Wiles, Edward Yarnold, and P.M. Parvis. Studia Patristica 38. Louvain, 2001.

Parkes, M.B. 'A Note on MS Vatican Bibl. Apost., lat. 3363.' In *Boethius: His Life, Thought and Influence*, ed. M. Gibson, 425–7. Oxford, 1981.

Parsons, D. ed. *Tenth-Century Studies: Essays in Commemoration of the Millennium of the Council of Winchester and Regularis Concordia*. London, 1975.

Passalacqua, Marina, and Leslie Smith, eds. *Codices Boethiani: A Conspectus of Manuscripts of the Works of Boethius*. Vol. 3, *Italy and the Vatican City*. London, 2001.

Payne, F. Anne. *King Alfred and Boethius: An Analysis of the Old English Version of the Consolation of Philosophy*. Madison and London, 1968.

Pelikan, J. *The Christian Tradition: A History of the Development of Doctrine*. Vol. 1, *The Emergence of the Catholic Tradition (100–600)*. Chicago, 1971.

Petersen, Joan M. *The Dialogues of Gregory the Great in Their Late Antique Cultural Background*. Toronto, 1984.

– '"Homo omnino Latinus"? The Theological and Cultural Background of Pope Gregory the Great.' *Speculum* 62 (1987): 529–51.

Pigeon, Darryl J. 'Cyprian, Augustine and the Donatist Schism.' *Ashland Theological Journal* 23 (1991): 37–47.

Pits, John. *Relationum historicarum de rebus Anglicis*. Paris, 1619.

Plummer, C. ed. *Venerabilis Baedae Opera Historica*. 2 vols. Oxford, 1896.

Pope, John C. *Homilies of Ælfric: A Supplementary Collection*. EETS 259 and 260. London, 1967–8.

– 'Ælfric and the Old English Version of the Ely Privilege.' In *England before the Conquest: Studies in Primary Sources Presented to Dorothy Whitelock*, ed. Peter Clemoes and Kathleen Hughes, 85–113. Cambridge, 1971.

Portalié, Eugène. *A Guide to the Thought of Saint Augustine*, trans. R. Bastian. London, 1960.

Powers, Patrick J.C. 'St. Augustine's Transformation of Platonic Political Philosophy, Christian Will and Pagan Spiritedness in De Libero Arbitrio.' *University of Dayton Review* 22.3 (1994): 117–32.

Pratt, David R. 'The Political Thought of Alfred the Great.' PhD dissertation, University of Cambridge, 1999.

Pristas, Lauren. 'The Theological Anthropology of John Cassian.' PhD dissertation, Boston College, 1993.

Quentin, H. *Les Martyrologes Historiques du Moyen Age*. Paris, 1908.

Rädle, F. *Studien zu Smaragd von Saint-Mihiel*. Munich, 1974.

Rambridge, Kate. '*Doctor Noster Sanctus*: The Northumbrians and Pope Gregory.' In *Rome and the North: The Early Reception of Gregory the Great in*

Germanic Europe, ed. Rolf H. Bremmer, Jr, Kees Dekker, and David F. Johnson, 1–26. Louvain, 2001.

Ramsay, N., et al., eds. *St Dunstan: His Life, Times and Cult*. Woodbridge and Rochester, 1992.

Ramsey, Boniface. 'John Cassian: Student of Augustine.' *Cistercian Studies Quarterly* 28 (1993): 5–15.

Ray, Roger. 'What Do We Know about Bede's Commentaries?' *Recherches de Théologie Ancienne et Médiévale* 49 (1982): 5–20.

– 'Bede.' In *The Blackwell Encyclopedia of Anglo-Saxon England*, ed. Michael Lapidge, 57–9. Oxford, 1999.

Recchia, Vincenzo. 'Gregory the Great.' In *Encyclopedia of the Early Church*, ed. Angelo Di Berardino, 1:365–8. Oxford, 1992.

Rettig, J. 'The Dates of the *Tractates*.' In *St Augustine: Tractates on the Gospel of John 1–10*, 23–31. Fathers of the Church 90. Washington, 1995.

Richards, J. *Consul of God: The Life and Times of Gregory the Great*. London, 1980.

Richards, Mary. 'Wulfstan of York.' In *Medieval England: An Encyclopedia*, ed. Paul E. Szarmach, M. Teresa Tavormina, and Joel Thomas Rosenthal, 820–1. New York, 1998.

Riches, John K. 'Readings of Augustine on Paul: Their Impact on Critical Studies of Paul.' In *Engaging Augustine on Romans: Self, Context, and Theology in Interpretation*, ed. Daniel Patte and Eugene TeSelle, 173–98. Harrisburg, PA, 2002.

Ries, Julien. 'Le jugement porté sur le Manichéisme par saint Augustin à la lumière de son expérience relatée dans les *Confessions*.' In *Papers Presented at the Thirteenth International Conference*, 264–74.

Rist, J.M. 'Augustine on Free Will and Predestination.' *Journal of Theological Studies* 20 (1969): 420–47. Repr. in *Augustine: A Collection of Critical Essays*, ed. R.A. Markus, 218–52. Garden City, NY, 1972.

– *Augustine: Ancient Thought Rebaptized*. Cambridge, 1994.

– 'Augustine of Hippo.' In *The Medieval Theologians*, ed. G.R. Evans, 3–23. Oxford, 2001.

Robinson, Bernard P. 'The Venerable Bede as Exegete.' *Downside Review* 112 (1994): 201–26.

Rotelle, J.E. 'Chronological Table.' In *Sermons*, ed. Rotelle, *The Works of Saint Augustine*, 3.1:138–63. Brooklyn, 1990.

Roti, Grant C. 'Anonymus in Boetii Consolationem Philosophiae Commentarius ex Sangallensis Codice Liber Primus.' PhD dissertation, State University of New York at Albany, 1979.

Rousseau, P., 'Cassian, Contemplation, and the Coenobitic Life.' *Journal of Ecclesiastical History* 26 (1975): 113–26.

– *Ascetics, Authority, and the Church in the Age of Jerome and Cassian*. Oxford, 1978.

– 'Cassian: Monastery and World.' In *The Certainty of Doubt: Tributes to Peter Munz*, ed. M. Fairburn and W.H. Oliver, 68–89. Wellington, New Zealand, 1995.

Rowe, William L. 'Augustine on Foreknowledge and Free Will.' *Review of Metaphysics* 18 (1964): 356–63. Repr. in *Augustine: A Collection of Critical Essays*, ed. R.A. Markus, 209–17. Garden City, NY, 1972.

Rowley, Sharon. 'Shifting Contexts: Reading Gregory the Great's *Libellus Responsionum* in Book III of the Old English Bede.' In *Rome and the North: The Early Reception of Gregory the Great in Germanic Europe*, ed. Rolf H. Bremmer, Jr, Kees Dekker, and David F. Johnson, 83–92. Louvain, 2001.

Rush, A.C., and K. Hester. 'Gregory (the Great) I, St. Pope.' In *New Catholic Encyclopedia*, ed. Thomas Carson and Joann Cerrito, 6:478–84. 2nd ed. London, 2003.

Rydstrøm-Poulsen, Aage. *The Gracious God: Gratia in Augustine and the Twelfth Century*. Copenhagen, 2002.

Saarinen, R. *Weakness of the Will in Medieval Thought: From Augustine to Buridan*. New York, 1994.

Sage, A. 'Praeparatur uoluntas a Deo.' *Revue des Études Augustiniennes* 10 (1964): 1–20.

Sauer, Hans. 'The Transmission and Structure of Archbishop Wulfstan's Commonplace Book.' In *Old English Prose: Basic Readings*, ed. Paul E. Szarmach, 339–93. New York, 2000.

Scalise, Charles J. 'Exegetical Warrants for Religious Persecution: Augustine vs. the Donatists.' *Review and Expositor* 93 (1996): 497–506.

Scarfe Beckett, Katharine. 'Source Summary for Anglo-Saxon Text *Historia ecclesiastica gentis Anglorum*.' 2002. In *Fontes Anglo-Saxonici*, ed. Joyce Hill et al., http://fontes.english.ox.ac.uk, accessed September 2004.

Scharer, Anton. 'The Gregorian Tradition in Early England.' In *St Augustine and the Conversion of England*, ed. Richard Gameson, 187–201. Phoenix Mill, Gloucestershire, 1999.

Scheible, Helga. *Die Gedichte in der Consolatio Philosophiae des Boethius*. Heidelberg, 1972.

Schepss, Georg. 'Zu König Alfreds Boethius.' *Archiv für das Studium der neueren Sprachen und Literaturen* 94 (1895): 149–60.

Schröer, A. See above under Benedict of Monte Cassino.

Schumann, O. *Lateinisches Hexameter-Lexicon*. 7 vols. MGH 4 – 4.6. Munich, 1979–89.

Scott, T. Kermit. *Augustine: His Thought in Context*. New York, 1995.

Scragg, D.G. *The Vercelli Homilies and Related Texts*. EETS 300. Oxford, 1992.

Seeberg, R. *Lehrbuch der Dogmengeschichte*. Basle, 1953.

Sedgefield, Walter John. Introduction in *King Alfred's Old English Version of Boethius*, ed. Sedgefield, xi–xliii. Oxford, 1899.

- Preface in *King Alfred's Version of the Consolations of Boethius, Done into Modern English, with an Introduction*, vii–ix. Oxford, 1900.
Sharples, R.W. *Cicero, On Fate, and Boethius, The Consolation of Philosophy IV 5–7, V.* Warminster, 1991.
Shimmyo, Theodore T. 'Free Will in Saint Augustine's Doctrine of Predestination.' *Patristic and Byzantine Review* 6 (1987): 136–45.
- 'St Augustine's Treatment of the Donatist Heresy: An Interpretation.' *Patristic and Byzantine Review* 10 (1991): 173–82.
Silk, E.T. *Saeculi noni auctoris in Boetii Consolationem Philosophiae commentaries.* Papers and Monographs of the American Academy in Rome 9. Rome, 1935.
Silvestre, H. 'Le commentaire inédit de Jean Scot Érigène au mètre IX du livre III du *De consolatione Philosophiae* de Boèce.' *Revue d'Histoire Ecclésiastique* 47 (1952): 51–65.
Smetana, C. 'Ælfric and the Early Medieval Homiliary.' *Traditio* 15 (1959): 163–204.
- 'Ælfric and the Homiliary of Haymo of Halberstadt.' *Traditio* 17 (1961): 457–69.
- 'Paul the Deacon's Patristic Anthology.' In *The Old English Homily and Its Backgrounds*, ed. P.E. Szarmach and B.F. Huppé, 75–97. Albany, 1978.
Smith, Leslie, ed. *Codices Boethiani: A Conspectus of Manuscripts of the Works of Boethius. Vol. 2. Austria, Belgium, Denmark, Luxembourg, the Netherlands, Sweden, Switzerland.* London, 2001.
Smyth, A.P. *Alfred the Great.* Oxford, 1995.
Souter, Alexander. 'Contributions to the Criticism of Zmaragdus' *Expositio libri comitis.' Journal of Theological Studies* 9 (1908): 584–97.
- 'Further Contributions to the Criticism of Zmaragdus' *Expositio libri comitis.' Journal of Theological Studies* 23 (1922): 73–6.
- *Pelagius's Expositions of Thirteen Epistles of St Paul.* Texts and Studies 9. 3 vols. Cambridge, 1922–31.
- *The Earliest Latin Commentaries on the Epistles of St. Paul: A Study.* Oxford, 1927.
- 'A Further Contribution to the Criticism of Zmaragdus' *Expositio libri comitis.' Journal of Theological Studies* 34 (1933): 46–7.
Stalnaker, Aaron. 'Spiritual Exercises and the Grace of God: Paradoxes of Personal Formation in Augustine.' *Journal of the Society of Christian Ethics* 24 (2004): 137–70.
Stancliffe, Clare. 'The British Church and the Mission of Augustine.' In *St Augustine and the Conversion of England*, ed. Richard Gameson, 107–51. Phoenix Mill, Gloucestershire, 1999.
Stark, J.C. 'The Pauline Influence on Augustine's Notion of the Will.' *Vigiliae Christianae* 43 (1989): 345–61.
- 'The Dynamics of the Will in Augustine's Conversion.' In *Augustine: Second Founder of the Faith*, ed. Frederick Van Fleteren and Joseph C. Schnaubelt, 45–64. New York, 2000.

Stead, Christopher. 'Augustine's Philosophy of Being.' In *The Philosophy of Christianity*, ed. G. Vesey, 71–84. Cambridge, 1989. Repr. in *Doctrine and Philosophy in Early Christianity: Arius, Athanasius, Augustine*, ed. Christopher Stead, 71–84. Aldershot, UK, 2000.

Stewart, C. *Cassian the Monk*. Oxford, 1998.

Stewart, H.F. 'A Commentary by Remigius Autissiodorensis on the *De consolatione Philosophiae* of Boethius.' *Journal of Theological Studies* 17 (1916): 22–42.

Straw, C. *Gregory the Great: Perfection in Imperfection*. Berkeley, 1988.

– 'Purity and Death.' In *Gregory the Great: A Symposium*, ed. J.C. Cavadini, 16–37. London, 1995.

– *Gregory the Great*. Aldershot, 1996.

Stump, Eleonore. 'Augustine on Free Will.' In *The Cambridge Companion to Augustine*, ed. Eleonore Stump and Norman Kretzmann, 124–47. Cambridge, 2001.

Sweet, Henry, ed. *King Alfred's West-Saxon Version of Gregory's Pastoral Care.* EETS os 45 and 50. London, 1871. Repr 2006.

Symons, T. Introduction in *Regularis concordia*, ed. Symons, ix–lii. New York, 1953.

Szarmach, Paul E. 'Another Old English Translation of Gregory the Great's Dialogues?' *English Studies* 62 (1981): 97–109.

– 'Meter 20: Context Bereft.' *American Notes and Queries* 15 (2002): 28–34.

Tax, Petrus. 'Die althochdeutschen "Consolatio"-Glossen in der Handschrift Einsiedeln 179: Grundtext- oder Glossenglossierung? Ein neuer, systematischer Ansatz, Teil I.' *Sprachwissenschaft* 26 (2001): 327–58.

– 'Das Längezeichen e im Fränkischen und Alemannischen schon um 1000? Eine neue Hypothese.' *Sprachwissenschaft* 27 (2002): 129–42.

TeSelle, Eugene. 'Nature and Grace in Augustine's Expositions of Genesis I, 1–5.' *Recherches Augustiniennes* 5 (1968): 95–137.

– 'Engaging Scripture: Patristic Interpretation of the Bible.' In *Engaging Augustine on Romans: Self, Context, and Theology in Interpretation*, ed. Daniel Patte and Eugene TeSelle, 1–62. Harrisburg, PA, 2002.

– 'Exploring the Inner Conflict: Augustine's Sermons on Romans 7 and 8.' In *Augustine: Biblical Exegete*, ed. Frederick Van Fleteren and Joseph C. Schnaubelt, 313–45. New York, 2001. Repr. in abbreviated form in *Engaging Augustine on Romans: Self, Context, and Theology in Interpretation*, ed. Daniel Patte and Eugene TeSelle, 111–46. Harrisburg, PA, 2002.

– *Augustine*. Nashville, TN, 2006.

Teske, Ronald J. 'Augustine, the Manichees and the Bible.' In *Augustine and the Bible*, ed. Pamela Bright, 208–21. Notre Dame, 1999.

– 'Augustine, St.' In *New Catholic Encyclopedia*, ed. Thomas Carson and Joann Cerrito, 1:852–68. 2nd ed. London, 2003.

Torchia, Natale Joseph. *Creatio ex nihilo and the Theology of St Augustine: The Anti-Manichaean Polemic and Beyond.* New York, 1999.

Trapè, Agostino. 'Augustine of Hippo.' In *Encyclopedia of the Early Church*, ed. Angelo Di Berardino, 1:97–101. Oxford, 1992.

Troncarelli, F. 'Per una ricerca sui comenti altomedievali al *De Consolatione* di Boezio.' In *Miscellanea in Memoria di G. Cencetti*, 363–80. Turin, 1973.

– *Tradizioni perdute: la 'Consolatio Philosophiae' nell' alto medioevo.* Padua, 1981.

– 'Boezio nel circolo d'Alcuino: Le più antiche gloss carolinge alla *Consolatio Philosophiae.*' *Recherches Augustiniennes* 22 (1987): 223–41.

Tugene, Georges. 'L'histoire ecclésiastique de Bède le Vénérable.' In *L'historiographie de l'Église des premiers siècles*, ed. Bernard Pouderon and Yves-Marie Duval, 259–70. Paris, 2001.

Tunberg, Jennifer Morrish. 'Physical Description.' In *The Copenhagen Wulfstan Collection: Copenhagen Kongelige Bibliotek Gl. Kgl. Sam. 1595*, ed. James E. Cross and Jennifer Morrish Tunberg, 24–8. Early English Manuscripts in Facsimile 25. Copenhagen, 1993.

– 'Scribes, Scribal Habits, Abbreviations, and Word-Separation.' In *The Copenhagen Wulfstan Collection: Copenhagen Kongelige Bibliotek Gl. Kgl. Sam. 1595*, ed. James E. Cross and Jennifer Morrish Tunberg, 31–49. Early English Manuscripts in Facsimile 25. Copenhagen, 1993.

Van Fleteren, Frederick. 'Principles of Augustine's Hermeneutic: An Overview.' In *Augustine: Biblical Exegete*, ed. Frederick Van Fleteren and Joseph C. Schnaubelt, 1–32. New York, 2001.

Van Oort, Johannes. *Mani, Manichaeism and Augustine: The Rediscovery of Manichaeism and Its Influence on Western Christianity.* Tbilisi, 1998.

Van Oort, Johannes, Otto Wermelinger, and Gregor Wurst, eds. *Augustine and Manichaeism in the Latin West: Proceedings of the Fribourg-Utrecht Symposium of the International Association of Manichaean Studies.* Leiden, 2001.

de Vogel, C.J. 'Boethiana I.' *Vivarium* 9 (1971): 49–66.

de Vogüé, Adalbert. 'Les Mentiones des Oeuvres de Cassien Chez Saint Benoît et ses Contemporains.' *Studi medievali* 20 (1978): 275–85.

– 'Les Sources des Quarters Premiers Livres des Institutions de Jean Cassien: Introduction aux Recherches sur les Anciennes Règles Monastiques Latines.' *Studia Monastica* 27 (1985): 241–311.

Von Hagel, Thomas. 'A Preaching of Repentance: The Forty Gospel Homilies of Gregory the Great.' *Homiletic* 31 (2006): 1–10.

Wallace-Hadrill, J.M. *Bede's Ecclesiastical History of the English People: A Historical Commentary.* Oxford, 1988.

Walsh, Maura, and Dáibhí Ó Cróinín, eds. *Cummian's Letter De controversia paschali, together with a Related Irish Computistical Tract De ratione conputandi.* Toronto, 1988.

Walsh, P.G. *Boethius: The Consolation of Philosophy.* Oxford, 1999.

Ward, Benedicta. *The Venerable Bede.* Harrisburg, PA, 1990.

– Preface in *Homilies on the Gospels,* trans. Lawrence Martin and David Hurst, 1:iii–ix. Kalamazoo, MI, 1991.

– 'Bede the Theologian.' In *The Medieval Theologians,* ed. G.R. Evans, 57–64. Oxford, 2001.

Watson, G. 'Commentary: Soliloquies.' In his *Saint Augustine: Soliloquies and Immortality of the Soul,* 165–97. Warminster, 1990.

Weaver, R.H. *Divine Grace and Human Agency: A Study of the Semi-Pelagian Controversy.* Macon, GA, 1996.

Webber, T. *Scribes and Scholars at Salisbury Cathedral, c. 1075 – c. 1125.* Oxford, 1992.

Weismann, F.J. 'The Problematic of Freedom in St. Augustine: Towards a New Hermeneutics.' *Revue des Etudes Augustiniennes* 35 (1989): 104–19.

Wetzel, James 'The Recovery of Free Agency in the Theology of Saint Augustine.' *Harvard Theological Review* 80 (1987): 101–25.

– *Augustine and the Limits of Virtue.* Cambridge, 1992.

– 'Pelagius Anticipated: Grace and Election in Augustine's *Ad Simplicianum.*' In *Augustine: From Rhetor to Theologian,* ed. J. McWilliam, 121–32. Waterloo, Ontario, 1992.

– 'Snares of Truth: Augustine on Free Will and Predestination.' In *Augustine and His Critics: Essays in Honour of Gerald Bonner,* ed. Robert Dodaro and George Lawless, 124–41. New York, 2000.

Whitelock, Dorothy, 'Wulfstan and the So-Called Laws of Edward and Guthrum.' *English Historical Review* 56 (1941): 1–21.

– 'Archbishop Wulfstan, Homilist and Statesman.' *Transactions of the Royal Historical Society.* 4th series, 44 (1942): 25–45.

– 'Wulfstan and the Laws of Cnut.' *English Historical Review* 63 (1947): 433–52.

– 'Wulfstan's Language.' In *Sermo Lupi ad Anglos,* ed. Dorothy Whitelock, 37–45. 3rd ed. London, 1963.

– rev., *Sweet's Anglo-Saxon Reader in Prose and Verse.* 15th ed. Oxford, 1967.

– 'The Authorship of the Account of King Edgar's Establishment of Monasteries.' In *Philological Essays: Studies in Old and Middle English Language and Literature in Honour of Herbert Dean Meritt,* ed. James L. Rosier, 125–36. The Hague, 1970.

– ed. *English Historical Documents, c. 500–1042.* 2nd ed. London, 1979.

Whitelock, D., M. Brett, and C.N.L. Brooke, eds. *Councils and Synods with other Documents Relating to the English Church, I: AD 871–1204.* Oxford, 1981.

Wilcox, Jonathan. 'The Dissemination of Wulfstan's Homilies: The Wulfstan Tradition in Eleventh-Century Vernacular Preaching.' In *England in the Eleventh Century: Proceedings of the 1990 Harlaxton Symposium,* ed. C. Hicks, 199–217. Stamford, 1992.

- *Ælfric's Prefaces*. Durham, 1994.
- 'Wulfstan and the Twelfth Century.' In *Rewriting Old English in the Twelfth Century*, ed. Mary Swan and Elaine M. Treharne, 83–97. Cambridge, 2000.
- 'The Wolf on Shepherds: Wulfstan, Bishops, and the Context of the *Sermo Lupi ad Anglos*.' In *Old English Prose: Basic Readings*, ed. Paul E. Szarmach, 395–418. New York, 2001.
Wilken, Robert L. 'Interpreting Job Allegorically: The *Moralia* of Gregory the Great.' *Pro Ecclesia* 10 (2001): 213–26.
Williams, Ann, Alfred P. Smyth, and D.P. Kirby, eds. *A Biographical Dictionary of Dark Age Britain: England, Scotland, and Wales, c. 500–c. 1050*. London, 1991.
Wills, Garry. *Saint Augustine*. New York, 1999.
Wittig, J.S. 'King Alfred's *Boethius* and Its Latin Sources: A Reconsideration.' *ASE* 11 (1983): 157–98.
- 'Boethius.' In *Sources of Anglo-Saxon Literary Culture: A Trial Version*, ed. F.M. Biggs et al., 74–9. Binghamton, 1990.
- 'List of Mss and Sigles.' Handout from 'What Early Glosses on 3 M IX Suggest about the "Remigian Commentary" on *Consolatio Philosophiae*,' presented at the Second Annual Symposium of the Alfredian Boethius Project. English Faculty, Oxford University, 27 July 2004.
Wormald, Patrick. 'Æthelwold and His Continental Counterparts: Contact, Comparison, Contrast.' In *Bishop Æthelwold: His Career and Influence*, ed. B.A. Yorke, 13–42. Woodbridge, 1988.
- 'Alfred (848/9–899).' 2004. *Oxford Dictionary of National Biography*, Oxford University Press, http://www.oxforddnb.com/view/article/183, accessed September 2004.
- 'Wulfstan (d. 1023).' 2004. *Oxford Dictionary of National Biography*. Oxford University Press, http://www.oxforddnb.com/view/article/30098, accessed September 2004.
Yorke, B.A., ed. *Bishop Æthelwold: His Career and Influence*. Woodbridge, 1988.
- 'Æthelwold and the Politics of the Tenth Century.' In her *Bishop Æthelwold: His Career and Influence*, 65–88. Woodbridge, 1988.
Zanna, Paolo, ed. *Alfredo il grande re e filosofo: La versione in inglese antico dei 'Soliloqui' di Agostino; Introduzione e traduzione italiana*, Milan, 2001.
Zinn, Grover A. 'Gregory I the Great (ca. 540–604).' In *Encyclopedia of Early Christianity*, ed. Everett Ferguson, Michael P. McHugh, and Frederick W. Norris, 1:488–90. 2nd ed. New York, 1998.

Index

ability (or capability, inability), 6, 9, 21, 23, 25, 27, 34, 44, 51, 53–4, 79, 88, 111, 115, 119, 140, 150, 154, 156, 158, 160, 163, 177–8, 181, 184, 188, 190, 198, 210, 213, 218–19, 269, 288n29, 317n134, 336n38, 338n51. *See also* capacity

Adam, 6, 9, 25, 32, 35, 48, 50–1, 69, 79, 81, 181, 101, 136, 174–5, 178, 183, 186, 193–4, 201, 213, 218, 275, 317n128, 323n62, 347n27, 348n54, 350n86, 353n121

Ælfric, ix, xi, 3, 8, 12–19, 21, 24, 29–33, 37, 39–40, 44–8, 61, 63–5, 75, 77–8, 81, 97, 110, 122–3, 126, 134, 148, 150, 164, 166–212, 215, 217–19, 283nn1 [Introduction], 2 [Chapter 1], 293n68, 294n75, 298n138, 300nn2, 4, 302n22, 304nn33–5, 305nn44, 50, 310nn26, 35–6, 312n64, 315n110, 321n44, 330n48, 345n1, 346nn12, 15–16, 347n26, 347–8n41, 348nn46, 54, 56, 59, 350nn80, 98, 352nn108, 109, 113, 352–3n118, 353n27, 357n160
- Works:
  De temporibus anni, 63, 206, 294n91, 310n26, 311n44

First Latin Letter for Wulfstan, 148
Grammar, 189, 203, 206, 349n72
Hexameron, 207, 356nn151–2
Interrogationes Sigewulfi in Genesin, 63, 206, 294n91, 310n26, 356nn151, 154
In xl de penitentia, 356n149
Letter to Sigeweard, 205, 208, 356n150
Lives of Saints, 205–7, 210, 330n48; *LS* **I.1**, 356nn151–3, 155; *LS* **I.17**, 210–11, 331n58, 357n161; *LS* **I.22**, 123; *LS* **I.23**, 209; *LS* **II.23b**, 209; *LS* **II.30**, 209; *LS* **II.33**, 209
Preface to Genesis, 63, 294n91, 310n27
Second Latin Letter for Wulfstan, 148
Sermones catholici, 14, 16, 19, 24, 39, 45, 63, 81, 166–204, 206, 211–12, 217, 293nn65, 67, 300n4, 303n27, 304n34, 310nn26–8, 33, 346n12, 352n112; *CH* **I.praef.**, 16, 293n67, 321n44, 346nn10, 14, 350nn85, 98, 355nn143–4, 356nn146–7; *CH* **I.1**, 294–5n91, 353nn119–20, 355nn143–5; *CH* **I.6**, 345n2, 355nn143–4; *CH* **I.7**, 32, 110, 182–4, 201, 347nn24, 26, 348nn54–5, 57–8, 350n86, 352n115, 353n129, 355n143;

Toronto Old English Series